Leonid Grossman

DOSTOEVSKY

A Biography

Translated by
Mary Mackler

The Bobbs-Merrill Company, Inc.
Indianapolis / New York

Published in the United States
by the Bobbs-Merrill Company, Inc.
Indianapolis   New York

Originally published by Molodaya Gvardia Publishing House,
Moscow, 1962

Published in Great Britain by Allen Lane, 1974

ISBN 0-672-51912-7
Library of Congress catalog card number 73-11809

Manufactured in the United States of America

First U.S. printing

Contents

Most Important Dates
in Dostoevsky's Life and Work

1821   30 October: born in Moscow, son of the army doctor Mikhail Andreevich Dostoevsky, in the Mariinskaya Hospital for the Poor.

1833-7 Years of study as a day-boarder in Moscow schools.

1837   27 February: death of his mother Maria Fyodorovna Dostoevskaya (*née* Nechaeva).

May: Dostoevsky and his elder brother Mikhail move to Petersburg.

Autumn: at Captain K. F. Kostomarov's preparatory school.

1838   16 January: enters Engineering Academy.

1839   8 June: father murdered by his serfs.

1840-41 Works on historical dramas *Maria Stuart* and *Boris Godunov*.

1841   5 August: commissioned as an officer.

1843   12 August: completes course in higher officers' class and is enrolled in Engineering Corps.

1844   June–July: his translation of Balzac's *Eugénie Grandet* published in sixth and seventh issues of the magazine *Repertoire and Pantheon*.

19 October: discharged from the service for family reasons with rank of lieutenant.

1845   May: completes *Poor Folk*. Meets Nekrasov and Belinsky.

Autumn: member of Belinsky's circle.

1846   15 January: *Poor Folk* published in Nekrasov's *Peterburgsky Sbornik* (*Petersburg Miscellany*). (Dates of all Dostoevsky's works given as of publication.)

1 February: *The Double* published in *Otechestvennie Zapiski* (*Notes of the Fatherland*).

October: *Mr Prokharchin*.

October–December: *The Landlady*.

1847   Beginning: breaks with Belinsky.

April–July: four *feuilletons* published in *Peterburgskie Vedomosti* [*Petersburg News*] under heading 'Petersburg Chronicle'.

Spring: begins to attend meetings at Petrashevsky's house.

1848   December: *White Nights*.

1849   January–February–May: *Netochka Nezvanova*.

Beginning of year: takes part in N. A. Speshnev's revolutionary circle.

March–April: attends Durov's circle on Saturdays.

15 April: reads illegal 'Letter from Belinsky to Gogol' at Petrashevsky's.

23 April: arrested and imprisoned in Alexeevsky Ravelin of Peter and Paul Fortress.

29 April–16 November: inquiry and trial of Petrashevskyites. 'Ringleaders', including Dostoevsky, sentenced to death.

19 November: The General Auditoriat's conclusion on Dostoevsky: 'penal servitude in fortresses for eight years'. The final resolution: 'Four years, and then a common soldier.'

22 December: ritual preparations for execution of death sentence on Semyonovsky parade ground. Reading of imperial 'pardon'.

24 December (night): departure of group of fettered prisoners, Dostoevsky among them, for Siberia.

1850   9–16 January: stay in Tobolsk. Meeting with wives of Decembrists in transit prison.

23 January: arrives at Omsk fortress to serve term of penal servitude.

January 1850–February 1854: penal servitude.

1854–9 Army service in Semipalatinsk. Makes the acquaintance of Wrangel, Valikhanov, the Isaevs. Meetings with P. P. Semyonov of Tien-Shan.

1856   24 March: letter to E. I. Totleben requesting assistance in restoring rights.

1 October: re-commissioned as officer.

1857   6 February: marriage to Maria Dmitrievna Isaeva in Kuznetsk.

1859   18 March: resigns from army.
       March: 'My Uncle's Dream'.
       November–December: 'The Village of Stepanchikovo
       and Its Inhabitants'.
       2 July: leaves Semipalatinsk for Tver, where he spends
       autumn.
       December (latter half): moves to Petersburg, with
       permission to reside there.

1860   1 September: beginning of *Notes from the House of the
       Dead* in the newspaper *Russky Mir* (*Russian World*)
       First collection of Dostoevsky's works published in two
       volumes in Moscow by P. A. Osnovsky.

1861   January: appearance of first issue of Dostoevsky
       brothers' magazine *Vremya*, carrying the beginning of
       The Insulted and the Injured.

1861–5 Friendship, correspondence and travels with A. P.
       Suslova.

1861–2 *Notes from the House of the Dead* printed in *Vremya*.
       May (middle): appearance of P. G. Zaichnevsky's
       'Young Russia' proclamation, concerning which
       Dostoevsky calls on Chernyshevsky.
       7 June: leaves for first journey abroad. Sees Herzen and
       makes acquaintance of Bakunin during travels.

1863   February–March: *Winter Notes about Summer Impressions*.
       24 May: imperial order to suppress the magazine
       Vremya because of N. N. Strakhov's article 'The Fateful
       Question'.
       August–October: travels abroad.

1864   January: Mikhail Dostoevsky receives permission to
       publish magazine *Epokha*.
       21 March: first issue of *Epokha* with beginning of *Notes
       from Underground*.
       15 April: death of Dostoevsky's first wife in Moscow.
       10 July: death of Dostoevsky's brother Mikhail in
       Pavlovsk.

1865   'An Extraordinary Event, or A Passage Within a
       Passage,' published in *Krokodil*.
       March–April: acquaintance and meetings with the
       Korvin-Krukovskaya sisters.

June: closing of *Epokha* announced.
July–October: abroad.

1866   *Crime and Punishment.*
4 October: begins to dictate *The Gambler* to stenographer A. G. Snitkina.

1867   15 February: marriage to A. G. Snitkina.
14 April: the Dostoevskys leave for travel abroad. Dresden. Baden-Baden. Bâle. Geneva.

1868   *The Idiot.*
12 May: death of three-months-old daughter Sophia in Geneva.
Summer: in Vevey.
Autumn: moves to Milan. *En route* the Dostoevskys stop at Bâle to see work of Hans Holbein the Younger. Winter in Florence.

1869   July: return to Dresden.
December: plan for novel *The Life of a Great Sinner.*

1870   *The Eternal Husband.*

1871   8 July: return to Petersburg. *The Devils* (completed in 1872).

1872   The Dostoevskys spend the summer in Staraya Russa, which becomes their regular summer home.

1873   Editor of weekly magazine *Grazhdanin.* Dostoevsky's articles appear under the heading *The Diary of a Writer.*

1874   19 March: hands in request to Chief Administration for Affairs of the Press asking to be relieved of duties as editor of *Grazhdanin.*
April: Nekrasov calls on Dostoevsky and asks him to write a novel for *Otechestvennie Zapiski.*

1874–5   Winter: lives in Staraya Russa and works on *A Raw Youth.*

1875   January: *A Raw Youth* begins to appear in *Otechestvennie Zapiski.*

1876   *The Diary of a Writer* revised as a separate publication. November issue contains 'A Gentle Creature'.

1877   November: frequent visits to the gravely ill Nekrasov, who reads his last poems to him.
2 December: elected Corresponding Member of the

Russian Language and Literature department of the Academy of Sciences.

30 December: delivers speech at Nekrasov's funeral.

1878   31 March: attends trial of Vera Zasulich, who shot and wounded the Governor of Petersburg, Trepov.

1879–80 *The Brothers Karamazov.*

1880   23 May–10 June: attends ceremonial unveiling of monument to Pushkin in Moscow.

8 June: delivers memorial speech on Pushkin at the second public meeting of the Society of Friends of Russian Literature.

1881   January (latter half): works on first issue of *The Diary of a Writer* for that year.

28 January: death of Dostoevsky, at 8:38 p.m.

1 February: funeral at Tikhvin Cemetery of the Alexander Nevsky Monastery.

Introduction

At the time of the Russian revolution in 1917, Leonid Grossman was already an established literary scholar. Born in Odessa in 1888, he had his first work published in 1903, at the age of 15. He graduated from the Law School of Odessa University in 1911, but his true love was literature and literary history. Among his early works was 'A Russian Candide (on the Influence of Voltaire on Dostoevsky)', which appeared in *Vestnik Yevropy*, No. 5, 1914. From 1921 he taught the history of literature and literary theories in Moscow, first at the Bryusov Institute of Literature, then, for many years, at the V. P. Potemkin Pedagogical Institute. He was the author of a large body of work, dealing with poetry, drama, the theatre, questions of literary form, and the relationship between Russian literature and social thought, and was an authority in the fields of bibliographical studies and textual criticism. When his *Complete Works* were published in Moscow in 1928, they already included *Seminars on Dostoevsky, Materials, Bibliography and Commentary* (1922), *Portrait of Manon Lescaut* (1922), *The Theatre of Turgenev* (1924), *The Poetics of Dostoevsky* (1925), *From Pushkin to Blok: Studies and Portraits* (1926), *Bakunin and Dostoevsky* (1926), *Pushkin in the Theatre* (1926), and *The Crime of Sukhovo-Kobylin* (1928). So high was the esteem in which he was held that the first edition of the *Great Soviet Encyclopedia* (1930) carried an entry for him, albeit a critical one. He is given his due as a distinguished scholar, but it is noted that while 'many of his historico-biographical and literary-descriptive sketches are interesting in concept and realization . . . as a disciple of Taine, Apollon Grigoryev and

Vyacheslav Ivanov, he displays extreme subjectivism and inconsistency of methodology in all his works, which weakens them considerably.' The 1930 edition of the *Literary Encyclopedia*, published in Moscow, also has an entry for him and criticizes him for 'emphasis on style and evasion of the question of the social causes of specific styles'.

In the thirties, Grossman continued to write prolifically. His works of that period include several biographical novels and stories, among them *Notes of D'Arshiac* (1930), derived from an episode in the life of Pushkin, and *Roulettenburg* (1932), based on Dostoevsky's *The Gambler*. He produced several studies of Dostoevsky, the most important of which was the Akademia edition in 1935 of *The Life and Works of F. M. Dostoevsky. Biography and Dates in Documents.*

However, though all the entries on Leonid Grossman – in the 1930 and 1964 editions of the *Literary Encyclopedia*, in the first and third (1972) editions of the *Great Soviet Encyclopedia* (he is not mentioned in the second, 1952, edition) – stress that Dostoevsky was the writer who interested him above all others, he did not publish a single work on Dostoevsky between 1935 and 1959. He wrote on *Balzac in Russia* (1937), *The Theatre of Sukhovo-Kobylin* (1940), *N. S. Leskov* (1945), *Versification in Lermontov* (1948), and *Belinsky's Poetics* (1954). Then, in 1959, came two works on Dostoevsky: *Dostoevsky, the Artist,* and *Dostoevsky and the Chartist Novel.* He published *Pushkin* in 1960, and *Dostoevsky* in 1963. This translation is of the second edition of the biography of Dostoevsky, which appeared in 1965 with much new material added. It was Grossman's last major work. He died in December 1965.

The gap of nearly twenty-five years in writings on Dostoevsky by Grossman must be examined in the light of the history of official attitudes to Dostoevsky in the USSR.

Long before the 1917 revolution, in fact, even in his own

time, Dostoevsky had a reputation among the Russian liberal intelligentsia as a pro-Establishment, conservative, anti-democratic writer. Later, Marxist intellectuals labelled him a reactionary and obscurantist. Both Lenin and Gorky attacked his writing in 1913. Lenin came out against the 'arch-noxious imitation of the arch-noxious Dostoevsky by writers who paint all kinds of horrors and frighten themselves and the reader.' Gorky, who always made a point of stressing that Dostoevsky was a genius, criticized the Moscow Art Theatre and its director Nemirovich-Danchenko for producing a dramatization of *The Devils*, which, he declared, was 'socially harmful'. Not surprisingly, when Lenin and his party came to power and put into practice the Marxist tenet that art and literature must serve to educate the masses, Dostoevsky, though never banned, was published very selectively and hardly mentioned in school programmes and textbooks on literature. The only separate editions of Dostoevsky's novels published in those years were *Poor Folk*, *The Insulted and the Injured*, and *Crime and Punishment*, and these were equipped with extensive commentaries emphasizing the author's portrayal of the oppressed masses in a capitalist society.

By the mid-1920s the official attitude towards Dostoevsky had relaxed somewhat. This was a period of ferment and excitement in Russian literature and the arts. While Dostoevsky had been played down in the land of his birth, in other countries the interest in his work had been growing. Apparently, there was a reluctance to let this great Russian writer be lost to modern Russia altogether. This paved the way for the decision to publish the first Soviet edition of Dostoevsky's *Complete Works*, which came out in thirteen volumes between 1926 and 1930. Dostoevsky was conceded his place among Russia's and the world's greatest writers, though always with reservations about his religious and political philosophy. The first edition of the *Great Soviet Encyclopedia* (1931) carried an article on Dostoevsky of about 6,000 words, as well as an extensive bibliography. The section on Dostoevsky's world outlook and creative work was written by A. V. Lunacharsky, the first People's Commissar of Education of the Russian Soviet Republic and one of the most cultivated men in the Soviet leadership. Lunacharsky wrote of Dostoevsky's literary genius, his psychological insight, his extraordinary portrayals and his impact on Russian and world literature. At the same time, he called attention to the role of Christian ideology and the contradictions in Dostoevsky's novels, his dualism, his lack of faith in human nature. In conclusion, Lunacharsky issued what might be taken as a serious warning: 'Dostoevsky's greatness stems from the dynamism of his work, from the wealth of his emotions, from his unquestionably sincere and impassioned struggle with himself and the whole world . . . To experience Dostoevsky critically is necessary. It is good self-discipline. But to pass through this fiery haze, across these dark abysses, beneath these lowering black clouds, before these rows of faces, distorted with rage and suffering, through the high-pitched noise of these quarrels and imprecations, the reader must be clad in the armour of mature class consciousness. Such a reader will emerge from Dostoevsky wiser with a fresh knowledge of life, especially of those elements with which the proletariat must deal, either by fighting against them or for them. But to submit to the direct influence of Dostoevsky in anything is out of the question. This would not only be harmful to the proletariat, it would be shameful and is, in fact, hardly possible. Should such influence be observed in anyone, it would be proof of philistine individualism in the person thus influenced, whether he be a writer or merely a reader.'

The situation remained much like this until the mid-thirties, with Dostoevsky recognized as a genius, the majority of his works not readily available, but with Dostoevsky studies continuing.

In January 1935 there was an interesting exchange

between David Zaslavsky, a prominent party journalist, and
Maxim Gorky. Zaslavsky wrote in *Pravda* on 20 January
1935: '*Literaturnaya gazeta* has announced with glee the
forthcoming publication by Akademia of *The Devils*. The
novel *The Devils* is the filthiest libel against the revolution
... One could understand its appearing in an edition of
complete works, not so much to be read, as to be studied.
But separately! Why *The Devils*? Why not *Notes from the
House of the Dead*? Or *The Insulted and the Injured*? Or even
The Brothers Karamazov? Gorky, remember, protested against
its production by the Moscow Art Theatre before the
revolution ...' Gorky, who had approved the Akademia
edition, replied in the 24 January 1935 issue of *Pravda*:
'Zaslavsky has really gone to extremes in his evaluation of
The Devils ... It seems to me that his loudly proclaimed
fright is out of place. The Soviet government has nothing
to fear, least of all the publication of an old novel ...
Incidentally, it is not true that *The Devils* is weak artistically
...' To which Zaslavsky replied in the next day's issue by
quoting Gorky's own words in 1913 (from his articles 'On
Karamazovism' and 'Once More on Karamazovism') and
concluding: 'Of course, one should not frighten others or
take fright oneself. But neither should one ... open wide the
sluice-gates of literary sewage ... The question of what and
how our young people read is a very important question ...
Confidence in our young people does not under any
circumstances release us from vigilance in that question ...'
Zaslavsky knew what he was doing. This was the beginning
of the period of party purges and the screws were being
tightened. It marked the end of any relaxation in the
official attitude towards Dostoevsky. From now on and until
the mid-fifties, after Stalin's death, Dostoevsky was presented as a reactionary, counter-revolutionary writer, all the
more dangerous because he was so talented. And whereas
other scholars tried to toe the line, some, such as A. Dolinin
and V. Kirpotin reluctantly, others, such as V. Yermilov,

with vicious attacks on colleagues, Leonid Grossman stopped writing about Dostoevsky altogether.

In this period Dostoevsky was even denied the qualities of humanity and compassion. *The Insulted and the Injured*, hitherto praised for those qualities, was now deemed a betrayal of humanism because it praised meekness (Yermilov, in *Against the Reactionary Ideas in the Works of F. Dostoevsky*, 1948). In that same pamphlet Yermilov engaged in some breast-beating, saying that he had overestimated Dostoevsky in his writings in 1939 and 1942. The second edition of the *Great Soviet Encyclopedia* (1952) carried an unsigned article of about 2,000 words on Dostoevsky in which the emphasis was on his anti-revolutionary and religious ideology and which concluded: 'Soviet writers and Soviet literary criticism are continuing to fight against the reactionary aspects of Dostoevsky's works and their canonization by the arms-bearers of foreign reaction.'

The seventy-fifth anniversary of Dostoevsky's death came in 1956, during the thaw that followed the twentieth CPSU congress, and served as an occasion to reclaim Dostoevsky. A new ten-volume edition of Dostoevsky's *Complete Works*, one of the editors of which was Grossman, appeared in 1956–58. Yermilov gave Dostoevsky back his humanism in the introduction to his 1956 book on *F. M. Dostoevsky*. And B. S. Ryurikov, writing in the influential journal of party theory *Kommunist* (1956, 2), stated the then official position on Dostoevsky, which did not, actually, differ very much from the one stated by Lunacharsky in 1931: 'Dostoevsky was a great realist artist, a sharp-eyed and impassioned student of life, an inspired psychologist, who knew the human soul. His novels were a giant step forward in the history of literature.' But, 'We do not idealize Dostoevsky. To minimize the contradictions in his work, to ignore what is unacceptable to the revolution in it, would be to betray the fundamental interests of the work of educating the working people . . .'

After 1956 there was a surge of scholarly works on Dostoevsky. The 1964 edition of the *Literary Encyclopedia* concluded its entry on Dostoevsky with: 'However, in the thirties and forties, the period of the personality cult, dogmatism and authoritarian thinking had a negative effect in Soviet literature on the study of Dostoevsky. There was a sharp decline in the number of works about him. Scientific research was hampered by statements in which Dostoevsky's work was characterized one-sidedly. After the exposure of the Stalin cult, the extensive study of Dostoevsky was resumed.'

The extensive study of Dostoevsky reached its culmination in 1971, the year of the 150th anniversary of the writer's birth, when the press and periodicals were full of articles about Dostoevsky and publishing houses vied with each other to publish the greatest number of books about and by him. In issue No. 16, 1971, *Kommunist* carried a long article by M. Khrapchenko, a high party official, entitled 'Dostoevsky and his Literary Heritage'. The following quotes from it will give the reader an idea of how far the official attitude to Dostoevsky has changed: 'The view that the writer's [Dostoevsky's] world outlook was conservative in all important respects is not true. It is disproved by the ardent protest against social injustice that imbues the writer's artistic creations, a protest that was not merely spontaneous, but was closely linked with his profound awareness of social disasters, his inner emotionality and torments.' And, 'While he did not accept the ideas of revolutionary socialism, Dostoevsky portrayed with extraordinary depth social conflicts from which the only escape was a basic reorganization of social relationships.' 'Dostoevsky's finest artistic creations are an enormous contribution to Russian and world literature. Imbued with the ideas of humanism, they attract the hearts and minds of readers of diverse countries and nationalities. All progressive people in the world highly appreciate Dostoevsky's works, their enormous role in the spiritual development of mankind. The Russian people, all the peoples of the Soviet Union, are deeply proud that Russia nurtured this literary genius – along with other great cultural figures – this incomparable master of literature. Dostoevsky's word burns with the flame of inspired intelligence and ardent feelings. It is inextinguishable, it has lived intensely, lives, and will live for ever and ever.'

Grossman's biography of Dostoevsky appeared in the 'Lives of Notable People' series. This series originated before the revolution, ceased publication in 1917, and was revived at Gorky's suggestion in 1933. The biographies in this series are intended for the mass reader and are written in a popular style. *Dostoevsky* presents the results of a lifetime of research and contains a great deal of material that was new at the time of publication, much of it based on conversations Grossman had with Dostoevsky's widow in the 1920s.

Mary Mackler

DOSTOEVSKY'S YOUTH

I

At the Hospital for the Poor

THE ARMY DOCTOR'S FAMILY

AMONG the Moscow students called up to work in army hospitals just before the Battle of Borodino in 1812 was one Mikhail Andreevich Dostoevsky, who had been attending the Academy of Medicine and Surgery. Mikhail Andreevich Dostoevsky was to spend many years in the army. It was December 1820 before he was discharged from military service with the rank of regimental medical officer, first class. During those years the young doctor attended a hard school. Working in overcrowded rear-line army hospitals amid the fetid odour of blood and decomposition, he performed countless operations and amputations, observing war not in heroic defence actions or great battles but in the mass of its trampled victims. He was only thirty when the campaign ended, but he had lost all zest for life. He never laughed.

In March 1821 the demobilized doctor was appointed to a post at the Mariinskaya Hospital for the Poor in Moscow, to which he moved with his young wife and infant son, Mikhail, their first-born. Some six months later, on 30 October, the Dostoevskys' second child was born in the new apartment the hospital had provided. They named him Fyodor.

The neighbourhood to which the doctor's new appointment had taken him and where his famous son was born had long been considered one of the most squalid in old Moscow. At the beginning of the nineteenth century there had been in this part of the Sushchevskaya district a cemetery for society's outcasts – tramps, suicides, criminals and their unidentified victims. The whole district was called 'the poorhouse', and the custodians of these wretched grave-yards of the poor were called 'poorhouse keepers', or *bozhedoms*. Here too there was a home for abandoned infants and a lunatic asylum. In 1806, on this site of suffering and sorrow, the architect Gigliardi had built a magnificent structure in the empire style with a pediment and Doric columns. The building was turned into a hospital for the indigent, a charity institution, and the street leading past its fence was called Bozhedomka.

It was in this neighbourhood that, while he was still a small boy, the man who was to portray the life of the big city first got to know the people who were its dregs. These drab creatures attracted his attention and sympathy and became important subjects in his later work.

*

The Dostoevskys came of an old noble family, whose names are mentioned from the sixteenth century onwards in various documents of south-western Rus'. Many of them advanced to prominent positions and became well known as members of the high court, marshals, judges, standard bearers*, and bishops. In 1506 the family was granted the village of Dostoevo in Pinsk District, between the Pina and Yatsolda Rivers; they then took the name of Dostoevsky, after their estate. In the course of five centuries the frontiers changed hands many times, and the Dostoevsky family, which lived on Lithuanian-Belorussian and Ukrainian territory, found itself sometimes in Poland, sometimes in Russia.†1

Imperious, quick-tempered, and with untamed passions and lusts, they figure repeatedly in the records of old court cases, which have been published by the Vilna Archeo-graphic Commission. At the end of the sixteenth century, for example, Maria Stefanovna Dostoevskaya was charged

* Polish *chorçży*, literally one who bears the standard
† Notes appear on pp. 609–621

with having hired one Jan Tur to murder her husband
Stanislav Karlovich, with having attempted to murder her
stepson Christoph Karlovich, and with having forged a will
to gain possession of their property. This Lady Macbeth of
Pinsk was sentenced to death, but the King of Poland
granted a stay of execution. In the middle of the seventeenth
century Filipp Dostoevsky, a warrior, was accused by the
sons of a local dignitary named Rechitsky of stealing their
property and beating their peasants. But at the same time
the family chronicle mentions distinguished historical
figures, too. One was Fyodor Dostoevsky, a sixteenth-
century *domovnik*, one of the Polish gentry who served the
famous Russian *emigré* Prince Andrei Kurbsky, celebrated
for the thunderous philippics he sent to Ivan the Terrible
from Lithuania and Poland.

By the eighteenth century the Dostoevsky family, which
had not accepted Roman Catholicism in place of Russian
Orthodoxy, had been excluded from the ranks of the western
nobility and had become impoverished and insignificant.
The novelist's grandfather, Andrei Dostoevsky, was merely
a humble archpriest in Bratslava, a remote town in Podolia
province. One of his sons, Lev, became a village priest. Of
six daughters, three married provincial priests and three
married Ukrainian minor state officials.

Only the youngest of the Bratslava archpriest's sons,
Mikhail (father of the writer), structured his life differently,
and went his own way. While still a youth he left the
seminary in Kamenets-Podolsk and ran away from the
paternal home. This obscure priest's son entered the Moscow
Academy of Medicine and Surgery, worked in army
hospitals, and ultimately became a doctor among Moscow's
poor. But his temperament, which had become quarrelsome
and callous in the struggle for existence, was poorly suited
to this humane profession. Mikhail Andreevich, according
to members of his family, was an exceedingly irritable,
quick-tempered and arrogant man. He was a hard worker

who grimly did his own duty in life and was impossibly demanding of everyone around him. His fits of anger were terrible. Moreover, he was extremely miserly and was an alcoholic.

The father's disposition and the unbearable atmosphere he created in the home cast a deep shadow over the novelist's childhood and adolescence. From the age of four onwards Fyodor already felt the despotic yoke of the head of the family. He later told a Petersburg friend, to whom he confided the story of his life, a great deal about the oppressive joyless atmosphere of his childhood. 'He was decidedly unwilling to talk about his father, and begged me not to ask questions about him.' It was of himself that Dostoevsky was thinking in the following passage from the manuscript of *A Raw Youth*:

There are children who from childhood already start to wonder about their families, *who from childhood are offended by the unattractive nature of their fathers*, and their environment, and, what is most important, who begin in childhood to understand the haphazard and disorderly foundations of their whole lives, the absence of established forms and family tradition.

A portrait of Mikhail Andreevich Dostoevsky that has come down to us shows a cold face with quite regular features, thin lips pressed tightly together, and eyes that gaze sternly from beneath Mephistophelean eyebrows. The high, gold-braided collar of his civil service uniform, which is tightly fastened and fits closely around his neck, completes an impression of cold and unfriendly reserve.

In 1819 this morose physician chose as his wife Maria Fyodorovna Nechaeva, a girl of radiant spirit and joyous disposition. Maria Nechaeva came from humble folk – old-fashioned artisans, the obscure, anonymous Russia of craftsmen and tradespeople. Her father, Fyodor Timofeevich Nechaev, had moved to Moscow from an obscure village in Kaluga Province at the end of the eighteenth century, and had gone to work as manager of a small shop.

Later he entered the third guild and became an independent merchant* in the cloth market. After a time he bought a house and married off his elder daughter to a member of Moscow's merchant aristocracy, Alexander Kumanin.

From early childhood Maria Nechaeva, the younger daughter, experienced through her mother the cultural influence of a different environment. Varvara Mikhailovna Nechaeva, *née* Kotelnitskaya, Dostoevsky's maternal grandmother, came from the *Raznochintsy*, as educated members of the unprivileged classes were called in the eighteenth century. Her father had been a proof-reader in a Moscow ecclesiastical printing-house in the days of Novikov†, and was reputed to be an intelligent and well-read man. Evidently his character had had an effect on the family's way of life and the children's upbringing; it was reflected in the personality of his youngest granddaughter. Dostoevsky's mother was fond of poetry, appreciated Zhukovsky and Pushkin, and was an avid reader of novels. She was musical and sang to her own accompaniment on the guitar. She had a gift for expressing her deep emotion as a loving wife and mother in vivid letters, imbued with lyricism and humour. She was all her children's first teacher. Dostoevsky always referred to her lovingly and was probably thinking of her sad countenance when he created the gentle, doomed heroines of his later works.

An old pastel, dating from the year Pushkin's *Eugène Onégin* was published, shows Maria Dostoevskaya in a white open-necked dress, her hair falling in silken curls around her cheeks. It is the dress and coiffure of Pushkin's heroine

* The merchant class was divided into three 'guilds' according to the amount of capital each man possessed. Entry to a guild implied that Nechaev had ceased to be a wage-earning employee and had started a business of his own.

† N. Novikov (1744–1818). Celebrated journalist, publisher and educationist in the reign of Catherine II. Thrown into prison for his progressive views in the reaction following the outbreak of the French Revolution.

Tatiana. The young woman's gaze is affectionate and pensive, the forehead is high and prominent; an almost imperceptible smile enlivens the thin lips. It is a spiritual, intelligent face, a little sad and full of maternal affection. Fyodor had his mother's forehead, the elongated shape of her eyelids and her penetrating gaze, except that his was filled with inquiring and sorrowful reflection.

*

In 1823, when Fyodor was two, the family moved into a different wing of the hospital building; this was where his childhood was spent. He and his older brother Mikhail were soon given a small room of their own, partitioned off from the entrance hall. Very little light penetrated that dreary nursery, which was painted, moreover, a dingy shade of 'off-white'. When Dostoevsky later described the cupboard-like or coffin-like Petersburg garrets where even thought lost its capacity to soar, he was surely thinking of the gloomy cupboard on Bozhedomka, where his poetic vision first began to develop.

Life soon began to disclose its genuine tragedies to the boy, prompting him to wonder and reflect. Fyodor liked to pass the time in the hospital garden, talking with the patients in their camel-coloured hospital gowns. He would observe the pale, sad men and women, half-crushed by hidden suffering. These were the people referred to in incomprehensible Latin words in the 'records of sorrow', the case histories that his father spent his evenings poring over in morose silence.

The Dostoevskys seldom had visitors. Of the family's close relatives their mother's elder sister Alexandra, wife of the 'eminent citizen and commercial counsellor' Kumanin, was the most highly regarded. 'My late aunt,' Dostoevsky recalled, 'played an enormously significant role in our lives from the time we were children until we were sixteen. She helped a great deal in our development.'

From this influential aunt the young Dostoevsky boys ab-

At the Hospital for the Poor 9

sorbed the views and traditions of the Moscow merchant class at all levels – from the small artisans in Syromyatnaya Sloboda to the hereditary nobility and shareholders in large enterprises, associated with the Russian-American Company. The younger Dostoevskys absorbed from her the archetypal views of the entire group concerning the absolute power of money in human affairs and worldly relationships. The ornate Kumanin house, situated in a quiet street off Pokrovka on a picturesque bluff sloping down to the river and adorned with porcelain, paintings and mirrors, was incontrovertible evidence of this material power. Alexandra Kumanina would arrive at the doctor's modest quarters in a carriage drawn by four horses, with a footman at the back and a postillion on the box. The family conversations in the hospital wing's small parlour imperceptibly instilled in the boys' minds the rules of piety that had evolved over the ages in the patriarchal world of tradespeople's Moscow. Devotion to the church and loyalty to the Tsar, observance of Russian Orthodox religious custom and constant filling of the safes – these were the ideals of this world of shopkeepers and rich merchants.

Such were the diverse social influences that shaped Dostoevsky's early attitudes; the traditions of an impoverished family of south-western Russo-Polish gentry mingled with the worldly shrewdness of third-guild Moscow merchants who had managed to marry into the families of some of the capital's biggest businessmen. But perhaps more powerful than all of these was the influence exerted by the tradition of intellectual culture going back to the writer's maternal grandfather, Mikhail Kotelnitsky. It was from this eighteenth-century Bible reader, who corrected proofs of philosophical treatises and codes of theological law in a Moscow ecclesiastical printshop, that love of books, poetry, speculative thinking and quaint speech entered the Nechaev shopkeeper milieu.

*

There was also a poet in the Dostoevsky family. 'When my ancestors emerged from the dark forests and swamps of Lithuania,' the writer's daughter wrote, 'they were probably blinded by the light, the flowers and the Hellenistic poetry of the Ukraine. Their souls warmed to the southern sun and poured forth in verse.' There is, indeed, a 'Penitential Song' by a Dostoevsky. It appeared in a late eighteenth-century hymnbook in Volhynia and was written, the writer's brother Andrei believed, by their grandfather, the Bratslava archpriest. The vocation of poet attracted the ex-army doctor's elder sons at an early age. Life had brought them into contact with art from childhood.

One of the first important influences in Dostoevsky's childhood was his early introduction to folklore. There was always a wet-nurse, brought in from a near-by village, in the large, prolific Dostoevsky family. The lowly names of these serf women have come down to us: Darya, Katerina, 'Lukeria, the bast sandal weaver'. It was they who introduced the boy to the legendary Firebird and Alyosha Popovich and, thereby, to literature. The writer often recalled his own nanny, a Moscow girl, 'an unassuming woman', amazingly noble in spirit, hired from among the petit bourgeoisie, who with dignity called herself 'citizenness'. She knew how to enthral the doctor's children with poetic fantasies about Ostrodum and other heroes of oral poetry. 'Our nursemaid Alyona Frolovna had a bright and merry disposition and always told us such wonderful fairy tales!' Dostoevsky wrote in 1876.

Serfs and without rights, these women inconspicuously performed an important and vital task: they awakened the boy's interest in the oral poetry of his people and at the same time fostered the development of that beautiful language – free-flowing, emotionally charged, profoundly Russian and memorably expressive – in which, in time, his world-famous books would be written.

Because of the patriarchal family's reverence for old customs and religious rituals, Dostoevsky became familiar with certain monuments of Russian architecture and painting at an early age. 'Every visit to the Kremlin and to Moscow's cathedrals was a solemn occasion for me,' he wrote towards the end of his life.

In 1859 Dostoevsky made a detour, *en route* from Siberia to Tver, to take another look at the art treasures of Sergiev Posad, which he had loved from childhood – the Byzantine halls, the collections of precious jewels, the 'clothes of Ivan the Terrible, coins, old books, all kinds of rarities – I could have stayed there for ever'. As a boy he had already seen one of the supreme achievements of medieval Russian painting, Andrei Rublev's 'Trinity', a genius's embodiment of the age-old folk dream of the 'beautiful man'. In an article written in 1847 Dostoevsky mentioned Moscow's Arkhangelsky Cathedral, 'the rarities of the Granovitaya Palata' in the Kremlin and Boris Godunov's grave as monuments that had made indelible impressions on his adolescent mind.

*

Sometimes the younger Dostoevskys had a chance to see the lively folk spectacles of old Moscow. They had a great-uncle, Vasily Mikhailovich Kotelnitsky, who was a source of family pride: he was a professor of 'medical toxicology', that is, pharmacology, at Moscow University, and for a time was even Dean of the medical faculty. Vasily Mikhailovich Kotelnitsky was not much of a scientist though, and N. I. Pirogov, the celebrated physician and medical scientist, as a student wrote a very humorous description of the comical nonsense in Kotelnitsky's lectures on drugs and potions and the amusement of his young audiences.

However, the good-natured professor was regarded as a 'champion of the students'. Childless himself, he was very fond of his great-nephews, who were usually brought to visit him at Easter. His small house was close to Smolensky marketplace, and at holiday time the boys could look from

the windows and see the marvellous show booths at Novin-
skoe with their red calico curtains and colourful homemade
placards. Great-uncle Kotelnitsky used to take his little
guests from distant Bozhedomka to see the entertainers and
magicians, the trained dogs and monkeys, the wax figures
of kings and marshals. Here the boy, who later wrote so
vividly of a theatrical performance put on by a group of
convicts, first felt the charm of folk theatre and glimpsed in
the troupes of 'jesters, clowns, strong men, and such like
tomfoolery' the vivid, untrained talent of old Russia's
itinerant buffoons.

It was not long before he discovered in the classical
theatre, too, a world of keen aesthetic pleasure. 'I was ten
years old when I saw a Moscow production of Schiller's *The
Robbers* with Mochalov,'* Dostoevsky recalled half a century
later, 'and I assure you that the extremely powerful impression I carried away with me then had a very fruitful effect
on my spirit.'

Dostoevsky's early literary impressions came from many
sources. A variety of works filled the bookcase that stood in
the family parlour, virtually the principal ornament in their
modest government-owned quarter.

The book of stories from the Old and New Testaments
from which his mother taught him to read had an extremely
strong impact on him. All his life the great novelist appreciated the literary significance of these legends, which he
regarded as outstanding folk epics, filled with drama and
lyricism.

Of these myths, the one he found especially fascinating
was the Book of Job, with its story of an innocent sufferer
who meekly accepted the harsh trials God sent down to
him – the death of his family, ruin, leprosy and poverty –
and was then rewarded; his health and wealth were restored,
he again fathered a large family, and he 'died being old and
full of days'.

* Mochalov (1800–1848). A celebrated tragic actor.

'I am reading the Book of Job,' he wrote to his wife in 1875, 'and it moves me to painful ecstasy. I stop reading and walk around the room for as long as an hour, on the verge of weeping. Strangely, Anya, this book was *one of the first in my life to affect me deeply. At the time, I was still practically an infant.*'

Dostoevsky was introduced to the art of the novel by the now almost forgotten eighteenth-century authoress Ann Radcliffe, once well known as the first exponent of a type of novel new in European literature. This was the 'Gothic' novel, so called because its authors were attracted to the medieval traditions of chivalry, as depicted in the sculpture and stained glass of Gothic architecture; it was also called 'black' because its subject matter was invariably gloomy and its atmosphere mournful. It was sometimes described as the 'novel of nightmares and horror' because it dealt in prophetic dreams, premonitions and omens of disaster. This whole atmosphere of fantasy was nourished, however, by instances from life. The unusual and the shocking were presented with the same subtle skill in realistic portrayal as the English novelists of social manners, Fielding and Smollett, had displayed.

Mrs Radcliffe was not only the pioneer but the complete mistress of the technique of the thrilling horror story.

As a small boy Dostoevsky, not yet able to read, would listen in the long winter evenings before bedtime, his heart 'hammering with excitement and terror', as his parents read him to sleep with the English novelist's many volumed epics, and then he would rave deliriously in his sleep.

Evidently the Moscow merchant's daughter Maria Nechaeva had been fond of stories of this genre since girlhood. Like her contemporaries, the provincial young ladies of the 1810s and 1820s,

> She* had early become fond of novels
> Which took the place of everything for her.

* i.e. Tatiana, the heroine of Pushkin's *Eugène Onégin*, from which these lines are quoted.

She can have had no inkling that her liking for this literature of adventure was already influencing the future work of her restless and highly strung son, whom the family called 'real fire'. Could anyone have foreseen the conflagration of ideas and emotions in world culture that would some day be kindled by this boy from Bozhedomka.

THE TULA ESTATE

In early childhood Dostoevsky knew no open horizons. Closed in by the hospital fence, he was a stranger to the Russian countryside until he was almost in his teens. The borders of lime trees around the hospital buildings and Marina Grove with its marquees and 'comedy players' were the first scenes of nature that he saw.

He was in his eleventh year when he got to know the Russian countryside, full of its own superstitions, rituals and customs.

In 1827 Dostoevsky's father, then an insignificant civil servant in the medical department, was promoted to the rank of collegiate assessor,* a rank that carried with it hereditary gentility and the right to own land with serfs. In 1828 he and his family were registered in the book of gentry of the Moscow District, and shortly afterwards agents for the purchase and sale of estates began to appear in the Dostoevsky home. In 1831 the doctor from Mariinskaya Hospital purchased the village of Darovoe in the Tula District, and the following year he purchased the adjacent hamlet of Cheremoshna. Together they constituted an estate of some fourteen hundred acres inhabited by a hundred souls. It cost Mikhail Andreevich Dostoevsky twelve thousand silver roubles and made him part of the ruling class of the Russian empire.

Darovoe, however, proved hardly more cheerful than

* Collegiate assessor, the eighth grade in Russian Civil Service hierarchy, equivalent to Major in the army.

Bozhedomka. The tiny mud-walled manor house with its thatched roof resembled a Ukrainian peasant hut. Beyond the orchard stretched what the writer's brother described as a 'rather gloomy and wild terrain, pitted with gullies'.

Contemporary scholars who have done research on the Dostoevsky estate have reconstructed a dreary picture: poor soil, no rivers or forests, a monotonous landscape of gullies and scrub, huts with thatched roofs that were removed in bad years to feed the livestock, and terrible poverty, backwardness, and mortality among the population, whom the *corvée* had ruined completely. Eloquent testimony to this state of affairs is also to be found in the letters of Dostoevsky's parents and in observations made by the last visitors to the small, neglected estate, where Dostoevsky used to spend his school holidays.

Poverty, oppression, brazen horse-stealing – the local *muzhiks* were notorious for horse-stealing – such were the evil elements he encountered during the years when the heart opens up to meet life. Even then he shuddered in the depths of his soul. In his last novel, half a century later, he mentioned the Cheremoshna his parents had once owned, and portrayed it as being in the possession of the dissolute and cruel Fyodor Karamazov. The Russian countryside, even in this poor area, was stamped forever on Dostoevsky's memory. 'This small and unremarkable spot made an extremely strong and profound impression on me that stayed with me throughout my life.' In the summer of 1877 Dostoevsky made a point of stopping in Moscow so that he could spend two days in Darovoe, visit Cheremoshna, and talk with the peasants, among whom he still found some he had known in his youth.

Dostoevsky's mother and father differed in their attitudes towards their new property. Maria Fyodorovna avoided harsh measures in administering the estate and was even remembered by the Darovoe peasants as their intercessor with the stern landlord; but the head of the family, the newly fledged owner of souls, flagrantly abused his power over the serfs who tilled his land. Even in the letters he wrote to his wife he instructed her to whip them – a measure that he himself, according to the recollections of the people on his estate, employed unrestrainedly. It is not surprising that the peasants hated him, nursing their anger and resentment and waiting for an opportune moment to take revenge.

A major disaster occurred soon after the purchase of the Tula estate. Early in the spring of 1832 both villages were destroyed by a fire that broke out, fanned by a strong wind. When the Dostoevskys arrived later they found a wasteland, dotted with charred timbers. Nothing was left standing except the mud-walled manor house. The peasant huts, farm buildings and even the charred and blackened centuries-old lime trees formed a vast landscape of sterility and sorrow; their skeletal outlines seemed to embody the cheerless lives in those enslaved villages, with sovereign Death hovering over them. Dostoevsky probably recalled this event half a century later, reviving the melancholy impressions of his childhood in Dmitry Karamazov's anguished questions: 'Why do these fire-stricken mothers stand here? Why have they turned black from black disaster? Why don't they nurse their infants?'

There were other figures of woe, in keeping with the doleful landscape. Agrafena, the homeless village idiot-girl, roamed the fields, calling incoherently to her dead baby. No one knew who the baby's father was. The unfortunate woman had been violated, Andrei Dostoevsky relates. Andrei later recognized the story of Lizaveta Smerdyashchaya and Fyodor Karamazov in *The Brothers Karamazov* as a reworking of the Darovoe beggarwoman's sad history.

In August 1831, when Dostoevsky was ten years old, he met a *muzhik* named Marei at the edge of the deserted Brykovo or Fedino woods. Marei comforted the child, who had been frightened by aural hallucinations. The sketch of the grey-haired ploughman who left his wooden plough and with dirt-stained fingers made the sign of the cross over the weeping boy is one of the finest pages in Dostoevsky's fragmentary autobiography. As the novelist himself informed us, the ploughman Marei was the first to reveal to him 'what deep and enlightened humane feeling' could fill the breast of a Russian peasant. Dostoevsky recalled this meeting when he was serving out his term of penal servitude and also described it almost half a century after the event in a celebrated chapter of his *The Diary of a Writer*. This was one of the vital sources of his ardent love for his people, a love that remained an outstanding characteristic of his work until the end.

IN MOSCOW BOARDING SCHOOLS

Two teachers from the near-by Yekaterininsky Institute were asked to tutor the boys. One was a deacon, and the Bible stories he recounted to his pupils about the Flood and the adventures of Joseph fascinated them. The other was a French teacher, Souchard, who was the first person to acquaint Dostoevsky with the school examples of his native literature.

Their father taught them Latin, of which he had acquired a good knowledge at the Podolsk Seminary and the Medical Academy. With his usual sternness, he would interrupt their recitals of declensions and conjugations at the slightest error with shouts of 'Sluggards!', 'Dolts!', and, pushing aside the old Bantyshev textbook, would stalk out in anger. It is no wonder that Dostoevsky never manifested any interest in Latin language or literature and that the only classical Roman poet he ever mentioned was Juvenal – and even that was in quoting someone else.

Dostoevsky absorbed the culture of ancient Greece and Rome chiefly through later poets, Racine, Schiller, Goethe and Pushkin. On the other hand, he very early displayed an interest in the novel, that variable, multifaceted, wide-ranging and profound genre that had evolved in the Middle Ages and the Renaissance and had become the predominant form in the newest European literature. The novel reflected the new questions being raised by the disenfranchised city-dwellers of the thirteenth to sixteenth centuries. It was the personal enterprise of the Third Estate that first raised in this form questions of individualism, the struggle for social ascendancy, rejection of religious authorities, sceptical analysis and freethinking irony, all of which gave to stories of manners the character of ideological battles or philosophical dramas.

The elder sons' education at home was completed in 1833, and Mikhail and Fyodor entered the Frenchman Souchard's school as day-boarders. (Souchard had Russified his name, and was by then called Drashusov.)

Some features of the Souchard school are reflected in one of the finest episodes of *A Raw Youth*, recounting a poor peasant woman's visit to her son, who is a pupil at a foreign boarding school in the capital. The boy is ashamed of his humble parent in front of his aristocratic schoolmates, but to her he boasts of the school's good food, his French vocabulary and the pompous director Touchard, who hypocritically tells his lowly visitor that in his school the illegitimate son of a serf woman is on an almost equal footing with the children of senators and counts. Of course, this has no real parallel in the writer's own life, but it authentically conveys the class atmosphere of the 'gentlemen's boarding school' where Dostoevsky first became aware of the caste spirit of aristocratic education; this was to weigh on him throughout his years as a student.

In the autumn of 1834 the brothers were transferred to Leopold Chermak's boarding school. The staff there included eminent Moscow teachers and scholars: the distinguished Russian mathematician D. M. Perevoshchikov, subsequently Rector of Moscow University and a member of the Academy of Sciences; I. I. Davydov, doctor of literature and a well-known follower of Schelling; A. M. Kubaryov, master of Latin literature and author of *The Theory of Russian Versification*; and the classicist Taider, apparently a disciple of the German school of philology.

One of Dostoevsky's schoolmates, Kachenovsky, has described him: 'He was a serious, thoughtful boy with blond hair and a pale face. He was not much interested in games. During breaks he hardly ever left his books, and when he did, it was to talk with the older pupils.'

As in the *lycée* Pushkin attended, the emphasis was on literature. The writer Grigorovich noted in his memoirs that all Chermak's pupils were exceptionally well-read in classical and contemporary poetry.

While Dostoevsky was at Chermak's school, Russian literature suffered a number of blows. Polevoi's *Moskovsky Telegraf* (*Moscow Telegraph*) was shut down and so was the young Belinsky's *Teleskop* (*Telescope*). Chaadayev was declared insane, Nadezhdin was exiled to Ust-Sysolsk, Pushkin was killed in a duel, Lermontov was exiled to the Caucasus, Gogol went abroad with a melancholy heart.

But this onslaught of reaction could not stifle all literary output. These years saw the publication of *The Captain's Daughter*, *Taras Bulba*, *The Inspector-General*, *Literary Dreams*, *The Death of the Poet*, *Borodino*, and poems by Koltsov and Tyutchev. The schoolboy Fyodor Dostoevsky began to be aware of himself within this irresistible flow of time. It began 'from about the time I was sixteen,' he wrote in the 1870s, recalling his first stirrings of inspiration; or, to be more exact, 'when I was but fifteen years of age.' '*There was a kind of fire in my soul, and I believed in it*; as for what would come of it, I did not much care.'

His parents subscribed to *Biblioteka dlya Chtenia* (*Library for Reading*), a magazine edited by O. I. Senkovsky, a professor of Oriental studies and author of some amusing short stories. The magazine published works by Pushkin,

Gogol, Lermontov, Zhukovsky, Krylov, Odoevsky, Bara-
tynsky and Vyazemsky. It carried or reviewed in detail the
early novels of Balzac, Victor Hugo and George Sand. As a
boy in Moscow, Dostoevsky had already discovered *Père
Goriot*, *Han d'Islande* and *Indiana*. All these works marked the
end of the romantic period and the emergence of a new
artistic style – realism.

Vanechka Umnov, a *gymnasium* student who was a contemporary of the Dostoevsky brothers, introduced them to
Ershov's *Hunchbacked Horse* and Voeikov's *Madhouse*. These
gave Dostoevsky his first contact with literary satire; he
even learned them by heart. He appreciated the genre
highly and was attracted to it time and again. The majority
of writers in this form were archaists and imitators of
Karamzin, but there were also Zhukovsky, Batyushkov,
Kozlov and Polevoi. Voeikov had mastered a laconic, epi-
grammatic style and could draw a biting caricature in a
few lines.

His sketch of one of the writers of the twenties is amusing:

> He writes nothing, he publishes nothing,
> He draws three salaries and accepts a dinner allowance.

The Dostoevskys' favourite authors also included Karamzin, whom Dosteovsky valued for his lyrical novella *Poor
Liza*, his sensitive travel books and vividly written history;
Sir Walter Scott, for his novels of political convulsions and
thrilling adventures, which heightened the future novelist's
imagination and impressionability; and Zhukovsky, for his
Anglo-German ballads that read like the Russian poems the
young dreamer loved so well. Particularly striking was his
interest in Pushkin. Dostoevsky was at boarding school when
Biblioteka dlya Chtenia and *Sovremennik* (*The Contemporary*) published the prologue to *The Bronze Horseman*, as well as *The
Queen of Spades* and *The Covetous Knight*.

But it seems that Dostoevsky, when still quite young, also
liked heroes of a different type – moral heroes with pure

hearts and lofty ideals. The notes for his novel about a great sinner contain an extremely significant passage about a man who has gone astray but towards the end of his life purifies himself morally and becomes another 'Haas'. This is a reference to Fyodor Petrovich Haas, a celebrated Moscow physician and philanthropist, whom Dostoevsky also mentions in the rough drafts of *Crime and Punishment* and about whom he wrote an inspired passage in *The Idiot*.

Dostoevsky had apparently known the name of this 'friend of the poor' when still in his teens. In the mid 1820s, Dr Haas was appointed city physician of Moscow, in charge of hospitals and the government-owned pharmaceutical dispensary, and his name was surely well known to the doctor's family on Bozhedomka.

In 1828 Dr Haas was appointed to a new post as head physician of Moscow's prisons. Horrified by the shocking conditions in the crowded gaols – those 'schools for mutual training in depravity and crime' – the new prison doctor waged an unremitting struggle against this frightful social evil. He succeeded in introducing a number of reforms in the punitive system itself, such as prohibition of the monstrous 'iron whip'. He was present whenever a group was dispatched on the journey to Siberia and saw to it himself that the convicts were properly shod. He kept many of the convicts in Moscow for medical treatment and accompanied others far along the road to Vladimir, providing them with clothing and money. He died a pauper in 1853 and was buried at police expense yet his name was well known among 'convicts and gaolbirds' and was uttered with reverence in the farthest corners of Siberia.

He was probably Dostoevsky's first model for the 'beautiful man'. In *The Idiot*, where the 'beautiful man' is the basic theme, Dr Haas appears for an instant, accompanying a group of convicts from the deportation point on Sparrow Hills* outside Moscow. In Dostoevsky's imagination this

* Today called the Lenin Hills.

unassuming humanitarian, whose motto was 'Hasten to do good', belonged in the same rank as Don Quixote, Mr Pickwick and Jean Valjean.

DOSTOEVSKY'S MOTHER

The situation of Dostoevsky's gentle mother, subjected as she was to her despotic husband's constant suspicions and accusations, steadily worsened as the years passed. Though Maria Fyodorovna was completely devoted to her family, worshipped her husband, and was willing to forgive him anything, she had to listen to his charges of unfaithfulness and defend herself against his prejudices and suspicions. Striking passages in her letters to her husband reveal the depths of her despair over her tragic lot. On 31 May 1835 she wrote to him:

I swear to you, my friend, by God Himself, by heaven and earth, by my children and all my happiness and my life, that I have never been and never will be a violator of my heart's vow, given to you, my dear friend, my only one, before the holy altar on the day of our marriage, I swear to you, too, that my present pregnancy is the seventh tight bond to be tied by our mutual love, a love that on my part is pure, holy, chaste and passionate, unchanged from the day of our marriage.

This vow of fidelity was made in 'the sixteenth year of our union'. Wrongly and grievously insulted, she concluded her letter:

Farewell, my friend. I can write no more nor can I collect my thoughts. Forgive me, my friend, for not having concealed the agonies of my soul from you. Do not grieve, my friend, take care of yourself for the sake of my love. As for me, command me. For you I am sacrificing not only my peace of mind but my very life.

In her next letter, dated 8–10 June 1835, she tells her husband how she felt when she read his charges of unfaithfulness:

I was filled with hatred for God's world. Nowhere could I find a place for myself, nowhere could I find comfort. For three days I walked around as if I had lost my mind. Ah, my friend, you will not believe how tormenting this is . . .

The despair of a ruined life comes through even in the letter's fervent assurances:

No one sees my love, no one understands my feelings; people regard me with base suspicion, whereas my love is my life. Meanwhile time and the years go by; my face grows all wrinkled and yellow, natural cheerfulness turns into melancholy – that is my sad fate, that is the reward for my chaste, passionate love. And if it were not that my clear conscience and faith in Providence sustained me, the end of my life would be lamentable. Forgive me for writing the harsh truth of my feelings. I do not curse you, I do not hate you – on the contrary, I love and adore you, my only friend, all that is in my heart.

Even now these intimate letters continue to move one by their profound sincerity of feeling and their striking power of expression. As one reads their faded pages, one can see why one of Maria Fyodorovna's sons became a famous writer. However, it was not only her undeniable literary gifts that led her son to his vocation, but also her sad lot. In the person of his mother the future great moralist first encountered in real life the problem of innocent suffering, of undeserved martyrdom, of the slow psychological exhaustion of a pure and self-sacrificing soul. Ethics became the foundation of Dostoevsky's creative thought, and the image of his mother became the supreme embodiment of moral beauty and goodness.

The strange scenes between his parents that Andrei Dostoevsky describes become understandable in the light of the couple's letters to each other. In that dark front room one evening 'mama' informed his father that she was 'pregnant again'. Father's face clouded and he expressed such displeasure to her that she 'broke into loud, hysterical sobs'. Their son was never able to forget this confrontation between husband and wife.

Another scene that impressed itself on young Andrei's mind was also probably caused by his father's jealousy, though it took a different direction. His mother's younger brother Mikhail Nechaev, who sang and played the guitar, began to pay attentions to the chamber-maid Vera, 'a pretty young girl', who lived in the house. In the family conflict that this situation provoked, the 'infuriated father struck Uncle in the face, I think'. Young Mikhail never appeared in the Dostoevsky home again.

In this emotional climate Maria Fyodorovna, who was sickly to begin with, slowly faded away. Her chest weakness, for which she needed peace of mind above all else, turned into 'malignant consumption'.

At thirty-five this frail woman had borne eight children (of whom one daughter, Lyubov, born in 1829, had lived only a few days). After the birth of the last child in July 1835, her lung disease took a sharp turn for the worse. In 1836 her hair was cropped short. Dostoevsky recalled some of her slow agony when he described, in his unfinished novel *Netochka Nezvanova*, written in 1849, the dying of his consumptive heroine, gentle, unhappy Alexandra Mikhailovna, crushed by her husband's jealousy and vindictiveness.

'See, it is already late autumn; soon the snow will fall. With the first snowfall I shall die – yes, but I don't mind. Farewell!'

Her face was pale and thin, and an ominous red spot burned on each cheek; her lips were trembling and parched from high fever. She spoke with difficulty. Her voiceless inner pain was reflected in her face, her eyes filled with tears.

'Well, enough of that, my friend, enough. Bring in the children.'

I brought them in. She seemed to draw repose from looking at them. After an hour, she let them go.

'When I die you won't abandon them will you?' she whispered to me as if afraid someone might overhear us.

'Enough, you will kill me!' was all I could say in reply.

'But, listen, you'll love them when I die? Won't you?' she asked seriously, and then added with a mysterious look, 'As you would love your own children?'

'Yes, yes,' I replied, not knowing what I was saying and choking with tears and confusion.

This is both a vivid sketch of the writer's dying mother and also, apparently, an echo of her deathbed conversations with her childless sister Alexandra Kumanina, who later did, in fact, act as a mother to the orphaned Dostoevsky children.

From the beginning of 1837 Maria Fyodorovna never left her small darkened bedroom. Daily consultations by physicians failed to provide relief. At the end of February the doctors informed their colleague that their efforts were futile and the end was near. On the night of 26 February the dying woman took leave of her children and fell into a coma; on the following morning she died. She was buried at the Lazareskoe Cemetery on 1 March.

This family tragedy almost coincided with a national tragedy, the death of Pushkin, the shocking news of which had reached Moscow early in February that year. But among the circle of relatives who had gathered at Maria Fyodorovna's deathbed, there was little interest in the murder of a Petersburg writer. Mikhail and Fyodor did not learn about it until they returned to school after their mother's funeral. Fyodor told Mikhail that if the family had not been in mourning already, he would have gone into mourning for Pushkin.

It was at about this time that the two brothers' literary inclinations began to manifest themselves. Mikhail, the elder, wished to become a poet and wrote 'three poems every day', Dostoevsky recalled forty years later in *The Diary of a Writer*. He himself, however, had already turned to prose, which seems to have consisted primarily of fantastic stories. These were what he was referring to when he told his brother in 1838: 'My dreams have abandoned me, and my lovely *arabesques*, which I once created, have lost their gilt.'

'Once' meant one year before; in 1837 he had written 'a novel of Venetian life'; this may be taken as the earliest example of his interest in the school of Ann Radcliffe, whose books were usually set in Italy.[2]

The mother's death brought about the complete disintegration of the family. The Kumanins took two of the children to bring up. The father took his four eldest sons to Petersburg and placed them in the Military Engineering Academy there. *En route* to the capital, Fyodor Dostoevsky caught a glimpse of the face of Russian officialdom. From the window of an inn in a large village somewhere in Tver Province, he observed a remarkable scene. A government courier, who had obviously just had a drink at the station, jumped into a troika and began worldlessly, methodically and calmly to hit the coachman in the back of the head with his enormous fist. The startled coachman set to frantically whipping his horses, which, from fright and physical pain, galloped off as if gone mad. All his life, Dostoevsky remembered this revolting scene as an example of pointless cruelty and innocent suffering. The powerful description of Raskolnikov's dream about a tormented peasant nag, dying as its frenzied master beat it with a crowbar, is associated with this recollection. A note in the rough drafts of *Crime and Punishment* reads: '*My first feeling of personal insult* came from the horse and the courier.'

Thus did Dostoevsky's childhood and boyhood years draw to a close. They were not without some bright and joyous elements – his mother, 'brother Misha', Pushkin, the countryside, fairy tales, books, the literature teacher, the Kremlin, Mochalov, his first poetic projects. But all this took place against a background of family drama, which remained a dismal memory throughout his life. The childhoods of Dostoevsky's heroes are usually joyless, and in this respect reflect a great deal of his own experience. The author of *A Raw Youth* was undoubtedly referring to himself when he wrote of the pure ideal that '*the proud young spirit, melancholy, lonely, stricken, and wounded even in childhood*, nurtured in his dreams'.

II

The Engineering Academy

'My brother and I were taken to Petersburg to the Engineering Academy and our futures were ruined,' Dostoevsky recalled towards the end of his life. 'In my opinion, this was a mistake.' The future writer had no vocation whatever for military engineering. From the classrooms on Basmannaya Street he should have gone directly to Moscow University, where he would have studied with Ostrovsky, Pisemsky, Apollon Grigoryev, Fet and Polonsky, soon to be his literary colleagues. But the elder Dostoevsky was unwilling to take his sons' artistic inclinations into account. He wrote to Fyodor that Mikhail's 'verse-scribbling' angered him because it was a complete waste of time. He intended his sons to have brilliant and lucrative careers in military engineering, considered an extremely profitable field at the time because increasing numbers of fortresses were being built on the western frontier. The young writer dared not even dream of the philology department with the modest teaching prospects it offered. He was handed a flintlock in place of classical texts, given a shako for his head, and placed in the ranks.

The Moscow boarding school had hardly prepared him for military service. On the training ground when the ranks stood facing the sun and the bayonets began to waver, the infuriated commanding officer would foam at the mouth and shout, 'Attention! There's no sun at the front. Atten-tion!'

Neither was there sun in the lecture-rooms of the majestic Mikhailovsky Castle, with its harsh military discipline and life lived to the beat of drums. The students dreamed of

nothing but finishing school and escaping from the unbearable routine.

The year 1838 marked the beginning of a period in
Dostoevsky's life of secret and strenuous struggle to safe-
guard his vocation as an artist. Dostoevsky made his own
creative amendments to the programme of military education: to engineering subjects he opposed the study of world
literature. Topography and fortifications could not divert
him from Hamlet and Faust. The theory of the construction
of crownworks and batteries could not obscure the goal he
had set himself – to serve 'mankind's spiritual thirst', as he
expressed it later. Now, he valued only the nights, which
he spent in the embrasure of a secluded window above
the Fontanka Canal, writing down his early reflections on the
enormous theme that possessed him: 'Man is a mystery
that must be divined!'

He was surrounded by noisy cadets, but the school could
boast certain intellectual traditions, and these he valued. In
the 1820s some of the students at the Engineering Academy
had formed a circle of admirers of 'holiness and honour'.
The group included D. A. Bryanchaninov, M. V. Chikachev
and N. F. Fermor, described by N. S. Leskov in his
story 'The Unmercenary Engineers'.

The memory of these seekers of righteousness lingered on
at Mikhailovsky Castle for a long time. When Dostoevsky
entered the Academy in 1838 he found that the traces of
moral enthusiasm were still preserved in the traditions of
that grim institution. And, following the example of those
earlier ascetic schoolfellows, he held himself aloof from the
new generation of mercenary engineers who, as he recalled
in 1864, 'reckoned intelligence by rank' and who 'at
sixteen already talked about nice warm jobs'.

The magnificent architecture of Mikhailovsky Castle
formed one of the deepest artistic impressions of Dostoevsky's
student years. Built by the French architect Brenne on the
basis of a design by the celebrated Russian architect V. I.

Bazhenov, Paul I's 'abandoned and forgotten palace', which had inspired the young Pushkin's ode to freedom, was considered to be an outstanding event in the history of Art because of its beauty and grandeur. Soon after it was built it was the scene of a conspiracy of the Guards. Afterwards the Tsar's bedroom was turned into a palace chapel. The iconostases and icon-lamps brought to mind the fearful political events of the not so distant past – the silent night in March 1801 when Alexander ascended the Russian throne after having given his consent to a palace *coup*: in effect, to the murder of his father. Here, Dostoevsky first encountered the theme of intellectual responsibility for parricide, as a historical fact, a theme that he embodied forty years later in the tragedy of Ivan Karamazov.

Dostoevsky worked conscientiously at his studies, but his favourite subjects, the ones he studied with interest and pleasure, were literature, history, drawing and architecture.

Professor V. T. Plaksin, a critic, student of the theatre and author of a pedagogical novel entitled *The Upbringing of Women*, taught Russian literature at the Academy. Belinsky mentioned his name in a number of articles, usually attacking him. Plaksin stuck to old-fashioned models in his teaching and ignored Gogol, but he paid a great deal of attention to Pushkin, Lermontov and Koltsov and provided a good selection of folk poetry in his textbooks. Josèphe Cournand, a Frenchman, taught his subject at a high level. This excellent lecturer received high praise from I. M. Sechenov,* a junior schoolfriend of Dostoevsky's at the Academy. Young Dostoevsky's admiration for Racine, Corneille, Ronsard and Malherbe, which is reflected in the letters he wrote at the time, stem from the lessons and textbooks provided by this sensitive teacher. Cournand included

* Ivan Mikhailovich Sechenov (1829–1905), eminent Russian physiologist.

contemporary writers in his syllabus, too: Balzac, Hugo, George Sand and Eugène Sue, all of whom became favourites with his gifted pupil.

The course dealing with the history of architecture he considered 'beautiful' and interesting; it gave him a thorough knowledge of the major styles in the plastic arts and instilled in Dostoevsky a lifelong love of architecture and a subtle understanding of its laws. Scattered throughout Dostoevsky's books and letters there are informed comments about buildings, about their 'physiognomy' and character. He collected pictures of well-known masterpieces of the art of building and used to cover his manuscripts with drawings of Gothic towers.

Though he did not associate with the mass of students and, as later in his life, preferred solitude and seclusion, he nevertheless gradually attracted a small circle of friends, among whom were Alexei Beketov, brother of the famous scientists with whom Dostoevsky became friendly after leaving the Academy; the artist Konstantin Trutovsky, who painted an inspired portrait of the writer as a young man and who later became a well-known genre painter and illustrator of Pushkin, Gogol and Shevchenko; and, finally, Dmitry Grigorovich, the author of *Anton-Goremyka* (*Anton the Unfortunate*), who soon left the Engineering Academy for the Academy of Arts.

*

The crucial events of young Dostoevsky's inner life during this period centred around his meetings, conversations and discussions with Ivan Nikolaevich Shidlovsky, whose acquaintance the Dostoevsky brothers and their father had made in the hotel at which they stayed when they arrived in Petersburg.

Shidlovsky was the first in the series of Dostoevsky's philosopher friends, whose conversations stimulated the development of his ideas and views. He was five years Dostoevsky's senior, had already graduated from the university, and was employed in one of the ministries. He wrote poetry and was considered an outstanding reciter and speaker.

The image of him that emerges from Dostoevsky's letters is an image of the young poet of the 1830s. His portrait is stylized in the romantic spirit:

> To look at him is to know he is a martyr! He is wasted, his cheeks are hollow, his shining eyes are dry and fiery. The spiritual beauty of his face increased with his physical decline.

The fate of this new Werther was described in the same style:

> He suffered! My God, how he loves the girl (Marie, I think), but she married another. Had he not loved as he did he would not have been the pure, exalted, disinterested priest of poetry that he was.

The description of the inner life of this thinker and visionary is even more expressive:

> He is the embodiment of the 'right' portrait of a man that Shakespeare and Schiller have given us; but even then he was quite capable of sinking into the gloomy mania of Byronesque characters.

Dostoevsky had a very high regard for the *Moskovsky Telegraf*, the organ of young Russian romanticism; he even called it the 'holy icon-case of my library'; 'I owe to it my whole spirit.' Shidlovsky was personally acquainted with the editor of the publication, Nikolai Polevoi, who might have impressed Dostoevsky as well with his romantic stories and his novel *Abadonna*. Verses by Shidlovsky that have come down to us bear the imprint of the late romantics' typical striving to identify inner stress with formidable cosmic elements:

> The storm is howling, the thunder rumbling,
> The sky is ready to fall.
> Over its steep waves
> Now here, now there a flame is dancing.

Now in a swift movement it breaks up.
Now it sprays out in a pattern,
Now it vanishes, and now again,
It begins to leap and wander.
Ah, if I could roam away on wings of freedom,
Away from life's troubles, up in the heavens,
Choose a place on a cloud,
Settle there, and now and then
With playful hand
Waken the responsive thunder.

Lines such as these fired the imagination of the twenty-year-old Dostoevsky, and their author's personality made an enormous impact on him. 'Last winter I was in a state of exaltation. My friendship with Shidlovsky gave me so many hours of the finest kind of life.'

Shidlovsky's complex nature did not manifest itself in full until later. He soon abandoned poetry for large-scale scholarly research and began a history of the Russian Church; and Ordynov, the hero of Dostoevsky's *The Landlady*, did the same. 'But academic research could not absorb all his spiritual energy,' Shidlovsky's sister-in-law told Dostoevsky's second wife, Anna Grigoryevna Dostoevskaya, in 1901. 'Inner disharmony and dissatisfaction with everything around him are presumably what motivated him to enter the Valuisk Monastery in the 1850s.' A man of strong passions and turbulent nature, Shidlovsky was unable to find peace of mind in the monastery either, and, discarding his monk's habit, went back to live in the country, remaining there as a lay brother until he died in 1872.

In the late 1870s Dostoevsky still spoke of the 'beneficial influence' exerted on him by that 'tremendous intellect and talent', who had so futilely dissipated his energies. 'To me he was a great man, and he does not deserve that his name be forgotten.' The conversations with Shidlovsky, the walks with him in Petersburg and its environs, the reading

together of beloved authors, the magazines, verses, mono-
logues and philosophical disputes – all this constituted a real
'romantic school', as opposed to the 'rotten, meaningless
studies at the Military Engineering Academy!'

*

Misfortune where those studies were concerned befell
Dostoevsky after the summer of 1838, which he had spent in
a fever of reading. Despite his excellent record in the autumn
examinations, he was kept back for a year by the algebra
teacher because of a rude answer he had given in the middle
of the term. Exactly what happened is not entirely clear, for
the punished cadet had always been described in school
records as 'extremely diligent in duty', and 'good in
conduct and practical management', and he was noted for
his restraint and reticence, even timidity, in school life.

He finished the rest of the course satisfactorily, receiving
the usual official recognition of his success in science and
military exercises. However, though outwardly industrious,
he never for a minute surrendered his intellectual position
and steadfastly continued his solitary creative work.

Dostoevsky's wide reading gave him prestige among his
colleagues and friends. That same autumn of 1838 he was
visited at the Engineering Academy by his brother Mikhail's
friend Riesenkampf, who came from Revel and was a
student at the Academy of Medicine and Surgery in
Petersburg, Riesenkampf was fascinated by his new
acquaintance, who read aloud to him enthusiastically from
Pushkin's 'Egyptian Nights' and Zhukovsky's 'The Baron
of Smalholm' (a translation of Sir Walter Scott's 'The Eve
of St John'). At that time Dostoevsky was at the height of his
romantic phase. 'He had a passionate love of poetry,'
Riesenkampf recalled, 'but he wrote prose exclusively because he lacked the patience to produce poetic form. Thoughts
rose up in his head like spray from a whirlpool. His splendid
natural gift for declamation burst the bonds of artistic
self-control.'

As for his friend Dmitry Grigorovich, Dostoevsky guided his reading, introducing him to Sir Walter Scott's *The Astrologer*, Hoffman's *Kater Murr*, Fenimore Cooper's *Lake Ontario*, and Thomas de Quincey's *Confessions of an English Opium-Eater*, 'a sombre book that Dostoevsky highly valued at the time' for its graphic portrayals of human suffering, poverty and crime. Dostoevsky also interested his friends in the celebrated *Melmoth, the Wanderer*, praised by Pushkin as 'a work of genius', in which the Faust theme was treated in the manner of an adventure novel. Grigorovich relates that

Dostoevsky's literary influence was not confined to me. It extended to three other comrades: Beketov, Vitkovsky and Berezhetsky. We formed a circle that kept aloof from the others, and we met whenever we had a free moment.

The members of the group never forgot their leader's 'inspired stories'.

It was long past midnight. We were all very tired, but Dostoevsky stood there, holding onto the door and talking with nervous excitement. His low, very husky voice was electrifying and we were unable to tear ourselves away.

None of Dostoevsky's literary efforts in Moscow had been more than juvenile trials, but in the four years he spent at the Engineering Academy, he acquired a broad knowledge of Russian and world literature. Association with young poets such as his brother Mikhail and, especially, Shidlovsky substantially widened his horizons and introduced him to new genres. The first things to take shape from Dostoevsky's creative activity were some romantic dramas, in which political and moral ideals are embodied in famous figures, placed by the forces of the age in a position of great internal and external conflict. Such were the historical tragedies *Maria Stuart* and *Boris Godunov*, which have not survived for us to read. Evidently the young Dostoevsky was fascinated by the problem of criminal rule and usurpation of power, as it was embodied in the lives of great characters of the past.

According to Pushkin, and to Karamzin too, Tsar Boris was an outstanding statesman but was defeated by his moral failure – the fact that he had committed a crime. Pushkin's tragedy contained in outline themes later used by Dostoevsky: does a strong personality have the right to commit murder in the name of the general good? Can the happiness of the many be built upon the suffering of a tormented child? What is the value of power obtained by usurpation? In Schiller's *Maria Stuart* two women struggle for the throne in a ruthless single combat that leads one of them to the execution block. The rivalry of two women possessed by uncontrollable hatred for one another was to become a favourite theme of Dostoevsky as a novelist, a theme he was to deal with in terms of the manners of his own day. But in 1842 such a subject for him still required the distance of centuries and the emotional setting of romantic tragedy.

Some of Dostoevsky's later writing casts light on his early years. Though he defined *A Raw Youth* as the autobiography of its hero, this novel reveals much about the author himself as a young man – not in specific instances or events but in the overall psychological pattern presented. Like his hero Arkady Dolgoruky, Dostoevsky, between the ages of sixteen and twenty-one (while he was at the Military Engineering Academy) strove to attain solitude and seclusion by withdrawing from everyone into his own vision, a vision that welled up from a profound source, but did not survive the test of reality. 'I learned the monologue from *The Covetous Knight* by heart when I was still a child; Pushkin never produced anything superior in terms of ideas,' says Dostoevsky. A dramatic picture of the unlimited authority of a single person, built upon the power of gold and subordinating everything else to it – this was how the powerless yet power-hungry boy interpreted the idea of Pushkin's 'little tragedy'. 'Power! . . . Almost from my earliest childhood I could never imagine myself except in the foremost place, always and in all of life's situations.' In Arkady Dolgoruky's mind this vainglorious dream takes the prosaic form of a project 'to become a Rothschild'. But for Dostoevsky, the young genius, the supreme aspiration was to rise to the summit of world art, to become a Shakespeare, a Balzac, a Pushkin.

Among the great names in literature, young Dostoevsky regarded Gogol as one of the greatest. That powerful satirist came to represent a whole epoch in the budding novelist's development and growth. Long before Dostoevsky's own works began to appear in print, he knew basically the 'whole' of Gogol – his Ukrainian stories, the Petersburg tales, *The Inspector-General* and *Dead Souls*. They all fascinated, inspired and taught him, but they taught him in different ways. Gogol's Petersburg tales – 'Nevsky Prospekt', 'The Portrait' and 'Diary of a Madman', which had already appeared in 1835, 'The Nose', which appeared in 1836, and 'The Overcoat', which appeared in 1842 – had a genuinely creative influence on the engineer and dreamer. They were the starting point of Dostoevsky's early work. The great originator of the school of naturalism had opened for him a new road into literature by the complexity of his realism, the unprecedented combination of physical portrayal with romantic story-telling, of everyday prose with disturbing fantasy, of images of the outer beauty of the empire's capital city with the details of its hidden workaday dramas involving petty civil servants and obscure actors.

It was on the basis of social contrasts such as these that young Dostoevsky's artistic method began to take shape. His early work was largely an assimilation of Gogol's Petersburg series, but in addition had the avowed aim of surpassing that master of the plastic style by the depth of his psychological studies. What boldness and what confidence that he would succeed! Yet all the same, what led him to that success was the principle laid down by Gogol himself, the creator of 'Arabesques', and formulated long afterwards by the genius who was his pupil. 'Out of a civil servant's lost overcoat he created a horrifying tragedy.' That was written by Dostoevsky, in 1861. But it was while he was inside the walls of the Mikhailovsky castle that he had come to perceive in the destinies of the Poprischins and the Chertkovs that element of tragedy in everyday life that in time led him to create a genre new to the world – the tragic novel.

THE MURDER OF DOSTOEVSKY'S FATHER

The harshness of Mikhail Andreevich Dostoevsky's character was imperceptibly preparing disaster for him. Having gone into seclusion in Darovoe with the younger children after his wife's death, he let himself deteriorate and became crueller than ever. 'One summer day', Lyubov Fyodorovna Dostoevsky's daughter, wrote:

He set out from Darovoe for his other property, Cheremoshna, and never returned. He was later found halfway there, suffocated by a cushion from the carriage. The driver had vanished along with the horses. Several peasants from the village disappeared at the same time. Other of my grandfather's serfs testified that this was an act of revenge: the old man had always been very hard on his serfs. The more he drank the more savage he became.

There are other family versions of this event, one told by Dostoevsky's younger brother Andrei, who was living with his father at the time:

His passion for alcohol was apparently growing more intense, and he was almost always in an abnormal state . . . [On 8 June 1839] a gang of about ten or fifteen men were working together in a field in Cheremoshna on the edge of a forest. Infuriated by something the peasants did wrong, or perhaps it only seemed so to him, Father lost his temper and began to shout very angrily. One of the bolder peasants said something extremely rude in reply and then, fearing the consequences of this, called out: 'Come on fellows, let's do him in!' With this exclamation, all fifteen peasants fell upon Father and, of course, finished him off in an instant.

This account presents a general picture of the event, but it remains in the realm of supposition and cannot be considered authentic. No witnesses to the murder came forward, no evidence about it was preserved, none of the murderers was discovered, no judicial enquiry took place. The son wanted to make his father's horrible death seem as presentable as possible; but the facts were apparently quite different.

Almost the only important step taken by the law officers who investigated the crime was to order an autopsy, as Andrei Dostoevsky himself reported. The autopsy record has not come down to us but the family knew what it contained, and not everyone kept silent about it. Dostoevsky's niece, Maria Alexandrovna Ivanova, who lived in Darovoe at the end of her life, told V. S. Nechaeva in 1926 that the murder had been committed without bloodshed and that therefore no signs of violent death were to be found on the body. At that time Danila Makarov and Andrei Savushkin, who had been serfs in Darovoye, gave the same testimony.[1] A staff member of the newspaper *Krasnaya Niva* (*Red Ploughland*) reported that same year, 1926, that he had been told by some Darovoe peasants that three peasants from Cheremoshna had made up their minds to kill their cruel master. 'As soon as he came through the gate the three men fell upon him. They did not beat him, of course; they did not want to leave marks. They had a bottle of spirits ready, poured the whole bottle down the master's throat and then gagged him with a kerchief. This suffocated him.'[2]

The records concerning this crime make clear that apart from the general hatred all peasants felt for proprietors, there were some who had special grounds for personal enmity against Dostoevsky's father.

One of the conspirators, Isaev, had a daughter, Akulina, who was only fourteen at the time of the murder. She had been taken into the master's house by his wife; so it must have been prior to 1836, when she was no more than ten or eleven. She was very pretty. The master kept her on in the house after Maria Fyodorovna's death and even had her assist him in his medical practice.

Another participant in the murder, the peasant Yefimov, had a niece named Katya, who grew up with his own children. Maria Fyodorovna had taken her into the house as a chambermaid when she was fourteen. Katya was, in Andrei Dostoevsky's words, 'full of fire'. After his wife's death the doctor made sixteen-year-old Katya his mistress and fathered a child by her, which died soon afterwards.

Mikhail Andreevich Dostoevsky's murder can be interpreted as *vengeance for a woman.*

When one considers that two of the murderers, and perhaps all four, had close female relatives among old Dostoevsky's house serfs and that the name of Katya's uncle is first among the persons named as murderers (the murder took place in the yard of the house in which Katya was raised), this interpretation seems to be confirmed.[3]

However, this was probably not the only motive for the crime. The 'abnormally quick temper and suspicious disposition of the alcoholic proprietor who vented his misfortunes and depression on his peasants' probably served as the chief cause.[4] What we know about his end from these records brings out very clearly the theme of the dissolute conduct of old Dostoevsky (his behaviour towards peasant girls).

The murdered man's body lay in the field for two days. The law officers who came from Kashira to investigate made no discoveries. They had probably been bribed by the murdered man's relatives, who were at pains to cover up his disgraceful end.

According to family tradition (reported also by Fyodor

Dostoevsky's daughter), when the news of his father's death reached Dostoevsky, he had his first serious attack of convulsions and fainting, a condition that was diagnosed much later as epilepsy.

Only a glimpse of his reaction to the murder in Cheremoshna has come down to us directly. It is contained in a letter he wrote on 16 August 1839 to his older brother Mikhail about the misfortune that had befallen the family. The future of the younger children – three sisters and two brothers – remained uncertain. Mikhail had expressed his resolve to become a father to them; he had said he would retire as soon as he finished the military engineering school, go to live in Darovoe, farm it, take care of the orphaned children and bring them up. Fyodor was impressed by these altruistic intentions and declared his readiness to help his brother in every possible way.

I shed many tears over our father's end, but now our condition is even worse. Is there anyone in the wide world more unfortunate than our poor brothers and sisters? The thought that they will be brought up by strangers devastates me.

There was already a plan afoot for the young Dostoevskys to be brought up by their rich relatives, the Kumanins. Fyodor did not approve this plan. He disliked his high-class relatives, whom he called 'paltry little souls', and did not correspond with them. Mikhail was the only one to whom, he felt, his brothers and sisters could be entrusted. 'You alone will be their salvation!' Here, for the first time in Dostoevsky's life, we encounter the Raskolnikov motif: 'My sisters will be destroyed!'

But things went the usual, practical way. The wealthy and childless Kumanins assumed responsibility for the younger Dostoevskys. They supported the boys until they completed their education and the girls until they were married. Within six months the eldest girl, nineteen-year-old Varvara, was married off to P. A. Karepin, a businessman who soon afterwards became the guardian of his entire new family, and his brother-in-law Fyodor's chief correspondent regarding money matters.

This was one of the most tragic chapters in Dostoevsky's family chronicle. The writer's daughter spoke of it in her memoirs:

All his life long he analysed the reasons for that horrible death. When he was working on the characterization of Fyodor Karamazov, perhaps he recalled his father's miserliness, which caused his sons so much suffering and angered them so, and his drunkenness and the physical revulsion he inspired in his children.

The celebrated novelist said nothing about this for forty years. But in the novel he wrote before his death he expanded his father's obituary into a shocking tale of sin, vice and crime.

FIELD ENSIGN

The autumn of 1841 marked the beginning of a new chapter in Dostoevsky's life. Promoted to the rank of field ensign-engineer, he became an external student at his school. He had to study the higher branches of military construction for two more years, but now he was a day student and free to live in his own apartment in the heart of the seething imperial capital.

Half student, half technical specialist, he felt himself to be a 'free, solitary, and independent' poet, as he wrote his brother in 1841. Above all he valued 'freedom and [his] vocation'. He lived for his dream of creative artistic achievement. Twenty years later he wrote of this period:

I was a terrific dreamer then. In my youthful fantasies I was fond of imaging myself now Pericles, now Marius, now a Christian in Nero's time, now a knight in a tournament, now

Edward Glendenning in Scott's novel *The Monastery*. What didn't I dream of in my youth! What didn't I experience with all my heart, with all my soul, in golden and inflamed daydreams that resembled opium-induced hallucinations!

But Dostoevsky the dreamer was already Dostoevsky the writer, though he had yet to discover his hero and his narrative form. Everything in him was still in a state of ferment. When several years later he wrote the story *White Nights*, notable for its strongly autobiographical psychology, he portrayed a solitary dreamer in whom one could already sense the genuine artist of ideas and words. This unknown poet fully realizes the profound drama of his vocation – the romantic isolation from surrounding reality; the destructiveness of his excessive idealism, his condemnation to loneliness, to rejection of personal happiness, to the fact that his rosy fantasies should be stillborn.

As always, reality forced its way into the meditator's cell. He might daydream about Schillerian heroes, but life capriciously wove its own narratives around him, drawing him into the circle of the events of the passing hour. He recalled one such brief drama twenty years later and related it in a carefree *feuilleton* form, that does not however conceal a sense of continuing sadness and ever-present pain.

But I had also overlooked the real Amalia. She lived right next to me, on the other side of the screen. Together we read the story of Clara Mowbray[5] and were so overcome with emotion that even now I cannot recall those evenings without experiencing a nervous shock. To repay me for reading and relating the novels to her she darned my old stockings and starched two false shirt-fronts. Towards the end, when we'd meet on our dirty staircase, where there were more eggshells than anything else, she would suddenly begin to flush in a strange manner and turn quite red. And she was so pretty, so good, so meek, with secret dreams and suppressed impulses like myself. I did not notice a thing. Or, perhaps, I did notice, but – I enjoyed reading *Kabale und Liebe* or the *Tales of Hoffmann*. Ah, how pure and innocent we were then! But Amalia suddenly married one of the poorest creatures in the world, a man of about forty-five with a bump on his nose; he lived for a while in corners of rooms in our house but the day after he found a job, he offered Amalia his hand and – utter poverty.

I remember how I said good-bye to Amalia. I kissed her pretty hand for the first time in my life, and she kissed my forehead and smiled strangely, so strangely that the smile scratched at my heart for the rest of my life. Why has all this left such an agonizing impression on my memory?

This may well be lyrical improvization, of course, and probably owes much to artistic invention, yet something in it seems to come from the author's own experience. The details may have been different, but behind them can be sensed young Dostoevsky's very real emotional life, which, along with the everyday details of its setting, was soon to become part of his early stories.

*

Fyodor's brother Mikhail continued his education in the Revel Engineering Command at Revel (now Tallinn, Estonia). In 1841 he married a local German girl, Emilia Ditmar, and by the mid 1840s he already had two children. Fyodor liked to visit his brother's family. He spent two summers with them and wrote part of *The Double* and *Mr Prokharchin* there.

He found Revel very interesting. It was the first Gothic city he had ever seen, though his studies at the engineering academy had given him a theoretical knowledge of the complex and powerful style of medieval buildings. In *Winter Notes* he recalled how in his youth, when he was studying architecture, he had so reverently made a drawing of the cathedral at Cologne, a famous example of German 'High Gothic'. In his later manuscripts he set down extremely detailed drawings of granite portals, rose windows and towers; these attested his unchanging interest in lancet architecture. Students of his work have, in fact, compared the laws of construction governing this type of architecture with the principles of structural design evident in his novels.

Gothic was the favourite style of the Romantics and was much admired by the young Goethe and by Chateaubriand. In Revel, Dostoevsky saw for the first time actual examples of western European medieval architecture, the ancient castle, the town hall, the exchange, the twelfth-century cathedral, the large guildhall and the churches and private houses with their steep-pitched roofs. He long remembered the strange, gabled skyline of this city of the Teutonic Orders and the Hanseatic League, and as late as 1869 planned a story laid in Revel.

A different city, however, was to serve as the arena and background of his work: Petersburg, in the reign of Nicholas I; a city of striking and frightening contrasts, a 'sick, strange and melancholy' city, seeming, to this impressionable observer, to be full of the dramas, trivial in their detail but far from trivial in their despair, that are the basis of his early stories.

*

Dostoevsky completed the senior officers' course on 12 August 1843. He was confronted by the unfriendly realities of life under Nicholas I. Absorbed as he had been in his literary projects, he did not graduate anywhere near the top of his class and instead of being assigned to one of the state's first-class forts, he was appointed to an exceedingly modest post under the Petersburg Command, 'to be employed by the drafting section of the Engineering Department'. His superiors would trust him only within the narrow, desk-bound limits of projective geometry and field cartography.

This did not bother the young engineer much, for he was already engrossed in constructive tasks of a different sort. His job did not satisfy his intellectual needs. He felt that he was a 'poet, not an engineer', as he recalled in 1877. He had no doubts as to his vocation: 'On the contrary, I was firmly convinced that the future still belonged to me and that I was its master.'

'BUT, LOVING LIFE . . .'

But, loving life, and to its momentary blessings
Attached by habit and environment,
With hesitant step I moved towards the goal.

Nekrasov

Dr Riesenkampf, whom Mikhail Dostoevsky had asked to keep an eye on his impractical brother, has described in his memoirs the daily life of the young writer, who had moved into his apartment with him.

The young doctor's patients were the 'proletariat of the capital'. This may have brought Bozhedomka to Dostoevsky's mind, but in this city, the seat of government, the contrasts of splendour and poverty were even more striking.

Dostoevsky used to talk with the doctor's wretched patients in the waiting-room, and there he made the acquaintance of the brother of a pianist named Keller. From him he learned how the lower strata of Petersburg's musicians lived, and this may have given him the idea for *Netochka Nezvanova*, a story about a great but unrecognized violinist, who vegetated in the orchestras of aristocratic patrons of music.

One day in the autumn of 1843 Riesenkampf returned to Petersburg from a trip to Revel and found Fyodor living on bread and milk, and in debt to a shopkeeper for that. Fyodor had recently written his brother Andrei: 'For God's sake, send me five roubles or so, or at least one rouble. I haven't had any kindling wood for three days and I don't have a kopeck.'

These dire financial straits lasted for about two months. Then in November he suddenly began to stride about the room in a manner unusual for him – loud, self-assured, with an air of pride. It turned out that he had received one thousand roubles from Moscow.

'But the very next morning,' Dr Riesenkampf wrote, 'he entered my bedroom with his usual soft, timid step and asked me to lend him five roubles.' He had lost at billiards part of the money earmarked for payment of urgent debts, and the rest had been stolen by a companion.

On 1 February 1844 Fyodor received another one thousand roubles from Moscow. As ill luck would have it, he stopped, merely out of curiosity, to watch a game of billiards at Dominique's, where he had gone to have supper. A gentleman called his attention to one of the players, who, as it happened, was a clever cheat who had bought the restaurant's entire staff. 'Now, dominoes is a perfectly innocent, honest game,' the stranger said. Dostoevsky immediately expressed his desire to learn this 'innocent' new game. It took twenty-five games, and his last hundred-rouble note was transferred to his teacher's pocket.

This episode explains a great deal about the young engineer's constant lack of money and prepares us for the drama of his mature years, portrayed so vividly in *The Gambler*, written in 1866.

Dostoevsky was far from being a hermit. He enjoyed variety performances, restaurants, cafés, officers' parties with punch, faro and other card games. Gay, pleasure-seeking Petersburg attracted him but it cost him 'terrific sums of money'.

It is not surprising that in his first years as an officer he became familiar with the special world of pawn tickets, loans, interest rates and promissory notes. The Petersburg usurer – a colourful and symbolic figure characteristic of an entire epoch, a sharp operator without heart or mercy, who made a rich living dealing in money and exploited the poor – now crossed his path for the first time.

He was a retired non-commissioned officer from an army hospital who loaned money at high interest with absolutely safe security. After obtaining from Dostoevsky a power-of-attorney, entitling him to receive Dostoevsky's salary for the next four months, and a special guarantee by the paymaster of the engineering administration, this Petersburg Gobseck* gave the young engineer a small sum from which he had deducted his enormous profit in advance. The deal impressed itself on Dostoevsky's mind and was evidently reflected some years later in his unforgettable characterizations of the usurer Alyona Ivanovna and of the owners of loan banks.

Dostoevsky hated capitalist man: the bourgeois, the philistine, the acquisitive person, the property-owner, the hoarder. He did not inherit his father's stinginess and was always generous, responsive and ready to share whatever he had. According to members of his family, he did not know how to handle money and never refused anyone who asked for it. But at the same time, contradictory as always, he very strongly desired independence, for which in his day having a great deal of money was the first prerequisite. He dreamed of material security so that he might attain artistic perfection. He was convinced that an artist must have financial security, for he must have freedom, and without sufficient money this was impossible. Like a number of other great artists, such as Balzac, Rubens and Richard Wagner, he was willing to accept wealth which would enable him to lead a full and vivid creative life. Like his Raskolnikov, he wanted to have 'all his capital at once'; he made plans to publish profitable editions of Schiller and Eugène Sue, went to law over large inheritances, aspired to become a landowner and dreamed of big winnings. These contradictions in the complex character of the author of *The Brothers Karamazov* contributed a note of high drama to his biography, and were resolved, ultimately, in tragedy. Dostoevsky not only wrote with absorption and self-oblivion, but also lived ardently, impulsively and passionately, as he admitted later

* Gobseck – a character from Balzac's novel of the same name, published in 1830.

in his life. 'Everywhere and in everything I go to the limit. All my life I have crossed the last line.' This 'maximalism' of character, this excess and extremity of feeling, this lack of emotional restraint, was an important part of his temperament and was fundamental to his work.

Love of life was strong in Dostoevsky and endowed his writing with the vividness and power that still breathe through it. In 1871, when he was nearly fifty, he wrote:

> In spite of everything I have lost, I love life ardently, I love life for life's sake, and seriously, I am still planning to *begin* my life. I will be fifty soon, yet I cannot make out whether I am ending my life or only beginning it. This is a principal attribute of my character and, perhaps, of my work.

But this trait, valuable though it is in a creative nature, produced a passionate fondness for the 'good things' of the moment, which often demanded substantial sums of money and impelled the writer to struggle hard to acquire them.

P. A. Karepin, the family guardian, reproached him thus: 'No sooner were the epaulettes on your shoulders than you began to write repeatedly in your letters of two things: the inheritance and your debts!'

Dostoevsky's financial situation became still more complicated. In 1844 he was ordered to take a trip to a distant fortress, Orenburg or Sevastopol. Such a trip would have cost him a considerable amount of money and would have taken him away from his writing for several months. Dostoevsky thereupon made up his mind to devote himself entirely to his writing, and handed in his resignation to the Department. He wrote his guardian a business letter, not concealing that he required money for a new career, namely literary work, which he felt was his vocation.

Dostoevsky's relatives did not sympathize with his desire to take up such an uncertain livelihood. Karepin argued in favour of a 'salary from the Tsar', and in his letters to his young relative he made ironical comments on the latter's admiration for Shakespeare. Dostoevsky called his guardian a Falstaff, a Chichikov* and a Famusov,† and declared that he, Dostoevsky, was unshakeable in his resolve to dedicate himself to his vocation: ' *To study people is both my primary aim and my primary amusement*!' His guardian gave in, and sent him five hundred silver roubles.

On 19 October 1844 Dostoevsky was discharged from the service at his own request, and on 7 November his name was removed from the lists of the Petersburg Engineering Command. This was an important date in his life, from then on he was free to be a writer, and to devote himself exclusively to his literary vocation. He was twenty-three years old, full of new plans and unclouded hopes. His first work had just appeared in print, a translation of *Eugénie Grandet*. 'A miracle! a miracle! The translation is unsurpassed,' he wrote to his brother.

Balzac had emerged from romanticism and had written in *Eugénie Grandet* a masterpiece of realistic art, portraying his protagonists' emotional lives in depth while at the same time developing a major social theme, namely the ruinous power of gold over the destinies of men and women.

As Dostoevsky worked on the translation he grew and matured as an artist.

It was an education for him, a practical seminar in the art of the novel. Dostoevsky's almost forgotten literary début proves that though still a novice he had already boldly and confidently mastered the medium of words, and this mastery entitled him to enter the world of writing.

That was what he thought himself. When he completed the translation and submitted the manuscript to the magazine *Repertoire and Pantheon*, he felt ready for independent creative work.

* Chichikov. An ingenious swindler, principal character in Gogol's *Dead Souls*.

† Famusov. The reactionary father of the heroine in Griboedov's comedy *Woe from Wit* (*Chatsky*).

The French novel it seems had re-educated him in many respects, and completed his formation as an artist. Gogol had disclosed to him the tragedy of everyday things. Belinsky had pointed out a whole new approach to the contemporary world. Balzac had revealed a devastating truth about life in depicting the inseparability of human characters from the social struggle of their age. His account of an orgy of rapacious instincts and the inaccessible beauty of one lonely woman's soul, the infinitude of whose emotions overcame all the horrors of a world of crime, was romanticism of a sort, but a romanticism that was at the same time profoundly realistic.

THE FIRST BOOK

In January 1844 Dostoevsky underwent an emotional experience that he called 'a vision on the Neva'. This was the inner realization of the world his dramas and images were to inhabit. He had found his heroes at last. He had begun to see a new art form that harmonized with his ideas. Now he could begin to create.

And I had a vision of another story; in some dark corner I saw the honest and pure heart of a ninth-grade civil servant,* and with him I saw a girl, insulted and sorrowing, and their whole story tore deeply at my heart.

This one sentence typifies almost all the subject matter of Dostoevsky's writing and his entire style, up to the time of his arrest. The lowly civil servant is a leading personage of the naturalistic school and can be traced back to Gogol's Petersburg tales. But the honest and pure heart in the breast of a grade-nine official and the insulted girl's heart-

* In spite of the rather high-sounding title of 'Titular Counsellor' the ninth grade was near the bottom of the fourteen grades into which the Civil Service was divided.

breaking sadness – that is the internal world of man, that is Balinsky's definition of Romanticism, a movement which, to him, was conceived first and foremost with the 'secret life' of the human personality.

Dostoevsky completed a first novel the length of *Eugénie Grandet* in the spring of 1845, and concentrated all his plans and expectations on it. ·

On the title page he wrote *Poor Folk*: this was to be the motto and the programme of all his future work.

*

In an article entitled 'Continental Affairs', written in 1843, Engels had noted the 'complete revolution' that had taken place in European literature in recent years: 'The place of kings and princes, who used to be the heroes, is gradually being taken by the poor man, the disinherited class, whose life and destiny, need and suffering form the substance of novels. This new direction in such writers as George Sand, Eugène Sue and Dickens is undoubtedly a sign of the times.' These were the authors whom, as we have seen, Dostoevsky had been reading avidly, and naturally enough these new protagonists appeared in his work too.

It is very interesting to observe the struggle between past and future styles in Dostoevsky's first story, where this novice at realistic writing is not strong enough to make the complete break with his older, romantic, manner, and firmly maintain the profound innovations in literary method that were to receive world-wide acclaim in his later works.

On all sides the demand was for everyday, prosaic, familiar characters. In 1845 the critic of *Finsky Vestnik* (*Finnish Herald*) wrote: 'Our favourite hero now is not a poet, not an improviser, not an artist, but a civil servant or, even more likely, a tax farmer, a usurer, in general, an acquisitive person.'

Dostoevsky responded to the temper of the times and centred his early work around the most ordinary people of the day, civil servants, tax-farmers, hoarders, serf-owners, and even the procuresses of Petersburg. But the young author was unable to give up his beloved characters – the poet, the improviser, the artist, 'Napoleons of every sort', as Belinsky expressed it. Hence his dreamers and admirers of Pushkin, who were the favourite heroes of the preceding generation. They were necessary to him, to convey and express his most cherished artistic aims, which were not to be stifled by the naturalistic techniques he had adopted. These heroes advance confidently to the foreground, and their proud images overshadow the minor civil servants and moral outcasts of the capital. A fountain of romanticism gushes forth from young Dostoevsky's naturalistic characterizations.

That is how his first novel is constructed, the everyday details and the social background against which his characters play out their hopeless dramas are reproduced with great precision. Petersburg under Nicholas I is depicted in the manner of the naturalistic school – big, black, soot-covered buildings, puffs of smoke in the fog; the slippery Fontanka Embankment where filthy women sell rotten apples and soggy gingerbread; Gorokhovaya Street, with its rich shops and luxurious carriages (a sketch in the manner of 'Nevsky Prospekt'), contrasted with close-ups of petit-bourgeois life; a dirty staircase crowded with rubbish and wash-tubs, clothes hung out to dry, giving off a sickly sweet smell of decay that pervaded the building and was 'enough to kill off the sparrows'.

The novel contained something else, to which the writers of the naturalistic school gave no thought – the tragedy of deep emotions, wounded and trampled by life. Dostoevsky's principal objective was to portray love as poor people are condemned to experience it. It was not the shabby civil service uniform or the dying sparrows that were frightening, but the stifling social atmosphere, in which the highest manifestation of the free human personality was doomed to destruction. The novel's basic theme is the spiritual relationship between noble, humble people in the cruel grip of the existing system. The mutual attraction between Makar Devushkin and Varenka Dobroselova is subjected to the ordeal of a pitiless world; a sensitive girl has been sold in advance to a wealthy rake and is then turned over to him to be his property for ever. Social contradictions are thus central to this psychological drama which in many ways anticipates Dostoevsky's later works.

This was the 'new world' that so amazed the young writer's contemporaries: the power and the right of love trampled by reality but retaining, even under the yoke of a despotic regime, its significance as the supreme value in life. Even Gogol had said nothing about this. *Poor Folk* was a 'sentimental novel' (as Dostoevsky himself once described his *White Nights*), except that it was set against the background of the terrible poverty in Petersburg in the 1840s: the romantic heritage reappeared in the new guise of realistic narrative. It was this that was to give some critics grounds for calling the young author's style 'sentimental naturalism'.

That was why this story about the poor of Petersburg posed problems that were quite unfamiliar to the sketch-writers of the 1840s. Conceived in a fervour of high morality, its theme is of supreme nobility, utter sincerity, selfless love and inner perfection. Makar Devushkin was Dostoevsky's first 'beautiful man', his earliest 'poor knight'. Like Prince Myshkin, Devushkin is not ridiculous but tragic. His is a pure and self-sacrificing soul, afire with love and compassion, but doomed to destruction in a heartless world of violence and universal commercialism.

Such was the new note that had been sounded in Russian literature. Devushkin mentions two stories, one by Pushkin and one by Gogol, that have given him fresh insight into the meaning of his existence. But 'The Overcoat' disturbs him because the object of the drama in it was not alive and because the downtrodden little man seemed to feel no profound emotional pain. 'The Postmaster' on the other hand, '*is my own heart*'. The ingenuous Devushkin expresses a perfectly correct judgement on this story of the bitter lot of a collegiate registrar* who has lost his daughter; indeed the pain of it reveals to him the innermost drama of his own soul. In *Poor Folk* the inner life of the hero is worked out by the method of the naturalist school. But Dostoevsky's subject is not everyday life but a human heart pining away from deep feelings for a creature as oppressed and unfortunate as itself.

The other leading theme of *Poor Folk* also has antecedents in the more distant past. The fate of a seduced girl was a common subject in eighteenth-century literature (*La Nouvelle Héloïse, Clarissa Harlowe, Poor Liza*); but Dostoevsky modernized the old story and developed it in an atmosphere typical of Petersburg in the forties. Years later, in *The Idiot*, he drew against this same background of the capitalist city the overwhelming and sorrowful image of a pure womanly heart destroyed in the frightful world of unbridled instincts and the omnipotence of money.

Poor Folk has still another characteristic Dostoevskian theme, one that gives his naturalistic portrayals the depth of genuine, great art. This is the theme of the creator, the thinker, the poet, which became his principal preoccupation. The first embodiment of this idea was the still sketchy but distinctive portrayal of the young writer Pyotr Pokrovsky, living in poverty among his books and manuscripts and worshipping Pushkin. Here we have an early portrait of the spiritual hero, who twenty years later, after the author himself had passed through philosophical struggles of agonizing complexity, was to emerge as Raskolnikov.

Dostoevsky's first novel took a long time to write. It was conceived and begun early in 1844. It was originally intended to be the story of a provincial girl's misadventures in

* Collegiate registrar. Civil servant of the lowest (fourteenth) grade.

the big city, and this concept was partially retained in the final version as the autobiographical notes of Varenka Dobroselova. ('I was only fourteen when father died.')

But apparently the ordinary diary form failed to satisfy Dostoevsky; the naïve style of a young girl's confessions did not offer sufficient scope for a Balzacian presentation of a contemporary drama, of a cruel struggle of instincts and lusts, played out against the vivid background of the period.

So Dostoevsky turned to the old form of the epistolary novel, which had been revived in the newest French literature, and found in it a genre flexible enough to express the most profound and the most subtle emotions. George Sand had used this method in her novel *Jacques*, the hero of which was associated by some Russian critics with Makar Devushkin.

Dostoevsky adopted this revived lyrical form of narrative prose and inaugurated his literary career with a simple and arresting epistolary beginning:

April 8. My precious Varvara Alexeyevna! I was happy yesterday, exceedingly happy, impossibly happy! For once in your life, stubborn girl, you listened to me.

What emotion, how much love and anxiety! This is the voice of a great writer. In the very first lines one can hear the authentic tones of the future novelist–poet. A new path was opening up. He had found his major emotional theme of selfless love, and in the lovers' letters he had found a means of expressing its depth and poetry.

This newly discovered technique transformed everything. He introduced unforeseen motifs into the original version of his story; he brought his meek and high-minded hero to the foreground, made the theme of sacrificial love central to his design, and created a series of epistolary confessions and declarations that revealed a lover's inexhaustible capacity for bringing his beloved happiness even at the cost of his own life. The action developed and gave flesh to the original image of an unhappy and 'beautiful man', and turned him into the hero of Varenka's radically transformed love story.

In this manner Dostoevsky's creative system took shape. It was a system that ultimately found expression in an inexhaustible abundance of plots and variations on plots, in a turbulent flow of themes and character types, in a dizzying sequence of ideas that led to endless rewriting and unflinching burning of entire chapters and sections; the incessant process of construction and destruction constantly in pursuit of a fleeting perfection, a perfection that he always had courage and insight enough to master in the end, though it brought him to the brink of despair.

IN THE LITERARY WORLD

III

The Belinsky Whirlwind

AFTER ten months of intensive work the story was ready. As Grigorovich, who shared an apartment with Dostoevsky at the time, wrote:

> One morning Dostoevsky called to me to come into his room. Before him on a small desk lay a rather thick notebook of large writing paper with turned down edges, covered with small handwriting.
>
> 'Sit down, Grigorovich, I only finished copying it yesterday. I want to read it to you, and don't interrupt,' he said with unusual animation.
>
> What he read to me at one sitting, hardly stopping at all, was soon to appear in print under the title *Poor Folk*.

The listener was 'impressed beyond words'. Grigorovich, who had already embarked on a literary career himself with his essay on 'The Organ-Grinders of Petersburg', knew from his contacts in the publishing world that Nekrasov was gathering material for a literary miscellany. He decided to show him Dostoevsky's manuscript.

That very evening Grigorovich and Nekrasov sat down to read the new story. They had assumed that ten pages would be enough to base their judgement on, but they could not stop, and read the entire manuscript of almost two hundred pages in a single sitting. The story's dramatic power amazed them. The scene of the student's funeral, with the old father, deeply anguished, running bareheaded after his son's coffin in the icy rain, his son's beloved books falling from his hands into the muddy street like farewell flowers, was shocking in its everyday tragedy. Grigorovich later told Dostoevsky:

Nekrasov was reading the part about the student's death, and suddenly, at the place where the father runs after the coffin, I noticed his voice break once, then again, and then he slapped his hand down on the manuscript and exclaimed: 'Ah, confound him!' Meaning you, and we went on like that all night long.

Soon afterwards, Nekrasov wrote about the 'incomparable characters' created by the budding writer. The story's denouement laid bare the depth of life's hopeless horror. The landlord Bykov, the helpless girl's seducer, had to get married for business reasons. He visited her unexpectedly and, accompanied by the suppressed sobs of the old civil servant, now doomed to a lonely death, he carried her off to his desolate house in the steppe. Grigorovich recalled:

I was reading. On the last page, when old Devushkin took leave of Varenka, I could no longer control myself and began to sob. I stole a look at Nekrasov. Tears were rolling down his cheeks.

The friends decided to go to Dostoevsky at once.

Dostoevsky was deeply touched by this unusual visit at so late an hour – towards the end of the bright white night – and in 1871 described the occasion:

They stayed with me for about half an hour. And in that half hour we talked about a vast number of things, understanding one another with half a word, exclaiming and hurrying; we talked of poetry, truth, the 'current situation', and Gogol, needless to say, quoting from *The Inspector-General* and *Dead Souls*, but chiefly we talked of Belinsky. 'I shall take your story to him this very day. Now, sleep, sleep, we are leaving, but tomorrow you must come to us.'

Dostoevsky could not fall asleep. The admiration of the very first readers of his tale filled his heart with a happiness he had never tasted before. He had set down his observations and thoughts 'with passion, almost with tears', and now they had reached other human hearts and struck them with untold force. Then anxiety took the place of this intoxicating joy. What would Belinsky say? How would 'that terrible and frightening critic' evaluate his manuscript? Besides, was it even possible for an unknown author to have a conversation with this authoritative judge of literary values, whose articles had already revealed to Dostoevsky so many secrets of the art of literature?

Nekrasov rushed into Belinsky's office that May morning and announced to the leader of 'naturalism' that 'a new Gogol' had appeared. 'Vissarion Grigoryevich! Read this, for God's sake, read this manuscript as soon as you can! If I am not mistaken, fate has sent our literature a brilliant new artist. In my opinion, it is a superb work.'[1] Belinsky listened to the young poet's eulogy with scepticism, but he yielded to Nekrasov's insistence and took the manuscript to read. From the very first page it captured his interest; increasingly fascinated as he went on, he read it through without stopping. When Nekrasov returned that evening he found Belinsky in a state of enthusiasm and feverish agitation. The critic declared:

The most striking thing about Dostoevsky is his astonishing ability to bring his characters to life before the reader's eyes and to draw their portraits in only two or three words. And then, what profound, warm compassion for the poor and the suffering. Tell me, is he a poor man who has suffered much himself? He must be. Only a genius with the insight to grasp in one minute what it takes an ordinary man many years to understand could write such a book at the age of twenty-five.

The two friends talked late into the night about the new story and its author, whom Nekrasov promised to bring to Belinsky the next day. Though it was very late, Nekrasov stopped by at Dostoevsky's and with boyish enthusiasm conveyed to him Belinsky's opinion of *Poor Folk*. The young novelist's pensive face lit up with extraordinary happiness.

Belinsky's first visitor the next day was P. V. Annenkov, a literary friend. Belinsky was standing by the window with a thick notebook in his hands, his face flushed with emotion.

He told his friend that this manuscript by a new talent was the first attempt in Russia to write a 'social novel'. He also called attention to the story's philosophical theme, the failure of idealism and the futility of sentimental dreaming in the harsh conditions of contemporary social existence. Belinsky described the story to Annenkov:

It is very simple. There are these kindhearted eccentrics who believe that to love the whole world is an exceptional pleasure and a duty for everyone. They cannot even begin to understand what is happening when the wheel of life, with all its contrivances, rides over them and crushes their bones and limbs in silence. This is all there is – but what drama, what characters!

And in nervous excitement Belinsky began to read aloud the places that had struck him most forcefully. These were, judging from his published reviews, the scenes in the director's office, at Gorshkov's deathbed, at young Pokrovsky's funeral, and Varenka's departure (Makar Devushkin's last letter). 'Everything here is true, profound, and significant!'

The day after this Nekrasov called for Dostoevsky at the appointed hour but found him in a state of great confusion. The shy and anxious author stubbornly refused to go to Belinsky's.

'What am I to him? What role shall I play there? What do we have in common? He is a scholar, a well-known writer, a famous critic, and I – what am I?'

'Fyodor Mikhailovich! Fyodor Mikhailovich! What humility! And towards whom? Haven't I read *Poor Folk*? Hasn't Belinsky read it?'

'So what, so what?' Dostoevsky asked softly and slyly, restraining a smile.

But a minute later the shadow of doubt and fear reappeared on his face, which 'used to change a thousand times a minute', Nekrasov recalled, 'sometimes resembling a dark cloud, then suddenly lighting up with a dazzling light, like sun sparkling in the frost'. Finally, after much persuasion,

Dostoevsky decided to try his luck, and the two young writers set out to visit the famous critic.

Belinsky lived in a big house on the corner of the Nevsky and the Fontanka, where he had a courtyard apartment whose two rooms, reached by a dark staircase, had windows facing the stables. The sun never penetrated as far as this.

But the critic's office was very clean and neat. There was not a speck of dust anywhere, the floors were polished to a mirror-like shine, the desk was in immaculate order, plants and flowers stood on the window sills, portraits of friends and favourite poets hung on the wall, and busts and statues of Voltaire, Rousseau, Goethe, Pushkin and Gogol were placed on the bookcases beside them.

The visitors were greeted by a man of somewhat less than average height with irregular features but a remarkable and original face. His blond hair fell over his forehead, and he had the hard and uneasy expression so frequently encountered in shy and solitary people. His manner was typically Russian, typically Muscovite. As he began to speak he started coughing, but he soon recovered and became animated. With a friendly smile he questioned the young author about his work on the story and spoke in passing about the tempo of creative work with Pushkin, Byron and Gogol. He showed his guests his collection of autographs of famous writers.

Belinsky's friendly reception calmed the embarrassed Dostoevsky. He listened avidly to the critic's words. Belinsky concentrated his analysis on the chief character in the new novel:

Take your unfortunate civil servant. Why, he has served so thoroughly and brought himself to such a point that he doesn't even dare to consider himself unfortunate, so humble is he, and he regards the slightest complaint as verging on freethinking. He dare not recognize even the right to his own unhappiness, and when that good man, his general, gives him those hundred roubles he is shattered, destroyed by amazement that 'his Excellency' could have taken pity on a person like himself. Or take the button that came off, or his attempts to kiss the general's hand – why, it is no longer pity that one feels for the unfortunate creature, but horror, horror! And there is horror in that gratitude of his! It is a tragedy! You have touched the very heart of the matter, you have gone directly to the chief thing.

Belinsky became more and more excited, and said finally:

This is the secret of artistic value, this is truth in art! *This is the artist's service to youth*! To you, as an artist, truth has been revealed and proclaimed; it has come to you as a gift; value this gift and remain faithful to it, and you will be a greater writer!

Dostoevsky left Belinsky's 'in ecstasy' and stopped at the corner, on Anichkov Bridge.

It was a bright day, and people hurried by along the Nevsky Prospekt. The Fontanka Canal reflected the clear, pale spring sky. The tamers of Klodt's bronze horses, mirrored in the barely moving water, shimmering slightly. 'This has been a solemn moment in my life, *changing it for ever*' – Dostoevsky felt through and through that it was 'something quite new, but something that I had not ever expected, even in my wildest dreams'. An unknown, boundlessly creative life lay before him. The foremost figure in Russian literature had initiated him into the brotherhood of Russian writers. He made a silent vow. 'This was the most exhilarating moment of my whole life. I used to recall it when I was undergoing penal servitude, and feel strengthened in spirit,' wrote the author of Russia's first 'social novel' thirty years later.

AT THE PANAEVS

Nekrasov and Grigorovich introduced Dostoevsky into the Panaev home. This was one of the centres of Petersburg's cultural life. Many readings, conversations and discussions took place there. For Dostoevsky this literary salon proved to be an important stage in his private life. It was here that he experienced his first love – a spiritual, idealistic, poetic, secret love. And, above all, an *aesthetic* love.

Panaev arranged a special evening at his house, to introduce an unpublished novelty, the story *Poor Folk*, to literary Petersburg. 'Dostoevsky read himself; he was a shy man in those days', one listener recalled, 'but his reading made a shattering impression on everyone.'

Ivan Ivanovich Panaev played a prominent role in Belinsky's circle and was one of the fashionable fiction writers of the 1840s. His tales *Onagr The Wild Ass*, *Aketon* and *Literary Aphid* were read with the liveliest interest. He was a good-natured and frivolous man, 'a child and a flighty creature', in his friend Belinsky's words. Dostoevsky valued straightforward natures of this kind and kept up his literary relationship with Panaev for a long time.

This entertaining but unprofound novelist had married a celebrated beauty, Avdotya Yakovlevna Bryanskaya, the daughter of a tragedian well known during Pushkin's youth. She grew up in the atmosphere of the theatre. The Karatygins, the Samoilovs, Martynov, Semyenov and Asenkov were friends of the family. On the advice of the celebrated choreographer Didlo, the girl trained to be a dancer, and this gave her figure a flexibility and her movement a grace that she never lost. The young writers found even more to admire in her sculptured features, her high colour and smooth olive complexion, her marble forehead, framed by smoothly combed black hair.

Despite her beauty she was unhappy. Her frivolous husband had one affair after another. She had no children. Stores of unspent love weighed heavily on her warm, responsive heart. Several years later Nekrasov, who became the companion of her life, described her passionate nature as manifested in a moment of jealous indignation:

> Her hair fell down about her shoulders,
> Her lips burned, her cheeks were flushed,

And unbridled speech
Poured forth in terrible reproaches.

It was on 15 November 1845, when his friends took Dostoevsky into the Panaevs' drawing-room, that he first met this dazzling beauty from the world of culture. Exceedingly responsive towards manifestations of triumphant, vital beauty, he apparently succumbed on sight to the finely moulded face of this Russian woman, then in the full flower of her extraordinary charm. She was twenty-five at the time. She loved life, festivities, entertainment and luxury, but at the same time she was unusually kind and sympathetic. It was this that made her so irresistible. Dostoevsky was overwhelmed by his first love, which opened up to him a new world of profound emotional experiences.

This was a major event in his life. 'Russians have a quite sensitive feeling for beauty and are susceptible to it,' he wrote from personal experience twenty years later. But in his early youth he had been so engrossed in his manuscripts and books that he had completely ignored his emotional life. And his literary activity had diverted him even more forcibly from romantic experiences. His second wife Anna Grigoryevna spoke of this:

I asked Fyodor Mikhailovich about his love affairs, and it seemed strange to me that, judging from his reminiscences, he had never been seriously and ardently in love in his youth. I believe that the reason for this was that he began to live an intellectual life too early. Creative work absorbed him completely and this was why his private life receded to the background. Next, all his thoughts were taken up with the political affair for which he paid so cruelly.

Evidently Mme Panaeva treated Dostoevsky with her customary warm attention and had no inkling of the role she was playing in his life. The day after the reception Dostoevsky wrote to his brother: 'Yesterday I was at Panaev's for the first time, and I think I have fallen in love with his wife. She is a celebrated woman in Petersburg. She is intelligent and pretty, and on top of everything else she is as kind and straightforward as can be.' And a few weeks later: '*I was seriously in love with Panaeva*, but it is passing now, although I'm still not sure . . .' Dostoevsky's instinct was right when he realized that Mme Panaeva was intelligent. She was soon to appear on the literary scene, and write several novels and (towards the end of her life) a well-known book of memoirs, *Russian Writers and Actors*.

While A. G. Dostoevskaya did not touch upon this episode in her *Reminiscences* (which covered a different period), she did attach some significance to it in private conversation. She once told me that

The infatuation with Panaeva was fleeting, yet it was his only infatuation in his young manhood. The not unintelligent and, apparently, sensitive Panaeva took pity on Dostoevsky, who was beginning to become an object of ridicule in her house, and he repaid her with deep-felt gratitude and the tenderness of sincere love.[2]

The note of sympathy and compassion for a painfully impressionable man, who had got into a circle of mocking young literary people, is heard again in Mme Panaeva's recollections of her meetings with the budding author of *Poor Folk*.

Soon after this, however, Dostoevsky stopped going to their house. His infatuation seems to have passed without affecting his work at all. That Panaeva's Christian name was given to one of the remarkable beauties in Dostoevsky's novels, Avdotya Romanovna Raskolnikova, might have been coincidence. But twenty years later, in his favourite work *The Idiot*, he immortalized this unusual Russian beauty, marked by deep suffering and suffused with spiritual strength. A mid-nineteenth-century watercolour of Panaeva shows a young woman with delicate features, smoothly combed black hair, and an expression of anxious reflection and inner pain on her face. This is precisely the impression

Prince Myshkin received from a portrait of Nastasia Filippovna: 'There seemed to be boundless pride and contempt,
almost hatred, in that face, and at the same time something
trusting, something amazingly ingenuous. As one looked at
the face these contrasts even aroused compassion of a sort.'

Beauty becomes a spiritual thing, reborn on the moral
plane, posing the problem of goodness. 'Is she good?'
Myshkin asked. 'Ah, if she were good all would be saved.'

The contrasts of Panaeva's nature were resolved in a
feeling of direct and active love (she demonstrated this later,
when, with uncommon selflessness, she took care of the dying
Dobrolyubov). Dostoevsky, with his inherent sensitivity,
understood this, and his heart was drawn to this woman, the
first he had ever met whose spirit matched her outward
beauty. But it was not for him to catch this free-spirited
society lady. This is how Panaeva described him in her
memoirs:

It was evident from the first glance that Dostoevsky was a
terribly nervous and impressionable young man. He was thin,
small, light-haired, with a sickly complexion. His small grey
eyes moved rather anxiously from object to object and his pale
lips twitched nervously. At first he was very shy and took no part
in the general conversation. But it was not long before he showed
himself to be an ardent debater. Because of his youth and
nervousness he was unable to control himself, and was too
obvious in showing his self-esteem as an author and his high
opinion of his own talent.

Dostoevsky's next story, *The Double*, served as the cause of
the first disagreements.

A POEM OF ST PETERSBURG

One evening at the beginning of December 1845 Belinsky
arranged a gathering at his home to read and discuss Dostoevsky's new story *The Double*. The author read aloud the
first three chapters, which unfolded the drama of a man

insulted by not being received at dinner in the home of State Counsellor* Berendeger – father of the charming Clara. Turgenev, Grigorovich, Annenkov and other members of the circle were present. Dostoevsky's second work was probably the most controversial thing he ever wrote. Though it had been conceived within the circle of ideas associated with Belinsky's magazine *Otechestvennie Zapiski* (*Notes of the Fatherland*), as a whole, it ran counter to the principles of the realistic school and evoked sharp objections. Belinsky himself gave a particularly detailed critique. Since we can learn from them something of the evolution of Dostoevsky's style, perhaps the antecedents of this story merit a closer look.

In 1845 an excerpt from Lermontov's unfinished story 'Stoss' had appeared in print. The hero, the artist Lugin, is a tragic figure, ugly and unattractive to women. He goes into seclusion and surrenders to his depression. His spleen increases until it becomes an obsession: the faces of the people surrounding him seem to be yellow, as in the canvases of Spanish portrait painters. He begins to have hallucinations. His mind is clearly breaking down.

This subtle sketch of mental illness was drawn against the background of an unsightly street in the capital: a November morning, wet snow, dirty buildings, purplish-grey figures passing quickly by in the fog, noise and laughter in a basement beer hall – all of which reappear in Dostoevsky's Petersburg. It is very interesting that Lugin moves into a big house with a dirty staircase and a multitude of apartments in Stolyarny Street at Kokushkin Bridge: exactly the same address as Raskolnikov's. In the Lermontov excerpt the address echoes Lugin's fixed aural hallucination.

Lermontov's story appeared in V. A. Sollogub's miscellany *Vchera i Segodnya* (*Yesterday and Today*), which Belinsky reviewed in the May 1845 issue of *Otechestvennie Zapiski*. With his usual perception he wrote of it:

* The fifth grade in the Russian Civil Service, equivalent to Brigadier in the Army.

Even though the content is fantastic, the reader is willy-nilly impressed by the story's skill and powerful atmosphere, as if laid on with a thick brush over an unfinished canvas.

Belinsky's review, printed about the time he made Dostoevsky's acquaintance, might have called the young author's attention to the story.

The Double was, apparently, conceived in May 1845; in the summer of 1845 Dostoevsky worked on it intensively while staying with his brother in Revel. We find the first mention of the new work in a letter written to his brother Mikhail from Petersburg in early September 1845: 'Golyadkin has gained something from my *spleen*'; precisely the word Lermontov had used to describe his sick hero's state.

But Dostoevsky, as always, went his own way and elaborated his own grand design. He always retained a special affection for his unrecognized story. 'Its idea was quite brilliant,' he recalled thirty years later, 'and I have never brought anything to literature more serious than this idea. But I had no success at all with the form of this story.'

The Double was a psychological study in depth of a split personality, that is, of the acute mental suffering of an unremarkable and harmless government clerk who had been roughly trampled on by life; he was mercilessly thrown out of his circle because, as he believed, of reports submitted against him by a secret spy, actually a creation of his own sick imagination and personifying, as it were, all his own weaknesses, shortcomings and vices.

This story of mental illness was closely interwoven with certain social phenomena of the period, indicating beyond doubt the depth and pertinence of the author's purpose. Dobrolyubov was the first to call attention to this theme: Golyadkin's madness, the perceptive critic noted, had social causes. He goes mad 'in consequence of the unfortunate disharmony between the poor remnants of his humanity and the bureaucratic demands of his position'. He falls in love with a girl from the upper civil service circle and is pushed aside as an undesirable suitor – 'and that was when all his concepts were turned upside down'. It is the drama of Golyadkin's social circumstances that grows into mental tragedy.

In the first versions of the story one of the main features of Golyadkin's insanity was, to use his own expression, *the historic idea*, 'In our age, Otrep'evs are impossible.'* The ancient political phenomenon of the impostor here takes on the character of moral lawlessness and bogus spiritual authority.

In *The Double* the timid little man had been frightened by imperial Petersburg, which watches him with its vigilant eye and encircles him with mysterious forces. This is what drives him mad. Dostoevsky's hero had a predecessor in Pushkin's 'poor Yevgeni', who is chased by bronze Peter, symbol of the relentless and vengeful autocracy:

> And all night long,
> Wherever the poor madman turned,
> The Horseman of Bronze galloped after him
> With heavily clattering hoofbeat.[3]

The system of Nicholas I, with its oppression and terrors, in fact produced many real persecution manias.

The young Dostoevsky himself was, according to one of his friends, extremely withdrawn, cautious, fearful and socially over-anxious. This must be why he called *The Double* a confession; it was the story of his own secret inner drama. It is significant that in 1866 he introduced into the plans for a second version one Antonelli, who had played a similarly destructive role in his own private life. Even in the early version of the story this theme was hinted at, and gave the tale sharp political overtones.

After the uprising of 14 December 1825 the political

* Grishka Otrep'ev was a runaway monk who pretended to be the Tsarevich Dmitri, son of Ivan the Terrible, and with Polish support led the rebellion against Boris Godunov.

police in Russia, already formidable in Arakcheev's* time, were reorganized and reinforced. Informing was widespread and continued to increase and become more sophisticated until, on the threshold of the revolution of 1848, it had reached an incredible scale. Writers, who suffered particularly under such a regime, sometimes ventured to note down those horrible 'grimaces' of contemporary reality. Vidocq Figlyarin in Pushkin's epigrams and *feuilletons*, Sprich in Lermontov's 'Masquerade' and Zagoretsky in *Woe from Wit* (*Chatsky*) perform this sort of satirical function. In Belinsky's well-known description, the period of Nicholas I was one of lies and deprivation of rights, 'where Pushkin lived in poverty and died a victim of baseness, and the Greches and Bulgarins manage all literature with the help of informers and live off the fat of the land'.

Lesser people also suffered under the system. Golyadkin in fear and trembling denies charges of free-thinking; but he knows that his enemies' machinations can not be halted. 'It's clear, they bribed, snooped, practised witchcraft, crystal-gazed, spied, and in the end what they wanted was to destroy Mr Golyadkin once and for all.'

In the early 1860s Dostoevsky planned a second edition to develop these ideas, which had been painstakingly camouflaged from the censors in 1846. In notes that have come down to us for an episode called 'Mr Golyadkin at Petrashevsky's' he developed the theme of secret persecution openly and directly, on the basis of his own experience as a young man.

He had planned a daring turn of plot that would bring the theme into broad daylight. The hero was to be followed into a political club by his crafty double, who warns the president that Golyadkin senior, who has inquired about the club's weekly meetings, is an *agent-provocateur* who will denounce the president (Petrashevsky) to the authorities. When

* Arakcheev, the reactionary minister of Paul I and his son Alexander I.

the slandered hero tries to frustrate the intrigue and open the Fourierist Petrashevsky's eyes to the real danger, Petrashevsky, already falsely warned against Golyadkin, says to him: 'You are the one who is the informer!'

From then on the slandered protagonist is not only unable to take part in the socialist circle but is even compelled to go into immediate hiding.

Dostoevsky's sketches for a new version of *The Double* express his intention clearly: 'Mr Golyadkin at Petrashevsky's. The younger man makes speeches. Timkovsky is a visitor. He insinuates himself into the confidence of the new member. *The Fourier system. Noble tears. They embrace. He will inform.*'

The most awful thing about this double was that his presence resulted in madness. Dostoevsky, who constantly talked with Dr S. D. Yanovsky about nervous diseases and was treated by him for unexplained fainting spells and brain seizures (an incipient form of epilepsy), could probably observe and describe complex cases of dual consciousness from his own sensations.

The idea of *The Double* continued to possess Dostoevsky's mind even after Mr Golyadkin's adventures were completed. In *The Landlady*, which he wrote shortly afterwards, he portrayed a Petersburg police detective:

His 'steely eyes' and attempts to get inside one's soul hinted at features typical not only of the Tsarist gendarmerie but also of Nicholas I himself, who, when with his victims, liked to play the role of their sentimental friend and an admirer of science and the arts.

The significance of this theme was apparent even upon the first reading of the story. According to Grigorovich, *The Double* made a strong impression on Belinsky, who sat opposite the author during the reading, 'hung avidly on every word, and in some places, unable to conceal his admiration, kept saying that only Dostoevsky could find such remarkable psychological subtleties.' Soon afterwards, Belinsky wrote of it:

> To anyone who understands the secrets of art, it is clear from the first glance that there is even more artistic talent and profundity of thought in *The Double* than in *Poor Folk*. This is a 'completely new world', discovered and recreated here for the first time. The story is striking for its 'emotional atmosphere and the author's skill in expressing a daring idea that is carried out with amazing artistry'.

The critic objected only to certain defects of form and a lack of sense of proportion, but in his view even the author's errors served only as 'proof of how much talent he had and how great that talent was'.

Dostoevsky listened to Belinsky's exhortations good-naturedly and indifferently, like a fully mature author. But he agreed with the critic's opinion that the form of *The Double* was a failure and was in need of reshaping. 'Why should I forfeit an excellent idea, *a character type of supreme social importance*, which I was the first to discover and which I heralded?' he wrote in 1859. Until the end of his life Dostoevsky continued to search for the appropriate embodiment of this 'brilliant and extremely serious' idea of his, trying again and again, and never ceasing to make the theme more complex and profound in each new novel he wrote.

Only in his last book was he to create the overwhelming image of Ivan Karamazov, an image distorted and exposed by his frightful companions, the lackey Smerdyakov and the Devil. Shortly before he died Dostoevsky realized his cherished plan; he reworked his early *The Double* in Ivan Karamazov's 'three conversations' and 'nightmare'. The agonizing search for a form that would suit the difficult design had ended at last. The hazy outlines of 1845, now including the story of the most horrible of crimes – parricide – are developed into the tragedy of a mighty intellect, beaten down by horror and despair at his own moral collapse.

REBELLION OR UTOPIA?

Dostoevsky had been reading Belinsky's articles with interest long before he met their author, in fact ever since the late 1830s and early 1840s, when Belinsky was undergoing an extremely profound crisis in his world outlook – overcoming his period of 'reconciliation with reality'. At that time Belinsky had not entirely abandoned his Hegelian position, something that attracted the young romantic. Belinsky's decisive turn soon afterwards to democratism and concern with social problems carried his zealous reader along with him too. In 1845 Dostoevsky could have read such articles by the mature Belinsky as 'The Secrets of Paris', 'Prince Odoevsky's Works', 'The Poems of Lermontov', 'The Adventures of Chichikov', and the celebrated 'Works of Alexander Pushkin' series still incomplete at that time. By 1844 Belinsky had already declared that it was a noble task to display to a depraved and egoistic society the spectacle of the suffering of those unfortunates whom contemporary civilization doomed to ignorance, poverty, vice and crime.

But young Dostoevsky did not regard socialism as a path to revolution; to him socialism was rather a new Sermon on the Mount, an appeal for brotherhood in the kingdom of universal war for power and money. The leaders of Utopian socialism compared their doctrine with Christianity and wanted nothing more than to revive the ancient doctrine in a manner appropriate to the current needs of society. The poet of the Petersburg poor accepted this, and it was his belief in altruistic 'morality' and personal 'saintliness' that was at the root of his subsequent ideological quarrel with that great rebel Belinsky, who by then had begun to seek in the latest theory of class struggle a strategy for the decisive battle against the doomed world that tolerated slavery and poverty.

While all this shows beyond doubt that Belinsky played a

major part in bringing the young writer into contact with the advanced social trends of the day, it also suggests the sharp differences in their political orientation. The lover of mankind who wrote *Poor Folk* and who himself called his early humanitarianism 'rose-coloured', 'heavenly-moral' and Christ-loving, rejected the Jacobin *coup d'état* methods that his teacher advocated. In 1849 Dostoevsky stated that he recognized Belinsky only for his earlier articles on aesthetics, 'which were written with truly great knowledge of the writing process'. Dostoevsky held dear the moral ideal of a community to come, with its poetry of love and cult of justice. Belinsky, on the other hand, was an advocate of early communism, which he had already begun to see as the system of the future, recognizing that it could not be established without revolutionary methods of struggle.

A statement that Dostoevsky made towards the end of his life about one such declaration by Belinsky has come down to us, though the novelist was never able to get it published. In 1873 he said to Vsevolod Solovyov:

'About Belinsky, for example,' he opened the issue of *Grazhdanin* [*The Citizen*] that contained his first *The Diary of a Writer* – 'did I say everything in this? Could I have said everything? They don't understand him at all, not at all. All I wanted to do was to cite his own words – nothing more – and I was not allowed to do so.'

'Why not?'

'Because they were unsuitable for publication.'

He recounted to me one conversation with Belinsky that indeed could not be printed and led me to remark that, after all, it was a long way from words to deeds, that anyone could briefly entertain the most monstrous thoughts yet would never turn them into deeds, and that there are people who occasionally like to affect cynicism and speak almost boastfully of some wild idea.

'Of course, of course, only Belinsky was not that sort of person – he meant what he said. His nature was a simple, integral whole in which words and deeds went together. Others might think something over a hundred times before venturing to do it and then still would not do it, but not he. And, you know, lately more and more such natures are being bred – what they say, they do: I'll shoot myself, and he shoots himself; I'll shoot you, and he shoots you. All this is wholeness, directness. Oh, how many of them there are, and there will be even more, you'll see!'[4]

In 1881 when Vsevolod Solovyov published this important passage, he was unable to express himself more explicitly, but it is evident that Belinsky's statement could only have been advocation of political assassination. It was not for nothing that Herzen called the author of the poem 'Dmitry Kalinin' a 'fanatic, a man of extremes' and concluded about Belinsky: 'Robespierre is an example of this breed of men.'[5]

This was how Belinsky, a revolutionary 'maximalist', appeared to Dostoevsky, who dreamed of social harmony and valued the early Utopians primarily because their system contained 'no hatred'.

*

A genuine struggle of ideas was waged in the study at Anichkov Bridge. The materialist, atheist, fighter and great herald of *exposé* literature and relevant art was opposed by the adherent of an evangelical morality, seeker of faith even when he himself doubted, supporter of idealistic aesthetics and 'fantastic realism', who refused to accept the overthrow of the values he had inherited from romanticism. 'My outlook was radically opposed to Belinsky's,' Dostoevsky himself said of their literary arguments. These words might serve as an epigraph to their entire impassioned and stormy dialogue.

'I found him a passionate socialist, and he immediately embarked on atheism with me,' Dostoevsky said in describing one of Belinsky's first 'lectures'. 'As a socialist he had to start by deposing Christianity,' the religion that gave rise to the moral principles of the society that he was rejecting. A militant innovator, Belinsky steadfastly blazed his own trail, affirming that the new literature must be concerned with advanced philosophical theory. This meant waging an implacable struggle against romanticism and mysticism, against 'stilted idealism' of any sort. The foundation of life was the movement of matter. 'To hell with metaphysics! Intellectual activity is the result of the activity of the cerebral apparatus.' Thus Belinsky anticipated by a quarter of a century one of the greatest works of Russian science, Sechenov's *Reflexes of the Brain*.

As early as 1841 Belinsky had informed his friends that in his mind the idea of socialism had absorbed not only history and philosophy, but also religion. Soon afterwards he wrote that he was 'enormously impressed' by the speeches about 'The Supreme Being' that Robespierre delivered on 18 Floréal and 20 Prairial in 1793. They represented a transition to a new revolutionary religion in which the cult of Reason, or 'The Supreme Being', freed from all 'mysteries', 'revelations', and 'miracles', demanded the worship of liberty, equality, the republic, the fatherland. This was the struggle against the Vatican, it was the 'de-Christianization' of France in the name of the revolutionary people's new political and social morality.

Robespierre's doctrine sought to transfer the worship and adulation of the masses from the millennia-old fetishes of antediluvian mythology to the great developments of contemporary civic life – to the Revolution, to the heroic personalities of mankind, to the martyrs in the struggle against tyranny.

In readings that Panaev conducted in his home in the winter of 1841 on the history of the French Revolution, his friend Belinsky spoke as a true champion of the extreme Left. Panaev recalled:

One had to see Belinsky in those moments. The whole of his noble and fiery nature was manifested here in all its brilliance, all its beauty, with all its infinite sincerity, and all its terrific energy. The speaker warmed up gradually and showed himself to be a real fighter.

All this is confirmed in Belinsky's letters, which formulate his programme for the organization of mankind:

The millennium will be established on earth not by the idealistic and noble Gironde's sugary and exalted phraseology, but by the terrorists, by the double-edged sword of the words and deeds of Robespierres and Saint-Justs.

Belinsky then read Feuerbach's *Das Wesen des Christentums*, which wrought a complete change in the younger generation's world outlook, and in 1844 he adopted the latest militant declarations of atheism. He was fascinated by Karl Marx's celebrated aphorisms: 'Religion is the opium of the people. The elimination of religion, which is the masses' illusory happiness, is a requirement for their genuine happiness.'[6] On 26 January 1845, shortly before Belinsky met Dostoevsky, he wrote to Herzen, probably under the direct influence of Marx's article 'Towards a Critique of the Hegelian Philosophy of Law', that he saw nothing but 'darkness, gloom, chains, and the knout' in 'the words "God" and "religion"'. This drew a sharp line of demarcation between the ideological orientations of Dostoevsky and Belinsky.

Dostoevsky described one of their most interesting arguments in *The Diary of a Writer* in 1873. In objecting to something Dostoevsky had said, Belinsky made a sharp criticism of Christianity, directing his fire with his usual accuracy against the chief bulwarks of the doctrine he opposed.

'But, look, it is wrong to charge man with sins, to burden him with debts and turning the other cheek when society is so evilly organized that man cannot help committing evil actions, when he is economically forced into evildoing, and it is ridiculous and cruel to demand of him what by the very laws of nature he could not do even if he wished to.'

We were not alone that evening. One of Belinsky's friends, whom he respected highly and whose opinion he often accepted, was present. There was also a very young writer, just starting out, who later gained literary renown.

'Why it touches me just to look at him!' Belinsky interrupted his own furious exclamations and, turning to his friend, pointed at me. 'Every time I speak of Christ in this way his whole face changes and he looks as if he wants to cry. Believe me, you are a naïve man,' he assailed me again. 'Believe me, if your Christ had been born in our time he'd have been the most obscure and ordinary man; he would have been effaced by today's science and the present forces of mankind.'

'Oh, no,' Belinsky's friend put in. 'If Christ were to appear today he would join the movement and head it.'

'Why, yes, yes,' Belinsky agreed with remarkable haste. 'That's true, he would join the socialists and follow them.'[7]

Dostoevsky never forgot these extreme and antithetical attitudes to the problems of religion. In his last book, in the 'The Grand Inquisitor', he continued his argument with Belinsky, contesting the latter's assertion that man is economically compelled to do evil. 'Do you know,' the Grand Inquisitor asks Christ, 'that centuries will pass and mankind will proclaim through the mouth of its wisdom and science that there is no such thing as crime and, therefore, no such thing as sin, that there are only the hungry? Feed them first, then demand virtue.' The Grand Inquisitor is represented as criticizing Christianity from the standpoint of socialism. Hence, his solidarity with Belinsky. Thus, on the eve of his death Dostoevsky was still fighting the old fight between Christianity and socialism, that had first arisen during the period of *Poor Folk* and that absorbed his mind and work throughout his life.

'THE KNIGHT OF THE SORROWFUL COUNTENANCE'

Dostoevsky was justly proud of the success of his first book, and did not consider it necessary to conceal this in public. He had unshakeable faith in his talent and vocation. As he wrote his brother on 1 February 1846:

I don't think my fame will ever again reach the peak it is at now. Imagine, all of our crowd and even Belinsky have found that I have gone far beyond Gogol himself. They find in me a new, original current, in that I proceed by Analysis, not Synthesis, i.e., I plunge into the depths and, while examining every atom, I search out the whole. Gogol, on the other hand, takes the whole right away and therefore is not so profound as I am. I have a most brilliant future ahead of me.

This innocent and naïve attitude prompted an ironical reaction among other young literati. Belinsky's circle was not only scholarly but also fun-loving. 'Arguments and serious conversations were not conducted methodically,' Kavelin recalled, 'but were always interspersed with witticisms and jokes.' Turgenev for one did not share Belinsky's enthusiastic opinion of Dostoevsky's literary talent and later openly declared his feelings in print: 'The excessive praise of *Poor Folk* was one of Belinsky's first errors and served to show that his powers had already begun to deteriorate.'

All this was reflected in the general opinion of the new writer. In conjunction with Nekrasov, who was a master of the *feuilleton* in verse, Turgenev wrote a rhymed missive, purportedly from Belinsky to Dostoevsky, in which Belinsky promises the young writer the highest place of honour in his huge *Leviathan* miscellany, but only on one condition – that he delivers his magazine from *The Double*, which was not popular with 'our crowd'. This satirical verse began with the publisher's address to the 'young writer', who had 'already plunged everyone into rapture'.

> Knight of the Sorrowful Countenance,
> Dostoevsky, dear wad . . .[8]

The satire contained such strokes of portraiture as 'cast aside your ashen glance' and others. The first four couplets did not transgress the bounds of literary jest; they made fun of the ordinary vanity of a rising star who was being lionized. But farther on the tone of friendly caricature became more deadly; an unfortunate choice was made of the incident used as the butt of this otherwise harmless ridicule.

Shortly before, Dostoevsky had appeared at a reception at the home of the well-known musician and patron of the arts Count Mikhail Yurevich Vielgorsky. Apparently, he had been invited by the host's son-in-law, the writer Vladimir Sollogub, who had visited the author of *Poor Folk* earlier and greatly admired his book. The home of this aristocratic grandee was frequented by luminaries of the artistic and political world, as well as by journalists and minor actors: Odoevsky, Vyazemsky, Bludov, Nesselrode, F. I. Tyutchev and the renowned 'cellist Matvei Vielgorsky, the host's brother. In this brilliant company Dostoevsky was introduced to a fashionable socialite, a girl 'with fluffy side curls and a grand name', as Panaev put it. This was the slim blonde Senyavina.[9] She was interested in theatrical and literary celebrities and had expressed a desire to make the acquaintance of the author of the fashionable novel. During the introduction the unsociable and easily embarrassed writer, stimulated and electrified by the atmosphere of the fashionable reception, suddenly felt ill and lost consciousness: he fell down in what was probably an epileptic fit (his condition at that time had not yet clearly manifested itself and had not been diagnosed). The derisive description of this 'faint' at the reception 'in front of this assembly of princes' and the 'blonde beauty' turned the epigram about the timid writer into a mockery of his grave illness, though the authors, admittedly, did not really know much about it.

Contemporary memoirs offer considerable evidence that people used to draw Dostoevsky deliberately into arguments that would cause him to cut the discussion short, leave the gathering in anger, and break off further relations with them. The distressing experience that the young Dostoevsky had to endure of first being praised to the skies and then too hastily and without sufficient cause being flung down from the heights and cruelly ridiculed, cannot but arouse our compassion for him.

Stefan Dmitrievich Yanovsky, his doctor at the time, gives a 'diagnosis' of his patient's emotional state in 1846:

> The suddenness of the transition that the author of *Poor Folk* experienced from admiration and acclaim as a virtual genius to complete denial that he had any literary talent at all, might have shattered a less impressionable and proud man than Dostoevsky. He began to avoid people from Belinsky's circle and withdrew into himself.

The only way he could see out of the situation was to break completely with the *Otechestvennie Zapiski* group.

Dostoevsky remained on good terms with Belinsky longer than with the others, but in the autumn of 1846 he became disillusioned with him too. 'He is such a weak person that even in literary opinions he changes his mind from one day to the next.'

On 7 October 1846, the year in which *Poor Folk* and *The Double* were published, he wrote to his brother: 'Petersburg is a hell for me. It is so hard to live here, so hard!'

Constant creative work at fever pitch had brought the impressionable and ailing writer, so skilled in portraying mental anguish, to the brink of despair. The following April he wrote again to his brother:

> You won't believe it, Here I am in the literary profession going on three years already. I seem to be in a daze. I have no life. I have not time to collect myself. My skill is diminishing because I lack time. I'd like to be able to consolidate. The fame that has been thrust upon me is of doubtful value, and I don't know how long this hell will go on – poverty, urgent work. Oh, if only I had some peace!

He never forgot this bitter early experience of sudden fame and rapid dethronement. The episode is first hinted at in his novel *Netochka Nezvanova* when the eminent violinist describes the ordeals of his artistic ascent:

Talent must have sympathy. It must be understood. But wait until you see the kind of people who flock around you after you have achieved even a little success. They will think nothing, even be contemptuous, of what you have developed through hard work, privations, hunger and sleepless nights. You will be one, and they will be many. They will torment you with pinpricks.

Netochka Nezvanova is the only one of Dostoevsky's early works that contains echoes of his own experience as a creative artist.

DIALOGUE ON ART. THE BREAK WITH BELINSKY

The decisive battle between Dostoevsky and Belinsky was fought on aesthetic grounds. The conflict between idealism and materialism that divided the two writers' views on fundamental ethical and political problems manifested itself most clearly where their philosophies of art were concerned. It was their aesthetic differences that decided the fate of their relationship.

The young Dostoevsky took an idealistic view of aesthetics. He felt a natural kinship with the concepts of the freedom of art, its disinterestedness, or 'uselessness', and the 'irrationality' of the poetic act. Kant's aesthetics with its doctrines are based, in the main, on such concepts.

Schiller's doctrine that art is a synthesis of poetry, philosophy and religion was bound up closely with Kantian aesthetics. It had already appealed to Dostoevsky in the early romantic period of his development, and he did not give it up later when he began to write his long novels. It is highly significant that by the early 1840s Dostoevsky was already familiar with Schiller's treatises on beauty, and he came to his aesthetic discussions with Belinsky prepared, and with a well-defined philosophical view of his own.

Hegel's aesthetics were a major contribution to the subject, regarding the absolute idea as the original source of art, and considering that the supreme manifestation of creativity had been achieved by the romantic tradition, one that embraced medieval Gothic, Shakespeare, Rembrandt, Goethe, Schiller. The romantic artist does not lecture and does not teach. He merely embodies an 'absolute inner life' and 'free concrete spirituality'. The most complete expression of these principles in Dostoevsky's time was the novel.

This was the kind of artist Dostoevsky wished to be, although, striving as he did to help solve the basic problems of his time through his art, his creative practice conflicted with this theory.

In the early 1840s Belinsky had already rejected the theory of 'pure art' and now he advocated analysis of artistic values, by the historical method: art expressed the life of the people. This new aesthetic was materialist and encouraged realism in art, a realism that not only analysed its world but expressed an opinion about it. This is why, the new theory of aesthetics declared, genuine art is always revolutionary – it demolishes the past; it rushes towards the future, it teaches, it moulds new people, and it issues slogans of liberation.

Such was the background against which the ideological conflict between the novelist and the critic was enacted.

In the last years of his life Belinsky was an irreconcilable enemy of romanticism, fantasy and idealism. He demanded that contemporary society be portrayed exactly as it was so that its evils might be combated. He declared war on all that was visionary, hypothetical or illusory.

Dostoevsky, the new portrayer of 'fantastic grade-nine officials', refused to accept the aesthetics of Belinsky's school unreservedly. He insisted on retaining his right to employ romanticism, fantasy and even psychology when it suited him to do so. For him the realistic descriptions of Petersburg were only useful in helping him express the philosophy of his hero. The descriptive reportage of the latest sketch-writers seemed to him to be superficial and lacking in perspective. He sought abstractions above all – ideas, problems, questions, Utopias, theories, dreams and hypotheses, which led to intellectual struggles and dramas played out against a background of everyday occurrences in modern cities.

His was a special kind of realism, profound, inspired and only partially influenced by the photographic technique of the *feuilleton* writers. 'Utopian realism', Henry Barbusse's term for Zola's style, could be applied equally well to Dostoevsky's.

Dostoevsky found Belinsky's system 'much too real' and for this reason incapable of appreciating properly the newest masters of the narrative form with their bold combination of the 'irrational' and the realistic. Twenty years later Dostoevsky was to write:

I remember my youthful surprise as I listened to some of Belinsky's purely artistic judgements. We were discussing *Eugène Onégin, Dead Souls, The Tales of Belkin* and *The Carriage*. His listeners felt that Belinsky was much less interested in Gogol's powerful delineation of character than in his power to expose. He rejected the ending of *Eugène Onégin*, that is, he disapproved of Tatiana's sacrificing herself to faithfulness and moral duty.

Dostoevsky stated that he had broken with Belinsky because of his 'ideas about literature' and the direction it should take. But ideas about literature included the central philosophical, historical, social and religious questions, which all converged in literature.

My views were fundamentally opposed to Belinsky's. I reproached him with trying to impose a specific and unworthy purpose on literature, reducing it solely to a description, if one may call it that, of newspaper reports and scandalous happenings. I protested that bile would never win anybody over and that you would simply bore everyone to death ... Belinsky became very angry with me and in the end we passed from coolness to a formal break, so that we did not meet at all in the last year of his life.

Dostoevsky said that his line of thinking was 'diametrically opposed to that of newspapers and the *incendiary*', that is, to the revolutionary (in the sense of the French '*incendiaire*').

Belinsky confirmed that the disagreement between himself and Dostoevsky concerned basic problems of creative art. From his own bitter experience in the 1830s he could sense that his young friend was taking a wrong direction and tried to prevent him from making a dangerous mistake, that is, succumbing to the 'pure art' theory.

'We ourselves were once ardent disciples of the idea of beauty,' Belinsky wrote, 'but with beauty alone art will not go far, especially in our day.' Dostoevsky could not take this new path. For him the 'aesthetic idea' remained the basis not only of creative thought but also of the entire historical process. A break was inevitable. It had been predetermined by the entire course of the two thinkers' ideological development.

One afternoon shortly before their final break Dostoevsky chanced to meet Belinsky outside Znamenskaya Church, which afforded a convenient spot from which to watch the construction of the new Nikolaev railway station. Their conversation in the street was brief, but, as always between them, meaningful. Belinsky had been thinking about the growth of Russian civilization, and about the happiness of its people, to be achieved not by theories and Utopias alone but by steel rails, iron locomotives and gigantic structures of metal and glass. He perceived the relevance of steam and electricity. As far back as 1845, he had written that by strengthening industry and trade, the new developments 'would weave together the interests of people of all categories and classes and compel them to enter into close and vital relationships with one another'. He visualized a strong and happy Russia, transformed by technology.

All his life Dostoevsky remembered Belinsky's words that day: 'I often come here to see how the construction is getting on. It does my heart good to stand and watch the work for a while: finally we will have at least one railway. You cannot imagine how much that thought gladdens my heart.' Dostoevsky was touched by the sincerity of that patriotic dream: 'It was well and warmly said. Belinsky never did things for show.'

But Belinsky did not win the young novelist over to his vision of the Russia of the future. At that time Dostoevsky was working on *The Landlady*, which Belinsky soon rejected for its romanticism and fantasy.

This last meeting between Dostoevsky and Belinsky at the construction site of the railway station crystallizes their differences and illumines the parting of two contrasting philosophical types: the revolutionary thinker and the Utopian poet.

IV

In New Circles

THE BEKETOVS AND THE MAIKOVS

As Dostoevsky remembered in 1861:

Valerian Maikov took over the criticism department of *Otechestvennie Zapiski* after Belinsky and set to work eagerly, brilliantly and with the radiant conviction of youthful enthusiasm. But he never got a chance to express himself. He died during his first year on the job. His was a beautiful personality and a very promising one, and it may be that we lost a great deal when we lost him.

This outstanding critic played a significant role in the history of Dostoevsky's early efforts to find himself. In 1846 he was the guiding spirit of a group of young writers and scientists whom Alexei Beketov, one of Dostoevsky's schoolmates at the Engineering Academy, had gathered together. Among them were Valerian's older brother Apollon Maikov; Beketov's two younger brothers, who were students of natural science; Pleshcheev, the poet; Grigorovich; Khanykov, an Orientalist; Dr Yanovsky, and others, and these became Dostoevsky's new associates.

After the electric atmosphere surrounding the literati, he found the company of these quiet students of nature and society restful. He wrote to his brother on 26 November 1846 that thanks to his new friends he had been completely reborn: 'They are active, intelligent people with wonderful hearts, honourable and strong in character. Their company has cured me.'

At Dostoevsky's suggestion the group rented a large apartment in the Vasiliev district of Petersburg and organized a household in common. For twelve hundred paper roubles a year, or thirty-five silver roubles a month, Dostoevsky had a private room in which to work undisturbed, and received dinner and tea as well. 'What a great blessing *association* is!' he concluded his report about his budget, employing a new term that socialist literature had taken up.

When the Beketov brothers left for Kazan at the beginning of 1847, Valerian Maikov invited Dostoevsky to the literary salon of his father, Nikolai Maikov, an eminent member of the Academy of Fine Arts.

The walls of the spacious reception rooms in Nikolai Maikov's large apartment on Morskaya Street at Sinii Bridge were covered with his paintings. His cathedral murals, his ceilings and medallions on mythological subjects, and his neo-classical female figures had made him well known. He painted an interesting romantic self-portrait in the style of Kiprensky and several good portraits of writers who were family friends, particularly one of Solonitsyn (now in the Tretyakov Art Gallery) and one (in the sixties) of Goncharov, a later work in good realistic style and probably the best portrait of the author of *Obryv* (*The Precipice*) and *Oblomov*.

Contemporaries valued Nikolai Maikov's canvases for the freshness of their colours and the clarity of their composition, but considered him a dilettante. Grigorovich, who was a connoisseur of the Arts, praised the tasteful gaiety of his palette, which brought to mind the old Venetian masters. Nikolai Maikov's academic style was alien to Dostoevsky, who believed that a painting must have a 'moral core', inner drama and maximum expressiveness. The bacchantes and bathing girls of Maikov's second period the 1840s when Dostoevsky knew him, had none of the qualities he demanded from painting.

The Maikov family's Hellenistic frame of mind was reflected not only in the father's canvases but also in the poetic efforts of his elder son Apollon, who in the dismal Petersburg of Nicholas I sang of:

> tympans and the sound of flutes,
> and the splashes of Bacchanalias.

Yet Dostoevsky maintained friendly ties with this 'cameo' poet to the end of his life, despite the profound differences in their creative temperaments and artistic inclinations.

Dostoevsky's real friend in this family of neo-classicists was the elder Maikov's second son Valerian, whom he had previously known in Beketovs' circle, an outstanding young author and literary critic of the new 'research' type. He was the founder of experimental aesthetics and demanded that art should propagate practical knowledge. He tried to introduce into his appreciations and reviews the spirit of scientific–philosophical analysis, to show the humanizing effect of art upon reality. He had a high opinion of Herzen, for whom life and learning were 'absolutely identical', and he recognized that Koltsov was a great poet, capable of rising to a scientific understanding of contemporary life; hence such an example of *economic poetry* as the lines beginning 'Why do you sleep, little *muzhik*?', which he described as 'the manifesto of a passionate politico–economist, dressed in artistic form'. But it was Dostoevsky who became Valerian Maikhov's real star. The young critic saw in Dostoevsky's very first works first-class material for the new literature, based on exactly observed sociological and psychological data. Valerian's opinion was new among the early evaluations of Dostoevsky's work and turned out to be correct in many respects.

Most people regarded the author of *Poor Folk* as a disciple of Gogol. Valerian Maikov asserted that there was a profound difference between the two writers: 'Gogol is mainly a social poet; Dostoevsky is mainly psychological.' Gogol, one might say, is the statistics of Russia transformed into art; Dostoevsky, on the other hand, is amazing for the vastness

of the characters he created. The scientific writer was
travelling his own road; he was not repeating *Dead Souls* in
any way and was creating characters that were no less significant than those of Gogol: Golyadkin, as a type, 'is just as
expressive and at the same time just as universal as Chichikov
or Manilov'.

Later, in the statement he made after his arrest,
Dostoevsky declared that he liked reading and studying
social questions. 'Socialism is the same thing as political
economy, but in a different form. And I like studying
questions of political economy.' This represented an enormous step forward, by comparison with his previous dream of
universal happiness. It was already an approach to a scientific interpretation of the most recent social problems.

In 1846 Valerian Maikov began to prepare a long article
about Dostoevsky's published works. This article might have
been the first scholarly monograph on Dostoevsky's early
writings; but he never completed it. On 15 July 1847 he died
of sunstroke, after bathing in a pond while overheated from
a long walk in the countryside around Petersburg. He was
not yet twenty-four years old.

*

At their meetings in the Maikov salon, guests used to
break up into smaller groups in different rooms, where they
would read aloud or discuss various subjects. 'I could tell
you a great deal about these groups,' Dr Yanovsky once
wrote. 'I could tell you, for example, how Dostoevsky, in the
group of which he was the centre, would discuss the nature
of the writings of Gogol and Turgenev or his own Prokharchin, with the minutely detailed analysis characteristic
of him.'

Prokharchin was the hero of Dostoevsky's third story, on
which he worked intensively in 1846. The censor had so
badly distorted this little tale of a civil servant frightened to
death that when it appeared Dostoevsky renounced it in
horror: 'All the life has gone out of it. Only the skeleton is

left.' Belinsky was critical of this 'incomprehensible story', though he conceded that it contains 'sparks of talent'.

Dostoevsky had certainly found a good plot, developed from a newspaper report about an impoverished civil servant 'who had died in rags with half a million roubles among his effects'. It was a tale to suit his style and the over-all pattern of his ideas. With that creative concentration on the eternal images of Russian and world literature that afterwards became characteristic of him (e.g. 'to write a Russian *Candide*'), when he came to draw his miser from the Petersburg lodging houses he took his bearings (as he him-self said) from the classical types of Molière and Pushkin, from the images of Harpagon and the Covetous Knight.

The design had dramatic breadth and subtleties of tone worthy of Rembrandt. Dostoevsky saw the miserly grade-nine official as a 'colossal person', demoniacal, omnipotent, like Pushkin's rapacious knight:

> I am above wishes and all care;
> I know my power ...

The neighbours of this power-hungry civil servant sense something Bonapartean about him, something superhuman and titanic: 'What do you think you are, a Napoleon or something? Do you think you're the only person in the world?' Later on, Dostoevsky developed these motifs with tremendous power in his long novels, where he displayed on a broader canvas the problems of the omnipotence of money and the boundless pretensions of an arrogant, self-centred personality. However, even this first sketch contains pages of astonishing power.

One outstanding fragment in the story is Prokharchin's dream, the vision, with its hidden echoes of Pugachov's peasant uprising, in which Dostoevsky depicts with power-ful strokes the terror the frightened miser feels when con-fronted by the spectators at a fire, a huge mob which envelops him like a boa constrictor. This scene foreshadows

The House of the Dead, Raskolnikov's dream of a carousing mob in a cemetery, and the conflagration of the village in *The Brothers Karamazov*. The qualities of a truly great writer can already be discerned in that early 'distorted' and underestimated story, with its vision of Russia in homespun cloth advancing menacingly against the hermit-like miser. This is the stuff of epic, and it lays bare the very roots of Russia's history.

DR YANOVSKY

Valerian Maikov introduced his friend Dr Stepan Dmitrievich Yanovsky to Dostoevsky, who soon welcomed him as both physician and friend. Dr Yanovsky was then a young man of twenty-eight who worked in the Medical Department and acted as a physician to his friends, probably free of charge. In a letter Dostoevsky wrote to Yanovsky in the early 1870s he called him 'one of the unforgettables', a friend 'who had had a marked effect' on his life: 'You loved me and you concerned yourself with me, with a mentally ill person (after all, I realize that now), up until my departure for Siberia.'

At first their relationship was a purely professional one. Yanovsky treated Dostoevsky for general ill health due to scrofula and scurvy, 'attacks of hypochondria', which is what Dostoevsky himself called his illness, and finally, for a brain disease. That this was incipient epilepsy is evident from Yanovsky's description of a falling fit Dostoevsky had in the street on 7 July 1847. Dostoevsky's pulse rate was over one hundred and he had slight convulsions. The doctor observed a strong rush of blood to the patient's head and extraordinary stimulation of his entire nervous system. He took the sick man home with him and bled him.

Yanovsky's letters to Dostoevsky show that he sympathized deeply with his patient, and that his treatment was successful. When he later moved to another city, he continued from a distance to try to instil optimism and peace of mind in Dostoevsky and to overcome his 'peculiar inclination towards pessimism, his despondent and constantly anxious state of mind', his tendency to doubt and despair. Dostoevsky had great respect for the doctor's observations.

For all that, it was the great psychological novelist himself who most accurately described his mental state, explaining, ten years later, how for two successive years, in the mid 1840s,

I was sick with a strange disease, a psychological disease. I was overcome by hypochondria. There were times when I would actually lose my reason. I was exceedingly irritable, painfully impressionable and had a knack of distorting the most ordinary facts.

Doctor Yanovsky, as we have seen, correctly characterized the drama of a man setting out to be a writer, as experienced by Dostoevsky. The doctor has left us a good description of his patient. Dostoevsky was not tall, but had a broad chest and broad shoulders, 'his head was well-shaped, though the forehead was unusually high with very prominent protuberances. He had small, light grey, extremely lively eyes; his lips were thin and always pressed together, lending his entire face an expression of concentrated kindness and affection'. The finely formed skull with the broad forehead and prominent frontal sinuses made him like Socrates.

Above all else Dostoevsky liked to discuss with his physician medicine, social problems, art, literature and – again and again – religion.

He was interested in Yanovsky's library, especially in the works of Gogol, who had been a favourite of his since the 1830s.

Besides works of fiction F.M. often borrowed medical books from me, especially books dealing with diseases of the brain and the nervous system, mental illness and the configuration of the skull according to the then popular old Gall system.

Thus passed the winter of 1846, a turning point in Dostoevsky's life and work, when he forsook Belinsky's literati for the friendly circle of young scientists, renounced the commonplace types of the naturalist school for themes with major characters and strong passions, and followed his stories about poor civil servants with a long adventure story that anticipated his long novels, with their plots of crime and their apocalyptic finales.

A ROMANTIC TALE

Dostoevsky was tireless in his efforts to find his own artistic style. 'Repetition is disaster in my position,' he wrote to his brother in October 1846.

He strove to recapture his early system of poetics and to get away from descriptions of the life of petty civil servants. By dint of a tremendous effort of creative will, he broke through to the form that he would in future make his own – the novel of passion, moral quest, acute psychological struggle and grandiose 'eternal' types, such as 'the great sinner', 'the beautiful man' and the 'penitent Magdalene'.

It was along these lines that he constructed *The Landlady*, a long story on which he worked intensively for over a year from October 1846 to December 1847. Begun as a realistic study, it developed into a strange story of mystery and horror, rooted in the newest psychological themes (the ambivalence of women's emotions, expiation of imaginary sin, the power of hypnotism, and so forth). His creative method was transformed; inspiration, in design and in style (one of the main elements in Dostoevsky's poetics), now entered into its full rights. The denizens of the outskirts of Petersburg took on the coloration of a romantic tale (in this connection Belinsky talked, and with good reason, about Hoffmann and Marlinsky). Dostoevsky himself remarked on the lyrical character of his prose-poem – 'my pen was guided by a stream of inspiration rising straight from the heart', he wrote to his brother at the beginning of 1847.

The plot of this adventure story unfolds against the background of contemporary Petersburg. A gentleman named Mikhail Vasilevich Ordynov, with a candidate's degree in Canon Law, not employed by the Government, is working on a dissertation, and experiences a tragic passion, which forever rends him away from the ordinary world of practicality and success.

Realizing the personal catastrophe that has overtaken him, he becomes a lonely seeker after the moral significance of life. Here now we see the evolution of that psychological, spiritual, internal realism which was to win for Dostoevsky a special place in the whole brilliant constellation of critical realists.* The author tries to keep his characters viable, and to make the collisions between them true to life. Everything is fundamentally credible, familiar, commonplace even. There is nothing unusual about the urban landscape – a view of a working-class district – long fences, 'wretched hovels', taverns and corn chandlers, 'gigantic, ugly, blackened red factory buildings with tall chimneys'. The principal character is surrounded by typical figures from Gorokhovaya Street and Voznesensky Prospect. The police-sergeant, the Tatar hall-porter, the poor German with his daughter Tienchen – all this is the authentic physiognomy of Petersburg. Even Murin, the 'sorcerer-magician', turns out to be simply the leader of a gang of thieves who have got away from the police in time.

But the customary features of naturalist stories of this kind are here overshadowed by extraordinary events. *The Landlady* is compounded of a powerful plot, intricate situations, crime on a grand scale and an intense inner struggle that draws strong-willed and masterful natures into its vortex. A strange style is used for the confessions made by the

* Critical realists. A Russian literary term for non-socialist realists.

principal characters – a compound of folk poetry, old Russian and ballads, with echoes of robber songs and erotic love lyrics, and with passages in the spirit of sectarian poetry, or of the chants of the Old Believers, rising to the heights of exaltation and extremes of enthusiasm. Nothing but this kind of intense, overwrought diction could measure up to the broad epic sweep of the story. This is romanticism with a vengeance, but it is romanticism confined within the clear-cut framework of one of the naturalist school's descriptive tales of Petersburg.

At the centre of the action there is an ex-brigand from the Volga, a fiery-eyed old man named Murin. He was once the lover of the mother of a beautiful girl called Katerina, and later fell passionately in love with Katerina herself – his stepdaughter – still quite a young girl. He set fire to her parents' factory, ruining them, and carried Katerina off. Now he has become a soothsayer, telling fortunes out of mysterious folios in black bindings that look like statute books of the Old Believers. This magician suffers from the 'black disease' – epilepsy; he is old and frail but more than anything else in the world he treasures his companion Katerina. In order to keep a hold on her he has implanted in her mind the notion that she is guilty of the death of her mother, and has committed the greatest of all deadly sins. He demands that she purge her guilt, and drives her to madness. The sick girl believes that only the wizard–soothsayer can absolve her from the fearful sin and give peace to her tormented conscience. But when Ordynov appears she begins to believe in him as her rescuer.

A complex psychological struggle ensues. To keep his beloved by his side the old man is even prepared to make the dreadful concession of forgiving this 'loving, rebellious' passionate nature for her 'sweetheart'. But the sacrifice is too much for him; in a frenzy of jealousy the former river pirate (who drowned Katerina's betrothed, a merchant lad named Alyosha, in a deep pool in the Volga) is ready for murder again. But it is neither Murin's bullet nor Ordynov's dagger that brings on the denouement. The heroine herself decides her own fate.

The elements in this story were to be developed fully in Dostoevsky's later work. The central situation of *The Landlady* anticipates that of *The Idiot*, where the heroine experiences the same agonizing emotional ambivalence and rushes back and forth between the angelic Myshkin and the criminal Rogozhin, finally running to the sombre, jealous Rogozhin from the altar to accept death at his hands.

All this had already been foreshadowed in *The Landlady*. Katerina confesses to Ordynov that she has fallen in love with him because his soul is 'pure, radiant, transparent'. But the Volga brigand's iron will dominates her. She loves both men and she fears both. 'I love you both, you are both dear to me,' she says to them, expressing her strange double feeling. In the end she rejects her dreamer and remains, though at the price of death, with the melancholy ruler of her destiny.

The character of Ordynov is in essence a precursor of Raskolnikov. He is a young thinker who has become a recluse. He is unsociable and melancholy. His 'mind, oppressed by solitude, sharpened and uplifted only by intense, frenzied activity', is concentrated on a single purpose: he is devising a new system of knowledge which will reconcile art and science, poetry and philosophy. He wants to be a scientific artist. He wanders, absorbed by this idea, through the back alleys of Petersburg, looking for a corner in which to live among the virtual beggars who inhabit a huge, dark, crowded tenement. Passers-by take him for a madman.

A path to the spiritual resurrection of Ordynov is adumbrated at the end of the story. As in Dostoevsky's later work the hero's catharsis is not completed, only indicated. The external world loses its savour for the young historian and his former creative activity becomes closed to him. But his inner life is not over; it has merely taken a new path. This story, rejected by contemporaries and soon condemned by the author himself, is one of the harbingers of the kind of work Dostoevsky was to produce in his maturity.

THE PROPAGANDA SOCIETY

V

The Petrashevsky Circle

DOSTOEVSKY, A FOLLOWER OF FOURIER

IN the spring of 1846 a stranger, wearing a cloak and a broad-brimmed hat, approached Dostoevsky on Nevsky Prospekt and said suddenly: 'May I ask what the idea of your next story is?'

This stranger was Petrashevsky, who liked to be original in manner and eccentric in conversation.

He was a prominent figure in the libertarian movement of the 1840s, a disciple of the French socialist thinker Charles Fourier, organizer of the first social circle in Russia, a magnificent speaker, a scholar and a propagandist, whose erudition in social questions was as remarkable as his political courage in the Petersburg of Nicholas I.

In 1845 he published an entire encyclopaedia of socialism disguised as *A Pocket Dictionary of Foreign Words*.

That same year he began to invite young people interested in the newest socio-economic problems to his home off Pokrovsky Square. The gatherings took place on Fridays in his small wooden house, with its crooked porch, creaking staircase and cheap furniture. Akhsharumov, a member of Petrashevsky's circle, describes them in his memoirs:

The meetings offered an interesting kaleidoscope of the most diverse opinions on contemporary events, government ordinances and the latest in various fields of knowledge. News of what was going on in the city was discussed here; people talked loudly and without restraint about everything. Now and then some expert would give a sort of lecture.

According to Pyotr Semyonov of Tien-Shan, 'a large part of the evening was sometimes spent talking about Robert

Owen's *New Lanark*, about the *Voyage en Icarie* of Etienne
Cabet and especially about Fourier's "phalanstery" and
Proudhon's progressive tax theory.'

Dostoevsky began to attend these meetings in the spring of
1847. The principal subjects discussed were serfdom and
reformation of the courts and of the Press. Talks were given
on Utopian socialism, atheism, the struggle against censorship, public trial, and the family and marriage. 'We have
sentenced the present social order to death,' Petrashevsky
had said. 'Now we must carry out the sentence.'

What was this new libertarian doctrine that captured
young Dostoevsky's mind?

Fourier taught that the existing economic system was a
regime of injustice, anarchy and poverty. It was a mortal
danger to mankind. A basic reorganization of society was
necessary, first of all, for the urban and rural proletariat,
that is, for the poorest and most deprived, those most
entitled to sympathy and assistance.

To ease the lot of these people, everybody must unite in
one single, grandiose, experiment. They must form the first
'phalanx' in the world; that is, an agrarian–industrial
association for community life in a spacious and magnificent
building, called a 'phalanstery', which would have halls for
concerts and dances, auditoriums for lectures, a theatre, and
reading rooms. This living together would reorganize the
structure of labour, would unite agriculture with industry
and would increase production tenfold.

Universal well-being would be promoted through the
skilful utilization of all the diverse qualities of human nature
– tastes, interests, passions – and in the sphere of morality
would create a new Newtonian law of gravity. Because the
people would like one another and combine their energies,
there would be no onerous labour but only work made
enjoyable by the attractiveness and diversity of the entire
production process.

In depicting the ugliness of contemporary 'civilization',

Fourier sharply criticized capitalist society. Engels called him one of the great satirists of all time. He pilloried bankers, merchants, colonialists, exchange dealers, bankrupts, usurers, rentiers – all the parasites pullulating in contemporary bourgeois society. This terrible world of antagonisms and suffering would be succeeded, according to Fourier, by a radiant kingdom of reason and happiness – by *social harmony*. This transformation of the social system would be accompanied by an improvement in the natural conditions of our planet and even of the entire universe. The road to universal happiness would also bring supreme beauty to the universe; it would lead to milder climates and bring new constellations into existence.

On becoming familiar with Fourier's teachings at Petrashevsky's Friday gatherings, Dostoevsky openly expressed his admiration for this 'political romance', as Fourierism was called in Russia. Even when he later had to testify before the Commission of Inquiry on charges of conspiracy brought against the group, he could not bring himself to belittle the doctrine that had won his heart.

Fourierism is a peaceful system. Its grace charms the soul. The love of humanity that inspired Fourier when he conceived his system warms the heart and the harmony of his system astonishes the mind. Its attraction does not derive from bilious criticism but from the love of mankind it inspires. There is no hatred in this system. Fourierism does not require political reform; the reform it calls for is economic. It does not encroach on the government or on property.

Dostoevsky did not desire a violent revolution that would transfer power to the new vanguard social class. As Pyotr Semyonov (a Petrashevskyite who knew him well and afterwards became the famous Russian geographer Semyonov of Tien-Shan) correctly pointed out, Dostoevsky was no revolutionary, not even in his youth, and could never have been one. He had merely taken part in a Propaganda Society and in a 'conspiracy of ideas'. According to Dostoevsky's own subsequent statement, his only guilt was his faith 'in theory and Utopia'. Like the authors of the French social novels popular in the 1840s, he exposed the wealthy and sympathized with their victims, but his intentions went no further than 'patching up' society that is, than expounding philanthropic doctrines and social dreams.

One of his favourite dreams went back to the poems of ancient Greece and Rome, the dream of a Golden Age, an era of innocence and bliss, justice and eternal peace, an era when mankind had not yet known private property, war, sin or evil. 'The Golden Age,' Dostoevsky was to write in 1876, 'is the most improbable dream, yet people have dedicated their whole lives and all their energies to this dream; prophets have been killed for it; it is a dream that people do not wish to live without, or even die without.' In the 1840s he believed that this 'improbable dream' was possible, and he was prepared to serve it by his writing.

True, these sympathies were not immediately reflected in his work. He hardly ever expressed ideas of this sort in his writing in those years and it is not surprising that Petrashevsky openly reproached him for not studying socialist literature more diligently. Only one story in that period, 'A Christmas Tree and a Wedding', can be construed as containing overtones of Fourierism, in that it presents a contemporary marriage as a kind of commercial transaction. But this motif is overshadowed by the theme of an elderly libertine choosing as his bride a sixteen-year-old girl with large dreamy eyes that seem to be begging for mercy.

In his fervent speeches at Petrashevsky's Friday gatherings, however, Dostoevsky often spoke on Utopian socialism, the problems of poverty and wealth, power and oppression, enslavement and freedom. According to Ippolite Debu, the members of the circle regarded the writer's passionate nature as ideally suited for propaganda. Dostoevsky used to make a powerful impression on listeners.

I can see Fyodor Mikhailovich at one of Petrashevsky's evenings as if it were today. I can still hear him telling how a sergeant major of the Finland regiment was forced to run the gauntlet for having taken vengeance on a company commander for barbarous treatment of his comrades, or describing the way landlords treat serfs.

Many believed that 'at times of such outbursts Dostoevsky was capable of going out into the street and carrying a red flag'. From what we know of Dostoevsky's subsequent intellectual history we recognize that his interest in Fourier's thinking was a manifestation of his fascination with a new 'cycle of ideas' – powerful and heroic. It must not be forgotten that even in the 1840s Dostoevsky was already first and foremost the great artist, a true poet, as he was fond of calling himself. And the enthusiasm of his speeches was not evidence of a desire for revolutionary action. He was a master of words, and was concerned only to popularize ideas that could lead to emancipation, to disseminate those new 'magnanimous' doctrines which called for the abolition of serfdom, censorship, inequality, oppression and poverty. The only means that Dostoevsky recognized for achieving this end was the powerful and sublime weapon which he could wield to perfection, the printed and spoken word. He was willing to take part as a writer and speaker in a protracted campaign for the reorganization of contemporary society. This is what he learned from the Fourierists. It is not for nothing that Lenin called Fourier's theory of renewal of the world a 'socialism without struggle'.

This in fact was what Dostoevsky's belief in Utopia amounted to. He was shortly to write of his judges: 'Let them try to prove that I desired changes and upheavals *by violence, by revolution and stirring up bile and hatred. I am not afraid of such charges.*' These words have a ring of sincerity, and are supported by the documentary evidence that is available.

Dostoevsky enjoyed the respect and friendly sympathy of

the Petrashevsky group, and he, for his part, had a very high opinion of his new friends for their outstanding talents and knowledge. In 1877, when a newspaper wrote that the type of Russian revolutionary had deteriorated from the Decembrists to the Petrashevskyites, Dostoevsky warmly took up the cudgels in defence of the public-spirited companions of his youth. He wrote in the Press that among the Petrashevskyites there were people 'who had come from the highest educational institutions' and who had later become eminent scientists and public leaders.

It is true, however, that these men were not the 'steel soldiers' of the Decembrist movement for whom Herzen had such admiration. This was a generation that had experienced the defeat of the revolutionary movement of the 1820s and had been drawn by the romantic magnet of Utopian socialism. But Dostoevsky knew intuitively and at once that they were the progressive heroes of his time. Among his papers there is a short but fascinating note:

> A novel about the Petrashevsky circle.
> The Alexeevsky Ravelin. Rostovtsev.
> Filippov, Golovinsky, Timkovsky.

This brief note indicates that Dostoevsky never forgot the young Russia of the 1840s and that he dreamed of re-creating it in the free form of the novel. The second line of it refers to the destruction of the Propaganda Society in 1849, and the third names some members of the circle who made a great impact on him.

Who then were these three Petrashevskyites whom Dostoevsky would have placed in the foreground of his novel about a Russian Revolution?

Pavel Filippov was a student of physics and mathematics at the university. 'He is still a very young man,' Dostoevsky wrote of him. 'He is ardent and very inexperienced. He is ready to commit the first mad deed that enters his head.' But he made a very serious proposal to this circle of like-minded people, namely, that they print anti-government articles on a secret lithographic press. He himself prepared the drawings for a printing press and ordered the parts for it in different workshops. In putting forward the plan he managed to interest Dostoevsky, who was attracted by the nobility and purity of his young friend's motives. 'He has many very good qualities for which I have become fond of him: he is honest, exquisitely polite, truthful, fearless and forthright.'

Twenty-year-old Vasili Golovinsky was one of the youngest members of the Petrashevsky circle. He was a jurist, son of a Freemason, an enthusiastic advocate of the emancipation of the people, and a fine speaker, whose logical thinking and staunch convictions inspired respect. Apparently Dostoevsky first met him in Durov's circle in the winter of 1849 and brought him into the Petrashevsky group. Golovinsky was present at only two meetings before the arrests, and made only one speech, which was about the fall of serfdom and was delivered with his characteristic fervour and persuasiveness. For this he paid with a sentence of death and – after the sentence was 'commuted' – with deprivation of his civil rights and with long years of service as a private in the army.

Konstantin Timkovsky was a lieutenant in the Black Sea Fleet, who had sailed the high seas for many years and knew many European and Asiatic languages. He loved the literature of all nations and had written a book entitled *The Spanish Theatre*. When he joined the circle, he was deeply religious, offering to prove the divinity of Jesus Christ by science alone, and was dedicated to social change by legal means.

In the company of the Petrashevskyites his views underwent an incredibly swift change. At one meeting he called for a popular insurrection without delay and declared that he was willing to go out into the streets and sacrifice himself to the sacred cause of freedom. He proposed that the world be divided between the communists and the

Fourierists so that their theories might be compared in practice, though he himself was already inclining towards communism.

Timkovsky fascinated Dostoevsky. 'He has one of those extraordinary minds which, once it has accepted an idea, is completely in its sway. The only side of the Fourier system that he saw was its pleasant side. His speech was written with feeling. It was evident that he had laboured over its style.' Dostoevsky pointed out that Timkovsky had a 'natural sense of elegance' and 'a mind eager for knowledge and constantly demanding food. Some thought him a photographically exact copy of Don Quixote, and perhaps they were not wrong.'

Although Dostoevsky never wrote the novel about the Petrashevsky circle, twenty years later he did revive in some of the characters in *The Devils* those of his contemporaries who had impressed him most, such as Petrashevsky himself, Speshnev and Timkovsky. The latter apparently was the model for one of the most memorable in the novel, the engineer Kirillov. Kirillov's swift change from religious faith to atheism, his willingness to blow up the whole world even while seriously working for the government, his peculiar revolutionary temperament and need for self-sacrifice, and his monomania, can all be traced back to Timkovsky.

*

Dostoevsky was well acquainted with the many attacks made upon the old order by various Utopians. He made use of the library of the Petrashevskyites, which was an arsenal of anti-feudal literature. In addition to the principal works by the French social thinkers, such as Fourier, Saint-Simon, Considérant, Cabet, Louis Blanc, Proudhon and Pierre Leroux, it contained Voltaire, Rousseau, Diderot, Helvetius, d'Holbach, George Sand, Feuerbach, Robert Owen and Karl Marx's *The Poverty of Philosophy*.

Dostoevsky was too absorbed in his own creative work to have made a special study of all the predecessors and classics of socialism; nevertheless, he was very knowledgeable about them. One of the books Dostoevsky borrowed from Petrashevsky's library was Cabet's *Le Vrai Christianisme*, the basic thesis of which is that communism is 'the reign of God on earth', that is, a reign of mercy, fraternity, equality, liberty and justice, and that peaceful propaganda is the only means by which communism can be achieved.

Books such as these tell us something of the young Dostoevsky's views. It seemed to him that only unlimited dissemination of the Utopian socialists' great ideas could save Russia from the terrible scourges of pauperism, slavery, prostitution and Arakcheevism. Waging the social struggle meant giving the masses the books, pamphlets, magazines and newspapers that exposed the system, such publications as *The Phalanx, Independents' Magazine, Peaceful Democracy* and other Fourierist organs, to oppose *Severnaya Pchela* (*The Northern Bee*). Dostoevsky dreamed of having Russian editions of these publications.

The information available about his attitude towards peasant insurrection is conflicting. In the early 1880s Alexander Palm recalled that when Dostoevsky had been asked, 'Well, what if it proves impossible to liberate the peasants without insurrection?' Dostoevsky had exclaimed: 'All right then, with insurrection!'

On the other hand, according to Alexander Milyukov, Dostoevsky agreed with those Petrashevskyites who believed that emancipation of the peasants must come from above. When, after Dostoevsky had given an enthusiastic reading of Pushkin's *The Village* ('slavery, collapsing by order of the Tsar'), someone expressed doubts as to whether it was possible for the peasants to be liberated by legal means, Dostoevsky said sharply that he did not believe in any other way.

The question is decided by Dostoevsky's testimony at the trial of the Petrashevsky group in 1849. He said that he believed that emancipation of the serfs must be accompanied by compensations to the landlords, who 'by losing their right to the peasants were losing workmen and, therefore, capital'. Advocates of this viewpoint 'do not want revolutionary or other violent types of action ... they stop at peaceful, possible, not cataclysmic measures.' Dostoevsky had spoken of this with Golovinsky in March or April 1849, not long before the members of the Petrashevsky group were arrested, that is, in the period when he was closest to the circle's left wing. Even at that time he did not entertain the thought of peasant rebellion.

In the two years that he attended socialist gatherings, Dostoevsky's chief activity was participation in discussions which were mainly on literary subjects, and this could not have provided the authorities with material for serious charges.

It was only in the highly charged atmosphere of 1849 that he became, for the first time and only time in his whole life, *a fellow-traveller of the revolution*, sympathized with its basic ideas, and was willing to take part in realizing them. This was a reflection of his burning protest against the system under which he lived and of the dream he had as creative writer of an ideal community of the future. Yet even then he was not willing to employ force of arms to achieve that great goal: a printing press was the means by which he wished to serve the revolutionary people.

SPESHNEV'S CONSPIRACY

Of all the gifted, intelligent, cultivated and brilliant members of the Petrashevsky circle the one who made the deepest impact on Dostoevsky was Nikolai Speshnev, who was the furthest of them all from literary magazines and the rostrum. Speshnev, more than any of the others, was the embodiment of the image of a political leader. Pleshcheev, the poet, thought him 'the most remarkable of us all'.

Speshnev's life and character were indeed extremely interesting. A Kursk landowner, who had spent several years in Paris and Switzerland, well-educated and highly intelligent, he was one of the first Russian communists. Handsome, wealthy, leader of the extreme left wing of the Propaganda Society, he was an ideal example of the 'aristocrat, espousing democracy', as Dostoevsky described him. According to an account by Ogaryova-Tuchkova, he was strikingly good-looking: 'He was tall and had chiselled features; dark brown curls down to his shoulders; his large, grey eyes seemed touched with quiet sadness.' Mombelli, one of the Petrashevskyites, said that Speshnev behaved 'somewhat mysteriously', 'was always cold and unruffled'; 'the expression on his face never changed.'

There is a good portrait of Speshnev in one of the letters of Mikhail Bakunin, the founder of the anarchist movement:

Speshnev joined [Petrashevsky's circle] in 1848,[1] in the early days of the Western revolution. He was a remarkable man in many respects: intelligent, rich, educated, good-looking, most aristocratic in appearance, though calm and cold inspiring confidence, as strength in repose always does; a gentleman from top to toe. Men were not drawn to him – he was too dispassionate and self-satisfied and did not seem to need affection from anybody. But women, young and old, married and unmarried – probably any woman he wanted – were all mad about him. Speshnev is a most impressive person, he is especially adept at wrapping himself in a cloak of thoughtful calm and mystery.

The history of his youth reads like a novel. Immediately after he graduated from the *lycée* he met a beautiful young Polish woman, who left her husband and children for him and got him to go abroad with her. She bore him a son. After a while she became jealous of him and in a fit of jealousy poisoned herself.[2] What traces this event left on his heart I do not know; he never spoke of it to me. I only know that it greatly enhanced his value in the eyes of the female sex, enveloping his beautiful head in an aureole of sad romance.[3]

Afterwards in Siberia 'everybody spoke of him with great respect, but without any affection'.

Speshnev belonged to the extreme left wing revolutionaries of the 1840s. The Commission of Inquiry regarded him as the most important of the accused criminals. Semevsky believed that he may not have been alien to the 'influence of revolutionary-proletarian communism in the spirit of Marx and Engels'. Some scholars have noted how close Speshnev's communism was to the French revolutionary materialist Desamis and the famous Swiss communist Weitling. Speshnev was a convinced atheist. He spoke openly against religion, and some notes denying the existence of God were found among his papers. As leader of the left wing of the Petrashevsky circle, he was planning to form a secret group that would carry out an uprising.

For quite a long time Dostoevsky kept his distance from this brilliant figure. 'I don't know him well,' he told Yanovsky, 'and to tell the truth, I don't want to get any closer to him: the gentleman is far too strong; he is not at all like Petrashevsky.'

But major political events soon brought them close together.

*

The political storms in Europe in 1848 reverberated widely in Russia. From the very first they were viewed with the deepest emotion among all groups in society, though with varied reactions. It was near the end of Shrovetide, but the news from France stunned Petersburg so that most people (according to a contemporary) completely forgot about plays, shows, dances, pancakes, and masquerades. Nicholas I received the first reports about the events in Paris on Friday 20 February, during a palace ball. An unexpected messenger broke up the festivities with a dispatch about the first barricades and the fall of Guizot's ministry.

The Tsar's court was plunged into complete confusion.

On Saturday 21 February, at 11 a.m., the Tsar heard a report from his Chancellor, Nesselrode, about a packet marked 'extremely important' he had received from the Russian envoy in France. The message was dated 12 February and said: 'Everything is over! The King has abdicated.'

But it was not yet clear what form the new French government would take. Only on the next day, Sunday 22 February, did Nicholas I appear at the Crown Prince's ball, during the mazurka, with the latest dispatches from Paris and cry out: 'Saddle the horses, gentlemen! A republic has been proclaimed in France!'

Though these words are regarded as apocryphal, they accurately reflect the Russian Emperor's attitude to revolutionary Europe. Given his foreign policy, military intervention was the only course open to him in a situation like this.

On 24 February Nicholas ordered the Minister of War to mobilize the army. That was his response to the fall of the July monarchy in France.

However, the plans to send an expeditionary force to France were not carried out. By mid March a wave of popular uprisings had swept Austria, Prussia, Hungary, the southern German states and a number of Italian duchies and kingdoms; and by April 1848 the face of feudal Europe had been transformed. In his manifesto of 14 March O. S. 1848 Nicholas I proclaimed: 'An insane and unbounded impudence now threatens our Russia, which God has entrusted to us. But may it never have its way!'

The Tsar made another response to the February revolution, but this time he did not aim to impress the world or to restrain France. It was highly confidential and concerned Russia alone, and in the end it caused Dostoevsky's life to take a grim turn.

On 27 February 1848 the Third Department of the Emperor's Private Office noted that 'every Friday *lycée* students, jurists and university students' gathered at Petrashevsky's. Orders were issued that steps be taken 'to discover his behaviour and way of thinking'.

Thus was the foundation laid for the 1849 political trial, which, though conducted secretly, soon became notorious throughout Europe for the cruelty of its sentences.

Meanwhile Dostoevsky was following the events in Paris with deep emotion. He wrote shortly afterwards:

A frightful spectacle is unfolding in the West; an unprecedented drama is being enacted. The age-old order of things is cracking and falling apart. The most fundamental principles of society threaten to collapse at any moment and drag the whole nation down with them. Every day thirty-six million people are risking their entire future, their property, their very existence and the existence of their children as if in a game of cards. Is this not a picture to excite attention, curiosity and interest, and to overwhelm the soul? This is the self-same country that gave us science, education, European civilization. This spectacle is a lesson! This is, after all, history, and history is the science of the future. . . . Who can blame me for taking a serious view of the crisis which is causing unhappy France to groan and break in two, for regarding this crisis as historically necessary to that nation's life, feeling that perhaps it is a transitory condition (who can tell now?) and will bring better times in the end.

This does not tell us everything about Dostoevsky's attitude to the situation in France, but it makes it clear that his heart ached for it.

In the Russian literary circles opinion was divided. Belinsky, Granovsky, Herzen, Turgenev and Saltykov saluted the great event: 'France seemed a land of miracles' (Saltykov-Schedrin). But Annenkov, Botkin and the Slavophiles made no secret that they were afraid of the storm that had broken over the world. S. T. Aksakov wrote about the 'frightful event which may change the order of things in all of Europe'.

Dostoevsky's statement is not so explicit. His words reveal

the pain and grief of a writer who is trying to understand the essential nature of a historical tragedy.

*

The events in the West marked the beginning of a new era for the Petrashevsky society, too. The Propaganda Society turned into a political club with set-piece lectures, regular discussions, a chairman and even a little bell: a bronze hemisphere with a statue of Liberty marking the Equator. It was rung to calm passions and maintain order during arguments.

At Petrashevsky's request N. Y. Danilevsky delivered a series of lectures about the teachings of Fourier, Speshnev reported on 'The communists' view of religion', Ivan Yastrzhembsky conducted a brief course in political economy, and a retired midshipman from the Black Sea Fleet, Balasoglo, spoke of family happiness in the phlanastery.

It was probably during this period that Dostoevsky delivered his three talks – he himself was to give an account of them, later, to his judges – two on literature and one 'on a subject by no means political, namely, the human personality and egoism'.

His talks on literature were controversial and challenged the advocates of militant, utilitarian, didactic art. Dostoevsky defended the autonomy of creative art as he had in his argument with Belinsky. The poet Durov was on his side, but the majority disagreed with him. Dostoevsky stated before the judges:

> I remember very well that he supported me warmly during my two arguments about literature at Petrashevsky's. In this argument I claimed that literature *needs no direction except a purely artistic one* and that it certainly does not need the kind of direction that exposes *the root of evil*; the reason why literature does *not need* such direction is that direction restrains the writer's freedom and is, in addition, bilious and abusive, which is fatal to artistry.[4]

Dostoevsky's third talk, 'Personality and Human Egoism', was apparently an analysis of Max Stirner's *The Ego and His*

Own, which Belinsky had found so interesting; there was also a copy of the book in Petrashevsky's library. According to Pavel Annenkov, this treatise about boundless individualism 'was much talked about' in 1849; just the time when Dostoevsky became close to Durov's circle.

It deals with 'the philosophy of the spirit', or the inner culture of the individual, but it also touches on the issues of anarchism, democracy, communism and revolution. According to Stirner, the human individual is the supreme and absolute value of the universe; all categories, such as God, world history, the state, law and morals, dissolve in it completely. This sort of extreme cult of the 'ego' led to a rebellion against God and to self-deification of the individual, to whom 'everything is permitted'.

This presages the rebellious declarations of Raskolnikov, Kirillov and Ivan Karamazov. 'If there is no God, then my will is my own and I am obliged to assert self-will,' declared the bridge-builder Kirillov in *The Devils*, perfectly willing to blow up the whole world.

*

The writers in the Propaganda Society constituted a special group and in the autumn of 1848 two of its members, Dostoevsky and Pleshcheev, approached Speshnev with the suggestion that they start their own salon, distinct from the Friday group. The meetings at Petrashevsky's were really too socio-political and there were too many strangers – 'one is afraid to say a word'. Besides, Petrashevsky was not at all interested in art. And so it had occurred to them to form a non-political circle centred on literature and music, where poetry and narrative prose would be cultivated and chamber concerts held. The pianist Kashevsky and the violoncellist Shchelkov, both of whom were 'completely indifferent', as Dostoevsky wrote, 'to anything outside the realm of art', had already joined them. Of the writers, Pleshcheev, Durov, the Dostoevsky brothers, Palm and Milyukov had joined the new group. They planned to publish a miscellany or a magazine. This closed group of artists was initiated in November 1848 by the action of Fyodor Dostoevsky.

This project, however, did not meet with Speshnev's approval. The revolutionist had his own interpretation of this withdrawal from politics. He considered the projected association 'a society of fear of the police'.

Under the influence of the past year's events in Europe, Speshnev had lost all interest in pure art. He wanted more energetic revolutionary action. And so, with characteristic vigour, he immediately set about imparting to Dostoevsky and Pleshcheev's artistic meetings a direction that was well-nigh the opposite of what had been intended. Sergei Durov, a poet of the Lermontov school and a member of the radical wing of the Petrashevskyites, was named head of the new group, but Speshnev was its actual leader.

In addition to writers from the Propaganda Society's moderate majority, the Durov circle was joined by Mombelli, Grigoryev, Lvov and Filippov, who gave the group a strongly rebellious colour and aimed it unequivocally towards struggle and protest.

It was in this atmosphere that for the first time Dostoevsky's views became more radical, through his closer contact with the practical revolutionary and political conspirator Speshnev.

Nikolai Speshnev had for several years been training himself to lead a nationwide insurrection in Russia. In 1845, when he was abroad, he had made a study of secret societies. He had studied the history of early Christianity and had been astonished at that ancient brotherhood's influence on the world. He had begun to think about creating a similar association to achieve social goals in his own day. He drew up a special oath for members of a Russian secret society, requiring of them unquestioning subordination to a 'central committee', active preparation of insurrection through communist propaganda and, what was most important, 'direct participation in the rebellion and fighting with firearms and other weapons and without sparing oneself'.

In one of his speeches Speshnev declared that since he was unable to write in Russia he was determined to make wide use of the spoken word 'in order to spread socialism, atheism, terrorism – everything good in the world'. Before long, these generalizations began to crystallize into clear-cut concrete plans. In November 1848 there appeared at Petrashevsky's Friday meetings a heavily built man who looked as if he had been in the Forces – thick-set, clean-shaven, with a wooden leg, animated, loquacious, gay, full of wise-cracks and stories, very well informed about remote regions of Russia, and having an inexhaustible fund of personal impressions, particularly of the Far East. This was a retired second lieutenant named Chernosvitov, a veteran of the Turkish and Polish campaigns who had afterwards made a name for himself gold mining.

Intelligent, cheerful, with a wide interest in every aspect of the contemporary world, its organizations and the types who lived in it, Chernosvitov was fond of visiting the taverns, drink-shops, slums and thieves' kitchens of Petersburg, observing the manners of the bottom levels of society of a great city, listening to their complaints and protests, interesting himself in their needs, and taking note of their muttered threats.

He was particularly fond of telling stories about his native land – Eastern Siberia – a grand, rich, fertile country with a wonderful climate and a way of life of its own, thinly inhabited and with inexhaustible possibilities for the future.

He used to say that a popular revolt was brewing in the Urals and Eastern Siberia. Everything was ready. The workers from the mines and the deportees from the goldfields were going to come thronging down to the south. The governments' forces in those remote regions would be too insignificant to stop the thrust of these countless crowds; the lower classes of the province would join the insurgents.

A new Pugachov revolt would begin! Then all that would be needed would be to start revolts in Moscow and Petersburg and produce a general conflagration in which the whole imperial system would collapse in ruins.

In February 1849 the Durov circle began to meet every week and this brought Dostoevsky into more frequent contact with Speshnev. They became closer politically and the influence of the revolutionist's strong will and dominating personality on the Utopian poet's meditative nature steadily deepened. As a pure Fourierist, however, advocating peaceful reforms as the only possible method of action, Dostoevsky was afraid of Speshnev's dangerous political path and even in the new climate of 1849 attempted to preserve his independent position as a writer, thinker and speaker. He rejected armed struggle. The most he would concede was to expand libertarian propaganda to the extent of organizing a secret printing press. This act, however, made him a political conspirator. He worried agonizingly about this radical change in his life, and Dr Yanovsky observed his patient's depressed state of mind with anxiety.

Dostoevsky invented a story to the effect that Speshnev had done him a great financial favour by lending him five hundred silver roubles and had thereby put him in great debt and deprived him of his peace of mind. 'Now I am with him and belong to him,' he told Yanovsky. 'Do you realize that ever since then I have had my own Mephistopheles?' Dostoevsky never forgot his spiritual subordination to Speshnev, nor the man's irresistible charm. When he was faced with the artistic task of portraying a Russian revolutionary, he included some of Speshnev's traits in his 'mysterious' Stavrogin.

The exact nature of the Petrashevskyites' revolutionary programme is unknown, but the tactics of the new organization that Speshnev had formed within the Propaganda Society included three elements: a managing committee, made up of the most intelligent and influential members of

the Propaganda Society; a secret printing press; and a
future insurrection. In the spring of 1849 Dostoevsky spoke
of the new group to Apollon Maikov, whose account,
extremely pertinent to an understanding of Dostoevsky's
life, has fortunately been preserved.

One evening Dostoevsky turned up at my apartment in the
Anichkov house in a state of excitement and said that he had an
important message for me.

'Of course, you understand that Petrashevsky is a chatterbox,
that he is not a serious person and that nothing can possibly come
of his undertakings,' he said. 'And for that reason several serious
persons from his circle have decided (secretly and without telling
the others anything) to form their own secret society with a
secret printing press in order to print various books and even
magazines, if that works out. We had our doubts about you, for
you are too proud' (imagine! Fyodor Mikhailovich reproaching
me with pride).

'What do you mean?'

'Well, you don't recognize authority. For instance, you do not
agree with Speshnev.'

'I am not particularly interested in political economy. And it
does indeed seem to me that Speshnev talks nonsense. But what
of it?'

'For the good of the common cause one must exercise self-
control. There are seven of us now: Speshnev, Mordvinov,
Mombelli, Pavel Filippov, Grigoryev, Vladimir Milyutin and
myself. We have chosen you to be the eighth. Do you want to
join our society?'

'But what is its purpose?'

'Its purpose is to organize a *coup* in Russia, naturally. We've
already got a printing press designed by Mordvinov. It was
ordered in parts, in different places. It is all ready.'

'Not only do I not wish to join the society, but I advise you
to get out of it. What sort of political leaders would we make?
We are poets and artists, not practical men, and we haven't a
penny. Surely, you don't think the likes of us are suited to be
revolutionaries, do you?'

Dostoevsky, who was wearing a red nightshirt with the

collar unbuttoned, began to preach passionately and for a long time, waving his hands. We argued for some time until we finally got tired and went to bed.[5]

In the morning Dostoevsky asked: 'Well, what about it?'

'Why, the same as yesterday. I woke up before you did and thought about it. I, myself, will not join and, I repeat, if it is still possible, give them up and get out.'

'Well, that's my own affair. And, listen, only seven people know what I told you. You are the eighth – there must be not a ninth.'

'As far as that is concerned, here is my hand. I won't say a word to anyone!'

I do not know whether the Commission of Inquiry knew about this faction in the Petrashevsky society. It said in Dostoevsky's sentence, among other things: 'For intending to start a secret printing press.' The printing press, which was at Mordvinov's, escaped notice when the house was searched because it stood in Mordvinov's physics laboratory among all kinds of machines, retorts, and the like. A seal was put on the door and that was all. By removing the hinges the family managed to get rid of the ill-starred printing press without breaking the seal.[6]

This newly published version of Maikov's letter shows how strongly political Dostoevsky was in the spring of 1849. It also explains the remarks Dostoevsky made with regard to a book, entitled *The Propaganda Society*, published in Leipzig in 1875. 'True,' he said, 'but not the whole truth. I do not see my own role in it. Many circumstances have been ignored completely. A whole conspiracy has vanished.' The reference is to Speshnev's conspiracy and his own participation in it.

In Durov's literary–musical circle, meanwhile, political discussions superseded Chopin concerts. By the middle of April Palm and Durov took note of the dangerous direction their 'artistic' meetings had taken and called them off. At this time the Petrashevskyites were having what proved to be their last and most significant meetings. It was as if the unquenchable torch of the libertarian ideas that had inspired them had flared up before their catastrophe with a final brilliant flame.

'ONE WOMAN'S STORY'

At the beginning of 1849 *Otechestvennie Zapiski* began to publish a new long novel by Dostoevsky enchantingly and poetically entitled *Netochka Nezvanova*.[7] The Petrashevskyite Ippolite Debu recalls that Dostoevsky told *One Woman's Story* (the novel's sub-title) at the Friday gatherings in much greater detail than appeared in the printed version: 'I remember that lively compassion he felt even then for the social 'stratum' which Sonya Marmeladova would later personify in his work (of course, Fourier's doctrine had some influence here).'

The following, from one of the manuscripts of *Netochka Nezvanova* that has survived, is apparently connected with the Sonya Marmeladova theme: 'You still have my engraving of 'Christ and the Woman' by Signole.[8] It has an inscription that reads: "*Qui sine peccato est vestrum primus in illam lapidem mittat.*"[9] My poor, poor darling! Are you that sinner?' The 'fallen woman' and 'righteous man' theme, subsequently to become a favourite with the mature Dostoevsky, appeared in his work for the first time in these two works of the late 1840s, *The Landlady* and *Netochka Nezvanova*. The drama of sin and expiation, however, is not the principal theme of *Netochka Nezvanova*; it merely touches on the main story line. The principal idea that Dostoevsky was trying to express in the novel was apparently that of the emancipatory mission of a great artist in the corrupt society of the day which is unexpectedly regenerated by the radiant power of the heroine's art.

Netochka Nezvanova marked a new stage in Dostoevsky's tireless artistic exploration. He had been dreaming of a novel constructed on the lines of Lermontov's *A Hero of Our*

Time, that is, a novel made up of five or six separate stories all centred on one protagonist. He was to set forth the theory of this unusual 'Lermontov' form much later, in letters he wrote in 1856 and expounded it again to his friends in 1868, when he was working on a plan for *The Life of a Great Sinner*. But it was in 1846 that he first turned his attentions to this complex but spacious and interesting form, when he was planning his first big novel, on which he worked mainly in 1848 and 1849.

The first part of *Netochka Nezvanova* is entitled 'Childhood' and is consistently written in the tone of a romantic tale about an outstanding musician with a tragic fate, a violinist and composer, inventor of a new music theory, crushed by poverty, dependence and failure, which is only aggravated by his excessive pride and vanity.

Out of this theme there imperceptibly emerges and unfolds a second theme – his main one. Netochka, the violinist's small stepdaughter, is growing up in an environment saturated with interest in art, among obscure actors, dancers and orchestra musicians. She adores her stepfather for his unrecognized genius and is waiting for her suffering mother to die, for then, she believes, their troubles will end and the road to happiness and fame will open up. But disaster shakes her out of this hopeful fantasy. Her mother dies on the day of a concert given by a celebrated guest virtuoso. That evening the self-taught Efimov plays his violin besides his wife's already stiffening body, testing his own talent, but his impotent bow can hardly manage even to repeat the virtuoso's musical phrasing. Efimov dies in an insane fit of rage.

The second part is entitled 'A New Life'. Netochka is taken into the wealthy home of Prince X. The poor little orphan becomes the friend of Princess Katya, the proud and domineering young daughter of the house. This is Dostoevsky's first story, incidentally, about children and their secret dreams. Princess Katya's unclouded childhood has had no resemblance whatsoever to Netochka's own dismal early years. The healthy, graceful, proud, rich girl is a complete contrast to the timid and shy dreamer from the lower strata of the urban intelligentsia. Katya is surrounded by a whole bevy of serf girls, whose enforced servility encourages her love of power. The quiet and meditative Netochka submissively accepts her new friend's outbursts of passionate friendship and unbending wilfulness. Dostoevsky's portrayal of the two young girls, so different in background, upbringing and character, is an early study of the 'meek' and the 'proud' and brings out admirably the social principles that produced two such contrasting natures – for one, life in a wretched attic; for the other, life in a princely palace. This part of the book is one of the finest in Dostoevsky's early work.

The magazine version contained an interesting portrayal of the 'unfortunate boy' Larinka, a lonely, sickly child, lost in the palace's empty halls. The critic Druzhinin associated Larinka with sick little Paul in *Dombey and Son*. It is true that Dickens was one of Dostoevsky's favourite authors at that time, but the portrait of Netochka's little friend Larinka was Dostoevsky's own characteristic image of a young creature whom life has injured at an early age and who dreams of revenge. Dostoevsky was to create such a character again some thirty years later in Ilyusha Snegirov in *The Brothers Karamazov*.

The third and final part is called 'The Secret' and depicts Netochka's life against the background of the domestic tragedy of a society woman. Prince X's stepdaughter, who has undertaken to be Netochka's guardian, a spiritually refined and morally sensitive woman, has fallen in love with a man beneath her station, and is slowly being killed by the contempt of the salon riff-raff and the hatred of her heartless bureaucrat of a husband. It is in the course of the development of this domestic conflict that the main story line is defined: Netochka becomes an outstanding singer, destined for triumph and fame. The parallel stories – the love of a society woman, enslaved by the conventions of marriage, and the confessions of a sixteen-year-old girl, elated by her youthful talent – reveal the influence of the early novels of George Sand, of whom Dostoevsky had a very high opinion. The third part of *Netochka Nezvanova* is an example of how well the young Dostoevsky developed a genre that attracted him, always with his own undeniable and inimitable touch.

It is interesting to see in *Netochka Nezvanova* Dostoevsky's first attempt at what was subsequently to become a favourite form of his, the philosophical dialogue (or monologue); the more so since it is on so important a theme as the creative method of an artist. Like Balzac, the young Dostoevsky believed that tireless, unceasing, persistent work was the basis of art. In his letters written to his brother in 1845 he expressed admiration for 'the old school', whose masters worked slowly and created little, but produced what they did with finality and for eternity. 'Raphael painted a picture for years, polishing it and removing from it, and the result was a miracle.' This became the basic law of construction for Dostoevsky's work. His attitude to the work of a creative artist was expressed in 1849 in his portrayals of the two violinists in *Netochka Nezvanova* – the 'cold, methodical B.', a tireless worker, and the gifted, quick-tempered and dissolute Efimov, who had a disorderly imagination and boundless self-esteem. The former reaches the pinnacles of art by dint of inflexible will; the latter dies, having dissipated his considerable talent ingloriously and fruitlessly.

Netochka Nezvanova has survived as a fragment of a long novel, which the author was prevented from finishing by his forced departure from public life. Even so it reveals a remarkably clear plan, originality of composition and extraordinary dramatic power in its delineation of character. It is one of the most mature and well-written works of Dostoevsky's youth. At the same time it contains contradictions and divergences that foreshadow Dostoevsky's ideological retreat from his progressive views. Though written at the height of the European Revolution of 1848-9, it was not touched by it. On the contrary, some of the situations in the story indicate that Dostoevsky was very remote from the revolutionary–democratic culture of Belinsky and Herzen. In this novel about a famous singer Dostoevsky is influenced not by the George Sand who was a socialist and a herald of future phalansteries, but by the George Sand of her 'first period', with its vague prophesies of a better future and graphic expression of the omnipotence of love, freedom in love, the beauty of creative art, songs and poetry and the enchanting inspiration of Chopin and Alfred de Musset.

In *Netochka Nezvanova* Dostoevsky has much to say about the serf-born intelligentsia, performers who were the protégés of landowners, and orchestras supported by the gentry. In 1848, a few months before the novel began to appear in *Otechestvennie Zapiski*, *Sovremennik* had printed Herzen's *The Thieving Magpie*, a deeply moving story about a 'great Russian actress', leading lady of a serf theatre company, who was hounded to death by the lecherous old Prince Salinsky, who owned the troupe. The story made a tremendous impression on contemporaries and remains an unforgettable masterpiece of Russian prose.

Dostoevsky seems to be giving his reply to *The Thieving Magpie*, which he must have known. All the social accents, so faultlessly and forcefully placed by Herzen, are inverted. The musician at Herzen's serf-theatre becomes, with Dostoevsky, a freely engaged commoner who can afford to display his intolerably arrogant and insolent manners; utterly immoral – a 'nasty' type. Conversely, rectitude and true humanity are the attributes of the aristocratic connoisseurs of this man's art – the generous landowner with his passion for music, who takes good care of his obstreperous clarinet player, and the good-natured prince, who rescues the poverty stricken girl. Magnanimity is here the prerogative of the upper social strata, while the negative traits belong to members of the lower social groups, for example, the unbearable Efimov, who is a direct predecessor of that '*bourgeois gentilhomme*' Foma Opiskin in 'The Village of Stepanchikovo'. In Dostoevsky's treatment Efimov is not destroyed by the monstrous social conditions that made serf orchestras possible, but solely by his own unbalanced temperament.

One of the brightest characters in *Netochka Nezvanova* from the author's point of view is Prince X., a well-known dilettante, a mystic and one who loves to do good. This is the first ideal prince in Dostoevsky's portrait gallery and anticipates the hero of *The Idiot*, though Prince X guards the traditions of his ancient family, represents the 'hereditary nobility' worthily and is a 'living chronicle of the ancient *boyars*' in his sumptuous life. Dostoevsky was to repeat these genealogical expressions more than once in his later apologias for the 'upper cultural strata'.

It is possible that the prototype for Prince X was Prince V. F. Odoevsky, whom Dostoevsky knew personally and admired. (*Poor Folk* has an epigraph from a story by Odoevsky.) Characteristically, Odoevsky wrote 'artistic' stories, such as *Beethoven's Last Quartet, Sebastian Bach, The Creations of Cavaliere Giambattista Piranesi*, and stories about the struggles and sufferings of 'great madmen'. This is in keeping with the leading motifs in *Netochka Nezvanova*, and Odoevsky's story *The Improviser*, which is about the death of an artist who tried to create without hard work, comes close to Dostoevsky's views as he expressed them in the conversations between the two violinists in his own story.

Netochka Nezvanova was the epilogue to Dostoevsky's literary youth. It was cut short before it could give us more than a glimpse of a major and serious purpose. To most readers it is a charming story about children, but its design is much broader. In it Dostoevsky was establishing himself as a portrayer of the dangerous path of the artist, creator and seeker; he was probably also establishing himself as poet of a distant Utopian ideal, which was to be realized through the influence of art on the masses. He combined profound psychological insight with nobility of theme in this tale of the celebrated Russian singer Anna Nezvanova, who came from the urban poor and whose talent brought joy to everyone.

THE LAST MEETINGS

It was assumed at the time that the destruction of the Petrashevsky circle was brought about by a banquet held on the occasion of Fourier's birthday; and the banquet did indeed bring nearer the disaster which was about to strike the great sociologist's Russian disciples. The meeting, although one of their last, was imbued with creative hope and unshakeable faith in the triumph of their doctrine.

On 7 April 1849 eleven Fourierists, with Petrashevsky and Speshnev at their head, gathered at the apartment of Alexander Europeus, a candidate for a degree at Petersburg University. A life-size, waist-length portrait of Fourier, ordered from Paris for the occasion, towered above the gathering. It was a picture of an extraordinary looking man with a huge forehead on which a light seemed to shine. The man's entire appearance, with lips pressed together commandingly and the fiery eyes of a prophet gazing into the distant future, conveyed great will-power. Before the great thinker's portrait, someone recited Béranger's famous poem about Utopian socialism:

> Should the sun
> Forget to light up our earth tomorrow,
> Some madman's mind would
> Light the world up.[10]

A copy of Fourier's celebrated book *The New World of*

Industry and Society was then torn into sections and distributed among those present for translation. Petrashevsky delivered a vigorous political speech. He proposed a toast 'for the knowledge of reality from the standpoint of social propaganda'. He said it was the task of the new generation of Russians to introduce into their land of Eastern stagnation and feudal barbarism the highest forms of human association as proclaimed by geniuses of the West. Socialism would triumph in Russia, a land exhausted by suffering that was the inevitable result of slavery and centuries of ignorance. The power of thought and science would cause the obsolete and unjust system to collapse and give way to the coming perfect organization of the masses that would provide every individual with all he needed for full development and complete happiness.

Akhsharumov, the orientalist, spoke of the cities in which people suffer all the time, live in constant agony and die of revolting diseases. Khanykov, a brilliant speaker and a friend and associate of the young Chernyshevsky, said that it was the society's task 'to restore the image of man in all its grandeur and beauty to liberate and organize the now repressed and suppressed noble, harmonious passions, to destroy capital cities and towns and use the materials therefrom to construct new buildings, and to turn this life of agony, trouble, poverty, shame and sorrow into a life of luxury and complete harmony, filled with joy, riches and happiness. To cover this entire impoverished land with palaces and fruits and decorate it with flowers, this is our aim, a great aim: never has this earth known a greater.' This contrast between existing poverty and suffering and the forthcoming Golden Age dominated the speeches and arguments of Fourier's Russian disciples, and aroused special fervour at this ceremonial banquet.

*

That anxious and restless winter the young Petrashevskyites who were especially interested in literature and music had an outstanding experience: they made the acquaintance of Glinka. The great composer had been living in Paris, Spain and Warsaw, during which time he had composed his *Aragonese Jota, Memories of Castile,* a Russian symphonic composition based on themes from wedding songs, with their wild gaiety and their melancholy – *Kamarinskaya,* and his charming lyrical miniatures to the words of Pushkin's 'Amber Cup' and 'I drink to Mary's health'.

Once back in Petersburg, he re-established his old friendships with Odoevsky and Vielgorsky and made the acquaintance of Serov and Stasov and other gifted young people. He was also very much interested in Petersburg's political circles, which were continuing the traditions of the Decembrists, so close to the heart of the composer of *Ivan Susanin.* He had been a pupil of Kunitsyn and of Galich at school, Kuechelbecker had been his tutor.* He had known Pushkin personally and never forgot the poet's verses against tyranny. He had heard about the secret societies and in many respects sympathized with their programme. He was interested in Ryleyev's *Thoughts.* Being a true artist, he hated despotism and loved freedom. Now he wished to meet the members of the Petrashevsky circle, and he invited some of them to his home one evening.

Among those invited was the author of the 'musical novel' *Netochka Nezvanova,* then appearing in *Otechestvennie Zapiski.* Dostoevsky had loved Glinka ever since the very first performances of *Ruslan and Lyudmila* in 1842, and he was overjoyed at the prospect of meeting the composer of that musical poem about ancient Rus. He saw seated at the piano a rather short man with small delicate hands, whose fingers seemed not to strike the keys but to drop on them like pearls dropping on velvet. Glinka had adopted this manner

---

* Kunitsyn, Alexander Petrovich (1783–1840), Russian jurist; Galich, Alexander Ivanovich (1783–1848), Russian philosopher and psychologist; Kuechelbecker, Vilgelm Karlovich (1797–1846), Russian poet, Decembrist. All three influenced Pushkin.

from the teacher he had had when he was young, the Irish pianist John Field, retaining its clarity and brilliance but adding great depth and genuine inspiration.

The atmosphere of the gathering was friendly and intimate. P. M. Kovalevsky has described that evening in his memoirs:

> The piano was tuned, a couple of bottles of Lafite were warmed and the composer asked a lady to stand by the piano.
>
> At first Glinka improvised rather lightly and without thinking. When all the guests had arrived, he took a drink out of his glass, lifted the lady's hand and patted it affectionately, then turned to the piano again. 'This is for you,' he whispered to the lady.
>
> 'When at times of merriment you open your pretty lips,' he sang, finally ending: 'I want to kiss, kiss, kiss,' with so much expression that the lady bent down to him. For Glinka, however, the impression he had made was sufficient.

That evening he played Chopin, Gluck, Bayan's lines from *Ruslan and Liudmila*, a fantasy on *Kamarinskaya*. 'There are only a few nights like this in a lifetime,' said the writer of the memoirs.[11]

Dostoevsky remembered this intimate concert all his life, his wife Anna notes. Twenty years later, in a story called *The Eternal Husband*, he drew in a few quick strokes a picture of a great musician seated at an open piano:

> Velchaninov selected a love-song of Glinka's that hardly anyone remembered any more.
>
> > 'When at times of merriment you open your
> > pretty lips
> > And you begin to coo to me more tenderly than
> > a dove . . .'

Velchaninov had had an occasion to hear this song for the first time about twenty years earlier, when he was still a student, from Glinka himself at a literary–artistic bachelor party in the home of a friend of the late composer. Glinka had let himself go and played all his favourite songs. Velchaninov remembered the extraordinary impression that this one love-song had made on him at the time. To have sung that short but extraordinary little song required truth, required genuine, complete inspiration, real passion or the complete poetic mastery of it.

Then follows a description of the performance of the song by Velchaninov, who had 'nearly mastered Glinka's manner of singing':

genuine inspiration could be heard in his voice ... cries of passion rang out as he sang the last lines, turning sparkling eyes to Nadya:

> 'Now I look more boldly into your eyes,
> I bring my mouth closer, I can no longer hear,
> I want to kiss, kiss, kiss!
> I want to kiss, kiss, kiss!'

Nadya was so startled she pulled back a bit. Her cheeks flushed pink, and in that instant Velchaninov saw a flash of response in her shy, almost timid little face.

Thus Dostoevsky recreated one of the most vivid musical experiences of his life.

*

The most famous of the Petrashevsky meetings, one that has gone down in the history of Russian literature and social thought, took place on 15 April 1849. At this meeting Dostoevsky read aloud Belinsky's 'Letter to Gogol', which astonished the audience by its boldness and power.

A few days before, about 10 April, Dostoevsky had called on Durov and had found a packet for him there from Pleshcheev, who was away on a visit to Moscow. The packet contained copies of the correspondence between Belinsky and Gogol. Prior to that, on 30 March, Pleshcheev had written to Durov that the deceased critic's 'article' was circulating in manuscript form in Moscow along with two other outstanding items of banned literature, Turgenev's *Hanger-On* and Herzen's *Before the Storm*, and that it invariably evoked general admiration in Moscow's drawing-rooms.

The intelligentsia of Petersburg had heard of Belinsky's letter but no one had actually read it. Dostoevsky had been wanting to read it since 1847, and now at last it was in his hands. He read the great journalist's indictment then and there to Durov and Palm, and while he was reading Petrashevsky dropped in. Dostoevsky promised him he would read all the literature he had received, including Gogol's reply, at the very next Friday gathering. A little while later Mombelli, Lvov, the Lamansky brothers, Filippov and Mikhail Dostoevsky, all members of Durov's group, arrived too. Dostoevsky read the 'article' aloud a second time. Belinsky's letter to Gogol made a tremendous impression on them all. They talked again about the need to spread anti-government literature of this kind among the people and to set up a secret lithographic press for the purpose. Mikhail Dostoevsky, who was a cautious man, objected to this.

A few days later twenty members of the Petrashevsky circle gathered at a regular Friday meeting. Among them was an agent of the Third Department, Antonelli, an Italian student who had attended all the Petrashevsky meetings since 11 March 1849. Dostoevsky read with his characteristic fervour. He testified soon afterwards at the investigation:

I read Belinsky's letter to Gogol, as I had volunteered to do when I saw Petrashevsky at Durov's. I read it, trying not to show any bias for or against either of the correspondents. I did not talk to anyone there about the letter after I had read it. I heard no one express an opinion about the correspondence. While I was reading I heard some scattered exclamations, some laughter, depending on the impression, but I could not draw any certain conclusions from this.

Dostoevsky did not say a word about the audience's enthusiastic comments, but Antonelli had reported them in detail: according to him the letter 'evoked general enthusiasm. The entire group seemed electrified.'

Dostoevsky told the Commission of Inquiry, 'As for myself,

I disagreed with literally every one of the exaggerations in it.'

This does not mean that he disagreed with the writer of the letter on everything. The social reforms that Belinsky proposed were entirely in keeping with Dostoevsky's political convictions. Dostoevsky undoubtedly agreed with Belinsky's 'minimum programme': abolition of serfdom and of corporal punishment and strict execution of the laws. But he worshipped Gogol and he must have been pained (as was Annenkov, who had made the copy of the celebrated letter when he was in Salzbrunn) by the personal accusations Belinsky made against Gogol. He did not regard Russian civil servants as a wholly corrupt group. On the contrary, he found among them many of his favourite protagonists with 'gentle' or 'meek' hearts. Makar Devushkin's chief, in *Poor Folk*, is the ideal of goodness and philanthropy. Nor did he agree with Belinsky's characterization of the Russian peasants as a deeply 'atheistic people without a trace of religious feeling'. All this patently conflicted with his views and could only have extended and deepened the philosophical controversy of 1946.

At the trial Dostoevsky stressed that he had read not only Belinsky's Salzbrunn message at the meeting, but also Gogol's reply to it. He insisted that he had never anywhere expressed agreement with Belinsky's famous indictment and declared that there were many witnesses who could corroborate his statement. The military tribunal, however, did not take much notice of these explanations.

*

The Propaganda Society met for the last time on 22 April 1849. The immediate tasks of contemporary literature were the subject of the discussion at that meeting. Petrashevsky urged writers to educate readers in the spirit of progressive ideas, as George Sand and Eugène Sue were doing in the West. Balasoglo assailed the writers present – the Dostoevsky brothers and Durov – and called upon them to write about the latest social movement in detail. Mombelli came to their defence. Then they discussed a plan of raising share-capital for the publication of a magazine. There were arguments and proposals and a programme was outlined.

But it was already a meeting of the doomed. On that very morning Nicholas I had given his decision on a memorandum submitted to him about the 'advocate of communism and new ideas' Petrashevsky, who had already been under surveillance for fourteen months, since the end of February 1848. The Tsar had written to Count Orlov, head of the Third Department:

I have read it all. It is an important case, for even if it were all lies, the lies themselves would be criminal and intolerable in the highest degree.

Start making arrests as you propose, only it would be better to avoid publicity as a result of the large number of people involved.

Give no advance notification to Nabokov.[12] It will be much better if he finds out directly from me. Arrange that.

God be with you. God's will be done.

On the same day Count Orlov signed an order for the immediate arrest of thirty-four Petrashevskyites. These were their last hours of freedom.

Dostoevsky had evidently called in late that evening to see Grigoryev, an officer of the Guards and author of the revolutionary book *Soldier Talk*. He borrowed a banned book by Eugène Sue, *Pastor of Cravant: Talks on Socialism*. It was after 3 a.m. when he got home. A little after 4 a.m. he was awakened by a strange noise. Someone was walking about his room. He heard the clank of sabres outside.

'What's the matter' he asked, sleepily.

'Engineer-Lieutenant Dostoevsky, you are under arrest by order of His Majesty,' the reply rang out.

A major of the gendarmerie uttered these words in tones

of great solemnity and then, changing to an ordinary tone of voice, ordered his squad:

'Seal the papers and books.'

Sealing-wax flamed and the state coat-of-arms was imprinted on Dostoevsky's boxes and bookcases.

A carriage was waiting at the entrance below. The prisoner was driven at a brisk trot to the Fontanka, to the well-known building near the Summer Garden that housed the Third Department of His Majesty's Private Office. The next day Dostoevsky was imprisoned in the Peter and Paul Fortress.

VI

The Court Martial

THE ALEXEEVSKY RAVELIN

THE walls were of fortress thickness. The whitewashed windows were covered by triple bars. Beyond were the high walls of the bastion. Only by pressing against the glass was it possible to get a glimpse of a scrap of the grey Petersburg sky and, at times, of a timid cloud floating by. In solitary confinement it is always twilight. The stool, the wooden bed, the table and the washstand melt into the damp darkness. A furry greenish-black mould covers the walls up to nearly seven feet from the floor. There is a hardly perceptible long narrow slit cut out in the body of the massive door. This is a peephole. It is impossible to tell whether it is blocked by its heavy cover or whether two eyes are staring through it, silently and watchfully: the Commandant's, the warder's or the guard's. It is damp, cold, bare. Hewn stone everywhere. The silence is complete. There is not another soul near by.

This was Dostoevsky's new habitation – the 'secret house' of the Alexeevsky Ravelin. It was the most dreadful place in the most dreadful of political prisons. Only the most important state criminals were brought here. The Decembrists – Ryleev, Pestel, Kakhovsky, Volkonsky, Trubetskoi – had languished in these cells. Now the Petrashevskyites had been thrust here. The 'secret' dungeon building was divided from the rest of the island area by insurmountable walls and a deep moat. The Ravelin's one entrance was accessible only by a bridge across the moat. In this citadel prisoners lost their names and were referred to instead by the number of their cell. Life was regulated by the Tsar's orders.

No restraints were imposed on the prison administration, there were no inspections and no controls. It was tantamount to being buried alive.

Flung into this prison without trial, the Petrashevskyites were now in the hands of the highest military authorities. The government had decided to make an example of them. A few days after the arrests, at the end of April, a secret Commission of Inquiry, consisting of high army officers and senators, under the chairmanship of General Nabokov, Commandant of Peter and Paul Fortress, went to work in the bastion on the Neva.

As one of the most important of the state criminals, Dostoevsky was among the first to be called before it. On 6 May three questions were put to him:

1. What was Petrashevsky's character as a man and, in particular, as a political person?

2. What took place at the gatherings in Petrashevsky's house?

3. Did the Petrashevsky society have a secret aim?

This was, in essence, a questionnaire on the whole activity of the socialist group. Dostoevsky submitted his testimony in writing, and even today that testimony is striking for its intellectual power, its independence and truthfulness, its dignity and its nobility. In it he strove to protect his comrades from the charges against them and took the responsibility for a number of actions that could lead straight to the scaffold. He was certainly justified when he wrote in 1854: 'I conducted myself honestly before the court and did not try to shift my own blame to others; I even sacrificed my interests whenever I thought I could possibly protect others by my confession.'

The documents of the case confirm this fully. Not only did the imprisoned writer openly state his convictions, ideas and interests in official testimony, but he also courageously criticized the system which his interrogators and judges represented. To their faces he condemned the oppression of thought and word that inevitably forced contemporary writers into insoluble conflicts. Dostoevsky was not afraid to disclose to the Tsarist executioners his own deep conflict as an artist with the system of Nicholas I. Even while imprisoned in the Peter and Paul Fortress he continued to defend his ardent young faith in the power of artistic creativity. He protested against the coercion imposed on his ideas by censorship and fought openly for the right to his own tragic style in Russian literature. A doomed but by no means spiritually broken man faced the inquisitors of the political dungeon. 'I love literature and cannot help being interested in it. Literature is one of the expressions of the life of the people; it is a mirror of society, what else has formulated new ideas in such a manner that the people can understand them if not literature?'

These are undoubtedly among the most memorable autobiographical pages Dostoevsky ever wrote. He set forth with extraordinary vividness the history of his political and aesthetic quests of the past three years. His masterly portraits of remarkable contemporaries like Belinsky and Petrashevsky shed light on the ideological struggle of the period and at the same time brought up major literary problems, boldly introducing into this document for the court names he loved so well, such as Pushkin, Griboedov and Fonvizin.* His pen turned his official testimony into a brilliant memoir.

The inquiry lasted four months. For a long time the prisoners were not permitted any contacts at all with the outside world. Finally, in July, they were allowed to correspond with relatives, receive books and magazines, and to write. By that time Dostoevsky 'had conceived three stories

---

* Griboedov (1795–1829), author of *Chatsky*, or *Woe from Wit*, one man's single-handed fight against the prejudices and corruption of Moscow society. Fonvizin (1745–92), author of *The Minor*, a comedy in verse about a satire on the ignorance of country gentry and their oppression of their serfs.

and two novels', and now he began to write down one of them. All he managed to finish, though, was a short story entitled 'The Little Hero', written in a new, brilliant and uncharacteristic style, about an adolescent's first love.

His brother sent him Shakespeare in a translation by Ketcher. The edition had not yet been completed but it included *Othello*, *Macbeth* and *Julius Caesar*. Dostoevsky was very pleased with this gift. He was also pleased to receive the latest issues of *Otechestvennie Zapiski*, which was serializing Charlotte Brontë's *Jane Eyre*: 'an extremely good English novel'. This was the story of a poor girl brought up in an orphanage and then employed as a governess in rich homes. Dostoevsky wrote to his brother that he suffered from insomnia, nightmares, nervous attacks and physical weakness. But the tone of his letters was invariably calm and cheerful. The Ravelin had not broken his creative spirit.

BEFORE THE COMMISSION OF INQUIRY

A narrow table stood on a raised platform in the smoothly whitewashed hall. From the smoothness of the gold-fringed blood-red cloth, the kind used on official occasions, rose a three-sided pillar inscribed with decrees of Peter I, surmounted by a two-headed eagle; an enormous bronze cross with a carved ivory figure flattened against its beams stood beside the table. At the foot of this carved image of an execution in ancient times lay heavy volumes of army decrees with their ruthless penalties of shooting and hanging. Above these paraphernalia of justice hung a dark varnished full-dress portrait of an unnaturally tall cavalryman, negligently crumpling a glove in one hand, and holding a white-plumed cocked hat firmly in the other, gazing down from his full height with a deathly look that turned the spectator cold. Just below the rowels of His Majesty's spurs were five frowning elderly faces with sideburns and smoothly combed hair: Dubelt's wolfish maw, Nabokov's heavy skull, the moon-like face, with shaved upper lip and bird-like eyes of grey-haired old Senator Gagarin, who was wearing a frock-coat with a white star; fat Rostovtsev's broad, sagging, face; and dried-up Dolgorukov's steely, cruel gaze. The blue and green uniforms and the silver of braid and the gold of orders were everywhere. The secret Commission of Inquiry was present in full strength.

They sat in silence, His Majesty's aides-de-camp and privy councillors – calm, withdrawn, inaccessible, elated by the powers they had been granted from above, proud of the servile exploits that had won them the right in their old age to shed rivers of young blood, and build their own splendiferous well-being upon death sentences uttered without hesitation and completed with the final flourish of royally ornate signatures.

From behind red cloth on the judges' table, fanatical eyes looked down from their dais curiously and avidly at the puny, sickly looking nervous young writer, who stood motionless before them in his prison clothes with heart beating and eyes open wide. Pale and round-shouldered, the genius who dreamed of a Golden Age and universal happiness stood before these Tsarist spies, clad in the broadcloth armour of their Guards' uniforms. Strange, clearly enunciated words fluttered down to him from the high platform. Old Nabokov, the chairman, was speaking. He was an ancient relic in honourable retirement. A participant in the battles of Borodino and Leipzig and in the assault on Warsaw, he had only recently resigned the command of a Grenadier Corps, and had been insulted with the resounding but hollow title of Director of the Chesmensk Home for Soldiers and Commandant of the Petersburg Fortress – in command of veterans and prisoners. For all that, he frowned threateningly and zealously strove to prove himself a worthy vehicle of His Majesty's wrath.

'Retired Engineer-Lieutenant Dostoevsky, the first,' he intoned in a hoarse, bass voice. 'You are charged with criminal membership of a secret society, which had begun to carry out its evil designs against the Russian Orthodox Church and the Supreme Authority. Kindly tell this secret Commission of Inquiry all you know about the matter. Come closer to the table.'

Dostoevsky took a timid step forward. He spoke with emotion and at length. His speech, confused at first, gradually gained coherence. Once more he was confronted by the agonizing question – why isn't everybody happy? The brilliant repartees in the debates and the inspired pages of Utopian books came vividly to his mind. He felt as if the great rebels and prophets were shedding the radiance of their wisdom. He spoke of the great drama being enacted in the West, causing unhappy France to groan and break in two. He spoke of the teachings of Charles Fourier, saying that though they were inapplicable to Russian conditions, they charmed the soul by their grace and harmony and love of humanity. He said that socialism had already greatly benefited society by the critical statistical research it had conducted. He spoke of the great Utopias, of a forthcoming world fraternity, which would bring back to our unhappy planet the blessed times of the Golden Age.

'And then all this around us today, all whom life has trampled, all the worn-out women and starving children, all the alcoholics, the dying villages, and the cities' horrible poverty and the diseases – all will disappear into one jubilant hymn of unknown, unprecedented, universal and boundless happiness!'

They listened to him attentively, without interrupting. But as soon as he finished they went into action. They exchanged fragmentary phrases with one another and agreed on the next moves in the inquiry. General Dolgorukov, assistant Minister of Defence, notorious pacifier of the mutiny in the Novgorod military settlements and most valiant suppressor of the Polish rebels, was the first to speak. He thrust forward his wizened face with its cold, colourless eyes. The narrow, crooked nose over the toothbrush moustache seemed to smell prey. The light glinted on the hollow temples beneath the thin hair. The broad webbed epaulets lifted slightly. In his bearing and gestures was the authority of one accustomed to command. He put his questions curtly:

'What was your rank when you left the service?'

'Field engineer-lieutenant.'

'Have you been at the front? Have you been on campaigns? How did you perform your service in the army Engineering Corps?'

He opened a slim notebook and leafed through it with a show of distaste.

'Are you familiar with these views?' He read with a grimace of repugnance:

It's a shame, fellows. They need us as long as we are fit, and then we'll be thrown out, into the ditches, food for the dogs. I served honestly and now I have to beg for alms on a street corner. And do you know how many of us there are? Everybody knows that soldiers don't even get decent cabbage soup; but take a look at *them, they* ride about on fast-trotting horses. Ugh, the scoundrels! But wait! The highest will be the lowest and, the lowest will be the highest. That's what the French did in their country, and others will do the same. Only with us and with the rotten Austrians things are different.

He pushed the manuscript away disgustedly. 'Are you familiar with this filth?'

'I myself have never read that manuscript.'

'But you were present at a dinner at the accused Speshnev's house in April of this year when Lieutenant Grigoryev read his revolting work with the ridiculous title *Soldier Talk* and you did not express indignation.'

'But it was not discussed and there was no occasion to state an opinion.'

'You, a graduate from a military school, a former officer of His Majesty, talk in this manner! For shame!'

Dolgorukov began to shout like an angry line officer. However, suddenly realizing that he was not at the front but in a court of law, he took himself in hand and even delivered a short speech, with the characteristic arrogance of a senior officer:

'You know that hard and fast order and strict discipline in the Russian army are based upon a carefully devised system of severe penalties. The knout, the rod and the cat-o'-nine-tails were introduced by the great reformer of Russia and are retained in our army's punitive practice to this day. Is it permissible to speak indignantly and provocatively in a company including military men about the just punishment by six thousand strokes of someone of a lower rank? Or do you deny that there was talk of this at your meeting, Retired Lieutenant?'

The last words rang out maliciously and venomously. Dostoevsky looked startled.

'There was talk of it. I spoke with indignation about the Finland regiment, about the brutal treatment by a company commander of his men, about the courageous action of a sergeant-major, who attacked that officer with a broadsword in retaliation for his comrades who had been tortured, about how he was sentenced to run the gauntlet of a thousand men six times until his corpse was finally dragged away from the place of execution. Yes, your information is correct. I spoke of all this at a meeting.'

'And when you finished your speech did not one of your listeners remark that you ought to march onto the square with a red banner?'

'I am speaking only of what I said myself. Surely, I am not obliged to say anything about anyone else.'

'You err. You are obviously unfamiliar with judicial procedure.'

Dolgorukov turned to Gagarin. The cleanshaven old

man with the silver star on his frock-coat stretched out his withered hand to the foot of the crucifix and took a heavy volume from the heap of law books there.

'According to the first clause of Article 137 of the rules on criminal and corrective penalties,' he read blandly, 'if the criminal makes a sincere and full confession and if, in addition, he provides correct information in time to prevent the implementation of further evil plans, the penalty for the crime may not only be reduced in measure but also in degree, and even in kind.'

'I have no information that can prevent any evil-intentioned actions. As for myself, I have nothing to hide,' Dostoevsky said.

'I am nevertheless compelled to inform you,' Gagarin continued in the same friendly manner, 'that in cases of special obstinacy on the part of a person being interrogated, the Commission of Inquiry has His Majesty's permission to bring him to his senses by putting him in irons.'

Pressing his thin clean-shaven lips together officiously, Gagarin darted a piercing look at the prisoner from his inquisitive, cunning eyes. He held his head a little to one side, as Catholic priests do during confession while they listen piously to the penitent sinner's voice. The old senator, in the tradition of the Gagarin family had once been a pupil of the Jesuits, and introduced some legacies of the brotherhood of Ignatius Loyola into the proceedings of the supreme court.

'You have forgotten that the state is a kind of Society of Jesus,' said he in the tones of a preacher. 'A subject is a staff in the hand of the ruler. Do not try to evade making a sincere confession as the law prescribes. Confess, repent, penitence is a great sacrament!'

Next, the stout General with the narrow, slanted eyes spoke.

'I am sorry for you, Dostoevsky,' he said melodramatically,

in the tones of the tragic actor Karatygin. 'I am sorry for you.'

He seemed about to deliver a solemn and impassioned monologue, but just then he grimaced desperately, screwed up his left eye wildly and stopped short, overcome by a frightful seizure of stuttering. The other judges waited patiently and sympathetically for the stout General's convulsion to come to an end. This was Adjutant-General Yakov Rostovtsev, a favourite of the Tsar's, the head of all military educational institutions. He had had to leave the ranks because of his speech defect and had entered the field of military education instead.

Slowly, he wiped away the excessive saliva with a silk handkerchief. His broad shiny face was puffed up and looked as if it would spread out like dough were it not for the straight, hard hair-line and the military uniform, which held the heavy and flabby human mask within their confines. The narrow eyes beneath the thin eyebrows glinted and shifted like a bobcat's, and the tuft of pomaded hair stood up like a rooster's comb, in the fashion of the celebrated military commanders of 1812. The cheeks were heavy and pendulous and there was a constant cunning smile beneath the silky, well-cared-for moustache, turned up artfully to meet the short wispy sideburns in imitation of the Tsar.

'I am sorry for you, Dostoevsky,' he said, stuttering frightfully but managing to impart a tearful tremor and sympathetic, imploring tone to his voice. 'After all, you are a poet, a writer. How could you have fallen so low? You know, I am a friend of writers. Bulgarin and Kukolnik are my best friends!'

Another spasm cut him short. After a pause, he continued without embarrassment: 'And here I, a friend of poets and artists, must interrogate you, a well-known writer, about a most horrible crime: you dared to forget that the Tsar's power is the instrument of Providence itself!'

Rostovtsev's face folded into a tearful grimace. He seemed about to weep then and there for his doomed friend.

Much later, when Dostoevsky was able to look up Herzen's banned writings in libraries abroad, he learned the whole truth about this stuttering dignitary. He read in *Polyarnaya Zvezda* (*Polar Star*) and *Kolokol* (*The Bell*) that this enthusiastic informer had been close to Ryleev, Glinka and Obolensky* in 1825, had taken part in their political discussion, and read them a tragedy he had written about 'pure ideal love of the fatherland'; but when he was invited to join the secret society he had hurried to the Winter Palace and said to Nicholas: 'Unrest is gathering against you. It will erupt when the time comes to take the new oath of allegiance and Russia may go up in flames.' He had even shed tears over it and the claimant to the Russian throne in turn had wept on his chest. This was 12 December 1825. On 14 December the informer took an active part in suppressing the insurrection. During the investigation that followed he threw himself about, repented and vowed that his loyalty to the throne was unwavering. Shortly afterwards he asked for and obtained the post of aide-de-camp to the Grand Duke. He climbed undeterred to the highest rungs of the ladder in the Tsar's service, but whenever the occasion arose, he was reminded of the sins of his youth. His participation in the investigation of the Petrashevsky case was one of these distant reminders: 'Here is another chance for you to atone for your closeness with Ryleev. After all,

* Decembrists, or members of the secret societies that staged an insurrection on 14 December O.S. 1825 with the object of replacing Tsar Nicholas I by his elder brother Constantine (see note † below). The Glinka mentioned here is not the well-known composer.

† Strictly, the heir to the throne after Tsar Alexander I was his brother Constantine, who had unknown to the nation (and even to the next brother, Nicholas!) executed a secret document renouncing the throne. On the death of Alexander I therefore, Nicholas was proclaimed Tsar, and immediately had to face an armed insurrection in favour of Constantine.

you have some personal experience in the matter of state conspiracies.'

Rostovtsev, continuing to stutter, grimace and blink, went on with his sentimental interrogation.

'Did you know the writer Belinsky?'

'I knew him, but I did not see much of him in recent years.'

'Tell the Commission why you parted company.'

'It was because of the difference in our views concerning the aims of art. Belinsky was very much upset by my statements that in his own way an artist serves and elevates mankind by striving for harmony and perfection in his work, and that is how he fulfils his mission to his contemporaries and to future generations. He protested heatedly that the starving, the poor and the labourers do not need abstract, self-sufficient beauty. I recall objecting that all people need art always, just as they need the air and the sun, because art is better able than any other means to bring people together, through supreme creative joy. I thought I could influence the artistic side of his nature by this Schillerian argument, that I could stir the poetic chord that never ceased to vibrate in his heart. But I was mistaken. He reproached me bitterly for an indifference unworthy of a writer to the burning evils of contemporary humankind. In return, I accused him of jaundiced thinking, and so we parted company for ever.'

'But if you parted company for ever, how is it that only recently,' he looked at a piece of paper, 'on April 15 of this year 1849, at a *big* meeting at the home of Counsellor, grade nine, Butashevich-Petrashevsky, you, sir, read a message from the writer Belinsky to the eminent writer Gogol?'

'I regarded this letter as a remarkable literary testament, even possessing artistic merit.'

'So you read it for reasons of literary merit alone, and then you gave the letter to others to copy?'

Rostovtsev glanced at the paper and continued: 'A document which calls the Russian clergy base and says there is in Russia a huge corporation of thieving and corrupt officialdom, that the Russian Church defends inequality, is servile to authority and is an enemy and suppressor of the brotherhood of man? You read all these things because of literary merit?'

Rostovtsev's face twitched. He closed his left eye as if taking aim, giving the impression of irony, and cunningly put his head on one side.

'I do not share all the ideas in the article, not by any means,' the prisoner replied.

'Oh, then you do share some of them?'

Rostovtsev turned to Nabokov. 'It seems to me that this point of the matter is clear enough.'

It was Dubelt's turn. He got nimbly to his feet, smoothed his luxuriant moustache with a parchment-like hand and, not without grace, as if entering the mazurka, plunged into the interrogation.

'Since you, sir, have embarked on the, for you, very important redeeming path of confession,' he said with the ceremonious air of the cavalry officer, 'won't you tell us' (at this point he began to drawl his words strangely, enunciating slowly) 'about the plan' (he hesitated, as if trying to recall something, then suddenly rapped out) 'to stab the Tsar to death with daggers during a public masked ball on the night of April 20 in the Hall of Assembly of the Gentry?'

Dostoevsky did not flinch.

'I never participated in any plans to kill the Tsar.'

'But surely, you heard your friends say many times that it is desirable to eradicate the sources of evil, to destroy, shall we say – an extremely stupid idea, incidentally, because it is absolutely unfeasible – to destroy the entire imperial family?'

He leaned across the table and fastened his eyes on Dostoevsky's face.

'I never urged anyone to do such a thing.'

'Then who did?'

The green phosphorescent eyes under the greying eye-brows drilled into him. The wretched prisoner stared as if hypnotized. His head whirled with thoughts. He strained to remember. He struggled to recall ... there had been some talk at Speshnev's ... 'this is obviously a phrase out of that conversation – "destroy the Tsar and his family" – that's just what he did say.'

Dubelt took a sheet of paper out of a folder and handed it to Dostoevsky. It was a plan of Petersburg with the barracks of the Guards units checked off on it, a revolutionary map of the capital with sites for barricades marked on it in india ink – the Palace Square, the embankments, the bridges and Nevsky Prospekt.

'I did not draw up this plan.'

'But as a military engineer you surely knew of it. After all, you are a topographer of the Engineering Department – could such matters as this have been decided without consulting you?'

'I made no preparations for an uprising or street fighting.'

'As one of the leading members of the society you must nevertheless have known about the plan for the Emperor's assassination by a group of masked conspirators. Did you also take part in designing the lottery tickets with appeals printed on them for an uprising and the murder of the Tsar?'

'No, I did not, and I am certain your information is false.'

'But it is hardly logical to preach Jacobinism and not to try to carry it out. It is customary for revolutionary societies to set up secret printing presses so as to disseminate new ideas. We know that your group, too, had plans of this kind.'

This was the question that Dostoevsky feared most. From the authorities' point of view this was, of course, his worst crime. The organization of a secret printing press to disseminate anti-government propaganda – this was no longer merely a conspiracy of ideas. This went further than discussions and poetry-readings. This was revolutionary action, very serious action. To confess to this was unthinkable. Besides endangering himself, such a confession would implicate several others, above all, Speshnev.

'It is useless for you to maintain silence on this point. We have in our possession drawings of a hand printing press with which you are no doubt familiar. We have obtained evidence from several craftsmen that they made some of the parts to order. If you tell us where the printing press was assembled and in whose house it was hidden you will greatly mitigate the guilt of your participation.'

The General lifted his hand in exhortation, and, not inelegantly, smoothed his moustache. The interrogation had reached its high point.

The chairman finally broke the dead silence.

'So,' Nabokov said in his hoarse voice, 'you stubbornly refuse to admit that you participated in a conspiracy to organize an uprising and to assassinate the Tsar?'

'I did take part in discussions on Fourierism, on serfdom and on military punishments. I did read Belinsky's 'Letter to Gogol' at meetings. I listened to *Soldier's Talk*. I believed in the coming advent of universal happiness and I shall never cease to believe in it. But I am not guilty of conspiring for a rebellion and for the murder of the Tsar.'

'You give us the opportunity to catch you out in lies. Read this.' Nabokov handed him a sheet of paper.

When the directing committee of the secret society, having evaluated the forces, circumstances and the situation, decides that the time has come for insurrection, I undertake, having armed myself in advance with firearms or cold steel, to participate fully and openly in the insurrection and in the fighting without sparing myself.

'I never signed such a paper.'

'Do you know the handwriting?'

'I couldn't say for sure.'

'What if we suggest that it is the handwriting of the accused Nikolai Speshnev?'

'I'm afraid I might make a mistake. It is possible that it is his handwriting, though.'

'You have no doubt that it is, for you were a member of the secret society he organized.'

'A small group of us did get together to read and to make music.'

'You must tell the Commission of Inquiry every single thing that you know about the secret society which Speshnev organized. You may do so in writing. You will be given questionnaires when you get back to your cell. If you lie or are obstinate your guilt will only be aggravated. By submitting detailed and complete testimony on the opinions expressed about the destruction of the Tsar and the royal family, and who expressed them, you can still save yourself. Do you know what is in store for you otherwise?'

'No, I do not.'

'Under military law, His Majesty's instructions to this secret Commission of Inquiry, and the powers granted to the auditoriat-general*, the penalty for conspiracy against the government is quartering or a shameful death by hanging.'

He stood up solemnly. The others followed suit. Five inquisitorial heads bobbed beside the massive bronze portrait of the Tsar in a bizarre pantomime: Dubelt's carnivorous jaw, Gagarin's Jesuitically pressed lips, Dolgorukov's hawk-like nose and leaden eyes, Rostovtsev's shiny Falstaff cheeks and Nabokov's cast-iron skull. They stood there, pompous and formidable, brimming with vanity and with the militant loyalty that they had proved over and over again in the course of several decades of zealous service to the Tsar and the fatherland.

---

* Civilian legal advisers called *auditors* were attached to military units to coordinate legal procedure at courts martial, etc. They were under the control of the *auditoriat-general*, which had functions analogous to those of the British Department of the Judge-Advocate General.

Nabokov spoke:

'In accordance with His Imperial Majesty's instructions' (the investigators straightened up) 'this secret Commission of Inquiry deems the charge for which you are being tried, Retired Lieutenant Dostoevsky, in the highest degree criminal and not to be tolerated. It will determine the degree of each participant's guilt and the penalties in all strictness of military law.'

The prisoner was led away.

*

The inquiry was completed on 16 November. The case of the Petrashevskyites then went to the auditoriat-general, that is, the supreme reviewing authority, which, on 19 December sentenced the twenty-one accused men to death by the firing squad. The sentence was accompanied by a recommendation that, since the condemned were so young and had repented, and since their activities had not had any harmful consequences, the death sentence be commuted and other penalties substituted in its stead. Nicholas I, in accordance with tradition, accepted their recommendation. He ordered, however, that his 'pardon' should not be announced to the condemned men until the original death sentences had been read to them publicly and all the preparations for their execution, short of the word 'Fire!', had been carried out. Then, and then only, were they to be informed of the commutation.

THE SEMYONOVSKY PARADE GROUND

On 22 December 1849 at eight in the morning Dostoevsky was bundled into a black carriage with frosted windowpanes and was driven to an unknown destination. After a while the carriage stopped and the guard sitting next to him opened the door.

'Get out.'

He stepped out and saw the others, all of them. A scaffold loomed black against the snowy expanse of a huge square. Petrashevsky stood next to the rampart. He was bareheaded, wearing a light summer cloak, his thick long hair was dishevelled, and he was unshaven. Where were they?

Dostoevsky looked around. He recognized the orange walls of the Guards regimental barracks and the five golden cupolas of the massive cathedral, rising above the rampart. This was the square where the Semyonovsky Regiment had its drills and parades. Infantry and cavalry troops stood in square formation in the exact centre of the parade ground. These were the battalions in which the condemned officers Palm, Grigoryev and Mombelli had served. The scaffold, a wooden platform covered with black cloth, was in the centre of the formation.

The condemned men were lined up at the rampart. There they were, thin, pale, unkempt, poets and jurists, engineers and officers, teachers and journalists – an entire Petrashevsky Friday – encircled by picked troops and mounted gendarmerie, with the military Governor-General of Petersburg, the Chief of Police, the Commanders of the Life Guards and the Tsar's aides-de-camp at their head.

After long months of solitary confinement the condemned men greeted one another joyfully and cheerfully, shouting friendly greetings and embracing warmly. This was a violation of the strict military ritual of carrying out the supreme penalty. Infuriated, Adjutant-General Sumarokov, Commander of the Guards' Infantry and master of the ceremonies, galloped up to them.

'Form a column!' the order rang out.

The major in charge formed the condemned men into a column. A priest in funeral attire stepped in front of the column and led the procession, escorted by Guards, past the troops towards the scaffold. They turned the last corner, having gone past all the troops, and stood in front of three narrow grey posts, dug firmly into the frozen earth. How much longer did they have to live? Ten minutes? Twenty minutes?

They were led to the short staircase leading up to the platform. They mounted the slippery steps to the scaffold.

'Present arms!'

Rifles darted upwards with a precise clang. The drums beat a nervous rat-tat-tat. An auditor* with a paper in his hands came onto the platform. In a thin, rasping voice he began to read the imperial sentence, shouting some of the words to the troops and some to the mob on the rampart, now pausing, now crying out shrilly with renewed energy. The wind howled. Words swept by like a whirlwind. It was impossible to catch a complete sentence. Phrases reached the brain in shreds – was the brain beginning to break under the strain, or was the blizzard drowning out the reader's falsetto?

'Having examined the case as presented by the army judiciary commission, the auditoriat-general finds all the accused guilty of planning to overthrow the state system and sentences them all to death by the firing squad.'

The auditor raised his crowing voice and lifted his hand to the brim of his uniform hat. The words reverberated through the square:

'His Majesty the Emperor has written in his own hand on the sentence: "So be it."'

Names, articles, resolutions flew over the square; over and over again, with menacing rhythm, came the words of the inexorable sentence. The dispassionate formula rang out for the tenth time:

'Retired Engineer-Lieutenant Fyodor Dostoevsky, twenty-seven, for participation in criminal plans, for circulating a private letter that contained infamous expressions about the Russian Orthodox Church and Supreme Authority, and for an attempt to disseminate writings against the

---

* *Auditor.* See note * p. 156.

government by means of a hand printing press – *to be put to death by the firing squad.*'

Again and again he heard familiar names of living and dear persons, followed by the same merciless phrase.

The auditor folded the paper twice, put it into an inside pocket, and went slowly down the steps. As the drums beat with an unbearable continuous roll the executioners in brightly coloured shirts and black pleated trousers mounted the scaffold, stamping their high boots. The condemned men were ordered to get down on their knees and the executioners broke filed-down sabres over their heads. The dry, hard snap of breaking steel rang out clearly in the icy air. The priest delivered the last sermon: 'For the wages of sin is death'; and held out a large cross for each man to kiss.

There was a church not far off, its gilded roof glittering in the bright sun. He remembered staring with awful intensity at that roof and at the sunbeams flashing from it; he could not tear his eyes from those rays of light; they seemed to him to be his new nature and he felt that in three minutes he would somehow merge with them. The uncertainty and the feeling of revulsion against this new thing which was imminent now were dreadful; but he said that the thing that was most unbearable for him at the time was the constant thought: what if I were not to die: what if my life were given back to me? What an eternity!

Thus did Dostoevsky put the memory of his execution scene into *The Idiot* twenty years later, in Prince Myshkin's story about a political prisoner he had known.

The time had come for the final ritual, being dressed for death. Their summer cloaks were taken from them and replaced by loose gowns of coarse linen with pointed hoods attached and long sleeves that reached almost to the ground. Suddenly the sound of lilting, insolent, prolonged laughter came from the scaffold. Everybody turned to look. Petrashevsky was shaking with uncontrollable laughter – this was surely deliberate – and was waving his clown-like sleeves.

'Gentlemen –' laughter choked him. 'How ridiculous we must look in these clown's shirts!'

By this laughter the great propagandist was striving to express, perhaps for the last time, his contempt for authority, and also to cheer his comrades. There they stood, tall, snow-white, uncanny ghosts, their outlandish garments flapping in the wind, their faces half-covered by the falling hoods.

They were formed up in threes. Dostoevsky was in the second row. The execution master called out:

'Petrashevsky. Mombelli. Grigoryev.'

Three white ghosts, summoned by the auditor and escorted by platoon commanders, slowly descended the slippery steps of the platform. They were bound to the three grey posts with ropes; their arms were pulled behind their backs and the long sleeves of the death shirts tied together.

Dostoevsky wrote later that same day: 'We were called out three at a time. Therefore, it would be my turn next and I had no more than a minute to live. I thought of you, my brother, and all yours. I also had time to embrace Pleshcheev and Durov, who were standing next to me, and to take leave of them.'[1]

Petrashevsky's face was tranquil. Only his eyes were extraordinarily wide. They seemed to glide over everything. He awaited the inevitable calmly. Mombelli was stony faced and pale as a sheet. Grigoryev's features were convulsed. An expression of anguished horror was on his face, and his eyes were glassy as a madman's.

The three platoons of sixteen men each, which were to carry out the sentence, detached themselves from their units and at the command of an N.C.O. took up positions along a chalk line about twelve yards in front of the posts, sixteen guardsmen in front of each of the three condemned men. They would all kill together, so that no individual would bear the responsibility for the bloodshed.

'Load!' the command rang out.

There was a thud of musket butts and a clang of ramrods.
'Hoods down over the eyes!'

Petrashevsky's wondering eyes, Mombelli's white mask and Grigoryev's insane grimace disappeared beneath the hoods. With a jerk of his head, Petrashevsky shook the white hood off his face.

'I am not afraid to look death in the eyes,' he cried.

'Aim!'

The platoons took aim.

'That was a fearful moment, indeed,' Akhsharumov recalled later. 'My heart stood still in anticipation, and the terrible wait lasted for a full half minute.'

Why didn't they fire? What was keeping them? One of the Tsar's aides-de-camp was galloping across the parade ground. He handed General Sumarokov a sealed packet. A staccato beat on the drums broke the dead silence. Sixteen aimed muskets all rose as one to point upwards. Something was going on at the posts. The prisoners were being untied. They were led back onto the black-shrouded platform. The *auditor* returned to the platform and began to read in his rasping tenor: 'Having read the report, submitted to him with loyal feelings, His Majesty . . . commutes the death sentence . . . deprivation of all civic rights . . . deportation to penal servitude . . . indefinitely . . . in the penalty companies of the Engineering Department . . . privates in the special Caucasian Corps . . .' and so on and so forth. Once more the name that was to be famous rang out on the Semyonovsky parade ground. 'Retired Engineer-Lieutenant Fyodor Dostoevsky . . . to penal servitude in fortresses for four years, and after that as a common soldier.'

Blacksmiths carrying a mass of clanging iron came up onto the scaffold. The platform shook as the chains dropped to the ground with a loud clank. Iron fetters were put on Petrashevsky's legs. Calm, contemptuous and scornful, Petrashevsky helped the smiths as they hammered the iron and riveted the chains. A government courier's carriage, drawn by three horses, drove up to the scaffold.

'By His Majesty's order the convict Butashevich-Petrashevsky shall set out for Siberia directly from the execution site, accompanied by a gendarme and a courier.'

'I wish to take leave of my comrades,' Petrashevsky said to the Commandant.

Swaying in his irons, he dragged his fettered feet clumsily from one man to the next, kissed each one and bade him farewell.

'Do not lose heart, friends. Let them put us in irons. These chains are a priceless bracelet, fashioned for us by the wisdom of the West and the spirit of the age, which penetrate everywhere, and placed on us by our love of mankind.'

He stepped back, bowed low, his chains clanking, and once more bade them farewell. He seemed to be asking their pardon for his involuntary guilt towards them. He was helped into the carriage. The troika, with a gendarme seated beside the coachman, took off and disappeared round a curve.

The remaining prisoners were escorted back to their cells. The crowd dispersed slowly and silently. Horsemen with white plumes on their cocked hats galloped off at full speed with reports to the Winter Palace. The Guards' regiments changed formation for the return march.

*

On the same day Dostoevsky wrote to his only close friend, his brother Mikhail:

My brother, I do not feel despondent and have not lost heart. Life is life everywhere. Life is in ourselves and not outside us. There will be men beside me, and the important thing is to be a man among men and to remain a man always, whatever the misfortunes, not to despair and not to fall – that is the aim of life, that is its purpose. I realize this now. The idea has entered into my flesh and my blood. Yes, that is the truth! That head which created, which lived the higher life of art, which experienced and had grown accustomed to the higher necessities of the spirit, that head has already been severed from my shoulders. What remains is memory and images, those I created and those I have not yet given form to. True, they will corrode me. But I have still got my heart and the same flesh and blood which can love and suffer and pity and remember, and that is also life. Never before have I felt such abundant and healthy reserves of spiritual life in me as now.

The strength of this creative mind and the courage of this sensitive man, who had just been put through the ordeal of a mock execution and would be departing to serve a sentence of hard labour in a few hours, are remarkable indeed. Dostoevsky was filled with optimism and unshakeable faith in his vocation and in his future renascence. 'After all, I spent three quarters of an hour with death today; I lived with the thought of it. I was at the very last instant, and now I am alive again!'

However, notes of suppressed despair came through in this deeply moving record of the feelings of a genius who has been at death's door:

Dear God, how many images that I have experienced and created will fade again, will die in my head or dissolve like poison in my blood! Oh, if I am not able to write I shall perish. I would rather go to prison for fifteen years and have a pen in my hand!

But the great poet's will triumphed over the terrible blows of monstrous reality. The horrible experience of the commuted execution gave him a new understanding of the meaning of life:

As I look back on the past and think how much time I wasted, how much time I lost in errors, idleness and not knowing how to live, when I think how little I valued it, my heart bleeds. Life is a gift; life is happiness, every minute of it could have been an eternity of happiness. Brother, I swear to you that I will not lose hope and will keep my spirit and my heart pure.

This fragmentary, hasty, disorderly confession, written in a cell, in the presence of gaolers, is one of the greatest confessions known to world art, and rings out like Beethoven's immortal behest: 'To joy through suffering.'

That same day Dostoevsky was informed that he was in the first group to leave for Siberia. He asked that his brother be permitted to pay him a farewell visit. His request was refused, but then the Commandant granted a petition submitted by the prisoners' relatives. On the evening of 24 December 1849 Mikhail Dostoevsky and Alexander Milyukov were admitted to the Commandant's house. Then Dostoevsky and Durov were brought in by an officer of the gendarmerie and guards. They were already dressed in the convict's travelling clothes: sheepskin jackets and felt boots. The meeting lasted half an hour. Milyukov wrote later:

There were tears in the elder brother's eyes and his lips trembled while Dostoevsky was calm and kept consoling him.

'Don't, brother', he said. 'You know me. After all, I'm not going to my grave. You are not seeing me into my coffin. They are not animals in prison, they are men, perhaps better men than I. And when I get out I'll start writing. I have been through a great deal during these months; within myself I have been through a great deal, and I expect I shall see and experience more – I'll have plenty to write about.'

At midnight he was taken to the smithy. The chimes of the Peter and Paul Fortress were playing 'Glory to the Tsar', as ten-pound irons were put on his feet. Then he was put into an open sledge with a gendarme (Durov and Yastrzhembsky were placed in two others) and the train of horse-drawn sledges headed by a government courier started on its long journey.

THE YEARS OF EXILE

VII

The Exiled Convict

THE JOURNEY TO THE PRISON FORTRESS

I T was Christmas Eve in Petersburg. The windows of the houses were brilliantly lit up. Christmas tree lights and ornaments glittered in many of them. The sledges drove past the house where Kraevsky, editor of *Otechestvennie Zapiski*, lived and where Mikhail's children were attending a Christmas party that evening. With pain in his heart Dostoevsky thought of his family, whom he would not see for many long years, perhaps never again. They reached Schlüsselburg in the morning and had hot tea there at an inn. The government courier, formerly a diplomatic courier, 'a nice old man, kind and humane', transferred the convicts into covered sleighs. Because it was a holiday the new coachmen were wearing festive cloaks tied with scarlet sashes. 'It was a glorious winter's day,' Dostoevsky recalled later.

This was his first trip across Russia. All he had known before was the road from Petersburg to Moscow and the sea voyage from Kronstadt to Revel. Now for two weeks Russian troikas carried him across the long snowy road from the Neva to western Siberia. His route lay through nine northern provinces: Petersburg, Novgorod, Yaroslavl, Vladimir, Nizhni-Novgorod, Kazan, Vyatka, Perm and Tobolsk. In the Urals the temperature fell to minus 40°C. 'I was frozen through to the marrow,' this Petersburg man wrote about his first journey across his boundless homeland.

Crossing the Urals was a sad moment. The horses and the covered sleighs sank in the snowdrifts. It was night. A blizzard was raging. We got out and waited for them to pull the sleighs out. All around us was snow and the blizzard. This was the borderline of Europe. Ahead was Siberia and a mysterious future there. Behind was the past – I felt sad and tears started to my eyes.

On 9 January 1850, the sixteenth day of the journey, Dostoevsky arrived in Tobolsk. Here he set foot for the first time in a regular prison, as yet only a temporary one. Tobolsk was a transit centre for convicts, and from it they were sent to the various Siberian mines, fortresses and factories. He saw people chained to the wall in a damp, suffocating cellar, convicts who had been sentenced to long terms of confinement without movement or air. He peered into the face of one of the most notorious brigands and saw in that face 'the most horrible spiritual obtuseness, a frightful combination of bloodthirstiness and insatiable carnality'. This was the threshold of the House of the Dead.

The newly arrived 'malefactors' were put in a narrow, dark, cold and dirty cell. Yastrzhembsky was in despair and resolved to kill himself. At times of crisis the nervous, ill, Dostoevsky always displayed remarkable courage. Now, too, he raised his dejected comrades' spirits. He took out a box of cigars he had managed to secrete among his things, a farewell gift from his brother. Tea and a tallow candle were brought to them.

'We spent most of the night in amicable conversation. Dostoevsky's pleasant, agreeable voice, his gentleness and mildness, even his several capricious outbursts, just like those of a woman, had a calming effect on me.' An atmosphere of inner warmth, solicitude and sympathy was created. Yaztrzhembsky abandoned the idea of suicide.

A surprise was in store for them in Tobolsk, an event they never forgot. Several wives of the Decembrists* came to the transit prison to see the 'politicals', to console them and help them in their misfortune. These were some of those obscure Russian women of unassuming grandeur of spirit,

* See notes * and †, p. 151.

of whom Nekrasov was to write in his famous poems about Trubetskaya and Volkonskaya:

> Perhaps, one day, continuing this story,
> We will mention others, too,
> Who left their homes
> And went off to die in snowy wastes.
> Enchanting images! You are hardly likely to encounter
> Anything more beautiful in the history of another country.
> Their names must never be forgotten!

Dostoevsky never did forget the four Siberian heroines who succoured him in that bleak moment: Polina Annenkova and her daughter Olga, Natalya Fonvizina and Z. A. Muravyova.

A. A. Annenkov, once a dazzling officer of the cuirassiers and a favourite of Alexander I, had made the acquaintance of Polina Hoebbel, a young Frenchwoman, in 1825, in the fashionable Petersburg shop where she was then employed. Shortly afterwards he was sentenced to penal servitude. Polina Hoebbel followed the man she loved to Siberia, overcoming incredible difficulties to do so since she was not formally married to him. Ten years of exile had not altered her lively disposition or broken her courageous spirit. Her daughter Olga Annenkova (subsequently Ivanova) settled in Omsk soon after that Tobolsk visit and took a close interest in Dostoevsky's life. Dostoevsky called her 'my own sister', 'a beautiful, pure soul, elevated and noble'. He also thought highly of Natalya Fonvizina, a woman with a 'good, human heart', 'who had sacrificed everything to her supreme moral duty'.

The four 'Decembrist women' had persuaded the inspector of the transit prison to allow them to meet with the political prisoners in his quarters. They had brought the men dinner and clothing and presented each with a copy of the Gospels, the only book they were allowed to have in prison. The cover of each book had been slit and a ten-rouble note placed inside. The Gospels were printed in large Old Slavonic script with abbreviations. Dostoevsky kept the book all his life and was reading it on the day he died. He recalled these events a quarter of a century later: 'We saw these great martyrs, who had voluntarily followed their husbands to Siberia. Though themselves guiltless of any crime, they had suffered the same privations as their convicted husbands, for twenty-five long years. Our meeting lasted an hour. They gave us their blessings for the journey ahead.' Apparently the exiles of 1826 had not been permitted to meet the new 'state criminals' themselves and so their wives had undertaken to do so.

Dr G. M. Meier, who was on the staff of the Tobolsk public almshouse in 1850, subsequently wrote in the Press that the Decembrists who lived in that town, Annenkov, Muravyov and Svistunov, were interested in the fate of the newly arrived Petrashevskyites and sent them underclothing and other things. They were particularly interested in Dostoevsky, who already had a reputation as the author of *Poor Folk*. The doctor used to see new arrivals in the prison and some of them in the hospital. Petrashevsky, Speshnev, Tol, Lvov, Mombelli and others passed through the Tobolsk prison as well as Dostoevsky, Durov and Yastrzhembsky. Dr Meier wrote in his memoirs: 'Dostoevsky was small, frail and seemed very young. He was extraordinarily calm, even though his arms and legs were in very heavy irons. . . . The arrivals were imprisoned in a very low-ceilinged, small, stifling room in the gaol.'

On about 20 January Dostoevsky and Durov were sent to Omsk. The instructions of the Governor-General of Western Siberia read: 'To be kept in irons and without any privileges.' The energetic and efficient Olga Annenkova managed to arrange for the two men to be driven the approximate six hundred versts from Tobolsk to Omsk by horses and sledges rather than marched by stages. Natalya Fonvizina decided to bid the 'Omsk convicts' farewell on the road just before they crossed the Irtysh River. She and another woman waited for them at a point five miles from Tobolsk in a frost of minus 30°C. Her companion wrote later:

At last we heard the tinkle of bells in the distance. A troika with a gendarme and a passenger came into sight round the bend at the edge of the forest. Another followed. We stepped into the road and when they came level with us we waved to the gendarmes to stop, as arranged in advance.

Dostoevsky and Durov jumped out of the Siberian sleds. They were dressed in convict sheepskin jackets and fur headgear that resembled hats with earmuffs attached. Heavy irons clanked on their feet. We bade them a hasty farewell and only managed to tell them not to lose heart and that good people would take care of them there, too.

This was the last greeting from the 'free' world.

THE HOUSE OF THE DEAD

Dostoevsky and Durov arrived in Omsk on 23 January 1850. The Omsk fortress had been built at the beginning of the eighteenth century to beat back the nomads of the steppes, but had soon been turned into a military prison. It was encircled by a moat and ramparts. 'And never before had a man with more hope, love of life and faith entered that prison,' Dostoevsky wrote thirty years later in his rough notebooks, apparently referring to that tragic moment in his life.

Their first encounter with Drill-Major Krivtsov, the chief warder, confirmed what they had heard about him, that he was a petty barbarian and cruel tyrant. Dostoevsky saw a half-drunk man with a brutish, purple face, wearing a soiled cap with an orange headband and an army uniform with dirty silver shoulder straps. 'The pimply and malicious face depressed us exceedingly: it was as if an evil spider were coming after a poor fly, already caught in its web.' As was his custom, Krivtsov shouted at the new prisoners in extremely abusive language and warned them that they would be flogged for the slightest offence.

Dostoevsky was taken to the guardhouse, where he was made to look like a convict: one side of his head was shaved, and he was given a two-coloured jacket with a diamond-shaped yellow patch on the back and a soft round cap to wear. He was then taken to the convicts' cells. These were in a dilapidated building, marked down for demolition, with rotting floorboards, a leaking roof and stoves that did not work properly. Fleas, lice and cockroaches abounded by the bushel. The bunks were bare shelves. One tub served everybody as a latrine from dawn till dusk. It was unbearably stifling, and the din of shouts, curses and clanking chains was incessant. 'It was hell and pitch darkness,' Dostoevsky wrote.

Here he saw the ancient, terrible penal code in operation: faces branded 'as eternal evidence of their rejection',[1] scarred backs that had been beaten with the rod, swollen black and blue, with splinters in the skin. The Omsk prisoners were mercilessly enmeshed in iron. In irons they washed in the bathhouse, in irons they acted on the stage, in irons they lay ill in hospital. A wasted prisoner died of malignant consumption one day and the first thing the N.C.O. did was to send for a smith to remove the irons from the corpse.

Dostoevsky was astonished at the hatred the mass of the convicts showed for the condemned gentlemen. Former serfs expressed their hostility to men who had till lately been landed proprietors and were now deprived of their unlimited power over them. 'You iron-beaked gentry have pecked us to death. Before, when you were the masters, you used to torment the people; now that you are the worst of the worst, you want to be our brothers.' Dostoevsky introduced this theme of class hostility into the epilogue of *Crime and*

Punishment. In Siberia Raskolnikov was aware of an unbridgeable gulf between him and the other prisoners. It was as if he and they were people of different nations, of enemy camps. A convict once attacked him in a fury and had it not been for the intervention of a guard there would have been bloodshed. As a rule though, class enmity among the convicts did not manifest itself so violently. Dostoevsky related that he had many friends and companions among the prisoners, and he was interested in their stories, songs and ethical problems.

Nearly all parts of Russia and all kinds of crime were represented among the motley prison population. Dostoevsky observed nearly every type of criminal, from smugglers and counterfeiters to child molesters and highway robbers. Judging from *Notes from the House of the Dead*, it was possible, using the method of Stendhal or Tolstoy, to divide the prison population into two basic categories: the naïve and rather simple babblers, and the silent ones. Among the latter group, which was much the larger, there were the morose and malicious, the kind and radiant, and the desperate ones.

It was the 'morose and malicious' in whom Dostoevsky, the painter of complex conscience-situations, was most interested. For four years he lived side by side with the ugliest celebrities in the annals of crime. There was Gazin, a Tatar, who had murdered children. There was a multiple murderer, the convict who took the writer's cherished Bible from him. And there was Aristov, the most repugnant of them all, a 'moral Quasimodo', a refined libertine, a parasite and a traitor. Such was Dostoevsky's environment of 'appallingly frightful criminals' in the convict barracks.

But there was also a handful of 'the kind and radiant', and Dostoevsky frequently unburdened his heart to them. Among these were a meek, simple-hearted youth; a grey-haired Old Believer, who was paying the price for his religious dissidence; and several mountaineers from the

Caucasus, who brought the knightly valour of their mountain customs to the filth and fumes of prison life. These Circassian mountaineers were not common criminals, not robbers or horse thieves, but political prisoners. They were valiant patriots and fearless guerrillas, who had fought singly or in small mounted groups against the advance posts of the innumerable forces of the Russian regular army. Russia's greatest poets, Pushkin ('Thus does speechless Caucasus wax indignant today, Thus do alien forces oppress it') and Lermontov ('The villages burn, they have no protection. A bonfire has been made of Cherkess freedoms') expressed admiration for the heroism of the mountain tribes. A war of liberation was being fought in Chechnya, Daghestan and Circassia against Tsarism's colonial oppression, and it had produced many martyrs and heroes. Dostoevsky's descriptions of the Caucasian prisoners conveys this, though for censorship reasons he had to refer to them as to common criminals. But historical truth irresistibly breaks through the conventions of this censor-ridden narrative.

The bullet- and sabre-scarred Nurra, nicknamed 'the Lion', was a strong, brave and noble fighter for his people's independence. The *Notes* say of him: 'In the Caucasus he lived in a peaceable village, but he used to go secretly to the mountain guerrillas and ride with them from their villages in raids against the Russians.' In the 1840s Shamil's* operations were at their height. By the time Dostoevsky arrived at the Omsk prison he found there exiled Lezghins, Chechens and Daghestan Tatars. Alei, Dostoevsky's bunk-mate, was a kind-hearted, extremely handsome Tatar youth. 'I think of my meeting him as one of the finest meetings of my life,' Dostoevsky wrote. He was an extraordinary creature 'of such great natural beauty that the very idea of anything evil could not be associated with him'. The picture is drawn with the lineaments of Dostoevsky's favourite moral heroes.

* Shamil (1798–1871). The leader of the Caucasian mountaineers' fight against the Russians.

Characteristic is the story of Alei's admiration for the Sermon on the Mount and the subtle desire of this Moslem to please his friend by praising his religion – 'Jesus is a holy prophet.'

The writer was also interested in the 'desperate ones' – men of steely will, untameably defiant, with the courage of despair. Orlov was one of these: 'We regarded him as the incarnation of infinite energy, of thirst for action and for vengeance, of determination to get what he wanted. His strange arrogance astonished me.' Petrov was another of these strong-willed types, a very determined and fearless man completely without self-restraint. It is from among people of this type, Dostoevsky wrote, that instigators and leaders appear at moments of crisis. 'They appear suddenly, in bold relief, dominating, coming into their own, at times of violent mass action or insurrection. And all plunge after them, follow them blindly, follow to the very last barricade breach, where they usually lay down their lives.'

Dostoevsky very soon perceived outstanding if undeveloped talents among the branded and abused population of the Omsk prison, bright sparks in the pitch darkness of incarceration. 'On that first joyless evening of my new life I saw only flashes of this, flashes in the smoke, the soot, the oaths and the inexpressible cynicism, in the mephitic air, amidst the clang of chains, the curses and the damnable, shameless laughter.'

THE STRUGGLE FOR EXISTENCE

Since Dostoevsky was not skilled in any trade, he was classed as a labourer. The Petersburg writer turned the clumsy grindstone wheel in the workshop, fired bricks in the factory, carried heavy hods to the construction site and standing knee-deep in the icy water, unloaded old state-owned barges on the Irtysh. He had to work in intolerable cold, when the mercury froze in the thermometer. The prison authorities kept to the letter of 'His Majesty's instructions' that the 'political' Dostoevsky was to be treated as a convict in the fullest sense of the word without any leniency whatsoever. A historian of the Tsarist prisons writes:[2]

It is amazing that the writer did not die there. The attitude of prison administrations in those days was that prison should be a place of nothing but deprivation and suffering. If the prison administration had been able to stick to its attitude consistently, the cemetery of the living would have become a cemetery of the dead. But the prisoners' instinct for self-preservation would not allow this. A persistent struggle for existence went on in prisons and punishment companies.

One of the manifestations of this struggle was the convict theatre. The authorities allowed the prisoners to give performances on holidays. The younger and more spirited men were the actors. They put on a triple bill. House painters did the curtain and sets, amateur musicians organized an orchestra of balalaikas, violins, guitars and tambourines. In a mixed programme that included pantomine and ballet Dostoevsky found the vaudeville and comedy most interesting. One number was a one-act comedy by the actor Grigoryev, entitled *Filatka and Miroshka*, about a village beauty, named Grusha, who preferred the love of a devoted orderly to the persuasions of a court clerk. The attraction of the simple story lay in its lively folk idiom, its couplets for each character and its hints of cheerful ribaldry. The convict Baklushin, a merry, excitable man, 'full of fire and life', played the simpleton Filatka. He was a brilliant actor and Dostoevsky considered his performance superior to those of the actors who played the part on the stage of the Imperial Theatre in Petersburg. Dostoevsky was also very much amused by *Kedril, the Glutton*, a farce which brought to mind the puppet theatre's Petroushka. The protagonist was a rogue of a servant, a stupid, sly, cowardly, deceitful and lascivious man. The play ended with both servant and master being carried off to hell by devils.[3]

The convicts' productions revealed the continuity of certain established techniques and concepts, traditions of the theatre preserved through several generations. These obscure stages, Dostoevsky said, are the source of 'our folk dramatic art' and deserving of special study.

The author of *Notes from the House of the Dead* remarked upon the zest, spontaneity, enjoyment and talent for invention shown in these performances. The convict actors showed a genuine flair for comedy and were brilliant in improvisation and free interpretation of their roles. The female parts were played by men. 'A shout of laughter greeted the lady of the manor,' who was the convict Ivanov, wearing a low-cut dress that exposed his neck, and carrying a parasol and fan. The dramatic talent of the common people gushed forth in a veritable fountain. 'How much energy and talent dies in Russia, almost completely wasted by enslavement and a hard life,' one of the spectators at the unusual performance was moved to reflect.

Dostoevsky was deeply moved by the songs, often sung by a chorus, accompanied by balalaikas and accordions. As he listened to the music of these instruments of the common people he 'understood for the first time the wild and rakish quality of Russian dancing songs'. Peasant songs, however, were rarely sung. Much more regularly sung were the special 'convict' and the 'brigand' songs, as well as city songs – songs of the urban poor, songs of servants – many of which were humorous and very close to the 'black love-song'. Sometimes a local steppe tune mingled with the prisoners' songs. The imprisoned writer also listened attentively to the plaintive Kirghizian melodies, wafted from the far bank of the river.

Dostoevsky subtitled his immortal book about convict life *Observations on a Destroyed People*. He concluded the history of his incarceration with the celebrated passage: 'You know, the people there were extraordinary people. They are perhaps the most gifted and strongest of our people. Mighty forces have been destroyed to no purpose, destroyed irregularly, illegally and irreversibly. And whose fault is it? Whose fault?'

The understanding of the prison population that Dostoevsky acquired in Omsk gave added depth to his portrayal of the common people in his subsequent work. While he was in prison he came to believe that the highest cultural strata of Russian society ought to merge with the common people, and this conviction became the programme of his writing once he was free again. 'How many native types and characters,' he wrote, 'did I take with me from my time in prison! How many tales of vagabonds, robbers and, in general, of the whole wretched existence! There is enough here for entire volumes!' Some of this material was utilized by Dostoevsky. In his *Notes* he told the stories of Private Sirotkin, who had knifed a company commander; of the talented Baklushin, formerly a non-commissioned officer, who had in a jealous rage shot a German for stealing his girl; of 'Akula's husband', who had killed his innocent, cruelly slandered wife; of a serf, whose bride had been taken from him by his dissolute landlord on his wedding night and who had used an axe to repay his master.

Dostoevsky also took with him from his time in prison a number of prototypes for characters in his long novels. Nor were these characters all 'vagabonds and robbers'. In his last novels the thinkers and men of strong passions, as well as the depressives who are disintegrating spiritually, take their beginnings from the inhabitants of the Omsk fortress.

Raskolnikov possessed the traits of those proud and power-hungry convicts, who unhesitatingly shed 'blood according to conscience', for the sake of higher aims. Svidrigailov has the complete amorality of Aristov, gentleman-born, a connoisseur of the arts and a portrait painter, who was nicknamed 'Bryullov' even in gaol. A handsome and educated man of refined intelligence, Aristov would not hesitate 'to sell the blood of ten men that he might immediately satisfy his unquenchable thirst for the coarsest and most depraved pleasures'. Stavrogin resembles Petrov in having enormous inner strength which he does not know how to use. Dostoevsky noted that natures such as these have something of Stenka Razin* in them. 'A boundless force, searching spontaneously for tranquillity, emotional to the point of pain, plunging joyously into bizarre bypaths and experiments in its quests and wanderings', it may nevertheless be seized by an idea powerful enough to organize it into 'unctuous silence'.

The gentleman parricide, Lieutenant Il'insky, who afterwards turned out to have been innocent of the terrible crime for which he was convicted, foreshadows the character and the fate of Dimitri Karamazov.

Finally, Lieutenant Zherebyatnikov, the prison flogger master of the birch and the stick, who reminded Dostoevsky of a patrician of the time of the Roman Empire, worn out with pleasures and enervated by every refinement of luxury and 'unnatural' vice, points towards the unforgettable image of the 'sensualist' Fyodor Pavlovich Karamazov who had the 'authentic physiognomy of an ancient Roman patrician of the age of decline'; that is of a period noted for dissolute morals and refinements of pleasure.

The prison-folk and their ways were growing up, together with Dostoevsky's musings, into the titanic figures of his late novels. Here, too, plans of tremendous philosophic profundity took their source; plans such as the *Confession*, conceived by him on the prison bunks, which grew ever wider and deeper till it emerged, ten years later, as one of the mightiest works of world literature – *Crime and Punishment*.

* Stenka Razin. Leader of the Don Cossacks. Famous for piratical exploits on the Don and Lower Volga and across the Caspian to Persia. Started a peasant revolt that swept over south-east Russia, but was ultimately captured and executed in Moscow in 1670.

TRANSFORMATION OF CONVICTIONS

It was while Dostoevsky was in his cell in Alexeevsky Ravelin, from which in fine weather it was just possible to see a scrap of sky, and absorbed in anxious reflections about his future, that he first began to have doubts about his recent ideological convictions. He began to feel that, in any case, it was not to be his role to put those convictions into practice and that his civil, not to speak of his physical, salvation would require painful renunciations of him. On 22 December 1849, after his return from the scaffold, he wrote to his brother: 'Perhaps we will recall someday . . . our youth and our hopes, hopes which at this very moment I am tearing from my heart with blood and am burying.' This is Dostoevsky's first suggestion that he might renounce his dreams of freedom. On the other hand, it is at the same time a testimonial to his deep devotion to those dreams, which he had to 'tear with blood' from the depths of his heart.

This sort of moral execution could not be effected in an instant. It took years for it to reach completion. The writer was not permitted to have pen or books, but his prodigious intellectual activity never ceased for a moment in his Siberian prison. Little by little, he subjected his early ideological interests to stern reappraisal. To the accompaniment of prisoners' songs and the clang of chains, the former Petrashevskyite re-examined in depth all the views of his youth. 'It would be very difficult for me to give the history of the transformation of my convictions,' Dostoevsky wrote in 1873, referring to the transition from his Utopian socialism of the 1840s to the reactionary views of his post-exile period.

However, he did leave a few indications for the future biographer. We know from his own statements that during the four years he spent in Omsk he thought over his entire past life, that he judged himself sternly and radically revised his earlier world outlook. This was a judgement pronounced in a dungeon in complete isolation from society and in profound spiritual solitude:

Completely alone spiritually, I re-examined my entire past life. I considered every last detail. I thought deeply about my past. Alone, I judged myself without mercy and in all strictness. At times I even thanked fate for having sent me this solitude, without which neither this judgement of myself nor the strict re-examination of my past life would have occurred.

Dostoevsky made a painful discovery in prison. He found that he was alienated from the common people. The convict sentenced to second degree penal servitude and, even more, the author of *Poor Folk*, was determined to overcome this alienation, whatever the price. The way to do this, he felt, was to renounce his socialist convictions, which he now, erroneously, believed to be anti-popular, cosmopolitan and un-Russian. He believed that for him, yesterday's Fourierist, the only way to the roots of the people was through the religious ideas of the serfs and the Russian Orthodox faith which they professed. This was a path back to the values of his childhood, to the old days in Moscow, to the traditions, the 'soil', the 'Russian and pious' patriarchal beliefs of his family.

That this reversal in Dostoevsky's views came about in Omsk is confirmed in a number of contemporary memoirs, which testify that in prison he already expressed conservative beliefs, clearly containing the seeds of his subsequent journalistic writing in favour of the establishment. His Siberian poems 'On the European Events in 1854', 'On 1 July 1855' and 'The Dread War is Over' may have been prompted by a desire to hasten his rehabilitation, but they nevertheless expressed his true feelings, which supported the new 'great power' school of Russian poetry of which his friend Apollon Maikov was the leader. And his *Notes from the House of the Dead* contain, as is well known, certain nationalist and religious-moralistic elements.

'Thoughts and convictions change, and the whole man changes too,' Dostoevsky wrote on 24 March 1856. There is sadness in these words. It is the sadness of parting with the convictions of one's youth, with the faith that mankind will be liberated from the chains of autocracy and with the belief that it is an artist's supreme mission to urge his generation to transform the world and to lead it to truth and justice. But there was no returning to the past. Other ideals had to be built, and for a person of Dostoevsky's temperament this meant opposite ideals. He admitted, with the ruthless sincerity characteristic of him, that he had changed his former convictions, as he explained in a letter to Apollon Maikov of 2 August 1868.

A letter he wrote to Natalya Fonvizina immediately upon his release was another summary of his reflections during imprisonment: 'About myself, let me tell you that I am a child of this age, a child of unbelief and doubts to this very day and shall be (I know this) to the day I am laid in my coffin. What terrible torment I have suffered and am suffering now because of this longing to believe, a longing that is all the stronger in my soul the more arguments I have against it.' Thus in 1854 Dostoevsky confessed to a lack of faith, that was mitigated only by a philosophical interest in Christianity.

The question arises – exactly when did Dostoevsky experience his religious crisis?

We think that the execution on 22 December 1849 was the turning-point. It brought a complete inner change in him, about which he himself wrote several times.

'That head which created, which lived the higher life of art, which experienced and had grown accustomed to the higher necessities of the spirit, that head has already been severed from my shoulders,' he wrote to his brother on the very day of the experience. And twenty years later, describing this ritual, he recalled that when the priest kept on presenting the Cross to his lips – 'almost every moment' – he, prepared for death 'made haste to kiss it, as if I were hurrying not to forget to snatch something to have in reserve – just in case. But I doubt if I was aware of any religious feeling at that moment.'

At this awful moment of ordeal Dostoevsky's religion had let him down. All the church's concepts about life after death, heaven, and immortality were opposed to the concept that a dead man dissolves in nature, that he merges naturally with the universe, perhaps with the rays of sunlight, which will become his 'new nature'. Unbelief was to remain for ever at the core of Dostoevsky's perception of the world, despite his keen interest in matters of religious controversy.

*

Dostoevsky's term of hard labour ended on 23 January 1854. In February he left the Omsk prison for ever. Early on the morning of his last day, before the convicts were led out to work, he walked through the barracks and in the semi-darkness of dawn bade farewell to his branded comrades. Durov was released from the prison at the same time. He had arrived there a young and cheerful man and was departing a grey-haired, short-winded semi-invalid, hardly able to drag his legs. The two men were taken to the smithy to have their chains removed. Durov was released first. Then the blacksmiths placed Dostoevsky's foot on the anvil, turned the rivet and brought the hammer down. The chains fell off. 'Freedom, a new life, resurrection from the dead. What a glorious moment!'

That same month, February 1854, Dostoevsky, having served the first part of his sentence, was enrolled as a private in the Seventh Siberian Battalion of the Line, stationed in a distant region of the steppe.

VIII

The Battalion of the Line

AFTER four years of imprisonment Dostoevsky found genuine rebirth in that early spring, the journey from Omsk to Semipalatinsk in a convict draft, across treeless expanses and along the banks of the Irtysh River. Towards the end of his life he told friends that he had never felt happier than he had during that enforced journey, after they had been picked up by a wagon train that they met on the road sitting on hard ropes 'with the sky above me, pure air around me and freedom in my heart'. Complete freedom was still far off, however.

Semipalatinsk was a remote town in the Kirghiz steppes, not far from the Chinese border. The monotony of the landscape of poor, squat buildings was enlivened by the graceful silhouettes of pointed minarets, scattered through the town. Once again Dostoevsky was quartered in a wooden barracks, but now he did not have to sleep on bare boards. His bunk was covered with felt. He had to attend parades with absolute strictness, but he had no other duties.

Here, too, he was in close contact with the common people, but of a different stratum – the soldiers. He never portrayed them in his works, as did Lermontov and Leo Tolstoy, but he acquired a warm affection for them. 'Those of us who have lived among soldiers,' he wrote in 1861, 'know how far removed they are from fanaticism. If you only knew what nice, likeable, dear fellows they are.' He recalled how he used to read aloud 'to the young soldiers and to others, to all sorts of Captains Polei, Panfilov, etc.'

After a short while Dostoevsky was granted permission to live in his own lodgings. He moved to the 'Russian town', located not far from his battalion, where he rented a dark, soot-covered cottage from a soldier's widow. The cottage stood in shifting sands that were dotted with thorn bushes. One of Dostoevsky's friends has described his way of life at that time:

The landlady's elder daughter, a girl of about twenty, took care of his simple needs – washing, mending and cleaning the room. She took care of Fyodor Mikhailovich lovingly, I think, cooked for him and was inseparable from him. I became so accustomed to her that it never surprised me when she and her beautiful sixteen-year-old sister, barefoot and wearing only shifts tied with red sashes and scarves, sat down to have tea with us in the summer.

The ex-convict was coming back to life. He had regained the right to read and write and now in spite of his military duties he flung himself upon books. He asked his brother to send him the European historians, economists, Church fathers, ancient authors, the Koran, Kant, Hegel, physics, physiology, even a German dictionary. The breadth of his plans and the variety of his intellectual interests after what he had undergone are astonishing indeed. Prison sentence had not broken the creative artist. In fact, it had given fresh impetus to his irrepressible desire to write. He read Turgenev, Ostrovsky, Pisemsky, Tyutchev, Maikov. He was sent the newly published edition of Pushkin's works, edited by P. V. Annenkov. He implored them to tell who was the L.T., whose *Boyhood* had been published in *Sovremennik**.

*

The autumn of that year saw a further improvement in Dostoevsky's situation. Alexander Wrangel, member of the Public Prosecutor's Supervisory Commission and Public

* L.T. stands for Leo Tolstoy; *Boyhood* is part of his early autobiographical trilogy *Childhood, Boyhood and Youth*.

Prosecutor for Civil and Criminal Affairs, arrived in Semipalatinsk in November 1854. He was a very young man – he had just reached his majority – and a recent graduate from the *Lycée*. Because of his passion for travelling and shooting he had decided to take a post in one of Russia's distant Asiatic possessions. Five years earlier young Wrangel had been present at the Petrashevskyites' mock execution and had felt very distressed for Dostoevsky, whom he already knew as a writer. The day after his arrival he sent a note to Dostoevsky, asking him to call that evening, and later described what happened:

Dostoevsky did not know who had summoned him or why, and when he came into the room he was extremely reticent. He was wearing a grey soldier's greatcoat with a red stand-up collar and red shoulder straps. He looked morose. His sickly, pale face was covered with freckles. His light brown hair was cut short. He was a little above medium height. As he examined me attentively with his intelligent grey-blue eyes he seemed to be trying to penetrate into my very soul, to discover what kind of a person I was. He admitted to me afterwards that he was very worried when my messenger told him that the 'Public Prosecutor for Criminal Affairs' wished to see him. But when I apologized for not having called on him myself first, gave him the letters, parcels and greetings, and spoke pleasantly to him, he changed at once, brightened and began to trust me. He often told me afterwards that on his way home from my house that evening he had felt instinctively that he was going to have a sincere friend in me.[1]

This marked the beginning of a new era in Dostoevsky's Siberian exile. His friendship with the district Public Prosecutor greatly improved his social situation. Although he was a private, serving an indefinite term in the line troops, he was welcome at the homes of the Battalion Commander Belikhov, Judge Peshekhonov and even of the Military Governor Spiridonov. Wrangel introduced him to a mining engineer at the near-by lead and silver factories, and to his officer friends; he took him along on trips to Kazakh villages; he showed him the town of Zmiev.

In the summer Wrangel and Dostoevsky moved in together to the only *dacha* in those parts, 'Cossack Garden', a summer house belonging to a rich local Cossack merchant, situated on the high bank of the Irtysh River. Here they gardened, went swimming and fishing in the river, and read. Dostoevsky worked on his prison memoirs and he read each completed chapter to Wrangel. The two men smoked their pipes and talked of Petersburg. 'Both daughters of Dostoevsky's landlady took an active part in our flower gardening efforts.' They watered the dahlias, sweet williams and stocks, the first ever to bloom in this sandy soil, where none but sunflowers grew.

Sometimes the two men took long rides on horseback, exploring the winter huts and the boundless steppe dotted with nomad Kirghiz tents. The Semipalatinsk region was rich in natural beauty, with broad steppes covered with feathergrass and wormwood, the waters of the wide Irtysh basin, pine groves and deep lakes. Wrangel has described the striking, mirror-like Kolyvan Lake, situated among gullies and cliffs, a spot that even Humboldt, who had travelled all over the globe, considered the most beautiful in the world. But Dostoevsky was indifferent to pictures of nature – 'they did not touch him, did not move him. He was wholly absorbed in the study of man.' Having always been interested in history, Dostoevsky turned to cultural archaeology and gathered a fine collection of ancient aboriginal objects, rings, silver and copper coins, bracelets, earrings, a variety of beads, broken spears and small silver, copper, iron and stone objects. He also made a collection of mineral samples. But most of all he valued remarkable people. Though Semipalatinsk society consisted almost entirely of provincial officials and army officers, there were among the arrivals from other parts of the country some highly cultivated people who treated the exiled writer with great respect and sympathy. These were his new friends, and they brought to mind the Petersburg circles of the 1840s.

In Omsk Dostoevsky had made the acquaintance of a Kazakh officer, Chokan Valikhanov, the first Kirghizian scholar, an ethnographer, folklorist and historian and they soon became friends. Valikhanov loved Arabic poems. He was an enterprising and courageous traveller and told Dostoevsky about his secret expeditions in 1858. 'Valikhanov is a most delightful and wonderful person,' Dostoevsky wrote to Wrangel. 'I am very fond of him and very much interested in him.' In letters to Valikhanov Dostoevsky foretold a great future for him: 'You are the first Kirghiz who has had a truly European education.' In Dostoevsky's opinion it was the duty of cultivated representatives of the Orient to serve their peoples by making every effort to promote rapprochement with Russia. He urged his 'dear Vali-khan' to try to make the Russians 'understand what the steppe is'.

Dostoevsky had met Pyotr Semyonov, afterwards known as Semyonov of Tien-Shan, in Petersburg at Petrashevsky's, but it was only in Central Asia that they became friends. 'Semyonov is a splendid person,' he wrote to Valikhanov. Semyonov was already an eminent geographer. He had recently toured Europe, conferred with Humboldt about a forthcoming expedition to Central Asia, climbed Vesuvius and the Alps by map and compass, without a guide, visited the ruins of Pompeii and Paestum, had been to the Louvre and other famous galleries, which had awakened in him a future connoisseur and author of studies of Flemish painting and old drawings. All these qualities in his gifted friend were valued by Dostoevsky, who visited him at Barnaul in the winter of 1857, and read his first studies for *Notes from the House of the Dead* to him. It was from Barnaul that Semyonov set out on his expedition to the inaccessible foothills of the 'Heavenly Range' (Tien-Shan).[2]

*

On 12 March 1855 the news of the death of Nicholas I in Petersburg on 18 February reached Semipalatinsk, and threw the town into a turmoil. Major political events had preceded the death of the Tsar. In the autumn of 1854 the Allies had managed to turn the course of the war. A party of Anglo-French troops had landed at Eupatoria in the Crimea; battles had been fought at Alma, Balaklava and the Inkerman Hills. The first bombardment of Sevastopol had taken place, Admiral Kornilov had been killed, and the main fire had been concentrated against Malakhov Hill. These events, which all took place between October and February, had greatly altered the picture of the war and presaged disaster. History was putting the entire system of Nicholas I on trial and preparing to deliver a terrible verdict on it.

The Tsar suffered agonies watching painfully the inexorable course of events. He had already said that the Austrian Emperor had 'twisted the knife in his heart' by his betrayal. The news of the defeat at Alma was a thunderbolt to him. The British Prime Minister Palmerston was threatening to dismember Russia and take away the Crimea, the Caucasus, Bessarabia, the Baltic provinces, Poland and Finland. Nicholas I, accustomed as he was to regarding himself as the Dictator of Europe (or 'Gendarme of Europe' as he used to be called in progressive circles at that time) was stunned by his unexpected humiliation and by the total bankruptcy of his whole policy. In thirty years as ruler of Russia, he had not been able to prepare his country adequately for war or to assure his own international influence. The verdict was about to be given against an entire epoch.

At the end of January the Tsar caught a cold and early in February he developed pneumonia. On 17 February his physician-in-ordinary Mandt stated that there was no hope. Nicholas died the next day. Russian opinion was convinced that the Tsar had taken poison. Historians consider that this can never be proved. However, such an act would not have been out of keeping with the Tsar's character and the logic of the situation. When the untenability of the system became obvious, the man who was its nerve-centre had nothing left to live for.

Dostoevsky and Wrangel attended a requiem at Semipalatinsk Cathedral on 12 March. Everybody was wondering whether the long, hard war would now end; and the exiled writer, like all the intellectuals under surveillance in Siberia, hoped for a change in his lot. Wrangel took immediate steps to help his friend. He wrote to close relatives in Petersburg, inquiring about attitudes in government circles and imploring them to find out whether a political amnesty would be announced at the coronation. Would it not be possible, he asked his sister in a letter dated 15 May 1855, 'to whisper a word about Dostoevsky to Dubelt or Prince Orlov? Surely, this remarkable man will not die a private here? That would be horrible. One feels sad and bitter for him.'

In prison the struggle had been to keep alive. Now the struggle was for liberation from lifelong service in the army. In this new, exceedingly difficult ordeal Dostoevsky once more displayed strength of character and a will to win. Dostoevsky had another reason for fighting this new battle with such determination. Since the spring of 1854, he had been involved in a personal drama.

MME ISAEVA

Dostoevsky emerged from his 'sad prison term', in his own words, 'with happiness and hope'. He arrived in Semipalatinsk avid for life, and in his very first year there he found a great all-absorbing love, a love that caused him much anguish but that also gave him some of the fullest and most unforgettable moments of his life: 'At least I have lived; though I suffered, I *lived*!'

On arrival in Semipalatinsk Dostoevsky had made the

acquaintance of a petty customs official named Alexander Ivanovich Isaev and his wife Maria Dmitrievna, *née* Constant (she was French on her grandfather's side). Her life had turned out unhappily. Daughter of the director of the Astrakhan quarantine, she had married an alcoholic. Incapable of regular work, hand in glove with all the riffraff of society, this man had condemned his wife and son to a life of acute privation. Dostoevsky found him already 'gone terribly to seed'.

When I made his acquaintance he had been retired from the service for several months and was looking for some kind of other job. As he had no property he was dependent on his salary, so when he lost his position the family gradually sank into frightful poverty. He had incurred many debts. He lived a very disorderly life, and his nature too, was disorderly, passionate, obstinate and rather coarse. He was irresponsible as a gipsy, vain and proud, and had no self-control whatever.

Dostoevsky found these contrasts of the man's nature interesting. 'Despite all the sordidness, he was an extremely honourable man,' he wrote. Isaev was, in part, the prototype for Marmeladov.

This was the beginning of Dostoevsky's first personal romance – an extraordinarily complex and painful one.

Maria Dmitrievna had tuberculosis, but, like many consumptives, she was passionately attached to life's joys and pleasures. Her home life was truly horrible. Her husband often became violent when he was drunk and she had to be on constant guard to protect her son from his father's rages. 'Respectable' society had turned away from them. All that remained were Isaev's companions, whom Dostoevsky described in one of his letters as unclean, disgusting alehouse types. Maria Dmitrievna, Dostoevsky wrote, was 'still young, pretty, educated, intelligent, graceful and kindhearted', and bore her burden with dignity and without complaint.

Later, in 1856, when he knew the complexity of her nature

better, he described her with more depth and comprehensiveness. 'Every minute reveals something original, sensible and witty, yet contradictory, infinitely good, truly noble – she has a chivalrous heart. She will destroy herself.' Dostoevsky saw his first love as a restless, impulsive, original, exalted, noble and courageous nature. He felt that she was on the brink of destruction, and his heart was filled with anxiety.

At that time she was twenty-six years old. Wrangel describes her as a pretty blonde of medium height, very thin, passionate and highly strung. 'Even at that time there was an ominous flush on her pale face, and a few years later consumption carried her off to the grave. She was well-read, fairly well educated, had an inquiring mind, was kind-hearted and *extraordinarily vivacious and impressionable*.' When Nikolai Strakhov met her briefly some time later in Petersburg, he was very favourably impressed by her pale and gentle features, though they already bore the mark, he noted, of her fatal illness. A portrait that has come down to us shows a young woman with an intelligent, strong-willed expression, a high forehead and sensuous lips. In animated conversation, in argument or in laughter, a face such as this might have appeared inspired or even beautiful.

From the outset Dostoevsky's relationship with Isaeva was based on a misconception and was mutually agonizing. Wrangel once explained how this came about:

She was kind to him. I don't think she really appreciated him, rather she took pity on an unhappy man, whom fate had treated so badly. It is possible that she even became fond of him, but she was never the least in love with him. She knew that he suffered from a nervous disease and that he was extremely short of money; he was a man without a future, she used to say. Dostoevsky mistook her feeling of pity and compassion for reciprocation and fell in love with her with all the ardour of a young man.

From the beginning of their intimacy Dostoevsky used to have fits of extreme jealousy, brought on by doubts as to whether she really loved him. Those doubts were especially strong at the time when the Isaevs left Semipalatinsk. After two years without a job and near beggary, Isaev was offered a post as 'assessor for the administration of taverns', a 'really very humiliating' offer, Dostoevsky remarked. This entailed moving to the wild Siberian town of Kuznetsk, in Tomsk Province, an awful backwater, four hundred miles away. But what could they do? They had hardly a crust of bread. They had to sell everything to pay their most pressing debts, borrow money for the trip and make the long journey in an open cart, not even in a covered wagon.

Dostoevsky's despair was boundless, Wrangel relates. He walked about like a madman, for the very thought of parting from Maria Dmitrievna made him feel that he had nothing left to live for. 'You see, she has agreed to go, she does not protest. That is what is so galling,' he kept saying bitterly. The Isaevs set out one evening towards the end of May. 'I shall never forget the scene of their parting. Dostoevsky sobbed like a child.'

Dostoevsky and Wrangel accompanied the Isaevs for a way along the forest road. It was a beautiful night. Wrangel got Isaev drunk on champagne and took him into his own carriage, where he fell sound asleep. Dostoevsky got in beside Maria Dmitrievna. They drove for a long while through a pine wood, bathed in moonlight. At last they stopped and took leave of each other. Then the horses galloped off, the cart disappeared from view, the tinkle of the bells died away. 'But Dostoevsky stood there as if rooted to the spot, speechless, his head bowed, tears rolling down his cheeks. We did not get home until daybreak.'

*

A correspondence developed between them that was even more agonizing than their personal relationship. Even at a distance Maria Dmitrievna constantly complained about deprivation, her illness, her husband's sad condition and the joyless future. Most of all Dostoevsky took to heart her complaints that she was unbearably lonely and had no one to talk to. But when the name of a new acquaintance in Kuznetsk, a 'likeable young schoolteacher' with rare qualities and a 'noble soul', began to appear in her letters with increasing frequency, he became very despondent, wandered about like a ghost and even stopped working on *Notes from the House of the Dead*, in which he had been absorbed.

In August 1855 Dostoevsky received a letter from Maria Dmitrievna, informing him that her husband had died. He had died in terrible agony, she wrote, their moving had been his undoing. He died of stone, Dostoevsky wrote later, 'solely because of the lack of medical assistance in the out-of-the-way place where he was employed'. The widow wrote that her little boy was frantic with tears and despair and that she herself was exhausted from sleeplessness and acute attacks of her own illness. She had had to borrow money for the funeral, and she had been left with nothing but debts. Someone had sent her three roubles and 'poverty pushed my hand to accept it, and so I have taken alms'. '*And so she was left after his death in a far off barbarous district, and she was left in such dire poverty that although I had seen many happenings of all kinds, even I could not find the words to describe her plight.*' Thus some years later, in *Crime and Punishment*, did Dostoevsky immortalize this commonplace tragedy of his Siberian past.

Dostoevsky dropped everything and devoted himself entirely to arranging Maria's affairs. He borrowed money from Wrangel; he tried to get eight-year-old Pasha admitted to the Cadet Corps; he petitioned for his rival, the Kuznetsk schoolteacher Vergunov ('a completely colourless individual', according to Wrangel) with heroic self-sacrifice: 'I am prepared to beg on my knees.' All this, apparently, was powerless to change Maria's friendly pity for Dostoevsky into love. In the summer of 1856, nearly a year after Isaev's death, Dostoevsky wrote letters to Wrangel full of despair:

'I am like a madman. It is already too late now! Things are horribly bad and I am practically desperate. It is hard to suffer as I have suffered. *I tremble lest she get married,* God help me, I'd drown myself or take to drink.' Before that, in a letter of 23 March, he had written: 'Oh, God save everyone from this fearful, awesome feeling. Great is the joy of love, but the suffering it causes is so terrible that it would have been better never to have loved at all.'

He soon came to know at first hand the atmosphere of mutual torment so typical of the plots of his novels. The letters he wrote to Wrangel in that period constitute a diary of the most passionate and agonizing love of his life.

13 April 1856. At Shrovetide I went to various houses for pancakes. I even danced at parties. I told Maria Dmitrievna about all this in a letter, about my even having danced, and about some of the local *ladies*. And she took it into her head that I was beginning to *forget* her and becoming interested in others. Later, when it was cleared up, she wrote me that the thought that I, her last and true friend, was already beginning to forget her had tormented her.

She writes that she was in torment and agony but she would not have let me know of her despair and doubts: 'I would have died rather than have uttered a word.' I can understand that. She has a proud and noble heart. And, she writes, that is why 'I involuntarily became cold to you in my letters; I was nearly certain that I was not writing to the same man who had so recently loved only me.'

I had noticed this coldness in her letters and was devastated by it. Then one day someone told me that she was getting married. If you only knew what became of me then! I was in agony. I re-read her last letters and because of their coldness I could not help doubting and therefore despairing.

In the midst of this he received a letter from Maria, asking 'what she should say if a man with some merit made her an offer of marriage'. He was horrified and ready to do something desperate. 'But a ghost of a hope stopped me. I decided to wait for her reply to my letters and was saved.

This is what had happened. Tortured by jealousy and sorrow because she had lost a friend, surrounded by vile, worthless people, ill and sensitive, far away from all her family and from all help, she had made up her mind *to find out for certain* how I felt about her, had I forgotten her, was I the same man I had been or not.' Dostoevsky had replied with 'despairing, terrible letters that tore her apart'. She then confessed that she had only been testing his heart.

There were grounds, nevertheless, for the rumour of her marriage. Someone in Tomsk is looking for a wife, and having heard that there was a widow in Kuznetsk, still quite young and, they said, good-looking, had offered her his hand through some old gossips in Kuznetsk (beastly people, who were always insulting her). She burst out laughing in the face of the Kuznetsk marriage broker. To me this is all melancholy, hell. Really, sometimes I think I shall go out of my mind!

In June 1856 Dostoevsky was sent to Barnaul on duty and, without asking for permission, he stopped off in Kuznetsk. ('I was prepared to stand trial, but I had to *see her*.') He spent two days with Maria Dmitrievna. She told him then about her feelings for Vergunov. The meeting was a sad one but not completely without hope.

She wept, she kissed my hands, but she loves another. I spent two days there. During those two days she remembered the past and her heart turned towards me again. In saying this, I do not know whether I am right or wrong. But she said to me: 'Do not weep, do not be sad, all is not yet decided. It is you and I and no one else.' This was positive. What two days those were for me! Bliss and unbearable torment! I departed at the end of the second day *full of hope*. But very likely the absent are always at fault. So it was! Letter after letter, and I saw that she was miserable again. She wept, and again she loves him more than she does me! I cannot say: so be it. I do not know what will become of me if I lose her. I am lost, but so is she. She is twenty-nine, she is educated, clever, she has seen the world, knows people; she has suffered, she has endured agonies; her last years in Siberia have made her ill; she is seeking happiness, she is capricious and strong-willed; now she is planning to marry a youth of twenty-four, a Siberian, who has seen nothing and knows nothing, who is barely educated, who is just beginning the first episode of his life, whereas she is, perhaps, finishing the *last episode* of hers – a man of no importance and without a thing in the world, a schoolteacher in a provincial school, who hopes (very soon) to have a salary of nine hundred paper roubles. Tell me, Alexander Yegorovich, isn't she ruining herself a second time? How can two people of such different characters, such different views of life and such different needs live in harmony? And what if he [reproaches] her a few years hence, what if he brings her to her death! What will happen to her, living in poverty, with a gaggle of children and condemned to remain in Kuznetsk? Who knows how far their future quarrels, which I foresee as inevitable, will go? What if he insults her by basely reproaching her for having taken advantage of his youth and for wanting to wear him out with sensuality, and she, she! beautiful angel, may have to listen to this from him!

My heart is breaking.

Maria insisted that Dostoevsky and Vergunov have a talk. Unable to make up her mind herself, she apparently thought the two men could cut the Gordian knot of her fate in her absence. But this did not happen. 'I met him,' Dostoevsky informed Wrangel. 'He wept in my presence, but that is all he knows how to do, weep.' Dostoevsky did not want to discuss the matter or use persuasion, aware of the futility of trying to decide affairs of human passion and human relationships by reason. However, when he got back to Semipalatinsk he wrote a long letter, addressed to both of them. 'I have pictured everything that may happen as the result of such an ill-matched marriage.' He pointed out the tragedy of the situation. He asked the young man 'to consider what he wished to do, whether he *was not about to ruin a woman's life for the sake of his own happiness*'. Vergunov took offence and replied with a sharply worded letter. Maria defended Vergunov heatedly, but after her first outbursts she addressed Dostoevsky 'tenderly again, affectionately again', again she loved them both. 'How this will end I do not know, but *she will destroy herself* and my heart sinks.'

Dostoevsky resolved to sacrifice himself and help her to be happy. This was putting into practice the noble ideal of self-sacrificing lovers such as Jacques Saxe and Devushkin. He appealed to the influential Wrangel to help Vergunov get a good post for the sake of Maria's happiness. 'She must not suffer. You know, he's only getting about four hundred paper roubles a year.' (This was only about ten silver roubles a month.) 'That is not enough to provide for a family, to make a woman like Maria Constant happy! It is necessary to talk with the Governor-General, to recommend Vergunov to him as a worthy young man, a fine young man of ability. It is also necessary to write about him to the Altai military governor. This is all for *her, for her alone*,' Dostoevsky concluded his desperate prayer. 'At least she should not live in poverty, that is all that matters!'

This letter to Wrangel of 14 July 1856 is an outstanding human document and provides valuable material about Dostoevsky's moral character. It is an indication of the heights to which his ardent and irrestrainable soul could soar. His moral beauty radiates from it in all its purity. Soon he would also display genuine courage, supreme vital energy, and the readiness of a strong man to do battle for the woman he loved.

*

Actually, the root of all the difficulties in the psychological situation that had arisen was Dostoevsky's position as a disfranchised state criminal still under sentence 'as a lifelong common soldier'. An indispensable condition for the marriage he so desired was that he be commissioned as an officer: 'After all, she cannot marry a common soldier, can she?' Early in 1856 Maria Dmitrievna had asked Dostoevsky what she should do if an elderly, well-off civil servant were to offer her marriage. He replied immediately that he would die if he lost her. 'I shall lose my mind or jump into the Irtysh.' At that time he was convinced that 'If my affairs succeeded, I would be preferred to anyone else.' It was necessary to speed up the processes of officialdom, it was necessary to put up a fight for his happiness. He decided on a bold and far-reaching plan.

At the Engineering Academy he had been acquainted with the Totleben brothers. Eduard Totleben, the elder, was now the hero of Sevastopol. At the most critical period of the war he had protected the city by a solid defence line that had compelled the Allies to give up the idea of a direct attack. Foreign specialists regarded him as the foremost engineer of the nineteenth century. Indeed, his ideas initiated a new era in the design of fortifications. His name was on everybody's lips, along with the names of Nakhimov and Kornilov. Dostoevsky resolved to write a letter, half confession, half request, to the defender of Sevastopol. He asked Wrangel, who was a very old friend of Totleben, to convey the letter to him personally.

On 24 March a member of the lower ranks, acting contrary to army rules, wrote a non-official letter to an aide-de-camp of the Tsar. This is one of the most important letters in Dostoevsky's epistolary legacy. Reminding Totleben that they had known each other a long time ago, Dostoevsky briefly set forth his 'sad story':

I was convicted of the intention (but no more) of acting against the government. I was convicted legally and justly. Long experience, harsh and agonizing, has brought me to my senses and greatly altered my views. But at that time, at that time I was blind. I believed in theories and Utopias. Penal servitude was frightful. But I swear to you, the worst agony was when I realized my errors, and realized at the same time that I had been cut off from society and exiled and could no longer be useful according to the measure of my strength, desire and abilities. I know that I was convicted for a dream, for a theory. Thoughts and even convictions change. The whole man changes. Imagine how it feels now to be suffering for what no longer exists, for what has changed in me to the opposite. . .

Dostoevsky speaks of his most cherished wish . . .

I do not regard army service as the chief aim of my life. There was a time when I was encouraged by the public's reception to take the path of literature. I would like permission to publish . . . I have always regarded the vocation of a writer as a most noble and most useful one. I am convinced that it is only as a writer that I can be useful . . .

Towards the end he alluded to his intimate personal affairs

I will not conceal from you that one circumstance on which, perhaps, my whole life's happiness depends (a purely private circumstance) has impelled me to . . . bring myself to your attention.

Wrangel had returned to Petersburg in February 1856, and as soon as he received Dostoevsky's letter he gave it to General Eduard Totleben. He also asked Adolf Totleben, the younger brother (who had been a class-mate of Dostoevsky's at the Engineering Academy) for his support. Both brothers expressed warm sympathy for their exiled former schoolmate and promised to do all they could for him.[3]

Shortly afterwards a resolution by the Tsar appeared in Dostoevsky's dossier.

His Majesty condescends to order that a memorandum be written to the War Minister, requesting that Fyodor Dostoevsky *be raised to the rank of ensign* in one of the regiments of the Second Army. If this is inconvenient, then he is to be discharged with the rank of 14th class and assigned to a civil service post. In either case, he is to be permitted to engage in literature *with the right* to publish on a legitimate basis.

This was not the complete pardon it seemed, for the Tsar's mercy stopped short at the point where he had added that Dostoevsky was to be kept under secret surveillance until his reliability was fully established, and only after that was the application for permission to publish his literary work to be submitted. Thus, permission to publish was put off indefinitely and the main purpose of the letter to Totleben had not been achieved; Dostoevsky had not obtained recognition of his rights as an author. Without permission to publish in the Press, he was a mere officer, and his position in the literary world was tenuous. It would take several more years before he won the right to work in the literary profession. Be that as it may, on 30 October 1856 Hasfort, the Governor-General of Western Siberia, received an imperial order from General Headquarters promoting Private Dostoevsky to the rank of ensign.

This major event, which changed his whole life, pleased him only because it enabled him to see Maria Dmitrievna the sooner. Dostoevsky wrote to Wrangel on 9 November: 'I think of nothing else. All I want is to see her, to hear her. I am an unhappy man. Love like this is a disease. I know it.' On the same day he wrote his brother: 'I still adore the same woman. She is an angel of God whom I met on my way, and suffering bound us.' He regarded this bond as inseverable.

At the end of November Dostoevsky arrived in Kuznetsk in the uniform of an officer. He explained his circumstances to her 'honestly and frankly': the absence of material security, the uncertainty of his rights as an author, but great hopes for a return to literature. His firm confidence persuaded Maria Isaeva at last that he was a man with a future. However, there was still the obstacle of her love for Vergunov, though that love had not entirely extinguished her feeling for Dostoevsky.

In *The Landlady*, written ten years earlier, Dostoevsky had portrayed the dualism of a woman's heart, unable to choose between two rivals – the brigand Murin and the righteous man Ordynov – a situation that had intrigued him because of its dramatic power. Now this very dualism confronted him in real life. Frenziedly, Maria Dmitrievna searched for a way out of the destructive vortex of conflicting desires:

should she choose the writer Dostoevsky or the impecunious but young and handsome schoolteacher in an out-of-the-way town?

Dostoevsky, who had a profound understanding of the human psyche, was convinced that this intelligent woman of strong character could not be truly in love with a shallow and colourless man, who was incapable of rising to her spiritual level. 'She loves me. I know this for certain. She quickly became disappointed in her new attachment. I already knew that from her letters in the summer. She was always frank with me. She never had any secrets from me. Oh, if you only knew what kind of woman she is! Surely, it would be desecration to lock away this rich emotional and intellectual world in a god-forsaken district school!'

Dostoevsky resolved to have another talk with Vergunov. This time life itself was on his side. Maria was evidently coming around to a decision in his favour. Vergunov withdrew. Dostoevsky was eager to make up to him for the sacrifice he had made. 'On my knees', he implored Wrangel to do something for the unfortunate schoolteacher. 'He is dearer to me now than a brother.' (It is interesting that rivals who grow as close as brothers make one of the principal themes in *The Idiot*.) Dostoevsky left Kuznetsk at the beginning of December with plans to have the wedding before Lent.

There was still much to be done before happiness could be achieved in a world where money decided everything; money was needed to rent and furnish living quarters, to pay for the journey by troika from Semipalatinsk to Kuznetsk and back (fourteen hundred versts), to purchase the rest of his officer's equipment, to dress his impecunious bride, and to pay for the marriage service and the wedding. And the bridegroom himself had only just come off N.C.O. rations. Dostoevsky displayed extraordinary energy. He wrote to relatives in Petersburg and Moscow, investigated the possibilities of borrowing money locally, talked with people, made the rounds raising money tirelessly so that he might arrange his home and his future. He acted with efficiency, energy, intelligence and without putting a foot wrong. The measure of an unusual man can be sensed in this battle for life, for work, for a family, and for happiness. In this, too, Dostoevsky was a builder and a creator.

His relatives were against the marriage, naturally. His Moscow aunt Alexandra Kumanina, who had had a hand in his upbringing, expressed the family's opinion: 'You have just emerged from unparalleled misfortune yourself. You have nothing, yet you are dragging another creature into your misfortune, and you are tying yourself down two and three times over.' Nevertheless, the Kumanins sent him six hundred silver roubles. His brother Mikhail and his elder sisters each sent him two hundred silver roubles. Captain Kovrigin, who held an important position at the Loktyev metallurgical factory, gave him a long-term loan of six hundred silver roubles. Several friends, General Khomentovsky and others, helped him, too. He had won the battle with honour.

THE WEDDING IN KUZNETSK

On 27 January 1857 Dostoevsky left for Kuznetsk to make arrangements for his wedding. Kuznetsk was a wretched town of hunters, trappers and prospectors, built round an old prison settlement. Dostoevsky wrote about places like this in *Notes from the House of the Dead*: 'In the distant regions of Siberia, in the steppes, mountains or impassable forests, one sometimes comes across small towns with a thousand, or perhaps two thousand inhabitants – and even that is a lot – wooden towns, colourless towns, with two small churches, one in the town and the other at the cemetery, towns that look more like the villages around Moscow than towns.'

This was where Dostoevsky had his first taste of happiness,

this was where one of the most important events of his private life took place. On 6 February 1857 he led the woman he loved so passionately to the altar of the local Church of the Holy Guide. The wedding was a very small one. Dostoevsky knew only a few people in Kuznetsk, and Maria Dmitrievna, as a poor widow, had lived a very quiet life. Their parents were represented by the local police officer and his wife, and the ceremony was performed by Father Yevgeni Tyumentsev. The best men were, Dostoevsky wrote, 'quite respectable people, simple and kindhearted', and there were two families, probably neighbours, as guests.*

One of the four official guarantors in the ceremony was the schoolteacher Nikolai Vergunov. This undoubtedly made for considerable tension at the marriage ceremony, springing from a complex of rivalry, jealousy, hostility and passion. Though all present were aware of these relationships, no one except Dostoevsky attached importance to them. It was only the great writer, who had set in motion this drama of love among provincial philistines, who perceived the deep undercurrents of this flow of passions, that were already stirring his imagination. Standing at the altar, Maria may have felt closer to her best man standing there beside her than to the bridegroom. As for the rejected man, who could guess his pain, his jealousy, his despair, his wrath, perhaps his thirst for revenge? What cruel and terrible end might have followed from such a white heat of passion? A bride fleeing from the altar? The murder of the martyred woman by her lover? The madness of the abandoned bridegroom?

For what Dostoevsky was dreading above all was that the excitable, headstrong Vergunov, with that ugly streak of cold-blooded savagery in his character, might commit some wild act and *cause the death* of Maria Dmitrievna.

---

* There are two 'best men' (Russian *shaferá*) at a Russian Church wedding. They hold crowns above the heads of the bride and bridegroom during the ceremony.

'*What if he brings her to her death?*' Dostoevsky had written in his letter to Wrangel of 14 July 1856.

Some 12 years later Dostoevsky was to immortalize this drama in his great novel about a fallen woman who came to love a righteous man and was killed by a libertine. And the wedding in Kuznetsk in 1857 was reflected in the deeply moving scene of Prince Myshkin's wedding night in *The Idiot*:

> Nastasya Filippovna came out looking as white as a sheet. Her enormous black eyes flashed at the crowd, like glowing coals. The crowd could not withstand her look. Anger turned to shouts of admiration. Someone was already opening the doors of the carriage. Keller had already offered the bride his arm, when suddenly she uttered a cry and ran down the steps and into the crowd. Her entourage were struck dumb. The crowd made way for her. Suddenly Rogozhin appeared five or six feet away from the porch. It was his eyes Nastasya Filippovna had caught in the crowd. She rushed to him like a madwoman and seized both his hands.
>
> 'Save me. Take me away. Wherever you wish, right now!'
>
> Rogozhin almost lifted her from the ground and practically carried her to the carriage.

A few hours later, towards the end of a white night in Petersburg, he would cause her death. The rivals would meet for the last time beside her body, with deep compassion for each other, before they both plunged into the night of insanity. Dostoevsky admitted that it was for the sake of this epilogue that he had written the entire novel. The novel had emerged from the writer's own shattering emotions at the time of his Semipalatinsk love, a love which he himself considered stronger than death. That perhaps is why the finale of *The Idiot* has a place among the greatest writing in world literature.[4]

*

A few days after the wedding the couple left Kuznetsk for Semipalatinsk. Their route lay through snowy pine forests, south-west across the Altai to the steppes of Kirghizia. They stopped off in Barnaul at Semyonov's. 'Here misfortune overtook me. I had a completely unexpected attack of epilepsy, which frightened my wife to death and filled me with sadness and despair.' It was a terrible sight indeed. The doctor in Barnaul diagnosed it at once as 'true epilepsy' and warned that he might suffocate from a spasm of the throat during one of his seizures. Dostoevsky regretted that he had married when he was afflicted with such a serious disease.

No doubt Maria felt the same way. Her new husband was incurably ill with a very grave disease of the brain which would certainly hamper his advancement in the army, and perhaps in any work he might undertake.

The Dostoevskys arrived in Semipalatinsk towards the end of February after a sad honeymoon. They set up a home but they felt that it was only temporary. They already sensed that they would soon leave Siberia for good. The company they kept in Semipalatinsk was mixed and rather modest. It included Geibovich, Commander of a company in the Seventh Siberian Battalion; Colonel Gultkevich; Lieutenant Snaxarev; Davydov, a clerk employed by a local merchant; Sitnikov, the assistant postmaster; Akimova, a major's wife; Popov, an assessor, and Mme Shmeister. This might be an exact copy of the town in Gogol's *The Inspector-General*.

Army service no longer interfered with his writing. Ensign Dostoevsky commanded his platoon, but he was already corresponding with the editors of *Sovremennik*, *Otechestvennie Zapiski*, *Russky Vestnik* (*Russian Herald*) and *Russkoe Slovo*. He was working on two long stories, 'My Uncle's Dream' and 'The Village of Stepanchikov'. In August 1857 *Otechestvennie Zapiski* published his story 'The Little Hero', under the pseudonym M—y (this was 'A Children's Fairy-tale', written in 1849 in Alexeevsky Ravelin, under a new title). Many of his literary friends offered help. The following from Pleshcheev is typical: 'Nekrasov and Panaev inquired about you with great sympathy and said that if you wished they would immediately send you money and would not bother you until you were able to write something for them.' This was already a return to literature, though Dostoevsky was still not allowed to cross the frontiers of Siberia.

Work diverted him from the unexpected trials of domestic life. He had not found the happiness he had desired and dreamed of in his marriage. 'Maria Dmitrievna was always ill, capricious and jealous,' Wrangel said of this unhappy marriage. The jealous scenes which later completely destroyed their married life began in Semipalatinsk. In 1857 it was already clear that Dostoevsky's love, which in December 1855 still shone out like a beacon in his letters, was undergoing a change. Before long he stopped mentioning it altogether. 'My life is hard and bitter,' he wrote in a letter of 13 December 1858. However, through the sadness and pain of profound disappointments, this strained and wearying love continued somehow to warm him and give him joy.

THE SIBERIAN NOTEBOOKS

After enforced sterility in prison Dostoevsky's need to create burst forth with great power. During the years he spent in Semipalatinsk he worked on *Notes from the House of the Dead* (completed in 1862) and some comic stories. He had many plans, some of which he partly carried out, to write patriotic poems, articles about Russia, art, the contemporary poets and, finally, 'a long novel', 'about the length of a Dickens novel', which would take many years to write, and was to be done on an epic scale.

Among these plans, *Letters on Art*, about which Dostoevsky wrote to Wrangel on 13 April 1856, is of major interest. Dostoevsky resolved to write a treatise on aesthetics because of an event of great academic and social significance. On 3 May 1855 Chernyshevsky's study *On the Aesthetic Relationship of Art to Reality* was published in book form. On 15 May the author presented it as a thesis for a degree at Petersburg University, thereby producing a considerable public reaction. N. V. Shelgunov, who was present at Chernyshevsky's disputation, wrote that the thesis 'was an entire sermon on humanism, a genuine revelation of love of humanity, which art was called upon to serve'. It was the first statement of the revolutionary democratic trend which would come into its own in the 1860s. Almost simultaneously with this public declaration, the June number of *Sovremennik* carried Chernyshevsky's own critique of his dissertation. In it he formulated the basic tenets of the materialist theory of aesthetics and gave a devastating critique of the Hegelian philosophy of art, which Dostoevsky had accepted in the 1840s and to which he remained true to the end of his life. Chernyshevsky acknowledged articles by Belinsky and Herzen, written in the 1840s, as sources of his work.

The official opponents objected to the candidate's views and defended the 'unshakeable ideal aims of art'. Shortly afterwards Turgenev, Leo Tolstoy, Grigorovich and others criticized Chernyshevsky's views in the same vein. Critics from the liberal camp – S. S. Dudyshkin in *Otechestvennie Zapiski*, the critic of *Biblioteka dlya Chteniya*, Annenkov in *Russky Vestnik* – also opposed the new revolutionary theory of aesthetics. They all sharply attacked the materialist philosophy of creative art and defended art for art's sake.[5]

Dostoevsky wished to define his own position in this great battle about contemporary ideas of beauty, and he drew up his own reply to Chernyshevsky's treatise. It was essentially a continuation of his own discussion on aesthetics with Belinsky. 'My article is the fruit of ten years of thought,' he wrote to Wrangel. 'I thought it all out to the very last word when I was still in Omsk.' Dostoevsky intended it to be a polemical ('hot') article, to conflict with many opinions – that is, with the opinions of the prevailing democratic programme of the Russian press – and even to support the official line (he was going to dedicate it to the President of the Petersburg Academy of Arts). It was in agreement with the conservative views of Apollon Maikov and was a denial of Belinsky's atheistic position. Dostoevsky formulated his idea clearly: 'Indeed, it is about Christianity's mission in art.'

Some years later, Dostoevsky, writing in his magazine *Vremya* (*Time*) (1862, No. 9) on the occasion of the first publication in Russia of *Notre-Dame de Paris*, stated what he considered to be 'the basic idea of all nineteenth-century art': '*the restoration of destroyed man*, who is crushed by the unjust yoke of circumstances, by the stagnation of centuries and of social prejudices; the *justification of the humiliated and all the outcast pariahs of society*.' Dostoevsky believed that by the end of the century a great work of art would surely appear which would express this idea as fully and immortally as 'Dante's *Divine Comedy* expresses the cherished ideals and beliefs of the Middle Ages'.

And so, in Semipalatinsk, Dostoevsky worked on the theory of aesthetics that he had conceived in Petersburg in 1846 at the height of his controversy with Belinsky. In 1856 he was not able to bring his plan to fruition, but soon afterwards, in polemics with Chernyshevsky[6], Dobrolyubov and Saltykov in the early 1860s, he defended his own Hegelian views concerning the essence of beauty[7], and he never ceased to present his theory of pure art forcefully on the pages of his ideological novels about contemporary Russia.

*

He could not write about these things while he was in Siberia. The profundity and tragic power of his cherished projects were quite inconsistent with the official requirements that the disgraced writer prove his loyalty by totally renouncing criticism of contemporary reality and by portraying Russian life in bright and happy colours. Dostoevsky had to put aside his beloved ideas and start writing harmless, even entertaining, stories, acceptable to the Press and the censor. Two of them, 'My Uncle's Dream' and 'The Village of Stepanchikovo', were completed in the late 1850s. He did not like the carefree stories he was forced to write while in Semipalatinsk, but they are still of interest, for they include sketches of characters drawn in depth in his later work. They are also interesting as examples of the tragic novelist's efforts at comedy. 'I began to write a comedy for the fun of it,' Dostoevsky wrote to Apollon Maikov on 18 September 1856. But he soon found himself writing in his accustomed novelistic form: 'In a word, I am writing a comic novel.' Actually, he had a gift for theatrical comedy. Both stories have been brought to life on the stage in the twentieth century and have provided outstanding Russian actors with a wealth of dramatic material.

'My Uncle's Dream' is structurally extremely interesting. Here for the first time Dostoevsky applied the law of composition that was to shape all his long novels. This is undoubtedly of the school of Gogol. Moskaleva's story resembles that of the town prefect, for the moment she announces her daughter's brilliant marriage all her vainglorious plans collapse right before the eyes of the whole assembly of enemies. This sort of vengeance at a moment of solemnity, 'the fool fooled' stage situation, is, according to Gogol, one of the most important laws of comedy. The ladies' meeting in 'My Uncle's Dream' where the company maliciously witnesses the sudden downfall of a hated despot, is precisely such a situation. One might call this compositional design the 'Inspector-General denouement'. Here, too, Dostoevsky first used the technique characteristic of his mature work of depicting turbulent and crowded scenes that literally shake the foundations in his novels, scenes of assemblages, arguments, brawls, hysterics, face-slappings and seizures.

'The Village of Stepanchikovo' is constructed according to the same law, but in this case *Dead Souls* was Dostoevsky's model. The painter of gloomy Petersburg now took life on a patriarchal estate for his subject. An enormous old orchard and boundless fields of ripening wheat indicate that all the inhabitants of the village of Stepanchikovo are well off and well fed. Nothing reminds the reader of the terrible events of recent years when the crop failed and the landlords, obliged by law to feed their serfs, gave them acorns, goosefoot and clay, and entire villages roamed the highways, begging. The numerous hunger riots that swept Russia during the reign of Nicholas I have not touched the village of Stepanchikovo. The Tsar's aides-de-camp, who were so startled by the peat-like appearance of the grain, have never passed this way, nor have cavalry squadrons come here to pacify starving mobs. The real geographical places where desperate uprisings of the poor were suppressed by armed force have nothing in common with the ideal province where Colonel Rostanev's estate is located. This island of the blessed among the dark elements of Nicholas's Russia has produced a special type of 'owner of souls', one who has little resemblance to the actual figures of the epoch.

If Dostoevsky had been able to choose his themes and to work on them 'in full voice', what mighty impulses for his profound and agonizing talent he might have found in the real facts of serfdom in its death-agonies! But in the late 1850s he was tied and chained. And so he drew his own 'ideal' landlord in opposition to the actual slave-drivers of the time. Colonel Rostanev, owner of a medium-sized estate, was a variation of his favourite image of a naïve and meek 'beautiful man'.[8]

Dostoevsky had always pictured the perfect government as a sort of paternal guardianship, and he regarded the problem of administration of the state as analogous to a family situation. According to his plan, the owner of the village of Stepanchikovo regards his *muzhiks* as small children, at times amusing, who know not what they do and who must be taught wisdom. It is no sin to laugh at them once in a while or to indulge them now and then; peasants adore this kind of a master.

To this representative of the ruling class Dostoevsky contrasted a type for which he always had a special hatred, the petty-minded upstart. Foma Opiskin is revolting. The writer spares neither colours nor words in depicting his ugliness. He is a moral and physical degenerate, in whom filthy ignorance is combined with despicable sycophancy, malicious envy with cruel tyranny. Unlike the well-bred, handsome Rostanev, who has an outstanding physique, Foma is hideous and 'unprepossessing': 'The most impudent conceit was evident in his face and in his entire pedantic little figure.'

Dostoevsky is precise about Foma's social origins. He remarks again and again that Foma did not belong to the gentry-class and that he had wormed his way into the privileged circle illegitimately. Because of this clear characterization, Dostoevsky is able, very cautiously, to touch on the unavoidable class question as it appears in this rural scene. The conflicts that arise with the peasants are not due to the owner's heavy hand but to the irrational despotism of a rascally hanger-on. The only reason why the village is restive is because the easy-going gentleman master has allowed himself to be bypassed by an ill-natured, vulgar little upstart. The peasants, who were so well off under the gentle reign of the owner of Stepanchikovo, begin to suffer at the hand of his boorish servant, an unexpected situation.

In fact their suffering, like everything else in Stepanshikovo, is more in the realm of humour than tragedy. In contrast to the actual historical situation of a serf economy, marked by torture and murder, Dostoevsky portrays 'moral' misunderstandings, arising from fortuitous causes: the house and field serfs of Stepanchikovo are not tormented to death; they are 'taught to death'. Foma Opiskin teaches them French by force, questions them about their dreams, and so on. Considering the chains, manacles and iron collars, the torture, secret executions and the 'right of the first night' that existed in the Russian manors of that day, the notebook of French words that old Gavrila is supposed to memorize does not horrify the reader. On the contrary, the author is obviously reckoning on getting a burst of laughter from his audience. For under the laws of Russia in the time of serfdom a peasant had no right to education, and Foma Opiskin's attempts to teach them astronomy, foreign languages and even to give them an idea of electricity and the divisions of labour are so incongruous as to produce a definitely comic effect.

Molière's immortal hypocrite and bigot is usually pointed out as one of Foma's prototypes. But Dostoevsky has given Foma a quality that Tartuffe never had. He has to a certain extent mitigated the character of clown and hanger-on by attributing to his protagonist suffering and unmerited humiliation. Foma is not just a vulture and money-grabber, who conceals his criminal plans behind outrageous hypocrisy; he is a member of 'the huge company of the embittered, from among whom all holy fools*, wanderers and pilgrims come'. He is not just a bully; he is taking revenge against society for the humiliations he has undergone. He is not only out for his own gain. He is a poet, capable of sacrificing utilitarian objectives for the sake of self-esteem. All this broadens and enriches the image considerably.

Foma's being a writer also makes him a more subtle character than Molière's ex-criminal. The lowest grade of writer, author of chapbooks for pedlars, a failure in literature, Foma is living proof that 'the snake of literary conceit stings deep and incurably'. Association with the Press has developed in him 'ugly boastfulness', a thirst for praise and marks of distinction, for admiration and respect, an inextinguishable need 'somehow to be first, to show off, to make

* 'Holy fools' (Russian *yurodivye*) were revered by the people of old Russia as having sacrified their very reason for Christ's sake, and thereby having attained a kind of wisdom. The 'Simpleton' in *Boris Godunov* is one of them.

prophecies, to boast'. Dostoevsky had a sharp eye for what went on in the lower depths of the literary 'bohemia' which he had observed in his time, and now he skilfully wove the specific traits of hack writers with small talent and boundless pretensions into this remarkable artistic variation on Molière's sanctimonious hypocrite. These qualities make the Russian Tartuffe a more complex figure than his prototype, and impart to him the atmosphere of humiliation and martyrdom so characteristic of the author of *Notes from Underground*.

Unfortunately, Dostoevsky does not depict Foma's metamorphosis 'from clown to great man', so that the entire period when Foma suffered insults and humiliations is concealed from the reader, who sees only a satirical picture of the protagonist when he has already gained power. In all his gestures and repartee Foma Opiskin sticks to the 'comic novel' tradition. The humorous treatment enables the author to draw a sharply defined portrait of the peculiar type that belongs neither to this group nor to that – capable of posing as a gentleman, when there are no real ones about – a provincial M. Jourdain, a Russian '*bourgeois gentilhomme*'. This innovation of interpretation has ensured the protagonist long life. Foma Opiskin has survived in the struggle for existence of literary types and his name has become a synonym for an insolent hanger-on in any environment or period.

That 'The Village of Stepanchikovo' met with several rejections is no doubt due to its refusal to treat the problems of the day and its wrongly chosen form: it was not possible to treat the festering and urgent theme of the Russian village in a comic way in the late 1850s. It was also wrong to have used manorial life as a background for a merry story of entertaining adventure at a time when the serf owners were making their last desperate stand to preserve their shaky title to the peasants' person and labour.

Despite a real desire to help the exiled writer, now re-entering literature, two magazines returned the manuscript to him and only a third, less influential and discriminating, accepted it; even that did so with a number of reservations which let the author know that humour was not his métier. Dostoevsky had never before met with such failure, nor was he to do so ever again. He learned this lesson thoroughly: in the future not only would he never seek to alter his artistic individuality, but he would strive to display it in all its unique distinction.

*

The political punishment meted out to the Petrashev-skyites was brought to an end in the late 1850s. In March 1859 Dostoevsky was permitted to retire from the army with the right to live anywhere in Russia except in the two capitals and to publish on general subjects. He chose Tver* as his place of residence because of its nearness to both Moscow and Petersburg. On 2 July 1859 he left Semipalatinsk for good. The journey back lay through Omsk, Tyumen and Yekaterinburg.†

One fine day towards evening, about five in the afternoon, as we were driving through the foothills of the Urals, we came upon the borderline between Europe and Asia in a forest. We got out of our open carriage, and I made the sign of the cross because the Lord had permitted me at least to see the promised land.

A whole decade of suffering was left behind. The resurrection of the man, the citizen and the artist lay ahead. The traveller carried with him notebooks that he had filled with writings that were as yet unknown but would shortly bring him world-wide fame. They were his first studies and sketches for *Notes from the House of the Dead*.

* Now called Kalinin.
† Now called Sverdlovsk.

THE 1860s

IX

The Magazine Vremya

THE 'POCHVA' PROGRAMME

RUSSIA was in a state of great ferment in September 1859 when Dostoevsky, after living a short while in Tver, stepped onto the platform of the Nikolaev Station in Petersburg. Compelled to demonstrate a new liberal orientation, the government had been making efforts to respond to the people's buoyed-up expectations. It had permitted the publication of new magazines, relaxed press censorship somewhat, and provided wider access to the universities. Young scholars and scientists were sent abroad more often. Fuller editions of Pushkin and Gogol were published, a volume of poems by Koltsov with a long introductory article by Belinsky (whose very name had been banned since the end of the 1840s) had appeared. 'Public opinion is spreading its wings ever wider,' the journalist Kavelin wrote at the beginning of 1856. 'The caravanserai of militarism, beatings, flogging and ignorance is collapsing.'

Dostoevsky, always exceedingly sensitive to dramatic turns in contemporary affairs, observed these historic changes, the rise of a new world from the ruins of the decrepit and wretched old (in the words of his beloved Schiller), with the excitement typical of a creative artist. He had watched the remarkable change while still in far-off Semipalatinsk and had tried even then to give expression to it in his work. In letters he wrote in May 1858 he mentioned a plan to write a novel that would have a new protagonist, a character pertinent to contemporary Russia, 'to the movement and ideas with which everyone seems concerned now'.

The all-important historical event of the emancipation of

the serfs, which people still thought would bring them complete liberation, was nearing. At the end of 1857 the Tsar had signed rescripts that gave the peasants a new status. They were published in the Press soon afterwards and took the most pressing issue of the day out of the secret committees and submitted it to public discussion. In 1858 the Russian Press was for the first time able to discuss serfdom, a topic about which it had maintained silence for centuries. This was regarded everywhere as the advent of a new era. Marx wrote at the time that the peasant movement in Russia and the emancipation of the slaves in America were the most momentous events of the day.

At the time of Dostoevsky's return to Petersburg the anticipated peasant reform was already going through a serious crisis. It turned out that the peasants were to be emancipated without land. 'This is emancipation into starvation and homelessness,' Herzen's *Kolokol* warned angrily. The publication of the Manifesto of 19 February* was followed by a wave of peasant uprisings throughout Russia. The democratic forces of Russia put forward leaders. Chernyshevsky, who had been a leader of the emancipation movement since the mid 1850s, denounced the gentry's reform and anticipated nationwide insurrection. The country was in a revolutionary situation, to use Lenin's expression.

Such was the galvanized atmosphere in which Dostoevsky resumed his interrupted labours, after a decade of enforced silence. It was the beginning of his return to the literary profession and he plunged into feverish activity. It was as if he were trying to catch up with all he had missed during his years of Siberian servitude. This was no broken or weary man. He did not seem to be disillusioned or crippled in spirit; his vitality and seething energy amazed everyone who knew him. He was more cheerful than formerly and he was gay and gentle with people, traits that abandoned him

* The Manifesto of 19 February O.S. 1861 abolished serfdom.

later. 'I do not feel as if my life is finished and I do not want to die,' he had written to Wrangel *en route* from Siberia.

*

Mikhail Dostoevsky had already in 1858 taken advantage of the government's more liberal policy to request and obtain permission to publish a literary and political weekly of up to sixty-five pages per issue, to be called *Vremya* (*The Time*). In the spring of 1860 this modest project was revived in a more extensive form. It was decided to publish a monthly magazine of about five hundred pages per issue, covering a range of subjects, including economics, finance and philosophy. Mikhail, who was the official editor of the new literary-political journal, undertook the business end of the publication. Fyodor Dostoevsky was the chief contributor and *de facto* editor. The announcement of the forthcoming publication, made in September 1860, was the manifesto of a new literary programme, known as the *pochva** movement, and at the same time a statement of Dostoevsky's position on the burning issues of the day.

The new magazine proclaimed as its ideological goal the reconciliation of civilization with its peasant roots, the synthesis of Russia's cultured stratum with the latent strength of the common people.

Since the reform of Peter I there has been only one instance of any closeness between the common people and ourselves, the educated class. That was in 1812, and we saw then how the people proved themselves! . . . We saw at last that we, too, are a separate, highly unique nationality, and that it is our task to create a new form for ourselves, a native form of our own, drawn from our own soil, from our national spirit and national resources. We foresee the nature of our future activity as belonging in the highest degree to all mankind, we foresee the Russian idea perhaps becoming the synthesis of all those ideas which Europe is developing with such persistence and such courage within its separate nationalities, and everything that is hostile to those

* *Pochva*: soil.

ideas, perhaps, becoming reconciled and receiving further development in the Russian national spirit.

The *pochva* programme was rooted in an idealistic conception of history, in a romantic view of the realities of Russia, and in the Slavophile view that the Russian peasants were completely submissive and obedient. It clearly repudiated *Sovremennik*'s materialism and revolutionary tendency. The *pochva* group assailed the militant ideas of democratic literature and rejected revolutionary methods of transforming Russia, for they regarded the emerging bourgeois monarchy, which they saw as a patriarchal idyll of the intelligentsia joined with the peasantry and of the Tsar joined with the people, as the most progressive form of government for Russia. On the peasant question, the *pochva* group took up a moderate position. They upheld the conservative view that there was no class antagonism in Russian history and that all was peace and harmony between the serfs and their landed masters. Some twenty years later Ivan Karamazov was energetically to deny this myth of class pacifism in Russia.

Dostoevsky welcomed the new juridical status of the common people under which it was now impossible to sell people or to gamble them away at cards. It was not enough of an achievement, but it was nevertheless a major event in the Russian people's unhappy history. 'The great reform was a feudal reform,' Lenin wrote, 'and it could not have been anything else, for it was carried out by the serf owners.' However, the fact remained that legally the peasants were no longer chattels. And in his journalistic writings, so remote from the militant positions of Chernyshevsky, standard-bearer of the peasant revolution, Dostoevsky supported the '*muzhik* Marei's' new civil status.

There was no trace of any revolutionary tendencies among the *Vremya* group, Nikolai Strakhov has noted. Ethical and intellectual interests, or pure liberalism, without a thought of violent insurrection, predominated. This suited Dostoevsky, who shunned coercion of any kind. However, Dostoevsky's literary talent, the fervour of his ideological quests, his journalist's militant temperament and his boundless love for the creativity of the Russian people, made his first magazine a major phenomenon in the history of the Russian periodical press. It is to the credit of *Vremya* that it perceived in Russian literature historical proof of the great future in store for the people which had produced it. 'Lomonosov, Pushkin, Lermontov, Turgenev – that is our claim to being a part of European life,' Dostoevsky wrote, anticipating the world recognition that would be given to Russian poetry and literary prose. It was in *Vremya,* too, that he wrote, 'The word, the word is a great thing!' a motto of his all his life. Pushkin was Dostoevsky's rallying standard. That great poet reveals the Russian spirit in all its completeness: 'The phenomenon of Pushkin is proof that the tree of civilization has already matured to the fruit-bearing stage, and the fruits it bears are not rotten, but magnificent and golden.'

Dostoevsky edited *Vremya* for about two and a half years (January 1861 to May 1863) and in that short period the magazine carried several outstanding works, apart from his own, that are still significant: two plays by A. N. Ostrovsky (*The Marriage of Balzaminov* and *There Is No One without Sin or Trouble*), the beginning of Nekrasov's *Red-Nosed Frost* ('The Death of Prokl') and the same author's poem 'Peasant Children', Saltykov's *Recent Comedies* and *A Day in Our Province*, Pomyalovsky's *A Winter Evening in the Seminary*, Nikitin's *The Master*, poems by Maikov, Pleshcheev, Polonsky, Mei and Vasili Kurochkin, travel notes by Grigorovich, and Apollon Grigoryev's *My Literary and Moral Peregrinations*. All these works were at the least genuine literature and some were of paramount interest. Dostoevsky was beyond doubt an outstanding editor.

*

The very first issues of the magazine began to serialize Elizabeth Gaskell's proletarian novel *Mary Barton, a Tale of Manchester Life.* This was the first Russian translation of a novel which Dickens and Carlyle had praised. Karl Marx, writing of the brilliant contemporary school of 'novelists in England, whose graphic and eloquent descriptions have revealed more political and social truths to the world than all the politicians, journalists and moralists taken together,' mentioned the then little-known Elizabeth Gaskell along with Dickens and Charlotte Brontë. Elizabeth Gaskell's first novel was an important landmark in the development of the new democratic literary form which later came into its own.

What was it that attracted Dostoevsky's attention to this book?

Dostoevsky's return to literature after ten years of banishment was at the same time a return to his 'old manner', to the subject matter and types of his glorious literary début – his stories of the 1840s, with their anxiety about social problems and their humanitarian concerns. This novel about Manchester's working people in the 1830s, published in 1848 but still untranslated because Nicholas's censors had found it unacceptable, presented an entirely new aspect of the *Poor Folk* theme – the theme of pauperism – which had moved Dostoevsky so deeply when he had first begun to write. It painted a frightful picture of unemployment, poverty, starvation and social oppression against the background of a big industrial city, with all its sharp contrast between the way of life of the factory owners and the workers. Russian fiction had not said anything about this yet.

Thus Dostoevsky boldly introduced a major new theme into the magazine prose of the 1860s, the theme of the disinherited in the capitalist world who are no longer passive and wordless but who take up arms against their oppressors. The conciliatory notes in the second part of Mrs Gaskell's novel and even the echoes of Christian morality in the denouement could not dilute the basic revolutionary quality of the theme and merely served to deepen the new poetics of love and compassion for the oppressed that Dostoevsky had evolved after the moral crisis he had undergone in prison.[1] But the most valuable contributions to the magazine were undoubtedly *The Insulted and the Injured* and *Notes from the House of the Dead*, by its *de facto* editor. And despite the magazine's general moderate political position, both these works were part of the new emancipation movement and recalled to its readers the socio-humanitarian message of Dostoevsky's early writing that Belinsky had so warmly welcomed.

As a critic and publicist, Dostoevsky entered into polemics with the major magazines on a variety of questions. His articles were especially vivid and forceful when he was defending his native language and literature. He fought his first battle against *Russky Vestnik*, at that time still a moderately liberal publication. Its editor, Katkov, had become interested in British state law in the early 1860s and after his return from a trip to England had become a champion of that • country's political institutions. The newly fledged anglophile's liberalistic criticism of the spiritual culture of his own backward country led him to declare in 1861 that Russian literature is 'small, scanty, has hardly begun to live, has hardly developed a language for itself'. This unwarranted attack evoked a forceful protest from Dostoevsky: 'It is not scanty at all. We have Pushkin, we have Gogol, we have Ostrovsky. There is continuity of an idea in these writers, and that idea is strong and is of the whole people. Is it possible that *Russky Vestnik* does not see the mighty personification of the Russian spirit and Russian genius in Pushkin's talent?'

When Katkov dared to describe *Egyptian Nights* as an erotic fragment, Dostoevsky wrote such an inspired and powerful commentary on that 'miracle of poetic art' that today, more than a hundred years later, it is still the sole and unsurpassed interpretation of Pushkin's immortal poem. It concluded: 'Yes, our understanding of art is poor. Even Pushkin, himself victimized and destroyed in our society, chiefly, it would seem, because he was the complete and consistent poet, was unable to teach it to us.'

Especially interesting in this series of articles in *Vremya* is Dostoevsky's extraordinary dialogue on art with Dobrolyubov in 1861. There were two camps in Russian aesthetic thought – the utilitarians and the advocates of pure beauty. Dobrolyubov belonged to the former, Fet to the latter. Dostoevsky proclaimed a third position, his own independent and catholic standpoint. He called for creative freedom, freedom of the poetic spirit and poetic forms, an art of unlimited possibilities and infinite aspirations, for, he contended, this was the kind of art that was of the greatest benefit to mankind. On the other hand: '*Art is always contemporary and effective, has never been otherwise and, what is most important, cannot be otherwise.*'[2] Dostoevsky does not go along with the champions of 'art for art's sake'. 'We feel that art should always be in keeping with man's goals, that it should not be at variance with his interest.'

But at this point Dostoevsky's essay takes an unexpected turn. 'If we desire *the greatest possible freedom for art* it is because we believe that the freer art is in its development, the more beneficial it will be to man's interests. Art must not be told what its aims and likings should be.'

But this 'highest freedom' of the artist precludes any requirement that his work should necessarily be topical and close to the demands of life.

Dostoevsky, who always brought together irreconcilable extremes in his political and religious views, did so in his aesthetic views too. He agreed with the utilitarianists that on the day of the Battle of Borodino, when the nation's very existence is at stake, a poet ought not to be absorbed in *The Greek Anthology*, and that on the day of the earthquake in Lisbon, a poet should not write verses about 'a whisper,

timid breathing, the trill of nightingales'.* Yet he protested
with equal vigour against the campaign that Dobrolyubov,
'the leading advocate of utilitarianism in art', was conducting against artistry, against Pushkin and Turgenev. Art,
Dostoevsky concluded, 'will always live man's real life with
him. Therefore, the most important thing is to refrain from
burdening art with all kinds of aims, from binding it by any
laws', from restricting its freedom of development. 'The
ideal of beauty, of normality, cannot die in a healthy society;
beauty is useful because it is beauty, because mankind
always has a need for beauty and for beauty's highest ideal.'

In this peculiar manner did Dostoevsky combine the two
opposing views on the essence of beauty to produce a synthesis of his own: beauty is useful simply because it is beauty,
without any preconceived goals. Corneille and Racine,
France's greatest seventeenth-century poets, were revived a
hundred years later and inspired the style of the great French
Revolution. That is the kind of free and perfect poetry mankind needs. By raising beauty to an absolute category in
this way Dostoevsky approached the 'pure art' theoreticians
and retreated from the principles of materialistic aesthetics
which young Dobrolyubov was developing consistently in
his articles as resident critic for *Sovremennik*.

NEW CONNECTIONS

As in the 1840s, Dostoevsky again found himself drawn
into literary circles and editorial offices. He began to
attend the Tuesday meetings at the home of A. P. Milyukov, the only friend of his youth who had come with his
brother Mikhail to say goodbye to him at the Peter and Paul
Fortress on 24 December 1849 before he started on the
journey to Siberia. Milyukov was now the editor-in-chief of

* The first lines of a poem by Fet that became a special butt for the
sarcasm of the radical critics.

Svetoch (*Torch*) and the contributors to his magazine used to gather at his home. Among them were Apollon Maikov, V. V. Krestovsky, D. D. Minaev, N. N. Strakhov, Dr S. D. Yanovsky, Apollon Grigoryev, Y. P. Polonsky, L. A. Mei, G. P. Danilevsky and M. I. Semevsky.

'Fyodor Mikhailovich, of course, held first place in the circle,' Nikolai Strakhov recalled. 'Everybody regarded him as a major writer and he took precedence not only because he was so well known, but also because of the multitude of ideas he had and the ardour with which he expressed them.' When he was particularly excited about something he would become very animated and his quiet voice would rise practically to a shout. His beautiful eyes, huge forehead and plain features were unforgettable when lit up by inspiration.

The circle's views had evolved under the influence of French literature and were determined by political and social issues. The creative artist was regarded as society's mentor and leader. The principle of service to the needs of the present prevailed, and Dostoevsky upheld that principle:

For him the most important thing was to move his readers, to state his idea, to make a specific impression. It was not the composition as such that was important but the moment and the impression, even though the impression might be incomplete. In this sense he was a true journalist and a renegade from the theory of pure art.[3]

Shortly afterwards the Milyukov group began to gather in Mikhail Dostoevsky's study on Yekaterininsky Canal, where a new *Vremya* editorial office was being organized. It was at this time that Dostoevsky established a close relationship with two thinkers who were to have a decisive influence on the development of his philosophical views. One was the remarkable Russian critic Apollon Grigoryev, the other was Grigoryev's closest disciple and heir, Nikolai Strakhov.

Apollon Grigoryev

This was a man of extraordinary brilliance, genuine creative inspiration and boldly original aesthetic views. Of the several groups that formed within *Vremya* one (probably the most gifted) gathered round Apollon Grigoryev, to whom young people were attracted by the qualities of his mind and heart and, above all, by his sincere interest in their literary efforts and his ability to stimulate them and make them work at maximum capacity. A product of late romanticism, Apollon Grigoryev was undoubtedly *en rapport* with Dostoevsky. The two men were about the same age, had gone through the same stages in their intellectual development and been stirred by the same heroes and the same works of art. Apollon Grigoryev always felt an affinity for the period of his early poetical interests, when young hearts were in a 'gloomy, anxious, ominous' mood and loved Lermontov and the tragic actor Mochalov. These interests had been succeeded by an interest in Utopian socialism; he valued the poetical aspect of this movement but remained aloof from its political conclusions.

In the early 1850s Apollon Grigoryev became the editor of a new magazine, called *Moskvityanin* (*Muscovite*), in which he developed a school of philosophical and artistic thought which undoubtedly influenced Dostoevsky in his post-Siberian period. It was a Slavophile trend that was reflected in all Grigoryev's most important mature works, such as his articles on Ostrovsky's comedies, on Russian folk songs and on Turgenev's *Nest of Gentlefolk*. It formed the basis of his essays in *Vremya* on Leo Tolstoy, Nekrasov, Shevchenko, and the Russian theatre, and of his theoretical studies on *Literature and Kinship with the People*, *Nihilism in Art* and *Our Literary Directions*. With Melnikov-Pechersky, Ostrovsky and Pisemsky, he appealed for the resurrection of Russian national art. Their manifesto was the 'song-prelude' of Mei, which

afterwards became widely known through two musical
settings, one by Balakirev and one by Glazunov.

> Och! 'Tis the time for thy freedom, song of Russia,
> Song of good news, song of victory, song of wide open spaces,
> Song that runs through the towns, the villages and the
>   fields,
> Song woven of storm and disaster,
> Song washed clean and baptised in blood and tears.

Apollon Grigoryev called the system he developed
'organic' criticism: 'Poets are the voices of the masses, of
peoples, of localities; they are heralds of life's great truths
and great mysteries; they bring words which contribute to the
comprehension of the organic unit of an epoch in time, and
the organic unit of a people in space.' Such enormous phenomena as the 'people' and the 'epoch', which produce the
poetry of great poets, also produce the criticism of that poetry.
'There is an organic kinship between art and criticism . . .
and criticism strives to be as organic as is art itself.' The
distinctive features of criticism are kinship with the people, a
sense of history, artistry and, following Carlyle, whom
Grigoryev regarded as his teacher, penetration into the
mystery of the human soul, belief in the primacy of ethical
issues over social issues, and a view of the artist as an inspired clairvoyant, a prophet and a preacher. Art should lay
bare 'the heart's idea' and combat 'the head's idea'. This
was an idealistic theory with its roots in Schelling, and it
ascribed to intuition the decisive role both in art and in
criticism.[4]

It is not surprising that *Vremya's* policy statements were
based on Apollon Grigoryev's favourite themes: kinship
with the people, the values of old Russian culture, of native
poetry and the artistry of native speech, the cult of art, the
theatre, folklore and music, the prime importance of
Pushkin and Ostrovsky to contemporary literature. All this
was united under the word '*pochva*', a term that had already

appeared quite frequently in Grigoryev's writings in the
1850s. In particular he considered Russian drama to be an art
form that belonged to the entire nation and he championed
this view in Dostoevsky's magazine. 'In our view, the
theatre is a great thing; it is great because by its very
nature it has to be the concern of the people. The
theatre has to remain close to the masses.' He expressed
this conviction in the many articles he wrote about Russian
actors of the day, articles which show him to be one of
the greatest of Russian theatre critics. They have left us a
gallery of portraits of such masters of the Russian stage as
Mochalov, Karatygin, Shchepkin, Sadovsky, Martynov and
Nikulina-Kositskaya. In 1864 Dostoevsky wrote in the same
vein, summing-up as it were on behalf of the great artists of
Russia: 'It was the direct power of art (theatre), and that
alone, which joined the serf Shchepkin with civilization,
that is, with us – so much for the question of art and even of
its material and social usefulness.'

Dostoevsky in fact made his own stage début shortly after
his return to Petersburg. (He subsequently acquired a
reputation as a public speaker.) He gladly accepted an
invitation to take part in a benefit performance for the
Literary Fund and chose the role of Shpyokin, the postmaster
in *The Inspector-General*. 'This is one of the most comic
roles, not only in Gogol but in the entire Russian dramatic
repertoire,' he declared. 'Moreoever, it has profound social
significance.' His performance on 14 April 1860 proved him
a superb comedian, 'what is more, a subtle comedian, capable of evoking purely Gogolean laughter,' said P. I. Weinberg, the director of that unusual production.

Not only did Apollon Grigoryev have a profound and
creative mind, but he also had a great deal of personal
charm. A member of the *Vremya* staff has left us a character
portrait of this 'last of the romantics', as he liked to call
himself, describing him as a sincere and forthright man with
a direct look, an intelligent, very Russian face, and bold

opinions. It was written at the time when Grigoryev joined the Dostoevsky brothers' magazine:

He lived in a small apartment not far from Znamenskaya Church. I found there several persons with whom I was not acquainted, among them A. A. Fet. The guests were drinking tea, while the host, who was wearing a red silk peasant-style shirt, strummed a guitar and sang Russian songs. Apollon Alexandrovich had a voice of great range and beauty, made even more beautiful by his warmth and subtle understanding of the nature of our folk poetry. He played the guitar superbly.

Once Strakhov objected during an argument: '"I do not agree with you but perhaps you know better." "Whether I do or not, I do not know," he interrupted me. "I am a current of air." That is what he used to call directions, schools and trends in contemporary art.' Strakhov concluded the memoir he wrote about his friend and teacher with a vivid if brief sketch:

Grigoryev was extremely handsome, possessing the striking combination of strength and grace. Indeed, he had a grandeur that very much suited his intense nature. His grey eyes were not large but they were set remarkably far apart and had an unusual brilliance that amazed me the first time I saw him. He had a Roman nose, his hands, which he treated most carelessly, were small, soft and beautiful, like a woman's.

Such was Apollon Grigoryev, one of Dostoevsky's strongest and most gifted contributors during his period as a magazine publisher.

The Actress Schubert

Fortune smiled upon Dostoevsky as this new chapter of his life began. A talented and attractive young Russian actress became his friend. Alexandra Schubert, *née* Kulikova, was married to Dr Stepan Dmitrievich Yanovsky, Dostoevsky's friend and physician of the 1840s. Her surname came from her first husband, an actor, and she had retained it after her second marriage. Dr Yanovsky now introduced his old friend and patient to this interesting young wife of his; he used to appear regularly with her at Mikhail Dostoevsky's literary-musical salon, at concerts and dances and discussions, and that was how Dostoevsky met her.

In her well-known memoirs Alexandra Schubert avoids giving a detailed account of her relationship with Dostoevsky. But her casual references to the great novelist, with whóm she was friendly in the winter and spring of 1860, are signicant:

F. M. Dostoevsky became very attached to me. He kept saying how sorry he was that nothing but nonsense was performed on the stage and kept urging (me) to undertake serious roles. But what roles? I asked Druzhinin to adapt *Polinka Sachs* but he would not. Dostoevsky spoke about *Netochka Nezvanova*. I was bored and listless and wanted to go to live in Moscow. I discussed this with my husband and he agreed to let me go. Everyone approved of my plan; F. M. Dostoevsky encouraged me particularly.

There is little doubt from the above about Dostoevsky's sincere feeling for Alexandra Schubert. Dr Yanovsky, who was an official at the Medical Department, was a kind but ordinary man and had nothing to offer his wife, either intellectually or emotionally. Plescheev observed rather aptly in a letter to Dostoevsky of 23 March 1860: 'I should think that it is a bore to live with Yanovsky – like being condemned for life to eat nothing but strawberry jam.' Alexandra Schubert moved in artistic and literary circles. She had always been especially interested in writers, many of whom she had met at the home of her teacher, the actor Shchepkin. She had known Gogol in Odessa and was acquainted with some of Russia's leading playwrights. And she no doubt found Dostoevsky, with his aura of heroism, the most interesting of all her acquaintances. Dostoevsky was then at the height of his creative powers. In his letters to her he wrote about his work on *The Insulted and the Injured*, about his forthcoming magazine and his plans to write for the theatre. This brings us to the artistic biography of Mme Schubert, without which the story of her friendship with Dostoevsky would be largely unintelligible.

*

Alexandra Schubert was the daughter of serfs and she grew up with a democratic view of life. She disliked the gentry and sympathized with the common people, and declared that nearly everybody who constituted the pride of the Russian dramatic theatre, opera and music was of serf origin. By the age of twenty-two she had a reputation as the finest ingénue on the Russian stage. She was expected to follow in the footsteps of the renowned Varvara Asenkova, but she went her own way and developed a style of her own even in vaudeville roles. From Shchepkin, whose favourite pupil she was considered, she learned theatrical realism. She had a very high regard for her most frequent partner, the 'sorrowful comedian' Martynov, who used to convey with subtle lyricism the suffering of the frightened, under-privileged 'little man'. The new school of artistic truth taught her to dislike routine effects and imparted to her acting a charming artlessness of interpretation and moving liveliness of diction. She once told Dostoevsky that he was a student of the heart, but he rejected this high praise, retorting: 'I do not accept your words for myself. What sort of student of the heart am I compared with you?' This as we shall see was entirely sincere.

Alexandra Schubert created a number of outstanding character portraits in the 1860s, chiefly in serious comedy, but also sometimes in drama. She played Lisa in Griboye-dov's *Woe from Wit* (*Chatsky*), Agnès in Molière's *L'Ecole des Femmes*, Maria Andreevna in Ostrovsky's *The Poor Bride* and, a little later, Mistress Quickly in *The Merry Wives of Windsor*. These were roles that demanded sure psychological delineation, lyricism and humour.

One can easily understand Dostoevsky's infatuation. His letters to her were very tender and solicitous. Everything in his new friend's life interested him. He wanted to be helpful in all her concerns, especially in her art. 'I wrote to Plesh-cheev, reminding him to be sure to announce your forth-coming début in *Moskovsky Vestnik* (*Moscow Herald*). I even suggested to him how in my opinion your talent might be described. You cannot imagine how much I would like to be present at your first performances.' Actually, Dostoevsky was planning to go to Moscow for this very purpose. He tried to dissuade the young actress from doing the usual kind of repertoire and encouraged her desire to work on serious roles: 'If I had the slightest talent for writing comedy, even just a one-act comedy, I'd write one for you. I think I'll try. If it is successful (others will decide that) I will present it to you as a token of my deepest esteem.'

There were franker declarations:

I'd like very much to earn your friendship. You are very kind, you are intelligent, you are a likeable person. To be your friend is a good thing. You have a charming disposition, too: you are an artist; at times you laugh so delightfully at what is prosaic, ridiculous, arrogant and stupid that it is a delight to listen to you.

The notes of deep emotion are not entirely concealed by the necessary restraint of a letter written to a married woman and well-known actress:

Farewell, I kiss your little hand once again and with all my heart sincerely wish you all that is brightest, clearest, most care-free and most successful in life. All yours, with infinite respect, F. Dostoevsky.

There is no exaggeration here. Many contemporaries echo Dostoevsky's opinion. V. N. Davydov, who con-sidered himself Schubert's pupil, said she was an unusually talented woman and a rare person. 'She followed everything that went on in Russia with a keen eye. Her attitude to art was serious and she loved the theatre deeply. She possessed native intelligence and had had a gentle upbringing. She was agreeable, unassuming and had a loving heart.' Her advice and guidance were highly appreciated by Streptova, Savina and Varlamov, then still very young. In the 1870s she was jokingly referred to as the 'conservatoire' because she had taught so many young actors and actresses.

*

In March 1860 Schubert made up her mind to break with her husband. She accepted an engagement at the Maly Theatre and moved to Moscow, where she could freely meet with the close friend who had openly encouraged her in her plan. In a letter of 12 June 1860 Dostoevsky wrote her an account of a talk he had had with her husband. Yanovsky kept saying that his wife was incapable of living alone and running a household and that he would have to move to Moscow to arrange her life.

'But it is not so difficult to fix up a house,' Dostoevsky objected 'especially if one has a little money, which your wife has from her salary at the theatre.'

'No, I will certainly move to Moscow where I have been offered a senior physician's post in a hospital,' Yanovsky insisted, with a touch of irritability towards Dostoevsky who, in fact, was already making plans to move back to the city of his birth. 'And if this should not work out I'll make my wife leave the Maly Theatre and return to Petersburg, to the Alexandrinsky Theatre.'

'Do you want to deprive a remarkable actress of her career in the theatre?'

'Well, what is to be done if that proves necessary?'

'Why, that is like taking the light, the air and the sun away from a person. Would you really do such a thing?'

'Michurina[5] manages to live without the theatre. One can act on private stages, too.'

'But that is tyranny. In Alexandra Ivanovna's place I would not obey you.'

'The laws are on my side. She cannot disobey me.'

'Are you capable of resorting to the law in such a matter? I confess, I did not expect this of you, with your humane code and convictions.'

'Well, of course, it won't go that far. I only meant in an extreme case. But aren't you defending Alexandra Ivanova too strongly? You evidently correspond with her constantly. Obviously, she is following your advice. You confide in her more than you do in me. You have betrayed our friendship. She said to me when I was in Moscow: "You don't know Dostoevsky yet. He is not your friend at all."'

Dostoevsky, between two fires, tried to explain the complexity of the situation to the young woman:

Stepan Dmitrievich knows that you have confided in me a great deal and have done me the honour of regarding my heart as worthy of your confidence. He knows that I myself am proud of that confidence and that I side with you more than I do with him in this domestic affair. Come to that, I did not conceal this from him. I disagreed with him on many things and thereby stood up for your rights.

Dostoevsky noted that Yanovsky was jealous of him: he thinks 'that I am in love with you'.

There was a large portrait of Alexandra on her husband's table. It showed 'a short, slim brunette with beautiful thick hair', as M. G. Savina described her later, 'fine but regular features and not large but very lively eyes'. The actress's appearance was wonderfully suited to her usual roles as a girl of seventeen. The gravity and meditative sadness of the expression of the portrait struck a responsive chord in the onlooker. It was the face of the actress of classical comedy and lyrical drama rather than of the vaudeville entertainer of lively manner and mimicry. Apparently, Dostoevsky could not tear his eyes away from the dearly beloved face. 'Noticing your portrait on his table I glanced at it. When I went over to the table a second time he suddenly, while talking to me, turned your portrait around so I that could not see it. This struck me as very silly. It was a gesture of vexation.' Dostoevsky advised the jealous man's wife to leave him. 'There is no life together for you, only torture.'

But soon afterwards circumstances compelled him to take a different course. He had to act cautiously, loyally and correctly to put an end to this dangerous romance without hurting the well-known actress and wife of his friend.

Shall I see you, my dear? I shall probably be in Moscow in July. Can we manage to have a heart-to-heart talk together? How happy I am that you are so noble and so gently trustful of me. That is true friendship. I tell you frankly: I love you very much and deeply, so much so that I told you myself that I am not in love with you, for it was important to me that you have the right impression and, my God, how I grieved when I thought you had withdrawn your confidence from me. I blamed myself. It was torture! But your letter cleared up everything, my infinitely kind one. God give you all kinds of happiness. I am so glad that I am quite sure now that I am not in love with you! That makes it possible for me to be even more devoted to you without fearing for my heart. I shall know that my devotion is entirely disinterested.

The novelist, who had apparently been enchanted by that lovely 'Agnès', refrained from reproaching her or quarrelling with her and chose the outward impeccability of a farewell, accompanied by a firm declaration that his heart was free and his devotion disinterested. The opening of his farewell letter is noteworthy: 'I read your letter with pleasure, especially as I had not expected to receive any more letters from you.' The whole of Dostoevsky's reply is a tactful break with his correspondent, couched in faultlessly polite language.

This marked the end of their relationship.

The comedy actress, who had flashed for a moment over Dostoevsky's horizon when he was just back from Siberia, left her imprint on his heart. M. G. Savina tells how

Dostoevsky exclaimed after the first time he saw her in the role of Verochka in *A Month in the Country*, 'You were wonderful, as wonderful as Schubert was in roles of that kind!' Apparently that name was still the highest praise in his eyes.

Alexandra Schubert kept three of Dostoevsky's letters for about half a century and parted with them only shortly before her death. She died in Moscow in 1909 at the age of eighty-two. Her funeral was a small ceremony and went unnoticed. Her name meant nothing to the young generation of actors and audiences. But there was a wreath on her coffin from the foremost Russian artistes of the day: Savina, Davydov and Varlamov. The inscription read: 'To our unforgettable teacher.'

Friend or Foe?

Of the principal contributors to *Vremya*, the closest to Dostoevsky was Nikolai Strakhov. A mathematician and natural scientist with a master's degree in zoology and a schoolteacher by profession, Strakhov had turned to literary work only in 1860 when his hopes for a professorship had been disappointed. He regarded himself as Apollon Grigoryev's pupil in journalism and as a follower of Dostoevsky's programme, and he wrote accordingly about problems of organic criticism, the 'soil', renewed Slavophilism and idealistic theories of aesthetics, carrying on a tireless debate against materialist philosophy and revolutionary action. His persistence in the ideological struggle and his scholarly skills in criticizing hostile trends made his journalistic writing relevant to the events of the day. Dostoevsky was influenced by his generalized analysis expressed in well-written scholarly prose. 'Special regards to Strakhov,' he wrote to his brother from Turin in the autumn of 1863. 'Tell him that I am reading the Slavophiles zealously and that I have found new things.' After he had read Strakhov's article about *Crime and Punishment* he said to him: 'You alone have understood me.' In 1873 he assured Strakhov: 'Half of my views are your views.'

At the time when the two men became acquainted Dostoevsky belonged to a group of writers for whom political and social issues completely overshadowed purely artistic problems. They believed that it was a writer's first duty to observe the development of society very closely and to subordinate eternal and universal interests to immediate, specific concerns. They considered environmental influences the chief factor in an individual's moral development and they made journalism the basis of their artistic creativity. Strakhov says that Dostoevsky shared closely in the thinking of the circle. If, indeed, a different and independent view concerning the artist's mission and the essence of creativity was fermenting in Dostoevsky's mind beneath all those current doctrines, this was unapparent even to so sharp-eyed an observer as Strakhov.

Strakhov brought a completely new breath of air to the Dostoevskys' magazine. He had come to the 'sociologists' from a close-knit literary association which worshipped knowledge, poetry and music, Pushkin and Glinka above all else. In that small circle he had developed a view of artistic freedom, arising from the theory of German philosophy that had come to Russia in Pushkin's time and in which he firmly believed. It is possible that in the course of his work with Dostoevsky – reading his articles to him in manuscript, talking and arguing with him constantly on aesthetic themes and acquainting him with many European doctrines – he won him over to his deep faith in the supreme importance of creative freedom to an artist. In many respects Dostoevsky's spiritual interests inclined him to accept this faith. At any rate, Dostoevsky did become imbued with it. To the end of his life Dostoevsky retained traces of the influence of both the poet and thinker Apollon Grigoryev and the logician and aesthete Strakhov.

Strakhov was an important contributor to *Vremya* and has left us masterly articles on *Fathers and Sons, War and Peace,* Herzen and Pushkin. Though as a militant follower of *pochva*'s backward-looking ideology he was a prisoner of reactionary theses, he was nevertheless a serious student of major phenomena of Russian spiritual and literary culture (which he, of course, interpreted in a specific and one-sided way). Incidentally, in evaluating his world outlook one should not forget that he was a convinced Hegelian and employed the dialectical method in his research. Leo Tolstoy had a high opinion of Strakhov's writings and corresponded with him and saw him over many years. Strakhov was at the beginning of his career when Dostoevsky met him. Dostoevsky said many times subsequently that he regarded him as a man of like mind and a comrade-in-arms.

Despite the principally intellectual nature of their friendship, Dostoevsky and Strakhov had a mutual liking for one another that became genuine affection. Strakhov was the only person with whom Dostoevsky felt at ease in the depression that followed an epileptic seizure, when he could not tolerate the presence even of the persons he loved best. The two men met constantly to talk. They worked side by side in the editorial office, frequently went on outings to the country together, travelled abroad together and wherever they happened to be – at the *Vremya* editorial table, in a scholar's book-lined cell, a coffee-house in Geneva, or an hotel in Florence – they carried on their endless animated and stimulating conversations, which Strakhov admitted to have been the best in his life.

*

The friendship cooled off in the mid 1860s for some reason we have never been able to discover. Strakhov hints obscurely at Dostoevsky's suspicious nature in his biographical writings about the novelist.[6] Only after the publication of Strakhov's letter to Tolstoy, that unparalleled denunciation in which the writer gives a murderous description of

Dostoevsky's personal characteristics, did it emerge that this colleague had been no friend of his editor, that he was hostile towards him, and capable of taking calculated and massive revenge for some disagreement and parting of the ways between them:

In 1881, when Dostoevsky died, Strakhov asked his widow to entrust him with describing the 1860 to 1881 period of Dostoevsky's life in the biography that was to appear in the first posthumous edition of the writer's works. (Orest Miller wrote the first part, up to 1860.) Strakhov had known Dostoevsky well while he was editor of *Vremya*, *Epokha* and *Grazhdanin* and his description of Dostoevsky's life, published in the form of memoirs in 1883 and entitled *N. N. Strakhov's Reminiscences of F. M. Dostoevsky*, is a valuable primary source of material about Dostoevsky. Written immediately after the great novelist's death, it contains a number of vivid, profound and even enthusiastic judgements from which emerges an indisputably authentic portrait of the great writer during the most important period of his work.

Yet at the very time of the book's publication, on 26 November 1883, its author wrote to Leo Tolstoy that he renounced his biography of Dostoevsky:

All the time I was writing I wrestled with myself. I wrestled against the revulsion that rose up in me. I tried to suppress this bad feeling. I cannot consider D. either a good or a happy man (which, in essence, is the same thing). He was spiteful, envious, dissolute and spent all his life in a state of agitation that made him appear pitiful and would have made him appear ridiculous if he had not at the same time been so spiteful and so intelligent. Like Rousseau, however, he considered himself the best and the happiest of men. While writing the biography I vividly recalled all these traits. In Switzerland in my presence he treated a servant so rudely that the man took offence and said to him: 'I am a man too, you know.' I remember being astonished at the time to hear such words addressed to one who preached humanity and thinking that they reflected the concept of the rights of man in a free country like Switzerland.

Referring to the theme of vice and sensuality, so common in Dostoevsky's works, Strakhov asserted that 'he had no taste, no appreciation of women's beauty and charm. This can be seen in his novels. The characters who are most like him are the hero of *Notes from Underground*, Svidrigailov in *Crime and Punishment*, and Stavrogin in *The Devils*.' Strakhov claims that Stavrogin's Confession is autobiographical:

With a nature such as this, he was very much inclined to cloying sentimentality and lofty and humane dreams, and these dreams constitute his direction, his literary Muse and his path in life. Come to that, all his novels are in essence self-justification and prove that all sorts of abominations can live together with nobility in a man.

He was a truly unhappy and bad man who imagined himself to be a happy man, a hero, and he loved tenderly only himself.

This is a brief commentary on my biography; I could have written and told about this side of D., too: there are many instances I remember much more vividly than those I have described and it would have been a much more truthful story. But let this truth die: let us show off only the façade of life, as we do everywhere and in everything.

Strakhov's letter was published for the first time in 1913, thirty years after it was written.

The reaction of Dostoevsky's widow when it appeared may be of interest to the reader. In one of the conversations I had with her about Dostoevsky in the winter of 1916–17 she was speaking of the unusually happy life she had had and of her love for her husband.

'Of course, I have had some hard knocks, too. The latest was very recent.'

The expression of her face changed as she broached the painful subject. She went on with noticeable emotion.

'You can imagine how painfully I reacted to the publication several years ago of Strakhov's letter, calling Fyodor Mikhailovich spiteful and dissolute and accusing him of

crimes against morality. Everything turned black before my
eyes from horror and indignation. What an incredible
slander! And from whom! From our best friend, a constant
visitor at our house, a witness at our wedding, from Nikolai
Nikolaevich Strakhov, who after Fyodor Mikhailovich's
death asked me to entrust him with the writing of his biography for the posthumous edition of his works. If Nikolai
Nikolaevich had been alive I would have gone to him at
once despite my advanced years and have slapped his face
for such baseness.'

Anna Grigoryevna's pale cheeks flushed with indignation
as she spoke. Her eyes sparkled with a youthful flame and
her voice rang out in anger and injury. At that moment the
young girl in Victor Bobrov's well-known sketch on the
margin of the finest engraving of Dostoevsky was clearly
visible in the sweet old woman's face. There was the same
burning look beneath finely drawn eyebrows.

'At the time I decided not to publish a denial. But I am
replying to Strakhov in my memoirs, which will be published only after my death. My book will explain a great deal
about my late husband's personality. I should like to say to
everyone what I said to Leo Tolstoy when he asked me what
sort of man Dostoevsky was. "He was," I said, "the kindest,
gentlest, most intelligent and generous man I have ever
known." And not long ago I had occasion to repeat this
under entirely different circumstances.'

Smiling, Anna Grigoryevna described the episode, which
was evidently important to her.

'You know, the Marinsky Theatre is preparing to produce an opera, by a young composer, named Prokofiev,
based on Dostoevsky's *The Gambler*. The young musician had
not inquired about our family's copyright, and we had to
issue a claim. The matter was then settled. But last Sunday
the maestro called on me to apologize for his error in person.
He brought me an autographed score of his opera. In
exchange, he asked me to write something in his album.

My attempts to refuse were in vain; in the end I had to give in. I already had the pen in my hand when he said: "I must warn you, Anna Grigoryevna, this album is dedicated exclusively to the sun. Anything you write in it must be about the sun." And do you know what I wrote?'

I thought of the slanting rays of the setting sun that Dostoevsky had loved so much, the great, colourful, wonderful sunset in the story about the itinerant holy man, and the setting sun above the English cathedral in *A Raw Youth*.

'No,' she said. 'I simply wrote: "*The sun of my life was Fyodor Dostoevsky, Anna Dostoevskaya.*"'

One had only to hear the pride in her voice to know how true her words were.

In spite of her advanced age Anna Grigoryevna did some very thorough research and produced a careful analysis of Strakhov's letter. She gathered many facts and arguments for the refutation of his grave and unsubstantiated charges, and one cannot help agreeing with her main arguments. Why, indeed, if Strakhov had disliked the man so much, did he offer to write his biography, why didn't he turn down the job? The incident with the waiter in Switzerland does not testify to Dostoevsky's 'spite' but merely to his exceeding irritability. Could a 'man with an evil heart, who loved only himself', have taken upon himself the burdensome financial commitments of numerous relatives, after his brother's death? Whom did Dostoevsky have to envy in contemporary literature? or even in classical literature? We have his admiring comments about Tolstoy, Goncharov, Nekrasov and Turgenev. Because of the nature of his talent Dostoevsky wrote a great deal about crime, cruelty and evil passion. By what right is autobiographical significance attached to this? Surely, an artist can portray a murderer without himself having committed murder! Is there any reason to suppose from Dostoevsky's material circumstances and way of life that he, who was always short of money and always working beyond his strength, was capable of committing Stavrogin's crimes?

Strakhov's charges are deeply amoral because they are the kind that cannot be disproved by facts or documents.

A FEUILLETON-NOVEL

Vremya started publication in 1861 with *The Insulted and the Injured.* The new novel's very title proclaimed its basic theme, genre and style. It was Dostoevsky's return to the social novel but, unlike *Poor Folk*, it moved on many levels, though it centred round a single, demoniacal figure, affecting the lives of all the innocent and suffering characters who play a part in this sombre drama of the big city. The plot was based on contrasts of vice and virtue, which heightened its excitement.

This story of unhappy love had many interested readers, but the critics, while they pointed out some excellent qualities, noted that the plan was unfinished and the story remote from life. Dobrolyubov called it the finest literary development of the year for its supremely humane ideal and sincere compassion, but he considered it beneath aesthetic criticism. Apollon Grigoryev, a critic of a different school, also pointed out the new novel's irreconcilable artistic contrasts. 'What a mixture of amazing emotional power and childish absurdities Dostoevsky's novel is!' The conversation with the prince in the restaurant rings false. 'The prince is out of a book', Katya and Alyosha are 'a child's invention', Natasha is sententious and prosy; but, on the other hand, 'what profundity in the portrayal of Nellie! . . . Altogether, what power in all that is visionary and exceptional, and what a lack of knowledge of life!' These comments were certainly astute and to the point. However, an accurate assessment is not possible without taking into account the nature of the author, who was setting off once more on his perennial quest. Dostoevsky had never ceased to experiment in his search for a satisfactory art form. For a long time the experiments were unsuccessful, sometimes for reasons over which he had no control, like the interruption of *Netochka Nezvanova*. Now, resuming his work after an interval of ten years, he was trying his hand at *a social novel, in the manner of Eugène Sue, a feuilleton-novel*.

This showed that the novel was intended for the big daily press, where it was serialized in short instalments over a whole year. A very special pattern was required, with each piece concluding on a note of rising interest, with theatrical effects, interrupted climaxes and symbolic, simplified, one-dimensional characters. The splintered novel resembled a current newspaper *feuilleton*, easily comprehensible by the readers. Some of the devices of the *feuilleton*-novel are common to many Dostoevsky productions. But this special type of fictional 'melodrama' is best seen in *The Insulted and the Injured*. Following the rules of adventure stories, Dostoevsky wrapped the principal events in mystery and grouped his protagonists at opposite poles of spiritual enlightenment and moral degradation – the villainous aristocrat and his submissive, noble victim; the scum of the big city and jewels like Nellie living in its basements. At the end of the novel Nellie turns out to be the natural daughter of Prince Valkovsky, who seduced her mother. This is reminiscent of the plot of Sue's *The Mysteries of Paris* in which a charming girl, abandoned to poverty and the big city's dens of vice, turns out to be Prince Herolstein's daughter. The fiendish Bubnova's ruthless exploitation of Nellie calls to mind the story of Fleur de Marie, tormented by the brothel owners L'Ogresse and La Chouette. Sue strove to portray his young heroine as one who retains her inner purity amidst the appalling wickedness surrounding her. Dostoevsky appreciated the drama and poetic quality of a concept such as this.

The narrative style of *The Insulted and the Injured* is nervous and spasmodic, with the unexpected turns of plot and shock

endings of sections and chapters that characterize the
feuilleton-novel. Episodes are completed at fateful instants,
at a sudden turn of events, at moments of high tension and
unexpected blows that plunge the heroes into anxiety and
whet the reader's interest: 'He seemed to be in a frenzy. I
moved the chair over to her. She sat down. Her legs would
not hold her.' 'I cried out in horror and rushed out of the
apartment.' 'Convulsions crossed her face and she fell down
on the floor in a terrible seizure.' These are typical chapter
endings in a *feuilleton*-novel.

Dostoevsky also followed the general principles that
govern the writing of this type of novel. Eugène Sue had
said that his 'epic' was not a work of art – that from the
artistic point of view *The Mysteries of Paris* was a bad book
but that it was good for the moral aims that it pursued. It
would be more correct to say that it was good for its narrative interest and for its relevance to contemporary society.

The Insulted and the Injured too was written in this style of
swift, excited narrative – unpolished but fascinating and
arresting.

Dostoevsky agreed with some of the things his critics said.
'I wrote a *feuilleton*-novel, peopled by a lot of puppets, but
no people, walking books but no artistically developed
characters.' However, he felt that his novel did contain
some poetry, two or three exciting, forceful passages and
two authentic well-developed characters! 'The book
turned out wild,' Dostoevsky concluded, 'but it has fifty
pages or so of which I am proud.' One of the 'authentic
characters' is the poetically fascinating image of little
Nellie. Dostoevsky writes with far more than ordinary
insight of a young girl heading towards ruin and lays bare
the social roots of the drama of her life. Nellie is a superb
drawing in Dostoevsky's gallery of portraits of children, yet
it did not win critical acclaim.

The lack of comprehension on the part of the reviewers
was undoubtedly due partially to the form Dostoevsky chose.

In the decade that the author of *The Double* had been away in exile, critical realism had fostered good fictional writing and was now established in Russian literature. Tolstoy's *Childhood and Boyhood*, Turgenev's *A Nest of Gentlefolk* and *On the Eve*, Goncharov's *Oblomov* and the *Provincial Sketches* by Saltykov-Shchedrin had already been published. To the writers of the 1860s the *feuilleton*-novel of the 1840s was an obsolete and outmoded form. Dostoevsky never again wrote an entire *feuilleton*-novel, though he used some of its devices in his compositional concepts.

'YOUNG RUSSIA'

One day in the middle of May 1862 Dostoevsky opened his door to find what he considered an amazing revolutionary proclamation stuck in the handle. It was, as he said later, 'one of the most remarkable of all the proclamations that appeared in those days'. It was entitled 'Young Russia' and called for immediate social revolution:

Soon, very soon, the day will come when we shall unfurl the great banner, the banner of the future, the red banner, and shall shout loudly: 'Long live the Russian social and democratic Republic.' We shall march against the Winter Palace and destroy those who live there.

Russia was entering the revolution, the unknown authors proclaimed. A battle with no quarter was about to be fought between the two parties into which the country was divided. One was the imperial party and consisted of the landed gentry, merchants and officials, and the Tsar. It owned the land, capital and the army. The other was the people's party, made up of the impoverished and plundered unarmed peasants, and it was opposed to these forces of the government.

Downtrodden and beaten today, it will rise tomorrow with Razin for universal equality and a Russian Republic; it will rise

with Pugachov to destroy officialdom and to distribute the land
to the peasants. It will cut the throats of the oppressive landowners, as it did in the eastern provinces in the 1830s. It will rise
up with the noble Anton Petrov against the entire imperial
party.[7]

Revolutionary Russia would demand a federated republic, the transfer of all power to a national assembly, the
socialization of the factories, the political franchise for
women, the destruction of the monasteries and abolition of
the family and marriage. It was possible that this would all
end in the destruction of the royal family, of a hundred
people or so. Very likely the entire imperial party would
come to the defence of this one hundred.

In which ... case, with full confidence in ourselves, in our
strength, in the people's sympathy with us, in Russia's glorious
destiny to be the first to put the great cause of socialism into
practice, we shall give one call: 'Take up axes', and then we will
kill the imperial party without mercy, as they now have no
mercy upon us; we will kill in the streets if those base scoundrels
venture to come out into the streets; we will kill them in their
homes, in the narrow lanes of towns, in the broad avenues of
cities, in hamlets and in villages!

The proclamation angered and upset Dostoevsky. Fires
had been raging through Petersburg in those days, and he
detected an ominous note in 'Young Russia'. He resolved
to talk with the leader of the revolutionary party. In the late
afternoon of the same day, he called on Chernyshevsky.

I found Nikolai Gavrilovich all alone. Not even the servants
were at home and he opened the door for me himself. He
welcomed me very cordially and showed me to his study.
    'Nikolai Gavrilovich, what is the meaning of this?' and I took
out the proclamation. He took it from me as something he had
never seen before and read it through.
    'Do you really suppose that I am with them? Do you really
think I could have had a part in the writing of this paper?'
    'Of course not,' I replied. 'And I don't even think it necessary to

assure you of it. But they must be stopped at all costs. Your word carries weight with them and, of course, they are afraid of your opinion!'

'But I don't know any of them.'[8]

'I am sure of that. But you don't have to know them or speak with them personally. You have only to declare your condemnation somewhere and it will reach them.'

'It may not have any effect. Besides, extraneous instances such as these are unavoidable.'

'But they do harm to everybody and everything.'

Just then another visitor rang the doorbell, I don't remember who. I left.

In 1888 Chernyshevsky recalled this meeting. As he told it, Dostoevsky had asked him to influence the revolutionaries because he thought it possible that they had started the fires in the city.[9] Probably, Dostoevsky and Chernyshevsky talked about both the fires and the proclamations.

The fires in Petersburg broke out on 16 May 1862 (as a result, researchers now believe, of government provocation). The weather was hot and dry and the flames spread and raged through entire blocks with extraordinary rapidity. The twenty-second and twenty-third of May were frightful; all of Bolshaya and Malaya Okhta and a huge section of Yamskaya burned down. The second-hand market and the Apraksin and Shchukin marketplaces with thousands of stalls were destroyed at the end of May. The damage to buildings and goods ran into many million roubles. Shelter could not be found for the multitude of the homeless.

Strakhov wrote of one incident:

It is hard to describe the horror that the fires inspired. I remember, one day Fyodor Mikhailovich and I started out for the country. From the steamer we could see clouds of smoke in the distance, rising above the city in three or four places. We arrived at a park where music was playing and gipsies singing. But hard as we tried to amuse ourselves, we could not shake off our dejection and before long I suggested that we go home.

Contemporary prints (in the French magazine *Illustration*, for example, which carried drawings by the Petersburg artist A. Kuznetsov) show a truly shocking picture of multi-storeyed buildings in the heart of the city, engulfed in flames that leapt to a blazing sky. They wove and spread like rivers of fire, and before their fury the bewildered authorities were helpless.

Vremya had prepared two articles about these events. Rumour had it that their author was the 'well-known writer' Dostoevsky. Actually neither Fyodor nor Mikhail had written them but of course they had read them and, being the editors, had probably inspired them. The articles emphatically rejected the slanderous charge that the fires had been started by 'students' and 'nihilists'. Such a point of view was 'seditious' and brought down a censorship ban. Both articles were ordered turned over to His Majesty's Commission of Inquiry under Prince Golitsyn. As publisher of the magazine, Mikhail Dostoevsky was summoned to testify before the Commission. This marked the beginning of the covert persecution of *Vremya*, the real editor of which was a recent 'state criminal'. Golitsyn submitted a report, proposing that the Dostoevskys' magazine be banned for eight months. At first Alexander II agreed, but after a report from the Minister of Internal Affairs, Valuyev,[10] he issued an order not to stop publication of the magazine now but 'to keep it under proper surveillance'. *Vremya*'s fate had, in fact, been decided.

The Petersburg fire of 1862 was the source for Dostoevsky's description in *The Devils* of burning Zarechye, fired on three sides, the incendiaries' criminal purpose suddenly revealed, and the crazed fire victims, like the octogenarian woman, who with palsied hands dragged a smoking and flaming featherbed through the broken windows of a burning house. The same work contains a remarkable 'philosophical landscape' of a conflagration. Several years later, Dostoevsky was to write:

A big fire at night titillates the senses and provokes gaiety. This is what firework displays are based on. But in fireworks the fires form graceful, symmetrical patterns and, since they are perfectly safe, have a playful, light effect, like that of a glass of champagne. A real fire is another matter. There is horror in it and, after all, a sense of personal danger, yet at the same time there is the thrill of flames in the night, causing a sort of concussion of the brain in the spectator and arousing his instincts. Driven with unbelievable force by the storm-wind, spreading terror and panic, the flame runs through the wooden buildings and poor villages, and through the little timber-built towns, making bonfires of entire streets.

The government accused the revolutionaries of having started the fires and took advantage of the 'favourable moment' to intensify its reactionary actions. It instituted unexampled persecution of the periodical press and its progressive representatives. *Sovremennik* and *Russkoe Slovo* were banned for eight months. The Chess Club, the second department of the Literary Fund (which assisted students) and the Sunday schools were shut down. Chernyshevsky, Pisarev, Serno-Solovyevich and others were arrested and gaoled.

NOTES FROM THE HOUSE OF THE DEAD

The last part of *Notes from the House of the Dead* appeared in *Vremya* in 1862. The history of this novel is long and complicated. During Dostoevsky's imprisonment in Omsk Dr Troitsky, head doctor there, did his best to lighten the manacled writer's burden. He used to prescribe long periods in hospital for 'manual labourer Dostoevsky' and permitted him to write there, though this was against the rules. In hospital Dostoevsky began to jot down figures of speech, conversations, convict poems and songs, then various episodes, scenes, incidents and confessions from which several years later, emerged his immortal book about prisoners in Russia under serfdom. The notes accumulated slowly, and were kept for him by a hospital *feldsher*.* When Dostoevsky went to live in Semipalatinsk the work progressed more quickly. He used to read his sketches to his new friends Wrangel and Semyonov of Tien-Shan. Gradually, an overall plan began to take shape. It would be a novel with a fictional hero and an eventful plot that combined 'the serious and the gloomy. It would be touching and would be of the people.'

The final draft preserved traces of that extraordinary personal drama that inevitably underlay these accurate and reliable notes. 'It was a description, albeit an incoherent one, of ten years penal servitude,' wrote Dostoevsky apropos of what he was publishing as the manuscript of a deceased Siberian convict. 'But in places the description is interrupted by another kind of story, by strange, horrible recollections, sketched unevenly, convulsively, as if by some compulsion. I reread these excerpts several times and have practically come to the conclusion that they were written in a state of insanity.[7]

Dostoevsky never developed this statement any further. But it provides important insight into his creative method and the intended scope of his Siberian plan. It appears that he had conceived these celebrated memoirs not simply as sketches of the Omsk prison, but in combination with another agonizing, terrifying story. According to Dostoevsky's compressed account of the matter, this exile's notebook contained the story of an unrestrained passion, of insane jealousy, of the inevitable murder of a greatly beloved woman – a remote harbinger, perhaps, of the story of Rogozhin and Nastasya Filippovna.

A novel of intense, out-of-the-ordinary experiences set against a background of accurately reconstructed reality, terrible but authentic and sociologically important – such

* A *feldsher* was a medical assistant, not fully qualified as a doctor but capable of a certain amount of unsupervised work.

it seems was the original idea for the future chronicle of penal servitude; a tragic episode on a firm, realistic basis, true sketches of the prison framing the confession of an untameable, jealous man.

But the romantic theme was eventually dropped, leaving the descriptive sketches of a Siberian prison which constituted the whole book. The novel that had been planned disintegrated into a series of pictures with psychological studies and interspersed stories.

The composition of *Notes from the House of the Dead* is highly original. Having abandoned his original theme (a story of wife-murder), the author constructed his chronicle out of three main components.

1. Life in a prison for criminals and political prisoners, that is, the life and customs of a prison barracks and of the *corps de gardes*, their clothing, their food, the way they washed, the shaving of heads, putting the prisoners into irons, the bathhouse, the hospital, a theatre production, drinking and card playing. These were superb scenes from life, snapshots, episodes, sketches, dialogues – first-hand reported from the world of the outcasts.

2. Character portrayals of convicts, expressive sketches of the social types within the narrow confines of a single prison, covering however a broad range of bold, strong folk types, collected by the Administration at Tobolsk from all parts of Russia. Dostoevsky once wrote from his Siberian exile: 'There are profound, strong and beautiful characters here, and what a joy it always is to discover gold beneath a rough outside', and this is the guiding principle of these psychological studies and descriptions of manners.

3. Interposed narratives by convicts about their past. These are in their own way tales of crime, prison folklore about passion and vengeance amidst the denial of rights and the tyranny of an ignorant, enslaved country.

In many respects this was a return to the naturalistic school, to his masterly realism of the 1840s, constructed from the raw materials of prison life into a new form of the tale of cruelty. His declared purpose was 'to present our entire prison and all I experienced in those years in one graphic, colourful picture'. The *Notes* derived both from true-life studies and the soaring flight of a great artist's quest for moral truth. The inimitable style of Dostoevsky's later work asserted itself here, and the unalterable law of his epic novels took shape, based as they were on exact data, on real-life incidents, crimes, political events and a variety of human documents, which give rise to the protagonists' extraordinary personal dramas. The novel, conceived at the height of the last fearful period of Nicholas I's reactionary rule, was completed in an already emancipated country. The press could at last write openly about the horrors of serfdom, and the suffering of the enslaved peasantry could be depicted in all its frightful reality. In the conclusion of *Observations on a Destroyed People*,* the author who had recently written of the idyllic Village of Stepanchikovo charges yesterday's state authority with having destroyed 'the most gifted and strongest of all our people'. This rings out as an indictment of a whole system and a whole epoch.

In this book Dostoevsky also attained genuine grandeur in the artistic expression of his own unique and agonizing theme. No wonder that it immediately captured the imagination of his contemporaries. The most sensitive and understanding readers of *Notes from the House of the Dead* were reminded of some of the greatest masterpieces of world art. 'The bathhouse scene is simply Dantesque', was Turgenev's widely known comment. And Herzen wrote with his usual expressiveness:

That epoch has left us one frightful book, a sort of *carmen horrendum* which will always decorate the exit from Nicholas's gloomy reign like Dante's inscription over the entrance to hell. That book is Dostoevsky's *House of the Dead*, a fearful narrative; the author himself probably had no suspicion, as with manacled

* The subtitle to *Notes From the House of the Dead*.

hands he drew the figures of his fellow convicts, that he was creating a Michelangelo fresco, fashioned out of the customs of a Siberian prison.

Indeed, the strictly realistic picture of the Omsk prison brings to our minds the symbolism of the Sistine Chapel's 'Day of Judgement', with its hundreds of writhing sinners whirling past a wrathful judge, who is threatening them with retribution and eternal suffering.

One of the basic laws of Dostoevsky's work took shape in this book: the study of physical realities develops into a philosophical poem; the ethnographic notes evoke an image of the fate of a great people, branded and enchained in Tsarist dungeons, but destined for future struggle, freedom and mighty creativity.

X

Abroad and at Home

WORLD CAPITALS

FROM the time he was a young boy Dostoevsky had dreamed of travel in Europe. Ann Radcliffe's novels had aroused a vague interest in Italy in him when he was still a child. In the 1840s he had dreamed of withdrawing to Rome for several years, as Gogol did, to write a long novel. But destiny willed that he spend a whole decade in Siberia. It was June 1862 before Dostoevsky's dream of seeing the cities of Europe and their wonders was fulfilled. Berlin, Dresden – Wiesbaden, Baden-Baden, Cologne, Paris, London, Lucerne, Düsseldorf, Geneva, Genoa, Leghorn, Florence, Milan, Venice and Vienna passed swiftly by in some ten weeks. Dostoevsky did his travelling in his own way, unlike other people's, as he did everything else. Except on rare occasions, he did not tour celebrated historical sights or look at famous scenery but was interested only in the crowd, the population, the types. Strakhov, who accompanied him on his journey through Italy, tells us that the important thing for him was to seize a general impression of street life. The moment they met in Geneva Dostoevsky began to explain to Strakhov 'that he despised the usual stereotyped manner of touring all sorts of places with a guide book'. He spent all his time observing people closely, and he also read a great deal.

Dostoevsky found Europe very disappointing. He wrote of this in *Winter Notes about Summer Impressions: A Feuilleton for the Entire Summer*, pages from a travel diary through Germany, Italy and England, which appeared in *Vremya* in 1863. Instead of showing the customary bubbling enthu-

siasm for the sights of old Europe, he wrote of its evil and
frightful aspects, and instead of the traditional landscape
descriptions and portraits of celebrities, he wrote of the
tragedy of the big city with its dissolute, sinful and stupefied
crowds. In social tenor, this is one of Dostoevsky's most
progressive works. Its criticism of the bourgeois world
and its bitter satirization of its wolfish manners are marked
by genuine anti-capitalist feeling, although the author does
not point the way towards the struggle. In form, these
are engravings of city life. Some of his sketches of London
evoke the merciless cruelty and hopeless gloom of Van
Gogh's famous painting of the inmates of a London gaol
taking their walk round the bottom of the well-like prison
yard.

Dostoevsky had known and loved Paris – the city of Balzac,
Hugo and Sue – from afar. He had revered the traditions of
the Great French Bourgeois Revolution, and when he found
himself for the first time in the arena where it was fought he
recalled the speeches of the leaders of the National Assembly,
the Convention and the clubs, and also l'Abbé de Sieyès'
celebrated aphorism about the future omnipotence of the
Third Estate. His *Winter Notes* cite the slogan of the insur-
gent city dwellers, which was later immortalized by history
and became France's motto: 'Liberty, Equality, Fraternity.'

The picture he draws of Paris focuses on the glaring contrast between the rise of the heroic bourgeoisie in 1789 and
the degradation of the present-day middle class. The
advance guard in the fight against feudalism have become
exploiters of the poor. The Parisian had adopted a new
creed, 'to accumulate money and acquire as many possessions as possible', for this is the only way to ensure political
tranquillity, that is, the continued sole rule of the property
owners. Hence comes their passion for picturesque eloquence in public affairs, and the loyal deputies of the Second
Empire, lecturers, lawyers and cicerones, have succeeded the
renowned speakers of the Gironde and the Montagne.

Dostoevsky heard Jules Favre, France's leading lawyer and later, in 1870, head of the provisional government, speak at a much-publicized trial. He conveyed the master orator's grandiloquent style, its melodrama and sentimentality, and aptly mocked his use of metaphor and his sing-song intonation. Shortly afterwards he heard the same sort of overwrought monologue from an elderly pensioner who was showing him round the Panthéon. 'Suddenly I wanted to laugh. An elevated manner of speaking can cheapen anything.'

The immortal French theatre of Molière, Racine and Corneille, favourites of Dostoevsky since his youth, he found had been vulgarized by sham magnanimity. The 'great Rachel', as she is called in *The Devils*, the last muse of tragedy, had died! Vaudeville and melodrama dominated the stage of the *Théâtre français*. Current plays raised aloft the banner of the all-conquering bourgeoisie, whose aim was to get rich and to astound the world by unselfishness and elevated rhetorics while doing so.

'A poor youth, named Gustav is standing before the footlights. He is in love with Cécile, who has no dowry. Cécile unexpectedly inherits a million. But Gustav proudly and contemptuously rejects the million. Why? For the sake of a fine speech, of course. But Mme Beaupré, a banker's wife, comes rushing in. She tells Gustave that Cécile will die this very minute for love of him. Gustave gathers up the million and goes off to Cécile and copulates with her. The banker's wife drives off to her estate. Beaupré has won out.' With this barbed satire against the current repertoire of plays by Sardou, Augier, Scribe and Dumas, Dostoevsky concludes his survey of the strange world where love is unknown and 'marriage is most often a wedding of bank accounts'.

It was only from the viewpoint of a civil engineer that Dostoevsky appreciated Paris. He wrote to his brother a year later, in 1863: 'This time the outside of Paris pleased me, that is, its architecture. The Lourve is imposing and the entire embankment as far as Notre-Dame is amazing.' But by and large, the world of acquisitiveness and hypocrisy made Dostoevsky feel uneasy about the future of European humanity. The French diplomat and critic de Vogüé mentions a conversation he had with Dostoevsky years later, when the Russian novelist expressed an inspired wrath that amazed him: 'A prophet will appear at the Café Anglais in the middle of one night and write three fiery words in the wall. This will be a signal that the old world is dead. Paris will collapse in blood and fire along with all the things that now constitute its pride, with all its theatres and coffee-shops.'

London, or present-day 'Baal', as Dostoevsky termed it, the centre of world capitalism, made an enormous impression on him. In Kensington he saw one of the largest edifices in the world, the new palace that housed the 1862 World Exhibition. The glass halls, the pointed pagoda-like towers and the two enormous many-faceted cupolas of the gigantic building were spread out across the royal parks. Products of human labour were gathered here from all corners of the world. In the evening, when all the buildings were lit up, it looked as if the capital of the colonial empire, having gathered the labour and thought of the entire globe in one place, were demonstrating its power, grandeur, arrogant pride and invincible strength. 'Crystal palace', as Dostoevsky called it in his *Winter Notes about Summer Impressions*, is one of the special terms Dostoevsky later employed in his *Notes from Underground*. 'Ant-heap' he used to imply the instinctive movement of living creatures, such as ants, bees or human beings, towards a social mechanism; 'chicken-coop' meant an inconvenient and ugly but not entirely useless temporary refuge from the rain; and 'crystal palace' meant an ideal community for mankind. These terms also appear in *The Diary of a Writer* and 'The Grand Inquisitor' Dostoevsky wrote shortly afterwards: 'Yes, the Exhibition is astonishing. You sense the terrifying force that has gathered all these countless people from all over the world here into one herd. You are aware of a gigantic idea; you sense that here something has already been achieved, here is victory, triumph.'

All the more horrible then were the streets of the city where the poor lived, corroded by the leprosy of hopeless poverty and the most frightful human indignities. Dostoevsky attended a 'white Negroes' sabbath' – Saturday night in London's working-class district. He was appalled by Whitechapel 'with its half-naked, savage and hungry population'. He visited Haymarket, thronged by thousands of street women – beauties, old women and adolescents. Incidentally, he drew some unforgettable sketches of the typical English girl. 'Nowhere in the world will you find a female type as beautiful as the Englishwoman.' But what is her lot?

Upstairs in the gallery I saw a young girl and stopped in astonishment. Never before had I encountered such perfect beauty! She was sitting at a table with a young man, who seemed to be a rich gentleman, and it was obvious that he was not a habitué of the casino... Their conversation was often interrupted by long silences. She was very sad, too. Her features were gentle and delicate; there was something secret and melancholy in her beautiful and rather proud gaze, some hidden thought, some yearning. I think she had consumption.

By her face Dostoevsky judged that she was a creature of the highest order, but swallowed up in Haymarket's frightful way of life. 'He left the casino soon afterwards and she, her white cheeks blotched with dark red from the strong drink, went off and was lost *in the mob of prostitutes*.' Here was the theme for an entire novel in the Dostoevskian spirit: a girl of remarkable beauty, proud heart and unendurable sorrow, abandoned among the prostitutes of a huge cosmopolitan city with its reprobates and wealthy men! Several years later Dostoevsky in fact wrote such a novel.

Another extraordinary encounter remained imprinted on

his memory, this time with a child among the crowd of sad women, dressed in finery:

In the Haymarket I saw mothers who had brought their little daughters with them to help in the hunt. Small girls of about twelve seize you by the hand and beg you to go with them. I remember seeing a little girl of about six, no more, among the crowd of people in the street; her clothes were in tatters; she was dirty, barefoot, hollow-cheeked and beaten: her body, which could be seen through her rags, was bruised. She was walking along as if in a daze, apparently in no hurry to go anywhere. God knows why she was roaming about in that crowd. Perhaps she was hungry. No one paid any attention to her. But what struck me most was the expression of such grief, such hopeless despair on her face; to see this tiny creature already experiencing so much damnation and despair was somehow unnatural and terribly painful. She kept shaking her unkempt head from side to side, as though debating a problem with herself, spreading her little hands, gesticulating, clapping them together suddenly and pressing them to her naked little chest. I turned back and gave her half a shilling. She seized the silver coin, then looked me in the eyes wildly, with frightened astonishment and suddenly started running off as fast as her legs would carry her, as though afraid I might take the money away again.

This briefly sketched six-year-old girl, beaten down by inexplicable despair among the dissolute and indifferent mob, will always remain one of Dostoevsky's great and immortal portraits.

AT HERZEN'S

Dostoevsky was confronted by a rather short, stocky man with animated gestures and burning eyes, a shiny, bulging forehead and a short beard in the manner of Garibaldi, aglow with the special masculine good looks of a man of fifty, active and creative. With the gay excitability of a student and a slight touch of the indulged aristocrat,

Herzen was talking in his usual sparkling style, making magic with his words. As he spoke he lightly tossed back his unruly hair, in which quite a lot of black still showed among the dense silver. What a contrast London, and England, must be for Fyodor Mikhailovich after the Omsk prison and the garrison in Semipalatinsk! Dostoevsky agreed, but bewildered and depressed as he was by the Exhibition, by the city's appearance, by the way the people looked, he spoke apprehensively about the proud and gloomy spirit that hovered above this enchanted and accursed place.

Herzen shook his head in disagreement. He smiled faintly and sadly. He had come to love London. He spoke of his love for the great city as he spoke about everything, using unexpected, picturesque and stimulating words. He liked to roam in the night through these stone passages, through the smoky alleyways, to push his way through the thick opalescent fog with its fleeting shadows. The Gothic stalagmites of Parliament are hardly visible in the darkness, and endless rows of lamps recede and vanish into the fog. 'One city, the well-fed city, has fallen asleep. The other, the hungry city, has not yet awakened – the streets are deserted and there is no sound except that of the measured steps of a policeman with his lantern. You sit for a while, you look, and your heart becomes calmer and more peaceful.

'And that is why I have come to love this frightful ant-heap, where each night a hundred thousand people do not know where to lay down their heads, and where the police often find women and children dead of starvation near hotels where you cannot buy a meal for under two pounds.'

'What is there to love?'

'Here you learn to know the Anglo-Saxon race – men of affairs, of practical poetry and of austere freedom . . .'

Dostoevsky observed the speaker attentively as he listened. Once upon a time, in his youth, he had followed with apprehension the brilliant victories of Iskander* that had threat-

* 'Iskander' was the pen-name used by Herzen.

ened to outshine his own early reputation as a novelist. Since
that time their lives and ideas had become even more sharply
contrasted. While Dostoevsky had languished in Asian
prisons, Herzen had become a European writer, a brilliant
politician and journalist and then the founder in London of
the first free Russian-language press. The charm of his name,
banned in Russia, was enough to surpass any literary fame.
The courageous independence of his activities, the stern
truthfulness of his militant writing, sharpened by an inimitable wit, galvanized young people. His grasp of the subtleties
of philosophy and culture, combined with his practical
revolutionary activities, constituted an extraordinary mag-
netic force.

They were driving through London in a hansom cab.

'All of England's history is here, hewn in stone.'

Before them loomed the Tower, fortress, palace, prison
and execution site, a fragment of the British empire in which
the bloodiest dramas in its annals had been enacted. They
drove to the docks where colossal depositories of goods that
London had sucked in from all parts of the world were being
loaded and unloaded, chains clanging, cranes screeching and
wagons creaking. The centre of world trade sprawled around
a complicated entanglement of ropes, blocks, chains,
bales, barrels, sacks, ladders, traps, hooks, gallows-like hoists
and innumerable masts with spikes that pierced London's
colourless sky.

This city was an unbelievably powerful pump, drawing in
goods produced for it from every quarter of the globe. There
was no end to the demand of this monstrous market. It was
for London that planters exploited Negroes mercilessly in
the American South and the West Indies. It was for London
that Australians and New Zealanders sheared huge flocks of
sheep and coolies cut sugar cane under the destroying sun. It
was for London that caravans moved drearily across deserts
in search of gold dust and ivory. It was for London that
weavers in far-off Kashmir made rich fabrics, and it was for

London that the most luscious fruits ripened and the most fragrant flowers bloomed under the Mediterranean sun. The insatiable giant devoured all.

Strakhov was the first to remark that *Winter Notes about Summer Impressions* 'somewhat reflects the influence of Herzen, towards whom Dostoevsky was very favourably inclined at the time'. He had in mind Iskander's three books: *Letters from France and Italy, From the Other Shore* and *Ends and Beginnings.* In these the brilliant *emigré* writer set out his observations of the mind and impressions of the heart, in letters from Paris, Rome and Naples to friends in Moscow. Their chief theme was the victorious bourgeoisie's struggle against the motive force of progress – the rising class of 'workmen'. They also expressed Herzen's sad reflections after the defeat of the June 1848 uprising and his hopes for the future revolutionary development of the proletariat. They suggested a solution to the dilemma of Russia and the West and constituted the author's spiritual return to his homeland and rejection of West European civilization, which, he felt, was incapable of rising to heights of creative activity and bringing about a new artistic renaissance.

However, while Herzen raised far more extensive political problems in his books than Dostoevsky did in *Winter Notes about Summer Impressions*, Dostoevsky rose to unsurpassed heights of tragedy in his portrayal of the city's horrors and agonies, especially in the chapter entitled 'Baal'. No doubt Dostoevsky felt a kinship with Herzen's ideas concerning the doom of Europe, with its 'autocracy of property', and the Russian people's mission to unite all mankind through the free spirit of its literature and philosophy. But all this is not solely attributable to Herzen's influence. The novelist and thinker drew on his own experiences and formulated his own concepts.

*

According to the information of agents of the Third Department which is normally very reliable, Dostoevsky also saw Mikhail Bakunin in London in 1862. There is no reason to doubt this, because six months before Dostoevsky came to London the celebrated anarchist had returned from long years of fighting and imprisonment and had moved in with his friend Herzen. Dostoevsky first heard Bakunin's name in Belinsky's circle. Belinsky often objected sharply to the statements of his friend Bakunin, who was a staunch propagandist of German philosophy, but as long ago as 1836 he had admired his 'vitality, restless spirit and lively striving for the truth'. After he left Russia in 1840 Bakunin moved from pure thought to political struggle, and in 1844 he was sentenced to permanent exile from Russia. It was not without a feeling of comradely pride that Belinsky used to read about his old friend's revolutionary activities far beyond the borders of his homeland. 'Just look at our Michel,' he would say over and over again, in astonishment at the scope of activity of this one-time member of a Moscow student circle who had made the whole world his arena. 'Come to that, it would have been ridiculous to have doubted him', he would remark with a radiant smile. He was impressed by the slogan formulated by Jules Élizar, as Bakunin was known, a slogan that had swept Europe: 'A destructive passion is a creative passion.'

Dostoevsky apparently remembered the oral legend that had arisen about Bakunin among his friends. With time he would become a subtle psychological portraitist, sometimes too a pamphleteer who could be hard on the 'men of the forties'. Behind the characters of his novels, and sometimes too in his journalistic memoirs, one discerns, transformed by fantasy or by criticism, the figures of Turgenev, Granovsky, Herzen, Belinsky, and among them that of the most active of propagandists of German idealism in old Moscow, the most outstanding of participants in the European revolution of 1849 on the barricades of Dresden – Mikhail Bakunin. Their personal meeting is incontestably an event in Dostoevsky's literary biography.

Since Dostoevsky had first heard his name, Bakunin had lived through an entire epic. In 1847 he had made a speech at a Polish banquet in Paris, condemning Nicholas I and predicting the imminent collapse of his empire. He had led uprisings in Prague in 1848 and in Dresden in 1849. He had been sentenced to death twice, in Saxony and in Austria, and had been imprisoned there in impenetrable dungeons (in Olmutz he had been chained to the wall), then turned over to the Russian government. After six years in solitary confinement in the Peter and Paul and Schlusselburg Fortresses he had been deported to Siberia, whence he had managed to escape. He reached England via Japan and America. On the evening of 27 December 1861, he walked into Herzen's house, where he found the whole family at the table. 'We must act,' were his first words after the greetings and exclamations of joy.

'There are nothing but demonstrations in Poland so far,' Herzen replied.

'What about Italy?'

'It is quiet.'

'Austria?'

'The same.'

'And Turkey?'

'It is quiet everywhere and there is nothing in sight.'

'Then what is to be done?' Bakunin cried out, in annoyance and anger. 'Surely, we don't have to go to Persia or to India to start something?' He could not live without work, that is, without struggle.

He soon sensed that Russia had awakened and was in a revolutionary ferment. Herzen wrote in *Kolokol* on 15 January 1862: 'Bakunin comes to us with redoubled love for the Russian people, with the indomitable energy of hope and strength, with health strengthened by the fresh, young air of Siberia. The shades and images of turbulent 1848 involuntarily come to life with Bakunin.' Bakunin had returned to his youthful dreams of a free Slav federation. In February

1862 he printed an appeal 'to all Russians, Poles and all Slav friends'; in July he wrote a pamphlet entitled 'Romanov, Pugachov or Pestel'. He called for a Russian popular revolution; he welcomed a peasant Russia and the vanguard of *déclassé* intelligentsia – 'seminary students and nihilists, the only fresh force apart from the common people'. He called for the destruction of the shaky foundations of the Tsarist empire and never ceased his efforts to guide from afar the revolutionary movement in his native land.

What could two thinkers as unlike as Bakunin and Dostoevsky, with diametrically opposed political positions, have talked about?[1] What common ground could the organizer of the Russian *pochva* movement have found with someone who proclaimed worldwide destruction? The only theme they had in common was the suffering past and heroic future of the Russian people. It is surely not coincidental that Herzen, who must have been present at their talks, wrote to Ogaryov: 'Dostoevsky was here yesterday. He is naïve and not altogether clear-headed but a very nice person. He has an enthusiastic belief in the Russian people.'

In the months since his arrival in England Bakunin was making up for nine years of silence and solitude. He gathered many of the Slavs living in London at his home and, according to Herzen, argued, preached, gave orders, shouted, made decisions, directed, organized and encouraged all day and all night. At any rate, 16 July 1862, the day that Dostoevsky talked with Bakunin and Herzen about the Russian people, remained one of the most memorable days in Dostoevsky's life.

'THE FATEFUL QUESTION'

A few months later unexpected disaster descended upon Dostoevsky's magazine. In the subscription announcement for *Vremya*, issued at the end of 1862, Dostoevsky had firmly reiterated his belief that 'Russia's salvation lay in the soil and the people' as the guiding principle of his programme in the coming year; but by the end of May 1863 *Vremya* had ceased publishing for ever, closed down by imperial order as an unpatriotic organ 'that offended national feelings'. This is what happened in the brief intervening period.

The international situation changed dramatically at the beginning of 1863, when, on the night of 22 January, the Central National Committee of Poland proclaimed an armed insurrection for the restoration of the *Rzeczpospolita* with the frontiers of 1772,* and detachments of insurgents then attacked Tsarist garrisons stationed in Poland. The scattered actions of the insurgents did not, however, develop into a popular war and Poland, receiving no support from the Western governments, headed towards inevitable defeat; the insurrection was finally suppressed in February 1864. The following May M. N. Muravyov, nicknamed 'the hangman' for his punitive actions in Poland, was appointed Governor-General of the six north-western provinces.

These extraordinary events created a great stir in Russia, and the country was soon in a ferment of conflicting attitudes. The reactionaries, headed by Katkov, gave their unconditional support to the government's military action. Within liberal circles there was a covert desire for a compromise solution to the conflict, while Russian revolutionary spokesmen came out openly in support of the insurgents' cause. Herzen spoke up vigorously in defence of Poland and, to quote Lenin, 'saved the honour of Russian democracy'. *Kolokol* carried a powerful appeal for international revolution: 'We want Poland's independence because we want Russia's freedom.'

* The *Rzeczpospolita* or 'United Republic' of Poland and Lithuania included up to 1772 (the year of the First Partition of Poland) large tracts of country where the majority of the population was Russian (Belo-Russians and Ukrainians).

Dostoevsky failed to find the right line. For three months after the insurrection began *Vremya* maintained complete silence about it, and when he finally decided that the magazine should express an opinion on this extremely important topic he commissioned the philosopher and literary critic Strakhov, who had had no experience in writing on international problems, to prepare the article. This choice proved disastrous.

It was decided that the article should have a general philosophical tone rather than a military–political one, and should deal with problems of national culture rather than with the concrete facts of the current war. The article appeared in the April 1863 issue of *Vremya*. It was signed 'A Russian' and entitled 'The Fateful Question', hinting at the famous verse Pushkin had written on an analogous occasion in 1830*:

> *Who will win the unequal argument?*
> The arrogant Polish gentry or the loyal Russian?
> Will the Slavic streams merge into a Russian sea?
> Or will that sea dry up?
> *That is the question!*

The 'Russian' declared that the present problem should not be solved by force of arms but by comparing the cultures of the two nations. Only when Russia had won 'a spiritual victory' over Poland would the rivalry between the two countries be decided in Russia's favour.

Moskovskie Vedomosti (*Moscow News*) was the first to attack *Vremya* for incorrect handling of the most burning political issue of the day. Dostoevsky answered with a long article, justifying the magazine's position, but by then it was too late to reverse the course of events. Valuev, the Minister of Internal Affairs, made a 'humble submission' to the Tsar about an outrageous article, entitled 'A Fateful Question', which had come out against all the government's actions

* i.e. The First Polish Insurrection of 1830.

and offended the feelings of the nation. As a result, the Tsar 'was graciously pleased to order on 24 May 1863 that publication of the magazine *Vremya* be stopped'.

Some time later Dostoevsky told his brother Andrei what really happened. The Governor-General of Moscow wrote in a private letter to the Tsar that Moscow was 'up in arms about an article entitled "The Fateful Question"'. Valuev had said nothing of the matter in his latest report to the Tsar, but when he finished presenting it, Alexander himself inquired:

'What's this "Fateful Question" that has turned up?'

'The magazine *Vremya* has already been banned, Your Majesty,' the wily Valuev hastily replied; and when he got back to Petersburg he issued a pre-dated order that the magazine be closed down.

Dostoevsky stoutly maintained that his magazine was patriotic, though he did blame Strakhov for having employed phrases so subtle and intricate as to give rise to ambivalent interpretations and lamentable misunderstandings: 'The writer was also partially to blame: he tried to be too subtle and he was completely misinterpreted.' In contrasting the two national cultures Strakhov had not given concrete historic facts and had thereby laid the article open to a charge of pro-Polish sympathies. Herzen considered that the article was, quite rightly, sympathetic to the Poles, and stated outright that Dostoevsky's magazine 'had printed *several humane words* about Poland that had outraged autocratic Russia.'

The attacks by reactionary circles and the semi-official press put the author of the article and the editors of *Vremya* in danger of further reprisals. But the editors of *Moskovskie Vedomosti* came to the rescue. They published an explanation in *Russky Vestnik* which, while it emphatically refuted the theses of 'The Fateful Question', denied that *Vremya* had had politically unreliable objectives in printing the article. There was no further repressive action. At the end of January 1864

Mikhail Dostoevsky received 'His Majesty's permission' to publish another magazine, to be called *Epokha* (*Epoch*). The Dostoevskys' group planned it as a revival of *Vremya* and expected it to have *Vremya*'s great success, but their hopes were never realized.

APOLLINARIA SUSLOVA

In the early 1860s Dostoevsky experienced one of the strongest passions of his life. The object of it was a young girl named Apollinaria Suslova. She was the daughter of one of Count Sheremetyev's serfs. She was born in a village in an out-of-the-way part of Nizhni-Novgorod Province and spent her childhood and adolescence there. This left a lifelong imprint on her. In 1864 she wrote how the political *emigrés* at the Paris salon of Countess Salias had angered her by not showing sufficient respect for the Russian people: 'No, I will not go along with these people. I was born in a peasant family and lived among the common people until I was fifteen, and I will live among the *muzhiks*. There is no place for me in civilized society. I will go to the *muzhiks*. I know that they will not insult me.' A little before this, when she first found herself in the centre of world culture she had been filled with hatred for the achievements of the brilliant civilization of bourgeois Europe and dreamed of fleeing from its temptations to the far-off villages of Russia, just recently emancipated. 'I think I shall settle among the peasants and be of some use to them,' she wrote in her diary of 27 August 1863.

Her father, Prokofy Suslov, a literate, intelligent serf, had apparently bought his freedom in 1855, when the system of Nicholas I had collapsed and emancipation was imminent, and had stayed on as chief manager of his former master's extensive estates. He then moved to Petersburg and was able to give his children further education. His elder daughter Apollinaria attended public lectures by eminent professors at Petersburg University and popular concerts including readings in which Chernyshevsky, Nekrasov, Pisemsky, Anton Rubinstein, Wieniawski and two recent political exiles, Shevchenko and Dostoevsky, took part.

Dostoevsky's impassioned readings from his *Notes from the House of the Dead* aroused great enthusiasm among the young and evoked stormy ovations from the 'new people' who packed the halls. A report by an agent of the Third Department describes a celebrated literary evening in the Ruadze Hall where, the agent said, Dostoevsky 'treated the audience to revolting stories of criminals serving sentences of penal servitude, in punishment companies, prisons and so forth, describing the deeds for which these criminals had been exiled or imprisoned after having been knouted, whipped or made to run the gauntlet.'

It is not hard to imagine the admiration this aroused in the young narodnik* Apollinaria Suslova. To a girl still so inexperienced and full of naïve enthusiasm, Dostoevsky must have seemed a hero and a martyr – the victim of an idea, a political criminal who had come through penal servitude, a sufferer for the revolutionary idea, a celebrated writer, who had brought with him from that legendary decade in the House of the Dead great hope, and had been crowned with the deathbed blessing of Belinsky himself. Though ill, puny, short, morose, with rough hands and feet that had worn a convict's heavy manacles, he must have looked taller and more handsome to her than anyone else she knew. And as he read, in the throaty voice of a weak-chested man, heartrending pages about the convicts' hell, he seemed to grow taller and broader and to tower above the shaken, silent audience, like the legendary heroes of old who carried great sinners up to the stars in their arms. Dostoevsky captured

* The *narodniks*, or populists, believed that Russia's salvation lay in the peasantry and went among the people to bring them enlightenment through education, and to learn from them the true Russian way of life.

Apollinaria's restless imagination: his pain and his glory dazzled her; the image he presented of a persecuted and suffering artist matched her impassioned desire to idolize and dedicate herself to the great and the heroic.

There is no reason to question the statement of Dostoevsky's daughter that her father had received a love letter from Apollinaria and was deeply touched by its sincerity and poetic spirit, though no such letter has been found in the Dostoevsky archives. Apollinaria, dazzled by his literary genius, told him of her boundless admiration, and Dostoevsky welcomed this ardent young love. He was very grateful for the new happiness that had entered his life, so burdened with intensive work on his novels and with the proof-reading of his magazine. 'Your love descended to me like a gift from heaven, unawaited and unsuspected, after fatigue and despair. Your young life near me promised so much and has already given so much. It revived my faith and what little was left of my former energies.'

Apollinaria Suslova attributes these words to Dostoevsky in her story 'Someone Else's and My Own' in which she gives a very realistic picture of their romance and expresses her own attitude to their love in the early stages of their intimacy. She wrote in her diary that she had never loved anyone or been intimate with anyone before she met Dostoevsky. This was her first passion. 'I gave myself to him in love, without asking and without expecting anything in return,' she wrote subsequently. On 16 November 1864 she recorded this fragment from a conversation in her diary:

> Speaking of a handsome Greek one day, I said that in my early youth I had not paid attention to good looks and that my first love was for a man of forty.
> 'You were sixteen then, weren't you?' he asked.
> 'No, twenty-three.'[2]

The idealistic girl felt no need for dazzling good looks or youth. She had been looking for an intellectual Titan and she had found one. She regarded their love as beautiful, as a grand passion. She was happy. Dostoevsky gave her an entrée into the literary profession by publishing a timid effort of hers in his magazine alongside *The Insulted and the Injured*, a story entitled 'For the Time Being'.

But ominous cracks soon appeared in their relationship. Rebellion began to rise in her young heart and she began to feel a need to break with Dostoevsky. She had begun to suspect that Dostoevsky's interest in her was merely the result of a need any busy man might feel, to find escape momentarily in sensual pleasure. Apparently Dostoevsky one day jokingly mentioned to her Balzac's well-known aphorism that even a philosopher must go on a wild orgy once a month. This was a deadly blow to her hero worship and her admiration for the creator of *The House of the Dead*. She 'blushed' for her relationship with him and wished to break it off for good.

Thus even the first period of their romance brought pain and conflict. 'I do not like it when you write cynical things,' she said to him. 'Somehow, it does not suit you. It does not suit the picture I had of you'; a picture, that is, of a great martyr, a mighty poet, and an inspired teacher. It was this vision of him that had quickened her original feeling for Dostoevsky in all its purity and depth and she could not but reproach him, as it were, now that her love could no longer maintain its original elevated level. Soon it turned sour and withered. No amount of talent could in her eyes excuse the 'petty sides of character'. She 'rebelled fiercely against anything she felt was a shortcoming or weakness and her hostility was the greater because this man had once seemed perfection to her'.

Her inner protest became more vehement as the years went by. In September 1864 she wrote in her diary:

People talk to me about Fyodor Mikhailovich. I hate him. He made me suffer so much when there was no need to suffer.

I now feel and see clearly that I cannot love, that I cannot find happiness in the pleasures of love, because men's caresses will remind me of insults and suffering.

And in December of the same year: 'When I think of what I was two years ago I begin to hate Dostoevsky. He was the first to destroy my faith.' We shall never know just what Suslova had in mind, what suffering he caused her, how he insulted her, what faith he destroyed. Even granting that she exaggerated, we dare not declare her accusations to be entirely groundless.

Dostoevsky was already thirty-four when he fell in love for the first time, with Maria Dmitrievna Isaeva. His passion for her was then very strong, but marriage to the woman he loved very quickly changed his passion to pity. Apollinaria Suslova was the first pure and cultured girl in his life; she had come to him with a noble dream of his genius lighting up her personality, and of her love giving sustenance to this man who had lived through the convicts' hell; she saw him as a new Dante, saved by the love of Beatrice. Dostoevsky had never before been the object of so deep a feeling, and was apparently unable to pass this exceedingly difficult test.

Another cause of the constant discord between these incongruous lovers was their opposing social views. A member of the movement of the 1860s, Suslova belligerently rejected the 'old world' and its art, religion, national culture and idealistic ethics, which constituted the principal spiritual values of Dostoevsky's philosophy. The differences between the *pochva* writer and the young nihilist, whose guiding light was Nekrasov ('Lead me on to the thorny road') and Pushkin's lines from *The Demon*:

> And nothing in all Nature
> Was he willing to bless

could not be reconciled. Hence the arguments about the emancipation of women, which Suslova mentions in her diary, defending her right to freedom and independence in love. Hence the heated discussions about revolution, for the energetic and impulsive Apollinaria often took up with the most extreme political trends and even expressed a willingness to participate in the anti-government terror, so characteristic of the reign of Alexander II. This tense and agonizing love–hate relationship lasted, with interruptions and separations, for six or seven years.

*

In the winter or spring of 1863 Dostoevsky invited his proud friend Apollinaria to go to Italy with him the coming summer. But then in May *Vremya* was banned and he plunged into the laborious task of liquidating a well-known magazine that had some four thousand subscribers, and at the same time attempting to save or revive it. Dostoevsky was unable to leave Russia for a long time. Suslova, weary of the complications of their relationship, departed for Paris at the beginning of the summer with the understanding that Dostoevsky would follow her there shortly and that they would then go on to Rome and Naples together.

The numerous matters to be taken care of and the complexity of the magazine's affairs kept delaying Dostoevsky's departure. He wrote 'A Reply from the Editors of *Vremya* to the Attack by *Moskovskie Vedomosti*', but the censor would not allow it to be printed. His attempts to revive the banned magazine or get permission to publish a new one were meeting with opposition from the authorities, who feared the former Petrashevskyite's possible influence on readers of a publication that dealt with social and political affairs. The difficult and sad days dragged on.

One evening he stood on the edge of Yekaterininsky Canal and peered into the dark water where the reflected flames of the gas lamps flickered dully, thinking of the best that still remained to him in life, Apollinaria. He took out of his black moiré briefcase a large photograph of a young woman in a smart light-coloured dress with a Parisian cut. A sharp pang pierced his heart. He looked closely at the

serious face. A young woman in a white blouse with a slightly
open neck gazed at him from the dark background. The
elongated oval of her face and her bright forehead were
strikingly pure. The dark hair, parted smoothly and lifted
high in a tight braid that encircled the head, shone like silk
in the sun. Huge, reflective, deep-set eyes looked out with surprise and almost naïveté, as if asking a question or sympathizing with someone's sorrow. The face was cloudlessly
serene. Intense thought and, perhaps, secret suffering had
given the features a refined spirituality. Only the lips had a
touch of the common people, of the peasantry, in fact.

This was the essence of Russian beauty, even though
dressed in Parisian clothes, this village girl with sorrowful
eyes and a high bosom. Of late he had come to love this type
of beauty as being part of him, of his native land, like the
gullies and forests of Cheremoshna, like the broad, full, rapid
Irtysh River. He could not bear being separated any longer.
In the middle of August he tore himself away from
Petersburg.

He found the journey through Europe, with the acrid
smell of coal and the ugly railway stations with their hum-
ped roofs, exhausting. All was fatigue, loneliness, thaler and
silbergroschen, and then all those depressing glass tunnels of
railway stations . . . but at last he reached Paris. Was he
really about to have the good fortune of enjoying this
legendary centre of Western art, of history and science, of
political struggle in the company of the woman he loved?

Paris! The city of Bonaparte and of Balzac! The bell of
Quasimodo, the hills of Père Lachaise, from where Rastignac
had flung his challenge to the whole of society.

The moment he arrived at his hotel he dispatched a note
to the Latin Quarter, but he was too impatient to wait for a
reply. He hired a *fiacre* and sped off to the Jardin du Luxem-
bourg. Here at last was her room. But why was she making
him wait so long? It was almost unendurable. And then,
her low 'How are you?', was hardly audible above the

agonized beating of his heart. All of a sudden he was overcome by an oppressive feeling of embarrassment, joylessness,
shame, pain. She said, 'I had given up expecting you.
Didn't you get my letter?'

That letter, which he only received the next day, remained
engraved on his memory for ever:

You have arrived a little late. A short while ago I still dreamed
of travelling in Italy with you and had even begun to learn
Italian. Everything has changed in a few days. You said to me
once that I could not easily give my heart away. I have given it
away in one week, at the first call, without struggle, without
assurance, almost without hope that I am loved. I was right to be
angry with you when you started to express admiration for me.
I am not engaging in self-condemnation, do not think that. I am
merely saying that you did not know me, yes, and I did not know
myself. Farewell, my darling.

But he did not need a letter to tell him that something irre-
vocable had happened.

'I've got to know everything. Let us go somewhere and
talk, or I shall die.'

The *fiacre* started back to his hotel. They sat in silence in
the closed carriage. When they reached the commonplace
room in a second class hotel on the Left Bank – he had
wanted to be near her – she finally replied to his sobs,
reproaches and supplications. She could hardly speak
through her tears.

'Are you happy? Are you happy? Just one word, tell me,
are you happy?' he kept saying, without rising from his
knees.

Her 'no' was hardly audible.

'How can that be? You are in love and you are not
happy? Is it possible?'

'He does not love me.'

'Who is he? A poet? An artist? A philosopher?'

'Oh, no.'

Finally, she calmed down and told him the whole story.

His name was Salvador, he was a medical student, very handsome, a dandy. His parents had settled in the Antilles in the last century. He came from a celebrated family of gold-seekers, sailors, *conquistadores* and colonizers. They had subdued an entire archipelago and enslaved the natives. The men came home to supper from their sugar and tobacco plantations with broken whips and blood-stained trousers. Though Salvador had acquired a little polish in Europe, you could nevertheless sense the schemer, hunter, *conquistador* and slave-owner in him.

'Just think, he had no understanding of books at all – something we can't possibly imagine!'

One might have thought that she was offering him consolation, so touched was she by his grief.

It did console him a little.

That he had no understanding was good. A foreign student was not a hero, not a poet, not a cynical thinker, not a demoniacal Lermontov. Thank goodness! This would not last long. Russia would call her back and she would not be able to resist the call. After all, in Petersburg she had become infatuated with a writer, primarily because he had been a martyr for his country, a bard singing of its sorrows, a courageous champion of an oppressed people.

A few days in Paris had upset everything. The dazzling dandies in the medical school, the wealthy foreign students with their southern tans and exotic names, in their tight frock coats and patent leather shoes, with riding crops in their bronzed hands and the sultriness of insatiable desire in their huge southern eyes, had at once pushed out of her mind the pale and sickly image of the Petersburg writer. Perhaps she had grown weary of his caprices, outbursts of irritation, constant worrying and despotic impulses of passion. Salvador! What a name. How could a Russian girl help falling in love with those triumphantly forceful syllables? Here was the subtle charm of a young and well-dressed foreigner in all the brilliance of his self-confident youth, elegantly dressed in strict accordance with the latest Parisian fashions. The very first time she had met him Dostoevsky's fate had been settled. He had lost her because he had no right to her, weak, sick, worn out as he was, the burning and momentary outbursts of his fading passion flickering across his senses like a flame across dry firewood. With her avidly grasping soul and the vigorous temperament of the common people, she needed other strengths and other passions.

Numbly, helplessly, despairingly, he begged for friendship, meetings, correspondence. 'Perhaps we can go to Italy anyway? My friend, do not fear, I will be only a brother to you.'

Once more his was the role of disinterested consoler, superfluous 'third party', the self-sacrificing friend. Was this preordained, was he never to be loved, never to reign over a woman in the fullness of passion, but always to be a sort of spouse, a disinterested guardian, even a mediator between lovers? Was he this time, too, destined to become his mistress's confidant and his rival's champion? Hadn't he had enough of being noble? Wasn't it time to stop playing the role of the eternal husband?

Apollinaria's hard character compelled him to take this path again. She did not conceal that she was madly in love with Salvador, while Salvador deceived her, considered himself under no obligation, avoided her and was trying to put her off. There had been an accidental meeting in the street and a cold exchange of words, after which the abandoned woman had made up her mind either to kill him or to commit suicide.

At seven in the morning she knocked on Dostoevsky's door. On that day she told him the whole story of her unhappy love affair without hiding anything from him.

'How can you settle human relationships by bloodshed?'

'I don't really want to kill him, but I would like to torture him for a very long time.'

'Enough,' Dostoevsky said. 'It's not worth it. He won't

understand anyway. It is senseless to destroy yourself on account of him.'

She agreed with some of the things he said but her heart long burned with a thirst for revenge that took unexpected, constantly changing, dangerous forms.

From her window Apollinaria had a superb view of Paris, especially of the district around the Place Sainte-Geneviève not far away. One day she called Dostoevsky's attention to the architecture of a medieval basilica right behind the revolutionary Panthéon.

'I confessed to a very evil plan in that church the other day.'

He was startled.

'How could you slander yourself to those celibacy-corrupted Catholic priests?'

'It wasn't slander. I told the truth. And why is a Catholic priest worse than one of our archdeacons?'

He was overcome with anxiety. His heart ached for her. She smiled affectionately.

'Do not grieve. Just look at the beauty of that chapel. It is considered one of the loveliest in Paris – Saint-Étienne du Mont. Really, it makes a confession to the most awful sins worthwhile. You were not here then, so I went to the chapel to confess to the *abbé*.'

'To confess to what?'

Then she admitted that she had harboured a secret plan. She had been possessed by a terrible and bloody scheme, that had held her in its tight grasp and would not let her go. She was not yet entirely free of its clutches.

'What is it? To kill Salvador?'

'No, not him.'

'Not him? Who then? Me?'

'Oh, no!' she said, so lightly and calmly that he was filled with bitterness at such contemptuous indifference. 'No, not you. I tell you it is a grand and extraordinary design.'

Her eyes burned with heroic resolution.

'Tell me. Unburden your heart.'

'Yes, I will tell you.' Clearly, she was finding it difficult to confess, even to him. 'Listen. I was simply dying from melancholy and anger. I felt that I must kill someone, but you are right that he is not worth it. He is petty. He is not worth committing a great sin for. You are probably right about that. To destroy oneself for an obscure student – no, I would turn my vengeance into heroism. In avenging my defiled love I would sacrifice myself, would become famous and go down in history.'

'Whatever have you concocted?' he asked, greatly alarmed. He had a feeling something terrible beyond belief was coming.

'What difference does it make which man pays for the outrage that has been perpetrated against me? You are all guilty. All of you have betrayal and carnality on your consciences. So if vengeance is to be wreaked, let the whole world hear of it. Let the revenge be unique without precedent, unrepeatable!'

'Apollinaria, come to your senses! Do you really think you could kill a man?'

'Without a qualm.'

'Whom?'

She looked at him with complete indifference, almost with contempt.

'Haven't you guessed? The Tsar.'

He started. Was it possible? How much this woman must have suffered to be willing to face such agony!

'Swear to me that you will never again even harbour such a thought.'

His eyes implored her. Through his mind flashed the discussions of 1848; Speshnev, Dubelt's office, the Ravelin, the awful road from the prison cell to the scaffold, three stakes sticking out of a depressing empty whiteness, a solid wall of soldiers, the death shrouds, the words 'Death by the firing squad!' echoing inexorably over and over again.

'Do you want to grovel at the executioner's feet like Du Barry, shrieking: "One more minute!"?'

She looked at him, tired, apathetic.

'No, I have already given up the idea. It has let go of me.'

He breathed a sigh of relief.

'What made you give up that monstrous idea?'

'I was wandering through the streets of the neighbourhood recently, thinking about my plan. After all, this was not the sort of thing that had been discussed in the clubs of Petersburg. I decided to take a look at the little cemetery over there, behind the railings of Saint-Étienne, where the bodies of Marat and Mirabeau were buried when they were thrown out of the Panthéon. There was this beautiful chapel with garlands and roses. I went in. A service was in progress. In the pulpit a Catholic priest was finishing his sermon. All of a sudden I felt drawn to him. I resolved to confess everything to him. The next day I knocked at his door. "Amen, come in." By day he looked altogether different: a big fat man, writing at a rolltop desk. He scarcely turned his head. "What do you want?" he said, quite rudely and annoyed. I didn't know what to do. "Well?" the same sharp impatience. I lost control of myself and burst into tears. He turned away. Finally, I mumbled a few words. He said: "If you are Russian you should go to a Russian Orthodox priest." "But I have heard so much about you," I said. "What can I do for you? Are you looking for a job? Don't you have any money? Don't you have a family or friends? Have you sinned against morality?" Those last words were uttered very sternly. I said to him: "There is so much suffering and crime in the world, especially in my country, Russia, and I have made up my mind to kill the source of my country's evils." "Nonsense!" he shouted. "There are laws; only idlers and drunkards suffer. Emperor Alexander is an ideal ruler and an ideal man!" It was all so crude, so common. It was as if someone had thrown a bucket of cold water over me. After that the whole thing was over.'

'But how could you have conceived of such an idea?'

She fell into a reverie.

'It is a fascinating thought,' she said finally. 'Such an enormous step after all, it is so simple. Imagine, one gesture, one movement, and you are among the celebrities, the geniuses, the great, the saviours of mankind.'

'Fame is won by hard work,' he remarked gloomily.

'Or by unprecedented daring.'

'Have you thought of the agony afterwards?'

'That is what stopped me. I suddenly thought: they'll execute me, and, after all, to live peacefully somewhere in the sun by a southern sea until the age of eighty wouldn't be so awful.'

Her frankness verged on the almost shameless. Depressed by this unexpected talk of regicide, which seemed to follow him wherever he went, Dostoevsky turned away and did not continue the conversation.

*

They left Paris at the beginning of September. Dostoevsky spent four days in Baden-Baden, haunted by the dream of winning a fortune at roulette. He lost three thousand francs and had to send to Russia for a hundred roubles in order to continue his journey. In Geneva he staked his last two hundred and fifty francs and lost. He pawned his watch and Suslova pawned her ring so they could go on to Turin. Sweltering Turin, then the capital of the Italian kingdom, appeared gloomy to the penniless travellers as they waited for the hundred roubles to arrive from Petersburg. Dostoevsky found Turin 'extremely boring', even an 'accursed' city. Suslova disliked the monstrous architecture of the ornately painted buildings.

However, in this uninteresting city a reconciliation unexpectedly took place. Suslova described it in her diary:

Tenderness for Fyodor Mikhailovich has come over me again. I reproached him one day, then felt that I was wrong. I wanted to smooth over my reproach and become tender towards him.

He responded so joyfully that I was touched and became doubly tender. When I sat down beside him and looked at him with affection, he said: 'Now that's a familiar look; I haven't seen it for a long time.' I leaned against his chest and burst into tears.

When they were in the Gulf of Genoa a storm came up and their ship began to pitch and toss. 'I thought this was the end,' said Suslova. The next day they dropped anchor at Leghorn and remained there for a whole day. On 28 September they arrived in Rome. Writing to Strakhov two days later about his literary affairs and plans, Dostoevsky said: 'It is strange, here I am in Rome and there is not a word about Rome in my letter.' However, the travellers had already seen the Forum, the Coliseum and most memorably St Peter's: 'A tremendous impression, Nikolai Nikolaevich. It sends shivers down the spine.' The letters Dostoevsky wrote during his travels contain only a few lines about famous cities. 'Rome and Naples made a strong impression on me. But . . . I'm dying to be back in Petersburg,' and all that Suslova noted in her diary was the animation of the motley Neapolitan crowd.

They arrived in Naples at the beginning of October. All along the way there from Rome they were searched frequently and were constantly being asked for their passports. In Naples they met Herzen and his family on board a ship. This was the most important event of the entire journey. Suslova was introduced to the celebrated *emigré* and to his twenty-four-year-old son Alexander, who later became a well-known physiologist.

The two of them travelled as far as Berlin together. Two days after their arrival there Dostoevsky began to feel the irresistible pull of roulette and took off for the gambling resort of Homburg.[3] Suslova, expecting nothing more from this joyless trip, returned to Paris. A few days after she arrived a letter from Dostoevsky caught up with her. He had lost all his money in Homburg and asked her to send him some. She borrowed three hundred francs from friends and sent it to him. Thus their journey ended: they separated, almost for good.

Many years later when Apollinaria was married, her husband asked her why she and Dostoevsky had parted.

'Because he did not want to divorce his wife. She was consumptive and "was dying anyway".'

'But she *was* dying, wasn't she?'

'Yes, she was. She died six months later, but I no longer loved him.'

'But why?'

'Because he did not want to get a divorce.'

I was silent.

'I had given myself to him in love without asking or expecting anything and he should have done the same. He did not, and I chucked him.'

Suslova places their separation in the autumn of 1863, but they did not break off entirely then. In this connection an exchange of letters in the spring of 1865 between Dostoevsky and Apollinaria's younger sister, Nadezhda, who was studying medicine in Zurich at the time, is of interest.

Dostoevsky had known Nadezhda Suslova at the beginning of the sixties when she attended lectures as an external student at Petersburg University and later at the Army Medico-Surgical Academy, and he respected her deeply. She was a revolutionary and his meetings and conversations with her left him with a number of *positive* impressions, rather unusual for him, of the new generation of young Russians, members of the '1860s movement'. These impressions were of great significance in his subsequent attempts to understand and even to justify the progressive people of that group. This episode of brief but very serious and pure friendship with this outstanding representative of Russian medicine (she was the first woman doctor in Russia) does much to explain the political judgements and positions of his later years and explain his constant close attention to and profound interest in such figures as Karakozov and Vera Zasulich.*

Writing to Dostoevsky in April 1865, Nadezhda Suslova accused him of having behaved unworthily with regard to her elder sister. She said he was inclined to enjoy other people's suffering and tears and had been rude and cruel to the girl who loved him. Dostoevsky defended himself in his reply to her. Apollinaria was a great egoist, he wrote. 'She always treated me with disdain . . . She does not admit equality in our relationship . . . She has no human feeling whatever.' In Paris she had greeted him with the words: 'You have arrived a little late.' She had tormented him constantly. 'I pity her because I foresee that she will always be unhappy.' Those words, incidentally, turned out to be the truth.

He contrasted Nadezhda to her sister. 'At every painful time I used to come to you to rest my spirit. You have seen me in my most sincere moments. You are dear to me as one young and new, and besides, I love you as a favourite sister.' He stressed what made her basically different from her sister: 'You have a heart. You won't lose your way!' Life soon proved these words also to be true. Dostoevsky informed his niece Sonya Ivanova on 31 January 1867: 'A few days ago I read in the newspapers that my old friend Nadezhda Suslova has passed the exams for doctor of medicine at Zürich University and has presented a brilliant thesis. She is still a very young girl: she is a rare individual, noble, honest and honourable.'

On 2 November 1865 Apollinaria Suslova wrote in her diary:

Fyodor Mikhailovich was here today and we kept arguing and contradicting each other. He has been offering me his hand and his heart for a long time now and it only makes me angry. Speaking of my character, he said: 'Should you get married you

* Karakozov. See Chapter XX. Vera Zasulich. See Chapter XVIII.

will come to hate your husband by the end of the third day. You cannot forgive me for having given yourself to me and you are taking revenge for this.'

One has to think that Apollinaria Suslova was the strongest passion in Dostoevsky's life. She was a woman of extremes, always seeking intensity of sensation, and she made the demands on life of a passionate, impulsive and emotion-hungry nature. Equally characteristic of her were the tendency to divide people into saints and scoundrels and the incessant sensual excitements, the strong will, the domineering nature and (apparently) a genuine 'infernalism'. She had a heart capable of noble actions but no less capable of outbursts of blind passion, furious persecution and revenge.

THE RED AND THE BLACK

Dostoevsky's travels in Europe with Apollinaria Suslova provided him with material for one of his finest stories, *The Gambler*. The idea for this story did not come to him in 1863, as is generally believed, but much earlier. In 1859, while still in Semipalatinsk, he read a lively and interesting article entitled, 'From the Notes of a Gambler'. This was a study of customs in foreign casinos and at the same time a tale about the personal drama of a man who loved the hazards of the gaming tables of Europe's resorts. The author's name, Fyodor Dershau, was undoubtedly known to Dostoevsky. Dershau, Finnish by birth, was a prominent Petersburg writer who published magazines and miscellanies, chiefly about the Russian and Scandinavian North. Taking his cue from the articles of Belinsky and Herzen, he had invited contributions to his publications from leading journalists, among them Valerian Maikov, Apollon Grigoryev, Palm and Durov. At one time Petrashevsky had even dreamt of turning the *Finsky Vestnik*, one of Dershau's publications, into an organ of his own political circle.

Dershau's article on roulette appeared in the April 1859 issue of *Russkoe Slovo*, which had only a month earlier printed Dostoevsky's 'My Uncle's Dream'. The editors of *Russkoe Slovo*, Apollon Grigoryev and Y. P. Polonsky, most likely sent their magazine to the exiled writer, whom they already regarded as a regular contributor, at Semipalatinsk. The sketch entitled 'From the Notes of a Gambler' was a primary source for Dostoevsky's short novel *Roulettenberg*, the name of which was changed to *The Gambler* by the publisher Stellovsky. The novel was published in 1866 with the sub-title *From the Notes of a Young Man*.

It was in the summer of 1859, as we suppose, that Dostoevsky read Dershau's article, in which a detailed description of a foreign casino is combined with the classic story of the gambler who wins a huge fortune at roulette only to lose every penny of it again soon afterwards. We even have him nearly committing a terrible crime. A barber by trade, he is tempted to cut the throat of a customer and rob him of a large sum he had won the evening before.

This edifying tale reeked of melodrama, but the introduction to it was of more than ordinary interest. The progressive journalist described a world of easy money that was little known to the Russian reader and epitomized the money-oriented, private-ownership civilization of the West. This friend of the Petrashevskyites conveyed the tragedy that lay behind the glitter of gaming tables in Homburg, Wiesbaden, Nauheim, Baden-Baden and Geneva, where the seeds of frightful human disasters – poverty, dishonour and suicide – were unwittingly sown. He wrote with unfeigned satirical indignation of gambling dens, masquerading under the respectable name of recreational halls, where immaculate gentlemen, wearing medal ribbons in their lapels, sat down next to winning players and adroitly picked bills and gold from their pockets, then withdrew, whistling carelessly. He described some shocking episodes:

In Wiesbaden only very recently a desperate young man, who had lost his entire fortune, shot himself there in the casino before the eyes of numerous spectators, crowding round the roulette table. It is noteworthy that this sad event did not even interrupt the gambling. The man calling out the numbers went on turning the wheel with the same cold-bloodedness with which he ordered the attendant to clean off the green baize of the treacherous table onto which the brains had spurted from the dead gambler's shattered head.

All of this answered Dostoevsky's requirement for a contemporary plot with a strong social content and sudden changes of fortune. Dershau also depicted fortune's skilled favourites. Among the casino's avaricious, thieving crowds there were inventors of infallible systems for winning. These people were content with a moderate daily sum, a few friedrichsd'ors, but they always managed to win that sum by coolness, calculation and self-control. The English were particularly adept at this and they made a living in the resplendent gambling towns of south-western Europe for years by their skill at roulette. To Dostoevsky this was a revelation. So there was a safe way to win! He avidly read thousands of descriptions of roulette. From then on he dreamt nightly of breaking the bank at the fickle wheel. He was certain he possessed the cherished key to the secret of getting rich quick: a cool head, low stakes, no taking risks. Some fifteen years later he was to write in *A Raw Youth*: 'I am still convinced that by keeping a completely cool head and preserving acuteness of intelligence and calculation in gambling it must be possible to overcome the crudity of blind chance and win.'

Dostoevsky was not only interested in the techniques of winning. Gambling also gave him a new literary theme, full of passion, struggle and danger. He dreamed of writing a masterpiece, to be inspired by the unpredictable turns of human lives dictated by the evens and the odds, the red and the black, the zero and the first twelve. The subject opened up broad possibilities for philosophical reflection and the portrayal of bold characters. It was then that the story of an outstanding Russian in the international crowd at a fashionable European resort began to take shape in Dostoevsky's mind.

Dostoevsky remained an intemperate gambler for nearly ten whole years. As far back as in the 1840s he had been so fascinated by billiards that he had lost large sums of money and had come into contact with professional sharpers. In Siberia, after his release from hard labour, his dormant passion for gambling manifested itself still more strongly. One of the girls he tutored in Semipalatinsk recalled that: 'At one time Dostoevsky seemed addicted to gambling. People used to gamble a great deal here then.' Once Dostoevsky told his companions about an extraordinary game he had watched the previous evening. The game had made a strong impression on him. He paced the room rapidly as he talked about it, finishing excitedly: 'My, that was a hot game! It's rotten not to have any money. A devilish game like that is like quicksand. I see and understand how vile this monstrous passion is . . . yet it draws me, it sucks me in.'

The quicksand did indeed suck him in.

On his first trip abroad in the summer of 1862 he immediately went off to one of Germany's notorious gambling resorts and won ten thousand francs there before he even reached Paris. This was apparently in one of the small towns not far from the French border – Wiesbaden, Homburg. Baden-Baden – which became part of Dostoevsky's life for a decade and where he underwent the most overpowering and at times extremely painful experiences. The power of the passion that possessed him was stronger than any of the arguments of his mind: 'The worst thing is that my nature is base and too passionate. Everywhere and in everything I go the limit. All my life I have crossed the last line.' Gambling drew him irresistibly. It was a dangerous and destructive temptation: 'The important thing is the game itself. Do you know how it sucks you in? No, I swear to you that it is not only greed, although first of all I did need the money as money.'

On 8(20) September 1863, he wrote to his brother:

Dear Misha,

In Wiesbaden I *devised a system of playing*. I used it in the game and I immediately won ten thousand francs. The next morning I strayed from the system in the heat of the game and immediately lost all my money. In the evening I returned to the same system in all strictness and I soon won three thousand francs again without difficulty. Tell me, how could I help being carried away after this, how could I help believing that if I followed my system strictly I would have a fortune in my hands? And I need money so badly. For me, for you, for my wife, to write a novel. People win tens of thousands here without even trying. Yes, I went with the hope of saving us all and protecting myself from disaster.

In 1863, while Apollinaria Suslova waited for him in Paris, he again stopped in Wiesbaden for a few days, dreaming of winning a hundred thousand. He won ten thousand, four hundred francs immediately and made up his mind to leave the very next day without even calling at the casino, But his resolution failed and he lost more than half his winnings. He transferred a considerable part of the remaining five thousand francs to Petersburg, asking that it be turned over to his wife who was gravely ill. But several days later he wrote from Baden-Baden to his family that 'I have lost everything at roulette, literally everything', and asked them to return the money he had sent them as quickly as possible. His brother Mikhail did not conceal his indignation: 'Why send your winnings to Russia if the very next day they have to be sent back so you can lose them again?' And then: 'I cannot understand how you can gamble while travelling with a woman with whom you are in love!' Dostoevsky was to deal with this psychological problem in his story.

His first impressions began to settle into a clear-cut plot. He devised a 'rather good plan for a story' on his new topic and jotted down the first notes for it on odd scraps of paper. He wrote to Strakhov about it in a letter from Rome dated 18(30) September 1863. He was interested in a 'type of Russian expatriate' – a man of spontaneous nature, many-sided, although he had not yet completely found himself:

The chief thing is that all his vitality, all his strength, and all his reckless courage are extended in roulette. He is a gambler, and not a simple gambler, just as Pushkin's Covetous Knight is not a simple miser. In his own way, he is a poet, but he is ashamed of this poetry, for he is profoundly aware that it is base, though the necessity of risk ennobles him in his own eyes. The whole story is the story of his gambling in casinos for going on three years.

This is the first outline for *The Gambler*. Although it mentions *The Covetous Knight*, from which Dostoevsky drew inspiration more than once, the final version shows the even stronger influence of Pushkin's *The Queen of Spades*. The aged woman in this story, who knows a secret for winning fabulous sums, and the penurious gambler, who demands that fate hand him a boundless fortune, are reflected in the protagonists of *The Gambler*. In his memorial speech on Pushkin delivered in 1880 Dostoevsky explained Herman's character: 'what and how he must have felt when he staked his happiness on a single card, believing profoundly in that card, yet panting and trembling with intense emotion.' This is how Alexei Ivanovich, the hero of *The Gambler*, plays, staking his life on a card.

Dostoevsky did not regard gambling as shameful, particularly for an artist, who has to learn all aspects of life He was on the gambler's side, and as he told his second wife he had himself experienced many of his hero's emotions and impressions. He claimed that it was possible for a person to have a strong character, to prove this by his life, yet to lack the strength to overcome a passion for gambling. This was a drama in itself. He saw that the turning of the 'wheel of fortune' in the Rhineland towns held as much human interest as the Siberian 'convict bathhouse'.

The author of *Notes from the House of the Dead* saw in the gambling scene the same frightful world of vice and crime he had observed so closely, only it was not hemmed in by the airless convict barracks, filled with the clank of chains and the roar of fearful oaths, but flourishing beneath the gilded arches of an enormous palace, where huge fortunes were lost and lives were ruined in the course of a few hours, to the intoxicating strains of dance and concert music.

He wrote to Strakhov from Rome in the same letter of 18 September 1863:

> If *The House of the Dead* won the public's attention because it was a portrayal of convicts, who had never been depicted graphically before, then this story will be sure to win attention as a graphic and very detailed depiction of roulette. It may turn out not a bad story at all. *The House of the Dead* was interesting, you know. And this is a description of a kind of hell, a kind of convict bathhouse. I would like to paint such a picture and will try to do so.

In the summer of 1866 Dostoevsky outlined a new plan for *The Gambler*, very different from the one he had devised in 1863 while he was abroad. At that time he had planned to write a story of about forty pages; now it was to be a novel of about three hundred pages. The short novel had been a favourite form of his since he wrote *Poor Folk*. He preferred it to the short story, found it more congenial, and did better at it. Only this extended form gave him enough scope to develop the material derived from his own experience in the casinos, and the agonizing image of Apollinaria Suslova. 'I have drawn up a plan for an extremely satisfactory little novel with even some signs of character portrayal,' he wrote.

The 'little novel' became a psychologically profound story, and the 'signs of character portrayal' developed into

finished pictures of real live Russians and Europeans typical
of their day. The life and customs of a German gambling
house provided the social background and the framework for
a portrayal of unrestrained passions. Dostoevsky exploded the
myth about the splendour of these international clubs and
the irreproachable self-control of the financial aristocracy
who filled them. 'There is no splendour in these disgusting
halls; and there are no heaps of gold lying around on the
tables; in fact, there is hardly ever a glimmer of gold to be
seen.' The general impression is not of 'splendour' but of
shame. Everything is 'somehow morally corrupt and
filthy'. 'This roulette scum', 'all these dregs, trembling over
a gulden', looking for an opportunity to steal someone's
stake, are revolting. And so are the croupiers, as they maintain order and protect the interests of the bank, with its
traps and thievery. Dostoevsky repudiates the notion of any
aesthetic values connected with this den of thieves, with its
cynical exposure of the jungle instincts of the capitalist
world and its unbridled lust for easy money, for fortunes
quickly snatched, for big piles suddenly amassed. In a
society built on the cult of money, and held together by
the fever for gold, the amorality of this cunningly organized
mass pillage takes away any beauty or grandeur from these
Rhineland palaces.

The Gambler, dictated in twenty-six days, between the
writing of the fifth and sixth parts of *Crime and Punishment*, is
one of Dostoevsky's finest works. It bears the imprint of the
extraordinary surge of his creative energy in 1866, a crucial
year for him, for it marked the beginning of a new period in
his private and professional life. The story, though concise,
raises major contemporary issues of the day, highlighting
the pernicious role of money in bourgeois society and its
get-rich-quick market – the gambling houses. It contains
brilliant satirical sketches of Western capitalist man,
'obsessed with acquisitiveness', and contrasts him with the
broad and free nature of the Russian, whom chance has

brought to a foreign country but whose temperament remains true to the vastness of his native land. It is also one of the most interesting of Dostoevsky's autobiographical sketches; its characters and plot embody his own intense and gloomy impressions of England, Germany and France. It was a companion piece in fiction to his angry journalistic 'Essay on the Bourgeois' and 'Baal'.

*

The most powerfully drawn image in *The Gambler* is Polina,* a Russian girl with an unique character, proud, courageous, independent, in love with life, intelligent and passionate, a tigress and torturer. 'She is capable of all the horrors of life and of passion.' Such was Dostoevsky's view of Apollinaria Suslova. The Polina in the story is a General's stepdaughter and remains in her stepfather's house after her mother's death as governess to her young half-brother and half-sister. She is attracted to the children's tutor, Alexei Ivanovich, a witty and gifted young man, a university candidate, who is very much in love with her. The General is planning to marry Mlle Blanche, a dazzling Paris courtesan, with whom he is infatuated, but his affairs are in complete disorder and he appeals for financial assistance to a young French moneylender, named de Grieux. De Grieux lends him large sums of money on the security of the houses and estate of the General's elderly aunt, who is expected to die any day. In Alexei Ivanovich's absence Polina agrees to marry de Grieux, whose 'perfect, beautiful build' has captivated her. This provokes a great diatribe from Alexei Ivanovich on 'The Frenchman and the young Russian lady'.

The Frenchman soon reveals his vile and calculating nature. He abandons Polina when he discovers that his expectations of a big dowry were unfounded, explaining that he has deducted fifty thousand roubles from her stepfather's debt to him as a present to her. Polina is outraged and

* The name Polina is actually a diminutive of Apollinaria.

resolves to return an equivalent sum to him. Her only salvation now is the chivalrous Mr Astley, who has succumbed to her beauty and intelligence. Alexei Ivanovich warns Polina's new English friend that, 'It will be a long time before Miss Polina is able to make up her mind to prefer you to the blackguard de Grieux. She may appreciate you, become your friend, open up her heart to you, but it will nevertheless be the detestable blackguard, the vile and petty usurer de Grieux who will reign in that heart.'

Such was Dostoevsky's new study of the West European bourgeois. Through his Gambler's lips Dostoevsky satirizes 'the German method of getting rich through honest labour'. At a *table d'hôte* at a German health resort, the Russian wanderer and carefree spender ridicules the systematic way Goppe and Co. save gulden from generation to generation so that five generations hence they will have accumulated many millions and feel entitled to 'judge the whole world and promptly condemn the guilty, that is, those who are not quite like them'. To the Franco-German type of businessman Dostoevsky contrasts Russians with their generous and unrestrained character. There is Polina, and Alexei Ivanovich, and, most remarkable of all, the truly epic figure of 'granny' Antonida Vasilievna Tarasevicheva, a magnificent old Moscow lady of merchant stock, cheerful, active, imperious, generous and domineering. This is a masterly portrait of Dostoevsky's maternal grandfather's second wife Olga Yakovlevna Antipova, an elderly lady who still enjoyed spending extravagantly. In *The Gambler* the old lady's fascination with roulette costs her a hundred thousand roubles; having on the very brink of the grave tasted the temptations of gambling, she then returns to her native land to expiate her sin through prayer.

The shadow of roulette also haunts the life of the humble tutor. To save Polina, who has asked him to get her the money she needs, he gambles desperately. He feels as if his life is breaking in two: 'My whole life was at stake.'

The fearless gambler is victorious, and he wins two hundred thousand francs. But a frightful emotional let-down is in store for him. His absorption in gambling, winning and gold has dimmed his formerly boundless love for Polina! 'I swear I was sorry for Polina, but, strangely, the moment I touched the gambling table yesterday and began to rake in packets of money, my love seemed to recede to the background. I could not stand the money and became dizzy.'

This had been the tragedy of Dostoevsky on his Italian travels with Apollinaria Suslova. In amazement, Apollinaria watched the great man become obsessed with a mania for gambling and carried away by the all-out battle in this pitiless kingdom of money. Dostoevsky himself noted with horror that his passion for the enchanting woman was weakening and dwindling away, and that roulette with its spell-binding numbers was taking complete possession of his life.

In the story Polina, perceiving this terrible change, rejects the help of the man she really loves and who has just won two hundred thousand francs for her.

'I won't take your money,' she said contemptuously.

'What do you mean? How is that?' I cried. 'Polina, why not?'

'I do not accept money without giving something in return.'

'I offer it to you as a friend. I offer you my life.'

She turned a long, penetrating gaze on me, as if wishing to stab me with a look.

'You are offering too much,' she said, smiling. 'De Grieux's mistress is not worth fifty thousand francs.'

The night passes in stormy changes of mood. In the morning she resumes the previous's evening's conversation.

'Now give me my fifty thousand francs.'

'Polina, you're starting again,' I began.

'You haven't changed your mind, have you? Perhaps you regret it now?'

The twenty-five thousand florins, counted out yesterday, lay on the table. I took them and handed them to her.

'Well, it's mine, now, isn't it?' she inquired fiercely, holding the money in her hands.

'It has always been yours,' I said.

'Good, then, here are your fifty thousand francs.' She swung her arm and flung the packet at me. It struck me (painfully) in the face and the money scattered on the floor. Polina ran out of the room.

Thus did Dostoevsky combine the story's two basic themes: the power of money in contemporary society, and the power of love in the souls of his chosen few. Polina loves no one but her 'gambler', and she loves him with all her heart and for all time. In the last conversation that Mr Astley has with Alexei Ivanovich he tells him that he has 'come to Homburg at Polina's express request to see you, to have a long, heart-to-heart talk with you so I can tell her everything – your feelings, thoughts, hopes and recollections! Why, she loved you. She still loves you!'

In the year and a half since their parting, the modest tutor of a general's children has gone completely downhill. He has worked as a valet, as a servant, has been in a debtors' prison, from which he was delivered by an unknown benefactor, has sought employment as a teacher of Russian, has gambled, risked, lost, gambled away whatever he won, and kept hoping that his luck would change some day. The end of the story may be open to conjecture and the future unpredictable, but the hero's destruction is as inevitable as an ancient tragedy.

Polina falls dangerously ill on the day on which Alexei Ivanovich has an unprecedented win, and she takes refuge at Mr Astley's. Astley calls a doctor and summons a relative to care for her. He says to the gambler, 'If she dies I will hold you responsible.' Shortly afterwards, Astley takes her to Switzerland, where she is ill for a long time, then to the north of England, where she stays with his mother and his sister. The old lady dies and leaves Polina a sum of seven thousand pounds. It seems as though Polina will soon become Mrs Astley. But the only man to whom her heart has ever belonged is the impecunious Russian of outstanding talents and noble heart, the unfortunate Alexei Ivanovich, a character who is especially dear to us, because in him Dostoevsky drew one of the finest portraits of himself in the turbulent decade when he was obsessed with roulette.

XI

The Demise of Epokha

THE SECOND MAGAZINE

THE whole story of the Dostoevsky brothers' second magazine is one of a lingering death. The attempt to preserve the
excellent *Vremya* under a new name proved futile. *Epokha*
came into the world still-born, and all Fyodor Dostoevsky's
editorial talent could not make it as brilliant a magazine as
the first.[1] But he put up a hard and courageous, even
dramatic, fight for the life of the second journal of the
pochva movement.

On 15 November 1863 Mikhail Dostoevsky submitted an
application to the Minister of Internal Affairs, Valuev, for
permission to publish a magazine, to be called *Pravda*
(*Truth*), in 1864 so that the subscribers to *Vremya*, which had
been compelled to stop publication in May 1863, might be
reimbursed. The policy of the new periodical, the application said, would be 'fully Russian', that is, patriotic and
nationalist. This was a promise that the magazine would
adhere to official views. The government took up an
equivocal attitude. They gave Mikhail permission to
publish the new magazine (under a different name, *Epokha*)
but it was the end of January by the time this came through,
and it was no longer possible to obtain subscriptions for the
entire year. The permit required the new magazine to be
'irreproachable in direction' and put it under special
surveillance. Under the circumstances *Epokha* was unable to
get out its first issue before 21 March 1864. This was an
important factor in the early and inevitable collapse of the
magazine.

Epokha's fate was inevitably affected by the major

historical crises of the time. Nikolai Strakhov has pointed out that a profound change took place in the public mood in 1863: 'The tremendous intoxicating upsurge of progressive feeling produced by the emancipation of the serfs in 1861 had been succeeded by an abrupt sobering-up and some perplexity.' There was a decisive turn towards reaction on the part of the government and of the public, and this determined the policy *Epokha* was to follow – that of a complete break with nihilism and open debate with *Sovremennik*.

The new magazine announced that it was the editors' firm intention to pursue a policy in the spirit of 'M. Dostoevsky's former publication', and to discuss social and zemstvo* developments from a Russian, a national, standpoint. This was in the tradition of the 'soil' movement, but moving further towards right-wing Slavophilism. *Epokha* sharply opposed any attack on the existing system, rejected social criticism and would not publish political satire. It stressed what it considered Russia's unique place in history and it regarded the 'all-obliterating' civilization of the West warily: to succumb to abstractions and try to live in an alien way (that is, according to the teachings of socialism) was wrong. All this reinforced the magazine's pro-establishment tendencies, and left no room for new, fresh, vital judgements on the painful features of real life.

However, in one respect *Epokha* played a positive role. It held that Russian literature is the medium through which uniqueness and originality of the people's life find expression, and it adopted a policy of publishing works by distinguished writers and favourites of the reading public, such as Turgenev, Ostrovsky, Fyodor Dostoevsky himself, Apollon Maikov and Plescheev. The political viewpoint of *Epokha* may have been conservative, but its attitude to Russian literature was a creative one. In general, though, *Epokha*'s objectives were mistaken, and the magazine hardly managed

* The *Zemstvos*, or elective councils for local self government of provinces and districts, were instituted by Imperial *Ukase* (edict) in 1864.

to survive the first and only year of its existence. It died a natural death with its thirteenth issue, for February 1865, which did not appear until 22 March.

Such was the short life and speedy demise of *Epokha*. 1864 was the 'terrible year' Dostoevsky's life, and the magazine's failure was only one of the reasons. He suffered severe personal bereavements in the course of that year. It also brought the definitive turning-point in his ideology. He took a stand which has always proved disastrous, even for the greatest of writers: he came out in defence of reaction and against the progressive forces of his day. This was probably the ultimate tragedy of his whole tormented life. As an artist, Dostoevsky retained his creative talent, but as a fighter and political thinker he had been blown back by the gale of history into the camp of the dark and sinister forces of the age.

This change represented more than the private tragedy of one great writer. It is possibly one of the greatest disasters to have befallen Russian literature. To grasp fully the magnitude of the tragedy and the lamentable consequences of the loss to socialism one need only imagine for a moment what a mighty epic someone with Dostoevsky's understanding of human passion and of tragedy might have left the world had he continued to live by the socialist principles that he cherished in his youth. But Dostoevsky was destroyed by the epoch in which he lived. He no longer had it in him to follow the free path of a Herzen, a Heine or a Victor Hugo. The death grip of Tsarism had stifled the freedom-loving dreams of Dostoevsky's youth, had cruelly destroyed that youth, and had tied him imperiously to its own ironbound cause. The Russian autocracy probably won its darkest victory when it succeeded in tearing this tremendous creative talent away from the literature of the 'forthcoming rebirth of the world', in which he had believed so ardently as a young disciple of Belinsky and Speshnev embarking on his literary career.

A DECLARATION OF PRINCIPLE

The first issue of *Epokha* carried the first instalment of *Notes from Underground*. In it Dostoevsky seemed to have resolved to abandon restraint for the moment and to express the agonizing scepticism that had been growing in him for two decades. *Notes from Underground* is one of his most revealing works. Never again did he expose so fully and so frankly the most secret recesses of his soul. It is his first criticism of socialism and his first open proclamation of egocentric and amoral individualism. With contempt and blasphemous ridicule, he desecrates everything that he had revered in the years of his closeness with Belinksy and Petrashevsky. It is as if he were venting the bitterness of his cruel experience as a convict on the spiritual leaders of his youth, attacking them with epithets and political diatribes. He says that the romanticism and socialism that fed his imagination and mind when he was a young man was 'beauty and nobleness, pressing hard against the back of my head for nigh on forty years'. He describes the leaders of Utopian socialism ironically as 'lovers of the human race', well-behaved and sensible men and other-worldly romanticists; he dubs their teachings 'systems for happiness', theories that try to make men believe that certain interests are their true, normal interests, whereas in reality such interests conflict with the irrepressible instincts of man's inner freedom and inborn independence. He denies once and for all that people can be organized in accordance with a preconceived plan because, he says, man's nature is irrational. He opposes to the Fourierists' Utopian systems a belief in unlimited freedom for human desires, the legitimacy of man's passion for destruction and chaos, the inviolability of the caprices and destructive arbitrariness of individual will. Once again Fourierism is in confrontation with Stirner, but this time the victory goes to the latter.

Dostoevsky conceived *Notes from Underground* as a

polemic against Chernyshevsky. The revolutionary democrats believed in the construction of a rational society
through the establishment of a socialist system. The *pochva*
adherents valued above all things the inner culture of the
individual, the ethical standards of behaviour and moral
suffering. The 'theory of rational self-interest' could not
satisfy all the needs of human nature, they believed life
could not be regulated by reason alone – there were also
freedom and will. The underground man would instinctively
refuse to accept the social theories, systems and classifications
which are supposed one day to benefit everybody. Dostoevsky
has no time for such utilitarianism and prefers 'freedom of
desire', 'the most advantageous advantage'.

None of this could do anything to shake the revolutionary
doctrines of Chernyshevsky – the principle of mass-struggle,
of philosophic materialism as the active force of life, of the
liberation of the toilers from every kind of slavery, of the
transfer of state power into the hands of the people, of new
foundations for the imaginative work that would create a
realistic art belonging to the whole people. A doctrine of
such majestic dimensions could not be shaken by the
critical efforts of the leaders of the 'soil' movement, which
only served to show that it was impossible for them to refute
the theory of rational self-interest, the new ethnic and
aesthetic of a 'prophet of genius'.

The ferocity and bitterness with which Dostoevsky
attacked Chernyshevsky's novel *What Is To Be Done?* stemmed
from the same acute crisis in his political thinking that had
caused him to reject the socialist humanism in which he had
believed in the 1840s. Dostoevsky now stood for untrammelled individualism; he now opposed his own individual
will to world history. Dostoevsky's hero regarded Utopian
socialism, with its promise of universal happiness, as a
beautiful lie, divorced from reality, from contemporary
Petersburg with its dismal streets, wet snow and ruined
girls.

Dostoevsky's attack on the revolutionary democrats culminates in the episode of an encounter between the underground 'paradoxalist' and a 'fallen woman'. Nekrasov had addressed a noble invitation to one of these outcasts:

> Come to my home, boldly and freely
> With your full rights as lady of the house.

The men-of-the-soil movement did not share these ethical notions of the revolutionary democrats. It was their new morality more than anything else that had provoked the conservative groups into their violent attack on *What Is To Be Done?* The rejection of antiquated forms of feudal marriage had been represented as the destruction of the family, the cornerstone of contemporary society.

Dostoevsky knew of a similar episode in which Apollon Grigoryev had been involved not long before. He had fallen in love in 1859 with a girl from the world of the rejected. Her name was Maria Fyodorovna Dubrovskaya and she was known as the 'young lady from Ustyng', after the town of her birth. Daughter of an alcoholic provincial schoolteacher, a sceptic and freethinker, she had an inquiring mind and passionate nature. Grigoryev was as much attracted by her desire for a new life as by her unusual looks, of which he wrote:

> A profile like a gipsy's
> A sorrowful beauty.

For a long time he dreamed of 'saving' her, of reforming her and making her part of his own life. In 1861 he carried her off to Orenburg, but the past, as well as the clinging mire of the present, proved too much for him. His last hope of happiness vanished. They parted in 1862, apparently for ever.[2] In an epilogue to his poem dedicated to that greatly sinning Maria there is a description of a 'Nekrasov Night' (the expression is Grigoryev's own) – winter, hunger, a sick child . . . in the style of 'Whether I am driving down a dark street at night'.*

In *Notes from Underground* the motifs of impassioned searching and hopeless separation acquire overtones of cruelty, ridicule and harshness. Dostoevsky does not direct his polemical attack against the wretched girl, for whom he clearly feels compassion, but against her irritable and weak-willed companion, who, intelligent as he may be, is helpless in the face of the universal phenomenon of human suffering. Who is the nameless hero of *Notes from Underground*? He is a solitary, secretive and cynical thinker, who hates all the highly successful 'progressivists' who win fame, he says, for advanced principles in which they themselves do not believe and which he, inhabitant of the underground, regards as a trap and a lie.

Dostoevsky wrote in his manuscript notebooks:

I am proud to have been the first to have portrayed the real man of the *Russian majority* and to have exposed the ugly and tragic side of his nature . . . His tragedy is in his awareness of ugliness. I alone depicted the tragedy of the underground, which is the suffering, the self-condemnation, the knowledge that there is something better and that it cannot be achieved, and, what is more important, the intense conviction of these unfortunates that all people are alike and that there is therefore no point in trying to improve.

Dostoevsky labelled his unprecedented protagonist an 'anti-hero'. The underground man's story is the story of how he 'shirked away his life in a corner in the underground because of moral debauchery, the deficiency of the environment, dissociation from the living, and carefully nurtured malice'. This solitude increases his mistrustfulness and hardens his heart. 'They won't let me – I can't be good.' At last this man, who has deprived himself of the right to

* A well-known poem by Nekrasov. For text and English translation, see *The Penguin Book of Russian Verse*.

simple human happiness, has found the key to his drama. That is the reason why he has been cut off from everything heroic, from everything human, from the struggle, from righteousness, from altruism, from everything whereby life derives strength.

There is a heroine in the story. She, too, is contrasted to the 'lofty and the beautiful'. She belongs to all men, but she has fallen in love with one man, even though, as it happens, he is the most unworthy of them all. This is her redemption; it leads her to 'living life', to the hope and dream of a better life, of a family. Her name is Liza and she deserves to be remembered.

On one occasion the underground 'paradoxicalist' is insulted publicly, and he vents his mortification on Liza. He torments her with descriptions of scenes from a pure life and of maternal happiness, forever denied to her because of her profession. He paints a compelling picture of what is in store for her: progress from one den of vice to another, from bad to worse, until she ends up in a cellar on Sennaya, prey to incurable diseases, beaten, in debt to the brothel keeper, ill with malignant consumption – then death and a pit filled with water. She bursts into terrible sobs as she listens to these predictions. Even her pitiless tormentor feels confused and embarrassed.

A few days later she comes to him with words of hope, with a yearning for a pure life with the whispered confession: 'I want to get away from this altogether.' All this strikes him as sentimental play-acting and infuriates him. He belongs entirely to the 'underground' and frenziedly reproaches the unhappy girl for her good impulse.

But then a strange thing occurred. Liza, whom I had insulted and crushed, understood much more than I had guessed. She understood from all this what a woman will always understand first of all if she is sincerely in love; she understood that I myself am unhappy.

In his portrayal of Liza, Dostoevsky transcends satire and shows himself a master at conveying the subtlest qualities of a person's inner life. Liza has become the heroine, and the underground man has been abased and crushed. But he replies to her elation and tenderness with new insults, now very much like revenge. Liza goes out, ignoring his appeals and retaining her own dignity as a human being. Only after she has gone does he notice the crumpled banknote she has thrown on the table, 'the very money he had pressed into her hand a moment ago' so as to cut off her path to hope, purity, resurrection, humanity and love.

Notes from Underground was a prologue to Dostoevsky's long novels. It was a direct study for *Crime and Punishment*, which it immediately preceded. It is not surprising that it made a strong impression on Apollon Grigoryev, who felt that in it Dostoevsky had at last found his own individual style. 'Keep on writing in this manner', was the dying critic's advice to his novelist friend.

Dostoevsky followed that advice. *Crime and Punishment* was a more profound and elaborate version of the 1864 *Notes from Underground*, written in the same style, with philosophical problems woven into the protagonist's private drama. Like the underground man, Raskolnikov withdraws from the world so that he can freely criticize the world's unshakeable laws in accordance with his own unrestrained desires. Exhausted intellectually and emotionally by his isolation from people, he seeks salvation in a street girl, from whom he receives the great gift of sympathy and compassion in return for the mental tortures he inflicts on her. Several of the basic situations in *Crime and Punishment* are direct descendants of *Notes from Underground*, complicated by the tragedy of a murder and all the complex of psychological and moral problems arising from it. From now on all Dostoevsky's novels would be constructed in this fashion – ideologically and tragically.

The author himself defined the rules of composition of his

story: 'It is exceedingly strange in tone, and sharp and savage, too; people may not like that. Therefore it must be softened and carried through by poetry.' *Poetry* is Liza. Her image brings light to all the dark corners of despair.

Originally, the story was to have been divided into three chapters, each differing in content but internally united. The first chapter was to have been a polemical and philosophical monologue, the second a dramatic episode, preparing the ground for the third, the disastrous conclusion. In a letter to his brother about the forthcoming publication of *Notes from Underground*, Dostoevsky wrote:

> The story is divided into three chapters. The first will be something like thirty-six pages. Do you really think it can be printed separately? It will evoke ridicule, for it has no juice without the other two (main) chapters. You know what modulation is in music. It is exactly the same here. The first chapter appears to be idle chatter, but in the next two chapters the chatter suddenly erupts into unforeseen disaster.[4]

Dostoevsky uses great finesse in applying the metaphor of musical modulation to the plan of a literary composition. The story is constructed on the basis of an artistic counterpoint. The psychological torture inflicted on the fallen girl in the second chapter answers to the insult inflicted on her tormentor in the first, and at the same time her meekness is in contrast to his feelings of offended and angered vanity. This is indeed contrapuntal. It is different voices singing the same theme, with a difference. It is polyphony, displaying the manifold images of life and the manifold complexities of human existence. 'Everything in life is counterpoint, that is, contrast,' as M. I. Glinka (one of Dostoevsky's favourite composers) says in his memoirs.

Thus did Dostoevsky present his rejection of his early dreams of a future socialist system. *Notes from Underground* was the first of several long novels which expressed his ceaseless search for some principle of a renewal of the old world other than the great social ideas that had illumined his youth.

THREE OBITUARIES

The move in 1859 from Semipalatinsk to Petersburg turned out to be a real disaster for Dostoevsky's wife, Maria Dmitrievna. She found herself regarded as an invalid and a poor relation by her husband's family, and treated with suspicion and hostility. Keenly aware of their dislike, she responded with all her resources of irritability and malice. All her life she was convinced that her brother-in-law Mikhail was her secret enemy, and only on her deathbed did she express a desire to make peace with him. Her husband's intensive activity during publication of his two magazines passed her by entirely. Dostoevsky had his own companions, with whom she did not belong.

Worst of all, however, was the effect on her health. In the dry air of Siberia the incursion of her illness was comparatively slow. In damp Petersburg the pulmonary process took a sharp turn for the worse, developing into 'malignant consumption', to use the medical terminology of the time. By the winter of 1862-3 her condition was considered dangerous and the doctors insisted that she go somewhere else to live. 'Having survived the spring, that is, not having died in Petersburg,' Dostoevsky wrote, 'my wife left Petersburg for the summer, and perhaps for a longer time, and I accompanied her away from Petersburg, where she could no longer stand the climate.'

At first Vladimir, at that time a sparsely populated, quiet provincial town, situated in a forested area, was selected as the place where her already doomed life might be prolonged. But apparently here, too, conditions were unsuitable for her treatment, and in the autumn of 1863 the dying woman was moved to Moscow, where Dostoevsky's brother-in-law Dr A. P. Ivanov undertook to care for her. At that time koumiss* was standard treatment for tuberculosis, but it could no longer help Maria Dmitrievna. Towards the end the sick woman's mind was affected: 'She had strange hallucinations. At times she would begin to whisper: "Devils, see the devils!" And she would not calm down until the doctor opened the window and pretended in her presence to drive the "devils" out of the room.'

Spring came and with it the customary aggravation of the disease. In the middle of April Dostoevsky wrote his brother: 'Yesterday Maria Dmitrievna had a very bad haemorrhage: blood gushed from her throat and flooded her chest and she began to choke.' Dostoevsky's wife died on 15 April 1864. This was the epilogue to Dostoevsky's most agonizing romance. He later wrote of it:

She loved me boundlessly, and I, too, loved her immeasurably, but our life together was not happy. Although we were positively unhappy together – because of her passionate, over-sensitive and morbidly imaginative nature – we could not stop loving each other. In fact, the unhappier we were, the more attached we became to each other.

As he sat beside the cold body of his wife on 16 April 1864 Dostoevsky jotted down in his notebook some reflections on the meaning of love, marriage and the individual's mission on earth:

April 16. Masha is lying on the table. Will I ever see Masha again?

To love another as one does oneself, as Christ's teachings require, is an impossibility. The law of the individual on earth prevents it. *Ego* is the obstacle.

And so, on earth man strives for an ideal that is contrary to his nature. When he finds he cannot achieve the ideal, that is, if he has not sacrificed his Ego to love of people or of another being

* Koumiss is a drink made out of fermented mare's milk, used by the nomads of the steppes.

(Masha and I), he suffers, and he calls this condition sin. And so a man must suffer constantly; this suffering is counterweighed by the heavenly pleasure of striving to carry out the behest, that is, of sacrificing. This is what earthly equilibrium is, otherwise the earth would be meaningless.

There is a lot of mysticism here, but one thing is clear – in his own way Dostoevsky had truly loved the dead woman and her death was a tragedy for him. Some eighteen months later he said his final requiem for her in his portrait of Katerina Ivanovna Marmeladova in *Crime and Punishment*, one of the finest passages he ever wrote.

Dostoevsky repeated many of the circumstances of Maria Dmitrievna's life in the story and character of Marmeladov's tormented spouse, though as always art transmuted the raw facts of reality. Katerina Ivanovna's carefree youth, her marriage to an inveterate alcoholic, 'hopeless poverty', the contraction of tuberculosis, the outbursts of malice and floods of penitent tears, were drawn from a reality that he knew well. He even included touches from Maria Dmitrievna's letters from Kuznetsk; for example, on the day of Marmeladov's death Katerina Ivanovna accepts 'alms', a green three-rouble note. Even in appearance Katerina Ivanovna resembles Dostoevsky's first wife in the period just before her death:

This was a woman who had become appallingly thin. She was slender, rather tall, and shapely. She still had beautiful brown hair, and her cheeks were flushed with red spots. She paced her small room, pressing her hands to her breast. Her lips were dry and cracked, and she breathed nervously and unevenly. Her eyes glistened as if she had fever, but the look in them was sharp and fixed. This consumptive, overwrought face made a painful impression in the last light of a flickering candle end.

This was how Dostoevsky remembered his first helpmate, in the Rembrandt lighting of a Petersburg apartment, with deepening shadows flitting across her hollow cheeks, setting off her fixedly gazing, burning eyes, a martyr, dying on life's scaffold – such was Dostoevsky's funeral offering on his wife's grave.

'A Few Words About Mikhail Mikhailovich'

'Troubles walk in long lines,' says a Russian proverb that goes back to the days of serfdom. This peasant wisdom often applied to Dostoevsky's life, but especially in 1864. Hardly had Dostoevsky's wife been buried than it was discovered that Mikhail was seriously ill. The illness had crept up on him slowly and unobserved. At first his liver inflammation had not alarmed anyone and he had continued to work hard on current issues of *Epokha*. But gradually the pain grew worse. He became worried and irritable. In June the doctors warned that there was danger, but the editor-in-chief of the resurrected magazine would not stop working. 'He kept on working even on the eve of his death; and the disease suddenly became hopeless.' Mikhail Dostoevsky died on 10 July 1864. Of all his family Dostoevsky had been closest to his elder brother, his chief helper and associate (except during the years of exile, when Mikhail was extremely cautious in his relations with this younger brother, who had been 'deprived of all civic rights').

They were not alike in character. It was only when he was very young that Mikhail had been interested in poetry and had believed it to be his vocation. He wrote to his father in 1837: 'Let them take everything away from me, let them leave me naked, but let them give me Schiller and I will forget the whole world. He who believes in beauty is already happy.' But life very soon cut this romantic period short. He married young and, burdened with a family, turned from writing intimate lyrical poetry to earning money as a contributor to the fiction and criticism columns of Petersburg magazines.

The turbulent year of 1849, when his brother was convicted, affected his life, too. Dostoevsky referred to this in a short article he dedicated to him in the June 1864 issue of *Epokha*, entitled 'A Few Words About Mikhail Mikhailovich Dostoevsky'. The article contains the praise customary under the circumstances, and is by no means authentically biographical. 'Once upon a time, in his youth, he was a most impassioned and dedicated Fourierist,' the younger brother wrote, though passion and opposition were always alien to Mikhail, who, while he attended the Petrashevsky Fridays, never spoke in the discussions and was considered extremely restrained, calculating and cautious.

Mikhail's role in the Petrashevsky trial is not at all clear. He was arrested in May 1849 but was released in June on the basis of a Police Department resolution that read: 'Not only did Retired Second Lieutenant M. M. Dostoevsky not commit any crimes against the government, but he even counteracted them.' He was rewarded for this by His Majesty's Chancery. A letter he wrote to the Chief of the Third Department, Dubelt, has come down to us:

Your Excellency
Leonti Vasilievich,
    Sir,
It is my privilege to reply to Your Excellency's kind letter of the 16th of this month. I received your most generous grant of two hundred roubles in silver on the 28th of this month.
With deep respect,
Your Excellency's most obedient servant,
                    Mikhail Dostoevsky
                    July 30, 1849

Andrei Dostoevsky, the third brother, also arrested in April 1849 but soon released because he had nothing at all to do with the affair, wrote in his memoirs that there had been rumours in public and even civil service circles that one of the three brothers had betrayed his brothers in the Petrashevsky case and had thereby come out of the affair untouched. This could not have been Fyodor, who was deported to hard labour. It could not have been Andrei, who had never had anything to do with the Petrashevsky society at all and never received a Tsarist reward for wrongful arrest.[5] There are several mysterious pages in the records of the political trial that have still to be researched and elucidated.

In the obituary Dostoevsky wrote he praised highly his brother's skill as editor of serious monthly magazines. Actually, he was attributing to Mikhail, whose literary talents were modest, his own lively, ardent and creative qualities as a brilliant journalist, philosopher-publicist, powerful satirist and debater, an often trenchant pamphleteer and a master of parody. The man officially designated as editor and publisher of *Vremya* and *Epokha* was mainly the business manager of those publications and had very little to do with their policies or ideological leadership. Mikhail did not claim to be more than a merchant. (In the 1850s he was in fact the owner of a tobacco factory.) Dostoevsky once described the real structure of the editorial board in a letter to Wrangel: 'You know, I was the one who started *Vremya*, not my brother. I directed it and edited it.' This was even more true of *Epokha*. Mikhail Dostoevsky was merely a capable translator who in his day produced good Russian versions of Schiller's *Die Raüber*, *Don Carlos* and *Reineke-Fuchs*. This was the extent of his contribution to Russian literature.

His death spelled complete ruin for his family and was a fatal blow to the great literary enterprise that had been created by the talents of his brother, Apollon Grigoryev, Strakhov and Serov, who had now lost their publisher.

Only three hundred roubles remained after my brother's death, and that was used to bury him. There was a debt of nearly twenty-five thousand roubles. The magazine's credit dried up. There wasn't a kopek with which to publish it, and six issues were still due and would cost a minimum of eighteen thousand roubles, in addition to which fifteen thousand roubles were needed to satisfy creditors. That was a total of thirty-three thousand roubles just to finish the year and survive until the next subscription campaign. His family was thrown on the world literally destitute – I was their sole hope and they all, widow and children, clustered round me, looking to me for salvation. I had loved my brother infinitely – could I have abandoned them?

The only practical thing to do, Dostoevsky himself realized, was to stop publication of the magazine and make a living by his pen. Yet because he wished to save his brother's honourable name and satisfy the creditors in full, he decided to continue publishing *Epokha*, hoping by sheer will-power to make it one of the best magazines in Russia.

He recalled in 1868: 'Everything depended on the magazine then. If it were successful all debts would be paid and the family would be delivered from poverty. Not to have continued the magazine would have been a crime.' The writers who had been working with the Dostoevsky brothers on both their magazines resolved to help.

'*A Russian Hamlet*'

Apollon Grigoryev worked with special enthusiasm. In less than six months he contributed to *Epokha* articles on the Russian theatre, two open letters to Fyodor Dostoevsky on 'The Paradoxes of Organic Criticism', and new chapters of his *My Literary and Ethical Peregrinations*, remarkable literary memoirs about the ideological and poetic currents of the day. In July 1864, however, he was thrown into a debtor's prison, not for the first time. He tried to continue to work for *Epokha* there, but found prison life unbearable. He fell ill and 'was going mad' from melancholy. Dostoevsky visited him on 21 August. Grigoryev implored his editor and friend to purchase his freedom, for which some one hundred roubles were required. 'If *Epokha* needs me, then make the sacrifice. Save me, get me out!' A few days later he sent a note to Dostoevsky asking for at least a little money as advance payment for literary work because his clothes were in tatters and he would have to pay a tailor fifteen or twenty roubles to make it possible for him to appear in the street.

On 2 September he summed up the sad results of his twenty years as a writer in 'A Brief Service Record as a Remembrance to my Old and New Friends'. The brief autobiography read like a will or deathbed farewell to 'dear friends'. It concluded with the words: 'Of course, my purpose in writing this was not to arouse pity for myself, a superfluous man, but to show that this superfluous man has always been fanatically loyal to his obdurate convictions.' The eternal Don Quixote, or the hero of La Mancha as he called himself, a wandering sophist, the last romanticist, was about to depart from literature, and from life. On 21 September, after two months in prison, Apollon was told that an unknown woman had purchased his freedom for him. He left the Tarasov debtor's prison on 22 September. On 25 September 1864, he died of a stroke.

On 28 September the man who had founded 'organic' criticism and the author of *A Hungarian Gipsy Girl*, which a great poet of another generation, Alexander Blok, called 'the only jewel of its kind in Russian lyric poetry', was buried at the Mitrofaniev Cemetery. There were only a few people at the funeral – Dostoevsky, Strakhov, D. V. Averkiev and Y. P. Polonsky of *Epokha*, P. D. Boborykin, editor of *Biblioteka dlya Chtenia*, several of that magazine's writers, the actors P. V. Vasilyev and Vladimirova and a few other actors who appreciated the reviews of one of Russia's finest theatre critics, as well as some strangers in shabby clothes, Grigoryev's acquaintances from the debtor's prison. Someone noticed a young girl in a kerchief, standing in a corner of the almost empty church. She seemed to be trying to avoid the others and was weeping softly.

It was a cloudy day. Afterwards the funeral party went into a nearby restaurant. Among them was a general's wife, named Bibikova, an elderly woman, who informed the company that it had been she who had obtained Grigoryev's release from Tarasov debtors' prison and that in return he had given her the rights to the royalties from his translation of *Romeo and Juliet*. The mixture of lies and gossip made a distressing impression. 'All the helplessness and all the benightedness of a writer's position in Russian society were revealed here in a merciless glare,' Strakhov wrote later.

There were no speeches over the open grave but the autumn 1864 issues of *Epokha* carried Grigoryev's literary letters, as well as articles about him by Strakhov, Dostoevsky and D. V. Averkiev. In his obituary note Strakhov wrote of his last meeting with Apollon Grigoryev in the debtor's prison some ten days before the latter's death: 'His pale, eagle-like figure was radiant with the light of thought.' He started talking about his favourite subject – the need to preserve the uniqueness of the regions that had rebelled against Moscow's authority back in the Troubled Times. One could clearly see his deep kinship with the people in his views of history and his boundless love for Russian songs, legends and poetry, whose breadth and freedom always attracted him.

Our conversation took place on the morning after one of these sleepless nights that Grigoryev had to endure. On these occasions he used to pass the time in a kind of imaginary dialogue with the thinkers that were his closest friends.

This time Grigoryev was very animated and intensely stimulated. One could not help thinking at this point that there are more important things in life than personal suffering. This man, ill, wearing shabby old clothes, and incarcerated in a debtors' prison, yet wholeheartedly absorbed in the common interest and concerned with nothing else throughout a sleepless night, could make anyone, who is too concerned with his own private interests feel ashamed.

This is a moving and graphic portrait of this knight of literature, who had been plunged into beggary but who, while in the horrible 'pit', nevertheless retained his enthusiasm for philosophy, literature and art.

Dostoevsky wrote of a different aspect of the man. He wrote of Apollon Grigoryev's magnificent letters on history, which show him to have been a modern Russian Hamlet. 'Undeniably, a literary critic must be a poet, too. Grigoryev was undoubtedly a poet, and an impassioned one. He was a straightforward man and in many respects, though he may not have been aware of it, was of the soil, strong as a rock. Of all his contemporaries he was perhaps the most Russian in character (I am not speaking of the ideal Russian, of course).' Many of Dostoevsky's ideas about the common people, the 'soil', about Pushkin and art came from Apollon Grigoryev. But the poet–critic was also close to the novelist as a person, as a type, as a talent. Dostoevsky liked open-hearted Russian natures such as Grigoryev's, freedom-loving, rakish, inspired, creative. He may have been thinking of him when he created his ungovernable Russian characters, one of the first examples of whom is the passionate, noble, fiery and inspired Dmitri Karamazov.

Three deaths in the course of six months left Dostoevsky with a deep feeling of loneliness. He wrote to Wrangel on 31 March 1865:

Suddenly, I was left all alone, and I felt really frightened. Life has broken in two all at once. Everything around me has become cool and empty. . . .

Side by side with the emotional drama was the total bankruptcy of Dostoevsky's journalistic concerns.

In addition, I am now responsible for ten thousand roubles in bills of exchange and five thousand roubles in debts of honour. Oh, my friend, I would willingly go to penal servitude again for as many years if I could thereby pay the debts and feel free once more.

But it was not Dostoevsky's habit to give way to despair. He was prepared to put up a struggle to continue his creative work.

MARTHA BRAUN

In a letter to Apollinaria Suslova, Dostoevsky, writing of his unbearable melancholy after the deaths of his wife and his brother, admitted that the desire for life and love had not been extinguished in him: 'I still hoped to find a heart that would respond to me, but I did not find one.' His quest for reciprocated love led him into a very brief and unusual romance in the autumn of 1864. It appears that his interest had been aroused by an unknown woman with an original personality and an extraordinary history who had happened to cross his path.

Pyotr Gorsky, a sketch-writer for Dostoevsky's magazines, brought to the *Epokha* office one day his friend Martha Braun (Panina), who was looking for literary work. She was a young Russian woman of common stock with some refinement and capability. She had a good knowledge of English, was energetic and venturesome, and wrote in a lively trenchant style. 'I always believed that life was created for excitement,' she told Dostoevsky.

In her youth she had apparently plunged into the swift and muddy stream of international intrigue. Penniless, she had risked her life in a game of chance and agreed to go abroad in an emigrant ship. This was in the late 1850s. She had become one of a noisy crowd of foreign adventurers, fortune-seekers and racketeers of all sorts. She remarked upon her return:

Though I lost nothing by leaving Russia, I gained nothing by going abroad. It makes no difference to me at all where fortune deigns to drop me. I am prepared this very minute to go anywhere. I have had to struggle with poverty everywhere; everywhere there was nothing but work for me and no time for philosophical reflections, even when adventures diverted me against my will from whatever I was doing.

It is evident from a bundle of Martha Braun's letters that have come down to us that she sought the company of educated people and that she wished to get into an intellectual profession but had been unable to do so because of unremitting poverty.

After the emigrant ship had cast her up on the shores of England she tried to get some order into her spiritual life, but without success. She was buffeted about from country to country and city to city and fetched up for a while in Austria. Four years passed in this way.

An unforeseen circumstance obliged me to seek refuge in Turkey. I was illegally arrested in Vienna and never reached my destination.

And so on with the same pointless and purposeless wanderings through all the countries of Europe in the company of suspicious characters; she was always in flight, as if running away from pursuit, arrest and disaster.

I swept through Austria and Prussia like a whirlwind in the company of a certain Hungarian. Then for seven months I travelled with some Englishmen, adventure-seekers. I had to criss-cross all of Switzerland, Italy, Spain, and finally, southern France, never resting from morning till night, sometimes on foot, sometimes on horseback. I parted from them in Marseilles, went to Gibraltar, but then some vapid notoriety-seeker, a Frenchman, for a certain sum took me (it was sheer masquerade) to Belgium and then on to Holland. We were deported from the former and driven out of the latter and after spending some time in a military prison in Rotterdam, I found myself in England without any money and with no knowledge of the language. I spent two days in the police station for attempted suicide, then two weeks with London's vagrants under bridges and in the sewers under the Thames. Then I unknowingly went to work for a distributor of counterfeit money, becoming an associate of counterfeiters. My poor knowledge of the language attracted the attention of all sorts of missionaries with religious tracts, who vied with one another to preach to me so zealously and diversely that I not only learned to speak English in two months but also became familiar with all kinds of English religious sects. Finally one Methodist took me away with him to the island of Guernsey, where a little later I married a sailor from a ship that had come there from Baltimore. With my patron's blessing, I went off to find a job first in Wyemouth, then Brighton and finally in London.

This was, of course, one of the most interesting human documents ever to come into the hands of Dostoevsky. He had never known a woman who had lived such an unusual life and told of it with such truthfulness, even with desperation, as she herself admitted.

Her situation became still more appalling when she got back to her native land, in 1862. She was completely alone – no family, friends or acquaintances: 'No one knows me, not one friendly voice answers me.' Hardly anyone believed her to be Russian. She attempted again to realize her dream of obtaining intellectual work. She finally managed to get into a generally accessible bohemian literary group that hung around the shabby editorial offices of third-rate magazines. There she met Karl Flemming, editor of popular dictionaries. Flemming lived in extreme poverty, 'because he drank the cup of death', yet she decided to move in with him and to 'manage his affairs', that is, his household.

A year later she moved in with Pyotr Gorsky, a talented writer of sketches and fiction, whose work Dostoevsky willingly printed in his magazines ('Poor Tenants in Hospital and the Cold', 'Honourable Love'). Gorsky, who was apparently sincerely in love with Martha Braun, also lived in semi-starvation and was also afflicted with alcoholism. 'With Flemming I descended into beggary,' she wrote to Dostoevsky on 24 December 1864. 'Gorsky and I were utter and absolute vagrants, at times no better than my English ones.' When she was once in hospital, the poor man begged her to write a *Journey through England* or else to postpone her discharge, although her recovery was complete, for he feared hunger and poverty might force her into vice, and that he would not have been able to bear. 'I feel pity for him and I am afraid of him,' the long-suffering woman said. What moving emotional conflicts, what material for a great novelist!

Now, after long years of unrelieved trouble and oppression, here was brief but immeasurable happiness within reach. Like Mahadeva descending to the *bayadère* in Goethe's ballad, a genius descended to her with deep and fervent feeling. He understood everything and responded to everything with love and compassion. Despite the distressing state of affairs at the dying *Epokha*, Dostoevsky gave his new friend financial assistance and commissioned her to write something. She no doubt answered his questions expansively and frankly, and she told him in her letters the moving story of her chequered life, a story that could well have come from one of his great and gloomy novels.

He talked to her of the spiritual harmony that might develop in their friendship. He told her that if the struggle for existence became harder she should leave the hospital without hesitation and come to him. Despite the frightful conditions in the Peter and Paul Hospital, despite the anthrax, typhus and other contagious diseases there, the nervous and hypochondriac Dostoevsky did not hesitate to go to visit her, and had a long friendly conversation with her. She acknowledged his visit with a letter. Her polite epistolary style does not conceal the boundlessness of her gratitude to this unusual man.

Forgive me for writing such a long letter and permit me to thank you sincerely for your kindness towards me and for the pleasure and honour your visit gave to me. I never dared hope for such flattering attention from you. As for myself, if I can ever be of any use to you through my work and my devotion, I am ready with all my soul to serve you.

By mid-January she was no longer signing her letters with the full formality of her surname, but only with her given name. This too, is an indication of her desire to show heartfelt devotion to the man who had 'such high prestige among clever people', and among Russian writers. She felt warmed and brightened by his very name. This was the greatest event in her unhappy, chequered life.

The general tone of her letters is remarkable. She does not expect a prolonged relationship and is grateful for even the briefest happiness. Dostoevsky had mentioned once, in an intimate talk, the possibility of prolonging their friendship. This had brought a ray of hope for future happiness, revitalized her and given her great hope. But he did not follow it up, and so Martha Braun wrote her last letter to him some time in the second half of January 1865:

Most gracious Fyodor Mikhailovich!

Perhaps I take advantage of your kindness and write to you too often, but you have given me so much attentive sympathy and so much of your confidence that I would consider it shameful ingratitude not to be entirely frank with you. From my letters to Mr Gorsky you could have obtained some idea about me and about my circumstances. At any rate, whether or not that spiritual harmony on which the continuation of our friendship depends arises between us, believe me that I will always be grateful to you for having given me your friendship and your good will for a single minute, for any length of time. I swear to you that I have never dared to be as frank with anyone as I have been with you. Forgive me this egoistical absorption, but so much sorrow, boredom and despair have accumulated in my heart in these two awful years in Russia that, as God is my witness, I am happy and joyful to have met a man with tranquillity of spirit, tolerance, common sense and truthfulness, such as I have not encountered either in Flemming or Gorsky. At this moment it makes absolutely no difference to me whether your connection with me lasts for a long or a short time. I swear to you that much more than the financial assistance, I value the fact that you did not disdain the sinful aspect of my person, that you esteemed me

more highly than I deserve. And, venturing respectfully to ask you
to return my letters to Mr Gorsky after you have read them and
wishing you well in every possible way, I remain, dear sir, your
humble servant,

                                                Martha Braun

This apparently marked the end of their relationship. Not a
reproach, not a protest, not a complaint. It brings to mind
the motifs of Dostoevsky's earlier story *White Nights* with its
epigraph from Turgenev:

> Or was he perhaps created
> To be close to your heart
> For a moment only?

And that story's lyrical ending: 'A whole minute of bliss! Is
that not enough even for a lifetime?'

Such then is this bundle of a woman's letters. They are
written in a simple, assured, strong and expressive style.
There was nothing sentimental in them. She knew life with
all its horrors and cruelties too well to be affected, to com-
plain, or to hope for anything. She wrote laconically, in an
almost formal manner, about her years of suffering. It was
not a man's style, however. These were letters from a
woman who had been through a great deal and who had
faced humiliation every day. Dostoevsky was fond of saying
'To write well it is necessary to suffer, to suffer!' Under other
circumstances Martha Braun might have become a writer.
She had enormous experience, emotional perception, 'the
memory of the heart' and aptness of expression. Her letters
are probably the finest in Dostoevsky's private archives.
Though Dostoevsky never mentioned her anywhere, she cast
her shadow on his work.

They parted in the winter, and by the spring Dostoevsky
had already started thinking about what proved to be one
of his most forceful compositions, one that was not entirely
unrelated to his winter encounter. That summer he began
to write down, in an *Epokha* ledger with a lot of unused pages,

a short story, which soon developed into a full-length book. This was a monologue by an elderly drunkard, such a one as collegiate counsellor* Flemming or junior captain (retired) Gorsky, by a father telling the story of his young daughter, who goes out into the streets when darkness falls because she has nowhere else to go. Such was the beginning of *Crime and Punishment*.

THE KORVIN-KRUKOVSKAYA SISTERS

In 1864 *Epokha* received two stories from a town in far-off Vitebsk Province. They were written in a woman's hand and signed with an abbreviation of the names of somebody called Yuri Orbelov. The first story was written in the vein of the latest fiction and might have been inspired by Dobrolyubov's† celebrated verse:

> I fear that all that I wanted so avidly
> And so vainly while I lived,
> Will smile down upon me happily
> Over my gravestone.

It was about a society girl who becomes interested in an impecunious student, refuses to surrender to her love for him and only after his death realizes that she has forfeited her happiness.

The second story dealt with a more complex theme and could not but have attracted Dostoevsky's attention. It described the complicated emotional crisis of a rich young nobleman who has been impressed by the idea of moral perfection at an early age and whose search for truth leads him to the cell of a monk. The hero becomes a disciple of Father Ambrose, an ascetic, and submits to harsh monastic

---

* The sixth grade in the Civil Service, equivalent to full colonel in the Army.

† Literary critic of the radical magazine *Sovremennik*.

discipline. An unexpected encounter with a young princess arouses his longing for another world and another life. He leaves the monastery to go among people and seek the higher meaning of life there. He is disillusioned, returns to his Elder and dies, crushed by profound disillusionment about the possibility of attaining righteousness. Despite some immaturity of literary style, the story showed a considerable talent for emotional portrayal. The hero's inner crises (in the Cathedral of the Assumption, at the monastery on the Tverskoy Boulevard) were conveyed surely and dramatically. Though the narrative was uneven, the psychological contrasts were presented with thorough understanding of compositional effects.

Dostoevsky found both stories worthy of attention. He replied to the accompanying letter, and, while he pointed out the novice's shortcomings, he praised the unknown author's talent warmly and promised to print the stories in the next issue of his magazine. Shortly afterwards, Dostoevsky made the acquaintance of the young girl behind the pen name of Yuri Orbelov. And it must be said that Anna Vasilievna Korvin-Krukovskaya, sister of the subsequently renowned mathematician Sophia Kovalevskaya, was one of the most outstanding and most talented of the women to whom Dostoevsky was attracted.

Anna Korvin-Krukovskaya possessed unusual beauty and a proud nature. Tall, graceful, with delicate features, sparkling green eyes and long blonde hair, she had been accustomed 'practically from the age of seven to being the queen at all children's balls'.[6] As a young girl she went through a number of intellectual states in her quest for a philosophy. The daughter of a lieutenant-general of the artillery and wealthy landowner, she spent her childhood years in Palibino, the family's estate near Vitebsk. Bored with the backwoods, she had at the age of fifteen devoured the old English novels in the large library of the old house, and was fascinated by the medieval knights they portrayed.

Sophia Kovalevskaya relates in her reminiscences:

To make matters worse, our huge and massive country house with a tower and Gothic windows had been built a little in the style of a medieval castle. During her 'chivalry' period my sister never wrote a letter without heading it: Château Palibino. She ordered the upstairs room in the tower, which had not been used for so long that the steps of the steep staircase that led to it were shaky and covered with mould, to be cleaned of dust and cobwebs. She covered its walls with old carpets and firearms that she dug out of the rubbish in the attic, and she spent all her time there. I can still see her graceful, slender figure in a tight-fitting white dress and her two heavy braids falling below her waist, seated before an embroidery frame. She was embroidering the family coat-of-arms of King Matthias Corvinus* in beads on canvas and gazing out of the window, watching for a knight to come riding up the highway.

One of Bulwer Lytton's novels about the lovely Edith Swan Neck and her beloved Harold had a strong impact on the emotional sixteen-year-old. Its presentation of the problem of love and death made a deep impression on her and plunged her into a moral crisis: 'Everything ends in death – the most wonderful happiness, the most passionate love.' She lost interest in the knights and the beautiful ladies for whose love they fought in tournaments. Now her purpose in life was to eradicate her new doubts through self-torture and self-sacrifice. Her new handbook was Thomas à Kempis's *Imitation of Christ.* Shortly after that, an amateur stage production at home revealed that she had dramatic talent, and so the young zealot's thoughts turned to drama school and triumphs on the stage. But this interest did not amuse her for long.

The son of the local parish priest, an extremely modern young man just out of a recently established seminary, one day visited the landowner's house. He had rejected a career in the church and entered the natural sciences

* Matthias Corvinus, King of Hungary 1458–90.

department of the university and when he came home for vacations he used to astonish his father with statements to the effect that man was descended from monkeys and that there was no such thing as a soul, only reflexes, as proved by Sechenov. The recent knight's lady, Christian zealot and renowned actress became very much interested in the conversation of the student from Petersburg. She began to wear black dresses with plain collars and comb her hair back, so as to look like a man. She disdained dancing, gathered the peasant children in her house in the mornings and taught them to read, and had long conversations with the peasant women. She began to read the books and magazines that were exciting her contemporaries in Petersburg. *Sovremennik, Russkoe Slovo* and Herzen's *Kolokol* appeared in the landowner's house, where only such semi-official organs as *Revue des Deux Mondes, Athenaeum* and *Russky Vestnik* had been seen before. New books, such as *The Physiology of Life* and *The History of Civilization*, arrived by the crateful. She confronted her parents with an unexpected demand: she wanted permission to go to Petersburg to study medicine.

She was refused permission, and in this new mood resolved to dedicate herself to literature. Without telling anyone, she sent the first manuscripts from Palibino to *Epokha* in Petersburg. Dostoevsky printed both the stories that had been sent to him by the daughter of the Marshal of the Gentry of the Province of Vitebsk. 'The Dream' and 'Mikhail' (originally entitled 'The Novice' but changed by order of the church censorship). He sent her the payment for them by post, and this provoked an explosion in the Krukovsky family castle. The new-fledged writer's father declared: 'A girl who can accept money from a man without the knowledge of her father and mother is capable of anything!'

But Anna prevailed on her father to let her read her stories to the family. The General was moved by his daughter's literary talent. He gave her permission to correspond with Dostoevsky and to make his acquaintance when they next visited Petersburg. 'But remember,' he added, turning to his wife, 'you will be responsible. Dostoevsky does not belong to our social circle. What do we know about him? Only that he is a journalist and an ex-convict – and that's not much of a recommendation!'

At the end of February 1865 Elizaveta Korvin-Krukovskaya and her two daughters went to visit relatives in Petersburg, and early in March the 'young Palibino ladies' made Dostoevsky's acquaintance. The first meeting was strained and unsuccessful. Dostoevsky felt awkward in the presence of the prim relatives and was clearly out of sorts. He looked old and ill and 'kept pulling at his fair, scanty beard and biting his moustache, and his whole face twitched'.

However, Dostoevsky's next visit, when he found nobody but the two sisters at home, consolidated the friendship at once. The novelist soon became a friend of the family. He was strongly attracted to Anna, the elder sister, and, surprisingly, became the object of the younger sister's first love. The adolescent Sophia would never forget her feeling of deep affection for the 'first man of genius that she had ever encountered in her life'. 'She venerated him not only for his genius, but also for the sufferings he had endured,' wrote Sophia Kovalevskaya about this early but deep feeling of hers, when she had become a professor at the University of Stockholm and laureate of many European academies.

Alone with the sisters, Dostoevsky grew animated, his conversation became picturesque and graphic; he spoke to them about his most cherished literary plans.

'Yes, life has hit me quite hard,' he would say, 'but then it suddenly turns kind and begins to spoil me, so that I grow nearly breathless with happiness.'

Once Dostoevsky told the young girls the psychological outline of what was to become Stavrogin's Confession, horrifying their mother, who was present.

At large gatherings he obviously felt ill at ease. He was

embarrassed and awkward in the society of the family's visitors, the important dignitaries, elderly academicians and dazzling Guards officers, and their German relatives from distant streets on the Vasilevsky Island. To camouflage his shyness, he behaved aggressively. He turned up at one such gathering in an ill-fitting frock coat, which tormented him the whole evening, and monopolized Anna's attention at once, not letting her move a step away from him. The girl's mother tried to convey to him that he was not behaving according to the rules, but he refused to understand. She finally came over and said firmly: 'I beg your pardon, Fyodor Mikhailovich, but as hostess here, Anna must entertain the other guests, too,' and led her daughter away.

He retreated to a corner and maintained an obstinate silence, darting angry looks at everyone. He was especially angry at a young General Staff colonel, a distant relative of the Krukovskys. Andrei Ivanovich Kosich, a veteran and hero of the Crimean War, a handsome man and interesting raconteur, was already accepted as his Palibino cousin's future fiancé. One look at the tall, self-satisfied officer filled Dostoevsky with raging hatred, Sophia Kovalevskaya recalled. 'The young cuirassier, settled gracefully in an armchair and bending slightly towards my sister, was telling her something amusing. Anyuta, not completely recovered from the embarrassing episode with Dostoevsky, was listening to Colonel Kosich with a rather stereotyped party smile, "the smile of a meek angel", her English governess used to say with acerbity. The sight of this group put a whole novel into Dostoevsky's head: Anyuta hates and despises the 'self-satisfied impudent fellow', but her parents want her to marry him and are making every effort to bring them together. Having conceived this story, Dostoevsky began to believe in it, and he became very indignant.

A fashionable topic of conversation that winter was a recently published book by an English clergyman, who drew a parallel between the Russian Orthodox Church and

Protestantism. In that Russo-German company this was a subject that interested everyone and the conversation became lively when it arose. Suddenly the hitherto silent Dostoevsky burst out:

'Surely, the New Testament was never written for society ladies! Here's what it says in it: "In the beginning God created man and wife", and again, "Man shall leave his father and his mother, and shall cleave unto his wife." This is how Christ understood marriage. What will all the mothers who are thinking of nothing but how to get their daughters married off to the best advantage say to that?'

His voice shook with emotion. The effect was startling. The well-bred Germans fell silent and stared. He glared back at them angrily, then retired to his corner and did not utter another word the entire evening.

That evening was an indication to Anna that it was time to break with her insufficiently polished suitor. She found herself always wanting to contradict Dostoevsky and this made him very nervous and captious. They argued constantly and heatedly about nihilism, says Sophia Kovalevskaya. They would sometimes quarrel about it far past midnight, and the longer they argued the angrier they became, expressing extremist views in the heart of argument:

'Today's young people are all obtuse and under-developed,' Dostoevsky would scream. 'Polished boots are more important to them than Pushkin.'

'Pushkin is out of date,' my sister would reply calmly, knowing that nothing infuriated Dostoevsky more than dis respect for Pushkin.

Enraged, Dostoevsky would sometimes pick up his hat and leave, first announcing solemnly that it was a waste of time to argue with a nihilist and that he would never darken our door again. But, of course, he would turn up again the next day as though nothing had happened.

However, the end was near. Sophia, who was in love with Dostoevsky, had learned the Sonata Pathétique of Beethoven for him. Absorbed one day in playing the difficult piece, she did not notice that he and her sister had left the room.

Lifting the curtain that covered the doorway to the small corner parlour, I saw Fyodor Mikhailovich and Anyuta, seated side by side on the small sofa there. The room was faintly lit by a lamp with a large shade. My sister's face was in the shadow and I could not see it clearly, but I saw Dostoevsky's face clearly: it was pale and excited. He held Anyuta's hand in his and was bending over her and speaking in the ardent, excited whisper that I knew and loved.

'Darling Anna, please understand, I fell in love with you the moment I saw you. Even before, in fact. I had a feeling from your letters. And I do not love you as a friend but passionately, with all my being.'

Everything blurred before my eyes. I suddenly felt bitterly lonely and deeply resentful, and the blood seemed to rush first to my heart and then in a hot stream to my head. I let the curtain fall and ran out of the room.

A feeling of bitterness, resentment and shame such as I had never known before filled my heart, above all, shame and resentment. Until that moment I had not even in my most secret thoughts realized my feeling for Dostoevsky and had not admitted to myself that I was in love with him.

Anna, however, had no doubts about her feelings. She already knew that one can appreciate a man's talent highly yet not want to marry him. With feminine intuition this eighteen-year-old girl sensed that Dostoevsky's wife would have to dedicate herself to him completely, give him her whole life and subordinate any personal feelings of her own. In the three months that she had known the nervous and demanding man he had already seized complete hold of her, had 'swallowed' her, so that she could not be herself any more. The only reply she could give to his proposal of marriage was a refusal. The winter season ended and the Krukovskys left Petersburg. Late in the autumn of the same year Anna Korvin-Krukovskaya heard that Dostoevsky was betrothed to 'a remarkable young girl with whom he had fallen in love and who had consented to marry him'.

Yet Dostoevsky's infatuation with this ardent nihilist of noble family left its mark on him. 'Anna Vasilievna is one of the finest women I have ever met,' Dostoevsky later told his second wife. 'She is extremely intelligent, sophisticated, well-read and has a wonderfully kind heart. She is a young woman of fine moral qualities. But her views are diametrically opposed to mine and she cannot give them up; she is much too direct. For that reason we could hardly have had a happy marriage.'

In 1869 Anna Korvin-Krukovskaya went abroad to study and shortly afterwards she married a French revolutionary, named Jaclard. She found her mission in life in France. During the Paris Commune she was a member of the Central Committee of the Women's Alliance, made public speeches, wrote for the Press, and worked as a sister of mercy in hospitals. When the Commune was destroyed, the Jaclards managed to escape to Switzerland, thanks to the arrival in Paris of Sophia with her husband V. O. Kovalevsky and of General Korvin-Krukovsky, who was acquainted with Thiers himself. After a few years in Switzerland the Jaclards took up residence in Russia. Dostoevsky renewed his friendship with Anna Jaclard in the 1870s. In 1879 the Dostoevskys and the Jaclards spent the summer in Staraya Russa and were on friendly terms.

Anna Korvin-Jaclard's literary career, begun in *Epokha* in 1864, ended in *Severny Vestnik* (*Northern Herald*), where her last story was published in 1887. She died in 1887 in Paris, where she had been working on her reminiscences about the siege of Paris and the Commune (they have not been preserved). Four years later in 1891, her sister Sophia Kovalevskaya, the world's first woman professor and a corresponding member of the Academy of Sciences, who when she was fourteen had been in love with the ex-convict and writer, died in Stockholm.

XII

A Novel of Confession

HISTORY OF A DESIGN

THE artist had travelled a long road to get to his master-piece. The beginnings of *Crime and Punishment* go back to the early 1850s. Its main character lived within Dostoevsky for some fifteen years. He wrote to his brother on 9 October 1859:

In December I shall start a novel. Do you remember that I told you about a novel of confession that I wanted to write after I had written all the others, saying that I had to live through it myself first? I made up my mind definitely a few days ago to write it without delay. All my heart's blood will go into this novel. I conceived it in prison as I lay on my bunk in a heavy-hearted moment of sadness when I felt I was losing grip of myself. The *Confession* will establish my name conclusively.

Allusions scattered through Dostoevsky's letters and note-books indicate that by the *Confession* he meant the story of Raskolnikov.

Dostoevsky's life among the outcasts in prison gave him a new insight into human nature. He was astonished by the integrity of the inner world and the case-hardened will-power of the murderers who surrounded him. He wrote of a convict named Orlov: 'It was evident that this man had absolute control over himself, that he felt contempt for all torture and punishment, and feared nothing in the whole world. We regarded him as the incarnation of infinite energy.'

Dostoevsky for the first time put into philosophical and ethical terms the sharply controversial problem of a man's right to commit a crime. The image that had begun to take shape in the writer's mind was of an amoral, titanic individual, who claims the right to 'shed blood according to conscience'. The design, that was afterwards to be noted down, is confidently developing.

The idea of excessive pride, arrogance and contempt for this society is expressed in this character in the novel . . . He wants power and he does not know how to obtain it. If only he could gain power quickly and get rich. And the idea of murder comes to him complete.

This variant of the main design of *Crime and Punishment*, as happens almost always with Dostoevsky, is interpreted and affirmed by one of Pushkin's central images.[1] An invaluable note in one of Dostoevsky's manuscript notebooks reads: 'Aleko* killed. Awareness that he is himself unworthy of his ideal, and this torments his soul. This is crime and punishment.' Dostoevsky wrote this in the 1860s, but the idea apparently originated in his Semipalatinsk period, when he received Annenkov's new edition of Pushkin's work and re-read Pushkin's poems. Therefore, Aleko's act of murder and his sense of rejection are among the most important sources of Raskolnikov's act of bloodshed and of his loneliness.

'The Gipsies' is one of Pushkin's most freedom-loving poems. In it the poet's protest rings out forcefully against the oppression of the despotic state of his day, founded on the unbreakable bond that welded together 'money' and 'chains'. Aleko of 'The Gipsies' cannot breathe in 'the slavery of suffocating cities'; he flees from their enclosures and joins the outcasts. But this protester himself invalidates his exploit by his boundless self-deification and all-embracing worship of his individual will, which leads him to claim

---

* Aleko is the hero of Pushkin's poem '*The Gypsies*'. He goes to live with the gipsies and marries Zemphira and afterwards kills her and her lover out of jealousy. The gipsies take no revenge, simply ask him to go away and leave them.

for himself the right to pass judgement on others. Pushkin sharply condemns this rapacious individualism of his hero in the simple words of the murdered Zemphira's father:

> 'Leave us, proud man.
> We are savages.
> We have no laws.
> We do not torment, we do not kill.
> We do not need blood or groans,
> But we do not wish to live with a murderer.'

Aleko's concept of untrammelled emancipation and rebellion brings him to moral collapse, by prompting him to commit an act of revenge, of ruthless murder. Pushkin's hero falls far short of his own high ideal of freedom and justice. This same unworthiness, in Dostoevsky's view is the essence of the tragedy of sin and vengeance that brought Raskolnikov too to his downfall.

Dostoevsky's original plan for *Crime and Punishment* was continually enriched, adding new impressions and interpretations as the years went by. At the end of 1860, when he was preparing material for the first issue of *Vremya*, he read a number of books about criminal trials in France, looking for thrilling accounts of famous crimes to stimulate readers' interest in future issues. He was struck by an article on the Lacenaire trial, and the second issue of *Vremya* carried a detailed account of that notorious courtroom drama.

Pierre-François Lacenaire, son of a Lyons merchant, was a rather refined, aristocratic-looking young man, with a sarcastic remark always ready on his lips. He had planned to study law, but in 1829 he killed the nephew of the celebrated political orator Benjamin Constant in a duel and was sent to prison. This duel, which concluded the First Act of his life, gave him the idea that he was one of the élite, an exceptional person with an extraordinary nature. Upon his release from prison Lacenaire embarked on a literary career. He wrote lyrics and verses. But this did not satisfy him, and he renewed his ties with his prison associates. Impelled by an insatiable desire for money and pleasure, he began to join them in burglaries. After a while he made up his mind to commit a major crime. He committed a murder with intent to rob, was apprehended and was imprisoned again. In prison he wrote a book of poetry and spoke to a gathering of writers, lawyers and physicians about his ideas on literature, morals, politics and religion, amazing all his listeners by his perception, the originality of his opinions and his remarkable memory.

Dostoevsky's interest was aroused by the psychological contrasts of this philosopher-cum-criminal, thinker-cum-murderer, which were he felt excellent novel material. As the *Vremya* editorial explained: 'The trial deals with a phenomenal, mysterious, fearful yet interesting individual. Base instincts and cowardice in face of poverty made him a criminal, yet he dares to depict himself a victim of his age. And withal, he has boundless vanity.'

The image that had been taking shape in Dostovesky's mind for a long time now acquired new traits and was given an added depth by the concept of a criminal of bourgeois background with pretensions to the role of romantic titan. As the critics correctly pointed out when the novel appeared, Raskolnikov was one of that vanishing race of heroes that romanticism loved so well – the poet, the painter, the musician, of 'élite' and 'mysterious' natures. This type found its expression, exaggerated and monstrously distorted, in the person of the real murderer Lacenaire, whose image was so intently studied by Dostoevsky.[2]

*

The difficult and dismal year of 1864 provided Dostoevsky with an abundance of real-life material for the main design of his novel. Financial disaster loomed after his brother's death. He tried feverishly to raise money. He signed promissory notes and paid off creditors, repulsed solicitors' claims and fought distraint of his property. The threat of debtors' prison was with him every minute of the day. For a whole year he had constant dealings with Petersburg's moneylenders, police inspectors, petitioners and racketeers of all types and ranks. His creditors included tradeswomen, court clerks, retired military men, and even a peasant. Never before had the usurers and the police played so large a part in his life. The problem of money, in all the ramifications typical of Petersburg in 1865 – the moneylenders, detectives, police, Raskolinkov's petty dealings with pawnbrokers, Alyona Ivanovna's practically worthless currency, and Luzhin's and Svidrigailov's five per cent per thousand notes – pervades the novel Dostoevsky was to start writing as soon as he had liquidated his ill-starred enterprise. For the first time in Russian literature the theme of capital, broached clearly and placed right in the centre of a novel, acquires the fascination and depth of a compelling social tragedy.

In that very difficult year Dostoevsky borrowed ten thousand roubles from his elderly aunt Kumanina in Moscow. This encounter was a true-life version of Raskolnikov's dilemma. On the one hand there were his late brother's impoverished young children, among them musically gifted boys and pretty girls, on the other, a senile old woman, who controlled the enormous Kumanin fortune and had willed huge portions of it to the Church for its embellishment and for prayers for her soul – exactly like the moneylender Alyona Ivanovna in the novel.

Dostoevsky found the literary sterility imposed on him that year, from Mikhail's death to his own departure abroad, extremely oppressive. 'In a whole year I have hardly written a single line.' But he was observing intently and absorbing impressions of this hitherto unfamiliar environment in which the struggle for money was ruthless and unconcealed. Just as after his release from prison he had set to work on *Notes from the House of the Dead*, so did he now, after his release from the grip of financial problems, start writing a novel in which the entire background is filled with figures of shady operators and Petersburg officials.

Alyona Ivanovna, who let furnished rooms in the Resslich and loaned money for interest, Chebarov, a debt collector, and Koch, a swindler, who made a living by purchasing promissory notes from usurers, were clearly portraits of Dostoevsky's creditors (his wife later described these 'buyers of promissory notes – civil servants' widows, landladies of furnished rooms, retired army officers, petitioners of the lowest order'). Pyotr Petrovich Luzhin, who used to do errands connected with litigation of all kinds and who was planning to open a public advocate's office of his own in Petersburg, is surely a portrait of the 'court clerk and attorney Pavel Petrovich Lyzhin', to whom Dostoevsky owed four hundred and fifty roubles and who attempted to place Dostoevsky's property in distraint on 6 June 1865. In his drafts for the novel Dostoevsky actually calls him Lyzhin. There is also reason to believe that the original of the local police inspector in the novel, Nikolai Fomich, was the inspector of the third block of the Kazan section, with whom on that same 6th of June Dostoevsky came to an arrangement over the delicate matter of distraint and who gave him a lot of valuable information about the police.

The desperate efforts Dostoevsky made to raise money in 1864 – having work printed by three printers at the same time, reading proofs, correcting other people's articles, sitting up till six in the morning and sleeping no more than five hours a day – did not produce the hoped-for results. By the spring of 1865 it was clear that his enterprise was absolutely and completely bankrupt. Publishing funds had been exhausted and *Epokha* had to close down. Dostoevsky now owed a personal debt of fifteen thousand roubles. He had to cease his feverish attempts to edit a magazine and get down to his basic and most important work – writing.

Dostoevsky was planning a novel about drunkenness,

which was then a topical subject. On 1 January 1863 a new system of excise duty on liquor had been introduced. Under the old system publicans and wine merchants had purchased concessions for the sale of alcoholic beverages from the Treasury and had encouraged drinking shamelessly. Now alcoholic beverages were sold in government-controlled shops. A dense network of such shops had spread rapidly across the whole country, and by 1865 it was clear that the 'drink reform' had not brought about 'sobriety of the masses'.

Dostoevsky had already discussed the more dramatic aspects of the problem of alcoholism, such as its effect on the children of drunkards. He had carried a long article in *Vremya* about a book by the French writer Jules Simon, entitled *The Working-class Woman*, which described the Saturday night drinking bouts of Parisian factory workers in the public houses in the suburbs of the city and the dismal home life of factory hands whose 'children lay dying of starvation or of consumption in unheated houses on beds without mattresses or blankets'.

As soon as *Epokha* was closed down he started work on this project, and by 8 June 1865 was offering A. A. Kraevsky, editor of *Otechestvennie Zapiski*, a novel called *The Drunkards*, which 'will deal with the current problem of drunkenness (pictures of families, the rearing of children under such conditions, etc.)'. It was from this beginning that the immortal portrait of the Marmeladov family in *Crime and Punishment* was developed. But Kraevsky was not in a strong enough financial position to accept Dostoevsky's offer. So Dostoevsky resolved to go abroad, where, far away from business matters, creditors and the police, he hoped to be able to concentrate on creative work.

Dostoevsky's financial situation did not improve abroad, in fact, it got worse. In Wiesbaden he lost all his money and even his watch at roulette in the course of five days. In Petersburg he had been besieged by creditors and been in constant danger of distraint and debtors' prison, but here he faced real poverty and real hunger. His letters from Wiesbaden in 1865 are poignant:

> They told me early in the morning at the hotel that they had been ordered not to serve me dinners, tea or coffee . . . I still have no dinners and for the third day now have kept going on morning and evening tea – and, strangely, I don't feel very hungry. What is bad is that they keep harassing me and sometimes even refuse to let me have a candle in the evening.

It was under these conditions that Dostoevsky set to work on his greatest creation.

Never before had he had such acute experience of hunger and want. Afterwards he used to say that it was at this precise moment that *Crime and Punishment* was conceived. It was after his losses at Wiesbaden in 1865 that he 'invented' *Crime and Punishment* and thought of getting into touch with Kafkov. This must be understood in the sense that ideas which had been long fermenting in his consciousness now at this critical moment of financial ruin formed a kind of new combination and thrust up into the foreground a design for a crime story.

This is what Dostoevsky wrote to Katkov in September 1865:

> Can I count on having my story published in your *Russky Vestnik*?
>
> It is a psychological account of a crime. The action is contemporary, this year. A young man of petit-bourgeois background has been expelled from the university and is living in extreme poverty. Lacking seriousness and stability in his mental makeup, he has given himself over to certain strange, 'half-baked' ideas in the air at the time, determines to escape from his vile situation at one stroke. He resolves to murder an old woman, widow of a titular councillor, who lends money for interest, and with that money to bring happiness to his mother, who lives in the provinces, and deliver his sister, who is employed as a companion in a landowner's family, from the threat

of imminent ruin due to the lascivious attentions of the head of the house. He will then complete his studies, go abroad, and for the rest of his life be honest, steady and unswerving in fulfilment of his 'humane debt to mankind', whereby he will, of course, 'redress his crime', if, indeed, the word crime can be applied to his deed against a deaf, stupid, evil, sick old woman who does not know herself what she lives for in the world and who might, perhaps, have died a natural death in a month's time.

Although crimes such as this are extremely difficult to carry out, that is, the murderers nearly always leave the most obvious clues and so forth and leave an awful lot to chance, which nearly always gives the culprit away, he succeeds by pure luck in doing the deed quickly and successfully.

He carries on for nearly a month before the final disaster. No suspicion of any sort is attached to him, nor can there be. At this point the whole psychology of crime unfolds. Unanswerable questions arise in the murderer's mind and unsuspected emotions torment his heart. The truth of God and the law of the earth take their toll and in the end he has an inner compulsion to go and confess. He is compelled to do this, for even if he is to perish in prison, he will be in touch with people again; the feeling of being isolated and separated from mankind, which he began to experience immediately after he had committed the crime, had tortured him beyond endurance. The law of truth and human nature has won out. The criminal himself resolves to accept suffering and thereby atone for his deed.

As we have seen, the design for the great novel was set out, in the autumn of 1865, with such remarkable clarity that even in the short letter the author grips us by the profundity of the problems he is posing.

Pushkin once wrote of Dante: 'The plan for "Inferno" alone is the fruit of great genius.' The same may be said of this letter. When the restrained and cautious Katkov read this brilliant outline in which all is catastrophic and all is tragic he immediately sent Dostoevsky an advance payment of three hundred roubles.

Dostoevsky worked at full stretch all through the autumn

of 1865. 'By the end of November I had a great deal written and ready, but I burned it all . . . I got interested in a new form, a new plan, and I started from the beginning again.' This was taking a chance, but it worked. In February 1866 he wrote to Wrangel: 'The first part of my novel appeared in the January issue of *Russky Vestnik* about two weeks ago. It is called *Crime and Punishment*. I have already heard many enthusiastic comments. There are bold and new things in it.' Dostoevsky was right. This was in fact the first Russian novel to base the action and the dramatic conflict on the economic crisis that was causing great ideological clashes and personal tragedies at that time.

When Dostoevsky had returned to Petersburg after ten years of exile, he had found a completely different city with a new way of life and new social relationships. A new social order was rising out of the disintegration of the feudal system. Raskolnikov's drama was played out against the background of the severe financial crisis of the 1860s. The periodical press, Dostoevsky's magazines in particular, wrote constantly about the economic difficulties of the post-war period. In one of the first issues of *Vremya* Dostoevsky carried a long article by Schiel, entitled 'Where Has Our Money Gone?' 1865 was in fact the year in which the commercial, industrial and financial crisis reached a particularly high level. It affected Dostoevsky's own affairs, compelling him to give up publishing. Magazines were closing down; credit generally was being withdrawn at an unbelievable rate; the government issued one loan after another; the money market was flooded with paper bills; the state Treasury was 'depressed' by a deficit.

Such was the state of affairs in the year when kind-hearted passers-by offered kopecks to the student Raskolnikov, and the titular councillor Marmeladov invented his own version of the popular saying, 'Poverty is no vice', by declaiming 'Poverty is not a vice, but begging, begging, sir, *is* a vice.'

Raskolnikov's 'razor-sharp dialectics' can only be understood fully within the framework of the panicky conditions
of the 1865 financial crisis. The whole action of the novel
stems from the problem of money, and one of the characters
explains Raskolnikov's crime simply in terms of economics,
and in particular the economic upheaval of the early '60s:
'There have been a great many economic changes,' replies
Dr Zosimov when Luzhin asks: 'What is the reason for the
corruption and incitement to crime of the civilized section of
our society.' From the book's very first lines we learn that
the hero is 'crushed by poverty', and the very first dialogue
is his conversation with a moneylender over a pitifully small
loan. A completely new linguistic style is ushered in by the
vocabulary of bookkeeping, or discounting, and the phrases
of these extraordinary conversations about interest and of
the petty calculations at a small loan office ('at ten kopecks
per month per rouble it will be fifteen kopecks for a rouble
and a half, one month in advance, please,' and so forth).

Poverty, hopelessness, sordid profiteering, miserable
greed – these are the novel's first, deliberately jarring, notes.
A few pages later Raskolnikov, in a conversation with a
servant girl, formulates his ideas: 'What can one do with a
few kopecks?' 'Oh, you would like to have all the capital at
once, would you?' she says. He looks at her strangely. 'Yes,
all the capital at once,' he replies emphatically, after a
moment's silence. And further on: 'What can I do with five
kopecks?' Shortly afterwards, in a billiards hall, another
student formulates this basic idea, putting the financial
problem on a new plane – claiming the right to money in
the name of the just distribution of the national wealth.

A hundred, a thousand good deeds which could be done,
enterprises which could be set up or saved with the old woman's
money, doomed to go to a monastery! Hundreds, perhaps
thousands, of lives put on the right path; dozens of families
saved from beggary, from disintegration, from ruin, from
corruption, from venereal hospitals – all with her money!

Raskolnikov's resolve is deepened and intensified by the harsh economics of the period, which continually confront him in the sombre episodes and tragic scenes of the big city – young girls violated, prostitutes, drunkards, suicides, and then the prospering usurers, the Luzhins and the Svidrigailovs. The encounters with these people constantly strengthen and stiffen his rebellious will. He resolves to carry out his plan and thereby to defeat that terrible monster that menaces all young creatures – the new capitalist city, where the power and strength of an entire empire are concentrated, the octopus whose tentacles are seizing hold of Sonya, the girl from Konnogvardeisky Boulevard, the whole Marmeladov family, and Raskolnikov himself.

*

Since the early 1860s the Russian novel had been concerned with portrayal of the advanced representatives of the younger generation. Some six months before Dostoevsky began to work on *Crime and Punishment*, *Epokha* pointed out that the most significant development of contemporary Russian literature was its preoccupation with the new breed of young people. In 1865 Dostoevsky, who was extremely sensitive to the pulse of the times, was getting down to work on the latest problem that life had thrown up. In *Crime and Punishment* he both shows us the tragedy of nihilism by his characterization of Raskolnikov, and satirizes the entire school of radical thought in the episodic figures of Lebezyatnikov and, to a lesser extent, of Luzhin. His portrayal of these characters was a continuation of the ideological struggle he had conducted in his magazines. The philosophies of the 'soil' and of revolutionary democratism cross swords in the novel's discussions, carrying on, as it were, *Vremya*'s and *Epokha*'s debate with *Sovremennik* and *Russkoe Slovo*.

As we have seen, the polemics in *Notes from Underground* were Dostoevsky's reply to Chernyshevsky's celebrated novel *What Is To Be Done?* published in *Sovremennik* in 1863. In

Crime and Punishment he tried using artistic generalizations to combat nihilism. Besides his wonderfully profound and dramatic portrait of Raskolnikov he drew caricatures of Chernyshevsky's radical young followers.

The novel *What Is To Be Done?* had been immediately recognized as the manifesto of revolutionary democracy. Dostoevsky had chosen as the principal target for his polemics the central production of the enemy party.

Chernyshevsky's theories were based on the same Fourierism which had once been a large part of the young Dostoevsky's creed. The Utopian vision of a coming Golden Age and universal happiness had left a deep imprint on Dostoevsky's creative mind, but he could not accept the ways in which these ideas were developing. Fourierism had led to revolutionary democratism, and this went against Dostoevsky's beliefs. Dostoevsky's opinion of Chernyshevsky's novel is expressed by Stepan Trofimovich Verkhovensky in the *The Devils*:

I agree with the author's basic idea, but that makes it even more horrible. It is our idea, ours! We were the first to plant it, to tend it, nurture it – what can they say that is new after us? But, my God, how they distort and mutilate it! Were these the ideals to which we aspired? Can anyone recognize the original idea in this?

Verkhovensky does not accept the new phase of the movement, when 'the peaceful democracy of the 1840s', having passed through the materialism of the 1860s, turned into revolutionary struggle. His anger at the socialist novel was undoubtedly Dostoevsky's anger.

In *Crime and Punishment* Dostoevsky uses Chernyshevsky's revolutionary doctrine as the jumping-off point for his own philosophical concept of a pointless 'ideological' murder and the frightful psychological penalty it exacts. To the Kirsanovs, Lopukhovs and Rakhmetovs* Dostoevsky con-

* Kirsanov, Lopukhov and Rakhmetov are names of characters in Chernyshevsky's novel *What Is To Be Done?*

trasts Raskolnikov – a nihilist of a special kind. Among Dostoevsky's contemporaries Nikolai Strakhov, his closest associate, understood the essential nature of Raskolnikov best. He made the acute observation that *Crime and Punishment*

shows us for the first time a nihilist who is unhappy, a nihilist who suffers deeply and humanly . . . The author has taken nihilism and carried it to its extreme, to a point from which there is hardly anywhere else to go . . . His aim was to show how life and theory struggle within a human soul, to depict that conflict in a situation in which it has reached its highest pitch, and to demonstrate that in the end life wins out. Such was the object of the novel.

Most critics associated Raskolnikov with Bazarov, in Turgenev's *Fathers and Sons*.

Dostoevsky's negative attitude to nihilism is even more obvious in the satirical characters, who parody some of the themes of *What Is To Be Done?* When Lebezyatnikov declares: 'Everything that is useful to mankind is noble. The only word I understand is "useful",' Dostoevsky is pushing Lopukhov and Kirsanov's theory of utilitarianism to the point of caricature. And when he says in discussing the views of radical journalism, that cleaning out rubbish dumps 'is much nobler than anything created by Raphael or Pushkin because it is more useful' and, in another place, referring to the word 'cuckold': 'Pushkin's disgusting hussar expression is unthinkable in the vocabulary of the future', Dostoevsky is parodying *Russkoe Slovo*'s and, to some extent, *Sovremennik*'s 'destruction of aesthetics' and critical re-evaluation of Pushkin.

Lebezyatnikov is particularly concerned with the problem of contemporary marriage and relations between the sexes. His wife's unfaithfulness does not upset him: 'My friend, until now I only loved you; now I respect you as well, because you have it in you to protest.' This is a paraphrase and a parody of Lopukhov's declarations to Vera Pavlovna. The problems of marriage and new forms of love were in fact central to the plot of Chernyshevsky's novel. Thus were the great ideas of Chernyshevsky's novel distorted in the mirror of parody, turned on to the views of the ragtag of nihilism, ideas which were nevertheless seen as a grave threat to Dostoevsky's 'idealization of the irrational'; these ideas were reason, the power of theory and the merciless directness of intellectual formulae, all of which were said to ignore the laws of living life and freewill.

'Theory as such must be cold. Intelligence must judge things coldly,' Lopykhov proclaims in Chernyshevsky's novel.

'But that is merciless, isn't it?' asks Vera.

'Towards fantasies that are empty and harmful,' Lopukhov replies firmly.

When Dostoevsky submits his hero to the crisis that liberates him, so that 'life, instead of dialectics, takes the offensive and something entirely different has to develop in the mind', he is fighting against the domination of cold and ruthless theories and for the individual's right to creative impulses. The movement of the 1860s never claimed, of course, as does Raskolnikov, that impecunious students have the right to murder usurers; but cold theory, according to Chernyshevsky, would teach people to keep warm: 'This theory is merciless, but by following it people will cease to be wretched objects of idle compassion. This theory is prosaic, but it lays bare life's true motives; poetry is to be found in life's truth.'

It is this doctrine that Dostoevsky attacks, preferring as he does the concepts of free will and the diverse 'motives of life', arguing that murder for ideological motives is the logical consequence of the chill theories and ruthless abstractions of revolutionary thinking. Thus *Crime and Punishment* represents a decisive engagement in the continuing struggle between the devotees of the 'soil' and of nihilism, between *Epokha* and *Sovremennik*, and between Dostoevsky and Chernyshevsky.

THE ANATOMY OF A NOVEL

Dostoevsky's unique style took definitive shape in *Crime and Punishment*, his first philosophical novel with a criminal setting. At the same time it is also a typical psychological novel, to some extent even psycho-pathological, with noticeable traces of the police-court *feuilleton*-novel and the English 'black' adventure novel. But, above all, like Dostoevsky's first work, it is a social novel; it places major and sensitive questions about the contemporary political situation in the forefront of events and subjects them to the fire of dialectics.

Dostoevsky's first short social novel, published in 1845, had been cast in the traditional form of a series of letters. His first long social novel, written twenty years later, has a complex and original structure: the hero's inner monologue on various topics alternates with philosophical dialogues, and both are set within a detective-story plot. Raskolnikov's prolonged and profound self-analysis, his arguments with Porfiri, Svidrigailov and Sonya, and the constant interplay between the murderer and the investigating authorities, are the fabric of which *Crime and Punishment* is made. The supreme artistry of the author is shown by the way this fabric is interwoven with the most sensitive themes of contemporary journalism, turning a novel of crime into a panoramic social epic.

It took Dostoevsky some time to piece together this structure. He considered three possible choices: 1. A first-person narrative, that is, the hero's confession; 2. The usual narration by the author; 3. A combined form ('the story ends and the diary begins'). The first form (the first-person story) had two possibilities: reminiscences about a crime committed some time ago ('It was exactly eight years ago') and testimony during trial ('I am on trial and will tell all'). In the end Dostoevsky rejected the first and third forms, since it would be difficult to cover all possible aspects of the plot if episodes in which the narrator was not himself a participant had to be excluded. However, the second form ('the usual type') did not completely satisfy him either. He devised a new plan in which the story is told directly by the author but concentrates exclusively on the protagonist. 'Another plan. Narration by the author, who is a sort of invisible omniscient being, never leaving Raskolnikov's side for a single minute.' This plan, of course, prevailed, except that the protagonist, who is indeed within the reader's field of vision nearly all the time, drops out of several episodes of the Svidrigailov story.

This principle of narrative by an author who so far as possible is never separated from his principal character, evolved by Dostoevsky in the course of his experiments, imparts a consistency, unity and concentration of action that make *Crime and Punishment* the best constructed of all his novels. Traces of the form originally contemplated still show in the final version, in that the events are nearly always presented from the subjective position of the hero, and this makes the entire novel a sort of inner monologue by Raskolnikov, imparting an extraordinary wholeness, tension and interest to the story of the crime.

The whole vast novel is concentrated on a single theme, which permeates it through and through. Everything is connected to the centre and circumscribed by a single circle. The reader learns in the very first paragraphs that a murder is being contemplated. For six chapters he is completely absorbed in the ideological motives and the material preparations for the crime. The moment the murder has been committed, the reader is drawn into the exceedingly complex psychological drama presented by the inner conflict between Raskolnikov's design, his theory, and his conscience, and the outer conflict between Raskolnikov and the authorities in the person of his strongest adversary, the investigator Porfiri Petrovich, and, to some extent, the police. Gradually, all the characters are drawn into the murder drama. To some of them (Razumikhin, Sonya, Dunya) Raskolnikov tells his secret himself, from others (Zametov, Svidrigailov, Porfiri Petrovich) he is unable to conceal it. The three conversations with the investigator are masterpieces of intellectual single-combat. The 'psychological' ring, which Raskolnikov's insuperable rival in dialectics begins imperceptibly and confidently to draw around him from the very first days after the murder, closes surely and precisely on the stormy evening of their last conversation, so calmly begun. Raskolnikov has no choice but to submit to Porfiri's logic and Sonya's moral influence. He gives himself up.

The progress of the drama is never interrupted, never broken by unrelated episodes. Everything is subordinated to a single deed; everything serves to bring that deed into stark relief and deepen its significance. The tragedy of the Marmeladov family is a strong argument in favour of Raskolnikov's theory and action. So is the influence of Svidrigailov in his sister's life, which emerges from his mother's letters, revealing the power the poor girl's employer has over her, a theme which the novel explores in depth. Svidrigailov is by no means a separate or episodical character; the part he plays makes the protagonist's destiny and personality even more plain.

*

We have noticed a certain influence on Raskolnikov's theory coming from Napoleon III's *History of Julius Caesar*, (published in Paris in 1865 and 1866). Napoleon III declares Caesar, Charlemagne and Napoleon Bonaparte, play an exceptional role in history because they chart a path for nations and perform the work of centuries in a few years. Exiles, executions, triumvirates, *coups d'état* are the tools with which history's heroes do the job Providence has imposed on them. In applying that theory to himself, Raskolnikov was thinking not so much of conquerors and rulers as of scholars, savants, legislators and reformers – persons who shape a nation's spiritual culture. He had in mind Newton, Kepler, Lycurgus, Solon, Mohammed; the only great general or ruler he mentions is Napoleon I, and even then, in his conversation at Porfiri's, he refers to Napoleon's progressive codification and the enlightenment that stemmed from the revolutionary principles of 1789. He asserts that a leader and reformer has the right to 'step over other obstacles' only in order to implement a grand design, and, furthermore, only 'if it is necessary to the execution of his idea (which might one day mean salvation for all mankind)'. Dostoevsky's young thinker allows sacrifice, but only if it is necessary to achieve a supreme human goal, if it is aimed at saving and renewing the world.

All through his declaration Raskolnikov never for one moment gets away from the category of *people with a new idea*, whom he considers the genuine leaders of mankind. These are not selfish, vain people, but great martyrs to their emancipatory ideas about the happiness of men. Erroneous though the Petersburg student's theory about the permissibility of shedding blood for conscience' sake, to use his opponent's words, may have been, it is imbued with a sense of historical tragedy and has nothing in common with the dynastic machinations and political place-seeking depicted in the book by Napoleon III, whom Karl Marx dismissed as a 'mediocre and ridiculous figure'. To Dostoevsky, and to his Raskolnikov, great men must above all have a broad intellect and compassionate heart, and must feel strongly about the suffering that people of every age and every nation have undergone. Pisarev understood this idea of Dostoevsky's. In his article on *Crime and Punishment* he said in refutation of Raskolnikov's theory: 'Men like Newton and Kepler never resorted to bloodshed as a means of popularizing their doctrines.'

Dostoevsky's real sources for Raskolnikov's theory, apart from his own observations in prison, were Balzac's novels, especially *Père Goriot* and *Les Illusions perdues*. In the rough draft of his 1880 speech on Pushkin, Dostoevsky mentions a character in a novel by Balzac, a 'beggar student' who, depressed by a moral problem he cannot solve, tells a friend a parable about a decrepit, sick mandarin, in which he raises the question of a person's right to kill a useless creature. The dilemma is presented very clearly: 'Would you, a beggar, have wanted to say, "Die, mandarin"', so you could have his million?' The Parisian student's question sums up the moral dilemma of the penniless Petersburg student Raskolnikov. The passage quoted by Dostoevsky comes from *Père Goriot*. The story of Balzac's Eugène Rastignac is the story of the development of a 'superman', whose final tempering is achieved in a crime. One of the main ideas of the Balzac novel is the conceit of the hero, who is convinced that he is entitled to step over corpses to gain his goal.

Although these elements reappear in the tale of Raskolnikov, the composition of Dostoevsky's novel is wholly original. In *Crime and Punishment* a motley company has gathered for Marmeladov's funeral breakfast. The dead man's entire family is present. His widow Katerina Ivanovna, in a 'paroxysm of pride and vanity', is very anxious to have a proper funeral feast, attended by prominent and respected people. But the esteemed guests do not come. The only guests are three Polish women, whom no one knows, a drunken provisions official, the German landlady Amalia Lippewechsel, and a deaf little old man. The mood is nervous and worried. Everyone is expecting a scene. The widow's growing irritation erupts into a quarrel with Amalia Lippewechsel, who starts screaming about 'a yellow card'.* Pandemonium breaks out – screeching, threats, the cries of frightened children. The prevailing tension is snapped by a terrible blow – Luzhin accuses Sonya of

* A yellow card was the required identification of a prostitute.

having stolen a hundred-rouble note from him. The note is found in Sonya's pocket, where the blackguard cleverly put it himself. The scene culminates in this thoroughly theatrical brawl.

At this point the vulgarity of the episode turns into genuine pathos. The sobs of a tortured soul rend the heart. Amid the general uproar Katerina Ivanovna is pressing Sonya to her, as if determined to shield her with her own life against all enemies. 'Sonya, Sonya,' she says, 'I do not believe it. See, I do not believe it!'

The weeping of poor, consumptive, bereaved Katerina Ivanovna had an effect on the company. There was so much misery, so much suffering in that pain-distorted, parchment-like, consumptive face, in those cracked lips, covered with dried blood, in that hoarse scream, in those uncontrollable sobs that sounded like a child crying, in the trusting, childlike, yet despairing prayer for protection, that everyone took pity on the unfortunate woman.

The tragic interlude is sustained by Raskolnikov's forceful speech in Sonya's defence after Lebezyatnikov has, in fact, exposed Luzhin. The law student's fervent intercession makes an enormous impression. Public opinion acquits the slandered girl.

But the drunken brawl continues, until finally Katerina Ivanovna runs out into the street in search of immediate and complete justice. The vulgar anecdote acquires a quality of high tragedy; her quest is a quest for truth, and the only outcome of such a quest is death. The exhausted woman falls to the pavement, blood gushing from her throat. The titular councillor's fretful widow becomes a genuinely tragic heroine, crushed and reviled, but majestic in her maternal despair and in her protest against the world's evil. We know of no scene, even in Shakespeare, to rend the hearts of the audience as this does.

Dostoevsky strove to impart a sense of palpitating immediacy to his story, to make the reader feel that all this is happening very much in the present day. The kaleidoscopic events of the 1860s are suggested throughout the novel by echoes from the most diverse sources, scientific, judicial, financial, economic, social and political, with the development of one psychological case illuminated by the most pressing issues of the day, and the protagonists' arguments and dialogues accentuated by catch-phrases from the contemporary press. Just as Stendhal originally intended to call *The Red and the Black* simply *1830*, on account of its reflection of the intellectual tendencies and moods of the moment Dostoevsky might equally well have called *Crime and Punishment* simply *1865*. Despite the timelessness of Dostoevsky's theme, the novel was firmly rooted in its own day and age.

The image of Marmeladov has features in common with a lot of material in Dostoevsky's magazine on the topical problem of alcoholism. Against a background of numerous articles exposing the connection between alcoholism and prostitution, tuberculosis, unemployment, mendicancy, abandoned children and the physical extinction of entire families, the main lines of the Marmeladovs' story are made to stand out clearly. Here is a story with all the basic features of the anti-alcohol journalism of the sixties – consumption, the yellow card, the lost job, black poverty, starving children, parents dying in the streets – set out with almost poster-like clarity, and at the same time etched deeply with genuine tragic artistry by the novelist. This was probably the first time the simple and horrifying story of the disintegration and ruin of a whole family, destroyed by the 'government-owned poison', had been told in all its oppressive hopelessness. Literary tradition had usually treated drunkenness as an attribute of a merry and carefree Falstaff. The Marmeladov theme not only greatly enhanced the pervasive tragic atmosphere of *Crime and Punishment* but at the same time related the novel to one of the problems with which progressive public opinion was concerned, thus setting upon the story of Raskolnikov the 'date stamp' with which Dostoevsky used always to try to mark his pages.

The image of Sonya serves a similar purpose. Her parents' alcoholism, lack of necessities, her mother's early death, her father's second marriage, scanty education, unemployment – and at the same time the eager hunt for young bodies in big capitalist centres, with their dens of vice and their procuresses – here we have the principal causes of the development of prostitution. The keen artistic vision of Dostoevsky has taken the exact measure of all these social factors, and made them determine the course of the life story of Sonya Marmeladova.

But the great poet–novelist has risen far above material taken from public-health statistics and has revealed, in the fate of his unfortunate girl, the well-springs of a love so deep, so self-sacrificing, as to place this image besides that of the loveliest heroine of spiritual courage – Antigone.

The image of Svidrigailov stems from the general system of construction of the characters in the novel, sharpened by the social topicalities of the period.

Svidrigailov is also a figure Dostoevsky's readers would instantly recognize. He is a big landowner, whose material wealth and personal power have already been restricted by the peasant reform, though he has retained ownership of the woodland and the water meadows on his estate. Dostoevsky introduces into his story the episode of the torture of a house serf, who is driven to suicide. Svidrigailov appeared even more brutal in Dostoevsky's manuscript notes: he flogged the serfs and 'took advantage of his peasant girls' innocence'. One article that appeared in Dostoevsky's magazine told of a landlord whose outrageous behaviour had compelled a young girl, who had been a governess in his household for more than six years, to flee from his house. This episode is strongly reminiscent of Dunya Raskolnikova's departure from Svidrigailov's estate in a peasant cart in the pouring rain. The most interesting point about the characterization of Svidrigailov, however, is Dostoevsky's effort to depict a-dyed-in-the-wool villain transformed by strong feelings, to show Svidrigailov rendered capable of self-sacrifice and altruism by an all-conquering love that he experiences for the first time.

Finally, there is Porfiri Petrovich, a character who is also subtly but inseparably bound up with the progressive press of the 'reform' period. He is a virtuoso in psychological analysis. He believes that an investigator's work is 'a kind of art and tries to influence Raskolnikov not only through logic and cleverness but also (in their last conversation) by exerting moral pressure. His attitude to his charge is one of attentive liking and sincere compassion. Porfiri's artistic and humanitarian traits exemplify one of the aims of legal reform, current at the time, which was to replace the hidebound and corrupt investigating police officer, who had figured in the old outdated inquisitorial trials, by a new type of educated criminologist, who is an assistant to the judge and takes an individual interest in those involved in a case.* Porfiri draws a brilliant character-sketch of the young peasant who is suspected of Raskolnikov's crime and having saved him from trial and prison, concludes, 'I really like that Mikolka.'

In the monstrous city, among the fallen and the dying, the vultures and their victims, the lechers and the street women, among thinkers grown unfeeling and the triumphant bourgeoisie, this scion of the village, Nikolai (Mikolka) Dementyev, son of the native soil, nurtured by folk wisdom, forgotten among the stone buildings of the capital but not forgetting his own truth, represents to Dostoevsky the inextinguishable flame of salvation. He represents the firm

---

* The reform of the lawcourts (1862–5) had brought a completely new type of criminal procedure on Western European lines, with *juge d'instruction* in place of the old police investigator who was prosecutor and judge in one.

foundation upon which the new intelligentsia will erect the Russia of the future.

This boy, a peasant from the Zaraisk District of Ryazan Province, pits all his instinctive moral strength against the 'theoretician' Raskolnikov, who is divorced from the soil and has shed blood 'out of principle'. Dostoevsky depicts Mikolka as a simple-hearted giant of a fellow, a grown-up 'little child', but he gradually deepens the image and reveals the tragedy of the attitudes of the religious sect to which the boy belongs. Mikolka is prepared to accept suffering, to commit suicide, to go to penal servitude, even though he is innocent.

Thus, among the other contemporary themes he introduces into the novel in the persons of his main characters, Dostoevsky returns once more to the principal theme of his philosophical journalism, namely, the peasants, with whom he had come into direct contact in Siberia and who were the object of the attention, anxieties and hopes of the Russian intelligentsia in the reform period. In this manner, he combines burning contemporary problems with major moral issues about the rights of the individual, the limits of self-sacrifice, and the boundaries of good and evil. From the manuscript notes for *Crime and Punishment* we know that Dostoevsky set himself a very extensive task: 'to dig into all questions in this novel'. Surprisingly enough, he accomplished that task. 'All questions' were indeed 'dug up' – questions uppermost in the minds of the people of the mid-1860s and questions uppermost in the minds of people of every period of history.

*

In *Crime and Punishment* Dostoevsky is a 'fast' painter, to use a favourite expression of Pushkin's. The all-inclusive brevity of his portraits of 1866 is not to be found in *A Raw Youth* or in *The Brothers Karamazov*. A few lightning strokes of the brush take the place of pages of lengthy description. In the six lines of his portrait of the old woman Dostoevsky

gives us an image that is so astonishingly lifelike that much
that is unexpected in Raskolnikov's behaviour is explained
by this outwardly repulsive appearance of the revolting
moneylender. Concerning Svidrigailov we read:

> It was a strange face somehow, like a mask: white, pink, with
> bright crimson lips. The eyes were somehow too blue, and the
> look in them somehow too heavy and motionless; there was
> something horribly unpleasant in this handsome face, which was
> extremely young looking for his years.

Dostoevsky's philosophical novel presents a rich collection of Petersburg types, bringing to mind the albums, or
'panoramas', of the foremost artists of the middle years of
the century. An original and keenly observant painter from
nature, the novelist produced incisive, detailed portraits,
remarkably close to life despite the grotesque quality they
sometimes possessed. ('He got involved with those third-
rate clerks because they both had crooked noses: the nose of
one slanted to the right, the nose of the other slanted to the
left.') It was not for nothing that he admired Gavarni,
whom he mentions in *The Insulted and the Injured,* and had in
his youth thought highly of Agin, the illustrator of Gogol's
Dead Souls. There is something in the Petersburg sketches of
Crime and Punishment that brings to mind the engravers of the
period whose expert styluses put life into so many naturalistic studies of manners.

Almost every character, moreover, has his own appropriate peculiarities of speech. Innokenti Annensky has correctly
drawn attention to Luzhin's stylized bureaucratic language,
to the ironical nonchalance of Svidrigailov's speech, and the
bubbling colourful phrases of Razumikhin. It is not difficult
to detect the sarcastically business-like tone in the speech of
the lawyer Porfiri and the affected politeness of Marmeladov's civil service language, abundantly interspersed with
church Slavonicisms which make the sensational story of his
downfall and martyrdom more picturesque. Sometimes it is

the 'verbal gestures', the intonation patterns of the various speakers, that are brought out with marked originality, and are even more telling than the vocabulary itself.

Side by side with portrait and genre images, the novel gives descriptions of the central streets of the capital, with their evil smells and dirt, the guildsmen and the artisans, the drinking houses and other low establishments which are masterpieces of urban landscape. 'Sad, vile, stinking Petersburg in the summer suits my mood and might even give me a somewhat false inspiration for the novel,' Dostoevsky wrote at the height of his work on *Crime and Punishment*. But the inspiration turned out to be genuine, vital and powerful. The internal drama of the novel gains an added dimension from the populous streets and squares of the city; the action is constantly moved out of the narrow and low-ceilinged rooms into the noisy streets. It is in the street that Sonya sacrifices herself, that Marmeladov falls dead, that Katerina Ivanovna bleeds to death. It is on a boulevard in front of the fire watchers' tower that Svidrigailov shoots himself, and it is on Sennaya Square that Raskolinkov attempts to make a public confession. The entire vast, diversified, complex mid-nineteenth-century city – the many-storeyed buildings, the narrow side streets, the dusty parks and the hump-backed bridges – looms massive and unyielding above the man who dreams of the unbounded rights of the individual intellect, and what it might accomplish. Petersburg is an inalienable part of Raskolnikov's private drama. It is the canvas upon which his ruthless dialectics draws its patterns. The Tsarist capital sucks him into its drinking houses, police stations, taverns and hotels. And above these dregs, this scum of life, the inveterate alcoholics, the corrupters of children, prostitutes, loan sharks and detectives, above the tuberculosis and venereal diseases, the murderers and the madmen, rises the city with its austere buildings designed by celebrated architects and sculptors, its 'magnificent panorama' spreading out luxuriously and exhaling the hopelessness of a 'deaf and dumb spirit'.

Despite its thematic complexity, the basic tone of the narrative is amazingly consistent and complete. It absorbs and blends the sounds and hues of the individual scenes and characters, of the diverse motifs of Sonya, Svidrigailov, Raskolnikov, Marmeladov and the old woman, and by constantly returning to this succession of dominant themes it imparts to the novel the symphonic texture of the city itself, with its great variety of voices, the stifled sobs and the angry screams, merging into the single and forceful whole of Raskolnikov's tragedy.

The epilogue of the novel reveals new heights and depths. Raskolnikov had been on the brink of moral destruction, but his titanic individualism collapses when confronted by the simple laws of universal human wisdom. Working and suffering among deported convicts, he comes to understand how groundless are his pretensions to genius and supremacy. He perceives his guilt towards people and rejects his egocentric philosophy, to accept instead the living and radiant feelings of his generous heart. Comprehension of the supreme meaning of good and altruism makes him, the poor student, who once ran into a burning house to rescue two small children, feel that a new man has been born in his prison garb, a man who will deny himself and give away his personality and his fate for the happiness of all. The delusions that he had so sedulously cultivated retreat before the powerful emotion that brings the proud thinker to life again, and turns him into a new, unpretentious and humane person. The once vanquished fighter is not saved by the abstract or evangelical forgiveness that forgives on principle, but by the courage of a strong character and the life-giving impulse of a selfless woman's heart. 'Love resurrected them. The heart of the one contained infinite springs of life for the heart of the other.' The drama of ideas, begun in an airless coffin-like hole in Petersburg, ends on the shores of the deep

Irtysh River, in Russia's boundless steppe. The new Raskolnikov, purified by suffering and having absorbed 'the
kingdom of reason and light, will and strength', will now
serve his great country. This novel about a man's fall and
rebirth ends with a vision of paths to a new life.

SUMMER IN LYUBLINO

Dostoevsky spent the summer of the year he was writing
Crime and Punishment in the countryside near Moscow. It had
become necessary for him to come to an agreement personally with Katkov and his 'executive editor' Lyubimov about
the arrangement of further chapters of *Crime and Punishment*
in forthcoming numbers of their magazine. As had quickly
become apparent a serious conflict was brewing between
author and publisher. Dostoevsky arrived in Moscow in
mid June 1866 and put up at the Hotel Dussot, near the
Maly Theatre.

It was unbearably hot. The burning 'simoom' with its
clouds of white-brick dust had already driven all his friends
and acquaintances to their summer cottages. His favourite
sister Vera (married to Dr Ivanov, a physician and teacher
of physics at the Cadet Corps and the Surveyors' Institute)
and her family were living about five miles from the city in
the small village of Lyublino, near Kuzminki. At the end of
June Dostoevsky rented a vacant two-storey brick house in
the same village. He acquired a samovar, teacups and a
blanket, and moved from the Hotel Dussot's suffocating
rooms to the quiet estate, which, with its big lake, old park
and dense mixed woodland, seemed just made for creative
work. It was not far from the chalet-style house, with the
large orchard, in which his relatives lived.

Dostoevsky may have had an important personal reason,
which he kept to himself, for his sudden move to Lyublino.
His sister Vera had her sister-in-law Elena Pavlovna

Ivanova, the wife of Dr Ivanov's younger brother Konstantin, staying as a guest that summer. This charming, intelligent, sensible young woman, who was a favourite with everybody, did not have a happy marriage. Her husband was seriously ill and this had soured his disposition. He wore his wife out with his jealous suspicions and plagued her unmercifully. The doctors had already said that there was no hope for him, and all the Ivanovs openly hoped that their adored sister-in-law and aunt would marry the widower Dostoevsky, also the pride and joy of the entire family.

Dostoevsky was not averse to the plan. His latest loves – Suslova, Korvin-Krukovskaya and Martha Braun – had been disappointing and he was emotionally worn out. He yearned for a quiet mooring place, a kind, tranquil, educated and practical woman, who would be a friend to him. Elena Pavlovna, whom he liked and respected, was such a woman. He had often stayed in the furnished rooms she rented out in Moscow, had found her most kind and was entirely willing to spend the second half of his life with her. There was never any doubt about Elena Pavlovna's consent.

Circumstances seemed to favour the romance in every way. With both of them in the country at the same time among relatives the question of matrimony might have been clarified, though the final decision would have had to be postponed, until Elena Pavlovna's husband died. Hidden, complicated romantic motives were characteristic of Dostoevsky's passionate and secretive nature and they soon manifested themselves. Constant meetings and conversations in the 'country house' setting at Lyublino, with boating on the lake and walks in the woods, set the stage for a serious discussion of the matter on their minds. Dostoevsky asked Elena Pavlovna outright whether she would marry him if she were free. She did not give him a direct answer, no doubt because she felt this would be ill-timed while her husband was slowly dying, but neither did she reject the proposal. Apparently she implied consent, and she did not conceal the budding romance from the family who were so sympathetic to her.

All this came to light three or four months later when Dostoevsky suddenly became engaged to Anna Grigoryevna Snitkina in Petersburg. According to Anna Grigoryevna, Dostoevsky was very much disturbed by the thought that he had raised hopes in another woman that he could not now realize. In fact, he considered it necessary to inform Elena Pavlovna personally of the forthcoming change in his life and to obtain her permission.[2]

*

All this goes to show that the summer in Lyublino had given him emotional experiences concealed from strangers but bringing him the joy of an approaching new life, the prospect of happiness, soon to be realized, with an intelligent and educated woman from his family circle, loved by all and genuinely fond of him.[3]

In Lyublino a new working day was established for the author. Dostoevsky used to get up at nine in the morning, have tea, and sit down to work, which lasted till three in the afternoon.

That summer in Lyublino was trying, because he had a hard fight on his hands to save one of the most powerful chapters he ever wrote. But it was there too that he wrote another superb chapter of *Crime and Punishment*, the one about the funeral feast for Marmeladov and the death of Katerina Ivanovna – pages in which Dostoevsky strikes at our hearts like a mighty genius. All through the summer he worked at maximum intensity. At three o'clock he would leave the world of his heroes and go to the Ivanovs, where he would dine and stay until late in the evening, enjoying the company of the lively Ivanov children, for whom he had warm and genuine affection.

His sister's family, which at the time consisted of five daughters and three sons, was close-knit and fun-loving.

Dostoevsky was especially fond of the eldest, twenty-year-old Sonya, a girl of rare inner purity and infinite compassion. The second daughter, eighteen-year-old Masha, was a fine musician. She was a student at the Moscow Conservatoire and a pupil of Nikolai Rubinstein. Dostoevsky described her as all 'charm, grace, naïveté', with a 'vivid talent'. The third daughter, Julia, was only fourteen, but Dostoevsky used to send her 'a special regard' in his letters. The fourth daughter, Nina, was thirteen. Dostoevsky corresponded with her towards the end of his life when she had literary aspirations and was writing a novel. Two of the sons were home that summer – Sasha, already a young man, and Victor, an adolescent – and they contributed to the fun and merriment.

The young Ivanovs, accustomed to freedom and self-reliance from an early age, were growing up in an atmosphere of trustfulness and love. Their mother had every right to say, as she did in a letter to one of her daughters when she was already approaching old age: 'You are hardly likely to find another family such as ours in all Moscow, where the children were so free.' The principle of free upbringing, correctly understood and affectionately applied, was very successful. Dostoevsky wrote to his sister in 1868: 'Who is dearer and closer to me than your family? To look at your children now makes the heart sing. To be sure, it is lively, noisy, boisterous in your house. But the imprint of a close, good, kind and harmonious family lies on everything.'

There were other young people at the Ivanovs, too. Dostoevsky's sister Varvara's son Alexander Petrovich Karepin was staying there. He was a young physician, in search of an ideal bride. He was the object of a great deal of harmless ridicule, but he was in fact an unusual and attractive man. He had a remarkable memory and was extremely well-read. He could give an impromptu lecture on any subject and had learned Spanish specifically to read his beloved *Don Quixote* in the original. He was a man of an extraordinary gentleness, but he was not without his

freakish and eccentric ways, which gained him the appela-
tion 'idiot'. His naïveté and kindness reminded his cousin
Masha of Dickens's Mr Pickwick. Could it be that this
nephew of Dostoevsky's had something to do, if only a very
little, with the conception of Prince Myshkin?

The elder daughters' friends from neighbouring houses
gladly joined the Ivanov family's gay and boisterous circle.
Some three or four years later Dostoevsky portrayed this bevy
of young girls against a background of the garden at
Lyublino in his short novel *The Eternal Husband*. The
young Zahklebinins in that story are drawn, in part,
from the Ivanov circle. 'Girls started gliding out singly
and in pairs. There were an awful lot of them somehow –
ten, maybe twelve, Velchaninov lost count.' Katya, the
eldest, 'a charming creature' with an unusual way of doing
her thick hair, resembles curly-haired Sonya. In the story
the younger sister exclaims: 'Katya! Can anyone have a
kinder heart than hers? She is everybody's angel. I am in
love with her.' The second sister, Nadya Zakhlebinina, is
apparently partly drawn from Masha Ivanova. She is the
prettiest of the sisters, 'a petite brunette with the look of a
savage and the courage of a nihilist, a mischievous imp with
fiery eyes, a charming, although often malicious, smile,
wonderful lips and teeth. She was slender and graceful, and
the fervent expression of her still altogether childlike face
revealed a budding intelligence.' But she was already singing
love-songs, accompanying herself on the piano. Dostoevsky
drew an especially graphic picture of his nieces' pert and
sharp-eyed friend Maria Ivanchina-Pisareva, 'a scoffer and
very bright' (in the story she is called Maria Nikitishna). *The
Eternal Husband* contains the only portrait Dostoevsky ever
drew of his stepson Pasha Isaev, who had joined him soon
after and had been warmly received into the young Ivanov
circle. Pasha is described as having a 'handsome, self-
satisfied, pug-nosed face', 'thick black shaggy hair and
large, bold, dark eyes'.

This picture of gay, carefree young people is an unusual one for Dostoevsky and perhaps that is why it has so much freshness and poetry. So attracted was the novelist by this unfamiliar milieu that he adapted his strict working schedule so he might enjoy it. He improvised humorous dramatizations with the youngsters, for instance, of Pushkin's *Black Shawl*. He arranged a mock trial of his Karepin nephew and wrote 'odes' and couplets in honour of the supernumerary doctor of the Pavlovskaya hospitals etc. N. N. von Vogt, one of Dr Ivanov's pupils at the Surveyors' Institute, relates that:

The walks usually ended in a variety of games in the park, sometimes lasting until midnight. F. M. Dostoevsky used to take a most active part in these games and he displayed a good deal of inventiveness. Once it even occurred to him to organize something like an open-air theatre, with us giving improvised performances. In short, he enjoyed himself with us like a child, probably finding release and tranquillity after his intense intellectual and emotional work on his great novel.

Dostoevsky was very fond of music. He often hummed under his breath and when he did, it was a sure sign that he was in a good mood. His niece Masha's excellent playing gave him much pleasure. On one subject, however, they did not agree. Masha was a great admirer of Chopin (as were all the women), while he did not particularly like the Polish composer's music, which he described as 'consumptive'. His favourite composers were Mozart and Beethoven and, of the Russians, Glinka and Serov, especially the latter's opera *Rogneda*. Masha describes how:

I once played a German song after Heine's well-known poem *Du hast Diamanten und Perlen* in Fyodor Mikhailovich's presence. Fyodor Mikhailovich liked it very much and asked me where I had heard it. I replied that the organ-grinders of Moscow played it. Apparently, he had never heard it before and after that he began to hum it quite often. I do not venture to assert this, but perhaps it occurred to him later, when he was writing the fifth chapter of *Crime and Punishment*, to put the words of this song into the mouth of the dying Katerina Ivanovna Marmeladova.

Judging from *The Eternal Husband*, the young people at Lyublino played intellectual games too, such as proverbs, and performed serious music, such as Haydn. Naturally, Dostoevsky not only joked and played the fool but also held forth on his favourite artistic themes. This is attested to by the same N. N. von Vogt, who gives a vivid picture in his memoirs of Dostoevsky as a conversationalist:

Fyodor Mikhailovich spoke slowly and in a low voice, with concentration, and it was apparent that enormous intellectual work was going on in his mind. His penetrating, rather small, grey eyes pierced his listeners. These eyes always shone with good nature, but sometimes they would begin to sparkle with a sort of mysterious, malicious light, as when he mentioned matters about which he had deep feelings. But there was an air of mystery about everything he said. He would seem to want to say something directly and openly but at that instant would conceal his thoughts in the depths of his soul. At times he would deliberately relate something fantastic, something beyond belief, painting wonderful pictures that would later long remain in his listener's mind.

Once a week Dostoevsky went to Moscow to talk with his editors at *Russky Vestnik*. He always came away dissatisfied and upset. Katkov and Lyubimov, whom Dostoevsky called the 'real editor' in his letters, were reading the manuscript of his novel. Lyubimov's word was decisive in the magazine. As a doctor of physics and mathematics and an eminent figure in the academic world (a little later he became a member of the Council of the Ministry of Education), he was remote from *belles lettres* and his chief concern was the respectability of his publication. In this regard he was strict and unbending.

It was he who called attention to Part IV of *Crime and Punishment*, to the now celebrated fourth chapter,[4] in which

Raskolnikov kisses Sonya's foot ('It is not to you that I bowed down; I bowed down to all human suffering') and listens to her read the story of the raising of Lazarus which she has only agreed to read at his request. She had not dared at first to utter a text that for her was sacred because she was a great sinner, but was gradually carried away and came to believe that her reading of this poetic legend would renew her listener's hardened and blind soul. Her voice rings out with fervour and joy. She puts all the feeling she can into her reading and finishes loudly, elatedly, trembling and shivering with cold.

She was still trembling feverishly. The candle end had long since begun to sputter in the crooked candlestick, casting a dim light on the murderer and the fallen woman in this wretched room where they had come together so strangely over the reading of the eternal book.

Such were the fragments and debris of the chapter that Katkov and Lyubimov had bespattered with their red pencils and which Dostoevsky finally altered beyond recognition at their insistence, changing its entire atmosphere. The Gospel was the official foundation of Russian statehood. Professor Lyubimov could not allow anyone to take liberties with it. He objected categorically to the portrayal of a street woman enacting the role of spiritual counsellor and reading from the bulwark of Russian Orthodoxy. How could a prostitute be permitted to perform the function of a priest? The author had put his social outcasts above the supreme wisdom of the Church and the state authority. He had abandoned moral criteria and fallen into nihilism. He had idealized a fallen and outcast woman to the point of considering her holy and able to bring salvation to a wicked sinner, condemned by society and the law. The light and the dark were completely misplaced. In this chaos it was impossible to distinguish good and right from vice and crime. A magazine that supported the government programme dare not mislead readers with such confused values. The editor instructed the author to revise this episode thoroughly and make the religious and ethical categories he employed absolutely clear. Such was Lyubimov's view.

Katkov supported his co-editor and insisted on the elimination of Raskolnikov's philosophical dialogue with Sonya, describing it as 'moralization' that interrupted the consistency and artistry of the scene. This was a terrible blow to Dostoevsky. He fought, argued, reasoned, but he had to submit and to undertake an agonizing revision of the scene he held so dear. According to Lyubimov, 'it was not easy for him to give up his original, exaggerated idealization of Sonya as a woman who had carried self-immolation to such frightful lengths of sacrifice. Fyodor Mikhailovich abridged the conversation that took place during the reading of the Gospel, and the printed version was considerably shorter than his original.'

Dostoevsky wrote to A. P. Milyukov in the middle of July:

I cannot tell you anything about this chapter. I wrote it with genuine inspiration but perhaps it really is bad. But it is not the literary quality that they are concerned about; it is the threat to morality. About that I know I am right – there is nothing against morality in it, in fact, quite the contrary. But they see it differently; they even see traces of nihilism. Lyubimov declared positively that it must be revised. I accepted it, and this revision of a long chapter was at least as difficult and depressing as writing three new chapters. However, I revised it and turned it in. But the trouble is that I have not seen Lyubimov and therefore do not know whether he is satisfied with the revision or whether they will revise it some more themselves. This is what they did to another chapter (of these four) from which, Lyubimov told me, he omitted a great deal.

I don't know what will happen further, but this first sign of conflict of views between me and the editors, beginning to appear as the novel develops, worries me very much.

At the same time Dostoevsky wrote to Lyubimov about his revision:

Evil and good are separated absolutely and it is now impossible to confuse or misinterpret them. I have made all the other changes you have indicated and more, I think.

And now I have this great favour to ask of you: for Christ's sake, leave the rest as it is now. I have done everything you said; everything is separated, divided and clear, a different atmosphere has been given to the reading of the Gospel. In short, permit me to rely on you fully: take care of my poor novel, my good Nikolai Alexeyevich!

But the editors insisted on further cuts. Katkov wrote to Dostoevsky shortly afterwards:

My dear Fyodor Mikhailovich!

I am sending you the proofs of the ninth chapter and I beg you not to reproach me for having changed some of the explanatory lines you added about the conversation and about Sonya's behaviour. I cannot in this note convey to you the complicated reasons that made me do this after mature reflection. When I see you I will give you a complete report. But I will say only this, that not one essential element of the artistic portrayal has suffered. The elimination of the moralization has only enhanced the originality.

Your sincerely devoted,
Mikhail Katkov[5]

Hard as the editors of *Russky Vestnik* tried to smooth over their guilt towards the great writer whose manuscript they had altered unmercifully against his will and consent, the lamentable fact remains that we will probably never know the fourth chapter of *Crime and Punishment* as Dostoevsky originally wrote it. The version that we have of this central scene is the result of the interference of two reactionary professors, trying their best to graft in acceptability and seemliness that was quite contrary to the writer's own boundless and bottomless interpretation of the ancient legend about the resurrection of a sinner.

In Lyublino Dostoevsky's life was greatly enriched by another emotional experience, perhaps the only one of its

kind in his whole life. This was his deep and pure spiritual
love for his twenty-year-old niece Sonya (Sonechka, as he
was fond of calling her, always addressing her in the polite
second person plural as a token of special admiration and
love). She was the eldest of the family and had inherited the
positive traits of character that Dostoevsky admired in her
father, the doctor and the teacher: 'With this man duty
and conviction were always first.' He was always responsive
to people's sorrows and troubles. It was he who had undertaken the troublesome and difficult task of caring for
Dostoevsky's wife when she was brought to Moscow in a
hopeless condition to die.

It is probable that, as daughter of the doctor and niece of
the patient, Sonya, then seventeen, was directly involved in
caring for her sick aunt. At any rate, that was when Dostoevsky first took notice of her. He had not known her
at all when she was a child. When he got back from
Siberia she was already almost fourteen. 'I really got to
know you that winter when poor Maria Dmitrievna died. I
am especially fond of you and this fondness comes from a
special impression which is very difficult to anatomize or
explain. I like your restraint, your inborn and highly
developed dignity.' And he also liked her firm attitude to
honour, her firm views and convictions, and, finally, her
calm, clear and true intelligence. To analyse and formulate
a feeling of this kind is difficult indeed, even for a Dostoevsky,
but the spiritual affection that this man who never gave up
his search for inner beauty felt for the young and pure
Sonechka Ivanova is apparent enough from the scattered
allusions and tone of his letters.

There were ten children in the Ivanov family and Sonya,
as the eldest, had to start helping her parents at an early
age. After her father's death in 1868 she took over firmly and
efficiently. She perfected her English and made translations
of Dickens, earning as much as two hundred roubles a
month in this way. It was Dostoevsky's opinion that she had

inherited his literary gifts (at least within the limits of literary translation) and he admired her greatly for her tireless and selfless work (which, incidentally brought on attacks of tuberculosis).

She epitomized the intellectual Russian woman of that period who had a hard task to do in life and who willingly performed a simple, unnoticed and genuine act of heroism. It is not surprising that of all those whom he regarded as the finest of the new generation – people such as Apollinaria Suslova's sister Nadezhda, the first Russian woman to receive the degree of doctor of medicine (from Zürich University) – he put Sonya first, 'a rare personality, noble, honest and honourable'. In 1866 he wrote to Anna Korvin-Krukovskaya: 'In Moscow I had some beautiful moments with my eldest niece Sonya. What a lovely, intelligent, profound and warm soul and how happy I am that I may love her very much as a friend.'

Sonya had thick blonde hair that fell in curls to her shoulders. Her face was intelligent, open, serious and radiant, her gaze deep, reflective and sincere. This was a woman of infinite compassion and unshakeable will. Dostoevsky's letters to her are imbued with extraordinary feeling: 'You are the child of my heart. You are both my sister and my daughter.' 'My invaluable friend, I regard you as a superior being and I respect you infinitely.' 'You are the personification of my conscience.' 'Farewell, my darling, my treasure. Your complete, complete friend, father, brother, pupil – all, all.' And in 1873: 'I love you, my sweet monk Sonya, as I love my children, and perhaps even a little bit more.' Apparently, Dostoevsky's niece had a tremendous spiritual influence on him. At one time he hoped she might come to live with his family in Petersburg.

But their friendship came to a sudden end. On 29 March 1871 Dostoevsky's aunt Alexandra Kumanina died. The division of the inheritance produced dissension in the family and plunged Dostoevsky into a quarrel with his relatives, causing a breach even with his favourite sister Vera. Sonya took her mother's side. She stopped corresponding with her uncle. 'God be with her, if it is so easy for her to accuse a person and it is nothing to her to break with him,' Dostoevsky wrote on 5 June 1875 to Elena Pavlovna Ivanova. 'Anyway, let it be as she wishes: perhaps I am the only one who finds it so difficult to tear the past into little pieces; other people are really much more sensible than I am.' These bitter lines, so full of pain and reproach, reveal for the last time the depth of his feeling.

It was not until 1876 that Dostoevsky received another letter, or rather a short note, from his niece:

My dear Fyodor Mikhailovich,

If you still love me a little you will be pleased to know that I am getting married to a man whom I love and respect. His name is D. M. Khmyrov. He went to the *gymnasium* with my brother Sasha and he has loved me for a long time. Congratulate me, my dear friend (I still venture to call you that in spite of all the gossip and filth that has estranged us). I love him with all my heart and he loves me no less. We are happy and hope to be happy all our lives long.[6]

Such was the epilogue to Dostoevsky's brightest and purest love.

THE EMPEROR

It was during this period that Dostoevsky wrote one of his most extraordinary outlines for a novel. In 1866 he read an article by the historian M. I. Semevsky about an eighteenth-century officer, named Mirovich, who had tried to liberate the 'Emperor' Ioann VI*, pretender to the Russian throne,

---

* Son of Duke Anton-Ulrich of Brunswick and great-grandson of Ioann V, stepbrother of Peter the Great. Proclaimed Tsar in his infancy on the death of his great-aunt the Empress Anna, but deposed and imprisoned after the palace revolution that brought the Empress Elizabeth to the throne.

from incarceration in the Schlüsselburg Fortress, where Empress Elizabeth Petrovna had put him and where he was literally buried alive. He was confined in a dark, soundproof cell, had no contacts whatsoever with people, had never been taught anything and was 'completely ignorant'. In this way they had accomplished the spiritual murder of a dangerous pretender to the throne, virtually equivalent to physical destruction. However, as Semevsky wrote, the gaolers did not entirely succeed in accomplishing their monstrous task. The solitary prisoner developed through introspection. He might even have attained a certain intellectual level if he had not been killed by the guard during Mirovich's attempted *coup*.

This material attracted Dostoevsky, not because of the obvious plot of court intrigues, mysterious prisoner and rebellious lieutenant, but because of the picture of the extraordinary growth of a human soul that had been trampled and defiled, yet retained the will to live and to think. The ultimate in oppression and humiliation of the individual, to which the hero in this story had been subjected, offered unusual scope for Dostoevsky's dominant themes of man's unmerited and immeasurable suffering and of the unconquerable power of the intellect.

In a short outline Dostoevsky described an imprisoned twenty-year-old youth, who does not know how to talk but who develops by watching mice and domestic animals, acquires an understanding of life, has dreams. He built the plot upon a profound dramatic conflict. In his sketch the young officer Mirovich, aide-de-camp to the fortress commandant, to whose daughter he is engaged, plans a *coup* and manages to gain access to the prisoner. 'Meeting of two human faces. His amazement, joy, fear, friendship.' Mirovich begins to teach Ioann Antonovich, striving systematically to bring light and discipline to his darkened soul. A tremendous theme unfolds – the education of a man who has been turned into a savage and whose mental growth has been artificially checked, a man who must acquire all at once the cultural and intellectual skills usually absorbed slowly, over decades. The novelist depicts this unprecedented pedagogical experiment with precise strokes.

Mirovich explains to the prisoner the phenomena of the world around him. From the attic he points out the Neva River and the environs of the fortress. Then he sets about giving the dethroned prince a political education. He explains the meaning of authority and power to him and tells him that for the kind of ruler he will become 'everything is possible' (the usual motto of Dostoevsky's proud thinkers: 'Everything is permitted').

'Everything is yours. Anything you wish for.'

'Let us go ahead.' The prisoner is resolved.

'But failure means death!'

'What is death?'

Mirovich kills a cat. The prisoner is horrified at the sight of blood. He does not want anyone to die because of him.

'If that is the way it is, I do not want to live,' he says.[7]

His mentor persuades him to change his mind by telling him of the enormous amount of good he can do if he becomes emperor. The prisoner is kindled by his teacher's enthusiasm.

Then Mirovich brings in his fiancée, who is wearing a beautiful ball-dress and carrying flowers. The unfortunate Ioann cannot conceal his admiration. For the first time in his life he is infatuated, captivated, transformed by love. A crisis is brewing. Mirovich's fiancée, struck by the impression she has made on the Emperor, resolves to gain supreme power. Mirovich becomes furiously jealous. The prisoner meets his wrathful and angry looks with astonishment. He begins to understand the meaning of beauty, love, passion, jealousy, hatred, mortal enmity. The education of his emotions is almost complete.

At that moment Mirovich raises an insurrection, perhaps

for the purpose of bringing about the tragic end. In Dostoevsky's notes 'the Commandant runs the Emperor through with a sword. The latter dies majestically and sadly.' He has learned about treachery and about murder. And he has also experienced the enlightenment of wisdom at the moment of death. The cycle of emotional life, traversed so rapidly, is tragically cut short.

It is regrettable that Dostoevsky never expanded this remarkable plan into a novel.[8] But the great laws of his method of psychological portrayal are visible in this brief outline and all his favourite themes and profound motifs are included in the masterly construction of the plot – loneliness, boundless fantasies, purity of heart, primitiveness of mind, passion, hatred, jealousy, cruelty, martyrdom, the temptations of beauty, the attractions of supreme power, spiritual guidance and perfidious murder. How skilfully he developed the themes in which he was interested on the basis of an episode long past, and how skilfully he plumbed the bottomless abyss of the human mind through a portrayal of the life of one historical individual!

Dostoevsky's method is fully revealed by this one manuscript sheet. His proclaimed principle of historical realism, of portraying not only the event but its enduring meaning as well, its 'hidden word' and subsequent development, its legendary past and its future, is realized here, as is another canon of his literary system – the construction of the plot round a moral centre. Also worked out here is his basic theme of human suffering – and in one of its most remarkable and most moving manifestations. And it is all lit up by the grand idea of the inexhaustible possibilities for spiritual and mental education of a personality that has been forcibly deprived of all resources for development.

This kind of complete exposure of 'the man inside the man' was recognized by Dostoevsky as his main objective. It was also the all-embracing style of his interpretation of life, of history and of the present time, in all their depths, all their aspirations or (to use Dostoevsky's own formula) 'realism in the highest sense'.

In his brief sketches of one extraordinary, yet real person – the living, fantastic 'Emperor' – Dostoevsky has reached the height of artistic truth, achieved his highest reality and exposed the inexhaustible inner forces of the human consciousness, triumphing over all the injustices of the Iron Age. It was in this kind of penetrating portrait of a man that Dostoevsky saw the essence of his system. He strove to illuminate and interpret the events of the inner world as inseperable from history, politics and ethics. The shimmering images of the passing day – 'life's mouse-like running to and fro',* the daily round and reality – all were transfigured. In this sudden flash life exposed its deeper meaning, its moral value, its real humanity.

In this sense Dostoevsky considered himself a disciple of Pushkin, and his system was rooted in that great poet's style, the basis of which was to perceive the truth of life lyrically and to express it dramatically; to proceed from the ordinary and the commonplace to the historically significant, and to philosophical generalization. Dostoevsky found the profound images of the Little Tragedies, the daring problems of *The Queen of Spades* and the mighty poetic realism of *The Bronze Horseman* wonderful models for his art.

The motifs and the characters were related. Pushkin stayed extremely close to the facts in his 'Petersburg story' as he called his poem of 1833, *The Bronze Horseman*: the event was based on the truth, the details of the flood were taken from contemporary magazines, and Petersburg was shown at a specific time – November 1824. The terrain of 'poor Evgeni's' dramatic flight from the ringing gallop of the bronze horseman's steed through the streets and over the embankments is described accurately. The picture is absolutely true to life and fully consistent with the hero's state of mind. At the same time it is imbued with the great

* A phrase of Pushkin's.

poet's brilliant imagination and imparts a symbolic content to the details of current newspaper reports of the flooding, raising political and ethical problems of far-reaching significance to Russia's future.

This is indeed what Dostoevsky called 'the purest realism – realism to the point of the fantastic'. This realism is not supernatural or impossible; it presents a lofty pattern of bold ideas, it portrays the tragic disaster of human lives and treats personal problems in terms of world history.

A NEW LIFE

XIII

The Last Love

A DRACONIAN CONTRACT

DOSTOEVSKY returned to Petersburg from Moscow at the
end of September 1866. He had about three months in which
to finish the last part of *Crime and Punishment* for Katkov's
Russky Vestnik. This gave him enough time and he would
have had no worries, had it not been for one serious obstacle.
A. P. Milyukov describes this in his reminiscences:

On October 1 [1866] I dropped in to see Dostoevsky, who had
recently returned from Moscow. He was walking rapidly up
and down the room and was evidently very much upset about
something.

'Why are you so dejected?' I asked.

'You'd be dejected if you were on the brink of ruin,' he replied,
continuing to walk up and down.

'Why? What's wrong?'

'You know my contract with Stellovsky?'

'You mentioned it to me, but I don't know the details.'

'Here, take a look.'

He went to his desk, took a paper out of a drawer, handed it to
me and began pacing the room again.

I was puzzled. Not to mention the paucity of the sum which
Fyodor Mikhailovich had agreed to accept for a new novel of at
least one hundred and sixty pages, never published anywhere
else before, the terms included a clause under which if the novel
was not delivered by November 1 of that year, 1866, he would
have to pay Stellovsky a huge fine. And if he did not deliver the
novel by December 1 (Dostoevsky explained this in a letter he
wrote to Anna Korvin-Krukovskaya), 'then he, Stellovsky, will
be entitled to print everything I write in the next nine years for
nothing and in any form he wishes and will not have to pay me
a kopeck.'

The last condition was outrageously illegal, but Dostoevsky's signature gave to this oppressive document the character of a juridical agreement.

Dostoevsky (this is evident from other letters of his) had offered to pay Stellovsky the fine in June 1866, but Stellovsky had refused it. Then Dostoevsky asked for an additional three months but had again been refused. He was very well aware of the reasons for this refusal: 'Since he is convinced that I do not have enough time left to write a novel of two hundred pages, especially since I have only written perhaps half of the novel which is running in *Russky Vestnik*, he would rather deny me a postponement and not accept the fine so that he may own everything I write later.'

Milyukov saw that the situation was extremely serious and that something must be done urgently.

'Have you written much of the new novel?' I asked.

Dostoevsky stopped in front of me, spread his arms and said: 'Not a line.'

I was astonished.

'Now do you understand why I am on the brink of ruin?' he asked bitterly.

'But what is to be done? Something must be done!' I exclaimed.

'What can I do when I have only one month before the deadline? I spent the summer writing for *Russky Vestnik*,[1] and I had to revise what I had written, and now it is already too late. It is impossible to write two hundred pages in four weeks!'

We fell silent. I sat down at the desk and he paced the room again.

'Listen,' I said. 'You can't enslave yourself for all time. We must find a way out.'

'What way out? I don't see any way out.'

'You know what?' I continued. 'You wrote to me, from Moscow I think, that you already had a finished plan for the novel, didn't you?'

'So I have, but I tell you I haven't yet written a single line.'

'Perhaps you could do this: let's get several of our friends together right away. You will tell us the plot of the novel. We'll outline the sections, divide it into chapters and write it by our combined efforts. Then you will go over it, and smooth out the rough spots and inconsistencies. Working together we can get it done in time. You will give the novel to Stellovsky and escape from slavery.'

'No,' he said emphatically. 'I will never sign my name to someone else's work.'

'Well, then, hire a secretary who can take shorthand and dictate the entire novel yourself. I think you could do it in a month.'

Dostoevsky pondered that, then began to pace again.

'That is another matter. I have never dictated before, but I can try. Thank you. I must do it, though I don't know if I shall be able to. Where can I get such a secretary? Do you know one?'

'No, but it is not difficult to find one.'

Milyukov inquired of P. M. Olkhin, a well-known teacher of shorthand, who sent his brightest pupil to Dostoevsky two days later. She was twenty-year-old Anna Grigoryevna Snitkina.

DICTATING A NOVEL

A little after 11 a.m. on 4 October 1866 Anna Snitkina arrived at the house on the corner of Malaya Meshchanskaya and Stolyarny Lane, where the author of *The Insulted and the Injured* lived in a rented apartment. The very house brought to her mind the unattractive modern Petersburg rabbit warren, an investment property, subdivided into a multitude of tiny flats, inhabited by shopkeepers and artisans, in which Raskolnikov lived. Dostoevsky's study was dark and silent. The contrast between the noise outside and the silence inside was depressing.

Anna Snitkina's first impression of Dostoevsky was a painful one. The heartache was still there fifty years later when she spoke of that first meeting.

No words can convey the depressing and pathetic impression Fyodor Mikhailovich made on me at our first meeting. I thought he looked absent-minded, terribly worried, helpless, lonely, irritated, practically ill. He seemed so crushed by some kind of misfortune that he did not see one's face and was incapable of carrying on a coherent conversation.

He asked me to sit down at his desk and then he read a few lines from *Russky Vestnik* very rapidly. I could not keep up with him and I said that I could not follow him and that no one spoke or dictated that fast.

He read it again, more slowly this time, and asked me to transcribe the shorthand into longhand. He kept hurrying me, saying 'My, how long it takes, does it really take that long to transcribe?' I started to hurry and left out a full stop between two sentences. Though I began the next sentence with a capital letter and it was obvious that the full stop had been omitted accidentally. Fyodor Mikhailovich was extremely annoyed at the omission, repeating: 'How is that possible?'

Dostoevsky's anxiety and absent-mindedness were made even more obvious as his new assistant was leaving. He apparently wanted at least to say goodbye politely, but it was not a success.

'I was glad that Olkhin recommended a girl secretary rather than a man. Do you know why?'

'No, why?'

'Because a man would have surely got drunk, but you won't, I hope.'

That struck me as very funny, but I suppressed a smile.

'You can rest assured that I will not get drunk.'

Anna returned the next day at the appointed hour, bringing with her the transcription of the first episode of the new novel, written in her beautiful script. She was nonplussed, embarrassed and full of doubts. Would the author accept her work? Would he go on with the dictation? And, for that matter, why should she bother to continue taking this most difficult dictation from a nervous and demanding man?

She would have been very indignant, her daughter Lyubov later wrote about this episode, if anyone had told her that day that she would be taking dictation from Dostoevsky for the next fourteen years.

The atmosphere at those first sessions was strained and anxious. Apparently Dostoevsky did not expect the new method of writing a novel to succeed and was afraid that his case was lost. However, after he started receiving his secretary's conscientious and exact transcriptions he gradually calmed down. The story about a gambler was coming along well. He was discovering a new and extremely fruitful method of doing a first draft. The quality of the exposition was much better and the work went much faster. He became absorbed in his theme and kept deepening the original concept.

As it became more evident that all was going well and his confidence increased, his attitude to his assistant changed. He finally noticed that she was nice-looking, young and, in her own distinctive way, attractive. She had beautiful, intelligent, shining grey eyes, a broad forehead and a resolute chin. He began willingly to share his plans and reminiscences with this pleasant girl, who could talk so wittily. Anna noted that Dostoevsky was becoming warmer and more attentive every day.

Dostoevsky finished dictating the novel on 29 October. On 30 October Anna brought him the transcription of their last session. It was his birthday, but he devoted it to the final revision of *Roulettenburg*. On 31 October, he arrived at Stellovsky's house carrying a thick notebook under his arm. A servant told him that the master was out of town. Dostoevsky went to the publisher's office, but the manager refused to accept the manuscript because he did not know about the contract. It was evening by the time Dostoevsky finally managed to persuade the police officer in charge of the district where Stellovsky lived to accept the manuscript and give him a receipt for it.

He had triumphed through an extraordinary effort of creative will. He had completed a two-hundred-page book in twenty-six days. Surprisingly, the speed with which he had written it had a very favourable effect on the work as a whole, increasing its suspense and tempo. No longer was he in danger of having to pay enormous fines; and gone, too, was the depressing prospect of loneliness, of having to spend the rest of his days, sick and hard-working as he was, without someone who loved him by his side.

THE SECOND MARRIAGE

One day, while the work was still in full swing, Dostoevsky told his copyist that he was at a crossroad in life. He had three choices, he said: to go east, to Constantinople or Jerusalem, and remain there for ever; to go abroad for roulette and give himself up entirely to gambling; or to seek happiness in a second marriage. Anna advised him to take the last course.

Dostoevsky visited his employee at her home for the first time on 3 November to ask her if she would take dictation for the last part of *Crime and Punishment*. It was a long journey, about two and a half miles. Anna lived on the outskirts of Petersburg, at Peski, hard by the Smolny Monastery. At that time this outlying section of the capital was striking for its unusual contrasts. The richly ornamented Russian baroque and classical buildings with magnificent columns and pediments, designed by such architects as Rastrelli and Quarengi, were still surrounded by empty lots, vegetable plots and wretched hovels, where 'poor folk' of low degree, artisans and tradesmen, lived huddled together.

In the late 1840s Grigory Ivanovich Snitkin, an official of the imperial household, had purchased two small plots of land here on Yaroslavskaya and Kostromskaya streets. He had built a two-storey brick house and three wooden wings on one of the lots. The family lived in the brick house. Anna's recently widowed mother Maria-Anna Snitkina, *née* Miltopeus (of Swedish or Finnish descent), managed the repair and upkeep of these houses and was often influenced by dishonest estate agents and property dealers who were slowly but surely leading her to ruin. On the other lot were two wooden houses, built for income and worth fifteen thousand roubles apiece. These were the two daughters' dowries. Maria Svatkovskaya, the married daughter, had moved into one of them. Anna, though not yet of age, had been managing the other since 1865.

As she herself pointed out, circumstances had made her full mistress of her house at an early age. She rented out and maintained the apartments and kept the official house record of tenants for the local authorities. Consequently, she developed a practical sense, an understanding of money matters as the foundation of contemporary society, an ability to cope with legal cases and skill in the management of town property when still very young, and this shrewd and solid common sense remained with her to the end of her life. One may well believe her daughter who wrote: 'Dostoevsky was surprised by the ease with which my mother worked out involved sums and by her knowledge of dull legal terminology.'[2]

When Dostoevsky drove up to the two-storey Snitkin home the first thing that caught his attention was a large sign over a greengrocer's shop on the ground floor. He climbed the stairs and found himself in a huge room with an inordinate number of porcelain knick-knacks and ornaments. He discovered later that the late Gregory Snitkin's unusual job, which was concerned with the imperial palaces, had developed in him a taste for vases, statuettes, Sèvres, Saxony and Russian porcelain, and that he had gathered a large collection, which his daughters had inherited. On this visit the talk was of business. Dostoevsky arranged to start dictating the last part of *Crime and Punishment*, which he was committed to complete for *Russky Vestnik* by the beginning of the following year.

Anna reported for work once more on 8 November. She found Dostoevsky looking rather agitated.

I hastened to ask Fyodor Mikhailovich what he had been doing the last few days.

'I was making up a new novel,' he replied.

'Oh? and who is the hero of your novel?'

'An artist, no longer young, a man of my age, in fact.'

'Do tell me, please,' I begged, very much interested in the new novel.

The reply was a brilliant improvisation. Never before and never after did I hear Fyodor Mikhailovich speak with such inspiration. As he spoke, I realized that he was telling the story of his own life, only altering the names and the places. Here was everything that he had talked about to me before, fragmentarily. His detailed, coherent account gave me a great deal of insight into his relationships with his deceased wife and his relatives.

'And then,' Fyodor Mikhailovich was saying, 'at this decisive moment in his life the artist meets a young girl of your age or a year or two older. Could a young girl so different in character and in age fall in love with my artist? Wouldn't this be incorrect psychologically? That is what I wanted your opinion on, Anna Grigoryevna.'

'Why couldn't she? If, as you say, your Anya is not an empty-headed flirt but has a good, warm heart, why shouldn't she fall in love with your artist? What if he is sick and poor? Surely, one doesn't love a man for looks and wealth! And why should it be a sacrifice on her part? If she loves him then she will be happy herself and will never have cause for regret.'

I spoke with feeling. Fyodor Mikhailovich was looking at me agitatedly.

'And you seriously believe that she might love him sincerely all her life?'

He was silent for a while, as if unable to make up his mind about something.

'Put yourself in her place for a moment,' he said finally. 'Imagine that I am the artist and I have told you that I love

you and asked you to be my wife. Tell me what your answer
would be.'

Fyodor Mikhailovich looked so embarrassed, there was such
anguish in his face, that I realized at last that this was not
merely a literary conversation and that it would be a terrible
blow to his self-esteem and pride if I were to give him an evasive
reply. I glanced at that dear, excited face and said:

'I'd reply that I love you and will love you all my life.'

Dostoevsky took this new love of his calmly. It was nothing
like the stormy passion he had had for Maria Dmitrievna
Isaeva or Apollinaria Suslova. He wrote of his marriage
shortly afterwards:

> Towards the end of the novel[3] I noticed that my secretary
> was genuinely in love with me, although she had never said a
> word about it, and I, too, had become more and more fond of
> her. Since my life had been terribly lonely and depressing since
> my brother's death, I asked her to marry me. She consented, and
> now we are married. The difference in our ages is frightful
> (twenty and forty-four), but I am beginning to feel increasingly
> certain that she will be happy. She has a heart, and she has a
> capacity for love.

He was not mistaken about Anna Grigoryevna, although the
betrothal period of two such dissimilar personalities did not
go smoothly and had some dramatic moments.

Dostoevsky did not conceal from his fiancée the debts he
had acquired upon the failure of *Epokha*. The claims of his
late brother's creditors against the extinct *Vremya* and
Epokha were so many and the sum total of the promissory
notes so large that only in 1879–80, a year before his death,
did he manage to repay them all (and that was due entirely
to his wife's extraordinary and energetic efforts). In
addition, he was constantly surrounded by at least a dozen
members of his own family who looked to him as their sole
financial support. He had been left with the responsibility
for his brother's entire family, now literally beggars, for
his twenty-year-old stepson Pasha Isaev, in part for his

brother Nikolai and even for Mikhail's illegitimate son Vanya and his mother Praskovya Petrovna Anikeeva.

He had written *The Gambler* for next to nothing, and Katkov, too, was paying him very little for his masterpiece *Crime and Punishment* – one hundred and fifty roubles for every twenty-four pages of manuscript. It was a very difficult time and it seemed that poverty would never loosen its hold on him. Anna realized that this pattern of work would soon ruin her future husband and deplete him of the strength he needed to continue writing with his usual intensity. She was aware that he constantly pawned his belongings to pay urgent bills. He had pawned the silver dinner service, Chinese vases from Kazakhstan, even clothing. To such a practical and devoted girl as Anna, who would willingly have given all her own money to relieve the man she loved from the terrible burden of other people's debts, the situation looked bleak.

'One of our evenings at Peski, usually so peaceful and happy, unexpectedly turned out very upsetting,' Anna Grigoryevna recalled half a century later. Dostoevsky arrived at Peski one evening towards the end of November, chilled to the bone. He was immediately given hot tea.

'Do you have any cognac?'

'I don't think so, but we have some sherry.'

He drank three or four glasses of sherry straight off and then asked for more hot tea. The hostess became anxious.

'Aren't you wearing your winter coat?'

'No,' he replied hesitantly. 'I'm wearing my autumn coat.'

'But why didn't you wear your winter coat?'

'Someone told me it was thawing today.'

'I'll send a servant at once to fetch your winter coat. He can take this coat home for you.'

'No, please don't do that, please!'

'Why not? You will catch cold on your way home. It will get even colder by nightfall.'

'I don't have a winter coat.'

'What do you mean? Has it been stolen?'

'No, it hasn't been stolen. I had to pawn it.'

It transpired that his relatives had come to his house that morning, clamouring for money to pay pressing debts and for their immediate needs. Dostoevsky had no money to give them. An on-the-spot family council decided that since the thaw had set in he could pawn his winter coat. This would provide money for immediate expenses, and in a little while he would receive the money coming to him from *Russky Vestnik*. And so Pasha took his stepfather's coat to the nearest pawnshop.

There was a stormy scene.

I was deeply shocked by the heartlessness of Fyodor Mikhailovich's relatives. I began to speak quietly but with every word I uttered my anger and bitterness grew. I lost all control and spoke like one demented, saying whatever came into my head, arguing that he had obligations towards me, his fiancée. I kept saying that I would not survive his death. I wept, screamed, sobbed hysterically. Fyodor Mikhailovich was terribly distressed. He embraced me, kissed my hands and begged me to calm down.

'I am so accustomed to pawning my things that I did not attach any importance to it. Had I known you would take it so tragically I would not have let Pasha pawn my winter coat.'

Anna's mother suggested that Dostoevsky become his fiancée's guardian and thereby acquire complete control over her property. He refused.

'This house belongs to Anna,' he said. 'Let her assume ownership officially in the autumn when she turns twenty-one. I do not wish to interfere in her financial affairs.'

During our engagement Fyodor Mikhailovich consistently refused to accept financial assistance from me. I told him that if we loved one another everything we owned should belong to us both.

'Certainly that is how it will be when we are married,' he replied, 'but meanwhile I do not wish to take a single rouble from you!'

Dostoevsky went to Moscow and obtained an advance payment of two thousand roubles from Katkov. When he returned he gave his fiancée five hundred roubles for the wedding.

'Hold on to this tightly, Anya. Our future happiness depends on it.'

The wedding seemed taken care of; surely nothing could hinder it now. But, as the saying goes, there's many a slip 'twixt cup and lip. At one point misfortune nearly upset this precarious financial situation altogether.

Since her husband's death Anna's mother's affairs had got into a terrible state of confusion and were getting worse every day. Early in February 1867, a few days, that is, before the wedding an agent of one of the widow Snitkina's biggest creditors turned up at the Snitkina apartment, accompanied by a bailiff, with an order for distraint of Anna's property for alleged failure to pay a court order of five hundred roubles. This was patently illegal as Anna's mother, not Anna, was the debtor, but the plaintiffs were banking on the young girl's inexperience. They were wrong. Anna repulsed the imminent threat with courage and intelligence and in a businesslike manner. The agent retreated. The wedding invitations could be sent out.

On 13 February 1867, Dostoevsky wrote to his closest friends:

After a great many worries and all kinds of misunderstandings (even illness) fate has decreed that my wedding shall take place on Wednesday, February 15, in the Trinity Church in Izmailovo at 7 o'clock in the evening. And this seems to be certain.

I wish to remind you of your kind promise to be with me at the time. The very thought that you wish to witness the first moments of my renewed life gives me great pleasure.

It was just ten years since Dostoevsky's first marriage, which had taken place on 6 February 1857 in Kuznetsk, a town in an out-of-the-way region of feudal Russia, a settlement of trappers and prospectors. The church there was poor and the clergy impoverished. The bride was a penniless widow with a hectic flush on her cheeks. The witnesses were a state-registered peasant and a local school-teacher, who had almost the day before been regarded as the bride's fiancé. That wedding always remained one of Dostoevsky's saddest memories.

Now he was leading to the altar of the Izmailovo Cathedral a comely girl of twenty in a wedding dress of white watered silk and a long veil. Candles burned in the chandeliers. The solemn voices of the choir accompanied the ceremony. The witnesses, best men and guests included eminent writers and scholars, such as Apollon Maikov, Strakhov, Averkiev, Stoyunin, Lamansky, Milyukov, and many others who had been contributors to the Dostoevsky brothers' magazines. At home relatives and friends welcomed the newly-weds with champagne. The bride, smiling, young and in love, was happy and was enjoying the way her celebrated husband charmed everyone.

Dostoevsky's brilliant and fortunate second wedding was far less in keeping with his style of life than the modest ceremony in the Church of the Holy Guide in distant Kuznetsk. That perhaps is why that first wedding, so poor in ritual and so grand in tragic and emotional power, is reflected in his work, while the second is not.

THE HONEYMOON

There were receptions, visits and parties for the newly married pair. One day during that honeymoon period of their marriage Anna discovered that her husband was gravely and incurably ill. She relates:

On the last day of Shrovetide we had dinner with relatives and then drove to my sister's to spend the evening. We had a gay supper with champagne. We stayed on after the other guests had left. Fyodor Mikhailovich was very animated and was telling my sister an interesting story. All of a sudden he stopped short, leaving a word dangling in the air, turned pale, started to get up from the sofa but then began to fall slowly in my direction. I looked at his altered face in astonishment. All of a sudden a horrible, inhuman cry, more like a howl, broke forth from his lips and he began to fall forwards.

I caught him by the shoulders and pushed him back into a sitting position on the sofa. Imagine my horror when I saw my husband's senseless body slipping off the sofa. I did not have the strength to hold him up. I pushed away a table with a lighted lamp on it and let him slip to the floor and knelt down beside him. I held his head in my lap all through the seizure. There was no one to help me. My sister was in hysterics and my brother-in-law and the maid were attending to her.

Little by little the convulsions ceased and Fyodor Mikhailovich began to come to himself. At first he did not know where he was and had even lost the power of speech. He kept trying to say something but instead of one word another would emerge and it was impossible to understand him. It must have been at least half an hour before we were able to lift him and lay him down on the sofa. We decided to let him calm down before we went home.

But to my great sorrow, the seizure recurred an hour later, and this time it was so bad that Fyodor Mikhailovich screamed with pain at the top of his voice for over two hours after he had returned to consciousness. It was frightful. He had some double seizures later, but comparatively few. The doctor said that this one had been brought on by the excessive stimulation of the champagne.

We had to stay the night at my sister's because Fyodor Mikhailovich was so very weak, and, besides, we feared there might be another seizure. What a horrible night I had! This was my first sight of the terrible disease with which Fyodor Mikhailovich was afflicted. As I listened to his incessant groans for hours, as I looked upon his face, so distorted with suffering that it no longer resembled him, at his eyes, motionless as a madman's, as I tried to make out his incoherent speech and failed, I was afraid that my dearly beloved husband was losing his mind, and how that thought terrified me!

However, after a few hours of sleep Fyodor Mikhailovich was so much better that we were able to go home.

It was during that same sorrowful week that there began the unpleasantness and misunderstandings that make my memory of our 'honeymoon' sad and distressing and that poisoned the first weeks of our marriage.

Dostoevsky's closest relatives – his late brother's family and his stepson – were, with very few exceptions, jealous of and hostile to Dostoevsky's new wife. *Epokha*'s creditors kept turning up with court orders for large sums and threats of distraint. The young couple began to plan to go abroad, at least until the autumn. But even another advance from Katkov did not provide them with with enough money for such a major undertaking.

Anna resolved to sacrifice her entire dowry to save her marriage. She pawned the new furniture, the piano, furs, gold and silver objects and lottery tickets. 'We went abroad, intending to stay three months, and we returned more than four years later,' Anna Grigoryevna recalled. In their absence nearly all of her property vanished.[4] 'But a happy new life, which ended only with Fyodor Mikhailovich's death, began for us there.'

XIV

Beginning of Wanderings

DRESDEN

THE Dostoevskys' wanderings through Europe began in Dresden, which the writer liked very much for its quietness, its picture gallery and its beautiful gardens. Then to Baden-Baden, where the author of *The Gambler* surrendered to his gambling compulsion and where he had the memorable conversation with Turgenev about *Smoke* and about the problems of Russia and Europe. From Baden, Dostoevsky, an admirer of European painting, made for Bâle, for the sake of one of the greatest masterpieces of the late German Renaissance. Next came Geneva, where he saw a great deal of Ogaryov and attended the celebrated congress of the League for Peace and Freedom. He and his wife spent the summer of 1868 in Vevey and then they went to Italy, where they lived in Milan and in Florence for long periods. They stopped in Bologna and Venice on their way to 'golden Prague', centre of the Western Slavs, where they spent three days, and then returned to their beloved Dresden. They left for Russia from Dresden on 5 July 1871.

> Oh, I am sad, I am sad! A thick darkness is falling
> In the distant West, in the land of holy miracles!

These lines from Khomyakov,* who was a favourite poet of Dostoevsky's, must have come to his mind often. During the four years the Dostoevskys spent abroad the storm clouds were gradually gathering over the European continent. It was the eve of the Franco-Prussian war and of

* Alexey Stepanovich Khomyakov (1804–1860). Slavophil poet and religious writer.

the Paris Commune. For the first time Dostoevsky was in the midst of world events and able to observe them first-hand.

Dresden presented the lamentable picture of a recently defeated city. In the summer of 1866 Saxony, which had joined Austria in the latter's conflict with Prussia, had been routed along with her ally and was now occupied by the Prussian army. When the Dostoevskys arrived, less than a year had passed since this capital of Saxony had experienced the horrors of bombardment and the King had fled to Bohemia. The local people told the visitors of hospitals crowded with wounded and described the roar of battle at the city's walls. The Prussian officers, in red collars and with their hair parted all the way down the back of the head to the neck, whom the Dostoevskys saw in restaurants and on Brülow Terrace, were the real masters of the city and the exponents of Bismarck's policy of German unification 'through blood and iron'. The formation of the North German Confederation, in the territory of which our travellers now found themselves, was the event of the day, but this confederation did not mark the end of a campaign; it was the forerunner of new sieges and more large-scale battles.

Dostoevsky arrived in Dresden full of plans for new works. He had undertaken to write an article called 'My Acquaint-ance with Belinsky' for the Moscow miscellany *Chasha (Cup)* and was interested in everything associated with that great critic. He searched energetically in secondhand bookshops and in libraries for materials about Herzen, Bakunin, Ogaryov and the Petrashevskyites. He needed issues of *Kolokol* and *Polyarnaya Zuezda, Byloe i Dumy (My Past and Thoughts)* and a number of pamphlets that were banned in Russia. Now that he had completed *Crime and Punishment* his thoughts had turned to the types and characters of the people of the 1840s, the predecessors of nihilism and the present unrest, the fathers and sons of the Russian revolution, who were to figure largely in *The Devils*, *A Raw Youth* and *The Diary of a Writer*.

It is possible that by this time Dostoevsky had started thinking about a philosophical novel, focused on the relationship between ethics and aesthetics, even if the idea was still vague. Not long after this he began to talk about the spiritual exploit of a supremely moral individual – the ideally beautiful man – referring to it as a theme that had long been dear to him. And the very day he arrived in Dresden, 1 May 1867, he took Anna to the picture gallery to see a work of art that for him represented this cherished theme: 'My husband walked quickly through all the rooms and led me straight to the Sistine "Madonna", a painting which he regarded as the supreme manifestation of human genius.'

The representational art of the High Renaissance was a major influence on Dostoevsky's creativity in those years. The great fifteenth- and sixteenth-century masters gave expression in the traditional religious imagery of the Middle Ages to their own cult of the beautiful man, to their delight in the moral beauty of motherhood and the enlightening power of reason. Their interest in nature and in life, in the active man and his feelings and ideas, produced the powerful art of a new humanism, aspiring towards universal happiness and world harmony. The creations of world painting interested Dostoevsky primarily from their philosophical side, as powerful stimuli for his own future plans, as inspired embodiments of the eternal images, capable of incarnating the archetypes even in a modern novel.

Anna Dostoevskaya related that Dostoevsky admired Titian greatly, particularly his famous 'Christ with the Tribute Money'. He would stand in front of the painting for a long time without taking his eyes off it. 'It is a magnificent picture,' he said to his wife. 'It is the equal of Raphael's Madonna.' Dostoevsky was to draw a powerful contrast between two Titian images in his last novel, which incorporated parts of his previously conceived *Book of Christ*. In Ivan Karamazov's 'Poem', the prophet and the Inquisitor are, as it were, done in the manner of the famous picture by the Venetian master, a picture which Dostoevsky in 1873 contrasted with 'The Last Supper' of the Russian 'Mobile' painter Ge*, of which it was, he said, the archetype – if the contemporary artist, thought Dostoevsky, had given to his Teacher the face 'with which Titian had drawn Him in his celebrated "Render Unto Caesar"', much would have immediately become intelligible'.

That same first day in Dresden Dostoevsky also saw the mythological landscapes of Claude Lorrain. The idyllic landscapes that Claude used as a background for scenes of the happy life of primitive peoples were typified in his masterpiece 'Acis and Galatea', with its rippling waves and slanting rays of sun and innocent and beautiful people on the shore of a shining sea. The jagged profile of a mountain shows blue on the horizon, the shadows are thickening beneath the overhanging cliff on the shore, but in the distance all is bright and airy and festive. 'But I always called it "The Golden Age",' Dostoevsky remarked about Lorrain's painting, which was the inspiration for a beautiful short prose poem, immortalized in Stavrogin's Confession and Versilov's monologue.

Dostoevsky greatly admired the young Rembrandt's famous 'Portrait of Himself with his Wife Saskia on His Lap'. (The genre scenes in Dostoevsky's novels, with their dark shadows and bright highlights, have been compared with Rembrandt's works.) The novelist, in Dresden with his young wife, was especially responsive to the joy of life and cloudless happiness with which all the details of that painting are imbued – the huge goblet of sparkling wine,

---

* Ge. A Russian painter of the so-called 'Mobile' group of the 1870s, the best known of whom is Tepin. They got their name (Russian *peredvizhniki*) because they used to have mobile exhibitions of their works.

the brilliant plumage of the velvet headdress, and the jubilant painter's completely absorbed, adoring smile. There were two other portraits of the same model in the Dresden gallery's Rembrandt collection – 'Saskia van Eilenburg' and 'Saskia with a Red Flower'. Rembrandt's 'An Old Woman Weighing Gold' struck a chord in the creator of Raskolnikov, while the 'Portrait of an Old Man in a Black Beret', with his refined features and deepset eyes filled with sorrow and compassion, was surely after Dostoevsky's own heart. Dostoevsky must in fact have felt a special kinship with Rembrandt's style of inspired and poetic realism, though he has not left any record of his impressions of this master of tragic portraiture.

Hans Holbein the Younger, one of the greatest sixteenth-century painters, was another of Dostoevsky's favourites in the Dresden Zwinger. Dostoevsky regarded his 'Madonna of the Burgomeister Meyer' as the supreme embodiment of quiet and secret sorrow. 'And my Holbein Madonna, how pure she is, how beautiful,' he wrote in his notebooks for *The Idiot*, where he also made a perceptive remark about the letter of a certain Russian girl 'written in the manner of the Holbein Madonna'. Goethe called the Dresden gallery 'an eternal fountain'. That is how the creator of Prince Myshkin must also have felt about it as he searched fervently for a great theme and a heroic type.

Among all the masterpieces of Renaissance painting in this collection Dostoevsky was drawn above all to the embodiments of the poetic legend of the fallen woman, regenerated by the untainted inner beauty of a perfect man. This is one of the best-known episodes in the New Testament and it has been represented many times in art, particularly in painting. Titian, Veronese, Murillo, Rubens, Van Dyck, Rembrandt, Correggio, Ribera, Claude Lorrain, Fra Bartolommeo, Carlo Dolci, Greuze, Poussin, Delacroix and many other of the world's greatest masters have portrayed the penitent Magdalene. Dostoevsky had already been moved by this theme in his youth. He had mentioned 'Christ Forgiving the Adulteress', by the contemporary French painter Emile Signol, in one of the manuscripts of *Netochka Nezvanova*. Now, twenty years later, he was once again moved by the dramatic power and profundity of this ancient legend as he studied the canvases in the Dresden gallery. He saw Batoni's 'Regeneration of the Fallen Woman', which gave him 'great pleasure'; Bartolommeo Biscaino's 'Sinner', showing a festively dressed courtesan, overwhelmed by a death sentence passed against a wise and righteous man; and the 'Penitence of Mary Magdalene of Leys', in which a young woman, head thrown back, is wringing her hands, imploring her companions to help her at this moment of agony when her conscience awakens and rebels.

A new novel was slowly germinating in Dostoevsky's mind and during these anxious and exhausting weeks these images must have been all the more vivid to him, as he planned a new book, in which he would endeavour to present that ancient dramatic legend against the background of his own cruel age. In the autumn of the same year he began an outline of *The Idiot*. In his notes for the novel Dostoevsky repeatedly calls attention to the analogy between his theme and the legend, and explains his idea – 'The Prince is Christ'; 'A passionate and tender scene with the Prince (the evangelical pardoning of the sinful woman in the church)'; 'Aglaya goes to see Nastasia Filippovna, says that it is vile to play the role of a Magdalene', and so forth.

By the beginning of 1868 the idea of the new novel had taken more concrete shape in Dostoevsky's mind; he wanted it to portray positively a beautiful man. He admits that although he has long cherished this theme it is a difficult one to express. He associates it with the pure and beloved image of the charming and radiant girl, whom ties of blood and of the heart had made dear to him. He wrote to her: 'This novel is called *The Idiot*; it is dedicated to you, that is, to

Sophia Alexandrovna Ivanova. My sweet friend, how I hope that this novel turns out at least somewhat worthy of the dedication.' Chapters from Dostoevsky's new book *The Idiot* began to appear in *Russky Vestnik* in January 1868.

*

Life in Dresden was tranquil, even gracious, for the Dostoevskys. They strolled in the English-style parks and on the various promenades in that city of gardens. They attended open-air concerts and heard symphony orchestras play Mozart, Rossini's *Stabat Mater*, Wagner's march from *Rienzi*, Beethoven's overture to *Fidelio*. 'Nothing greater than this has ever been created,' Dostoevsky wrote in a letter to his wife a little later. 'In Beethoven there is passion and love everywhere. He is a poet of love, of happiness and of the melancholy of love.'

The Dostoevskys belonged to several libraries which had French and Russian books. Dostoevsky re-read Victor Hugo's *Les Misérables*, which he greatly admired, and *The Old Curiosity Shop* and *Nicholas Nickleby* by his beloved Dickens. He became a habitué of a café where he could read foreign and Russian newspapers, always an important source of material for him. Anna, who had been interested in porcelain from childhood, used to visit antique shops and special collections, where she admired the famous Meissen and amazed her husband by her tireless curiosity. 'It turns out that there is a definite lover of antiques in Anna's character (and I find this very sweet and amusing),' Dostoevsky wrote to Apollon Maikov on 16(28) August 1867. 'For example, she really enjoys looking at some stupid town hall, taking notes, describing it (which she does in shorthand and has filled seven notebooks), but the gallery has interested and amazed her most of all.'

They did not know anyone in Dresden and they both enjoyed the seclusion. They wrote a great many letters. Anna corresponded with her family and with her friend

Maria Stoyunina. Dostoevsky corresponded with his literary friends, Apollon Maikov and Nikolai Strakhov, with the editor of *Russky Vestnik*, Katkov, and with the friend of his heart, Sonya Ivanova.

But their married life was not all fair weather. One day Dostoevsky received a letter from Apollinaria Suslova. He replied to her from Dresden, telling her of the change in his life and addressing her in warm and tender terms:

Your letter made me sad. You write that you are very unhappy. I do not know what your life has been like in the past year and what has been in your heart, but judging by all I know of you, it is difficult for you to be happy. Oh, my darling, it is not the cheap, *necessary* happiness I want for you. I respect you (and I always respected you) for your uncompromising standards, but, after all, I know that your heart is *incapable* of not making demands on life, while you yourself regard people either as infinitely shining or from the start as scoundrels and boors. I am judging from the facts. Draw your own conclusions. Goodbye, eternal friend.

It is evident from Anna's Dresden diary that 'Polina's' (Apollinaria's) letters upset Dostoevsky. Her diary describes him reading one of these letters received in Dresden:

I watched his face all the time he was reading that fine letter. He re-read the first page many times as if unable to make out the meaning of what was written there; then at last he read it through and blushed crimson. It seemed to me that his hands were trembling. I pretended not to know and asked him what Sonya wrote. He replied that the letter was not from Sonya and smiled rather bitterly. I had never seen him smile like that before. It was a smile of either contempt or pity. I really do not know which, but it was a rather pathetic, forlorn smile. Then he became frightfully absent-minded and hardly understood what I was saying.

Anna was equally upset by Suslova's letters. She was afraid Dostoevsky might leave her for his former passion. 'I felt cold, I trembled and even wept. I was afraid that his old attachment might revive and that his love for me would vanish.

Lord, don't send me such a calamity. I was terribly unhappy. Every time I thought of it my heart would bleed. Lord, not that, it would ·be too painful for me to lose his love!'

Letters continued to arrive from Suslova and to fall into Anna's hands. Anna did not dare to bring the matter out into the open, but her hints became more direct and obvious. This infuriated Dostoevsky.

He walked over to me quickly and, his chin trembling, began to tell me that he had now understood my words, that he reserved the right to correspond with anyone he wished, that he had certain contacts and that I should not dare to interfere with him!

However, the Dostoevskys' prolonged stay abroad and their frequent changes of address made it difficult to keep up the correspondence. Gradually, even the exchange of letters with Suslova came to an end. At the beginning of July, after two months in Dresden, the Dostoevskys went for the summer to Baden-Baden, a fashionable resort where roulette was played.

BADEN-BADEN. THE ENCOUNTER WITH TURGENEV

En route to Baden-Baden the Dostoevskys passed medieval castles with round towers which brought to their minds the crusaders and their tournaments. In Frankfurt-am-Main Anna was charmed by the blossoming white acacia, which she had never seen before. They saw the monuments to Gutenberg and Goethe. Dostoevsky was impressed by an old Gothic church near the market, which he said was 'perfection in art'.

In Baden-Baden, they stayed at the large Hotel Zum Goldenen Ritter, but gambling losses from the very first day soon compelled them to move to an out-of-the-way section of the city. They rented two small rooms above a smithy.

The blacksmith's deafening hammering and the cries and screams of children filled the house all day long. Anna submitted to her fate uncomplainingly: 'I don't pay attention to the noise in the smithy, as I have already become accustomed to it. But Fedya, he notices it. He does not get enough sleep and this makes him irritable.' Their time in Baden-Baden was about the saddest period in their four years in Europe. Towards the end of their stay there they were in real trouble, but even at the very beginning a serious event occurred that left a lasting imprint on Dostoevsky's life and work. This was his ideological quarrel with Turgenev, which caused a breach in their relations for many years.

As the Dostoevskys were returning from the casino one evening they met Goncharov, who had recently arrived to take the waters. Dostoevsky introduced him to Anna. Goncharov told them that Turgenev was in Baden-Baden. Turgenev had in fact taken up permanent residence in this fashionable resort and was building himself a house next to Pauline Viardot's villa, and all the celebrities of Europe used to visit them. As if speaking for Turgenev, Goncharov told them that Turgenev had seen Dostoevsky at the roulette table the previous evening but had not gone up to him because he knew that players do not like to be disturbed. 'Since Fedya owes Turgenev fifty thaler,' Anna wrote in her diary after she heard of it from Goncharov, 'he ought to go to see Turgenev, otherwise Turgenev will think that Fedya does not want to see him for fear he may demand his money.' The debt was a debt of honour that Dostoevsky had incurred two years before.

Dostoevsky decided to call on Turgenev the very next day. They had been on perfectly friendly terms during the years of the publication of the *pochva* magazines, and Turgenev's *Phantoms* had been published in *Epokha*. Shortly after the demise of *Epokha*, in 1865, when Dostoevsky was in Wiesbaden with Apollinaria Suslova and had begun to work on

Crime and Punishment, he wrote to Turgenev, having lost money gambling, asking him for a loan of one hundred thaler, which he promised to repay within three weeks. Turgenev immediately sent him fifty thaler and a friendly letter. Dostoevsky thanked 'the very kind Ivan Sergeyevich' warmly, for even that sum was 'very helpful'.

Two years had gone by and Dostoevsky had not repaid the debt. Moreover, he had now been losing heavily and wanted a further extension of time to pay. The matter could, no doubt, have been arranged without much difficulty, but there was one circumstance that made the situation much more complicated. Dostoevsky had in recent months come to disagree completely with Turgenev, and he feared that if he went to see him now he was bound to have a heated argument with him. Turgenev's novel *Smoke* had appeared in *Russky Vestnik* in March 1867 and had aroused a storm of indignation among critics of all parties and trends. 'Everybody is abusive, both the reds and the whites,' Turgenev wrote to Herzen. Dostoevsky, too, found *Smoke*'s 'extreme Westernism' and 'denial of the national ideals of the Slavophiles and the soil' repugnant.

Dostoevsky called on Turgenev at noon on 10 July. His host immediately started talking about the vehement press campaign against his novel. He had written to Pavel Annenkov: 'It seems to me that no one has ever been abused so unanimously as I am being for *Smoke*. The stones are flying from all sides. In the English Club in Moscow the gentleman collected signatures protesting against *Smoke* and even suggested that I be expelled from the gentry-class.' He explained to Dostoevsky the principal idea of *Smoke*.

'There is one common and unavoidable road for all – that is civilization, and all the claims of Russianism to independence are nonsensical. I am writing a long article against all Russophiles and Slavophiles.'

'Why don't you send to Paris for a telescope for your convenience?'

'Whatever for?'

'You could train the telescope on Russia and observe us; it is difficult to see what is happening otherwise. Russia is a long way off.'

Turgenev frowned but did not reply.

'You know,' the visitor continued, 'I really did not expect that all the criticism (that is, attacks) against you and the failure of *Smoke* would have annoyed you so much. It really isn't worth it.'

'But I am not in the least annoyed. Where did you get that idea?'

Dostoevsky picked up his hat, but before he left he gave vent to all the dislike of the Germans that had accumulated in his heart in the last three months.

'Do you know what sort of scoundrels and cheats one comes across here? The common people here are much worse and much more dishonest than ours, and undeniably more stupid. You talk about civilization. Tell me, what has civilization done for them and what have they to boast about to us?'

'You offend me personally by that kind of talk. I want you to know that I have decided to settle here for good.'

'Though I have read *Smoke* and have been talking to you for a whole hour, I nevertheless did not expect to hear you say that. Forgive me for having offended you.'

They parted politely.

'I vowed never to set foot there again!' said Dostoevsky.[1]

Turgenev evidently felt the same way. He called on Dostoevsky at 10 o'clock the next morning (knowing that they never got up before twelve) and left his visiting card, to indicate clearly that their personal relationship was ended. They still met in the casino but did not even greet one another. Dostoevsky paid his Wiesbaden debt to Turgenev in March 1876 (we have Turgenev's receipt for it).

To the honour of both writers, their many years of enmity

ended in reconciliation at the Pushkin celebrations in 1880, not long before they both died.

*

Dostoevsky's wife felt that the impetuosity, impulsiveness and passion that so often plunged her husband into despair were inherent traits of his character. She has described his behaviour at an auction they attended in Dresden one day. Dostoevsky greatly admired a set of bowls and plates of dark cherry-red Bohemian crystal with a gold border. He could not afford to purchase all eighteen articles, but he persuaded a Frenchwoman there, who was admiring the same set, to go halves with him. He started bidding, going higher and higher, thaler by thaler.

'His gambling fever grew by the minute,' Anna recalled. 'I saw the price going up and I thought with horror: "What if the Frenchwoman changes her mind?"'

The Dostoevskys had very little money and were planning to leave for Russia soon. To transport nine fragile crystal objects in suitcases was out of the question. It was foolish to bid for them. The price threatened to leave them penniless. But Dostoevsky was in the grip of the gambler's irrestrainable passion and he was not satisfied until the precious bowls and plates were his.

Dostoevsky had first begun to gamble extensively during his trips abroad in 1862 and 1863. He tried his luck at roulette and won a big sum, but in subsequent sessions he twice got cleaned out. The mania that possessed him was stronger than any rational argument. He found the dangerous and destructive temptation to gamble irresistible. 'The important thing is the game itself. Do you know how it sucks you in? No, I swear to you, it is not only greed, although first of all I did need the money as money.'

Subsequently, Anna, having personally experienced the ruinous consequences of Dostoevsky's gambling passion, gave a detailed account of his condition when seized by that unconquerable fever:

Everything Fyodor Mikhailovich said about the possibility of winning at roulette by using his method was absolutely true, and success might have been complete if that method were being used by some cold-blooded Englishman or German, not by such a nervous man as my husband, who used to get carried away and who used to go to extremes in everything. In addition to cool-headedness and restraint, a roulette player must also have considerable sums of money so that he can sustain unfavourable luck in the game. Fyodor Mikhailovich did not meet the conditions in this respect either. We had comparatively little money and absolutely nowhere to obtain any in case of bad luck. Before the week was out Fyodor Mikhailovich had lost all his cash and had to start worrying about where to get some more so as to continue the game. We had to pawn our things. But even after he had pawned our things my husband could never restrain himself and sometimes he lost all the money he had got for the pawned articles. Often he lost every last thaler. And sometimes luck would suddenly favour him and he would bring home several dozen friedrichsd'or.

Once I remember, he brought home a full wallet in which I counted 212 friedrichsd'or (at twenty thaler each), that was about 4,300 thaler. But this money never remained in our hands for long. Fyodor Mikhailovich could not restrain himself. Before the excitement of the game had died down in him he would take twenty coins, lose them, come back for twenty more, lose them, and thus for two or three hours, returning for money several times, and finally he would lose it all.

I must say in fairness to myself that I never reproached my husband for his losses.

But my heart ached to see how he himself suffered. He would return from the roulette table pale, haggard, hardly able to stand on his feet, ask me for money (he used to give me all the money), depart, and come back half an hour later even more upset, for money, and so on until he had lost everything we had.

When he had no money to gamble with and there was nowhere to get any, he would sometimes become so depressed that he would begin to sob; he'd get down on his knees before me, implore my forgiveness for tormenting me by his actions and work himself into a state of extreme despair. It took much effort and persuasion on my part to calm him down, to make it appear as if our situation were not so hopeless, to devise a way out and turn his attention and thoughts to other things.

The story of Dostoevsky's incessant losses, hopes, insane risks, overpowering gambling fever, inability to cope with the gambling devil or to stick to the system he had devised ('As soon as I begin to win I immediately start taking risks. I cannot control myself'!) presents a picture of the extreme mental agony into which he constantly drew his wife by describing to her every detail of his bad luck. 'I have lost everything'; 'I have pawned my watch'; 'For God's sake, send me some money for the return ticket'; 'Save me for the last time'; – his letters to her were groans of penitence, self-accusation and attempts at self-justification, fervent vows and fresh requests for money. They are the stuff of tragedy.

Anna, abandoned in an alien city, without friends or family, alone, pregnant, extremely nervous, with hardly any money, used to strain her resources each time and send him the twenty imperials he asked for. She kept hoping that this hell would come to an end, that this loneliness, this separation, this gambling fever that had overcome her beloved husband would run its course. But then she would receive another letter. 'Anya, my darling, my friend, my wife, forgive me, do not call me a blackguard. I have committed a crime, I have lost everything you sent me, every last kreuzer. I received it yesterday and I lost it yesterday. Anya, how can I stand to look at myself now? What will you say about me?'

What would Anna say? She would send him some more money for the return ticket and would wait to hear that he had lost it again.

By half past nine I lost everything and I left in a daze. I was in such agony that I ran off to find a priest. (Don't worry, I didn't get there, I didn't get there, and won't go.) As I ran through unfamiliar streets in the darkness I thought: after all, he is God's pastor, I won't be talking to him as to a private person but as if at confession . . . but I lost my way and went home. It is midnight now, I am sitting and writing to you. (And I won't go to the priest, I won't go, I swear I won't go!)

Dostoevsky's expiatory letters, imbued with shame and anguish, are more moving than the most horror-ridden pages of his novels.

Baden-Baden was the first place Anna witnessed this daily, agonizing and hopeless drama, and each evening she wrote down her impressions in her shorthand notebooks. These notes must not be ignored, for they give us a vivid picture of a great man – a thinker and a poet – in the grip of an unconquerable passion which is causing him and the woman he loves unbearable agony. We shall give one instance characteristic of the whole of Dostoevsky's system of play, and of their whole life at Baden-Baden.

On the morning of 16 July they had amassed 166 gulden.[2] Dostoevsky gambled all day long, repeatedly dipping into the money put aside for housekeeping. By the evening they had 66 gold pieces left. The day's loss amounted to one thousand francs. By the end of the next day, 17 July, they had twenty gold pieces left. He lost all of it on 18 July and asked his wife for her jewellery to pawn. 'I took out a pair of earrings and a brooch and gazed at them for a long, long time. I felt I was seeing them for the last time. (And I was.) I felt dreadful. I was so fond of them. Fedya had given them to me.'

Anna kissed them good-bye and gave them to him, asking him to redeem them within one month. 'Fedya got down on his knees before me, kissed my breast, kissed my hands, said that I was kind and sweet, that here I was, not well, that there was no one the world better than I was.' He went away, and Anna burst into sobs. It was all so frightful, painful, hopeless, irremediable, unbearable. Her despair verged on madness, sobs choked her. 'Oh, Lord, how hard it is for me.

How many more dreadful times such as these am I to have in my life?'

Some three hours later Dostoevsky returned.

'He told me he had lost everything, even the money he had obtained for the pawned earrings (120 francs). Fedya sat down on a chair and pulled me to his lap, but I got down on my knees in front of him and tried to console him.' He began by saying that this was the last time, but he could not go on. He put his elbows on the table, leaned his head on them and began to cry. Yes, Fedya wept. He said: "I have stolen, taken and lost everything of yours." I tried to console him but he kept on weeping. How my heart ached for him. It is terrible, the way he suffers.'

But on the next morning, 19 July, he was at the gambling table again with the last of their savings (one gulden, one five-franc coin and four florins) and again he lost it all. He pawned his wedding ring for twenty francs and lost it. Anna gave him her expensive lace mantilla (a gift from her mother) and her wedding ring without the slightest hope that he might have a run of luck. She was miserable.

It was late in the evening when Dostoevsky came home. He was carrying a bouquet of pink and white roses for Anna. He handed her both wedding rings which he had just redeemed. He had won 180 francs and had actually got up and left the roulette table. The old German pawnbroker said to him as he returned the wedding rings: 'Never gamble again, if you do, you will lose everything.' Dostoevsky did not heed this advice. Within two days the roulette wheel carried away the 180 francs. 'Now we really have no money to live on,' Anna wrote in her diary on 21 July.

In Dresden she had enjoyed listening to music. Here even this simple pleasure was farther from her reach. The ladies were too well dressed! 'And all I had to wear was an old black dress in which I was awfully hot and which did not look too good either. But what can I do if this is the way it has to be!' Her shoes were shabby and she had to hide her feet. All she could do was to climb the hill behind the railway station and listen to the distant music 'which sounded wonderful' from there. As the Baden-Baden orchestra played Beethoven's *Egmont*, Mozart's *Don Juan* and *Magic Flute*, Donizetti's *Lucia di Lammermoor*, Anna tried to forget herself and the horrible realities of her life. 'Our situation is hopeless,' she wrote in her diary in August. 'It is dreadfully hot, the children cry, the sound of the hammers in the smithy is unbearable. We do not have a kopeck. All our things have been pawned and perhaps gone forever. The rooms are small. We are sick and tired of the sound of the bell. There are no books, and ahead is the possibility that we will have to stop having dinner.'

Besides, they were both ill. Anna suffered from nausea, vomiting and acute pains. Dostoevsky had epileptic seizures, which were accompanied by the fear of death. Anna's family sent her money and they were able to leave 'this accursed city', this 'hell', this gambling den that had caused them so much suffering. They left Baden-Baden for Geneva on 23 August 1867, turning aside on their way to visit Bâle to see the masterpieces of one of the greatest masters of the German Renaissance.

HANS HOLBEIN THE YOUNGER

One of the strongest impressions ever made on Dostoevsky by a painting was that of 'Christ Taken from the Cross', by Hans Holbein the Younger, whose work he had liked so much in Dresden. As a child Dostoevsky had read Karamzin's *Letters of a Russian Traveller*, one of which reports the author's interest in the 'paintings by the celebrated Holbein, who was born in Bâle and was a friend of Erasmus'. 'There is nothing divine in "Christ Taken from the Cross", but it is an extremely natural picture of a dead man.'[3]

Probably Dostoevsky had also read George Sand's preface to her book *La Mare au Diable*, which spoke of the enormous significance of Holbein for the newest, progressive art:

> The first impulse for the writing of this book came from Holbein's engraving 'Dance of Death', because of the very important thoughts it provokes about literature and its broad social base. In Holbein's time art depicted the poor and melancholy aspects of life. Unremitting pessimism, especially painful because it promises nothing but suffering to all the disinherited, colours Holbein's world outlook. The contemporary artist is confronted by the same problem of the starving and the ragged, of social enmity and inhumanity.

This of course was also Dostoevsky's principal theme.

Anna wrote that Dostoevsky had heard about Holbein's 'Christ Taken from the Cross' (probably in the 1860s) and was determined to go to Bâle while he was in Europe to see this work which even from a distance had appealed to him. So they changed trains on the way to Geneva and spent 12 August in the city of Erasmus of Rotterdam and of the celebrated painter of his portrait.

The day was overcast. They were surprised at how silent and gloomy Bâle was. But at the town museum they saw the satirical 'Dance of Death', in which people from all social groups, ranks and professions are following the implacable ringleader. And they saw the extraordinary painting Dostoevsky had come to look at and which he recalls in *The Idiot*:

> Hanging over the door to the next room was an unusually shaped painting. It was about six feet across and surely no more than eleven inches high. It showed the Saviour, just removed from the Cross.
>
> 'Why, this is a copy of Hans Holbein,' the Prince said after a close look at the painting. 'I'm not much of a connoisseur but I believe that this is an excellent copy. I saw the original abroad and I cannot forget it.'

'Incidentally, Lev Nikolaevich, I have been wanting to ask you: do you believe in God?' Rogozhin said suddenly, walking several steps.

'How strangely you ask that and . . . look!' the Prince exclaimed involuntarily.

'I like to look at this painting,' Rogozhin mumbled after a moment's silence, as if he had forgotten the question he had asked.

'At this painting!' the Prince cried, and, as if struck by an unexpected thought: 'Why, there are some that might lose their faith after looking at this painting.'

'There are some that might,' Rogozhin assented unexpectedly.

Dostoevsky had planned to include in the novel an interpretation by Prince Myshkin of Holbein's masterpiece (perhaps his talking about it to Rogozhin quoted in the above excerpt was an outline for this). Questions of atheism and faith, of realism and naturalism, would have had wide scope here. But in the end he did not write this philosophical commentary on Holbein, although he had been strongly affected and quite carried away by the picture in the Bâle museum.

A remarkable work (wrote Anna in her diary) but it simply horrified me. Yet it impressed Fedya so much that he proclaimed Holbein a wonderful artist and poet. Contrary to tradition, Christ is depicted in this painting, 'with an emaciated body, the bones and ribs showing, the hands and feet pierced by wounds, swollen and very blue, as in a corpse that is beginning to rot. The face is agonized and the eyes are half open but unseeing and expressionless. The nose, mouth and chin have turned blue. In general, this so closely resembles a real corpse that, truly, I don't think I would dare to remain in the same room with the painting. Perhaps it is amazingly exact, but, truly, it is not in the least aesthetic and in me it aroused nothing but revulsion and a sort of horror. But Fedya is full of admiration for this painting.

Anna probably wrote this the same day. Much later she returned to this memorable episode of her foreign travels in her reminiscences, adding a number of details about Dostoevsky's response to Holbein's extraordinary innovation:

The painting overwhelmed Fyodor Mikhailovich, and he stopped in front of it as if stricken. For my part, I was unable to keep my eyes on it. It was too painful, especially in my delicate condition, and I went into another room. When I returned about fifteen or twenty minutes later I found Fyodor Mikhailovich still standing there as if rooted to the spot. On his agitated face was the sort of frightened expression I had often noticed during the first moments of an epileptic seizure. I quietly took my husband's arm, led him to another room and made him sit down on a bench, expecting him to have a seizure any minute. Fortunately, it did not come. Little by little, Fyodor Mikhailovich calmed down, and when we were leaving he insisted on going to take another look at the painting that had made such an impression on him.

This magnificent study of the nude showed the legendary martyr as a rotting corpse, incapable of rising to new life. The painter's harsh realism guided him away from the conventional beauty and canonical piousness of the official Church interpretation. It is no surprise that in *The Idiot* Prince Myshkin remarks upon, and Rogozhin confirms, the anti-religious significance of the celebrated painting in Bâle.

GENEVA

Since the Austro-Prussian war of 1866 it had been feared in European political circles that a clash between France and Prussia was imminent and inevitable. Anti-militarist agitation had begun. Various pacifist groups decided to convene an international congress of progressive leaders of the West to demonstrate the ideals of peace and freedom of nations. The Congress was to meet in Geneva in September 1867 in the Election Palace under the banner of the League for Peace and Freedom. Victor Hugo, Garibaldi, John Stuart Mill, Herzen, Bakunin, Ogaryov, Louis Blanc, Pierre Leroux, Jules Vallès, Elise Reclus, Edgar Quinet, Jules Favre, Littré and Büchner accepted invitations to participate.

The Dostoevskys arrived in Geneva, where they had decided to spend the winter, about two weeks before the opening of the Congress. Dostoevsky wanted to go somewhere where he could speak the language during his wife's forthcoming confinement, and since French was the only foreign language he knew well he chose French-speaking Switzerland. This was a splendid opportunity to observe all the eminent figures of the contemporary revolutionary movement. At that time the environs of Lake Geneva, as well as the principal city of the canton, were a major centre for European and particularly Russian, political *emigrés*. Herzen had been in the habit of staying there for long periods since the mid 1860s, as he did the year the Dostoevskys lived there. Pierre Leroux, veteran of the socialism of the 1840s, was there that summer. Ogaryov, Utin, Ahl, Serno-Solovyevich, Karl Vogt, Nikoladze, Elpidin and Lev Mechnikov, 'Garibaldi's aide-de-camp', lived in Geneva in 1867.

Both Anna Dostoevskaya and Strakhov say that Dostoevsky saw a great deal of Ogaryov, who used often to drop in to visit the voluntary exile from Petersburg, bringing him books and newspapers and even lending him ten francs now and then. From the letters Herzen wrote to his son from Geneva it is evident that Dostoevsky often went to see Ogaryov, too, where he must have met the many Russian *emigrés*. Finally there was Bakunin, who arrived in Geneva at the beginning of September 1867, at about the same time as the Dostoevskys, and who used to be at Ogaryov's a great deal. Bakunin lived on the shores of Lake Geneva for about a year, at first in Geneva itself, then farther out, in Vevey and in Clarens, where Dostoevsky was also staying. On 27 February 1868

Herzen wrote to his son that Ogaryov was ill: 'The trouble is that he doesn't get any quiet – Bakunin, Utin, Dostoevsky, Merchinsky, Chernetsky, Danich, us.' Dostoevsky undoubtedly met Bakunin many times during his stay in Geneva and must have talked with him often; he also heard other people talk about him, and could observe him freely and at first hand, as one of the most celebrated representatives of the Russian revolutionary emigration. Now they were to meet at a political congress of worldwide importance.

The Congress was a significant demonstration by European progressive opinion. It was covered by the major political press of the whole world. Eminent public figures from different countries, Guillaume, Büchner, Cesar de Pape, spoke on behalf of various organizations. Ogaryov and Bakunin were elected to the group of vice-presidents. It is not surprising that Dostoevsky, who had been close to the Utopian socialists in his youth and then experienced a crisis that led him into the opposite camp, should have been interested in this Congress. These new leaders of socialism and revolution were still no more than names to him, but at the Congress, as he wrote to his niece Sonya on 11 October 1867, he could observe firsthand 'these gentlemen, whom I was seeing in the flesh, not in books, for the first time'. For a creative artist, philosopher and journalist such as Dostoevsky this spectacle was of course of paramount interest. His letters make it plain that his first direct observation of the figures of the contemporary Left, their declarations and their discussions had evoked from him heightened interest, though of an entirely negative kind. The theses calling for the extermination of the Christian religion and of the great monarchies, for the abolition of capital and 'the issuing of an order that everything belongs to everybody' – which is how Dostoevsky interpreted the views of his socialist contemporaries – conflicted basically with his own world outlook. And since ideas were important to him as stimuli to creative work, the Geneva Conference needs to be taken into account in the history of the novel he was writing at the time.

There was one speaker that must have interested him particularly. When it was the turn to speak of Mikhail Bakunin, the renowned soldier of the international revolution, the veteran of Prague and Dresden, the former prisoner in Saxony, Austria and Russia, who had been twice sentenced to death, who had escaped across three continents and become a legend in his lifetime, the whole vast auditorium of the Palace at Geneva shook under the impact of his explosive theses. He arrested the attention of the entire Congress. For the first time, after an interval of twenty years, Bakunin was making an appearance on a political platform, wearing the halo of a fearless fighter against despotism and martyr of the reactionary governments. His speech, according to eyewitnesses, was extraordinarily effective.

As he ascended the steps leading to the platform, where the Bureau was seated, in his heavy, clumsy gait, dressed with his usual carelessness in some sort of grey overall, a shout went up: 'Bakunin!' Garibaldi, who was in the chair, stood up, took a few steps towards him, and flung himself into his arms. The meeting between two veteran, tried soldiers of the revolution made an extraordinary impression. The audience rose and applauded enthusiastically.

Bakunin's speech was received with noisy approval. 'His majestic figure, his vigorous gestures, the sincerity and conviction in his voice, his short sentences, as if chopped with an axe, were very effective.'

He began by making an energetic protest against the very existence of the Russian empire, based as it was on the denial of all human rights and freedoms. He called for the abolition of centralized states and the establishment of a free federation of provinces and peoples – a United States of Europe. He predicted that there would inevitably be a frightful world war and certain return 'to the horrible times of Wallenstein and Tilly'. He concluded with his customary oratorical flourish: 'Woe, woe to the nations! Woe to the nations, whose leaders return victorious from the battlefield! The laurels and the haloes will become chains and manacles for the peoples who imagine themselves the victors.' Electrified, the crowd, six thousand strong, listened in tense silence.

Every event in the Geneva Palace had a strong impact on Dostoevsky. In letters that he wrote to Russian friends a few days later, about the work of the Congress, he laconically but effectively expressed his outrage at the projects for the abolition of the Christian religion, the destruction of large states and the forcible imposition of peace. 'All this without the slightest proof, all this learned by rote twenty years ago and not changed one bit. Fire and sword! and when all has been destroyed, then, in their opinion, there will be peace.'

That was Dostoevsky's summing-up of Bakunin's speech. He was familiar with the passionate and stormy doctrine about the collapse of the old world in a tremendous war. He understood correctly the main features of communistic anarchism with its basic principle of social revolution as a spontaneous insurrection and of the speedy destruction of states by the declassed elements – bandits, criminals, convicts and beggars. Now, too, he understood correctly the basic tenet of the Bakuninism of the sixties, according to which complete intellectual emancipation of the individual – the supreme aim of historical development – was possible only under the aegis of atheism and materialism. Bakunin's slogans, 'As long as God exists, man is a slave,' and, 'Man is rational, just, free, therefore there is no God,' anticipated the anti-religious aphorisms of the free-thinkers in Dostoevsky's late works.

He was also aware of the despotic, imperious note that Bakunin imparted to the anarchist movement. He sensed the extent of the worldwide destruction that was expected to precede the formation of the autonomous communes Bakunin advocated. That was why he expressed the essence of this strange summons to universal peace in the words

'Fire and Sword'. As a thinker and a writer he was angered
and horrified by this impassioned propaganda for the destruction of the great states, but as an artist, he sensed the
power and forcefulness of this remarkable man, so very
Russian, who had been a focus of attention among his greatest contemporaries for well nigh thirty years. That was why
he gazed so eagerly at the strong features of this giant, who
had been so long known to him – by report from stories told
in Belinsky's circle, and by face-to-face meetings at Herzen's
in London and at Ogaryov's in Geneva – and who now
stood before his eyes, aloft on the rostrum of world politics,
delivering his merciless verdict on the whole of contemporary civilization. The shattering gift of speech of this famous
emigré, his halo of heroism in revolt and martyrdom in
prison, the living legend of his exploits and his sufferings,
could not but have moved one who too had endured the
scaffold, prison and Siberia. And while those steely words,
calling for the destruction of religion and patriotism, sent
stabs of pain into his heart, the personality of the orator who
had pronounced them appeared, as it were, before him,
revealing the intricate secrets of the man's troubled and ever
insatiable spirit. As he gazed at the features of that face,
Dostoevsky began to feel the surge of agonizing anxiety
that presaged the conception of a new work of art. The
personality of Bakunin had somehow unleashed the dormant
elemental force of some kind of creative potential, and a new
image, still profoundly enigmatic yet already unbearably
disquieting, had begun painfully to erupt in his consciousness. On that day Dostoevsky was confirmed in his resolution
to portray Bakunin in a novel about the Russian revolutionary movement, a novel which he may well have begun
to think about writing in the early 1860s. Some two or three
years later he was to begin to create the image of Stavrogin.

*

The principal events in Dostoevsky's private life during
that period were additions to his family. His first child, a

girl whom they named Sonya, was born in Geneva on
5 March 1868. According to Anna, Dostoevsky was a most
tender and loving father and devoted a great deal of time
and attention to his infant daughter. He would sit by the
cradle for hours, sometimes humming to her, sometimes
talking to her in a language of his own. His first words
when he woke up in the morning or when he came home
were, 'How is Sonya? Did she sleep well? Did she feed well?'
He found paternal love, which he had come to know so late
in life – he was in his late forties – a source of infinite joy.

But it was not destined to last long. The shortest document, and one of the saddest, in Dostoevsky's whole life, was
always reverentially preserved in his private archives.

Geneva. Funeral department.

Dr Sylvester has been informed that the death of Mlle Sophia
Dostoevskaya occurred on 24 May, 1868 at the age of three
months and that the burial will take place on 26 May, 1868 at
four o'clock in the afternoon.

Dostoevsky's grief was overwhelming. In all his bitter life
this was the hardest blow, far worse than any of his former
hardships. As for Anna:

I was shaken and grieved by her death and terribly afraid for
my unhappy husband. His despair was violent. He wept and
sobbed like a woman as he stood before his darling's cold body
and covered her pale little face and little hands with hot kisses.
Such stormy despair I have never since seen. We both felt that
we would not be able to bear our grief. It was dreadful to look at
Fyodor Mikhailovich. He had grown so weak and haggard
during the week of Sonya's illness. A few days later cypresses
were planted on her grave and a white marble cross placed
among them. My husband I went to her little grave every day.
We brought flowers and wept.

A few days later Dostoevsky wrote to Maikov:

This little creature, three months old, so pale and tiny, was
already a personality and a character to me. She was beginning

to recognize me, to love me and to smile at me when I came up to her. She loved to listen as I sang her songs in my ridiculous voice. She did not cry and she did not pucker up her face when I kissed her. She used to stop crying when I came over to her.

Stricken by this loss. Dostoevsky opened his heart to his wife and told her the entire sad story of his life. On the deck of the steamer on which they left Geneva one warm but overcast day he talked to her about the sad blows fate had dealt him throughout his life.

Fyodor Mikhailovich was deeply moved and shaken by the leave-taking from Sonya's grave and then, for the first time (he rarely complained), I heard his bitter complaints against the fate that had pursued him all his life. He told me about his sad and lonely youth after the death of his tenderly beloved mother. He recalled the ridicule his literary colleagues had heaped upon him after having first recognized his talent, and the way they had so cruelly offended him. He recalled the time in prison and how much he had suffered in his four years as a convict. He told me of his dream of finding the domestic happiness he craved in marriage with Maria Dmitrievna and how that, alas, did not work out. He had not had any children by Maria Dmitrievna and her 'strange, touchy and painfully imaginative nature' was the reason why he had been so unhappy with her. And now, when the 'great and only human happiness of having one's own child' had come to him and he had had the opportunity to feel and appreciate this happiness, malicious fate had had no mercy on him and had taken the creature he loved so dearly away from him. Never before and never again did he describe in such great and touching detail the bitter wounds he had had to suffer from people who were close and dear to him.

The Dostoevskys spent the whole summer in Vevey. Anna was despondent and wept a great deal. Dostoevsky worked very hard, 'day and night', on the second and third parts of *The Idiot*. The town reminded him of the quiet Russian provinces (Bronnitsa or Zaraisk). At the same time it 'has some of the finest scenery in all Europe. The most lavish ballet does not have sets such as this shore of Lake Geneva. ... Mountains, water, sparkle – it is magic.' Prince Myshkin is depicted in this immense space. 'Before him was the brilliant sky, below was the lake, all around was the bright, endless horizon.'

However, the only possible life here was a solitary one, and Dostoevsky liked the big cities of Europe with their crowded streets. Early in September they left for Italy, where Garibaldi's long struggle for the country's unification was just coming to a successful end.

XV

A Poem-novel

THE PLOT

THE plot of the new novel *The Idiot* took shape slowly and agonizingly, but as a result of its creator's intensive work it acquired firmness, harmony, drama and grandeur. Gradually, the main lines of a mighty design emerged from the ramifications of the action and dominated all the episodes, digressions and set pieces. What then was the outline of Dostoevsky's favourite work?

Lev Nikolaevich Myshkin, scion of an impoverished princely family, with no means of livelihood, has just returned to Petersburg after a stay of several years abroad, where he had been sent by a benefactor to consult a celebrated physician about his epilepsy. At the house of General Epanchin, an aristocratic relative of his, Prince Myshkin sees a portrait of a dazzling beauty, Nastasia Filippovna, a gorgeous Petersburg 'camellia'.* Arrangements are being made to marry off Nastasia Filippovna to General Epanchin's secretary Ganya Ivolgin. Myshkin, a sensitive and impressionable man, is struck by the expression of hidden suffering he perceives on the lovely face. The portrait of Nastasia Filippovna is among the finest descriptive writing to be found in Dostoevsky's work. Alexander Blok took it as an epigraph for his dramatic poem 'An Unknown Woman'.

Nastasia Filippovna's lot had been a tragic one. A pretty child, daughter of an impecunious landowner, she was early orphaned and taken to be brought up in the home of a wealthy businessman, named Totsky, for whom she later became an object of pleasure. But the intelligent, serious,

* i.e. a courtesan, like Dumas' Lady of the Camellias.

talented and strong-willed young woman rebels against the
despotism and insult to which she is subjected. Protest
against all oppression and injustice wells up in her breast.
She determines to avenge herself against the society which
has defiled her dreams of happiness and purity. She is
seeking an escape from the stifling world of lies, cynicism
and baseness, so as to be reborn for true love and happiness.
Upon meeting Prince Myshkin, who is so different from the
Petersburg high society she knows, she falls in love with him.

Prince Myshkin is the embodiment of Dostoevsky's idea
of a beautiful man. He is unassuming, sincere and sensitive,
full of compassion for all the humiliated and insulted. He is a
friend of children and a champion of the sick and the 'fallen',
and his dream is of happiness and peace for all men. This
draws the contempt of the prosperous members of society,
who regard him as a 'holy fool', 'an idiot', a nonentity.

Dostoevsky conveys with great power his hero's super-
iority to the representatives of the ruling circle who surround
him. He puts him in the midst of landowners who are
philanthropists, generals who are tax-farmers, financial
tycoons and the place-seekers and shady manipulators who
fawn upon them. Among them are Totsky, member of
trading and joint stock companies; Epanchin, titled owner
of estates, factories and profitable apartment houses; the
'impatient beggar' Ivolgin, a man with a black, greedy,
envious soul and boundless conceit. In this den, in which
the profit motive, deception, the cult of money and contempt
for man rule supreme, every honest and decent person is
doomed to destruction. The tragedy of the gifted Russian
woman Nastasia Filippovna and the noble dreamer Prince
Myshkin is predetermined by the jungle laws of this heartless world.

When he gets to know Nastasia Filippovna, Prince
Myshkin is smitten by deep feelings of love and pity. 'You
have suffered and you have emerged unsullied from a hell
such as this,' he says to her, overwhelmed by her tormented

beauty. Wishing to remove her from the big city's luxurious and horrible demi-monde, he asks her to become his wife. Her love and admiration for him prompt her to an act of sacrifice. 'Totsky's mistress' will not 'ruin an infant' – she will drown her feeling for him in debauchery. As she drives off in a troika with Rogozhin she bares her whole soul to Myshkin: 'Adieu, Prince, for the first time in my life I have seen a man.'

Soon afterwards their relationship becomes more complicated. Rogozhin, an unbridled and lustful young millionaire merchant, is madly in love with Nastasia Filippovna. A man ruled by passion, this character in the novel is partially drawn from the famous trials of the day, brought into the novel by Dostoevsky in order to accent the picture of an evil and criminal epoch in which the struggle for money and power is universal and unrestrained. Rogozhin, however, differs from the run of common banditry; he has a capacity for loving to the point of self-oblivion. He has a generous nature, violent impulses and strong feelings.

Nastasia Filippovna, not daring even in her thoughts to bind her tarnished life with that of a pure and righteous man, accepts Rogozhin's attentions. But she is concerned about Myshkin and devotes all the energy of her warm heart and fine mind to arranging the happiness of her 'grown-up baby'. She believes that the best thing for him would be to marry Aglaya Epanchina, the General's lovely and intelligent daughter. She writes Aglaya beautiful letters, which reveal all the Prince's love for her and all her own determination to give him up for ever. But a meeting between the two women shortly afterwards end in a sharp breach between them. Myshkin is a deeply loyal friend to both, but at the critical moment he stays with the insulted and suffering Nastasia Filippovna.

They are on the threshold of happiness. Prince Myshkin leads Nastasia Filippovna to the altar. But Nastasia Filippovna is still agitatedly seeking a way out of her moral impasse. That is why when Rogozhin appears on the scene she loses the will to struggle. Prince Myshkin's bride is carried off by Rogozhin, who kills her out of despair and jealousy. The horrible world of money-grabbers and libertines has destroyed two beautiful people who happened to be drawn into its accursed circle.

The novel's principal scenes are forceful and dramatic. Take the episode that so graphically reveals the role of money in that society: Nastasia Filippovna flings a packet of one hundred thousand roubles into the fireplace, telling Ganya Ivolgin that if he pulls the money out of the flames he can have it. Or the scene when Rogozhin, jealous of Prince Myshkin, tries to kill him, and the Prince cannot believe that his friend and chosen brother wants him dead. Or the meeting between Nastasia Filippovna and Aglaya and their 'single combat' for the 'beautiful man', ending in victory not for the proud girl but for the unfortunate woman to whom the meek Prince had given all his love and compassion. Or the epilogue, which imparts the quality of genuine tragedy to the novel. These fragments all reveal Dostoevsky's mastery as a great realistic portrayer of the human heart, as a profound psychologist and inimitable lyricist.

The loving, kind and altruistic Prince Myshkin is the author's ideal man. But even he must submit to the universal law of suffering, hopelessness and ruin that rules the world of the Golden Calf. It is in this profound poetic symbol that Dostoevsky embodies his thoughts about the fate of spiritual beauty in the kingdom of money-making, lasciviousness and crime.

THE IMAGES

Prince Myshkin

Of all the other characters of fiction that Dostoevsky mentioned in connection with Prince Myshkin, the one that

exerted the most influence on his portrayal of his hero is
Cervantes's 'Knight of the Sorrowful Countenance'. What
particularly attracted the Russian novelist was the effort
made by the author of Don Quixote to give his hero an
exact and true social characterization, which predetermined and explained his personality and his exploits. Don
Quixote is an impoverished petty nobleman, a poor, rural
hidalgo, whose mind has been affected by the romances about
chivalry he has been reading and who imagines himself to
be a knight errant with a mission to fight for the salvation
of all the oppressed and disinherited in the cruel world of
feudal autocracy. An exalted humanist and admirer of
spiritual beauty, he fights for the triumph of justice and
universal happiness in the name of his chaste and knightly
love for the beautiful Lady Dulcinea de Toboso. Don
Quixote may appear ridiculous in his naïve ignorance of
harsh reality, but in his moral quest for supreme truth he is
a tragic figure. Victor Hugo was right to point out that deep
down in his heart Cervantes sympathized with Don
Quixote.

Dostoevsky was fascinated by this image. 'In all the world
there is nothing more profound or more powerful than this
book,' he wrote later. 'To this day it is the last and greatest
word in human thought.' It is the bitterest irony that a man
is capable of expressing, it is 'the greatest and the saddest
book ever produced by the genius of man'. Dostoevsky
gives a profound interpretation of the drama of Don
Quixote, who could not survive the collapse of his illusions
and who, when 'he was defeated by the commonsense barber
Carasco, a scoffer and a cynic ... died then and there,
quietly, with a sorrowful smile, consoling the weeping
Sancho, loving the whole world with the great power of
love in his noble heart, yet realizing that there was nothing
more for him to do in this world.'

This is, basically, the way in which the image of Prince
Myshkin is constructed – the last representative of an

ancient line, half-destitute and ill, imbued with boundless love for an enchanting luckless woman, he is powerless to protect her from the world's evil, and departs for ever, following her into the night of his madness.

This is the 'Poor Knight' as interpreted by Pushkin. Dostoevsky knew only an incomplete text of Pushkin's ballad, which at that time could not be printed in its entirety owing to a ban imposed by the ecclesiastical censorship. The third verse ('As he travelled to Geneva, by a wayside cross he saw the Virgin Mary', etc.) was cut out, as also was the last verse ('But Our Lady, of course, came to his defence'), which turned the whole poem into a cryptogram. All that was left were the beautiful and vague phrases 'He had the vision that is beyond mind's understanding' or 'Since then, his soul having been consumed, he never looked at a woman'. The mysterious initials A. M. D.* were passed by the censor, as were the liturgical Latin appellations *Lumen Coeli Sancta Rosa!* which did not mean much to a Russian reader. Yet Dostoevsky unerringly interpreted this fragment from Pushkin as he built his own image of pure love:

> Filled with pure love,
> True to a sweet dream.

Someone at Epanchin's house says: 'There is a strange Russian poem about a "poor knight", an excerpt without a beginning or an end.' Aglaya replies: 'I think the poet wanted to combine in one extraordinary image the whole tremendous concept of medieval chivalrous platonic love. Needless to say, this is an ideal. The "poor knight" is Don Quixote, only a serious Don Quixote, not a comical one.' And she goes on to recite: 'Once upon a time there was a poor knight' with a deep understanding of the spirit and meaning of the ballad. 'Her eyes shone, and once or twice a slight, hardly perceptible tremor of inspiration and admiration crossed her beautiful face.'

* A.M.D. stands for the Latin *Ave Mater Dei*–Hail, Mother of God.

To give more vitality to his hero Dostoevsky imparted several autobiographical attributes to him: his own illness, his own appearance, his own moral philosophy. The 'idiot's' genealogy is very similar to Dostoevsky's family history. His complex class psychology was meant to reflect that social group in contemporary Russia whose mission, in the author's view, was to produce the positively beautiful man, a man whose moral grandeur would eclipse even that of the immortal Knight of La Mancha.

Myshkin as we have seen is the last and only representative of an old noble family, now in complete decline. Some of his immediate forebears were single householders, that is, peasants in life and customs, but who, as members of the gentry-class, had a right to dispose of the fruits of their labour as they wished, and to own serfs. 'He ploughs himself, he shouts at himself, he takes the money himself,' was how a popular saying described the single householder. Because of their material decline these impoverished gentry were a source of anxiety to the Tsarist government. Dostoevsky took a deep interest in this portentous and depressing sign of the times and had written of it in an article in his magazine, entitled 'The Gentleman who Wants to be a Peasant'. It was from this stock that his favourite hero came, the penniless, epileptic Prince Myshkin. The Prince's father tried to stave off the extinction of the family. He rose from cadet to the rank of second lieutenant of the infantry, but he could not rise any further and died in an army hospital under arrest. On his mother's side, Prince Myshkin came from petty merchant stock. His mother was a commoner, daughter of a Moscow merchant of the third guild by the name of Papushin, who died bankrupt; in effect, that is a townsman.* However, social restoration comes from a

* In the rigid social class system of the old Russia, the urban population was divided into an upper class of merchants and a lower class of 'townsmen'. Merchants were further subdivided into three 'guilds' according to the amount of capital they possessed. Anybody who

branch of Myshkin's merchant relatives. His maternal grandfather's elder brother was a very wealthy merchant and all his money is unexpectedly inherited by the indigent young Prince, the last member of the family, opening up unlimited possibilities to him.

Dostoevsky imparts his own spiritual ideals to Myshkin. The Prince appears among the shareholders, dashing officers and shady businessmen of Petersburg as a righteous man among sinners. He is regarded as an 'idiot', but, Aglaya says, no man is like him 'in noble simplicity of heart and infinite credulity'. Dostoevsky succeeds wonderfully, especially in the first part of the novel, in conveying the captivating and irresistible charm of this 'beggar saint', who has risen, as it were, 'above the mêlée' of human passions and lusts. Prince Myshkin possesses the transparency and warmth that comes from that wisdom of the heart which is superior to the most refined and brilliant arguments of the mind.

In his manuscript notebooks for *The Idiot* Dostoevsky depicts Prince Myshkin with a zest for life, for the times he lives in, for his homeland. The Prince exclaims, in the spirit of Pushkin – not of 'The Poor Knight', but of the 'Bacchic Song' – 'Long live the sun! Long live life!' His main theme is Russia. His concern is constantly reflected in his conversation: the parallel 'of the foreign and Russian peoples' (Dostoevsky's favourite 'Russia and Europe' theme), 'the Prince's words at Aglaya's country house, when he draws a comparison between the West and the East', his description of Moscow and, most important, the tremendous impact of his new impressions of Russia.

As he himself admitted, Dostoevsky did not fully achieve his purpose. He loved his 'idiot' dearly but he realized that he had not fulfilled his intentions. Capitalist Petersburg of the 1860s, portrayed in the tradition of the naturalistic

---

possessed less than the minimum needed to qualify for the lowest or third 'guild' was ranked as a 'townsman' – a class that included petty shopkeepers, artisans, clerks, etc.

school, did not in real life provide sufficiently broad and deep perspectives for portrayal of a supreme moral ideal. The contradictions in Prince Myshkin's life and character – the homeless wanderer who becomes a millionaire and eligible suitor, the declassed and impoverished relic of a dying family, making speeches in defence and in praise of titled nobility and dignitaries – violate the essential nature of the image as it was first conceived. Besides, Myshkin is not a reformer, not an active figure, which a truly 'beautiful man' should be; Don Quixote, once he adopted an idea, took up arms.

But though Dostoevsky's portrayal of Prince Myshkin fell short of the 'higher meaning' of his realism, he did attain it in his magnificent portrayal of the 'fallen woman', who had loved greatly and paid with her life for her tempestuous emotions, striving towards unclouded spiritual beauty.

Nastasia Filippovna

Nastasia Filippovna, the focal point to which all threads of the plot lead and from which all the impulses of the action arise, is one of Dostoevsky's finest creations. There are two possible interpretations of this complex and profound female character. One regards Dostoevsky's heroine as a bacchante, a *hetaera*, 'possessed', in the grip of sensual passion, which is the cause of her destruction. It is no accident that she calls herself a 'street woman', 'Rogozhin's', 'shameless'. Her face wears an expression of 'boundless pride'. She is an avenger without mercy. One of the novel's main characters says that her beauty is 'fantastic and demonic'.

The other interpretation regards Nastasia Filippovna as the embodiment of moral sensitivity and chastity, of aspiration towards an ideal and love. She is fond of music, has read much poetry, possesses faultless taste and inborn culture. She dreams of a man who will understand her. She has a courageous and bold nature, capable of protest and struggle. It is the second, pure, Nastasia Filippovna who prevails in the final version of the novel. Dostoevsky 'acquits' his heroine. He depicts her against the background of the rotten high-ranking Petersburg society and portrays with great sensitivity the birth of her higher feelings for the first man of extraordinary inner radiance she has ever met. Reborn to a new life, she rebels against the world of the Totskys, Epanchins and Ivolgins. There is a ring of truth and justice in the protests that she flings in the faces of her flesh-hungry pursuers, men who took away from a girl her supreme right to love and happiness.

The image of Nastasia Filippovna is thrown into sharp relief by the contrasting image of Aglaya Epanchina. Aglaya is a strong-willed, intelligent girl. She is capable of appraising her surroundings critically and is trying to break out of her nest into freedom. 'I do not want to go to their balls. I want to be useful.' She is fascinated by revolutionary literature. She 'has read all the banned books'. In the epilogue to the novel Aglaya breaks with her aristocratic background, throws in her lot with a Polish revolutionary and joins him in the fight for the liberation of his enslaved homeland. Hence come Natalia Filippovna's sincere affection for the general's daughter, and the strange relationship between them that culminates in their 'duel', that memorable meeting of rivals from which the deprived, outcast woman emerges as the victor. Dostoevsky gives a masterly exposition both of the unshakeable sense of personal dignity of this 'ruined woman' and of the tempest of suffering that sweeps over her outraged soul at the end. The image attains the stature of high tragedy.

Dostoevsky's tragic heroine has rich spiritual resources. She has a reputation for being completely unmercenary. No man can boast of success with this notorious courtesan. In Petersburgh, her tie with Totsky now is only for appearance's sake. Actually, she has left him and withdrawn into a circle of her own, consisting of poor civil servant's wives, down-at-heel actresses, and an obscure schoolteacher's family. She has a fondness for the company of 'holy fools' and old women. She is drawn to the obscure, the submissive and the wretched. From time to time the connoisseurs of her dazzling beauty gather at her home. At such times she acts the role of Pericles' beloved. She is witty, lively, irresistible, is a subtle conversationalist, and is skilled in repartee and in arguments on controversial topics. Her guests are amazed at 'the brilliant intelligence and radiant feelings she revealed when she was interested'.

What strikes people about her appearance is the perfection of her features and a kind of sorrowful spirituality. 'Beauty such as this is power,' says another woman fervently. 'With such beauty it is possible to turn the world upside down.' Nastasia Filippovna's beauty is imbued however with an inner pain that seems to augur madness. Her portrait hanging on the wall arouses deep compassion in Myshkin and he reflects on how that tormented nature might be saved by goodness. Her dazzling features frighten and alarm him; he is terrified by that magnificent face that has in it something menacing, like the countenance of Apollo.

In spite of this Nastasia Filippovna turns out to be capable of warmth and self-sacrifice that shine through one of the finest scenes in the novel, her meeting with Prince Myshkin at night at the Epanchin country house in Pavlovsk.

Now, at last, she stood in front of him, face to face, for the first time since they had parted. She spoke to him, but he gazed at her in silence. His heart was filled to the brim and began to ache. He could never afterwards forget this meeting with her and he always recalled it with the same ache in his heart. She knelt before him, right there in the street, as if possessed. He drew back in fright, but she caught at his hand and tried to kiss it, and, exactly as in his dream the night before, tears sparkled on her long lashes.

'Get up, get up,' he said in a frightened whisper, lifting her up. 'Please get up at once.'

'Are you happy? Are you happy?' she asked. 'Say one word, tell me, are you happy now? Today? This minute? With her? What did she say?'

She would not get up, she would not listen to him, she kept asking questions hurriedly and hurrying to speak, as if someone were pursuing her.

'I am going tomorrow as you have ordered. I won't . . . this is the last time I am seeing you, the last time. This is really the last time.'

'Be calm, stand up,' he said in despair.

She peered into his face and seized his hand.

'Adieu,' she said, finally, and got up and walked away from him quickly, almost running. The Prince saw Rogozhin appear suddenly beside her, take her arm and lead her away.

It is because 'Totsky's mistress' cannot bring herself to besmirch the pure image of the Poor Knight by remaining near him that she feels compelled to flee from the altar to Rogozhin and to accept death at his hand.

Rogozhin

The novelist has set the image of Rogozhin on the same high artistic plane. This personification of impulsive, absorbing passion is transformed, in the struggle, into equally overpowering and elemental jealousy. He is dominated by passion 'to the point of pain'. To convey this welter of untrammelled instincts that turn so easily into pain and suffering, Dostoevsky chose to portray a primitive, direct and easily enflamed nature in all the primeval freshness of its desires and impulses. Nobody has ever told Rogozhin how to behave. No one has ever taught him the inhibitions of internal discipline. He sweeps through life like the wind through the fields. He is only semi-literate and has not read anything at all. He 'did not even know the name of Pushkin'. His manner of speaking is that of the common people and he uses illiterate expressions such as 'them there', 'these kind', 'ain't'. His clothes are in poor taste and loud – a brightly coloured tie with a jewelled pin, a massive diamond ring on a dirty finger.

Culture has never touched this 'millionaire in a sheep-skin coat'. His family is close to the more primitive sects that had broken off from the Orthodox Church. Though his father observes the 'law' for appearances' sake, he is drawn to the Eunuchs and Flagellants and religious sectarians of all varieties. His aunt, a nun by vocation, lives in Pskov, the heart of the Old Believer country. And even he, the youngest heir of the firm, has a tendency, as Myshkin notes, to the 'two-finger sign of the cross' and pre-Nikon scriptures.* Rogozhin's unpolished merchant family is remote from the innovations of the Europeanized way of life, from the businessmen with haircuts and coloured waistcoats. Rogozhin has strong ties with folk traditions and ancient beliefs. The harmony of old-fashioned piousness exists within him side-by-side with the frightening recklessness of the rebellious *streltsi*.†

In creating this broad and bold Russian character Dostoevsky drew on his memories of Othello, one of his favourite Shakespearean characters. Even Rogozhin's appearance is significant: he has black curly hair, a flat, wide nose, high cheekbones, a crude lower jaw and burning eyes. The author refers to him repeatedly as a

* The seventeenth-century Patriarch Nikon ordered a revised version of the Bible and service books of the church, based on comparison with Greek originals, to be used in place of the traditional versions current in Russia at the time. Many 'Old Believers' broke away from the Church, refused to read 'Nikon's scriptures' and continued to cross themselves with two fingers instead of using three, as Nikon had ordered. Later a number of strange sects developed among the 'Old Believers', some of whom practised various forms of self-mutilation.

† *Streltsi* were the garrison of Moscow, intensely conservative and always prone to mutiny against any innovations. They were put down by Peter the Great.

'blackamoor', 'black-haired', 'gloomy'. That his appearance calls to mind the Moor of Venice is no accident. Rogozhin is equally violent in love and hatred. When he becomes aware of the depth of Nastasia Filippovna's love for Myshkin, he determines to kill him. On the other hand, his naturally honourable heart is captivated by the Prince's charm. He is torn by an inner struggle and he nearly gives up his criminal design. In fact, he resolves to make that crime an impossibility by going through the folk rite of exchanging crosses with Myshkin. This makes them brothers in blood, and he asks his aged mother to give her blessing to his rival 'as if he were her own son'. He wishes thereby to impart the nature of fratricide, one of the most dreadful of crimes, to his contemplated deed and to make it impossible. All this is as simple and majestic as the catharthis of an antique tragedy. The way is open for Rogozhin to do a grand deed of heroic sacrifice. Condemning himself to the supreme agony, trembling and panting, he makes a titanic effort to hold himself back on the brink of the abyss.

'Take her then, if that is fate! She's yours! I give her up!...'

The sacrifice is beyond his strength; the attempt at murder is made, and it is only the terrible answering cry of the epileptic Prince, 'Parfyon, I don't believe it', that stays Rogozhin's hand.

Rogozhin's jealousy finally breaks out stormily and unrestrainedly in the dead of that white summer night, when he carries his 'queen' away from the altar at which she stood with Myshkin, and forever stops her turbulent heart, a heart at once filled with pure love and in the grip of sinful passion. He hears his sentence of penal servitude silently and reflectively, fully prepared to embark on the path of purification and resurrection.

These central images of the novel, with their complex interrelations and tense struggles express one of Dostoevsky's most cherished ideas, the grandeur of self-sacrificial love for a suffering human being, a theme which rings out with great clarity and power in his novel of the year 1868: 'Compassion is the main, and perhaps the sole, law of the existence of all mankind.'

THE STRUCTURE

Dostoevsky formulated a new structural principle for *The Idiot*, with a main story line and innumerable parallel stories, or side plots, all through the novel, which clarify or throw into strong relief the evolution of its central design and the basic development of the action. 'And that is the reason for the infinite number of stories in the novel ('*Les Misérables*' of all classes) accompanying the action of the principal story line.'

The monograph about Myshkin is accompanied by subordinate sketches about the dregs of various social groups, such as the seedy General Ivolgin, the civil servant Lebedev, the 'bawdy buffoon' Ferdyshchenko, the usurer Ptitsyn, the 'positivist' Burdovsky and his company, Rogozhin's gang, and all sorts of other characters, disreputable figures who contrast sharply with the basic parable of the righteous hero. The counterpoint contrasting these grotesque figures with the one saint, or moral hero, apparently takes its beginning from *Notre-Dame de Paris*, one of Dostoevsky's favourite books, which exemplifies Victor Hugo's method of romantic antithesis; the Cathedral of Notre-Dame in Paris faces on to the courtyard full of freaks, and the beautiful Esmeralda inspires passion in the monster Quasimodo. As we know, Dostoevsky in his realist novels sometimes used the devices of late romanticism, recast in the spirit of the new era and thrust unexpectedly and boldly into the thick of contemporary reality.

That is why the basic theme of *The Idiot* is accompanied by episodes that seem to parody the leading motif. The interpolated tale of Marie is a sketch in miniature of the novel's dominant story about the tragic lot of an unjustly defiled woman. Rogozhin's renunciation is anticipated and parodied by General Ivolgin's empty words: 'The Prince shouts: "Yours!" I shout: "Yours!"' and so on. Lebedev's incoherent story about the Countess Dubarry supplements Myshkin's moving reflections about the last day of a condemned man. Ippolit's note about Holbein's 'Christ Taken from the Cross' is an ironic interpretation of Myshkin's and Nastasia Filippovna's impressions of the same painting. Thus there are numerous correspondences, parallels, or 'thematic rhythms' in the novel, leitmotifs that constantly recur in different keys and with varying dynamics throughout this complex, epic orchestration of the events of the story.

Dostoevsky employs another favourite technique of his, the 'conclave' where he gathers his characters together for an important purpose and then produces unforeseen complications that reveal the main thread of the plot. The culminating scene of the first part is Nastasia Filippovna's birthday. As always in Dostoevsky's work, there is a sense of concealed and anxious anticipation here of an important event. The heroine's engagement to Ganya Ivolgin is to be officially announced. Outwardly all is calm and respectable. The company is entertaining itself with salon games. But the drama below the surface suddenly erupts. The Prince wants to marry Nastasia Filippovna. It is announced that he has inherited a huge fortune. Rogozhin brings his 'queen' a packet of a hundred thousand roubles. She flings the money into the fire to test her fiancé's disinterestedness. Ganya resists the temptation, but he falls into a faint. Through the entire scene Nastasia Filippovna is talking feverishly: Totsky's mistress does not want to ruin the righteous man. 'Prince, now you must have Aglaya Epanchina!'

When he was finishing *The Idiot* Dostoevsky wrote in one of his letters: 'It was for the final scene of the novel, practically, that the whole novel was written and conceived.' That final scene, where Prince Myshkin and Rogozhin meet beside Nastasia Filippovna's dead body, one of the most powerful episodes in all of Dostoevsky, was the kernel of the entire novel. The heroine's death and the mutual compassion of the rivals, of the brothers in blood, each sensing the other's hopeless end – penal servitude for one, the madhouse for the other – was the tragic denouement for which this novel about a beautiful man, doomed to destruction by a heartless epoch, was written.

The Idiot, the most lyrical of Dostoevsky's long works, is the closest he came to fulfilling his lifelong desire to produce a poem novel, by which he meant a production where the main images were distinguished by the special fullness and power of their emotions, where their relationships revealed a profound inner drama and pointed the way towards the great ideas of man and the world. Gogol called his *Dead Souls* a 'poem'; the characters of that work became eternal images, and in that picaresque anecdote the author could be heard weeping for his native land. It was for this kind of transformation of the petty and the vulgar into the tragic and overwhelming that Dostoevsky always strove. And, in this sense, the central images of *The Idiot* are deeply poetic. Their interaction rises to the heights of genuine tragedy, while the boldly and originally constructed plot enables the author to express a number of his basic views concerning the destiny of a pure and solitary man, surrounded by "*Les Misérables*" of all classes'.

Because of the abundance in it of artistic impressions about the works of celebrated Renaissance painters *The Idiot* is also a unique aesthetic treatise, containing many remarkable aphorisms about beauty. Beauty, in Dostoevsky's view, is a mighty force, capable of transforming the world of lies and crime into a kingdom of truth and perfect harmony. It is in this novel that Dostoevsky wrote the celebrated line: '*The world will be saved by beauty.*'

XVI

Before the Battle

ITALY. DRESDEN AGAIN

DOSTOEVSKY did not enjoy living in Switzerland. He liked open spaces; he felt hemmed in by the mountains that surrounded Lake Geneva. 'They limit my range of vision,' he told his wife. 'I could never write anything worthwhile here.' They decided to go to Italy for the winter. At the beginning of September the Dostoevskys set out across the Simplon Pass by horse and carriage. The early autumn sun warmed them gently. They used to get out of the carriage and walk up the footpaths, gathering alpine flowers along the way. 'The most vivid imagination cannot picture the beauty of the mountain road across the Simplon,' Dostoevsky wrote to his niece shortly afterwards. Anna walked slowly, leaning on her husband's arm. She had a feeling that they were leaving their sorrows behind, on the other side of the Alps, and that life would smile on her again in Italy.

Dostoevsky took a great liking to the peasants of Lombardy, who reminded him of the tillers of the soil in his distant homeland. In Milan he marvelled again at the cathedral. 'Enormous, marble, Gothic. It is as fantastic as a dream.' They climbed to the roof to look at the statues and admire the view of the Lombardy plain below. But it was a rainy autumn in Milan. The local libraries did not subscribe to Russian newspapers, which were a necessity to Dostoevsky during his sojourn abroad. In November they left for Florence.

In Florence they led the kind of happy life they had led in Dresden, visiting picture galleries and looking at famous buildings. Dostoevsky admired the architecture of the palaces, museums and cathedrals. Anna writes that he went often to the Palazzo Pitti, where he greatly admired Raphael's 'Madonna della Sedia'. In the Uffizi Gallery he fell in love with another Raphael, 'San Giovanni Battista del Deserto'. He regarded the Medici 'Venus' as a work of genius.

Dostoevsky's daughter Lyubov wrote that after going to the galleries:

they would stroll in the city along the Arno River. If the weather was fine they would go for a walk in the Cascine or Boboli Gardens. The roses blooming there in January captured their northern imaginations. My parents were accustomed to seeing snow-covered streets and people huddled in heavy coats at that time of the year. Flowers in January seemed an incredible phenomenon to them. My father mentioned the roses in Boboli Gardens in letters to friends and my mother writes of them in her reminiscences.

On sunny days Florence 'is nearly heaven', Dostoevsky wrote to his niece Sonya Ivanova on 6 February 1869: 'It is impossible to imagine anything better than the effect of this sky, air and light. The sun and the sky and the genuine *marvels of art*[1] are incredible, literally unimaginable.'

This constant immersion in art led Dostoevsky to suggest to Maikov in a letter from Florence in 1869 several themes for historical ballads of the type of Maikov's *Legend of the Cathedral of Constance*, most of them about Russia's past. Dostoevsky wrote to Maikov that he should then suddenly in another ballad.

show late-fifteenth- and early-sixteenth-century Europe, Italy, the Papacy, the art of the churches, Raphael, the worship of Apollo Belvedere, the first rumours of the Reformation, Luther, America, gold, Spain and England – a large, seething picture, to be drawn parallel to all the preceding Russian pictures – but with hints about the future destiny of it all, the future of science, atheism, *the rights of man*,[1] from a Western viewpoint, not ours, which is the reason for everything that is happening and that will happen.

Such was the vision of the Renaissance that Dostoevsky derived from his artistic peregrinations in Europe.

The city of Dante and Michelangelo put Dostoevsky in a mood for creative work. He worked hard on the last part of *The Idiot*, striving to finish it by the end of the year. It was in Florence, on 11 November 1868, that he planned the 'scene of the rival women', and made a note of Nastasia Filippovna's 'proud and lofty speech, simple and with great dignity'. In Florence, too, he wrote the chapters of Prince Myshkin's wedding and Nastasia Filippovna's death, and of the rivals beside her body.

In the spring of 1869 the Dostoevskys decided to leave Florence and go to Prague, intending to stay there for the next winter; Dostoevsky had a lively interest in fostering closer ties between Russia and the foreign Slavs. They left the Tuscan capital in July, stopped for a day in 'scholarly Bologna', the ancient university city, to see Raphael's 'St Cecilia', and spent four days in Venice. That unique city made a strong impression on Dostoevsky's artistic susceptibility and creative imagination. He was delighted with the architecture of St Mark's and spent hours looking at the mosaics. He admired the powerful structural design and celebrated ceilings of the Doge's Palace. This no doubt brought to his mind Venice's turbulent history – Casanova's flight from beneath the leaden roof of the ancient dungeon (the so-called *plombs*), a daring enterprise, described in the famous adventurer's memoirs, which Dostoevsky had published in *Vremya*, or the motley carnival crowds in the piazza, where, as Schiller describes in his *Geisterseher*, mysterious people in masks and cloaks wove bloody intrigues. 'Actually we never left St Mark's Square all four days, such a charming impression did it make on us both by day and by night'; thus Dostoevsky's wife concludes her description of their Italian travels.

The Dostoevskys spent only three days in Prague. There were no furnished rooms for rent there, so they went to near-by Dresden to settle for the winter. On 14 September 1869 their second daughter, Lyubov,[2] was born there.

'THE LIFE OF A GREAT SINNER'

Leo Tolstoy's *War and Peace* was completed in 1868 and received with acclaim by readers and critics alike. Soon after the publication of the fifth, and last, volume Strakhov wrote: 'This is an unprecedented phenomenon – *an epic in contemporary art forms.*' Dostoevsky was impelled to try his hand at this sort of 'Homeric' genre and to express his cherished ideas about modern man in a panoramic epic novel. 'The whole idea calls for something big, at least the length of Tolstoy's novel,' he wrote to Strakhov in the spring of 1870. However, from a letter he wrote to Maikov at the end of 1868 we know that he was already then planning an enormous novel, to be entitled *Atheism*. It was to be the story of a Russian sceptic who, after many years of moving back and forth among all sorts of theologies and popular sects, 'in the end finds the Russian Orthodox religion and the Russian soil'.

Dostoevsky felt that the central theme of his own spiritual experience and world outlook could only be encompassed by the extensive form of the newest type of philosophical epic novel. He would develop his theme on several planes, concentrating on different problems and employing different styles, but he would have to cover material just as extensive and substantiate the plot with thoroughly researched facts; before he started writing it he would, he said, 'have to read practically a whole library of atheist, Catholic and Russian Orthodox writers'.

Dostoevsky's idea for a work of this kind went back to his reading in his youth. George Sand's original and exciting novel *Spiridion* was very popular in the early 1840s, when Dostoevsky belonged to Belinsky's circle. Panaev had translated excerpts from it specially for Belinsky and Nekrasov and, considering Dostoevsky's interest in George Sand's work, it is very likely that he read the novel at the time and even then perceived it to be a new, original and bold genre, combining contemporary politics with religious and philosophical problems. It might even then have stirred his own dormant literary inclinations. He had appreciated this experiment in writing an ideological epic of contemporary times and turned to it when he was planning his own book about atheism and again, ten years after that, when he was planning his last novel, *The Brothers Karamazov*.

George Sand had written *Spiridion* with Pierre Leroux and had woven into it the most compelling theme of the era: socialism or Christianity? This theme had deeply interested Dostoevsky in his youth and it formed the basis of his last novel, though his approach differed from that of *Spiridion*, which was an extended critique of Catholicism from the standpoint of Utopian socialism. The action spans the second half of the eighteenth century up to the time of the French Revolution. Its hero Alexis is a young novice monk who is torn by struggle between two awesome forces, atheism and faith. 'A Catholic and a heretic at the same time, I turned with one hand to the authority of the Roman Church, while, with the other, I leafed through books filled with a rebellious spirit and free research.' Because he has profound doubts, the young novice leaves his monastic order and goes out into the world, 'to throw the monastic garb down upon the thorny road and go to people to seek freedom of conscience and knowledge'. The student of Catholic theology becomes an impassioned free-thinker and implacable opponent of the Roman Church. His religion is transmuted into philosophy: from a believer he becomes a scholar. 'It seems to me that Socrates was no less worthy of expiating mankind's sins than was Jesus of Nazareth.' Plato and Spinoza have taken the place of the saints in his mind and they, in turn, give way shortly afterwards to the exact scientists, to the fathers of geometry, Newton, Kepler and Descartes. At these heights of knowledge the former monk feels the 'dizziness of atheism'.

The intellectual peregrinations of a Catholic monk who has read all the volumes in the monastery's big library anticipate as it were, the conflict of Dostoevsky's great sinner. In George Sand's novel the theme of unbelief, which Dostoevsky so profoundly developed in *The Brothers Karamazov*, dominates the quests of the young Benedictine monk. Dostoevsky was strongly attracted by George Sand's main design, which had given rise to her peculiar creative method. According to her own explanation, the Abbé Spiridion is the embodiment of humanity passing through all the religious creeds. It was something like this artistic encyclopedia of beliefs that Dostoevsky dreamed of producing in his *Atheism*.

Dostoevsky thought constantly about this complex plan, so rich in ideas and drama. He returned to it in a letter to Maikov, dated 25 March (6 April) 1870, calling it *The Life of a Great Sinner*. It was to consist of five separate stories, connected only by the person of the hero – the structure Lermontov used in his *A Hero of Our Time*.[3] The first story was to be the introduction: the educated milieu of Russia in the 1840s or even the 1830s, the hero's childhood and adolescence, his life in a boarding school and his participation in a crime. The second story would take place in a monastery, where the Bishop Tikhon of Zadonsk* is living in retirement. The thirteen-year-old hero has been sent there by his parents to be educated and reformed. The corrupted 'nihilist child' comes under the influence of Tikhon, who teaches him self-restraint: 'Conquer yourself and you will

---

* The historic Tikhon of Zadonsk, a great religious teacher and a saint of the Russian Church, lived from 1724–83.

conquer the world.' Chaadayev* is serving a term of exile in the monastery and Pushkin, Belinsky and Granovsky visit him. There are also some members of popular sects there – the dissenters Pavel Prussky and Golubov and the monk Parfeny.

The third story would portray the hero's young manhood, his university years, his interest in positivism and in atheism. He has immeasurable pride and contempt for mankind and is convinced that he is a great man. A repulsive usurer instils in him the idea of accumulating money. Extraordinary contrasts of an unusual personality: heroism and dreadful crimes. In this volume the great sinner's criminality will reach its culmination.

The fourth story would depict a profound crisis in the hero's philosophy: out of pride, he becomes a hermit and wandering holy man and travels all over Russia. There is an unexpected turning point: 'Romance. Love. A desire to be meek.' The fifth book would portray the sinner's complete regeneration: 'He becomes meek and kind to all precisely because he is far superior to them all . . . He ends up in an orphanage and becomes another Doctor Haas.[4] Everything becomes clear to him and he dies, confessing his crime.'

One can only imagine the breadth and scope of a novel executed according to this design; embracing three decades of Russian life, the main currents of social thought and philosophical inquiry, with portraits of major historical figures, travels through Russia and studies of the common people's concepts of truth and sin, Christ and Antichrist; the profound development of an outstanding individual, from his committing murder to his inner enlightenment and fruitful activity to benefit the poor and the oppressed. What

* Peter Chaadayev (1797–1856) published a celebrated 'Philosophical Letter' in 1836 advocating thoroughgoing westernization of all Russian institutions. For this he was declared insane and placed under medical supervision.

an intensively detailed and all-inclusive picture of mid-nineteenth-century Russia such a sweeping canvas would have presented!

To write about this 'calvary' of a modern Russian seeking after truth Dostoevsky had to return to Russia, as he himself said in his letters. The novel he had already begun to write about the Russian revolution also required that he return home. The Dostoevskys started to make preparations for their departure. At this time a very important thing happened to Dostoevsky. He gave up gambling. He was cured of the 'accursed mirage', 'nightmare', 'accursed fantasy'. He wrote to his wife on 28 April 1871:

A marvellous thing has happened to me. The vile fantasy that has *tormented* me for nearly ten years has vanished. For ten years (or rather since my brother's death, when I was all at once crushed by debts) I dreamed of winning a large sum of money. I dreamed seriously and passionately. But now this is all over! This was *truly* the last time. Can you believe it, Anya? My hands are untied now. I was tied by the game. Now I will think about my work and will not dream of gambling whole nights long, as I used to do.

Just before they left for Russia an unnoticed but not undramatic episode took place: Dostoevsky burned all the manuscripts of the books he had written while abroad, that is, *The Idiot, The Eternal Husband* and the first parts of *The Devils*. His wife implored him to keep these precious manuscripts and to take them back with him.

But Fyodor Mikhailovich reminded me that he would certainly be searched on the Russian border and that his papers would be taken away and would get lost as were all his papers when he was arrested in 1849. It was also possible that we would be detained in Wirballen while the papers were examined. Sorry as I was to part with the manuscripts, I had to give in to Fyodor Mikhailovich's persistent arguments. We lit a fire in the fireplace and burned the papers.

The greatest loss was that of the numerous variant drafts that Dostoevsky always made of his manuscripts. But Anna Grigoryevna did save the most important papers: the manuscript notebooks for the novels, which contained so many plans, quick drafts, 'tests', early versions, studies, characterizations, excerpts, all of which are of exceptional importance to the study of that tireless writer's work. Anna Grigoryevna gave the notebooks to her mother, who was returning to Russia at a much later date, and so the notebooks were saved. The notes for *The Idiot* were published in 1931 and the notes for *The Devils* in 1935.

The Dostoevskys arrived in Russia at the beginning of July 1871. This marked the end of an exceptionally important period in Dostoevsky's life. The main concepts of all his subsequent work had taken shape and the artistic and philosophical ideas of his last three novels had taken firm root while he was abroad. But creative designs have destinies of their own. Pressing new themes crowded the plan he had made in 1868 out of the novelist's workshop, and only a few of the ideas from the series of novels Dostoevsky had conceived found expression: in *The Devils*, *A Raw Youth* and *The Brothers Karamazov*. It is perfectly clear from Dostoevsky's notebooks that these were all fragments of *The Life of a Great Sinner*.

A TERRIBLE YEAR

Dostoevsky's last year in Europe was one of the most important years in the modern history of Europe. Prussia's policy of conquest was turning the European war, begun in July 1870, into a just war on the part of the French, who were defending their territory and their nationhood

Dostoevsky kept a diary of the military events in his work notebooks.

The end of July: The army has taken over all transportation facilities. The post is not even being delivered. Yesterday the newspapers did not arrive from Berlin. A battle will probably be fought in about a week.

It is already the 3rd of August. About three hundred thousand troops have gathered on each side of the Rhine. They were already facing each other yesterday, each ready to attack the other at any moment. The exchange rates are falling. Prices are going up on everything. Neither side can stand a long war. Yet they are planning to fight for a long time. Something is sure to happen! The decisive engagement will probably take place tomorrow or the day after.

Today is the 11th [August]. The French were defeated on the 6th.

Today is September 14 and the troops may have reached Paris already.

October 10. Paris is besieged. In France there is inertia, the result of administrative procedures. There is no firm government.

His deep concern was matched by his accurate understanding of current events. On 17(29) August at the very beginning of the war, when it was still possible to make conjectures about its outcome, he wrote to his niece in Russia:

France has become too hide-bound and petty. Temporary pain does not mean anything. France will survive and be resurrected for a new life and new thought. For it has all been the old talk, on the one hand, and cowardice and pleasures of the flesh, on the other. Napoleon's name won't work again.

Our seventy-year-old Russian, European, German policy will also have to change, that goes without saying. Those same Germans will at last show us their true selves. In general, there will be great changes everywhere in Europe. What a shake-up! How much new life will be called forth everywhere!

Dostoevsky was living in Germany during the entire period of the Franco-Prussian conflict. He saw the German posters, announcing 'War is declared!' appear on all the walls. He witnessed the official welcome given to the victorious troops, returning from France a year later. He heard German professors demanding the destruction of Paris and read letters from German soldiers about the horrors of the campaign, a fragmentary diary of the army in the field. In the heart of Saxony he read Jules Favre's celebrated reply to Bismarck, the wrathful and despairing words which he recalled three years later in *The Devils*, where he used them as a leitmotiv to his fantastic 'Marsellaise': 'Not an inch of our land, not a stone from our bastions!' He followed with close attention the rise of the new people's state from the ruins of the decrepit empire and heard the new democracy appeal for a brotherhood of working people of all countries and for peace among all nations. The Paris Commune caused him to reflect anxiously about the destinies of mankind and the paths that history might take.

On 4 May 1871 Strakhov asked Dostoevsky in a letter: 'What do you say about the French events? Here, as usual, many enthusiastic adherents of the Commune have turned up . . . What do you think? Is this, perhaps, the beginning of a new era? Is this the dawn of the day that is to come?' Dostoevsky's reply was in keeping with his by now established convictions, which were remote from any support for revolutionary action but were passionately directed towards a quest for supreme social justice. Dostoevsky believed that there were certain special paths by which universal truth would be attained. 'The world will be saved by beauty' – this is the conclusion he drew from his travels in old Europe, 'the land of holy miracles', a conclusion borne out by the Zwinger and Uffizi Galleries, by the Palazzo Pitti and the Bâle Museum, and by the cathedrals towering above the squares in Milan, Cologne and Strasbourg with their lancet towers and fantastic sculptures.

What 'new word' could the contemporary revolution say in face of such priceless spiritual culture? 'The conflagration of Paris is an enormity, even though to the adherents of the Commune it appears to be *beauty*.' And so 'the aesthetic idea has grown confused in modern mankind'. This is not how an ideal society is created; these are not the paths that lead to social renovation. 'They have lost Christ in the West and that is why the West is toppling.' Amid the mighty new laws of historical struggle that were being revealed to mankind, Dostoevsky remained a captive of his moribund religious and aesthetic views.

However, he was soon to admit that the battle that had begun between the bourgeoisie and the proletariat would end in an inevitable victory for communism. In the manuscript notes for *A Raw Youth* he wrote the following astonishing lines:

Versilov on the inevitability of communism. The life of people has two sides: the historic, and that which ought to be (justified by Christ, who appeared in the flesh of man). Each side has immutable laws of its own. According to these laws communism will triumph (whether the communists are right or wrong). But their triumph will be the farthest point of removal from the kingdom of heaven. However, one must expect this triumph. Yet *none* of those who rule the destinies of this world *is expecting it.*

XVII

A Political Novel

THE HISTORY OF ITS GENESIS

'. . . *Even if it turns out to be a political pamphlet, I will have my say.*'
Letter to N. N. Strakhov, 5 April 1870

IN December 1869, at the time when Dostoevsky was planning *The Life of a Great Sinner,* he read startling news in the Russian and foreign newspapers he obtained in the Dresden library, where he used to spend his evenings. These were reports of a mysterious murder in Moscow, an ominous conspiracy that had spread its tentacles across all of Russia, a dangerous organization of political terror, a Society of People's Retribution, or Society of the Axe, and mounting Russian revolution. The dispatches repeatedly mentioned the terrible names of the now elderly Bakunin and a young man, named Nechaev, as threatening the peace of all Europe. The news from Moscow shocked Dostoevsky.

A student, named Ivanov, was found murdered in the Razumovsky Park of the Petrovsky Academy. The details of the crime are horrible. Ivanov's body was found frozen in a transparent block of ice. There was a bullet hole in the back of his head. The bullet had come out through the eye. It had apparently been fired point blank. His feet were wrapped in a hood that had been filled with bricks and a scarf was wrapped tightly around his neck. Apparently, the murderers had dragged the body to the pond from the site of the crime. The hat (not his) on Ivanov's head was very crumpled, as if from the heavy blows of a blunt weapon. Ivanov is said to have arrived at the Academy three years ago from Kazan Province. He was very well liked but was withdrawn and not very social. He was on an Academy scholarship and used to send most of his money to his mother and sister.

The background to the crime was soon common knowledge. It was discovered that several young men in Moscow, led by the underground conspirator Sergei Nechaev, a close friend and follower of Bakunin, had formed a secret society of terrorists, modelled after the Polish national revolutionary society (the *Rząd*) which had an axe for its emblem and was called the Committee for the People's Retribution. At the society's clandestine meetings Nechaev was constantly opposed by Ivanov, a student of the Petrovsky Agricultural Academy, who made no secret of his intention of splitting off from the circle and forming a new revolutionary society of his own. Nechaev persuaded his comrades to 'liquidate' their dangerous associate for fear that he might betray them to the authorities. And so, late on the evening of 11 November 1869, five conspirators enticed Ivanov to a deserted part of the Razumovsky Park, murdered him in the ambush, and flung his body into a pond. Progressive public opinion the world over, Marx and Engels included, condemned this unprecedented political lynching.

It turned out that Nechaev had been acting in accordance with the precepts and plan of Bakunin, at whose house he had lived in Geneva in the spring of 1869. Bakunin had recently printed several articles in his Geneva newspaper *Narodnoe Delo* (*The People's Cause*), calling for the establishment of ties between the Russian and world revolutionary movements for the purpose of liberating the many millions of working people from the yoke of capital, hereditary property and royal power: 'We must make the people aware of the boundless strength that has been slumbering in them since Pugachov's* day.' Young Nechaev had been appointed representative of the Russian branch of Bakunin's World

* Emelyan Pugachov, a cossack from the Yaik (or Ural) river, raised a great peasant revolt in S.E. Russia and proclaimed himself to be the murdered Tsar Peter III, husband of the reigning Empress Catherine II. He was captured and executed in 1775.

Revolutionary Alliance and it was his objective to bring about violent insurrection in Russia and to transform the despotic autocracy into an all-embracing alliance of free communities. The young rebel returned to Russia in August 1869 to carry out the political directive he had been given to raise a nationwide rebellion by 19 February 1870 on the quaking sands of the cankered empire, and to tear down the whole rotten system.

Dostoevsky did not waver for a moment; he perceived immediately that he could put many of his cherished ideas into a novel about Nechaev. He had before him once again, as he had in 1865, the image of a rebel student with a destructive philosophy on his lips and terrorist tactics in his actions: 'similar to *Crime and Punishment*', he wrote to friends about his new idea, 'but even more pertinent, even closer to reality and touching directly upon the most important contemporary problem'. He saw how fascinating he could make this story of an ideological crime, how many of the pressing issues then uppermost in the minds of all Europeans he could weave into the portrayal of this murder, committed 'for reasons of theory'.

He had more than enough material and data. He had seen the general headquarters of the Russian revolution in Petersburg in 1848 and in Geneva in 1868. He had known personally and seen the 'fathers and sons' of the Russian revolution in Kolomna and at Carouge, outside Geneva – at Petrashevsky's Fridays and at the sessions of the League for Peace and Freedom. He had known and seen the entire contingent of young *emigrés* at Geneva, which Nechaev had joined only a few months after the Dostoevskys had left Switzerland and where he had formed an alliance with the patriarch Bakunin, for the purpose of consigning mighty Russia to flames and destruction. When Dostoevsky learned that 'Geneva directives' were the source of Nechaev's conspiracy he felt that this was a theme he understood and knew firsthand. He resolved to incorporate the facts of the current political struggle in the symbolism of his novel and to make a fantastic juxtaposition of his impressions from newspaper accounts with his reflections on the Gospel texts. He determined to depict in his fresco of this underground hell a huge gallery of portraits of the leaders of two revolutionary generations, making his Stavrogins and Verkhovenskys composite studies of the major figures among the Petrashevskyites and the Nechaevites.

He put aside the notes he had made for *The Life of a Great Sinner* (already remarkable for their dramatic force and their profundity) and began to work rapidly and determinedly on this challenging idea of a political novel about the troubled times in which he lived. At the end of 1869, only one month after the shot was fired in the park of the Petrovsky Academy, he was already making notes for *The Devils* in his manuscript notebooks.

*

Contemporary newspapers provided Dostoevsky with quantities of information about the principal figures of the 'Russian revolution', primarily about the man whom journalists of different countries and political views called the inspirer of the murder, the organizer of the conspiracy, and the instigator of Nechaev – Mikhail Bakunin, 'Geneva leader of the Russian revolution'.

That notorious name had an electrifying effect on the powerful German press. Many newspapers in Prussia, Cologne and Frankfurt gave a great deal of space to the 'nihilist revolution in Russia'. This is not surprising, considering that Bakunin had been a leader of the revolution in 1848, had shown his skill in conducting revolutionary activities in Dresden (where Dostoevsky worked on *The Devils* for a year and a half) and had been a German political criminal. The *Allgemeine Zeitung* declared:

It is true that Bakunin is the founder and leader of this conspiracy, the aim of which is no more or less than the destruction of all state principles, the rejection of all personal property and the establishment of a reign of communism.[1]

The first article about Bakunin in the Russian press appeared at this time. It was written by M. N. Katkov, who had been a comrade of Bakunin's youth and later became his political enemy. The headquarters of the Russian revolution, wrote the editor of *Moskovskie Vedomosti*, had moved from London to Geneva:

It is from there that the appeals to take up axes are broadcast; it is from there that emissaries are sent to us; it is there that the Khudyakovs[2] and the Nechaevs run for inspiration and orders. Nobody talks about the publishers of *Kolokol* any more. The sceptre of the Russian revolutionary party has passed into the hands of another celebrity, of that same Bakunin who rioted on the streets of Dresden in 1849, who was gaoled in Austria, was later handed over to our government, was imprisoned in the Fortress, wrote touching and penitent letters from there and was pardoned and deported to Siberia, where he was given complete freedom, worked as a tax collector, married a very young Polish girl of an exiled family, associated with many of his wife's countrymen, and when the Polish disturbances broke out, fled from Siberia, setting out in 1863 with some hotheads among the Polish *emigrés* on a naval expedition against Russia but then preferring to land on the coast of Sweden. That is who he is, this leader of the Russian revolutionary party, organizer of the conspiracy which has spread its tentacles all across Russia. He is an interesting figure. His shadow falls across all of gigantic Russia.

The article referred to Bakunin as commander-in-chief of the Russian revolution and as its Geneva leader, who set up Stenka Razin* as a model for his young followers. Katkov's article had undeniable informative value, and for an experienced artist it was a treasure house. Dostoevsky did not overlook it.

Dostoevsky's return to Russia coincided with the begin-

* Stenka Razin. See note on p. 181.

ning of the sensational Nechaev political trial, which was held in open court in Petersburg from 1 July to 1 September 1871. The most important political document of the trial was the *Catechism of a Revolutionary*. Its analysis by the lawyers attracted universal attention. Dostoevsky made a thorough study of this code of rules for agitators, from the complete text, published in *Pravitelstvenny Vestnik* (*Government Herald*). The influence of the *Catechism* is obvious in the chapter of *The Devils*, entitled 'Pyotr Stepanovich is Busy', which appeared in *Russky Vestnik* in October 1871.

Something can be learned of Dostoevsky's method of handling historical documents from a comparison of the materials of the trial with the novel itself. Pyotr Verkhovensky, whom the author conceived as a swindler and adventurer, a sort of Khlestakov* of the revolution, is following the Geneva rules when he urges the establishment of dens of vice, association with local scandal-mongers and prostitutes, with the police and elderly civil servants, with bandits and criminals; he recommends that pressure be brought to bear on high-ranking personages through their mistresses, and so on and so forth (his own relationships with the governor and his wife, Karmazinov and Fedka the Convict are also dictated by these rules).

Dostoevsky assumes, as did those at the trial, that Bakunin was the author of the *Catechism*, though he never mentions Bakunin's name in the novel. In court the lawyers for the defence stressed this authorship. It was extremely important for the advocates who were appearing for the first group of defendants to prove that there was no conspiracy in Russia at all and that not only Nechaev's followers but Nechaev himself were guided by *emigré* leaders. They implied that it was not the defendants Uspensky, Kuznetsov and Pryzhov who were guilty, but Bakunin, the dangerous leader of the European revolution, whose proclamations and

---

* Khlestakov. The young scamp who is mistaken for a government inspector in Gogol's play *The Inspector-General* (*Revizor*).

appeals, coming from Geneva, corrupted gullible young Russians. Behind the cross-examinations and speeches of Spasovich, Urusov and the other lawyers one could clearly discern the efforts to prove that Bakunin was the invisible spirit on trial, that it was he who had shaped the principles of extreme revolutionary struggle into a menacing code of rules of insurrection.

'Ours is a fearsome cause, filled with universal and ruthless destruction. So let us join together with the savage world of bandits, with the true and only revolutionary force in Russia.' No one at the trial doubted that the author of this was Bakunin, and that was Dostoevsky's impression too. Pyotr Verkhovensky, speaking of the organization of the underground, says to Stavrogin: 'You wrote the rules yourself, there is no need to explain them to you.'

Certainly Bakunin's philosophy of revolution is concentrated in the *Catechism*, an extraordinary declaration which contains the essence of his political programme and method of struggle. It resounds with the heroic motifs of the destruction of the old world and the liberation of enslaved and enchained mankind. It contains forceful and correct instructions to soldiers fighting for the new life. But all this is smothered over by the principles of 'Machiavellian politics and the Jesuit system', to use Bakunin's own words; these instruct the aspiring rebel to suppress all human feeling – friendship, love and honour – and channel all his emotions towards universal, horrible, ruthless destruction.

It is very possible that Dostoevsky attended the trial and saw the principal defendants, who later became characters in his novel. It is quite certain that he went to see the actual site of the murder, for he says in the novel: 'It was a very gloomy place at the end of the huge Stavrogin park. *I went there later on purpose to take a look.* How gloomy it must have seemed on that autumn evening!' Dostoevsky was in Moscow at the end of December 1871 and the beginning of January 1872, and he surely took the opportunity to go to

Petrovsky-Razumovsky Park to get a firsthand impression
of its topography, which was reproduced exactly with all its
ponds and grottoes in 'A Night of Great Labour'. Dostoevsky
was highly selective in his use of the materials of the trial,
adapting them to his complex design and imparting to that
extraordinary criminal affair an inimitable atmosphere of
idea-fantasies and tragic destinies.

*

The focal chapter of the entire composition took shape as
Dostoevsky worked on the second part of the novel. This was
Stavrogin's Confession, the ninth chapter of Part II of *The
Devils*. Katkov however refused to print it in his 'family'
magazine and in the end Dostoevsky was compelled to re-
structure the novel, a large part of which had already been
published. He cast about in vain for a way out of this disaster.
He submitted compromise solutions, trying to save at least
the basic elements of his plan. But Katkov would have none
of the variations he offered on his profound treatment of a
crime against a little girl, a theme that he had already developed to some extent in the story of Svidrigailov. Dostoevsky argued that Stavrogin's sin was merely a figment of his
disturbed imagination, not an actual fact. But to no avail.
He had to omit the chapter entitled 'At Tikhon's', the
second section of which was Stavrogin's Confession, and was
therefore unable to carry out his plan to incorporate in *The
Devils* the fragment from *The Life of a Great Sinner* in which
Stavrogin, the underground revolutionary comes to a monk's
cell to expiate his moral lapses.

As in his other novels, Dostoevsky here, too, presents a
religious element, namely the Orthodox Church, in opposition to socialism and rebellion. This was the main theme of
his projected *Life*, or *Atheism*, the hero of which finally
comprehends the Russian Christ and the Russian God and
becomes a teacher of beggar children and a benefactor of
doomed prisoners, like Dr Haas, that noble friend of the
unfortunate.

It was fourteen months after this overwhelming blow to his cherished concept that Dostoevsky submitted the rest of the novel for publication. When the last part of *The Devils* finally appeared in *Russky Vestnik* at the end of 1872, the epic that was to have told of a redeemed sinner bore no resemblance to a novel–poem in the style of Dante's *Divine Comedy*, with its vision of Purgatory and the possibility of ultimate redemption, but was more reminiscent of a medieval morality play about the fearful end of an un-repentant criminal. Stavrogin's gradual degradation to new vices and sins ends in despair and suicide.

Though Dostoevsky outwardly submitted to his editors, inwardly he remained true to his concept of purgatory. As he finished *The Devils* he was still looking for a suitable setting for his original idea of the bringing of light to a blackened conscience through public penance. That he had not at the end of November and the beginning of December 1872 given up hope of publishing Stavrogin's Confession is evident from the concluding lines in the manuscript: '*Some notes, they say, were left after Nikolai Vsevolodovich Stavrogin, but no one knows what they are, I am searching for them very hard. Perhaps I will find them and then and if possible . . .*

Finis.[3]

This is a valuable piece of evidence about Dostoevsky's attitude to one of his pivotal themes, to which he gave an open-ended finale, with vistas of future realization.

PROTOTYPES AND TYPES

Originally, the protagonists of the novel were to have been the students Nechaev and Ivanov, the former as a Raskolni-kov type, the latter as a Myshkin type: the murderer devoted to theory and the destroyed 'beautiful man'.

Two historical contemporary figures – the student Nechaev
and the religious dissenter Golubov – were to have clashed
in the novel and struck the spark that fired the plot.

But, as we have seen, from their earliest reports of the
murder the newspapers had brought in, alongside Nechaev
and Ivanov, a third contemporary figure whose stature,
especially in 1870, greatly surpasses that of the student
principals – *Bakunin*. It was his personality, which as a result
of the Nechaev murder had assumed extraordinary importance as the topic of the hour in the Russian and
European press, that was taken by Dostoevsky as the
foundation for the central image of his novel – Stavrogin. It
is only in this light that the enigmatic image of the hero
emerges from the dusk of complex psychological mysteries
and gets its proper interpretation. Dostoevsky wanted to
embody in Stavrogin his own picture of the celebrated
Russian rebel and to show that all his noisy activities were as
fruitless and futile as was his much-discussed personality. In
Dostoevsky's version, the world-famous revolutionary is
a typical scion of the Russian nobility with all the built-in
reflexes of his class, a wanderer in Europe, torn from
his native soil, a captive of convoluted thinking, powerless
to accomplish anything and doomed to inactivity and an
inglorious end.

Stavrogin is the personification of exclusively intellectual
cerebral power. In him the intellect has swallowed up all
other spiritual manifestations, paralysing and sterilizing his
emotional life. Thought, developed to a monstrous degree,
devouring every spiritual quality that might have thrived
alongside it, had become an idol to which the entire
gamut of emotions, imagination and lyrical feelings
had been sacrificed. 'Some new formidable thought is
struggling in you,' 'a great thought is shaking you,' the
people around Stavrogin say to him, sensing a quality of
tragedy and greatness in this man who has been eaten up
by an idea. This naked, incredibly hypertrophied brain has

an astonishing capacity for devising sweeping conceptions that are doomed to collapse because of their exclusively cerebral nature. This is a genius of the abstract, a titan of logical abstractions, completely engrossed in wide-ranging but sterile theories, which derive their impact from a colossal force that kills everything that Stavrogin touches and are tragic because of their inability to be constructive, to convert destruction into construction. The quality of death that one feels in Stavrogin comes from the petrification of a brilliant theoretician, who cannot move from the idea of destruction into the category of creation, who cannot in practice turn the will to destroy into creative fire.

This is a huge, tragic image and it is not surprising that Dostoevsky, in the process of creating it, fell under the spell of his hero's prototype. He wrote in one of his letters:

Nikolai Stavrogin is a gloomy individual, too, a villain, too. But now he appears to me as a tragic figure . . . I have sat down to write a poem about this man because I have too long had the desire to portray him. In my opinion he is both a Russian and a human type. I have taken him from my heart.

Dostoevsky's feelings about Nechaev were very different. He was well aware of the destructive force of irony and it was with this weapon that he had decided to castigate Nechaev, belittling his image by derision, and denying his claims to the recognition of contemporaries and the admiration of young people by drawing a caricature of him. Dostoevsky was of course resorting to a tested political technique, dethroning a party opponent by ridiculing his reputation, by destroying his 'heroism', his 'grandeur' and depicting him as petty, laughable and comic.

The result was unexpected. A historical personage, who had impressed his contemporaries by the tragic quality of his nature and the intensity of his will, turned out to be a petty and insignificant figure in the novel. Dostoevsky achieved his satirical purpose but he missed the opportunity to portray a forceful personality, worthy of his lofty flights of artistic and philosophical imagination. Only once is Pyotr Verkhovensky allowed to step outside the limits of the clownish criminality allotted to him and rise to the heights of inspired prophecy. This belittlement was deliberate. Even the prosecutor at the Nechaev trial commented on the magnetism of this man for whose sake intellectually and socially diverse organizations had sacrificed everything and risked death, and who had managed to form a revolutionary society that was united 'in inner composition and in the spirit that vitalized it'. At the same time the satirical tone Dostoevsky adopted did not give him enough scope to make the most of the pernicious traits of the real Nechaev. The author's determination to draw Pyotr Verkhovensky as a swindler, adventurer and blackguard unbalanced him and prevented him from producing a portrait of a convincingly complex individual.

Some of the other characters in *The Devils* were able to withstand the onslaught of the creator's pamphleteering design. This is especially noticeable in the case of the figure, so much ridiculed by the author, of 'the respectable Mr Stepan Trofimovich' Verkhovensky, the father of Pyotr Verkhovensky. Conceived as an object of satire, he grew vastly in stature under Dostoevsky's pen; and, breaking through the lineaments of caricature, in the course of the work he came to have features of deep and beautiful humanity, which give the old dreamer kinship with the great images of world literature. Several years after the publication of *The Devils* Dostoevsky himself expressed deep compassion for old Verkhovensky and even for his historical prototype.* He wrote in *The Diary of a Writer* in 1876: 'Granovsky was the purest of men in those days. He was irreproachable and beautiful. He was one of the most honest of our Stepan Trofimoviches (the type of the idealist

* Timofey Granovsky (1813–55); a liberal professor of history at Moscow University.

of the 1840s whom I draw in my novel *The Devils* and whom our critics considered to have been correctly drawn. After all, I love Stepan Trofimovich and respect him deeply).'

It is Stepan Trofimovich Verkhovensky who presents Dostoevsky's most cherished ideas concerning art, Pushkin, Raphael, Shakespeare. It is he who is charged with expressing the novel's basic idea, namely, that the great invalid, Russia, will be cured of the maladies that have accumulated in her 'for centuries and centuries'. Thus, possibly contrary to the author's original design, Stepan Verkhovensky is the character around whom all the action revolves. He rises above the whirlwind of events not only as its original cause but also as its clearest-eyed analyst. The elder Verkhovensky, whom Dostoevsky scholars have studied very little, is entitled to go down in world literature as a distinctive and magnificent Russian Don Quixote.

Dostoevsky was very much interested in the destinies of the Old Believers, who had emigrated to Turkey, Austria and Prussia and had later rejected socialism and returned to the Russian Orthodox Church. To him these were truly 'new Russians' whom he envisaged in contrast to the Lopukhovs and Rakhmetovs,* and they were to be the positive heroes of his later novels.

N. Y. Danilevsky, a former Petrashevskyite, exiled from Petersburg in 1849 as a convinced Fourierist, had undergone this sort of political evolution. In 1869 he published a monograph about the cultural and political relations between the Slavs and the Germans, entitled *Russia and Europe*, which was an attempt to rebuild the doctrine of the Slavophiles on a new foundation. The character of Shatov in the novel shows the same pattern of experience. Dostoevsky, who had known Danilevsky in the 1840s, welcomed his ideological evolution warmly and even considered himself to be of like mind. He wrote to Maikov on 11 December 1868: 'To

* Characters in Chernyshevsky's novel *What Is To Be Done?*

turn from a Fourierist to Russia, to become Russian again and to love one's soil and essence! This is the sign of a wise man!'

Dostoevsky also parodied the literary world in his anti-nihilist novel, for instance in his satirical portrait of Turgenev as the 'great writer' Karmazinov. In his delineation of Karmazinov Dostoevsky expressed the attitude, prevalent at that particular time among conservative journalists who shared his view, that Turgenev was an extreme Westerner, a nihilist and an enemy of their 'Russian social cause'. Turgenev, derided mercilessly in the novel both as a literary artist and as a person, was particularly pained by the political implications of the caricature. He wrote: 'Dostoevsky has permitted himself something worse than parody; as Karmazinov he has portrayed me as secretly sympathizing with the Nechaev party.' Turgenev's meaning is clear: *The Devils* is a political denunciation.

Extraordinary as such a judgement may be, it must be admitted that Dostoevsky's novel contains some very incisive political lampoons. In his effort to depict the leaders of the enemy camp in a variety of unflattering guises Dostoevsky did not hesitate to dip his pen in acid. He was relentless in the pursuit of his purpose of degrading the eminent political figures of two revolutionary generations such as Petrashevsky, Speshnev, Bakunin and Nechaev in the eyes of their closest associates.

In any case Dostoevsky never restricted himself to completely faithful reproductions of his prototypes. He wrote to Maikov: 'After all, it is not Chaadaev in my novel. I have only taken the type.' In *The Diary of a Writer* he comments: 'Naturally, my Nechaev's face does not resemble the real Nechaev's face.' Dostoevsky's aim was to paint from his own carefully chosen palette a gallery of sarcastic portraits in the style of Goya, and this he succeeded in doing.

In choosing the locale for his novel Dostoevsky was also governed by artistic pragmatism, selecting a setting that

would allow maximum expressiveness. Analysis reveals that
in this case he has drawn an exact picture of Tver* the last
city he lived in as an exile, in the autumn of 1859. This was
strictly in accordance with facts; Bakunin had roamed that
city when he was a young landowner in Tver province, and
Tikhon Zadonsky had lived in a monastery on the shores of
the Tverets and Tmaka Rivers. By the author's will, two
different historical periods converge and two historical
personalities, who have captured his imagination, come
together to converse. Dostoevsky brings Bakunin into
Tikhon Zadonsky's cell.† This extraordinary encounter of
two contrasting figures resulted in some of the most highly
charged writing in world literature, Stavrogin's Confession.

With regard to the time of the novel, it practically coin-
cides with the actual date of Nechaev's residence in Moscow,
the autumn of 1869. Nechaev arrived there on 3 September
1869, and on 22 November 1869 he left for Petersburg.
Pyotr Verkhovensky arrives in Tver at the beginning of
September and leaves for Petersburg at the end of October.
In keeping with these chronological details, the landscape
is always an autumn one: rain, mud, washed-out roads,
'low, murky, ragged clouds', 'half-naked trees', 'a slow,
fine drizzle, as if coming through a sieve', 'long since
harvested fields', 'a damp, old garden, dark as a cellar'.

Dostoevsky departs from the real-life chronology in one
detail: the pond is not frozen when Shatov is murdered. In
the real murder Nechaev had to break the ice and drop
the body through the hole; in the novel the men swing the
corpse and throw it into the water, causing ripples on the
surface. The change of season, from the end of November to
the end of October, before winter set in, was probably not a
fortuitous one. The narrative is presented in consistently
dreary colours of dying and disintegration. The drab,

* Today called Kalinin.
  † The historical St Tikhon Zadonsky lived in the eighteenth century.
See p. 457 note.

colourless, gloomy north Russian autumn in an impoverished district and the dreary city were surely a deliberate expression of Dostoevsky's feelings about Russia's sickness, about the joylessness of that age and his premonition of approaching ruin. Like Raskolnikov in *Crime and Punishment* who, weighed down by his nightmarish designs, feels as if he is suffocating in the dust, heat, lime, sand and airlessness of Petersburg in the summer, so does Stavrogin disintegrate and die to the accompaniment of the hopeless sound of persistent autumn drizzle, amidst the darkened fields and muddy roads, under the cold, leaden sky and naked trees in his deserted family park, in whose thickets the murderers have just been sheltering.

*

To sum up the ideology of this complex novel: *The Devils* is a political satire against the revolutionary movement. Its purpose, as Dostoevsky described it in detail in his letters, is to rout the revolutionary movement as represented by the 'fathers' – the Utopians of the 1840s – and the 'sons' – the practical revolutionaries of the 1860s. Dostoevsky's aim was to defend Russian monarchism by attacking the forces that undermined and threatened it. But despite the vehemence of the denunciation Dostoevsky expresses in the novel, it misfires. He ignored a number of major developments of revolutionary history that took place in the end of the 1860s and the beginning of the 1870s. The formation of the Russian section of the First International, the socialist alliances of workers, the widespread movement of intellectuals to bring enlightenment to the people, the formation of the Chaikov circle, which set out to counteract Nechaev's influence among young people – none of these events was treated seriously in Dostoevsky's journalism or fiction.

Though it was the major trends of the contemporary revolutionary movement that provoked his satirical indignation, Dostoevsky dealt in his novel only with lesser, often secondary, developments. He directed all his criticism against Russian liberalism, individual rebellion and the excesses of the Nechaev movement. From his position in the reactionary camp he attacked only a few, perhaps the most exposed, but certainly not the strongest, of his adversaries' positions. Striking at what seemed the most vulnerable spot did not turn out to be good strategy.

An analysis of the novel will reveal that the very approach which Dostoevsky, the ideologist, adopted to this enormous theme condemned him and his political conclusions to defeat in advance. Having himself, in his youth been close to the ideas of the Utopian socialists, he apparently could not find it in himself to maintain the tone of castigation he had chosen, and towards the end of the novel he takes Stepan Trofimovich Verkhovensky through an 'apotheosis' of revelation. He also failed in his satirization of Bakunin, for Stavrogin, modelled after him, retains his significance and seriousness throughout the novel, and to the very end inspired in his creator close attention, bordering on reverence. Finally the real-life Nechaev, by the tragedy and force of his deed, overshadowed the clown, Pyotr Verkhovensky. The novelist's portrait is far inferior to the historical prototype.

Such was the gulf between the aim and its realization. There were also subjective elements that predetermined the failure of the political concepts of *The Devils*. As a great master of psychological portrayal, Dostoevsky could not be consistent in his adherence to the position of the Katkovs and the Meshcherskys.* In some parts of the novel, the artist and the thinker in him overcome the pamphleteer and supporter of the establishment's ruthless and prejudiced policy. While he criticized and condemned the Paris Commune, he did not take the extreme right-wing position of its detractors and denouncers. This is not the only instance of its kind in *The Devils*. In some places Dostoevsky departs

---

* Prince V. P. Meshchersky, proprietor of the conservative magazine *Grazhdanin*, afterwards edited by Dostoevsky. See Chapter XVIII below.

much further from the official line he supports. He endows most of his Nechaevite protagonists with real-life, attractive characteristics. In obvious contradiction to the novel's basic tendency, Dostoevsky expresses through the lips of Stepan Trofimovich a liking for the younger generation, whose value and grandeur the elderly scholar can perceive even through what he considers their errors.

Stepan Trofimovich, dying: 'Long live Russia, there is an idea in her, there is an idea in them, in the nihilists.

'Their idea is hidden. We were exponents of an idea, too. This eternal Russian urge to have an idea, that is what is so wonderful.

'*Je ne parle pas* that everything of theirs is fitting and proper: God's poor flock.'

In the draft of the foreword to *The Devils*, never completed, Dostoevsky noted that the Russian revolutionary had the capacity 'to *sacrifice himself and everything for the truth*' and to confess that truth openly, to the whole world. In this connection Dostoevsky contrasts the 'regicide' Karakozov* to the Italian terrorist Orsini, who flung a bomb into the French Emperor's carriage. The purpose of *The Devils*, he said, was to point out that truth for which the younger generation ought to fight.

The national idea is in Kirillov – to sacrifice oneself immediately for the truth. Even the wretched misled suicide of April 4† believed in his own truth at the time (they say he repented later – thank God) and did not hide, as Orsini did, but faced up.

To sacrifice oneself and everything for the truth – that is a national characteristic of the generation. May God bless it and send it undisputable truth. For the whole question is: what is to be considered the truth. This is why the novel was written.

As he finished writing *The Devils* Dostoevsky, like Stepan Trofimovich, sought in his own way to understand

---

* Dmitri Karakozov, a student, who shot at Alexander II. See Chapter XX below.

† i.e. Karakozov.

the younger generation, for he believed in the sincerity of their quests and felt that they had only by chance swerved from the correct path. Notes of sympathy of this kind are understandable and almost inevitable in Dostoevsky, for he had known the revolutionary movement from personal experience. In 1870 Dostoevsky admitted in a letter to Maikov that even in prison he had retained 'a very strong leavening of Russian liberalism', and a little later he announced publicly in *The Diary of a Writer* that in his youth he could have become a Nechaevite himself. He recognized in himself the same elements of opposition and even of active revolutionary deeds for which he was condemning his younger contemporaries.

In attacking the free-thinkers and rebels of two generations, Dostoevsky was committing to the flames all the political idols he had worshipped in his youth. At the same time, in the statements made by Stepan Trofimovich and in some of his own notes about Young Russia's urge to sacrifice, its sincerity and enthusiasm, he was paying a last tribute to that which he was burning on the bonfire of his pamphleteering wrath. While noting all the manifestations of Dostoevsky's barbed satire against the liberation movement, a student of *The Devils* must not ignore the writer's attempts to understand the revolutionary generation, and even the 'regicide' Karakozov. Such understanding did not come to Dostoevsky lightly, and it is our duty to call attention to and recognize the existence of this reverse trend in his pamphlet against revolution.

CONTEMPORARY CRITICISM

The last instalment of *The Devils* appeared in *Russky Vestnik* in December 1872 and the reviews followed shortly afterwards. Generally, civic-minded journalistic opinion condemned Dostoevsky for his opposition to 'Westernizing progress' and for his conclusively joining 'Katkov's orchestra'. It reproached the author of *The House of the Dead* for writing a new kind of anti-nihilist novel. All the critics compared Dostoevsky's new novel with N. S. Leskov (Steblitsky)'s reactionary novel *At Daggers Drawn*, which had recently caused a sensation. They criticized Dostoevsky for having kept too close to the transcript of the Nechaev trial: 'The author begins to copy the court report and imagines that he is creating a work of art.'

However, nearly all its detractors recognized some of the characters in the novel as being outstanding. There was unanimous appreciation of Stepan Trofimovich Verkhovensky, who was called a 'flesh-and-blood man, approaching such types as Onegin, Beltov* and Oblomov in artistic reality' (*S. Petersburgskie Vedomosti* (*Petersburg News*), 13 January 1873). Even N. K. Mikhailovsky, who was harsh in his condemnation of Dostoevsky for going over to the 'right-wing' camp, nevertheless considered a number of the personages in his new novel 'successful', and some even 'superb' (the Lembke couple, Karmazinov). Mikhailovsky made a special study of Dostoevsky's 'favourite heroes', who, he noted, are 'on the border of sanity and insanity', but who nevertheless deal with very important problems of life and morality. This line of the Raskolnikovs and the Myshkins is continued in different variations by Stavrogin, Pyotr Verkhovensky, Shatov and Kirillov, 'men devoured by an idea', frequently, moreover, a religious idea.

Mikhailovsky denies that such 'mystics' are typical of the revolutionaries of his day. But they are typical of Dostoevsky's work and they are therefore of interest to his readers. They pinpoint his distinctive literary style and the characteristic trend of his thinking, which is marked by interest in the major movements of history. 'Why doesn't Dostoevsky write a novel about fourteenth- or fifteenth-century Europe?' Mikhailovsky asked. 'All those flagellants, demo-

* Beltov, a character in Herzen's novel *Whose Fault?*

nomanes, were-wolves, all those macabre dances, banquets during plagues, and so on, the entire amazing inter-mingling of egoism with guilt feelings and an urge for expiation – what gratifying subject-matter this would be for Dostoevsky!' But no, he has to take material that is alien to him – the nineteenth-century Russian revolutionary move-ment – and doom himself to failure by imparting his own 'eccentric ideas' to his heroes.

Hence the lack of clarity of the protagonists, Stavrogin, Kirillov and Shatov. Hence, too, the unintelligibility of the novel's principal idea: the devils represent loss of the cap-acity to distinguish between good and evil. 'How is that!' Mikhailovsky exclaims. 'The sick and devil-ridden Russia that you have depicted is being covered with railways, fac-tories and banks, yet not a single characteristic of that world is to be found in your novel. Your novel does not contain the *devil of national wealth*, the most widespread of all devils and the one that can least distinguish between good and evil. *You have gone after the wrong devils.*' Mikhailovsky's idea is clear: devastating satire ought to be directed against the real evil spirits of the times – the monsters of accumulation of money, the bankers, the shareholders, factory owners and stockbrokers, capitalists of all types and ranks – not against the active and progressive fighters 'with consciences of crystal clarity and hardness'.

Mikhailovsky's is probably the best of the early articles about *The Devils*. Its basic theses were repeated by P. N. Tkachev in his book *Sick People*. Tkachev, who was, with Nechaev, a leader of the student movement in 1869, was later sentenced to imprisonment (he emigrated in 1873). He contributed an article about *The Devils* to the magazine *Delo* (*The Cause*) (Nos. 3 and 4 for 1873), in which he expresses regret for Dostoevsky's 'abdication' and 'peni-tence' and attitude towards Chernyshevsky. The young heroes of *The Devils* – Stavrogin, Verkhovensky, Shatov and Kirillov – were all 'knights of ideas', but their development and upbringing had given them artificial or 'wax' souls, torn from healthy nourishment and therefore inclined to emotional abnormalities. They constitute a gallery of insane young men with a variety of manias – suicide, destruction, the cult of the common people as God-bearers, and so forth. This is all abstract delirium, containing no reality. The characters are not real people but dummies for hackneyed ideas.

E. Markov, the *Russkaya Rech* (*Russian Speech*) critic, noted perceptively that Svidrigailov had already in *Crime and Punishment* lifted up a corner of the curtain that concealed Stavrogin's Confession (not yet published then) and that in the same novel Raskolnikov's dream while in prison already revealed the horrors of plague sores, which turn healthy people into devil-ridden madmen. 'But never, never did people consider themselves so intelligent and so inflexible in truth as did those who had caught the disease,' Dostoevsky's hero raves. This is clearly a precursor of *The Devils*, which merely elaborates the brief text with which Dostoevsky had been obsessed since the 1850s and 1860s.

The satirical picture of revolutionary youth – Shigalev's theory, the mad engineer Kirillov, the maniac Shatov – is not a picture of society but a biting political philippic. 'Dostoevsky's gloomy muse drives man away from the image of man, ruthlessly tears off the wings of his hope . . . and forcibly beats down his mind and heart in the fruitless solitude of personal suffering.' Nevertheless, Markov wrote in conclusion, we prefer 'this raw, clumsy, one-sided writer, a sinner in his way, but a genius in his way, too', a writer who does indeed deserve to be called 'Shakespeare's pupil', to many writers recognized and respected in the world.

Thus did literary criticism in Dostoevsky's lifetime look for methods and techniques to give adequate interpretation to his last works. A. M. Skabichevsky wrote more boldly and confidently than anyone else in 1876: Dostoevsky is '*a genius who belongs not only on the same level as Russian artists of the first rank, but even belongs among the greatest geniuses of Europe in this century'*; but he weakened this comment with a number of reservations.

But it was not until the publication of Gorky's article 'Once more on Karamazovism' in connection with the Moscow Art Theatre's production of *Nikolai Stavrogin* that young Russia heard an appeal for a new life. Gorky wrote: 'It is not the Stavrogins who ought to be shown to her [Russia] now but something quite different. Cheerfulness ought to be preached, spiritual health and action are needed, not introspection; it is necessary to return to the source of the energy – to democracy, to the people, to public opinion and to science.'

V. D. Bonch-Bruyevich, reminiscing about Lenin's reading habits, has given some of Lenin's opinions of Dostoevsky's works:

Although his attitude towards *The Devils* was sharply negative, Lenin said that the reader should not forget that the novel reflects events connected not only with the activities of S. Nechaev, but also of M. Bakunin. At the very time when *The Devils* was being written, Karl Marx and Friedrich Engels were waging a fierce struggle against Bakunin. It is up to the critics to sort out what in the novel refers to Nechaev and what refers to Bakunin.[4]

Today *The Devils* is being studied from all angles – historical, social, philosophical and artistic – so that the reader can now appreciate this complex and diversified book in its entirety.

THE LAST DECADE

XVIII

Dostoevsky as a Journalist

A PERIODICAL

SOON after Dostoevsky's return to Petersburg, his friends Apollon Maikov and Nikolai Strakhov introduced him to the aide of Prince V. P. Meshchersky, leader of the Russian conservatives and author of vapid high-society novels. Meshchersky had a great deal of influence at court; he recommended candidates for ministerial posts and was involved in the scandalous financial machinations of his henchmen. S. Y. Witte,* who knew him at a somewhat later period, wrote in his memoirs that Meshchersky used his acquaintance with the monarch and the powers-that-be to obtain subsidies for his magazine *Grazhdanin* (*The Citizen*) and the means to reward his favourites lavishly at the Treasury's expense.

To have become an associate of this kind of political manipulator was a lamentable event in Dostoevsky's life and probably the greatest mistake he ever made. When Dostoevsky met him, Meshchersky was in the process of organizing the new *Grazhdanin*, a weekly 'with militant conservative objectives', in Meshchersky's own words. Maikov, Tyutchev, Dostoevsky, Strakhov and B. M. Markevich were the godfathers of this new publication. A young journalist named Gradovsky was invited to be the editor, but by the autumn of 1872 he was at odds with Meshchersky's programme 'of putting an end to the reforms'. Dostoevsky took over and was the editor of *Grazhdanin* through 1873 and the beginning of 1874.

* Count Sergei Witte, Prime Minister of Russia under Nicholas II.

During that period he developed a new form of journalism – the reactions of an artist to the events of the day. This was his *The Diary of a Writer*, in which he wrote on a wide variety of current issues and interesting topics, such as his disagreement with Belinsky, his meeting with Chernyshevsky, his opinion of Nekrasov's 'Vlas', the mission of the Russian people, Leskov's fine story 'The Sealed Angel' (one of his best works), a play about factory life for the folk theatre ('this is a tragedy in the full sense of the word, and the villain is vodka'), and his interest in Utopian socialism. 'Bobok', a bitingly satirical story that appeared in *The Diary of a Writer* in 1873, was the first of a series of superb short stories 'A Gentle Creature', 'The Dream of a Ridiculous Man', 'A Boy at Christ's Christmas Tree'), which were a new achievement of his in the shorter forms of narrative art. This constituted Dostoevsky's invaluable contribution to Prince Meshchersky's otherwise shallow society periodical.

It was not long before Dostoevsky found his duties at *Grazhdanin* unbearable. The progressive press was condemning him for apostasy. The discussions with contributors, the reading of manuscripts and the editing of articles were time-consuming, and everything had to be adapted to the mediocre limits of a semi-official publication. Differences soon arose between him and Meshchersky, the unavowed director. Dostoevsky tried to oppose a programme of his own to Meshchersky's wretchedly petty political tendencies, which really amounted to an appeal for a return to 'the system of Nicholas'. 'My idea is that Socialism and Christianity are antitheses,' he wrote in a letter to M. P. Pogodin on 26 February 1873: 'I would like to discuss this in a series of articles, but I have not even begun working on them.' The 'main irritation', however, was that 'characters for stories and novels are swarming in my head and taking shape in my heart. I conceive them, write them down, add new features to the written plan every day, but then I find that all my time is taken up by the magazine, that I can no longer write anything – and I am overcome by remorse and despair.'

The only thing he valued in the magazine's stifling environment was the contact he had with the young members of the staff, mostly technical workers, who used to talk to him about their aspirations and dreams. One of these was Varvara Timofeeva, a young girl who read the galleys and page proofs of *The Diary*, often sitting at a big table where Dostoevsky was writing 'by the light of the same printshop lamp'. Dostoevsky often exchanged a few remarks with her on current topics. Once in a while, however, they had longer conversations:

The two of us stayed behind, waiting for the proofs. F. M. got up and, moving his chair closer to the desk at which I was working, asked:

'Tell me, why are you here? Do you have a purpose in life?'

It was so unexpected that at first I was confused. But I took hold of myself somehow and replied. I even told him my most cherished dream.

'I want to write, to be a writer,' I murmured timidly.

Surprisingly, F. M. did not laugh.

'You want to write? So that's it! And what would you like to write about? What exactly? Novels, stories, articles?'

'I like psychology . . . inner life,' I whispered, afraid to raise my eyes and feeling like a perfect idiot.

'Do you think it is easy to portray inner life?'

'No, I do not think it is easy. That is why I am studying and preparing myself.'

'There is only one woman writer in the whole world, worthy of the name,' he went on seriously. 'That is George Sand. Can you be somebody like George Sand?'

I froze in despair. He was depriving me of all hope. And, unaware of what I was saying, I kept repeating, as if in a daze: 'I want to write. I feel the need. That is all I live for!'

'That is all you live for? Well, if that is the case, write. And take my advice, never invent stories or plots. Take what life provides. Life is far richer than all our inventions. No imagination can invent what the most ordinary average life will sometimes provide. Respect life!'

At times he was morose and irritable. He would not say a word for evenings on end. When he left, he would offer a limp, lifeless, dry, cold hand. But at other times he would become animated and suddenly begin to read poetry – usually Pushkin's *Prophet* and Lermontov's *Prophet*.

'I put Pushkin's above all others. In Pushkin it is nigh on the supernatural,' he said 'But Lermontov's *Prophet* has something that Pushkin does not have. Lermontov has a great deal of bile. His prophet had a whip and poison. *They* are there!'
And he read it aloud with bile and poison:

> I began to proclaim love,
> And the truth of pure doctrines,
> And all my neighbours
> Threw stones at me madly.

Only once did the shy proof-reader venture to ask Dostoevsky about his work.

'I read your *Notes from Underground* all last night. And I could not rid myself of the feeling that man's soul is a horrible thing! But I also felt that this was the horrible truth!'
Fyodor Mikhailovich smiled a bright, frank smile.
'Apollon Grigoryev[1] told me that that was my *chef d'oeuvre* and that I should always write like that. But I do not agree with him. It is too gloomy, really. *Es ist schon ein überwundener Standpunkt.*[2] Now I can write more radiantly, more conciliatorily. I am working on something now.'

Among *Grazhdanin*'s most important contributors was K. P. Pobedonostsev, then a member of the State Council and teacher of law to the Grand Dukes. He was one of the most sinister government reactionaries in the period of the decline of Tsarism. He opposed emancipation of the peasants, trial by jury, the new *zemstvos* and town institutions and secular schools (which he wanted replaced by parish schools).

Pobedonostsev had a high opinion of the author of *Crime and Punishment*. He used to help Dostoevsky get out the issues of the magazine and tried to exert ideological influence on him. It is evident from the correspondence between them that the future Supreme Procurator of the Holy Synod was keeping a sharp eye on Dostoevsky's journalism, that he often gave him material for *The Diary of a Writer* and commented on the issues in detail.

But even this lofty patronage could not make Dostoevsky's position secure. At the time of his appointment to the editorship the Third Department declared it would 'not accept responsibility for this individual's future activities'. Administrative reprimands for violation of censorship rules hailed down on Meshchersky's magazine. In June 1873 the censorship committee indicted Dostoevsky and the Petersburg District Court sentenced him to a fine of twenty-five roubles and two days in the army guardhouse.

On 11 March 1874 the Minister of Internal Affairs charged *Grazhdanin* 'with opinions that tend to incite hostility against one section of the empire's population', and on 12 March it issued its '*first warning to the magazine in the person of its publisher–editor Fyodor Dostoevsky*'. Clearly, the editor of the 'political periodical' would have to be relieved of his duties, otherwise the publication would be closed altogether. On 19 March Dostoevsky submitted a petition to be released from the editorship of *Grazhdanin*, citing reasons of health, to the Chief Administration for Affairs of the Press.

THE GUARDHOUSE

But before he could get this release he had to serve his term of imprisonment in accordance with the sentence of the Petersburg District Court of as long ago as 11 June 1873. Dostoevsky had been sentenced as editor of *Grazhdanin* for printing information about 'August Personages' in his magazine without permission from the Minister of the Imperial Court. When he appeared in court he had pleaded not guilty but had been sentenced to a fine of twenty-five roubles and two days' imprisonment. No one had been in a hurry to see the sentence carried out. A. F. Koni had told Dostoevsky unofficially that he could serve it at his own convenience. Nine months elapsed, but now the forthcoming break with Meshchersky's periodical meant that he would have to finish up the 'court incident'. Dostoevsky submitted the appropriate application. On 21 March 1874 the district police officer called for him and escorted him to the local court, where he was informed that the place of his imprisonment was the guardhouse on Sennaya Square, to which he was taken forthwith.

He was put 'in a spacious and clean enough' room (described by Vsevelod Solovyov, who visited him there on 22 March) but with another prisoner, a young, poorly dressed artisan with a colourless face. 'Don't pay any attention to him,' Dostoevsky whispered to Solovyov. 'I have tried everything. He is made of wood.' Dostoevsky sat at a small deal table, drinking tea and smoking his 'cannons'. He had a thick French book, which he did not let out of his hands. It was Victor Hugo's *Les Misérables*, one of his favourite novels. 'See, it is a good thing that they have locked me up,' he joked with his wife. 'I would never have found the time otherwise to renew my earlier wonderful impressions of this splendid book!'

It was as if the characters that had moved Dostoevsky so deeply during his foreign travels in 1862 had come to visit him in prison: the convict Jean Valjean, protesting against the jungle instincts of the kingdom of evil that had destroyed him, but already seeing the light of the supreme truth of self-sacrifice and humanity; the pure and meek Fantine, whom dissolute society had purchased from beggary and hunger and flung into the prostitution of the big worldly city; Gavroche, the light-hearted gamin of the Paris streets, who was loyal to his people and laid down his life on the barricades for the Republic. Dostoevsky considered these well-known scenes of the epic novel among the finest in world literature ('It cuts the heart once, and the wound remains forever'). All of them came back to him, filling his poet's heart with emotion and pity and diverting him for at least a short time from Sennaya Square and the deadly official formality of his temporary military prison.

Dostoevsky's first visitor was his wife, who brought him a parcel. Then Maikov came, and after him Vsevolod Solovyov. Dostoevsky used to enjoy discussing serious subjects with young Solovyov. Now he reminisced about his Siberian prison term and expatiated on a favourite theory of his that an erring person can be saved by making a radical change in his usual way of life.

Fortune helped me then [that is, at the end of the 1840s], penal servitude saved me, I became a completely new man. Once the decision was made, my agony ended; that was still during the investigation. When I found myself in the Peter and Paul Fortress I thought that this was the end of me. I thought I could not stand it for even three days. Then, suddenly I felt perfectly calm. What do you suppose I did while I was there? I wrote 'The Little Hero'. Read it. See if there is any malice or agony in it. I dreamed quiet, good, kind dreams, and as time went by it became easier. Oh! what great good fortune for me Siberia and penal servitude were! I really learned to know myself there, my friend, I learned to know Christ, learned to know the Russian man, and I began to feel that I, myself, was a Russian, one of the Russian people. All my very best ideas came to my head then. They are merely coming back now, and not as clearly either. Oh, if you could only be sent to penal servitude!

'This was said so enthusiastically and so seriously that I could not help bursting into laughter and embracing him,' Vsevolod Solovyov recalled. Dostoevsky arrived home at noon of the third day, first having stopped off at a toyshop.

On 22 April 1874 *Grazhdanin* printed a statement to the

effect that 'F. M. Dostoevsky has been compelled by poor health to give up his duties as editor but will continue to contribute to the magazine as much as possible.' Dostoevsky did contribute occasional short anonymous articles right up to the end of the 1870s, mostly to a weekly feature called 'The Last Page'. But he never again worked on the magazine regularly.

Dostoevsky took with him from the stifling atmosphere of Meshchersky's magazine the new creative form he had devised there and it served him until the end of his life. He continued to publish his *The Diary of a Writer*, a new kind of literary journalism, in which he dealt with topical subject matter, improvised freely on current issues of public life, reminisced, wrote 'incidental stories', reportage, impressions and even several profound psychological short stories. Many of the articles in *The Diary* are equal to the finest scenes and dialogues in his novels. Despite *The Diary*'s conservative views, it gained wide recognition and many issues had to be published in larger than usual editions or to be reprinted.

Now that Dostoevsky was rid of his laborious editorial duties, he began to plan the writing of a new long novel, based on his materials and notes for *The Life of a Great Sinner*.

*

In April 1874 Nekrasov called on Dostoevsky, and to the latter's surprise invited him to write a novel for *Otechestvennie Zapiski*, to be published the following year. He offered him 250 roubles per 24 ms. pages, which was much higher than Dostoevsky's usual fee of 150 roubles. The editors of the progressive *Otechestvennie Zapiski* – Nekrasov, Saltykov and Mikhailovsky – considered it desirable to carry a new work by one of Russia's most powerful writers; they may also have hoped to bring him closer to progressive literature and keep him away from *Russky Vestnik* and *Grazhdanin*.

But Dostoevsky had strong feelings of loyalty to the political direction he had taken. He said to Nekrasov:

I cannot give you an affirmative reply for two reasons, Nikolai Alexeevich. First, I must get in touch with *Russky Vestnik* and find out whether they are counting on something of mine. If they have their material for next year, then I am free and can promise you a novel. I am a long-standing contributor to *Russky Vestnik*. Katkov has always treated my requests with kind attention and it would be indelicate on my part to leave them without first making them an offer. This can be cleared up in a couple of weeks.

Dostoevsky went to Moscow to see Katkov, who told him that *Russky Vestnik* had all it needed for the next year (Tolstoy's *Anna Karenina*) and was not in a financial position to buy another novel. Even after that Dostoevsky kept putting off his reply to Nekrasov, for he feared he might have ideological differences with the editors of the organ of the revolutionary democrats. It was six months before he finally gave his consent, in October 1874.[3] Even so, at the end of that year he was still full of anxieties and doubts.[4] The first issue of *Otechestvennie Zapiski* for 1875 began to print *A Raw Youth*, subtitled *Notes of a Young Man*.

IN THE FAMILY CIRCLE

Upon their return to Petersburg from abroad the Dostoevskys rented a four-room apartment on Serpukhovskaya Street, near the Technological Institute, and purchased the furniture they needed on credit. Now they could invite friends to their home and engage in the philosophical discussions which were the breath of life to Dostoevsky.

Their financial situation was extremely difficult. All the property they had left behind with 'reliable people' had vanished. Household goods, dishes, glassware, china, winter coats and other clothing, and the fine library that Dostoevsky had collected in the 1860s, had been taken away, stolen, lost for ever. As the result of inefficient management, the Snitkins' three houses in Peski (with the spacious wings and a large plot of land) had fallen into the hands of unscrupulous businessmen. There was nothing at all left for Anna, her mother and her brother. The Dostoevskys had to set up house from scratch. Furthermore, they were promptly besieged by creditors, whose demands would probably have ruined Dostoevsky if it were not for his wife's business acumen, intelligence and energy.

Anna Grigoryevna had changed very much, as all her relatives noted on her return to Russia. The timid, shy girl had become a determined woman, waging a successful fight against the bane of their existence – the creditors of the Dostoevsky brothers' magazines. At that time Dostoevsky's debts amounted to twenty-five thousand roubles, most of which had been taken over by dealers in promissory notes, some of whom were heartless, shameless loan sharks. The creditors were also demanding the return of large debts that Mikhail Dostoevsky had incurred when he was still running his tobacco mill, and were threatening to distrain Dostoevsky's property and have him thrown into debtors' prison.

'But how do you think I can write if I am sitting in a debtors' prison? How will I pay you if I am deprived of the opportunity to work?'

'Oh, you are a famous writer. The Literary Fund will buy you out of prison.'

Dostoevsky offered to pay his debt in monthly instalments but he met with a sharp refusal.

Without saying anything to her husband, Anna Grigoryevna went to negotiate with one of the inexorable agents. He greeted her with an ultimatum.

'Money on the table, or else distraint before the week is out. Your property will be auctioned off and your husband will be put into Tarasov Debtors' Prison.'

'Our apartment is rented in my name, not in Fyodor Mikhailovich's,' Anna replied. 'Our furniture has been bought on credit and until it is paid for in full it belongs to the furniture dealer, so you cannot distrain it. As for your threats of debtors' prison, I warn you, should this happen, I will implore my husband to stay there until the term of your debt expires. I will find a place to live near by, visit him with the children and help him with his work. And you won't get a copper, and not only that, but you will have to pay for his food. I give you my word that you will be the one who is punished.'

The agent thought about it and accepted Anna's terms.

Nor was this all that Anna did. She began to publish her husband's novels in separate editions and gradually became an experienced publisher. Only as a result of a decade of this kind of struggle and austerity were the debts paid in full – one year before Dostoevsky's death.

*

'Nowhere is a person's character expressed so vividly as in daily life at home with the family,' Anna Dostoevskaya writes in her reminiscences. And, knowing as she did all that there was to know about this side of Dostoevsky, she reveals unsuspected traits of his personality. Our picture of the writer as a man is rounded out by glimpses she gives us of Dostoevsky rocking the children to sleep, decorating a Christmas tree for them, dancing a waltz, a quadrille and even a mazurka with his wife, like a 'real Pole', to the accompaniment of a toy organ. The thinker and psychologist displayed excellent taste in women's clothes and selected his wife's dresses. He had a passion for beautiful things: crystal, Bohemian glassware, vases, *objets d'art*.

In Dostoevsky's letters to his wife one senses the tranquil happiness of a tired and sick man who has at last, after half a century of struggle and bitterness, achieved the cherished dream of having a family and settling down. Words from a letter he wrote to Nikolai Strakhov come to mind: 'Three quarters of a man's happiness is in marriage; there is hardly a quarter in all the rest.'

As the children grew older Dostoevsky sought to bring

them into contact with art, culture, poetry, novels, the theatre. In the summer of 1880 he read Schiller's *The Robbers* to them, a favourite of his, which his young audience, however, did not understand. In the last years of his life he began to take them to the opera, but exclusively to *Ruslan and Lyudmila*. Once, due to a singer's illness, Auber's *The Bronze Horse* was substituted for the great work of Pushkin and Glinka. Dostoevsky wanted to go straight home, but he gave in to the children's entreaties and they remained. 'We were delighted with the fairy-tale,' his daughter Lyubov relates, 'but father was dissatisfied. He wanted us to remain true to his beloved Lyudmila.'

He used to read them Pushkin's poems and stories, 'The Captain's Daughter', 'The Shot' and 'The Blizzard'. He always had tears in his eyes when he read 'The Poor Knight'. He also read them Gogol's 'Taras Bulba', Lermontov's 'Borodino' and 'Taman', Schiller's *Glove* in a translation by Zhukovsky, and in 1880 he read them Ostrovsky's *Poverty is Not a Vice*. He was fond of reciting Griboyedov's *Chatsky*, or *Woe from Wit* to them and was especially appreciative of the part of Repetilov, whom he regarded as a predecessor of the Western-minded liberals. The novels of Walter Scott and Charles Dickens were basic reading for his children.

Beginning with 1872 the Dostoevskys spent the summers in Staraya Russa, an ancient little town in Novgorod Province rich in history. Dostoevsky became very fond of this quiet, secluded place. The family usually rented a spacious manor house on the edge of the town, on the river bank, among age-old elm trees. When in the spring of 1874 Nekrasov asked him to write a novel for *Otechestvennie Zapiski*, Dostoevsky went to Staraya Russa for a whole year. He wrote *A Raw Youth* there. He also went to Staraya Russa in May 1880 to work on his Pushkin memorial speech. Staraya Russa was in fact reproduced in Dostoevsky's last novel. The writer described its narrow streets, cut by ditches, the Plotnikovs' grocery shop and the broad country view he had from his window, of a field turning green and a pine wood on the edge, where he imagined he could see the old white monastery from which (according to his plan for a second novel about the Karamazovs) the 'early lover of mankind' Alyosha was to go out into the world to fight for universal happiness.

From 1873 the Dostoevskys lived in a house belonging to a Lieutenant-Colonel Gribbe and in 1876 they bought it. It was a small house in German taste, set in an orchard, and it was full of surprises, such as secret wall-cupboards, trap-doors and dark spiral staircases. Dostoevsky reproduced some of the features of the Gribbe house in his description of Fyodor Karamazov's dwelling, with its tiny cell-like rooms, winding passages, dim chambers and scurrying rats.

In the spring of 1872 Dostoevsky, at the request of P. M. Tretyakov, founder of the Moscow art gallery, invited the painter Perov to his house and posed for a portrait by him. Perov, who was a keen-eyed observer and a methodical worker, had an unusual approach. Anna Grigoryevna relates:

> Perov visited us every day for a week before starting to work on the portrait. He would find Fyodor Mikhailovich in different moods. He talked with him, provoked arguments and succeeded in noting the most characteristic expression of my husband's face, the expression he had when he was absorbed in creative thought. One might say that Perov captured Dostoevsky's 'moment of creativity' in the portrait.

The portrait does indeed show a great thinker at the start of the late and final period of his work, when he wrote his last novels and his Pushkin speech. The pose is simple and restrained. He is immersed in thought.

Dostoevsky continued to be deeply interested in Russian art. He had a high opinion of young Repin, especially of his 'Volga Boatmen', in which he perceived enormous truth, power, directness and reality: 'I'll put it simply. The figures are Gogolean. One cannot help loving those defenceless creatures. One cannot help reflecting on what one owes yes, really owes, to the common people.' Dostoevsky welcomed the vital originality of the young painters who were taking native themes for their work. He remarked upon the two birch trees in Kuindji's 'View of Valaam'* and the national typicality of the three figures in 'Hunters At Rest'. He sympathized with the serious portrayal of Russian life in Makovsky's 'Admirers of the Song of the Nightingale'. Genre painting of this kind was, he felt, the path of true art, art that is lyrical and humane.

*

During the 1870s the Dostoevskys lived in several fairly large apartments, usually of five rooms, but poor and depressing. In the autumn of 1872 they moved into a two-storey wing set far back in the courtyard of the buildings of the second company of the Izmailovo Regiment. The young writer Vsevolod Solovyov visited him there, and in 1881 recalled the circumstances of their first meeting:

I climbed up a narrow, dark staircase, dropped my coat on some sort of trunk in the low-ceilinged entrance hall, passed through a dark room, opened a door and found myself in his study. But could this be termed a study? this wretched corner room in a tiny wing, where one of the most inspired and profound writers of our time lived and worked?

The apartments on Ligovskaya Street and on the corner of Yamskaya and Kuznechny Streets were very much the same. 'Since I have known him these past eight years he has changed apartments several times, and each was gloomier than the last, and he always had an uncomfortable room with not enough space to turn around in,' Solovyov wrote. It was in dreary studies such as these that Dostoevsky wrote his last three novels, his philosophical short stories, *The Diary of a Writer*, 'A Gentle Creature', the speech in memory

* Valaam. An island on Lake Ladoga, with a famous monastery.

of Pushkin and 'The Grand Inquisitor', the central chapter of his last novel.

His creative method never ceased to deepen and broaden, its all-inclusive neo-realism becoming more polished while retaining the basic features of the romanticism he had loved in his youth. Extraordinary interest attaches to the great master's last declaration,* written half a year before his death, and evoked by his meditations on *The Queen of Spades*.

It may be a fantastic story, but in art the fantastic has its limits and its rules. The fantastic must touch so closely upon the real that you must almost believe it. Pushkin, who has given us nearly all forms of art, wrote *The Queen of Spades*, which is the pinnacle of the art of the fantastic. You believe that Herman did indeed have a vision, and that it was a vision that harmonized with his world outlook, and at the end of the story, that is, after you have read it through, you still do not know what to think: was this vision a product of Herman's nature, or was he really one of those who have come into contact with another world, a world of evil spirits, hostile to mankind. That is art!

Such was the essence of Dostoevsky's own 'poetics', which continued to develop right up until the end of his life, raising his imagery to unattainable heights of bold truth and penetrating artistic perception.

In 1873 the twenty-year-old philosopher Vladimir Solovyov wrote Dostoevsky a letter, enclosing an article he had written about the negative principles of Western development. This marked the beginning of a friendship between the two men. The young scholar and poet became Dostoevsky's last philosopher friend and had an influence on the basic concepts of *The Brothers Karamazov*. When they first met, Vladimir Solovyov had only just completed his studies, having obtained a candidate's degree in science. Dostoevsky became very fond of him because of his intelligence and erudition. He used to say that his face reminded him of a painting he loved, Annibale Caracci's 'Head of the Young

* The Pushkin speech. See Chapter XXI.

Christ'. Once he told his young friend why he felt so close to him: 'You remind me of someone I once knew, a certain Shidlovsky, who had an enormous influence on me in my youth. You are so much like him in appearance and in character that at times it seems to me that his soul has trans-migrated to you.' They did not see one another often in the mid 1870s – Vladimir Solovyov taught at Moscow University and made a trip to Egypt – but in 1877 he came to live in Petersburg and then they became close friends.

In 1878 Vladimir Solovyov delivered a series of public lectures on religious–philosophical themes in Petersburg. Dostoevsky did not miss a single one. In 1880 he attended Solovyov's defence of his doctoral thesis on 'Criticism of Abstract Principles' and wrote approvingly of it to friends: 'The young philosopher Vladimir Solovyov (the son of the historian) made a profound statement at a recent debate here about his thesis for the degree of doctor of philosophy: "It is my deep conviction (he said) that mankind knows much more than it has yet had a chance to express in its science and in its art."'

NEW THEMES

In 1873 Dostoevsky paid a visit to the juvenile delinquent section of the Petersburg Prison, to gather material about the emotional state of an abandoned child. In the summer of 1877 A. F. Koni showed him around a children's colony on the Okhta River. Dostoevsky talked to the children for a long time and, his companion later related, made a very strong impression on all those that gathered round him: 'The faces of many who had already swallowed the big city poison became serious and lost their artificial expression of cynicism and bravado.'

Dostoevsky saw the inmates as 'young souls thirsting for beautiful impressions', and he pondered over the means of satisfying this longing. The author of *Netochka Nezvanova* was planning to write a novel exclusively about children, with a child as hero, and he wanted to portray juvenile criminals in it, as well as political plotters, Protestants and atheists. The tenth book of *The Brothers Karamazov*, entitled 'Boys', reflects this design in part and the studies for that novel contain notes about factory children. Until the very end of his life public events in Russia aroused a lively response in Dostoevsky. In *The Diary of a Writer* he commented extensively on current court dramas that had aroused his anger, especially several cases of maltreatment of children in which, he felt, the eminent lawyers who defended the tormentors were glib at finding excuses for their clients.

In this period Dostoevsky was very active in editorial, journalistic and literary work. Whereas his editorial activities at *Grazhdanin* in 1873 had provoked the polemical protests of progressive Russian journalists, his independently published *The Diary of a Writer* was acclaimed in remote corners of Russia. He received a large number of letters, corresponded with strangers about all kinds of private matters, saw obscure visitors in his home, listened to confessions, advised, taught, guided. At the end of 1877 the Academy of Sciences, made him a corresponding member of its Russian language and literature department. His readings at literary evenings from his own works or from the work of great poets invariably met with an enthusiastic reception.

This period of unprecedented success, which rewarded the long-suffering writer for the trials and tribulations of his past, had its negative aspects, too. Dostoevsky's creative powers, which never ceased to develop, were not equalled by his political thinking, which inclined more and more towards militant reaction. Consequently this last period of his life, the period when he wrote his *The Diary of a Writer*, is often painted over with joyless and gloomy shades, which diminish the doctrine of humanism that he preached and weaken even the cult of beauty to which he tried to remain true. In this respect Gorky's articles 'On Karamazovism' offer many fair and undeniable arguments against the author of *The Devils* and *The Brothers Karamazov*.

As a hard worker and a craftsman, however, Dostoevsky remained at an unprecedented height. He never tried to evade the enormous difficulties that confronted him in giving artistic expression to his ideas, and always surmounted them, though, as his letters indicate, the difficulty of the tasks be set himself often wore him down. The tensions of the creative process, which had him jotting dozens of plans, characters and episodes down on paper, would suddenly be discharged with long break periods, during which he would have agonizing doubts about his ability to realize his concept. He began to write *Crime and Punishment* in the summer of 1865; in November he burned everything he had written and started developing his ideas anew. He revised *The Idiot* eight times.

From letters to literary friends, it is evident that during the first half year of his work on *The Devils* he kept tearing up what he had written and starting all over again: he changed his plan at least ten times, drafted a huge number of variations, lost his reference files in the mountain of paper he had covered with writing, and at times was in complete despair at the complexity of the novel he had conceived. 'Never before have I had to put so much work into anything I was writing,' he wrote to Strakhov on 9(21) October 1870. 'I am afraid that I have undertaken a theme beyond my powers. I am seriously afraid. It is agonizing!' And he informed his niece that after long months of intensive work he 'had crossed out everything already written [about three hundred and fifty ms. pages] and started from page one again', concluding his literary martyrology with a despairing cry: 'Oh, Sonya, if you only knew how difficult it is to be a writer, to endure this fate!'

When he was in this state of mind he used to be very harsh towards himself as a writer. 'Having always been more of a poet than an artist, I constantly undertook themes that were beyond my powers,' he wrote to Apollon Maikov in 1870. 'I get carried away by poetic impulses and without considering my capacities. I undertake to express an artistic idea that is beyond my powers,' he wrote to Strakhov in 1871. That his anxieties were unfounded is evident from his superb literary achievements.

A NOVEL ABOUT UPBRINGING

From the mid 1870s a crisis is evident in the novelistic form used by the author of *The Devils*. That he was seeking new ways to portray the world about him is especially obvious in *A Raw Youth*, and, as always, his explorations were bold and dangerous. In that novel he discarded the central-crime technique, weakened the story line considerably, and presented the reader with a number of difficulties in finally unravelling the mystery of his philosopher-hero. Though he was a first-class master of the female portrait, his heroines lack expressiveness; their portraits are deliberately, it would seem, left unfinished. Despite the undeniable brilliance of some of the episodes and the philosophical depth of much of the dialogue, the novel dissolves in a feverish succession of incidents that blur the contours of his main design. The excuses and explanations Dostoevsky gives, especially at the end of the novel, indicate that he was engaging in intensive exploration. His quests were not always successful. Saltykov-Shchedrin called *A Raw Youth* a 'mad novel', and Turgenev, as is known, sharply condemned 'this chaos'.

Here was a distinguished writer, the critics remarked, who was failing to understand the hopes and aspirations of young Russia. Public opinion was astonished that the author of *Poor Folk* and *The Insulted and the Injured* should have become the champion of the Russian gentry and claimed for it the role of sole exponent of the finest concepts of world civilization.[5] The apologia for the aristocratic class that Dostoevsky offers in *A Raw Youth* (already apparent, incidentally, in Prince Myshkin's speech in *The Idiot*), so unexpected from a democratic writer, is vehement to the point of bellicosity. 'I, Versilov, come from a twelfth-century gentry family', 'the time is not far off when the whole Russian nation will become gentry', and 'I am a gentleman above all else and I will die a gentleman' (spoken in French in the original) are the slogans and vows of this 'gentleman of ancient lineage and at the same time a Paris Communard', as the author describes him in the concluding epistolary epilogue. This moralistic sermonizer expresses the idea that the Russian hereditary gentry is the sole group of cultivated Russians capable of providing *belles lettres* with a 'beautiful hero'. He looks to the Russian classics: 'Already Pushkin, in "The Traditions of a Russian Family", planned the plots of his future novels, and, believe me, everything beautiful in our country up till now is to be found there.'

Dostoevsky's manuscript notes for *A Raw Youth* contain references in the same vein to Leo Tolstoy:

> I have one favourite Russian writer, my dear, a novelist, but for me he is practically a historiographer of our gentry, or, to be more exact, of our cultivated stratum, which is completing the 'education period of our history' . . . Be that as it may, whether it be good or bad in itself, we already have here a long-established and clearly-defined group, with rules and its own kind of honour and duty – it has its heroic types, too – they die for the homeland; as fiery youths they rush into battle, and as veteran generals they lead the whole fatherland into battle.

To this elegant and picturesque epic of gentility Dostoevsky contrasts the disorderliness and amorphousness of an 'accidental family'. The story of the childhood and adolescence of the Irtenyevs and the Rostovs is followed by the family chronicle of a *raznochinets*.*

The form of the novel is didactic, like *Télémaque, Wilhelm Meister* and *David Copperfield*. Dostoevsky shows how his young hero is really educated by life, not by schools and teachers, and how the innate nobility of his soul refuses to submit to life's dark and evil forces but, instead, finds its path to a radiant world outlook and fruitful activity. Originally, *A Raw Youth* was conceived as part of *The Life of a Great Sinner*,[6] which could easily have taken the form of a peda-gogical novel, but Dostoevsky soon decided against hagio-graphy and turned to the usual form of a first-person narrative by a contemporary.

The illegitimate offspring of a land-owner and a peasant woman, Arkady Dolgoruky seeks out of hurt pride to shut himself off from other people and to carry out his eccentric ambition (to 'become a Rothschild' or even a Covetous Knight† – to acquire in isolation a sense of omnipotence), but he gradually comes under the influence of an outstand-ing thinker, his father, who is a 'higher cultural type, a type that is not to be found anywhere else in the world, *one who feels compassion for everybody, for the whole world*'. 'This is a Russian type,' Dostoevsky adds. According to the original concept, this aristocratic intellectual sympathizes with the Paris Communards and even predicts inevitable victory for communism (though Dostoevsky himself has no sympathy with this).

It is not in Touchard's French boarding school, which the gifted and charming young man attends, that his inner qualities develop, but against the background of the corrupt capitalist city, with its restaurants, gambling dens, and 'cesspools of filth' of all kinds, above which are the quiet attics, where thinkers and dreamers engage in wonderful

---

* *Raznochinets*. An educated Russian who did not belong to the gentry and who was not a member of a guild.

† Covetous Knight. See p. 36–7 above.

dialogues about the Golden Age, the Paris Commune, the decline of Europe, and the transformation of stones into loaves of bread. As always in Dostoevsky's work, these glimpses of history and legend are imbued with drama and poetry. The climax of these moral wanderings comes with the appearance of a Russian pilgrim who captivates the young seeker with wise sayings of the common people. But the 'new life', the approach of which the raw youth senses towards the end of the story, will not lead him to a monk's cell but to university lecture halls. A broad path will open up into science, work and life.

In his wanderings and seeking the raw youth comes into contact with a revolutionary circle, reproduced in the novel on the basis of the materials of the political trial of Alexander Dolgushin and his followers, who called for the destruction of the royal family. In Dostoevsky's eyes, regicide was the extreme manifestation of moral disintegration in contemporary Russian society, and it was a subject that required a separate novel if it were to be developed. He made the story of the Dolgushinites short in this book, and set aside the theme of regicide to be the foundation of his next novel, *The Brothers Karamazov*, which was to develop during the so-called 'assassination period'.

Versilov

Dostoevsky was unusually successful with the opening of this very elaborately constructed novel. He introduced into the action in the very first pages an event that determined the principal lines of the narrative and the destinies of its central characters. He showed how an 'accidental family' arises and how it raises its members.

Versilov, the young lord of the manor, whose wife has died, has come to live on his estate. Among his manor serfs is an elderly gardener, Makar Dolgoruky, a pious man, well-versed in the lives of the saints. He has recently married a pretty eighteen-year-old girl, named Sonya, also a manor serf. Sonya is an orphan. She has been taught to read a little. She catches the eye of the newly arrived master, and leaves her righteous husband to go to him, and stays with him for good. Versilov attributes his own sudden infatuation to a feeling of pity for the meek young woman, who is one of the *defenceless* and has 'humbly' given him a deep and pure love, sacrificial and infinite.

A son, Arkady, is born of this union. Officially he is the son of Makar Dolgoruky, but his 'illegitimacy' is known to all and causes him a great deal of secret anguish. His sense of social inferiority affects his character and even instils eccentric ideas in him. His aim in life, however, is to live in a purposeful and worthwhile manner. The boy has two unofficial mentors. One is his natural father, Versilov, a well-known salon preacher in the 1840s; the other is his legal father, the pious pilgrim Makar Ivanovich Dolgoruky.

Versilov, the raw youth's father, occupies in the novel the central position of a thinker, like Raskolnikov, Myshkin, Stavrogin and, later, Ivan Karamazov. However, he is not a creator of ideological systems or even of a bold theory. He is merely a gifted dilettante in the sphere of thoughts and words, an improviser of philosophical fragments that are brilliant in form but shaky in conclusions, contradictory and, in effect, devoid of realistic insights into the future.

The history of this image is interesting. Orest Miller, a professor of Russian literature who knew Dostoevsky well in the last years of his life, asserted that Versilov embodied many of the traits of Herzen, as Dostoevsky interpreted him in his *The Diary of a Writer* for 1873, in which he drew a critical and in part ironical picture of the celebrated journalist. Dostoevsky wrote there that Herzen was 'a product of our squiredom', in whom 'the last ties with the Russian soil and the Russian truth have collapsed', and a most graphic example of the upper classes isolation from the common people and their religion.

'Naturally, Herzen had to become a socialist, and to do so precisely in the manner of a Russian gentleman's son, that is, without any necessity or purpose and solely because of the "logical course of ideas" and the emotional emptiness at home,' Dostoevsky wrote in the chapter 'Old People'. 'Always, everywhere and all his life he was above all a *gentilhomme Russe et citoyen du monde*, or, in plain words, the product of serfdom, which he hated and from which he came, not only through his father but even more through separation from his native land and its ideals.'

To Dostoevsky Versilov was a born *emigré*, one who from his youth, has dreamed of England or France with their progressive political institutions and who has never thought the Russian people any better than 'the French rabble of ninety-three'. Actually, in these traits Versilov was very different from Herzen, for whom emigration was a patriotic exploit and the Russian people a spiritual shrine.

All that Versilov and Herzen had in common was the aestheticism which formed the basis of their philosophies of history. Herzen said that he had always had respect for beauty and considered art a very great value: 'Together with the flickering summer lighting of personal happiness it is our only indubitable blessing.' He told how he shed tears of love for all beauty when he 'gazed into the features of Raphael's Madonna, listened to Liszt's music or watched Taglioni's dances'. Dostoevsky had a high appreciation of Herzen's sensitivity to art and regarded him as a true poet always and in everything. There is a certain analogy here with Versilov, who apprehended the great and turbulent epochs through the world masterpieces of painting, and wrote short poems in prose about the mythological past and the tragic future of European mankind. The legendary early happiness of antiquity is embodied for Versilov in Claude Lorrain's 'Acis and Galatea', which he calls 'The Golden age'. It is significant that a 'large, excellent print of the Dresden Madonna' and 'a huge, expensive photograph of the cast bronze doors of the cathedral in Florence' hung on the wall of Versilov's favourite room, where he used to sit for hours. There is an element of autobiography here.[7]

Versilov's concept of history was close to Dostoevsky's own. He feels as Dostoevsky did at cruel moments of world crisis, when warring nations forgot about beauty in the heat of battle. Dostoevsky never failed to remember that the aesthetic idea was the supreme criterion of historical significance and the ultimate judge of contemporary battles and victories. He gave this idea to his Versilov so that through him he might condemn the bloody week in Paris in 1871.

For Versilov the defeat of the Commune was expressed in a series of events to which he gave the name 'Tuileries'. On a big area of Old Paris, on the right bank of the Seine, close by the walls and moats of the Louvre, there had stood, in the sixteenth century, a tile factory which has given to the neighbourhood the name that it keeps to this day.[8] The tile factory had been torn down by order of Catherine de Medici and a magnificent palace erected in its stead, which retained the name of the former factory. In 1572 the new palace was the scene of sumptuous festivities marking Henry de Navarre's marriage to Marguerite de Valois, four days before St Bartholomew's Day, 24 August. The grand celebrations were intended to divert the attention of the Parisians from the ominous preparations that the Queen Mother and her partisans, the Guises, were making for the massacre of the Huguenots on the night of 23/24 August. The Bourbons and the Bonapartes ruled France from this palace. The Convention met here. In February 1848 the revolutionary mob of Paris entered it.

In 1871 it was in this palace that the Communards put up a desperate defence. On 24 May 1871, as the Versailles troops were approaching the Tuileries after having recaptured the Maison des Invalides and part of the Champs-Elysées from the Communards, a fire broke out inside the Tuileries and spread rapidly. Other conflagrations broke out in different places. Flames licked at the palace on all sides. Where the thick fortress walls and iron roofing did not give way to the raging fire, explosions resounded and the walls collapsed. The reactionary press seized upon this event as its principal argument against the Communards. The Katkov press invented a pernicious neologism, which it used as a sort of counter-revolutionary banner when referring to the incendiaries of Paris – *petroleishchiki*.*

Even at this tragic turning point in history Versilov's feelings are seen to be uncertain and ambivalent. He is prepared to try to prove to Thiers and MacMahon that the Commune was a logical development. That is why this 'Russian European' feels that the conflagration in the Tuileries is the funeral bell tolling for old Europe, that it is the destruction of a whole world because 'the aesthetic idea has grown confused in modern mankind'. But he is wrong; the Tuileries was never a treasure-house of art as was the Louvre, which housed masterpieces such as the 'Venus de Milo', the 'Niké of Samothrace', Leonardo da Vinci's 'Gioconda', Michelangelo's 'Slaves' and canvases by Rubens. When he calls the Tuileries fire a symbol of contemporary barbarism he perhaps has in mind the destruction of the luxury of the Bourbon dynasty, the Gobelin tapestries and the bronzes, the full-dress portraits and the decorated ceilings, the state trappings of the French kings. There was undoubtedly a great deal of labour and beauty in this decorative art, but it was not a national art to be placed above the world-historical tasks of revolutionary struggle, nor was it a valid argument against the Communards, who were defending new proletarian Paris from the savage onslaught of counter-revolutionary troops.

* *Petroleishchiki*. A Russification of the names invented by the French for the incendiarists of the Commune – *pétroleurs, pétroleuses*.

At this moment of final and decisive conflict this Russian 'universal man' does not take his place on the barricades but displays the usual duality of his weak nerves and unstable character.

They had just burned down the Tuileries then; there was not a single European in all of Europe then! I alone could tell all those *petroleishchiki* to their faces that their Tuileries was a mistake. And I alone could say to all the conservatives, thirsting for revenge, that though the Tuileries was a crime, it was also a logical development.

Versilov remains *above the conflict*. His aesthetic views are powerless in the face of the sweeping social struggle of the day. He is not interested in the outcome of this titanic struggle or in the future of the world, but only in the logic of events, the philosophy of state and law, the idealistic concept of world history – anything that can provide material for the musings and visions of this exquisite sophist, for his designs and his preludes. He was never a fighter. He never fought under the banners of revolution. He is far from sympathizing with the Communards. To Arkady's questions about how contemporary states would end up and how society would be renewed, he replies: by universal bankruptcy. 'A struggle will begin and after seventy-seven defeats the beggars will destroy the stockholders, take away their stocks from them and of course take their places and become stockholders themselves. Perhaps they will have something new to say and perhaps they won't. Most likely, they will go bankrupt too.'

This is Dostoevsky, the journalist of the 1870s, speaking. Dostoevsky's last novels cannot be separated from his *The Diary of a Writer*.

Madame Akhmakova and Lady Byron

Versilov's private life is filled with turbulence and anxiety. He is very successful with women and this imparts excitement to the story. He is already 'at the halfway mark in his stay on earth' when he has his most complicated and passionate love affair, and it breaks up his life. This is a 'love-hate' relationship with Katerina Nikolaevna Akhmakova, a remarkable woman, beautiful and courageous, the daughter of his friend, the old Prince Sokolsky. He meets her during one of his trips abroad. Katerina Akhmakova, who is attracted to the young Prince Sokolsky (no relation to the old Prince Sokolsky) at that time, becomes interested in the new kind of religion, a sort of neo-Catholicism, that Versilov is preaching to the Russian aristocrats in Ems.

At the same time her young step-daughter, a sickly, intense girl, becomes touchingly attached to Versilov and soon afterwards announces to her immediate family that she intends to marry him. The result is a violent turmoil in the family, and implacable objections on the part of Madame Akhmakova, who from this moment hates Versilov. At the height of all this romantic imbroglio, the 'enflamed girl' apparently takes poison. She dies two weeks later. Young Prince Sokolsky slaps Versilov's face in public when he gets back to Ems after the funeral. Versilov does not accept the challenge. When he appears on the promenade the next day everyone turns away from him. Akhmakova refuses to see him any more. But they meet again, years later, in Petersburg, where Versilov's son Arkady is also infatuated by the dominant, strong-willed character of this woman. The key to this image is to be found in an early note Dostoevsky made: *Byron's wife.* Let us see what this means.

Fatigued by success and fame, by the admiration of contemporaries and the attentions of women, Byron dreamed of tranquil happiness with someone remote from the worldly and bustling circle of English high society. He became interested in young Annabella Milbanke – 'a fresh wild flower' – who had been brought up on an estate in a close-knit, patriarchal family, far from noisy crowds. Annabella was intelligent and capable, studious, well-read and searching for the meaning of life. Her charming face wore an expression of childlike surprise and trustfulness. She wrote poetry, which Byron praised. Because of her interest in mathematics she was dubbed 'princess of parallelograms'. Byron wrote to his friend Lady Caroline Lamb in May 1812, 'She certainly is a very extraordinary girl; who would imagine so much strength and variety of thought under that placid Countenance? . . . I have no desire to be better acquainted with Miss Milbanke; she is too good for a fallen spirit to know, and I should like her more if she were less perfect.' Nevertheless, he soon proposed marriage to her and was refused. He felt a somewhat surprised respect (André Maurois notes this) for the only woman who ever rebuffed him. He repeated his offer of marriage half a year later, and this time it was accepted. They were married on 2 January 1815.

This marked the beginning of tragedy for them both. Their views on religion, ethics and metaphysics (in which Lady Byron was interested) differed sharply. Lady Byron tried to reform her husband's stormy nature, giving him advice which he thought naive (for example, 'do good'). He had never liked 'intelligence in a skirt' and would not admit any sentimentality in marriage. He was despotic, capricious, proud, demoniacal and, towards the end, malicious and vengeful. The less his wife understood him, the more she loved him; she dreamed of being his slave and was willing to be his victim.

But after a while the darkest of all the wicked lord's secrets came to light. His wife had suspected that he had a hidden, shameful crime on his conscience. She soon learned beyond any doubt of Byron's criminal intimacy with his stepsister Augusta Leigh. Neither tried to hide their relationship from Annabella, and life together became impossible for the Byrons. On 10 December 1815 the poet's wife bore him a girl, whom they named Augusta-Ada. Early in 1816 the Byrons parted. On 17 March the poet accepted a separation 'by amicable agreement'. The same day he wrote a farewell elegy with the celebrated first verse:

> Fare thee well! and if for ever,
> Still for ever, *fare thee well*!
> Even though unforgiving, never
> 'Gainst thee shall my heart rebel.

On 25 April 1816 he left England, never to return.

Public opinion favoured the wife, who had not made any excuses or charges and lived in seclusion and silence. She engaged in charitable works and organized national schools. A short time before her death she gave to Harriet Beecher Stowe, the American author of *Uncle Tom's Cabin*, the family papers that exposed Byron, and explained to her her role as victim in their disastrous marriage. In 1868–9 Harriet Beecher Stowe wrote an article entitled 'The True Story of the Life of Lady Byron', which created a sensation at the time and was reprinted all over the world. Dostoevsky probably read the article; he could not but have been interested in information about the English poet, whose work he admired so much.

Dostoevsky's note discloses the analogy he saw between his Akhmakova and Lady Byron:

> The Princess – a rather morose, very impressionable character, though with flashes of radiance. The arrogance of the highborn; unbearable pride, English stubbornness and fastidiousness. (Byron's wife), petty vanity. Katerina Nikolaevna is a rare type of society lady, a type which may not even exist in this circle. She is a simple and exceedingly straightforward type of woman.[9]

The epilogue to Versilov's story is significant. On his deathbed the Elder Makar Ivanovich reminds his master of a promise he made long ago 'to cover up his sins with the altar', that is, to marry Arkady's mother if she were widowed. 'Versilov was deeply moved . . . He went over to Mama and embraced her warmly, without saying a word . . .

Never before had he seemed so mysterious and incomprehensible to me.' The concluding 'mad scene' follows. It is immediately after the funeral of the pilgrim Makar Ivanovich, who has bequeathed to Versilov a miracle-working icon, a family treasure. And now the excited and overwrought head of the family, as if impelled by an evil spirit, takes this relic, the object of everyone's devout veneration, and suddenly smashes it in two against the corner of the tile stove. There is a hidden allegory in this, he says, but he does not disclose the meaning of it.

But the symbolism of the scene is clear. Versilov is repudiating his own promise to marry 'Mama'. He is breaking with his Russian past, rejecting the drab people through whom Orthodox icons work miracles, and is turning once again in his dreams towards the images of Catholic art which captivated him and towards the ideas of Utopian communism. He is ready to become an *emigré* again, a Westerner, a tourist in Europe. He is torn away from his native roots and is doomed to destruction.

But the author commutes this sentence. After all his wanderings, Versilov's end is calm, sensible and poetic. He does not lose touch with his native soil. He does not go mad, does not commit suicide, though he has been close to doing so. The last time we see him it is spring and he is standing by an open window. 'Mama is sitting beside him. He is stroking her cheeks and hair and gazing into her eyes with affection. Now he never leaves Mama for a moment and will never leave her again.' The herald of world citizenry has entered his last period, the Russian period. He will spend it in his native land, among people and shrines that are dear to him. He has now taken into his heart forever 'the only tsaritsa', his 'martyr', his 'last angel', the quiet woman of the enslaved people, whose sacrificial love has illumined his turbulent life.

There is some resemblance here to Herzen's famous *spiritual return to his native land*: 'Faith in Russia saved me when I was on the brink of moral destruction.' But Herzen points out a complete way into life, into contemporaneity and into the future. Dostoevsky's enigmatic thinker, that refined sophist without dogma or programme, that sceptical observer of European revolutions, who repudiated his own country's stirred-up hopes in favour of a sterile quest for truth in foreign lands, gives us no such lead.

Such is the dualistic image of 'a Russian gentleman and citizen of the world', who never did find in the world of Gothic and Renaissance art a living shrine for his own impoverished and oppressed peasantry. Dostoevsky pardons him, but he does not justify him. His genuine hero is of the people and maintains unbreakable bonds with them.

A Peasant Pilgrim

He is the pilgrim Makar Ivanovich Dolgoruky. This image in the novel stems from a spiritual tradition that was close to Dostoevsky's heart – the tradition of the wandering Russian holy man.

A Tale of the Monk Parfyony's Wanderings and Travels in Russia, Moldavia, Turkey and the Holy Land, which was published in Moscow in 1856, was read widely and was very popular with the *pochva* group. Apollon Grigoryev, Strakhov, Dostoevsky and Leo Tolstoy had a high opinion of the book. Dostoevsky owned a copy and took it with him on his European travels in the late 1860s. In open letters to the editor (which Dostoevsky published in *Epokha* in 1864) Grigoryev compared Parfyony's account with the finest of the old Russian 'wanderings'. The style of that contemporary pilgrim to the Near East had something of the living and vigorous speech of the Archpriest Avvakum* and also

---

* The Archpriest Avvakum († 1681). An 'old believer', persecuted and eventually martyred for his beliefs. His *Life, Written By Himself* is a brilliant example of natural, racy, contemporary Russian.

of the *Dukhovnie Stikhi**, and this imparted the quality of folk tale to the story of his travels. Grigoryev was very much impressed by the remarkable poetical talent, combined with childlike simplicity which marked 'the humble monk's book'.

These were the qualities that Dostoevsky needed when he started to portray positive heroes from that circle in his writings of the 1870s. He was drawn to that spiritual figure from the obscure Russia of pilgrims and hermits, that naïve and poetic dreamer, who had written such a lyrical account of his journeys. His book was in Dostoevsky's library, and the author mentions him in his notebooks and letters. Dostoevsky planned to put a 'shorn monk from Mt Athos' alongside Pushkin, Belinsky and Chaadaev in *The Life of a Great Sinner*, the long novel which was to have been his final work.

The personality and preaching of the Elder Makar, and a little later of the Elder Zosima, are marked by the naïve poetic quality and pure heart, combined with folk wisdom, that distinguished Parfyony. Dostoevsky mentions this in his letters: 'This chapter,' he wrote to his editor N. A. Lyubimov on 7 August 1879 about the section entitled 'On the Role of the Scriptures in Father Zosima's Life', is elevated and poetic. The prototype derives from some of the preachings of St Tikhon of Zadonsk, while the naïveté of presentation derives from the monk Parfyony's book of travels.' The special style of Parfyony is reflected in the appearance and speech of Makar Ivanovich, a simple-hearted wanderer through contemporary Russia.

It is characteristic that Dostoevsky endows his righteous hero with artistic talent, with poetic skill even. The bard's inner world has tranquillity and beauty ('comeliness', Arkady calls it) and these unseen features have a greater influence for good on Arkady than do the philosophical

* The *Dukhovnie Stikhi* (spiritual verses) are traditional poems on religious subjects, dating perhaps from the fifteenth to seventeenth centuries.

vistas and refined aphorisms of the 'charming dialectician' Versilov. This is the point at which this novel about upbringing approaches its main theme and hints at the brilliant flashes of the finale. Young Arkady's attraction to this type of peasant thinker and artist in his quest for the truth is characteristic of the kind of hero Dostoevsky held so dear. To the very end of his life Dostoevsky believed that 'the Russian spirit' possessed 'the ability to bring the world new light if it is allowed to develop in its own way'. Nothing could shake his *predominating idea* that Russian culture would bring a great gift to the world through its literature, poetry and philosophy – through Pushkin and Tolstoy, through the treasures of Old Russian art, and through the national concept of truth and justice.

*

Dostoevsky was fond of mentioning in his works the literary masterpieces which to some extent he followed in his own design as he strove to produce meaningful new variations on the motifs current in Russian and world literature. It is on these grounds that he mentions *The Covetous Knight, The Old Curiosity Shop, Faust* and *Les Misérables* in *A Raw Youth*; so much is common knowledge. But some explanation is required for two celebrated tales of the '40s, which according to Dostoevsky 'had an unbounded civilizing influence on the generation that was growing up at the time' and which are both mentioned on the very first pages of *A Raw Youth – Anton the Unfortunate* and *Polinka Sachs*.

Polinka Sachs, as its author Druzhinin pointed out, was inspired by George Sand's celebrated novel *Jacques*, which championed freedom of love, especially for the oppressed and disenfranchised women. In George Sand's novel, young Fernande's husband is not outraged when he discovers that his wife loves Octave, but, on the contrary, feels that to object would be the crudest egoism. This is precisely the position of the husband in Druzhinin's story. When he discovers that his wife Polinka loves young Galitsky, he arranges for a divorce without informing the lovers, takes the blame on himself and sacrifices himself to create new happiness for the woman he loves.

Dostoevsky had a penchant for the theme of sacrificial love. He has several like motifs in *Poor Folk, White Nights* and *The Insulted and the Injured*. He gives an expanded variation on this theme in the fate of the saintly Makar Ivanovich in *A Raw Youth*. The Elder withdraws from all struggle against the young lovers, his wife Sonya and their master Versilov. A pilgrim by vocation, he goes off to wander from monastery to monastery, but he retains his right to protect the wife who has abandoned him. From time to time he comes home for short visits so that he can help, cheer and shield Sonya from sorrow and trouble (of which, considering Versilov's prolonged journeys and 'romances', she probably had plenty).

The portrait of the mother of the raw youth is warmed through and through by the author's sincere affection. Dostoevsky probably recalled his own mother and drew on the brightest image of his childhood to create this purest embodiment of motherhood. Yet it is not simply photography. Dostoevsky's mother was the daughter of a merchant, not a serf girl. She loved life, took pleasure in art, poetry and music, and had little resemblance to the silent woman of *A Raw Youth*. But she, too, was a martyr and her hollow cheeks, too, were a sign of the great love that had so mercilessly destroyed her beauty, as Versilov says in the novel: 'Russian women lose their looks quickly. Their beauty merely flashes by, and this is not due solely to ethnographical peculiarities, but also to their capacity for selfless love.'

The Russian serf woman, frightened and silent slave of her master, invisibly dominates the final text of the novel. The rough notes for *A Raw Youth* contain the following remark: 'The mother – a Russian type (tremendous character), oppressed and obedient, and firm as the saints.' This

Russian type of mother, submissive, one of the common people, practically a beggar, predominates in the final version. This is not a Catholic Madonna of the pre-Raphaelite painters. This is a Russian serf in the spirit of Tyutchev, 'weighed down by the cross she bears' (as one of Dostoevsky's favourite poems expresses it). This is not a Botticelli Virgin, but a real, flesh-and-blood 'Lukerya of the Bast Sandals', as one of the wet-nurses was called who used to come to Dostoevsky's father's house from the village and who fired the children's imaginations with fairy tales and songs.

This Russian mother is displayed to us by the author in all the grandeur of her spiritual beauty in one of the novel's finest episodes, the description in Chapter 9, Part II, of her visit to her young son at the French boarding-school, where the pupils mock him for his 'illegitimacy' and the director Touchard tries to make this child of common origins into his lackey. This chapter is a magnificent example of Dostoevsky's psychological insight and poetic realism which can bring to light the most secret dramas of the human heart. However, this superb realism is not characteristic of the general style of this novel about the troubled times the author lived in. Dostoevsky set himself trail-blazing tasks for which he required new forms.

The Problem of Style

In *A Raw Youth* Dostoevsky employed a principle that he had formulated in February 1870 in his plans for *The Life of a Great Sinner*: 'Not to explain the complete, predominating idea in words and *always to leave it a mystery*, but to do so in such a way that the reader is constantly aware that the idea is a solemn and religious one and that the life story is so important that it had to be started back in the childhood years. The man of the future is put on a pedestal all the time.'

This unusual and complex law of composition is in evidence throughout *A Raw Youth*. The protagonist unfolds before the reader in the process of his own development as the new man of the future. But the central figures, like the guiding or fundamental idea, remain 'a mystery' to the end; hence the unclear, confused, ambiguous and secretive tone of the narrative. Some of the episodes are riddles and some of the heroes are symbols. A variety of solutions and interpretations, guesses and approximations, is possible. The author has deliberately concealed the fundamental principles of the structure from the reader's eyes. Dostoevsky's cherished design – to portray the man of action of the Russian Revolution – would have emerged only in the second novel of *The Brothers Karamazov*, which death prevented Dostoevsky from writing. 'And now we are trying to solve this problem without him.'*

Hence the enormous difficulty for Dostoevsky to find the right answer to the problem of style for his novel about the formation of a young personality in the middle of an universal ferment. He had to find new forms to embody the emerging social–political themes that were going to remain uppermost in his mind till the end of his life.

Dissolution is the main visible idea of the novel. 'Russia's disintegration in the post-reform period' – 'Degeneration of the Russian family, general chaos, confusion and collapse, constant breakdown' – 'Our moral principles shaken to their foundations' – 'The right to be dishonourable' – 'Intellectual unrest and lack of moral direction' – 'The muddle that we are in at the present moment.' All these are posed as problems in the notebooks as early as 1874–5, but were not solved till just before the novelist's death.

With his usual boldness of innovation, Dostoevsky set himself an extremely difficult task – to depict this chaos prevalent all over Russia in a fittingly chaotic manner. He

* A quotation from Dostoevsky's Pushkin Memorial Speech. See Chapter XXI.

rejected the novelist's usual goal of a coherent plot where unity of action is achieved through binding together the main characters in emotional relationships that have a logical cause and sequence, a goal triumphantly reached in *Crime and Punishment*. Instead, he introduced unrelated paradoxical motives and brief, mysterious episodes, postponing explanations to a future date which never came. The resulting style is dynamic, even feverish, like a mirage or a whirlwind, or, as Dostoevsky puts it so aptly, 'delirious or foggy'. The novelistic genre with its hard and fast epic rules seems to dissolve and float away in fleeting visions or hazy pictures that never crystallize into regular shapes or obtain organic development.

Consequently the pace of the narrative is unusually rapid. The action moves swiftly and ends in an extravaganza of dizzying events – Lambert's brazen attempt at blackmail, Akhmakova fainting, Versilov trying to kill the blackmailer, an attempt to shoot the heroine, Arkady's sudden insanity, a revolver, wounds, blood, a fist fight and a spit in the face. This concentration of crimes and outrages serves as the denouement of this novel about an 'accidental' family and is supposed to indicate some sort of pointless and fearful collapse for a whole society that is unfit to live.

Dostoevsky is not satisfied with giving a coherent picture of the gradual formation of one character, as Goethe and Tolstoy do. His aim in his novel about upbringing is, in his own words, 'to divine what may be concealed in an adolescent's soul in times of unrest'. This is a different method and a different subject! Divining the secret of a young mind that has been stirred by terrorist acts is more than an account of 'years of study' or 'years of wandering'. It contains the seed of political tragedy; it shows the birth of titanic struggle and the choosing between life and death.

To draw so unusual a literary portrait, one so different from easily understood factual accounts and generally accepted patterns, required an inexhaustible well of artistic innovation, capable of enlivening the stultified forms of nineteenth-century classical realism. Much of the experimentation in this novel proved sound and provides us with samples of the distinctive, very complex style of the late Dostoevsky, a style which anticipated some of the trends that appeared in modern art long after Dostoevsky's death. In his last period Dostoevsky was very fond of contradictions, even of 'eccentricities', in structure, for he believed that it was not necessary for everything to be easily comprehensible and conveniently clear at first glance. He believed that an author was entitled to keep something back and to be mysterious. 'Let the readers do a little work themselves,' he wrote in 1872, proclaiming his right to write in a special, difficult, complex, intricate and even supernatural style.

A Raw Youth was not popular and puzzled the majority of critics, who used such expressions as 'Dostoevsky's gloomy underground', the life and morals 'of a prison or a house of prostitution', a world of ghosts instead of a society of people. But from the distance of a century we can now see the amazing courage of an ageing writer in search of new novelistic forms, a search that sometimes led him temporarily astray, as in *A Raw Youth*, but that soon led to the brilliant triumph of *The Brothers Karamazov*, a world masterpiece which emerged from the seething ferment of ideas and events in a period of a revolutionary situation, and which reflected in the very form of its artistic embodiment the disintegration of the decrepit empire.

THE TRAGIC SHORT STORIES
A Gentle Creature

The creative method he used in *A Raw Youth* not having met with sympathetic recognition, Dostoevsky tried new artistic experiments. At this critical moment in his literary career, he found a new path for himself and a new literary form; he

created a tragic short story of extraordinary power and
undeniable truth, and rose to new heights of narrative skill.
His lyricism and philosophy of life found forceful expression
in two short and perfectly fashioned stories that attained
the conciseness and profundity of Pushkin's work. These are
Dostoevsky's little tragedies, 'A Gentle Creature' and 'The
Dream of a Ridiculous Man'.

The history of the making of 'A Gentle Creature' is full of
internal drama, The period of its general development was
rather long. In 1869 Dostoevsky jotted down a plan for a
story on a subject unusual for him, domestic conflict and
rupture. A number of motifs in that plan anticipated the
1876 short story:

After the Bible he stabbed her to death (an underground type
who could not endure being jealous). Widower. First wife died.
Found and deliberately chose an orphan for greater peace of
mind. He himself is a real underground character, has been
knocked about by life. Has become bitter. Boundless vanity...
The wife cannot help noticing that he is educated; then she
sees that his education does not amount to much and that any
kind of ridicule (and he takes everything as ridicule) annoys him.
He is hypersensitive. When he sees that she has no intention of
laughing he is extremely happy. They go to the theatre once and
to the assembly once. He has experienced agonies. Quarrels with
a guest, who treated him superciliously. From the window he
watches the lover in the courtyard. He eavesdrops at a rendezvous. He is slapped in the face in front of his wife.

At one time there was even the beginning of genuine love
between him and his wife. But he destroyed her heart.

Though in this sketch the tragic end is different – the husband 'stabbed the guilty wife to death' – the contours of 'A
Gentle Creature' are perfectly clear in it.

A rash of suicides swept Russia in 1876. The writer L.
Simonova related that Dostoevsky took each suicide to
heart as if it were the death of someone dear to him. He
began to reflect on the situation of a suicide, to penetrate

into the mental state of so unfortunate a creature, and he gave expression to his feelings on the subject in an article entitled 'The Sentence', which appeared in the October 1876 issue of *The Diary of a Writer.*

In her memoirs Mme Simonova mentions a conversation she had with Dostoevsky about this article. The following passage is of interest:

'Where did you get that "sentence"? Did you make it up yourself or did you pick up the idea somewhere?' I asked him.
'It is my own. I wrote it,' he replied.
'But are you an atheist?'
'I am a deist, I am a philosophical deist!' he replied, 'Why do you ask?'
'Because you wrote "The Sentence" in such a way that I thought you had experienced it yourself.'

It will be recalled that Voltaire, Rousseau and other seventeenth- and eighteenth-century freethinkers called themselves deists and that they regarded this as a concealed form of atheism: God was recognized merely as an impersonal first cause of the world, which was otherwise left entirely to the operation of the laws of nature. An atheistic world outlook is expressed in 'A Gentle Creature', too. One day shortly afterwards Dostoevsky read a newspaper report about a young seamstress from Moscow, named Maria Borisova, who had come to Petersburg, where she had no relations and where she was counting on making a living solely by her craft. But the plans for a new life in the capital speedily collapsed, and one overcast day in autumn the desperate girl had taken a figure of the Virgin her parents had given her and, pressing it to her heart, had jumped out of the attic of a six-storey house on Galernaya Street and been killed.

Dostoevsky was deeply moved by this extraordinary suicide. The inner contrasts of the incident struck him – the unusual combination of despair and faith, of destruction and hope, death and love. 'That icon in her hands is a strange and unprecedented feature in suicide,' he wrote in *The Diary of a Writer* immediately after the event. 'There are events which, though they appear to be very simple, keep coming to mind for a long time, which you keep seeing, as if you were to blame for them. This gentle soul, who destroyed herself, involuntarily torments the mind.' Such was the great writer's obituary for an obscure seamstress.

The image of this poor, lonely girl, who had died in the big wealthy city, continued to trouble him. One day he put aside the manuscripts he was working on at the time and wrote his artistic commentary on what was an all too ordinary item of 'Russia's home news'. Instead of international current affairs, the November issue of *The Diary of a Writer* for 1876 consisted entirely of the story 'A Gentle Creature'. It was not Dostoevsky's aim to depict the unhappy fate of a suicide in a strange and heartless city. He had more than once portrayed the death of a humiliated young creature in capitalist Petersburg; only the year before he had inserted into *A Raw Youth* a short story about a girl, named Olya, who had come to the capital without any money, replied to advertisements in search of work and invariably encountered elderly libertines or procuresses, and finally hanged herself. There was no point in repeating the story. He took from his old notes the plan for a story about a wife-murderer and, while preserving its inner drama, gave the heroine new traits and devised a new ending that altered the entire tenor of the story. The death of Maria Borisova on the cobblestones of a Petersburg courtyard, as she pressed her parents' icon to her heart, served as a frame as it were, for his old idea of a despotic husband and a martyred wife.

Dostoevsky exploded the established form of the classical short story. He provided one outstanding event, as the form requires, but through that event he attempted, successfully, to portray the heroine's entire unhappy life. Parallel to it he developed a complex psychological story of an underground man whose profession of moneylender is his means of avenging himself against a society that humiliated him. The two lives are fully explored (a technique which goes beyond the normal bounds of the short story form), yet the action is sustained at that high level of tension that the form requires. As a result, the tale, with its tense plot and all the action finally coming together within one circle of disaster, is truly of the short story tradition. Dostoevsky ignored the canons that require the emphasis to be at the end and boldly started out with the denouement of the tragedy: 'The suicide wife lying on the table' and the husband trying to comprehend the reasons for her act. The end, becoming the beginning, determines the circular structure of the narrative; this is a 'spiral-story', to use Paul Heyse's well-known expression.

The winding coils get further and further from the point of departure, but the expanded spring is suddenly compressed towards the centre, the starting point, so that the denouement, the end of the spiral, comes right above its beginning – the introduction to the tale.

This ingenious device testifies to Dostoevsky's perfect understanding of the laws of the short story and to his intimate knowledge of its finest examples. And however erudite his knowledge of the form might be one thing he knew for certain: that the storyteller must use his skill to arouse interest in the characters and the action from the very beginning. He constructed 'A Gentle Creature' on this principle. The first chapter is called 'Who I Am and Who She Was'. This is the opening and the exposition. It tells the pre-history of this complex and moving drama and presents several of the motifs common to all Dostoevsky's work with high intensity and forcefulness.

The heroine was orphaned when she was twelve. Her health was always poor and she was predisposed to consumption. She was brought up by two embittered aunts, who made a slave of her, beat her, reproached her with eating their bread, and, finally, decided to sell her. Feverishly, the doomed girl started to advertise in the newspapers for a job that might save her. To pay for the advertisements she pawned the last few belongings her parents had left her. Among these was an old family icon with a silver overlay, which reappears in the finale of the drama and plays a decisive role in the working out of Dostoevsky's design. The hero's 'pre-history' also contains typical Dostoevskyan motifs. He was expelled from his regiment by a court of honour for not having fought a duel with someone who had insulted him, although he had not admitted the insult and had courageously disregarded public opinion and its tyrannical sentence. So this 'most generous of men' became a pawnbroker. Now he is middle-aged, solitary and withdrawn.

Despite the economy of the short story form, Dostoevsky does not forgo his customary description of the appearance of his principal characters. He was convinced, as he stated in *A Raw Youth*, 'that only in rare moments does the human face express a person's principal trait, his characteristic thought. The artist studies the face and divines the person's central thought.' The face of the 'gentle creature' expresses sadness and surprise at the horror of life, as well as the nobility of a young soul. In appearance she resembles Sonya Marmeladova: slim, blonde, with large, pensive blue eyes and a questioning smile. She has the generosity of youth 'Even on the brink of ruin, the mighty words of Goethe blaze out.' The hero's description of himself is, naturally, more generalized. He is a pleasant, impressive looking 'retired junior captain from a crack regiment', tall, slim and well-bred.

The romantic interest is also characteristic of Dostoevsky's style: the relationship between the moneylender, in his commanding position, and the girl, who is about to go under, is a typical 'Svidrigailov' situation ('I am forty-one, she is only sixteen . . . very sweet, very sweet'). She marries the pawnbroker. 'Of course, it is also a fact that she had nowhere else to go' – the Marmeladova motif again. The action is delayed by the technique of introducing interludes – digressions, reflections, descriptions of intentions and secret plans. The pawnbroker resolves to freeze his young wife's enthusiasm. Her heart yearns for deep love, but he is determined to preserve his way of life, which is cold, taciturn, calculated, measured, extremely economical, though adequate; he has set himself the goal of accumulating thirty thousand roubles so he can retire to the Crimea. But she 'wanted to love, was looking for someone to love'.

And the 'gentle creature' rebels; the pretext is insignificant, but the causes are deep. She determines to take revenge against her respectable torturer. For this purpose she arranges a rendezvous with a former regimental comrade of her husband's, the officer Efimovich, who was the main instigator of his expulsion from the regiment. This first rendezvous is observed by the husband, who is in the adjoining room with a revolver in his pocket. The wife retains her virtue and astonishes the secret watcher by her intelligence and honour. The husband interrupts the rendezvous and leads her away.

The commonplace situation takes an uncommon turn. The customary triangle is really non-existent, yet it impels the drama towards tragedy. At the culminating point of the story the young wife puts a revolver to her husband's head. She thinks he is asleep, but he is not. He is aware of everything but he makes no move to resist: 'Of what use is life to me if the creature I adore has pointed a revolver at me?' It turns out that the cold-hearted pawnbroker in his underground is really secretly and desperately in love with his wife. This also marks the rehabilitation of the one-time coward, who was expelled from the regiment, for he does not waver when a pistol is put to his head.

Dostoevsky constructed the central situation of the narrative with great skill and gave the plot the unexpected and surprising turn that highlights the profoundest crisis of the internal action. 'The marriage was dissolved. She was defeated but not forgiven.' Thus ends the first part of the tale. The rebellious 'gentle creature' becomes gravely ill. A pause in the plot follows. The distinctive features of the short-story form are already visible in this first part of the story – concentration of the plot, a minimal number of characters, a single place of action, suspense, an unusual or strange event of arresting interest and profound, vital significance. All of this predetermines the further development of this model tragic short story.

The second chapter deals with a new psychological conflict and determines the location of the finale. When the husband realizes that the 'gentle creature' has abandoned him for ever he is overcome with horror and tries to keep her: 'I kissed her feet in ecstasy and joy.' He urges her to come south with him, to the sea, to France, to Boulogne: 'That is where the sun is, our new sun.' The final disaster is approaching. The tormented woman is emotionally drained. Her husband's belated adoration horrifies and revolts her. The future holds no glimmer of light. Clasping her parents' icon, her last treasure, in her arms, she jumps out of the window to her death.

The tragic ending cuts the knot of confused relationships. The suicide's husband keeps trying to justify himself; he says it was an accident, a fatal coincidence, an unexpected oversight, a blind error, a trick played by indifferent fortune. 'Oh, it is unbelievable, unbelievable! It is a misunderstanding. It cannot be true. It is an impossibility!' he moans. He was only five minutes late! 'It is all chance, simple, barbaric, stupid chance. That is what's so awful!'

The epilogue portrays a lonely, desperate man from whom all has been taken. 'What do I care about your laws now? What do I care about your customs, your morals, your life, your state, your religion?' Culture has dried up. The universe is empty. The whole edifice of the world has collapsed. The sun at Boulogne has gone out. 'They say the sun gives life to the world. The sun will rise, and you will look at it, can't you see that it is a corpse? Everything is dead, corpses everywhere.' Nature, religion, ethics, the concepts of altruism and Christianity? Nothing can fill the bottomless void from which the only creature he loved has gone, having voluntarily removed herself from the power of the laws of life that so cruelly injured her.

This is one of the most powerful stories of despair in world literature. The author explains that the hero, overwhelmed by the disaster, is making his confession in an effort 'to collect his thoughts'; into his complex dialectical way of thinking come flashes of an agonizing quest for the truth which should at all costs be uncovered, but which remains hidden and unattainable.

This is probably the finest interior monologue in all of Dostoevsky's work. No wonder the hero says: 'I am a master of talking in silence. I have talked through my whole life in silence and I have lived through entire tragedies by myself, in silence.' Dostoevsky was always interested in the confessional form. He subtitled 'A Gentle Creature' 'A fantastic tale', noting in the preface that he regarded this experiment as 'realistic to the highest degree', the author merely taking dictation, recording the disorderly flow of thoughts of a man who is deathly tired, who appeals in his despair to imaginary judges and who realizes in horror that he is profoundly and completely alone.

This is a tremendous advance in the form of Dostoevsky's work. It is a turn from the free and unrestricted form of the novel to the controlled and circumscribed short-story form, with appreciation for its specific features of tense action, expressive imagery and intensity of plot. Everything is concentrated round one unprecedented incident, so that the unity of the drama is unbroken: all the threads of the story originate with the central character. All the episodes lead to the main idea, giving to real-life incidents the depth of a philosophical generalization. And all this is rendered in

Dostoevsky's superb, brilliant, and fearless manner of portraying the shaken soul of someone who has suddenly perceived an overwhelming truth. Intellectual tragedy, collapse of a world outlook, spiritual and physical death are all contained within the framework of a story in which every dialogue and every detail possesses hypnotic power.

The higher laws of a creative artist's method have transcended and transformed the limits of the classical form. Dostoevsky tells the entire life-story of the two protagonists in this short compass, discovering in it a way to disclose every facet of a troubled mind and present man's eternal tragedy through the prism of a topical episode from the newspaper.

The Dream of a Ridiculous Man

Like 'A Gentle Creature', 'The Dream of a Ridiculous Man', which appeared in the April 1877 issue of *The Diary of a Writer*, was subtitled 'A fantastic tale'. In this instance the subtitle referred to the Utopian content of this slight production – a description of an ideal society in the spirit of the Golden Age of the ancient poets, which the French nineteenth-century Utopian Socialists took for a symbolic image of a future socialist system. But, as always, Dostoevsky produces a highly original 'political short story'.

The story describes the transformation of a blessed kingdom of innocent and happy people into a frightful world of cruelty, malice, sin and violence when 'civilization' is introduced into it. The disaster is caused, according to the conservative-minded author of *The Diary of a Writer*, by a certain 'contemporary Russian progressivist', who contaminates the happy and sinless land with his views, 'like an atom of the plague that contaminates entire countries'. These 'children of the sun', as Dostoevsky calls them, come to know untruth, sensuality, jealousy, cruelty, bloodshed, sadism, laws, the guillotine and war. Their desperate attempts to recover their former happiness only intensify the general dissension and enmity. Everything is heading for destruction. But when the ridiculous man wakes up, he formulates his own law of salvation for people living together: 'The important thing is to love others as one loves oneself.'

In 'The Dream of a Ridiculous Man' the motifs and imagery of Dostoevsky's earlier work are developed with maximum economy – the Golden Age, the beautiful man, the question of the possibility of arranging 'universal happiness', the facts of unbearable human suffering, especially of children. The recurring images and 'reflections' of Dostoevsky's protagonists reappear in the brief sketches in this story – the mythological paradise that inspired Versilov's remarkable interpretation of Claude Lorrain's 'Acis and Galatea' in *A Raw Youth* (and before that, Stavrogin's Confession); the images of Kirillov, Raskolnikov, Lebyadkin, the man 'from the underground', despairing little girls in a big city (Netochka Nezvanova, Nellie, the London beggar-girl).

Like Dostoevsky's other works, especially those of the 1870s, this story contains contradictions. Here and there it gives the reader a glimpse into the future 'harmony' that the author was to write of in his later searchings: 'I have seen and I know that people can be beautiful and happy without losing the capacity for living on the earth. *I do not want to believe and I cannot believe that evil is the normal condition of man.*' 'I do not know how to build a paradise,' the 'ridiculous man' concludes, finally convinced that 'there can be no paradise' on earth. The scepticism that characterizes the late Dostoevsky is already vocal in this short story. Statements such as these rather weaken Dostoevsky's 'sorrowful observations' about the historical path of mankind and the prospects for its future development, and they do not give any concrete indications of how people should unite to produce a rational society.

TAKING LEAVE OF NEKRASOV

By the end of 1877 Nekrasov was a dying man. His life had recently been prolonged for a few months by an operation performed by the celebrated Viennese surgeon Bilroth, who had been summoned to Petersburg, but the end was nearing, and friends and admirers of the poet grieved deeply. Chernyshevsky expressed the feelings of all progressive circles in Russian society in a letter he wrote to a friend from Yakutia, where he was living in exile:

> If Nekrasov is still breathing when you receive my letter, tell him that I love him dearly for the man he is and that I am convinced that his fame will never die, that Russia's love for him, the greatest and noblest of all Russian poets, is eternal. I weep for him!

Dostoevsky did not belong to those circles, but he shared their grief. He never forgot that Nekrasov had shed tears over the manuscript of *Poor Folk*, and had been the first to express to him admiration for his talent. He never forgot how in the 1860s, when he returned from Siberia, Nekrasov had presented him with a volume of poems and read aloud an excerpt to him from 'The Unfortunates', a poem about a courageous and wise political exile, dubbed 'The Mole', who had understood and loved his fellow prisoners, taught them loyalty to their country and faith in the strength of the people, and had explained Russia's essential nature and mission to them:

> She knows no middle course.
> She is black, wherever you look,
> But vice has not eaten through to her core.
> *Within her breast*
> *There flows a pure and living stream*
> *Of the powers of the people that are living yet,*
> *Just as there are many gold-bearing veins*
> *Beneath Siberia's icy crust.*

'I was thinking of you when I wrote this,' he had said to Dostoevsky ('that is, of my life in Siberia,' the novelist explained), 'this was written about you.'[10]

There were moments of sincere and deep affection between the two writers, who frequently found themselves on opposite sides in literary and journalistic conflicts. (Dostoevsky recalled this not without sorrow: 'I remember how we later somehow went separate ways . . . This was helped by misunderstandings and by circumstances, and also by worthy people.') However, they were close in the most important and basic matters. Their work had many common traits. As young men both had adopted the principles of the naturalist school, which were in keeping with the latest and most progressive trends in Russian life; both had found that this school could not satisfy their profound spiritual requirements and had soon turned to the tragic side of the everyday life they portrayed. This was the 'human voice' in their work. Dostoevsky's sketches of the petty civil servants of Petersburg already gave an indication of the hopeless pattern of their lives – madness, illness, fear, rejection and early death. The path he took as a young writer anticipated his brilliant group portrait of the Marmeladovs in the 1860s. Nekrasov's early poems were also short naturalistic studies, imbued with the sufferings of the Petersburg poor. These were the scenes, sketches and characters in 'The Thief', 'The Drunkard', 'The Cabman', and 'Whether I am driving down a dark street at night', poems which 'drove Turgenev out of his mind'. This poetry of despair, with its background of Petersburg cellars and attics, gave the urban poet a kinship with the future author of *Crime and Punishment*. At the moment of final leavetaking both men felt this basic closeness.

Nekrasov's death was a slow one, yet he remained in complete control of his mental faculties and with a strikingly high level of creative activity. He made some of his most famous poems in that 'black year' and they have become part of the national heritage. The friends who visited him in that period have drawn a picture of a courageous poet, surmounting illness and death by sheer will-power. 'Work always gave me life,' Nekrasov wrote on his death-bed, and his work as a poet continued to nurture the forces of life in him practically to the very death agony.

On 4 March 1877 Nekrasov was very weak, but he read his new 'Cradle Song' aloud.[11] 'His manner of reading,' so A. N. Pypin related,

made the impression even stronger and more painful. Then he got out of bed, with our assistance, and went on talking. He was lethargic from the opium he was taking. He spoke of the thoughts seething in his cloudy brain, they come and go, come again, he said, and end up in a poem. He talked about a plot he had in his head [the plan for the poem 'The Tramp']. He explained his view of the character of the common people, that whatever their troubles, bad luck or unbridledness, they were at bottom basically gentle and humane.[12]

The poet's sister A. A. Butkevich wrote in her diary:

March 23 [1877]. F. M. Dostoevsky came. My brother is drawn to him by memories of their youth (they are the same age) and he [Nekrasov] loves him. He said. 'I cannot talk, but tell him to come in for a moment. It gives me pleasure to see him.' Dostoevsky sat with him for a short while. He told him that he had been surprised to see women prisoners with *The Physiology of Petersburg*[13] when he visited the prison. Dostoevsky looked unusually pale and tired. I inquired about his health. 'It is not good,' he said. 'My seizures are getting worse all the time. I have already had five this month.'

Nekrasov wrote his last poem, 'Oh, Muse, I am at the Doors of the Grave', at the beginning of December 1877, a few weeks before he died. Dostoevsky paid his last visit to the dying man about this time. Nekrasov was terribly exhausted but was completely lucid in mind. He was still composing those wonderful farewell poems, of which

Dostoevsky wrote shortly afterwards in *The Diary of a Writer*:

I have read Nekrasov's 'Last Songs' in the January issue of *Otechestvennie Zapiski*. Impassioned songs and unsaid words, as always with Nekrasov, but what agonizing groans of a sick man! Our poet is very ill and – he told me himself – is clearly aware of the situation.

Such a situation brings out what has been most important in human relations over the whole span of a lifetime, and affects both speakers alike. So it was on this occasion. Neither had ever forgotten their first meeting, which was an indelible experience in both their lives; for Dostoevsky it was 'the most exhilarating moment of my whole life. I used to recall it when I was serving my term of hard labour and feel strengthened in spirit.'

Dostoevsky's account of his last conversation with Nekrasov is as significant as his famous description of their first meeting on a white night in June 1845.

I recently dropped in to see Nekrasov, and he, ill and in pain, began immediately to recall those days. Something happened that day (it was thirty years ago) that was young, fresh, good, the kind of thing that remains forever in the hearts of those concerned. We were both in our early twenties.

The poet's youth had brought the sounds of spring into the atmosphere of slow agony. After all, it was Nekrasov who had led Dostoevsky into literature by introducing him to Belinsky and printing the timid novice's first story in his *Peterburgsky Sbornik*.

And now, thirty years later, I recalled that moment again, and it was as if I were experiencing it all over again, sitting at the sick Nekrasov's bedside . . . Yet we have lived our whole lives apart. On his bed of suffering he now recalled dead friends.

Their prophetic songs have not been finished
They fell victim to malice and betrayal

In the flower of their youth. Their portraits look down
At me reproachfully from the wall.

This is a painful word – *reproachfully* – but read these agonized
songs for yourself and let our beloved poet come to life again!
A poet with a passion for suffering . . .

This was written after Nekrasov's death.

Nekrasov died on the evening of 28 December O.S.
Dostoevsky learned of it the next morning and went to pay
his respects. When he came home he held an unusual
memorial service for Nekrasov – he re-read nearly everything the poet had written. Once again he felt the power of
Nekrasov's masterpieces, which he listed shortly afterwards
in an article about him: 'A Knight for an Hour', 'Silence',
'Russian Women', 'Vlas', rated as 'great' by Dostoevsky,
and 'On the Volga', that he called 'one of the most powerful and appealing of his poems'. 'That night I re-read
nearly two thirds of Nekrasov's writings and I realized
literally for the first time how great a part Nekrasov the
poet had played in my life all these thirty years.' Dostoevsky
decided he would speak at Nekrasov's funeral.

Several thousand of the poet's admirers, among them
many young students, gathered at the cemetery. Poems
were read and speeches were made, one by a working-man.
Dostoevsky recalled:

Deeply moved I pushed my way forward to his still open
grave, covered with flowers and wreaths, and in my weak voice I
said a few words after the others. I started by saying that this
was a wounded heart, with a wound that had never healed, and
this never-closed wound was the source of his poetry, of all this
man's agonizing love for those who suffered . . . I also expressed
my conviction that Nekrasov was the last link in the chain of
poets who had introduced their 'new word' into our poetry. In
this sense he . . . followed directly in the footsteps of Puskin and
Lermontov.

At this point a voice from the crowd interrupted with:
'Nekrasov stands higher than Pushkin and Lermontov. They

are only Byronists . . .' But this did not disconcert the speaker. 'Not higher, but not lower either,' was Dostoevsky's firm reply, as he turned towards the young people. 'Higher, higher!' continued to come from that group. In his memoirs Plekhanov relates that it was he and the group of revolutionaries with him who had made this objection. A comparison of Nekrasov with Pushkin seemed 'a crying injustice' to them. Dostoevsky did not pursue this discussion beside the open grave, but replied to his opponents in the next issue of *The Diary of a Writer*. He gave profound characterizations of Pushkin, Lermontov, Nekrasov and Byron, in the course of which he lets fall the brilliant aphorism: 'The word Byronist cannot be used as a term of abuse.'[14]

Dostoevsky printed the speech he had made at the funeral in the December 1877 issue of *The Diary of a Writer*, expanding it into a brilliant article and giving a serious characterization of Nekrasov as a man and a poet with all the contradictions of his complex nature, as a 'Russian historical type', who would always remain in the hearts of our people, for 'in his love for the people he found something unshakeable, an unshakeable and holy solution to everything that tortured him'.

THE TRIAL OF VERA ZASULICH

On Friday morning, 31 March 1878, Dostoevsky arrived at the district courthouse to attend the trial of Vera Zasulich, who was charged with having shot at the Governor of Petersburg, General Trepov. Zasulich had fired in protest against Trepov's outrageous order of 13 July 1877, under which the revolutionary student Bogolyubov was sentenced to be flogged for not having removed his hat in Trepov's presence. The arbitrary sentence had been carried out the same day and aroused a rumble of protest among the public and in the *emigré* press. The girl revolutionary, who did not know the victim personally, in fact had never seen him, came to Petersburg from the provinces to carry out an act of vengeance for the despotic and violent behaviour of the authorities. She shot at Trepov on 24 January 1878, injuring him seriously. She was seized on the spot and placed on public trial by jury. This was one of the late nineteenth century's most celebrated political trials. Progressive public opinion all over the world followed it very closely. Dostoevsky, too, was very much interested in the person of the accused.

He took his seat in the press box and looked around the crowded courtroom. 'The court is in session,' rang out, and the judges, headed by the chairman A. F. Koni, sat down in massive red chairs at a huge curved table. Adjoining the table were the benches of jurymen, apparently selected, for this occasion, from among intermediate grade civil officials ('a reliable element' for the decision that the government required). Behind them were the 'honorary seats' for dignitaries and high-ranking military men – members of the State Council, senators, General Staff officers, all in uniform and wearing medals, stars and ribbons. Then came representatives of the judiciary, prominent lawyers, and the capital's bureaucratic élite. The rows of chairs for the public were colourful with ladies' dresses and filled with the aristocracy of the literary salons. Among the celebrities present were the eighty-year-old State Chancellor Gorchakov, who had been a school-friend of Pushkin's at the *lycée*, 'a tiresome guest, superfluous and out of place among the new generation'; Professor Tagantsev, shining light of Russian criminologists; Sklifosovsky, the foremost surgeon; Karabchevsky, a brilliant young advocate. In short, 'all Petersburg' – government, public, scientific and artistic – had gathered as if at an official festivity.

Seated on the prisoner's bench on the far side, beyond the barrier, was the lonely, sorrowful figure of a young woman, encircled by towering gendarmes with unsheathed swords. This was the accused. She was wearing a dress of black lustrous cloth; her smoothly combed hair was parted in the middle; her intelligent brown eyes shone with sincerity and goodness. She inspired the sympathy, liking, love, even admiration, of the spectators. 'One feels like saying to the gendarmes,' the *Golos* (*The Voice*) reporter wrote from the court, '"Go away, leave this unhappy girl alone. Sheathe your swords, the cold shine of steel is not appropriate to the radiant look in her gentle eyes!"'

When her turn came she spoke only a few sentences, quietly and with restraint, but what she said was very significant and moving. She spoke of Trepov's mockery of Bogolyubov, who had already been through a long period of solitary confinement and had been sentenced to fifteen years of penal servitude.

'How cruel one must be to compel a tortured man such as this to endure the punishment cell, the whipping post, being beaten up! And for what crime? For not having removed his hat at a second meeting! To me this did not seem to be punishment but mockery, arising from personal malice. I felt that this sort of thing could not, must not, pass without something being done. I waited, but no one spoke up. There was nothing to prevent Trepov from perpetrating the same kind of outrage again and again. So, seeing no other way to alter this sort of thing, I resolved to prove, if necessary at the cost of my life, that no one who ruthlessly mocks another human being can be sure of doing so with impunity . . . I did not find, I could not find, any other means of attracting attention to the incident. It is a frightful thing to raise one's hand against another human being, but I knew I had to do it.'

The interrogation by the court was over. Arguments by counsel began. The prosecutor tried to dispel the very favourable impression the defendant's speech had made. With a show of emotion he pointed to the material evidence, lying on the table, a large-calibre pistol with a shining barrel.

'She held this revolver in her hands. She made her plans deliberately. It is a murder that failed for reasons beyond the perpetrator's control. She arbitrarily took upon herself the combined role of prosecutor, judge and executioner. The court cannot condone the use of whatever means are at hand to achieve political ends.'

Alexandrov, the advocate for the defence, ascended the platform. He was a nervous, 'truthful, courageous man, with a slightly hysterical note in his voice' (from newspaper reports). He had a reputation as a subtle analyst of the law and a persuasive courtroom orator. His defence of Vera Zasulich brought him fame throughout Europe. His speech was not only a defence of the accused, but a formidable indictment of the Petersburg government in the person of its representative, Trepov.

He described the emotional state of this courageous, fair-minded girl, shattered by the account of the shameful punishment meted out to an outstanding representative of progressive youth, how she suffered for the man whose human dignity had been insulted by police arbitrariness. Who would come to the defence of the insulted honour of a helpless convict? The press? Public opinion? The law? All were silent. And Zasulich resolved to perform with her weak, feminine hands the duty of a whole epoch. To kill or to wound – this was of no importance to her. What was important was to brand the torturer publicly. The conclusion of the defence speech rang out: 'Gentlemen of the jury! This is not the first time that a woman, accused of having shed blood, has come before the judgement of public conscience on this bench of crime and suffering. Many of them left here acquitted. But this is the first time that a woman being tried had no personal interest in the attempt to kill, no thirst for personal revenge, but associated her crime with the struggle for an idea, for the honour of someone who was merely a fellow unfortunate. However one may regard her deed, one cannot help perceiving the honest and honourable impulse behind it. She may depart convicted, but she will not depart in disgrace, and one can only hope that the causes that produce crimes and criminals such as this may vanish.'

An unprecedented ovation shook the courtroom. The Chairman's shrill bell could not restrain the spontaneous outburst. The jurymen were handed their forms and withdrew. Then came the agonizing wait for the verdict.

Dostoevsky followed the trial with bated breath. Before him unfolded a broad canvas of the government's unrelenting struggle against the younger generation, who represented the finest forces of his native land and who were giving their lives in the great cause of the liberation of the people. What was the right thing to do? He was still in the pro-government ranks, a champion of the Church and State idea, an enemy of the nihilists, of the democratic intelligentsia and of terrorists. Why, then, did this clear-eyed, fearless girl move him so profoundly? After all, a revolver with large-calibre bullets is not an argument with which to settle a moral issue. Bloodshed is not the path to the truth. It was the axe that destroyed Raskolnikov, and it was the rebirth of love for the people that saved him. Surely, it was the duty of a writer to protest against 'blood for conscience sake'.

Then why did the accused's person and every word she uttered shine with supreme humanity? Clearly, she represented the best, the good, the intelligent, the selfless and self-sacrificing youth who are the country's hope, who are Russia's future. How is it possible to accuse, convict, punish this courageous Russian girl who has such boundless love for her people? He leaned over to his neighbour in the press box, the journalist Gradovsky, and tried to tell him about the conflict within him.

'She must not be convicted. Punishment is not appropriate here; it is superfluous. But how is it possible to say to her: "Go, but do not do this again!" I don't think we have a legal formula of that kind, and likely as not they will go ahead and make a martyr of her . . .'

The jurymen did not confer long. An electric bell rang. The foreman of the jury read out the first question put to them by court:

'Is Zasulich guilty of having on 24 January, 1878 deliberately wounded Adjutant-General Trepov in the region of the pelvis with a large-calibre bullet from a revolver she had acquired for the express purpose of retaliation for the punishment of Bogolyubov?'

Tension was high. There was dead silence in the packed courtroom. Everyone was standing. The foreman read unhurriedly and clearly:

'The answer of the jury to the first question is "*No, not guilty*."'

The applause and shouts did not abate for several minutes. The public was enthusiastically expressing the country's opinion and condemning the system that brought pure girls such as Vera Zasulich to the prisoner's bench.

Dostoevsky was in agreement with the acquittal of the girl, whose courage had won over everyone. He went out into Liteinaya Street and made his way with difficulty through the crowd in front of the courthouse where happy shouts welcomed the unexpected acquittal. He came home late that night, shaken, moved, stimulated to creation, thinking deeply of the tremendous questions that had tormented him all his life and that the realities of Russia had now made all the more compelling.

A large notebook lay open beneath the lampshade on his desk. For several months now he had been drafting a plan for a sweeping epic about revolution and religion. It was to be about the new hero of these harsh and bloody times – a young terrorist, who has left a cell in a monastery to go out and attack supreme authority. The accused girl's simple and profound words ran through Dostoevsky's mind: 'It is a frightful thing to raise one's hand against another human being, but I had to do it.' He wrote down in his notebook Vera Zasulich's words about the moral difficulty of her bold act. Surely, this uncontrollable inner protest against killing was more estimable than her self-sacrificing deed!

He was again suffused by a glow of admiring love for his great nation and for his country's present-day young people, who were giving their lives in defence of truth and justice. Who dare say that our young people are decaying?

Nothing of the sort! They are *searching for the truth* with the courage of the Russian heart and mind and have merely *lost their leaders* . . .

Never before in all our Russian life has there been an epoch in which the great majority of young people (as if they sensed that all Russia had reached an end-point and was teetering over an abyss) were more sincere, more pure of heart, more eager for truth and reality, more willing to sacrifice everything, even life, for the truth and for a word of the truth. Truly, they are Russia's greatest hope![15]

Russia, teetering over an abyss – what a broad theme for a contemporary political novel!

In the summer of 1878 Dostoevsky began to write *The Brothers Karamazov* – a chronicle of his times – in which he would introduce and treat in a new way the burning theme of Russian life – young Russia's path to regicide.

XIX

Before Sunset

THE last decade of Dostoevsky's life was not particularly eventful, but the rather monotonous existence of a settled family man that he led in that period facilitated his work considerably. These were the years of his greatest achievements as a thinker and as a literary artist, and of full recognition of his vital contribution by the Press and the public. From the mid 1870s Russian critics began to associate Dostoevsky's name with that of Shakespeare. Dostoevsky was extremely active in editorial, journalistic and general literary work in this period. His influence grew steadily. His fame reached its acme when he delivered his speech in memory of Pushkin.

I. N. Kramskoi, one of the most profound and sensitive artists of the time, famed for his paintings 'Inconsolable Grief' and 'Nekrasov in the Period of "Last Songs"', wrote to P. N. Tretyakov on 14 February 1881: 'Dostoevsky has played an enormous role in the life of everyone (I think) for whom life is not a holiday but a profound tragedy. After the Karamazovs (and during the reading of it) I looked around in horror several times and was surprised that everything was the same, that the world had not turned over on its axis.'

After the hardship and tragedy Dostoevsky had experienced, he greatly appreciated the manifestations of his readers' love and drew fresh inspiration from them. 'In the last months he was in a state of elation,' one of the people close to him recalled. 'The ovations stimulated his nerves and fatigued his system. He regarded the laurels presented to him as the best of all possible rewards. People used to come to him as if to confession. They entrusted him with unbelievable confidences. Old and young had faith in the power of his word.'

But he never grew complacent or satisfied with his achievements. He never ceased to pursue the idea of a better future for his fellow-countrymen in his creative writing. Up to the end he was on fire with huge designs, which he only touched on in his last novel, but which retained, for him, the importance of inspired creative tasks. There was the writing of a Russian Candide – depicting, apparently, the martyrology of mankind as seen in the destinies of Russian serfdom. There was the book about Christ to be given to the world; not one that denies His existence, as Strauss had done nor an artistic poetization, like Renan's, but a book that would penetrate deep into the altruistic morality of His teaching, with fearless criticism of the high ideal proclaimed in the gospel, its limitlessness, and the impossibility for weak and vacillating man to carry it out. He wanted to write a book of literary reminiscences and create in it a unique gallery of portraits of Belinsky, Nekrasov, Valerian Maikov, Herzen, Apollon Grigoryev, Chernyshevsky, Turgenev, Goncharov, Vladimir Solovyov – pages about illuminating philosophical friendships and the irreconcilable struggle of ideas that had marked his whole career and had blazed up with special force during the last year of his life. He planned to write a book of polemics under the title *A Reply to My Critics*, and in it answer those who continued even in the period of his renown to object sharply to his literary and political ideas.

That there should have been such critics was inevitable, considering the restlessness of Dostoevsky's thinking, which allowed for differing and contradictory solutions to the basic problems of existence. Dostoevsky had never followed one set of commandments. Opposing forces struggled in his work, and his behests to posterity were frequently irreconcilable.

One might apply to him Dmitry Karamazov's despairing words about the awesome and mysterious phenomenon of beauty: 'Here, the Devil fights God, and the battlefield is the hearts of men.'

In 1883 Leo Tolstoy, who appreciated Dostoevsky for his 'deep heart', nevertheless protested against 'raising to the level of prophet and saint a man who died in the midst of a most heated inner struggle between good and evil. He is moving, interesting, but you cannot take *a man who was all struggle*, and set him up on a monument for the instruction of posterity.' The struggle within Dostoevsky was a product of the revolutionary epoch to which he could not reconcile himself because of his theoretical ideals and with which he could not find a common language. This was the final drama of his life and it sprang from the depths of his world outlook and his work.

THE PERIOD OF ATTEMPTED ASSASSINATIONS

Dostoevsky's favourite writers – Walter Scott, Victor Hugo, George Sand, Dickens – sympathized with the common people's movements for liberation, but they rejected revolutionary terror. Such, basically, was also the position of their great Russian admirer and pupil. In questions of social struggle Dostoevsky remained a Utopian moralist and a Christian, who wanted freedom and happiness for the people but insisted that they be achieved by peaceful means. He repudiated revolutionary terror as being the very opposite of mercy and humanity. Yet he was deeply moved by the courage, boldness and honour of the Russian revolutionaries, who sacrificed themselves so heroically for their cause. He had words of sympathy both for Karakozov and for Vera Zasulich. But he did not accept their militancy; he rejected the very principle of their struggle and sharply condemned 'street revolver-shooters'.

Until the 1870s, manifestations of individual terror were rare and seemed to be the exception, but the 1870s put this opponent of political violence to a formidable test. New forces and new historical events had brought about a transition to armed struggle in the formerly 'apolitical' *Narodnik* (populist) movement. Bakunin's ideas advocating insurrectionary tactics, denying all state control and defending banditry as 'one of the most honourable forms of Russian folk life', gained much influence. (Hence Stavrogin's association with Fedka the Convict, an association which horrified Dostoevsky.) It was Bakunin's belief that this sort of activity on the part of the advanced intelligentsia would bring about a national revolution. The secret circle of A. V. Dolgushin, in whom Dostoevsky evinced great interest and whom he portrayed, in part, in *A Raw Youth*, was also close to Bakuninism. The members of the Dolgushin group believed in seeking truth with a tinge of mysticism, but their main object was to organize a popular uprising, and they were prepared 'to destroy the imperial family' in order to win.

A revolutionary society called Zemlya i Volya (Land and Freedom) was active in the latter 1870s. Its members believed in agitation not only by words but, even more, by deeds – by insurrections and strikes. On 6 December 1876 Zemlya i Volya organized an impressive demonstration in the very heart of Petersburg, on the square in front of the Kazan Cathedral. Students and members of the democratic intelligentsia gathered in the semicircle of the wide Corinthian colonnade. They carried a red flag as a symbol of protest against the deaths in political prisons. The young Plekhanov made a speech appealing for struggle. The police hustled the demonstrators away from Nevsky Prospekt and arrested the leaders.

Dostoevsky denounced the 'Kazan affair.' He felt that the revolutionary youth had 'defiled the people's temple'. The forces of Russian insurrection had, he felt, for the first time struck a blow against the bastions of Orthodoxy. Actually, the authorities won that battle. The persons seized in the square were declared to constitute 'a criminal society' and were tried ruthlessly and harshly at a special session of the Senate.

The revolutionary impetus of the latter half of the decade kept mounting, but irreconcilable differences arose within the revolutionary camp. A great debate about the use of terror was in progress. A whole generation was confronting and reassessing Raskolnikov's problem: does a strong personality have the right to permit himself to shed 'blood for conscience sake' – for the good of the people? In the summer of 1879 Zemlya i Volya split over this problem into two organizations: Cherny Peredel (Black Repartition) and Narodnaya Volya (The People's Will). The former continued doing educational work among the peasants. The latter adopted the tactic of terror against individuals. Its first act was to pass a sentence of death against Alexander II, and in the autumn of 1879 it organized a number of attempts to assassinate the Tsar. This marked the beginning of a long period of 'single combat' by the revolutionary underground against the government and of the transition of the Narodnik movement to the tactics of political terror.

On 2 April 1879 there was a bold and audacious act of terrorism – A. K. Solovyov's attempt on the life of Alexander II when the Emperor was taking his morning walk near the General Staff building. The Tsar was hard put to it to escape from the continuous shooting, which he did by skilfully applying the Army Manual of Field Tactics, bending down nearly to the ground as he ran, and continually changing the target area by zigzagging. But even this could not save the supreme authority. On 5 February 1880 the Winter Palace was shaken by an explosion. Bushels of dynamite had been laid in the very walls of the Tsar's residence! It was members of the Palace Guard who received the blast and suffered the consequences.* This operation had been carried out by Stepan Khalturin, a working-man, with the help of the executive committee of Narodnaya Volya.

These terrorist activities took on the ominous quality of an inexorable personal threat, an inescapable death sentence, passed by unknown agencies. The government saw that it would have to make some concessions to society. On 15 February 1880 Count M. T. Loris-Melikov, Governor-General of Kharkov, who had a reputation as a liberal and a skilled administrator, was appointed chief of a special Royal Administrative Commission. Dostoevsky approved of this measure and was pleased at the anticipated 'pacification'. On 20 February, however, a young revolutionary named Mlodetsky made an attempt on the life of Loris-Melikov. This event upset Dostoevsky, who feared that it might cause the government to go back on its promises.

The revolutionary terror of those days confronted Dostoevsky with a critical ethical question: did a person have the right 'to prevent' a political assassination? He was very much upset by all the terrorist acts both in Russia and in the West – the shot fired by Vera Zasulich, the attempted assassination of the German Emperor, the actions of the anarchists in Europe. The political events of the day presented him with an agonizing problem involving individual duty, sacrifice and heroism. Suvorin has left us a most interesting note about a conversation he had with Dostoevsky on 20 February 1880 (that is, two weeks after the Khal-turin explosion in the Winter Palace and on the very day of Mlodetsky's attempt to assassinate Loris-Melikov), testifying to the great confusion in the writer's heart.

'Would we have gone to the Winter Palace to give warning

---

* Sixty soldiers were killed and thirty more wounded. The Tsar and his family were saved through being late for dinner.

about the explosion, would we have gone to the police, would you have gone up to a policeman on his beat, to ask him to arrest those men? Would you have gone?' Dostoevsky kept asking insistently.

'No, I would not have done such a thing.'

'Nor would I have. Yet why not? After all, it is horrible! It is a crime. What if we might have been able to prevent it? I was thinking about this before you arrived. I considered all the reasons why I ought to have informed. They are basic, serious reasons, and then I considered the reasons against it. They were quite insignificant. Simply the fear of being regarded as an informer.'

A comparison of Dostoevsky's vacillations now with his remarkably courageous and honest position at the political interrogations in 1849 reveals the regrettable deterioration of the great novelist's civic morals.

*

Politically, Dostoevsky's lot was a tragic one. Having been compelled by circumstances to take a second oath of loyalty to the autocracy in 1856 through the mediation of the hero of Sevastopol, Adjutant-General Totleben, he always felt obligated to keep that vow. Hence his adherence to government policy in *The Diary of a Writer* and in some of his novels, especially *The Brothers Karamazov*; hence his support of reaction and his closeness towards the end of his life to its most prominent ideologists – Katkov, Pobedonostev, Meshchersky, Tertii Filippov and Suvorin. In the 1870s he was accorded a measure of acceptance by the ruling circles of Russia, headed by the Tsar.

Pobedonostev's main idea about the need to establish a strong Russia by restoring the kind of church life that Russia had before Peter I is present in Dostoevsky's journalistic writings and is elaborated in his last novel. 'He conceived his Zosima at my suggestion,' Pobedonostsev, then already Chief Procurator of the Holy Synod, wrote in a letter. 'When he was writing *The Brothers Karamazov* he used to call on me on Saturday evenings and in great agitation give me an account of the new scenes in the novel.' From the correspondence between Pobedonostsev and Dostoevsky it is evident that Pobedonostsev kept a sharp eye on Dostoevsky's journalistic activities, providing him with materials for *The Diary of a Writer* and giving a detailed opinion of each issue.

Pobedonostsev introduced Dostoevsky into court circles and did all in his power to bring him closer to members of the imperial family. On his advice and with his assistance, Dostoevsky sent the heir to the throne (the future Alexander III) *The Diary of a Writer*, *The Devils* and *The Brothers Karamazov*. It was probably not without Pobedonostsev's participation that Dostoevsky was charged with the responsible and difficult task of giving spiritual guidance to the young Grand Dukes. At the beginning of 1878 Admiral Arsenyev, who supervised the education of Alexander II's younger sons, called on Dostoevsky. He told him he had come on the Tsar's behalf and that the Tsar wished Dostoevsky to exert a positive influence on the young Grand Dukes by his conversation and to 'touch upon the role they might have to play in view of the present condition of society'. Dostoevsky apparently performed this duty with his characteristic intelligence and talent, for he was soon requested to extend his activities as court pedagogue and hold conversations with the sons of the Tsar's brother, the Grand Duke Constantine Nikolaevich, and later to attend the small gatherings of his 'charges', the future poet 'K. R.' (the Grand Duke Constantine Constaninovich) and the Grand Duke Sergius Alexandrovich of lamentable memory* (Governor-General of Moscow from 1891).

Dostoevsky's closeness with members of the royal family opened doors to exclusive circles of Petersburg's aristocracy. Dostoevsky, who had never belonged to the highest nobility either by origin, profession, or way of life, now, at the end of

* Grand Duke Sergius, assassinated in 1905.

his life, had most of his social contacts in this set, and strove to become the exponent of its socio-political views. He was seen constantly in Petersburg high society, who willingly admitted the celebrated novelist to their exclusive circle . . .

Consequently, in the last years of his life Dostoevsky's Petersburg had no resemblance whatsoever to the impoverished quarters that he had portrayed in his early stories and in his first long novel. An enormous change had taken place in the setting and in the emphasis of his politics. The ornate décor of the imperial residences had succeeded the modest surroundings of his youthful writings in the poor neighbourhoods of the capital. Petrashevsky's crooked little wooden house in Staraya Kolomna with the smoking night lamp and the tattered couch, where young Dostoevsky had learned about socialism and sermonized, was now displaced by rooms in the Marble Palace and the reception halls of the Anichkov and Winter Palaces. The last chapter of Dostoevsky's life was set in a luxurious and official atmosphere, so uncharacteristic of his life as a wanderer, convict and toiler that he sought to conceal from his literary friends the unexpected turn of fortune that had brought him from prison and barracks, from gambling casinos and editorial offices, to Rastrelli and Rinaldi drawing-rooms, where the most exalted members of the royal family and dignitaries of the empire listened benignly to this poet of the insulted and the injured.

IN LITERARY SALONS

Among the Petersburg literary salons of which Dostoevsky was a habitué was that of Countess Sophia Andreevna Tolstaya, widow of the poet Count Alexei Konstantinovich Tolstoy. She used to gather together literary celebrities and intelligent ladies capable of appreciating them. There was no shortage of worshippers at this Mount Olympus, although the worship was purely intellectual. Among those who came to this salon were Goncharov, Turgenev, Vladimir Solovyov and Sollogub.

Viscount Melchior de Vogüé, a well-known student of the Russian novel, then a secretary at the French Embassy in Petersburg, frequently met Dostoevsky in Countess Tolstaya's salon, which reminded the Parisian diplomat of the drawing-rooms of the Faubourg Saint-Germain. His diary for 1880 mentions an 'argument with Dostoevsky', and contains the following entries: 'Self-adulation that gives one a glimpse how far Slavic thought will go in the big movement that is coming soon.' 'Dostoevsky says: "We possess the genius of all nations and the Russian genius as well. That is why we can understand you, while you are incapable of understanding us."'

Anna Dostoevskaya relates:

At Countess S. A. Tolstaya's Fyodor Mikhailovich used to meet many high society ladies: Countess A. A. Tolstaya (a relative of Count Leo Tolstoy), Mme E. A. Naryshkina, Countess A. E. Komorovskaya, Yu. F. Abaza, Princess Volkonskaya, Mme F. Vonlyarskaya, the singer Lavrovskaya (Princess Tserteleva) and others. These ladies were all extremely friendly to Fyodor Mikhailovich. Some of them were sincere admirers of his talent, and Fyodor Mikhailovich, who was so often irritated by literary and political arguments in male society, greatly enjoyed the ladies' always restrained and tactful conversation.

The literary salon of Yulia Denisovna Zasetskaya, daughter of the partisan poet Denis Davydov, had an entirely different atmosphere. Mme Zasetskaya was a kind-hearted, intelligent and gifted woman, very active in charity work. She was a chairman of a society that maintained over-night shelters and she gave Dostoevsky a pass entitling him to visit one of the shelters for the Petersburg poor at any time of the day or night. It worried Dostoevsky that this brilliant Russian lady should have deserted the Russian Orthodox Church and become a Lutheran. He felt that such a fine person ought to belong to the Russian church and the Russian people. He tried indeed to guide the errant woman back onto the correct path. They had heated and fierce arguments, as N. S. Leskov, who was present at their discussions, relates, but Dostoevsky was never the victor. Mme Zasetskaya had an excellent knowledge of the Bible and was acquainted with many of the best researches of English and German theologians, which Dostoevsky had never read. They argued incessantly and uncompromisingly.

'I cannot see that Russians are better than anyone else and that their religion is truer than any other. What does Russia have that is better than in other countries?' Mme Zasetskaya would say.

'Everything is better,' Dostoevsky replied.

'I don't see that.'

'That is because no one ever taught you to see things differently.'

'To whom shall I go to learn?'

'Go to the *muzhik* in your kitchen. He will teach you.'

Leskov noted that Dostoevsky tried to pronounce 'kitchen' the way it is pronounced by servants.

Countess Visconti, Zasetskaya's merry and easily amused sister, burst into laughter.

'*Comment*! Am I to go to my kitchen servant? Lord, what nonsense you talk!'

'What will he teach me?' Zasetskaya insisted, puzzled.

'He will teach you everything!' was Dostoevsky's reply.

'But what? What is everything?'

'How to live and how to die.'

Dostoevsky's tired eyes flashed with a pale fire, bringing to mind the look of the well-known Polish mystic Towianski. The argument broke off.

The view Dostoevsky expressed in this conversation anticipated Leo Tolstoy's teachings of ten years later, teachings which won over many contemporaries. Leskov continues: 'The question: What can the *muzhik* in the kitchen teach? was answered superbly by Count Leo Tolstoy in his story of the death of Ivan Ilyich. '*The muzhik teaches to live while remembering death*, he teaches to come *and serve the suffering*. To follow him is praiseworthy and not at all humiliating – such was Tolstoy's reply.'[1]

Among the habitués of Petersburg salons in the 1870s was a young scholar who shortly afterwards became a lecturer at Warsaw University, Alexander Lvovich Blok, an original, strange and gifted man. His son Alexander* later wrote of him: 'My father, who was an excellent musician, a connoisseur of *belles lettres* and a fine stylist, regarded himself as a pupil of Flaubert.' But 'he could not fit his constantly developing ideas into the concise forms he sought. There was something convulsive about his quests as there was in his entire emotional and physical make-up.' In his poem 'Vengeance' there are lines in which the sinister appearance of the poet's father, that had so struck Dostoevsky, is sketched against a background of the family chronicle of the Beketovs.†

> His features bear
> A rather unusual imprint.
> Once (when he was passing through the drawing-room)
> Dostoevsky noticed him.
> 'Who is that handsome man?' he asked
> In a low voice, bending down to Vrevskaya.
> 'He looks like Byron.'

The son admits the resemblance:

> The same expression of authority,
> The same impulse towards the abyss.

This kind of external appearance always interested Dostoevsky, and one may believe the family tradition that

---

* Alexander Alexandrovich Blok, the great twentieth-century poet and author of *The Twelve*.

† Beketovs. The family of Professor Beketov, whose daughter married the 'sinister' A. L. Blok and became the mother of the poet.

the novelist had intended to put this demoniacal scholar into the gallery of his heroes.

Dostoevsky also attended the salon of Countess Alexandra Andreevna Tolstaya, a close relative and personal friend of Leo Tolstoy and his correspondent for many years. In the 1870s Dostoevsky used to speak of Tolstoy as his favourite Russian writer and of *Anna Karenina* as our *new national word*, 'with which nothing in European literature can compare'. Strakhov wrote to Tolstoy that the chapters of *Anna Karenina* which appeared in the April issue of *Russky Vestnik* had caused a veritable explosion in Petersburg: Dostoevsky is waving his hands and calling you a *god of art.*'

In *The Diary of a Writer*, however, Dostoevsky condemned Tolstoy for the indifference one of his central characters, Levin, displays to the oppression of Slavs and to the horrifying Turkish brutalities in the Balkans. 'A great "teacher of society" such as the author of *Anna Karenina* ought not at the height of a terrible national tragedy to advocate the narrow path of personal convenience,' he wrote. Dostoevsky sensed in Tolstoy's new work a trend towards 'no use of force to resist evil', a doctrine that was alien to all his militant writing in *The Diary of a Writer*, and he had every intention of entering into battle against Tolstoy on this point in his monthly. Countess Alexandra Tolstaya wrote in this connection:

Knowing that I was related to Count Leo Tolstoy, he said to me that he had never met him but had a great curiosity about him as a writer and as a man.

'Perhaps you can explain his new direction to me, Countess. I see something special in it that I do not yet understand.'

The Countess offered to read him the latest letters she had received from Tolstoy. This was arranged a few days later. 'I can still see Dostoevsky before me,' wrote the Countess:

I can see him holding his head in his hands as he listened and repeating despairingly, 'That's not right, that's not right.' He did not sympathize with a single one of Leo's ideas. Then he asked me for permission to take the copies I had made of Leo's letters and many of the originals. From some of the things he said I concluded that he wished to confute Tolstoy's views.

A few days after that evening Dostoevsky was no more.

'THE HUNCHBACKED ANGEL'

Of all the Petersburg salons he went to, Dostoevsky found the Stakenschneiders' the most congenial. The eldest Stakenschneider daughter became the object of his last emotional attachment and he took her as a prototype for one of his most touching characters in his last novel. Elena Andreevna Stakenschneider was, in the words of Goncharov, 'a hunchback with an intelligent face'. 'She moved about on crutches and had bad legs, but she was intelligent, kind-hearted and friendly,' V. Mikulich (see below) tells us. Elena Stakenschneider wrote of herself: 'There are many things that others can do that I cannot do – I cannot dance, dress up, or flirt.' She read a great deal and enjoyed listening to talented and erudite people. In her mother's salon she met poets, journalists, novelists and, in the 1870s, Dostoevsky, whom she mentions many times in her well-known diary. She revered this 'very great man' and tried to make his life easier by her sympathy and attention. For his part, Dostoevsky felt deep pity for her and was so profoundly affected by the drama of her life that the suffering image of her came to be recreated in his writings.

There had been many turnings in the spiritual path of Elena Stakenschneider. Born in 1836 in the family of a wealthy court architect, she grew up in a house on Millionnaya Street in an atmosphere of German patriarchal piety. She was taught morals according to the lives of the saints and loyalty and patriotism according to the etiquette of the court of Nicholas I. But other influences of the period reached the Stakenschneider salon, too. The inquisitive, bright young woman became interested in the social trends of those turbulent times – in equal rights for women, the student movement, the Polish insurrection, Herzen's *Kolokol*. Her chief mentor was Pyotr Lavrovich Lavrov, an eminent sociologist, philosopher and writer. But this enlightening influence ended in 1866, when Lavrov was exiled from Petersburg and emigrated.

After the death of Elena's father the family moved to an apartment on Znamenskaya Street, where the literary 'at homes' continued but where the world outlook of this lonely, crippled woman took a new direction. In the 1870s our seeker for moral justice was losing sympathy with the 'movement of the 1860s'. Dostoevsky now became her mentor. She had a very high opinion of *The Diary of a Writer*, even considering it superior to *The Brothers Karamazov*, and she adopted a great many of its author's views. In the winter of 1879–80 Dostoevsky, his wife reports, often attended the Tuesdays at Elena Stakenschneider's house, where writers gathered and read their works and sometimes read classical plays or acted in amateur theatre productions.

Among the Stakenschneider family's young friends was twenty-two-year-old Lydia Veselitskaya, who used to come there to see Dostoevsky, whom she admired fervently. Veselitskaya dreamed of a literary career. She did indeed become a brilliant writer, but that was in the 1880s and 1890s, after Dostoevsky's death, when, under the pen name V. Mikulich, she wrote her lively and interesting trilogy *Mimochka as a Bride*, *Mimochka at the Waters* and *Mimochka Poisons Herself*, in which she portrayed with subtle humour a new type of middle-class girl, who is striving to get into high society. Leo Tolstoy noticed the second of these stories and wrote to its author approvingly.[2] Anna Dostoevskaya tells us:

I should like to point out as an indication of Fyodor Mikhailovich's sensitivity and foresight that after he had spoken to the young girl two or three times he perceived, despite her youth and understandable embarrassment, that she was not an ordinary young lady but had the seeds of something higher in her, a striving towards an ideal, and probably literary talent.

Dostoevsky felt comfortable and relaxed in this company. He told the girls' fortunes with cards, played simple card games with them, joked, teased and sometimes read aloud, as V. Mikulich describes in her reminiscences:

At one such 'concert' Verochka and I each took a volume of Dostoevsky – she took *The Karamazovs* and I took *Crime and Punishment* – and went over to him to ask him to read something aloud. He was already sitting with Elena Stakenschneider again when we came up to him with the books and Verochka told him the wish of the entire company.

He took the book out of my hands but, frowning at the title, gave it straight back to me, saying 'Only not that!' Verochka handed him her book but he frowned at *The Karamazovs*, too, and turned to speak to Elena. We stood there in front of him, disappointed, holding the rejected books and not knowing what else to say.

'If I am to read I will read something good,' Dostoevsky said. 'Give me Pushkin.'

'What will you read?' asked Elena.

'*The Covetous Knight*. The old Baron's monologue.'

Elena Stakenschneider called out for volunteers to read the other roles in the play. After some brief consultations readers were found and they sat down at the table.

They read the first scene and got up. Dostoevsky was left at the table alone. It became very quiet in the drawing room, so quiet you could hear a pin drop. And in that deferential silence he began to read in his low but clear voice:

'As the young scapegrace bides the trysting hour . . .'

He read the monologue through superbly. I for one had never in all my life heard anyone read it better. And when at the end of the third scene he began to whisper, breathlessly:

'I cannot stand. My knees are giving way.

'I am choking, choking, where, where are my keys,

'My keys, my keys!'

we feared he would have a seizure then and there. But all ended well. He drank a glass of water and bowed to the public, who were applauding loudly.

A full amateur stage production was also being prepared and Dostoevsky expressed a desire to participate.

'What part would you like to play?'

'Othello. I will be Othello.'

Othello was his favourite tragedy in the repertoire of his favourite tragedian. Towards the end of his life he wrote of 'the universality, the universal comprehensibility and immeasurable depth of the world types of Aryan man that Shakespeare portrayed for all time.' To the very end Dostoevsky liked playing a part in a tragedy.

A few days before his death he said he would play the monk who denounces the Tsar for executing his truest followers and murdering his son, in the first part of Alexei Konstantinovich Tolstoy's trilogy *The Death of Ivan the Terrible*. But he never played these tragic roles.

He continued to impress audiences by his platform readings. He was regarded as one of the finest speakers and readers of Russian. From the time he was a young man he had been reading his favourite poets to his friends. Little by little, he had developed into a genuine master of recitation. He read with highly original inflections and in inspired tones. In his last years he participated readily in literary programmes, electrifying his audiences by his vivid interpretations. An artist of Russian speech, he attached a great deal of importance to poetic melody and conveyed the musicality and rhythm of the language splendidly, 'of course, without violating naturalness', Strakhov remarks. Of his own works Dostoevsky willingly read Raskolnikov's dream about the peasant and his horse, Marmeladov's monologue, some excerpts from *The Brothers Karamzov* including the chapters 'The Confession of an Ardent Heart', 'Devout Peasant Women', 'The Grand Inquisitor', and 'Ilyusha's Funeral'. Of his beloved Pushkin he used now to read the scene in the

Chudov Monastery from *Boris Godunov*, 'In the Time of Spring Warmth', 'For the Shores of the Distant Homeland', 'The Wanderer', 'As Long as the Poet does not Require it', and *The Prophet*, evoking great enthusiasm in his audience. He also read Nekrasov's 'When from the Darkness of Errors' and excerpts from Gogol's *Dead Souls*. 'He had no equal as a reader,' one of his contemporaries declared. 'His manner of reading was unbelievably exciting.'

Professor Semyon Vengerov, an eminent historian of Russian literature, reported his impressions of a reading by Dostoevsky at a benefit performance for the Literary Fund on 9 March 1879, in which Turgenev, Saltykov, Grigorovich and Polonsky also took part. But the others 'merely read, while Dostoevsky in the full sense of the word uttered prophecies'. He read 'The Confession of an Ardent Heart' from *The Brothers Karamazov* (Mitya's account of how he pitied and saved Katerina Ivanovna), in a high-pitched but clearly articulated and incredibly thrilling voice. Nearly forty years later the listener still could not forget 'the complete emotional absorption of the crowd of thousands in the mood of one man'.

One of the particular admirers of Dostoevsky's readings was Elena Stakenschneider, whom he watched and studied as an artist.

The image of a luckless, sick woman, deprived of happiness and joy, yet able to meet all the blows of fortune with kindness, intelligence and sympathy, is perceived in the features of one of Dostoevsky's last (and little noticed) female characters – Ninochka Snegiryova, the younger daughter of the impoverished and humiliated Junior Captain Snegiryov. 'This was a pitiful creature,' Dostoevsky wrote. 'A young girl of about twenty, hunchbacked and unable to use her withered legs. Her crutches stood nearby in a corner, between the bed and the wall. The poor girl's wonderfully beautiful and kind eyes gazed at Alyosha with a sort of tranquil meekness.' As her father described her:

'This is God's angel in the flesh, come down to mortals – *my hunchbacked little angel*!' 'Ninochka's face wet with tears', imploring her father beside her brother's open grave: 'Papa, give mother a flower!' appears for the last time in the concluding chapter, entitled 'Ilyusha's Funeral'.

This image, as we see, stayed with Dostoevsky to the very end, and his last pages are illuminated, as it were, by the radiance of a noble character.

Dostoevsky finished *The Brothers Karamazov* in early November 1880. It was the completion of three years of work on the plan and the manuscript of a novel which had first been conceived while he was in prison in 1850 and which, apparently, began to take formal shape in 1874. He wrote to the editor of *Russky Vestnik* on 8 November 1880, when he sent him the epilogue of *The Brothers Karamazov*:

Well, at last the novel is finished! I worked on it for three years, printed it for two – this is an important moment for me. I'd like to have it out in a separate edition by Christmas. There is an enormous demand for it, both here and among booksellers all over Russia. They are already sending money. However, permit me not to bid you farewell. After all, I expect to live another twenty years and to write.

Ahead of him lay a new *Diary of a Writer* and the second novel about the Karamazovs.

At this 'important moment' Dostoevsky was in fact winding up his career as artist and novelist, begun almost forty years before.

To realize his huge new designs for the completion of the Karamazov epic, and to write the other works that he had conceived, Dostoevsky was asking Fate for another twenty years of creative work. He had just over two months left to live.

Yet he had had his supreme triumph – in 1880 – half a year before he died, at the Pushkin commemoration in Moscow.

XX

A Novel of Synthesis

SECOND-LIEUTENANT ILYINSKY

DOSTOEVSKY based the plot of *The Brothers Karamazov* on the life of a fellow-convict in Omsk, Retired Second-Lieutenant Ilyinsky, formerly of the Tobolsk Battalion of the line, who had been convicted of parricide and sentenced to twenty years' penal servitude. Of the two hundred prisoners in Omsk, this 'gentleman-parricide' aroused Dostoevsky's special interest. He is mentioned in the very first pages of *Notes from the House of the Dead* and is the first in the gallery of portraits in that celebrated book. 'There is one parricide that I just cannot get out of my mind,' Dostoevsky wrote. The *Notes* say that this was a dissolute man, with many debts, who had killed his father to gain an inheritance. But he had never confessed to the crime. Dostoevsky had learned the details of the affair from people from Tobolsk, his home town, and believed that his information was more or less correct: 'The entire town in which this parricide was formerly stationed tells the same story.'

There may have been former residents of Tobolsk among the Omsk prisoners, but it is more likely that Dostoevsky heard about the Ilyinsky affair from the Tobolsk Decembrists with whom he was in contact while he was in Siberia, especially the Annenkov family, for a long time residents of Tobolsk: 'The proof was so clear that it was impossible not to believe it.' Apparently, Dostoevsky was then already interested in the moral phenomenon of parricide. It was not until much later that he learned how tragic this man's fate had really been.

The first chapter of *Notes from the House of the Dead*, which contains the description of this parricide, was published in 1860 and was reprinted four times in the course of eighteen months. It is not surprising that it reached Siberia and, eventually, Tobolsk itself. In May 1862 Dostoevsky received a letter from Siberia, stating that the 'parricide' about whom he had written was innocent. In the May 1862 issue of *Vremya* Dostoevsky informed his readers in Chapter 7 of the second part of *Notes from the House of the Dead*, entitled 'A Pretension', that he had received incontrovertible information to the effect that the 'gentleman-parricide' of the first chapter of the *Notes* 'had suffered penal servitude for ten years without reason, and had officially been found innocent by the court'.

Dostoevsky never forgot this 'amazing instance', 'the deeply tragic' story of 'the destruction of a still-young life by such a horrible accusation'. He made a mental note of it as suitable for further literary development. Much later, in the autumn of 1874, he wrote in one of his manuscript notebooks:

13 September 1874. A Drama. In Tobolsk, about twenty years ago, similar to the story of Il—sky! Two brothers, an aged father, one brother has a fiancée with whom the other brother is secretly and enviously in love. The girl loves the elder brother, but the elder brother, a young lieutenant, lives a wild and fast life. He quarrels with his father. The father disappears. No sign of him for a few days. The brothers discuss the inheritance; suddenly the authorities find the body in the cellar. The clues point to the elder (the younger does not live with the father). The elder is tried and sentenced to penal servitude. (He had quarrelled with his father, boasted of his late mother's inheritance, and other foolishness. When he enters the room and even his fiancée turns away from him, he says drunkenly: 'Do you really believe this?' The younger brother has fashioned the clues flawlessly.) The public doesn't know for certain who committed the murder. A scene in prison. They want to kill him. The authorities. He does not tell any names. The convicts swear

fraternity to him. The chief gaoler reproaches him for having killed his father.

Twelve years later his brother comes to see him. A scene in which they understand one another without words. Another seven years go by. The younger has a high rank and title but he is suffering, he is a hypochondriac. He tells his wife that it was he who committed the murder. 'Why did you tell me?' He goes to his brother. His wife comes, too. On her knees she begs the convict to say nothing, to save her husband. The convict says: 'I have got used to it.' They make peace. 'You have already been punished,' the elder says.

It is the younger's birthday. The guests arrive. He comes into the room. I committed the murder. They think he has had a stroke.

The end: the elder has been released, the younger is in a prison transportation centre. He is being deported. (As a slanderer.) The younger asks the elder to be a father to his children.

'I have taken the right path!'

In the earliest notes for *The Brothers Karamazov* the elder brother is usually indicated by the name Ilyinsky. Later this name is mentioned in conjunction with Dmitry Fyodorovich, the name eventually given to the character. It is not difficult to perceive the resemblance between the story of Lieutenant Ilyinsky and this early outline for *The Brothers Karamazov*. In addition to the story of Dmitry Fyodorovich, the sketch also gives the plot of an interpolated short story, entitled 'The Mysterious Visitor'. The true murderer's confession before a gathering of guests who have come to wish him a happy birthday is developed in Zosima's story.

It appears from the Russian army orders for the 1840s that Ilyinsky retired from the army in 1845. Since he was already in the prison when Dostoevsky arrived there at the beginning of 1850, the crime on which *The Brothers Karamazov* was based must have occurred in the late 1840s. Unfortunately, the letter from Siberia attesting to the condemned man's innocence, which might have shed greater light on the history of one of Dostoevsky's most outstanding concepts, has not been found among the writer's private papers. However, the real-life source of the plot is obvious enough from the available materials.

In the mid 1870s Dostoevsky wrote down several plans in his notebooks, which reappeared in the finished novel. For example:

And so, one brother is an Atheist and desperation.
The second is a complete fanatic.
The third, the future generation, is the living force, new people.
(And – the newest generation – the children.)

This last theme, the children, had long occupied Dostoevsky's mind as one of the most important in his portrayal of contemporary society. His child heroes are unforgettable (Netochka, Nellie, Polechka Marmeladova) and highlight the drama of the life around them. Towards the end of the 1860s a new image, that of a capable and thinking adolescent, began to take shape in Dostoevsky's novels. There is Kolya Ivolgin in *The Idiot*, a bright boy who brings the clarity of his understanding to the confusion and chaos of his elders' relationships. Then the 'illegitimate' Arkady Dolgoruky, a much more complex character, for he develops his own ideas and programme for life; he dreams of power, yet is willing to give up everything to rescue an abandoned infant.

The theme of children on the road to destruction moved Dostoevsky deeply: 'Some froze to death in the baskets in which they had been abandoned on the doorsteps of Petersburg civil servants; others were suffocated by the Finnish wet-nurses the orphanages hired; still others died at their mothers' empty breasts (during the Samara famine), and others suffocated from the smoke in third-class railway coaches.' All these victims of dreadful reality came together, by Dostoevsky's fantastic design, at 'Christ's Christmas Tree'. Could such a thing have really happened? 'That is why I am a novelist, to invent', the author of *The Diary of a Writer* concluded his Christmas story. Dostoevsky's encounter among the night-time crowds in the Haymarket with a little girl of six, dressed in rags and looking as if she were crushed by a hopeless sorrow and struck down by an 'unnatural' curse, was no invention, however, and he was surely thinking of it in the scene in 'The Dream of a Ridiculous Man' which depicts a shivering little girl, rushing down a deserted street in horror and despair and calling for help.

In the mid 1870s Dostoevsky jotted down a plan for a 'novel about children, solely about children with a child for its hero', with chapter titles such as, 'Children arguing about a republic and a monarchy', 'Children establish contacts with child criminals in a prison', 'Child arsonists and train wreckers', and so forth. He never wrote the novel, but he put into *The Brothers Karamazov* the boy Kolya Krasotkin, apparently a budding revolutionary, for Kolya says: 'I am a socialist.' Kolya is certain that he knows the people well. He quotes Belinsky and Voltaire and declares that 'the Christian religion has served only the rich and the nobility, enabling them to keep the lower class in bondage'.

Unlike reactionary novelists, Dostoevsky portrays his young rebel as charming and gifted. This schoolboy engages in political arguments with the monk Alyosha and hopes passionately ' *to sacrifice myself for the truth some day*'. His idea is ' *to die for mankind*'. Apparently, this brave young boy was to have had one of the leading roles in the revolutionary events of a second novel about the Karamazovs.

Contrasted to this straightforward and courageous boy is Ilyusha Snegiryov, an insulted and embittered child, who is torn by inner conflict. But Ilyusha's conscience rebels and he struggles energetically for his father's honour. The novel ends with the chapter 'Ilyusha's Funeral' and a speech by Alyosha Karamazov, urging the children who have crowded round him to be generous and courageous in life as was their deceased comrade, as are Kolya Krasotkin and the shy and intelligent Kartashov. The epic of the Karamazovs and, with it, Dostoevsky's life work, end with the loud shouts of the excited children. The last novel sums up the whole tremendous cycle.

*

After completing *A Raw Youth* in 1875 Dostoevsky turned away for some time from literary work, as he had done after *The Devils*, and in 1876 and 1877 he worked mainly on *The Diary of a Writer*. But at the very beginning of 1878 he took temporary leave of his readers. 'In this year of respite from urgent publication I will really and truly get down to one literary work, which has imperceptibly and involuntarily taken shape in my head during the two years of publication of *The Diary*.' His wife confirms that at the beginning of 1878 Dostoevsky 'was absorbed in drafting a plan for the novel *The Brothers Karamazov*'. He was unable to get down to writing the novel at once, because various events and business matters required his attention, and he made only his usual preparations, in the form of preliminary notes, outlines, plans and research. After the sudden death of his three-year-old son Alyosha on 16 May 1878 this preliminary work apparently stopped too.

On 18 June Dostoevsky and Vladimir Solovyov left Petersburg on a journey to the Optina Pustyn Monastery, which they reached on 25 June, having stopped off in Moscow for four days. *En route* Dostoevsky told his companion the plan and the theme of the epic novel he had in mind. 'The church as a positive social ideal was to have been the central theme of a new novel or a new series of novels, of which only the first, *The Brothers Karamazov*, was written,' Vladimir Solovyov wrote. But, of course, this was not the sole idea of Dostoevsky's last novel, for in it the author dealt with a number of significant problems that had been in his restless and inquiring mind all his life.

AN EPIC NOVEL OF CONTEMPORARY RUSSIA

By July 1878 Dostoevsky had already started to write his enormous epic *The Brothers Karamazov*, a novel of synthesis, summing up almost the whole of the writer's work and striving to embody all his most cherished thoughts. With its multiplicity of places and of images, this vast novel about Karamazovism is heterogeneous in its points and in its components. Its essentially political nature tends to be obscured by the extraordinary incisiveness of its character delineation, the intensely tragic quality of the passions, vices and inspirations it reveals, the polished dialectics of its conversations and arguments, and, finally the brilliant theological criticism in the poem about the Grand Inquisitor. Yet this masterpiece of socio-psychological portrayal is marred by the reactionary and mystical views of its author, who depicted the Young Russia movement of the 1860s as an unmitigated disaster, corrupt and 'disorderly'.

In his 'history of one family' Dostoevsky the journalist dealt extensively with issues pertaining to the contemporary state, such as the law courts, the Press, schools, nationalities, the church, and revolutionary propaganda, and he invariably treated these fundamental issues of autocratic Russia's internal affairs strictly in the spirit of official policy, defending the ideas and trends of the government circle with which he constantly associated in the last period of his work. However, as the critics even then correctly pointed out, Dostoevsky's ideals were lofty and humane, though the doctrine he derived from them was erroneous and invalid The reader does not notice what he preaches but responds to his characters and to their drama because 'the author's passionate love for people, his deep compassion for suffering souls, covers up all else. In spite of his efforts to act as the champion of the powers of darkness, he is a lighted torch.'

The enormous quantity of material in the family chronicle of the Karamazovs is presented in a simple, clear-cut plan, divided into three main sections:

1. Rivalry in love between the father and his elder son Dmitry, making them mortal enemies.
2. The mysterious murder of old Karamazov.
3. A miscarriage of justice that dooms the carefree and impulsive Dmitry to long years in prison on a charge of parricide.

The turmoil of events draws into its vortex all the members of the Karamazov family as well as the two young women connected with it, Grushenka, a provincial 'infernalist', whose sensual beauty is the cause of the mortal hatred between the elderly libertine and his uncontrollable firstborn, and Katerina Ivanovna, the daughter of a colonel, recently out of a finishing school. Katerina Ivanovna is very grateful to Dmitry for an act of chivalrous generosity to her and she dreams of reforming him, of saving him from moral destruction so that he may begin a new life.

From this cauldron of untameable passions and lofty sentiments emerge the main conflicts of a sensational crimestory that echoed all over Russia.

The plot of Dostoevsky's last work is organized in accordance with his well-tried rules of composition, but at extreme high tension and with maximum expression, truly *fortissimo*. The novel is built upon sharp contrasts of persons and events. At one extreme are the moral degenerates – Fyodor Karamazov and Smerdyakov. At the other are the 'angels' – Alyosha and his spiritual mentor Zosima. The monastery is contrasted to Skotoprigonyevsk; the Russian monk is contrasted to the libertine, the Elder's teaching is contrasted to the conversation over the brandy, and the 'reverend father' is contrasted to the blackguard Karamazov senior. To the end Dostoevsky makes use of antithesis as his main structural principle.

Another of his favourite devices – confrontation of all the main characters – is also often used. The gathering of all the Karamazovs in the hermitage for the purpose of settling a family quarrel in a friendly fashion soon develops into a shocking squabble, first in the Elder's cell and then in the Father Superior's refectory. But when the atmosphere has been strained to the breaking point by old Karamazov's quarrel with Dmitry, the challenge to a duel and the insults directed against the monks, there is a sudden change. The Elder Zosima falls to his knees before Dmitry and touches his head to the ground as a mark of respect to one who will suffer a great deal in the future. The novel opens with this scene of transition from quarrel to drama.

His central chapters are actuated by similar 'assemblies' – for example the wild party at Mokroe. Here is how the fortunes of the principal characters lead up to this scene, Dmitry, who has fallen passionately in love with Grushenka. wants to marry her and is waging a desperate struggle against his father, who has promised the beautiful young woman three thousand roubles for a single rendezvous with him.

'But what if Grushenka goes?' Alyosha asks Dmitry.
'I'll break in and interfere.'
'But what if . . . ?'
'I'll kill.'
'Whom will you kill?'
'The old man. I won't kill her.'
'Brother, what are you saying?'

Dmitry makes no secret of his hatred for his father. Horror grips everyone as they sense that a crime is brewing in the quiet provincial town. An unforeseen event alters the situation. Grushenka learns that her 'first and rightful lover' the Polish officer Mussyalovich, 'her seducer', whom she has never ceased to adore, is on his way to her. And 'Grushenka flies off to a new life'. The despairing Dmitry, who is by now on the point of committing suicide, rushes after her to a disreputable tavern on the edge of town.

The company accepts him. They play cards. The Polish visitors are exposed as card-sharpers. Mussyalovich insults Grushenka. The Poles are thrown out. There is a wild feast with everybody invited – ribald songs, zithers, drunkenness, rustic dancing. Above the fumes and the din there rises, like a clear, ravishing song, Grushenka's declaration of love for Dmitry. Life is utterly changed. From somewhere has come the dawn of his moral regeneration. But disaster breaks into that moment of brightness and spiritual elevation: 'Retired Lieutenant Karamazov, you are charged with having murdered your father, Fyodor Pavlovich Karamazov this night.' The merciless intervention of the authorities precludes the new life which our hero was about to begin. Now he must face the prosecutor, the examining magistrate, the police and the district officer. He is accused of having committed a serious crime. The house which was a moment ago filled with singing and drunken noise is suddenly dead silent.

Old Karamazov's murder also reveals the tragic destiny of the second son. Ivan Karamazov's brilliant and creative intellect, which has grappled with the problems of his family and of the chaos in the world, is dragged down into the filth and the blood of a revolting crime, and falls from the summit of a lofty idea down into madness and death. Ivan is destroyed by the tragic conflict the crime produces in his great mind. This atones for an irreparable mistake, for it was he who put temptation in the path of his younger bastard half-brother, the manservant Smerdyakov, by speaking in favour of the anarchist slogan that 'everything is permitted'. Smerdyakov, offspring of the wretched idiot girl Lizaveta Smerdyáschaya, is a moral monster, a spiritual corpse, a cynical Westerner, and an enemy of Russia. He is the real parricide.

Smerdyakov transfers all responsibility for his crime to

Ivan, accusing him of being the intellectual murderer of their father: 'The chief murderer is you, sir, and you alone. I am of very little significance, even though it was I who did the killing.' Smerdyakov, condemned and blamed by his mentor, hangs himself on the eve of Dmitry's trial.

Towards the end of the novel the chief characters gather together in a grand *tutti* before the final catastrophe. The three brothers, the two women rivals, Junior Captain Snegiryov, Rakitin, the valet Grigory, the tavern keeper Trifon Borisovich and Dmitry's drinking companions of the orgy at Mokroe, all meet at the trial. Also present are celebrated lawyers, elderly dignitaries, fashionably dressed ladies, journalists from Petersburg, townspeople and peasant jurymen. This is an unprecedented gathering indeed. All Russia is watching the trial. The orderly investigation, the measured debates and the brilliant polemics of the opposing sides are the sequel to the previously depicted domestic brawls.

The examination of the witnesses is interrupted by 'sudden catastrophe' (the title of the chapter about the trial). Ivan declares publicly that Smerdyakov killed the old man, and 'I was the one who taught him to kill.' The witness loses his mind, becomes violent and is carried out of the courtroom. Overwhelmed, Katerina Ivanovna, who is convinced that Ivan, whom she loves, has destroyed himself by his testimony, determines to save him at Dmitry's expense. She shows the court a letter of Dmitry's in an attempt to show that he murdered his father. The distraught woman's statement turns into denunciation, a speech of extraordinary force, a ringing indictment of the prisoner. Grushenka, trembling with anger, screams across the courtroom: 'Dmitry, your snake has destroyed you!' Katerina Ivanovna is carried out in hysterics. Dmitry is convicted and sentenced to twenty years of penal servitude. But he is overcome by a feeling of radiance, such as he has never known before – a new man is being born.

DMITRY KARAMAZOV

As had been the case in real life, the novel's principal hero is a complicated and basically honourable character. He was the usual dissolute officer in everyday life, sensual, unrestrained and loose in morals, the typical arrogant army brute, always ready to insult and hurt someone, always ready for an 'orgy and a pogrom'. But beneath this rough exterior there beats a living, sensitive heart. Poised between deadly sin and life-giving beauty, he knows not only the fall into the abyss, but also the flight to the glittering summits. Dmitry is an intellectually and morally gifted individual, a profound and compassionate soul, a man of impulses and enthusiasms, an ardent admirer of Schillerian dithyrambs and Hamlet's soliloquies; he himself writes poetry and is in love with life and with art. He is instinctively quick to embark on heated discussions of intimate or general philosophical topics, a direct and naïve thinker with a gift for primitive, vividly expressive speech.

In his manuscript notes for *The Brothers Karamazov* Dostoevsky intended Dmitry to say in his final speech in court: 'I am one who loves Schiller, I am an idealist. Anyone who thinks that I am a blackguard does not really know me.' He had said that he would like to begin his 'confession of a passionate heart' by reciting Schiller's *Hymn to Joy*. But before speaking of jubilation and happiness he must speak of the suffering and sorrow that fill men's lives. And so he turns to *The Eleusinian Festival* with its gloomy beginning about the primitive times of the human race:

> Wild and fearful in his cavern,
> Hid the naked trogolodyte,

Dmitry begins, coming to the anguished lines about humiliated man:

> From the fields and from the vineyards
> Came no fruits to deck the feasts,

Only flesh of bloodstained victims
Smouldered on the altar fires,
And wherever the grieving goddess
Turns her melancholy gaze,
Sunk in vilest degradation
Man his loathsomeness displays.

These lines overwhelm Dostœvsky's hero: 'Sobs suddenly break forth from Dmitry's breast. He seizes Alyosha's hand: "Friend, friend, in humiliation, now, too, in humiliation. Man suffers frightfully on this earth, he has so many troubles."'

The fate of Dmitry is profoundly tragic. Though he is a man of lofty flights of the spirit, he has been unable to break out of the bondage of the sin and vice that have ensnared him. At the moment of disaster, however, his entire being lights up from within. He has a dream in which he sees a burnt-out village, blackened timbers, emaciated peasant women with hungry children, crying in their arms. He asks: 'Why are people poor? . . . Why is a child poor, why is the steppe bare, why don't they embrace and kiss, why don't they sing joyous songs?' And he wants to enter into battle against this evil 'so that from this moment on there may be no tears'.

Thus did Dostoevsky on the eve of his death express his eternal love for the Russian village. Dmitry Karamazov grieves over the poverty and the suffering of the peasants. He wants to be their champion and defender, to promote their happiness, to mourn for their sorrow. This is one of Dostoevsky's last great chapters about the infinite suffering of the people of Russia.

THE CULMINATION OF HIS CREATIVE ART

'Of all Shakespeare's heroes, only Hamlet could have written his creator's tragedies,' one Shakespearian scholar has remarked. We shall take the liberty of paraphrasing this statement. *Of all Dostoevsky's heroes, only Ivan Karamazov could have written his novels.*

Ivan Karamazov is a fine writer, philosopher and journalist. The reader is told of three outstanding works he has written. Let us call them tentatively; 'A Russian Candide', 'Book about Christ' and 'Dialogue with the Devil'. Dostoevsky's titles for them in the novel are 'The Insurrection,' 'The Grand Inquisitor', and 'The Devil: Ivan Fyodorovich's Nightmare'.

Ivan and Alyosha are seated alone in a room in a provincial tavern, discussing age-old problems.

'I accept God directly and simply,' but 'I do not accept this world of God's', Ivan says challengingly. He cites as his reasons for this declaration current events and annals of crime. In support of his charge against the 'Creator of the world' he quotes various 'petty facts' and 'petty anecdotes' from newspapers, pamphlets, historical magazines and court records. True stories from the press about war brutalities, executions and child-beating disclose the whole 'devil's vaudeville' of contemporary reality. The human tears with which the earth is soaked 'from crust to core', and, above all, the torture meted out to completely innocent children, force Ivan to conclude that the religious concept of a future harmony in which the voices of all the tormented and tortured will merge into a single song of praise, 'Thou art just, O Lord!', is invalid, improbable and unacceptable. 'And that is why I reject the higher harmony altogether. I do not want a mother to embrace the torturer whose dogs have torn her son from limb to limb. I do not want harmony, I do not want it because of my love for mankind.' This humanist principle compels him to protest against the traditional concept of God, to reject religious Utopias and to urge the protection of people against the cruelties of historic reality. This is Dostoevsky's 'Russian Candide'.

As the reader will recall, *Candide* is celebrated for the forcefulness of its protest against human suffering. In this philosophical masterpiece Voltaire, deeply shocked by the disasters of the eighteenth century – the rapacious Seven Years War, the earthquake in Lisbon, the cruelties of rulers, the rivers of blood and human hecatombs – rises in wrath against the doctrines that talk about well-being and beneficent mankind. By insisting that 'everything is for the best in this best of all possible worlds', his Dr Pangloss, who is the embodiment of Leibniz's consoling doctrine, highlights the contradiction between the existence of a merciful God and the suffering of man, and the ridiculousness of a theory under which all present suffering becomes great harmony in the future. His conscience protests against the fact of suffering, especially of children: 'What crime have these children, crushed and bleeding to death at their mother's breast, committed, what is their guilt?'[1]

Ivan then tells Alyosha about a poem he has composed, entitled 'The Grand Inquisitor'. Basically it is a critique of Christianity. The contemporary socialist declares that it is beyond the power of man to fulfil the lofty moral demands of the New Testament and that when Christ demanded impossible heroism he had an exaggerated opinion of human nature, which is in reality weak and cowardly. First, the hungry ought to have been fed. 'Feed them, then ask for virtues!'

This criticism is supposedly being presented from the standpoint of nineteenth-century progressive philosophy, presented by Dostoevsky in the image of the Spanish Grand Inquisitor: the irreversibility of instincts is contrasted to the values of the 'spirit'; the harsh truth about the masses is contrasted to the dream about heroic individuals; the inflexible laws of 'bread to eat' are contrasted to inner freedom, and, finally, the blood-stained monstrousness of historical reality is contrasted to the 'ideal of Beauty'. The conversation touches on Roman Catholicism, the Inquisition, the Pope and Jesuits, who 'corrected Christ's work' and substituted for Christ's unachievable moral behests the attributes of real power: the sword of Caesar, the miracle, the mystery and authority. But the Vatican is here constantly identified with the newest social doctrines, which as long ago as the 1840s called for the reorganization of mankind on the basis of the correct distribution of material wealth.

A. V. Lunacharsky,* criticizing the theses Dostoevsky set forth in Ivan Karamazov's poem, repudiates the implicit assertion in it that 'socialists are akin to the Grand Inquisitor – both bring plenty and chains'. Marx's doctrine says that 'socialism creates the conditions for the maximum development of all the potentialities inherent in man'. 'Socialism', Lunacharsky wrote in his article 'The Russian Faust', 'is based on boundless confidence in the working-man, placed in normal conditions . . .' Since Dostoevsky did not believe in man or in his social instinct, he rejected the truly humane atheistic revolutionary ethic. Throughout Ivan Karamazov's poem one senses the anguish, the sincerity, achieved through suffering and the pain of the author, for whom it is agonizing to reject the liberating ideas of socialism in favour of 'Caesar's sword', that is, the authority of the autocratic government.

Dostoevsky chose sixteenth-century Seville as the setting for his legend. He draws a laconic, concise sketch of the ancient Catholic city. Only the previous evening a hundred heretics were burned in the city squares as the King and his charming ladies looked on. The elderly Inquisitor in his purple cardinal's robe was master of ceremonies at that 'magnificent *auto da fé*'. The portrait of the Inquisitor is superb, bringing to mind El Greco's ruthless-looking Spanish rulers: 'Tall and straight, with a parchment-like face, sunken eyes that still burned bright as a flame'; he has the bloodless lips of a nonagenerian. The portrait is not only a characterization and a biography of the subject, but also

* A. V. Lunarcharsky (1875–1933): Soviet Commissar of Education in the years immediately following the Revolution.

conveys the ideological atmosphere of an epoch of high-sounding principles and burning bonfires.

The finale of the legend is sustained in the spirit of romantic drama. At night the Cardinal, wearing the coarse robe of a monk and carrying a torch, descends into the dungeon to visit his prisoner. For an instant the beauty of the world – the hot darkness of Spain and, in the words of Pushkin's poem, the night 'fragrant with laurel and lemon' – is contrasted to the old man's decrepitude and blood-thirsty vengefulness. The High Priest makes an accusatory speech which is a monologue about the destinies of mankind. He discusses world problems. Dostoevsky's cherished theme about the suffering and happiness of mankind supersedes the story of the Karamazov family, becoming a solemn chorale, an oratorio, or a *Dies irae*, a Day of Judgement. And an obscure tavern in one of Russia's out-of-the-way provinces rings with a critique of the New Testament that is almost a historical tragedy in itself.

Ivan's monologue, which takes up three chapters in the novel, provides great scope for Dostoevsky's narrative style. At first the conversation between Ivan and Alyosha is merely the 'getting acquainted', the start of understanding between the younger Karamazovs, who have come together in Skotoprigonyevsk to settle a family quarrel. But the immense problems of religion and socialism unexpectedly break into the ugly story of one family with its quarrels about money and sexual rivalry. As a skilled orator, Ivan bases his theme on current political material and develops it in terms of the latest echoes from Russia's inner life. Under his penetrating gaze, military dispatches and law reports become a picture on a world scale of the hopeless suffering of innocent creatures: he is shocked by the fate of dying children. The two legendary characters in the poem rise above the newspaper chronicles that form the fabric of this latter-day tragedy, and their meeting completes the philosophical conversation of two Russian boys about the principles and purposes of the world edifice.

KARAMAZOV OR KARAKOZOV ?

Dostoevsky intended to write a vast epic of revolutionary Russia in two novels. He informed his readers:

> The principal novel is the second one. It will be about my hero already in our time, at this current moment (that is, on the borderline between the 1870s and 1880s). The first novel took place thirteen years ago and is hardly a real novel, but rather only one moment of my hero's early youth. I couldn't have done without the first novel because if I had, much in the second novel would not have been comprehensible.

The action of the first part of the intended two takes place in 1866 (this is confirmed by the fact that trial by jury, which Dmitry is given, was only introduced into Russia in April 1866). The two novels were to have comprised the history of one life, that of Alyosha Karamazov. Dostoevsky completed the first novel in November 1880 and planned to return to the story of his hero in 1882, after an interval of a year. But he did not live to carry out his plan.

However, we have information about the idea and the theme of the second, unwritten novel and can reconstruct some of its main story lines.

We know from Anna Grigoryevna that:

> Twenty years were to have elapsed since the last pages of the first volume. The action had moved into the 1880s. Alyosha was no longer a youth, but a mature man, who had already gone through a complicated emotional drama with Liza Khokhlakova. Dmitry was on his way back from penal servitude . . .

Another indication concerning the second novel comes from Suvorin, who wrote in his diary that Dostoevsky had told him on 20 February 1880:

that he would write a novel in which Alyosha Karamazov would be the hero. He wanted to take him through the monastery and make him a revolutionary. Alyosha would commit a political crime. He would be put to death. *He would have searched for the truth and in his quest would naturally have become a revolutionary.*

Brief as this note is, it is very significant. Dostoevsky planned to make Alyosha the principal hero of the Karamazov epic. Alyosha was apparently to have been the image of a martyr revolutionary. An impassioned seeker for truth, he had as a young boy gone through infatuation with religion and with the personality of Christ. But he had left the monastery to go out into the world and come to know its passions and sufferings. He has a stormy and agonizing romance with Liza Khokhlakova. Emotionally exhausted, he seeks to make life meaningful by doing useful work for his fellow men. He has a need to be active and to perform heroic exploits. In the social atmosphere of the late 1870s, this meant being a revolutionary. He becomes fascinated with the idea of regicide as a means of inciting a nationwide insurrection which would end all the country's troubles. The contemplative monk becomes a very active political figure. He participates in one of the attempts to assassinate Alexander II. He finally ascends the scaffold. The protagonist of this epic about contemporary Russia represents the tragedy of an entire epoch with its doomed younger generation.

The prototype for Alyosha was Dmitry Vladimirovich Karakozov. Karakozov, a student from an impoverished gentry family, had joined a socialist propaganda circle but soon found peaceful opposition fruitless. On 4 April 1866 he came to the Summer Garden at the time of the Tsar's afternoon promenade and mingled with the crowd waiting at the gates for the Tsar's departure. As Alexander set foot on the carriage step a shot rang out. The bullet missed. Karakozov, for it was he who had fired the shot, was captured on the spot.

We have the testimony of a contemporary about Dostoevsky's reaction to the attempted assassination. P. I. Weinberg, who was visiting Apollon Maikov on the same day, describes it:

> Fyodor Mikhailovich Dostoevsky came rushing into the room. He was frightfully pale, looked terribly upset and was trembling as if in a fever.
> 'Somebody has shot at the Tsar,' he cried, without even greeting us, his voice breaking with emotion.
> We all jumped up.
> 'Did they kill him?' Maikov cried out, in a voice that did not sound human.
> 'No, they missed. All is well. But somebody fired, somebody fired, somebody fired . . .'
> We waited until he had calmed down a bit, although Maikov was on the verge of fainting himself, then the three of us ran out into the street.

In his outline for a preface to *The Devils*, Dostoevsky mentions Karakozov ('even the wretched, misled suicide of 4 April believed in his own truth at the time', and so on). References such as this have led scholars to suppose that Dostoevsky made use of the Karakozov affair in *The Devils*, too, for in many respects that affair was a prelude to the Nechaev case. Uspensky and Pryzhov, leading Nechaevites, had close contacts with the Karakozov group, and the methods of N. A. Ishutin, the leader of the movement to which Karakozov belonged, anticipated the characteristic techniques of Nechaev.[2]

It was discovered that Karakozov belonged to a secret society in Moscow, whose aim was to overthrow the existing state system. Some of the members of that organization advocated the gradual reform of the government, while others called for immediate revolution to be incited by regicide. Karakozov was one of the latter. The society had formed a secret group, known by the name 'Hell', whose purpose was to carry out these extreme measures. One of its members was designated to commit regicide and instructed to carry on his person a capsule of poison and a proclamation explaining the reasons for and aims of the overthrow of the government. Karakozov was in sympathy with this design, and presently made an attempt to realize it.

On 31 August 1866 the Supreme Criminal Court sentenced Dmitry Karakozov, twenty-five years old, to deprivation of civil rights and death by hanging. The sentence was carried out on 3 September 1866 at 7 a.m. on Smolensk Field.

This was one of the central acts in the tragedy of the younger generation on the threshold of the 1870s and 1880s. Dostoevsky's greatness is revealed in his ability to rise above his own convictions, spiritual inclinations and political views and to portray, naked and irrefutable, the depth of suffering of the entire epoch. The wretched 'suicide of 4 April' was in Dostoevsky's mind as he finished his novel about the Nechaevites, appearing to him as the exponent of some unattainable but higher truth. Alyosha Karamazov was to develop into this kind of courageous martyr – the personification of his epoch at the time of its most fearsome struggle. That is why Dostoevsky gave him the only slightly altered surname of a real historical personality, Karakozov.

REALISM AND SYMBOLISM

To the very end Dostoevsky defined his literary technique as 'realism in the highest sense of the word'. Realism, to him, meant basing a literary work on true concrete facts of real life, but raising them to the level of broad philosophical inquiry. That is how *The Brothers Karamazov* is constructed. Speaking of 'Pro and Contra', one of the most important books of the novel, Dostoevsky emphasized that 'even in such an abstract theme as this I did not go against realism'. Throughout the whole length of the novel he nowhere lowered his exacting standards of ample and reliable documentation.

To get the chapters about schoolchildren right, Dostoevsky read pedagogical literature (Pestalozzi, Froebel, Leo Tolstoy's articles about schools). To impart the correct atmosphere to the Russian Monk's teachings he read theology and church history (St Nilus of Sora, St John of Damascus, St Isaac the Syrian, St Sergius of Radonezh, St Tikhon of Zadonsk). To convey the feeling of the current moment he made use of court records (the cases of Kroneberg, Zhesing, Brunst and others) and of various incidents from contemporary public life, which he had already developed extensively in his journalistic writings. Dostoevsky's personal impressions of a whole lifetime, from his very early recollections of his mother's illness and his father's murder to his latest emotions in connection with the death of his son and his journey to Optina Pustyn Monastery, wonderfully increase the power and heighten the reality of the narrative. Even Ivan Karamazov's arguments in his talk with Alyosha are rooted in current or in historical reality. As Dostoevsky wrote to his editor: 'Everything that my hero says in the text that I have sent you is based on reality. All the instances involving children have actually taken place and have been recorded in newspapers, and I can tell you where – I have not invented anything.' Nothing is invented, but the vision of a genius has re-interpreted, illumined and deeply humanized everything.

By combining all these techniques Dostoevsky has imparted to his last novel an undeniable sense of vitality in presentation. In it the voice of the age can be heard above the author's incorrect views, telling of boundless suffering and exposing ugly sores. In places the novel has the authentic thrill of a fresh newspaper page, and the passion of the author's tone conveys this poignant immediacy to subsequent generations. For Dostoevsky, however, his main aim is to pose philosophical and psychological problems that go

far outside the bounds of empirical data and, in their ultimate conclusions, touch upon the world of Utopia and
'fantasy'. Dostoevsky's boundless 'poetics' and 'emotional-
ism' reached their peak in *The Brothers Karamazov*.

The intense vitality of the characters does not detract
from their symbolism and universality. The protagonists
are embodiments of abstract vices and virtues. Lust is
personified by Fyodor Pavlovich Karamazov (as the first
critics of the novel noted), egoism (egocentricism, we should
say) by Ivan Karamazov, unbridledness by Dmitry, and
moral purity by Alyosha. 'They resemble allegorical
characters in a medieval mystery play. But a mighty talent
has breathed life into these allegories, a broad intellect has
given this mystery play deep significance.' It should be
pointed out that the novel's central theme, parricide, is a
symbol of regicide, a historical phenomenon that always
excited Dostoevsky.

In his last novel Dostoevsky continued to search for a
unique form of composition devoid of the customary
narrative clichés. Here, as opposed to *A Raw Youth*, he
returned to constructing a wide-ranging narrative round the
central crime-story, which organizes the whole action of the
novel. All the characters have clear-cut, sharp contours and
leave no doubt as to their reality. The female characters are
unforgettable, for example the magnificent Grushenka with
her all-conquering Russian beauty. The distinguishing
feature of *The Brothers Karamazov* is maximum tension in
composition and in drawing. Everything here is taken to the
limit, to extremity, with the utmost acuity of expression, 'in
fever and synthesis' to use the author's own words.

As in *A Raw Youth*, Dostoevsky makes no attempt at unity
of construction or strict economy in means of presentation,
but once again strives to express in the very form of his
narrative his own horrified vision of the complete disintegration, disruption and decomposition of the great whole
that he so piously revered. Into his new myth about a

leprous but curable Russia he puts the entire fierce struggle of the political trends of the day, and he presents a revealing picture of the convulsive divisiveness and pathological disharmony of all the everyday components of that struggle. Dostoevsky required precisely this kind of complex deformation of the whole, the destratification and distortion of traditional beauty, the unnatural intersection of planes and the disorienting contrasts of the elements, in order to contrast the chaos of the present to his dream of a Golden Age and universal happiness.

The Brothers Karamazov is a mighty consummation of the work of a titanic master. It brings new life to Dostoevsky's favourite types and elucidates all aspects of his principal ideas. Governing the crowd of central figures, so closely related to one another yet so different, is their creator's concept of irreconcilable struggle between philistines and tragic heroes. Among the latter Dostoevsky includes obscure people, who possess the great gifts of love, compassion and self-sacrifice. It is this concept that determines which side his main characters take in the battle for life that he portrays. Dostoevsky condemns philistine actions and spirit in a whole series of portraits of negative types – from Bykov, Opiskin and Luzhin to Fyodor Karamazov, Rakitin and Smerdyakov. He strives to show how life's highest values, which the poets rescue and the 'meek' cherish, crumble before the onslaught of these dark forces.

Dostoevsky's true heroes are the creators of new ideas and the bearers of human warmth. Like everything beautiful, they are doomed to destruction in a world ruled by cruel lusts and criminal passions. Immolation is the lot of the fearless heralds of new ideas; and supreme moral beauty spells death to those who have detached themselves from the jungle law. It is these proud protesters and defeated martyrs whom Dostoevsky holds most dear and with whom he feels the closest kinship. It is they who convey the poignancy and poetry of his work. For, despite the backwardness of Dostoevsky's political programme, his early interest in Fourierism imbued his concepts with a lofty humanism and a desire for a better future, and the genius of his creativity with its unswerving artistic truth invariably triumphed over the biassed slogans of his journalistic polemics. These are the few 'bright' inhabitants of the monstrous city. They constitute 'a world of prophets among strongboxes',[3] to use the expression of a Dostoevsky scholar. They are the thinkers who have rejected contemporary reality, and the martyrs who have been trampled under its heels.

Hence the structural complexity of Dostoevsky's last novel. The abundance of themes and material divides the family chronicle into 'books', some of which can stand alone, with lengthy extraneous fragments interpolated. At times Dmitry's passionate romance, Ivan's intellectual tragedy and Aloysha's early quests are excessively complicated by Dostoevsky's political views. Not everywhere do the theory and the drama blend smoothly; sometimes they obviously clash. It is not however the ideologue of Pobedonostsev's Russia, or the preacher of theocracy, who triumphs, but the great master of the philosophical novel.

From the standpoint of Dostoevsky's own structural principles, *The Brothers Karamazov* is the completion of his development as a literary artist. It is the full synthesis of his creative experience and the expansion of a novel-poem into a novel-epic. Death prevented him from carrying his concept through, but in many respects he had already achieved his stated purposes. By an extraordinary surge of intellectual power and will, Dostoevsky created towards the end of his life a monumental novel resembling a choral tragedy, a multi-voiced yet harmonious epilogue to all his turbulent work.

XXI

Dostoevsky's Epilogue

THE PUSHKIN MEMORIAL

THE major literary and public event of 1880 was the unveiling of a monument to Pushkin in Moscow in June. Dostoevsky, who had always considered Pushkin to have expressed Russian national awareness more fully than anyone else, was interested in the forthcoming celebrations. Several months beforehand he had suggested that there ought to be a serious article about the poet in the Press. In fact, he wrote in a letter to a friend, he 'would love to make a short speech about him' in Moscow. This reached S. A. Yuryev, chairman of the Society of Lovers of Russian Literature and editor of *Russkaya Mysl* (*Russian Thought*), who wrote to Dostoevsky on 5 April 1880, inviting him to speak at the memorial meeting in Moscow and offering to print his speech as an article in his magazine. On 5 May 1880 Dostoevsky replied to Yuryev, accepting the invitation and saying that he would arrive in Moscow on 25 May.

Dostoevsky attached special importance to this speech 'in memory of the greatest of our poets and a great Russian'. He decided to go to Staraya Russa, where he could work on the speech in quiet and seclusion, far away from the distractions of Petersburg. The rough drafts of it have been preserved and the abundance of variations, added fragments and changes testify to the enormous amount of work he put into it. In that one concentrated and forceful speech Dostoevsky presented the essence of his doctrine on the role of artistic genius in the future of mankind. He compressed all the themes of world history, which had engaged his mind in the course of decades of travel and work, within the framework of a memorial tribute to the poet he loved above all others. The Pushkin celebrations were conducted in an atmosphere of high enthusiasm. In the words of the austere lines addressed to the poet's statue by the absent Fet:

> Your prophecy has come true,
> Our old shame has looked upon your bronze countenance.

A new generation in all its diversity of opinions and associations gathered before this 'bronze countenance', hoping to find in it solutions to all their pressing problems and doubts. Huge crowds attended the unveiling, which took place in Strastnaya Square at noon on 6 June. The statue of Russia's immortal poet stood on the square amidst the fresh green leaves of the boulevard. The poet seemed to be walking slowly forward, absorbed in thought, his head bent slightly, as if greeting the crowd and offering it the gift of his undying verse. As orchestras struck up, people formed lines and began to move past the bronze figure, laying wreaths at its feet. This moment marked the beginning of a spontaneous outburst of general enthusiasm, which continued undiminished through the three days of ceremonies.

After the unveiling the delegations proceeded to the official ceremony at Moscow University, where they heard tributes to Pushkin delivered by the Rector of the University Tikhonravov, the historian Klyuchevsky, and the Shakespearian scholar Storozhenko. At the municipal banquet in the Hall of the Assembly of the Gentry (now the House of Trade Unions) that afternoon N. N. Katkov, a leader of the extreme right wing, made a speech calling for the reconciliation of all warring social groups 'under the Pushkin monument'. Nobody joined him when he raised his goblet and Turgenev deliberately covered his glass with his hand. This incident received a great deal of attention in the Press. *Golos* wrote: 'It is painful to watch a man hoping to atone for twenty years of treachery by making a speech at a

banquet and being castigated.' In the evening Dostoevsky
made his first appearance; at a literary concert, where he
read the Chudov Monastery scene from Boris Godunov.
Pimen, the chronicler, was one of his favourite characters.

The next day, 7 June, Turgenev read a subtle paper
on 'A Magnificent Russian Artist' to the first public meeting
of the Society of Lovers of Russian Literature, but he
expressed some scepticism in it concerning the magnitude
of Pushkin's contribution: 'We hesitate to bestow on Pushkin
the title of a national and a world poet, though we dare not
deny him that title either.' At the second literary dinner the
same day Dostoevsky made a short speech on Pushkin.

The day after that, 8 June, Dostoevsky was the first
speaker, and his speech created a sensation. For his cherished
idea, the idea he had propounded as editor of *Vremya* – that
the intelligentsia must merge with the masses of the people,
that the 'historical suffering Russian' was to be healed by
the Justice of the People, and his thesis that the advent of
universal, worldwide happiness was necessary to the peace
of mind of the restless suffering Russian, were in keeping
with the audience's mood. 'Everybody was amazed and
captivated by the harmoniously expressed idea of the
Russian's inborn compassion for other people's troubles,'
Gleb Uspensky wrote in an article entitled 'The Pushkin
Celebrations'.

Dostoevsky appealed for self-restraint on the part of
proud individualists like Pushkin's Aleko and his own Raskolnikov. 'Humble yourself, *proud man*,[1] and above all *humble
your pride*. Humble yourself, idle man, and above all *toil in
your country's fields*.' This was not an appeal for silent submission; it was an appeal for self-education and work. However,
among Russia's uprooted wanderers, divorced from the
people and devoid of faith in the ideals of their native land,
whom he condemned, Dostoevsky also included the exponents of revolution and socialism. He considered socialism
and revolution sterile and destructive and declared that the

only escape from socialism lay in religious unity, in 'fraternal harmony of all tribes under Christ's evangelical law'. In Dostoevsky's view Pushkin was the first to portray, in his Aleko, 'that unhappy wanderer in his native land', who appeared in the early 1820s, even before socialism, 'among our educated community; he had rebellious tendencies in the spirit of Jean-Jacques Rousseau and was divorced from the people.' From this arose the subsequent movement of the Russian revolutionary intelligentsia, who, in Dostoevsky's opinion, had reached a dead end and whose only way out was in 'humble association with the common people'.

The very first press notices of Dostoevsky's speech objected to these views. Democratically minded critics pointed out that Dostoevsky's ideas were out of touch with current Russian life and that his declared principle of 'universal humanity' was an abstraction: the doctrine of moral self-improvement that he expounded in his speech completely ignored the political causes of 'wandering' in Russia. But the central idea of the great novelist's speech had been that Pushkin had early found his ideals in his own native land and had pointed out the way of salvation for all through fellowship with the people, together with the recognition of the universal ideas and eternal images of world literature, and that thereby he had kindled a new guiding light over the course of Russian history and had prophesied its future developments. This, together with the picture of a coming universal harmony, had roused the enthusiasm of the whole huge audience in the Hall of Columns. People felt themselves transformed by the genius of a thinker and an artist.

The extraordinary impact of Dostoevsky's speech was due in part to the speaker's eloquence. Dostoevsky had always been interested in rhetorical skills and had a superb command of all the techniques and rules of public speaking.

He loved to portray skilled public speakers in his novels. Strakhov wrote of that speech: 'Though he read from a written text, it was not reading at all, but living speech, direct, sincere, from the soul. The audience listened as if no one had ever said anything about Pushkin before.'

Dostoevsky highly appreciated a simple, almost intimate, conversational style in oratory. In his last novel he wrote of the famous orator whom he depicted: 'He began very directly, simply and convincingly, without a trace of arrogance, without any attempt at eloquence, at emotional intonations, at resounding words. This was a man talking with an intimate circle of like-minded people.' Dostoevsky began his speech in the packed hall of the Assembly of the Gentry in precisely this manner. He proceeded like a subtle and experienced orator, keeping his field of view inside a narrow, contemporary angle, and flung at his listeners impassioned words that expressed their own most troubling thoughts. He showed them Pushkin's greatness by demonstrating that they, the younger generation, had a spiritual kinship with the poet's prophetic concepts.

'The moment Dostoevsky finished,' Uspensky continues, 'the audience gave him – an ovation is not the word – they went into ecstasies of idolization. One young man was so overcome by emotion as he shook the writer's hand that he fell to the platform in a faint.' Ivan Aksakov, who was the next speaker, declined to speak, remarking: 'I consider Fyodor Mikhailovich Dostoevsky's speech an event in our literature. Yesterday it was still possible to argue about whether Pushkin is great, whether he has world significance. Today this question no longer exists. The true significance of Pushkin has been demonstrated.'

Admiring listeners crowned the victor in this difficult literary contest with a laurel wreath. Dostoevsky was elected an honorary member of the Society of Lovers of Russian Literature. The Mayor, S. M. Tretyakov, conveyed

Moscow's gratitude to him. At the concluding programme that evening Dostoevsky recited Pushkin's 'The Prophet' with awe-inspiring elation, Strahkov recalls. He began melodiously and solemnly and ended with an inspired cry:

'*And burn men's hearts with the word!*'

This was, in effect, the finale of the Pushkin celebrations. That same night Dostoevsky laid the laurel wreath that had been presented to him at the feet of his teacher's statue. Anna Grigoryevna relates what her husband told her:

It was a warm night, but there were very few people in the street. Fyodor Mikhailovich drove to Strastnaya Square, lifted the huge laurel wreath that had been presented to him at the meeting after his speech in the morning, laid it at the foot of the statue of his great teacher, and bowed to the ground before it.

What is the main significance of this famous speech, and wherein is the secret of its unprecedented success?

In his Pushkin memorial speech Dostoevsky expressed with great forcefulness his deep, lifelong yearning for a worldwide alliance of all men, which, he believed, it was Russia's mission to bring about. Hence the special attention he gave to those of Pushkin's works which 'shone with world ideas'; hence his profound admiration for Pushkin's sensitivity to the rest of the world, 'this most important national capacity of ours'. He presented his points in characteristically picturesque language. His tribute to Pushkin remains one of the most important events in Pushkin studies because it was composed and delivered by a great poet. It was not a scholarly report, a public lecture, or a critical study. In emotion, expressiveness and dramatic power it was a genuine ode in prose, and everyone who heard it was deeply moved. Dostoevsky knew how to give a festal character to a mighty dithyramb, full of light, illuminating with a blinding flash the immortal countenance of the author of the 'Bacchic Song'.

ILLNESS AND DEATH

Dostoevsky had written from Ems in August 1879: 'I lie here and think constantly that of course, I will die soon, in a year or two, perhaps, and what will become of my three little golden heads after I am gone.' At the end of 1879 a Dr M. N. Snitkin, a relative of Anna Grigoryevna, at her request examined Dostoevsky and, though he reassured the patient, he told Anna that her husband's illness had made ominous advances and in his present condition emphysema could be a danger to his life. The tiny blood vessels of the lungs had become so brittle that the slightest physical effort or emotional excitement might cause them to burst. All strain must be avoided.

In 1880 Dostoevsky had reached the goal of his life. He had won triumphant recognition, unprecedented influence and nationwide fame. The year of *The Brothers Karamazov* and of his Pushkin speech gained him a reputation as one of Russia's greatest thinkers and creative writers. The aim of his life, as once expressed in a letter to Maikov from Florence in 1868: 'to write . . . and though I die, I will have my say', had been achieved, in the main. He still had a multitude of plans, and what he said of his beloved poet on 8 June 1880 may be applied to him: 'Pushkin died at the height of his powers and undoubtedly carried away some great secret to the grave with him. And now we are trying to guess that secret without him.' Dostoevsky, too, carried with him to the grave the secret of a grandiosely conceived second novel about the Karamazovs. He died less than three months after he had completed the first volume.

*

In that short period Dostoevsky produced his last work, the first issue of *The Diary of a Writer* for 1881. He worked on it in the second half of January.

The times were tense and critical. The government had been compelled to make serious concessions. Alexander II had approved his Prime Minister Loris-Melikov's draft plan for the participation of representatives of the *zemstvos** and the cities in the government.

Dostoevsky, who was an unwavering supporter of the autocracy and opposed to the granting of a Constitution, was in complete agreement with the plan, for he favoured patriarchal forms of conferring with the 'Russian Land'. He wrote of this in the last issue of *The Diary of a Writer*: 'Summon the grey homespun coats and ask them about their needs and they will tell you the truth.' This was not, however, a concession to liberalism; in the same issue of *The Diary*, he wrote with his usual dislike of the 'European Russians', who dream about 'crowning the edifice', their 'endless talking-shops' and so on. In this article, on which he worked a few days before his death he wrote that the Tsar was linked to the people, 'as a father is linked to his children', and reiterated emphatically his belief that freedom would come to Russia differently, not as it did in the West; that it would come 'without revolutions, restrictions, treaties'. Sympathy with the new line of the government was not the slightest evidence of any 'internal political shift' in Dostoevsky. He continued to defend the power of the autocracy and the Russian Orthodox Church.

Nevertheless, Dostoevsky's progressive new ideas about Young Russia forming an indivisible alliance with the masses of the peasantry, obscured though they were by the establishment dogmas he had adopted, came through in his work:

Our radiant, fresh youth will, I think, immediately and primarily, give their hearts to the common people and will, for the first time, understand them spiritually. That is why I place my hopes so much and above all in the youth, for they, too, are afflicted with 'truth-seeking,' a longing for the truth, and

* *Zemstvos*. See p. 308

therefore they are the closest to the common people and will understand that the people are looking for the truth.

Dostoevsky believed that 'complete freedom is possible in our country'. In the last period of his life the great novelist was fond of reading Ogaryov's poems aloud, reciting them with enthusiasm and hope:

> I told my fortune by the Bible
> And I wept bitterly and sighed
> Hoping that fate would give me
> Life and grief and the death of a prophet.

To have given to his people, in his declining years, the chronicle of the Karamazovs and the Pushkin speech was indeed to have achieved the calling of an artist-thinker. In that sense the epilogue to the life of Dostoevsky seems to correspond to the best of his famous pages.

Dostoevsky's end was darkened by the evil passions of the heartless 'war of all against all'. The Kumanin inheritance, which had been causing family quarrels and mutual recriminations for several years, struck its last blow at him in January 1881, a fatal blow, as it turned out. Under his deceased aunt's will, Dostoevsky was at this time to receive a share of her Ryazan estate amounting to 1,200 acres on the condition that he pay his sisters, who did not share their aunt's landed property, compensation. This led to the sad denouement.

Dostoevsky's favourite sister Vera Tanova came from Moscow to ask him to let his sisters have the land instead of money, that is, to surrender his share of the Ryazan estate to them. The novelist's daughter relates that her father and her aunt discussed the matter at dinner on 26 January. They became excited as they talked. Dostoevsky got up from the table and went to his study. There he had a haemorrhage from the throat, but it did not last long. He tried to calm his family, and showed the children humorous pictures and verses from a subscription form for the magazine *Oskolki*

(*Splinters*). Towards evening the family doctor arrived. While he was being examined Dostoevsky had another haemorrhage and fainted. When he regained consciousness, he took leave of his family and, after sending away the children, thanked his wife for the happiness she had given him.

He had a quiet night and he had no haemorrhages the next day. The family felt easier. Dostoevsky talked to the children, and read the proofs for *The Diary of a Writer*, which was to appear on 31 January. He was worried about the censorship, spoke to the printer's make-up man and was told that the issue had been passed. Altogether, he was in an excited mood: 'One moment he was expecting to die quickly and soon, giving instructions, worrying about the family's future,' Suvorin wrote. 'The next, he was living, thinking, dreaming of future words, talking about how his children would grow up and how he would bring them up.' A specialist called and, finding the patient considerably improved, said that he would recover.

At seven o'clock the next morning, 28 January, Anna Grigoryevna awoke to find her husband staring at her.

'How do you feel, my dear?' she asked, bending over him.

'You know, Anya,' he whispered, 'I have been awake for the last three hours, thinking all the time, and I have just realized clearly that I am going to die today.'

'But, my dear, why do you say that? You feel better now. You haven't had any more haemorrhages. A "plug" has apparently formed, as Dr Koshlakov said. For God's sake, do not torment yourself so. You will live, I assure you!'

'No, I know that I am going to die today.'

He opened the Bible that the Decembrist wives had given him in Tobolsk.

'You see, it says "Do not restrain." That means that I am going to die.'

Anna Grigoryevna was weeping. He thanked her again, tried to console her, and told her to take care of the children.

'Remember, Anya, I have always loved you ardently and have never been unfaithful to you, not even in my thoughts!'

At eleven o'clock blood gushed from his throat. He became very, very weak. He summoned the children, took their hands and asked his wife to read the Parable of the Prodigal Son. This was the last story Dostoevsky heard. At seven o'clock in the evening he had another haemorrhage and lost consciousness. At thirty-eight minutes past eight he died.

The room was filled with friends and acquaintances, who had come in accordance with tradition to be present at the death of a loved one. Against the dark background of the couch, beneath a photograph of the Sistine Madonna, they watched freeze into motionlessness 'that face, exhausted by thought, as if burnt through from within by a passionate flame'.

Dostoevsky had expressed a desire to be buried next to Nekrasov, whom he considered his literary godfather. This wish was not carried out. He was buried two days later in the cemetery of the Alexander Nevsky Monastery near the grave of another poet whom he loved, Zhukovsky. Apollon Maikov, Grigorovich, the actor Samoilov, Averkiev, Orest Miller, professors, students and countless unknown readers o his immortal books were there. Some of his oldest friends, including the Petrashevskyite Palm, spoke beside the open grave. In his address to the huge crowd that had filled the cemetery, Vladimir Solovyov said that Dostoevsky was a literary genius who had striven to depict not only the everyday life of society but to portray a social movement as it advanced towards lofty moral ideals. Hence his condemnation of proud individualists with their 'self-deification' and his passionate demand that individuals who had separated themselves from the people return to the people.

CONCLUSION

Dostoevsky was fond of saying to young seekers: 'Elevate yourself in spirit and *formulate your ideal.*' These words express the aim of his whole life. He passed through various stages in his quest for a guiding truth – romanticism, Utopian socialism, Christianity (specifically, Russian Orthodoxy), the 'soil' and Slavophilism, the 'Golden Age' and the struggle against 'dying' Europe, and, finally, theocracy, that is to say, a State-Church. He considered himself weak in philosophy, 'but not in love of it, in love of it I am strong,' he said. And he surely proved this by the way he so richly developed his own world outlook, embracing so many theories, systems, doctrines and hypotheses.

Not everything here was coherent, and integrated. Many of his intellectual enthusiasms were transitory, superficial and accidental, though always sincere and impassioned. But he had one dogma of faith that never changed: the *Russian people* in all their historical magnitude and in the tragedy of the current struggle constituted his true ideal and the wellspring of his creativity.

Dostoevsky had studied Russian history extensively. He had never forgotten the peasant Marei and his family's obscure little village. He had lived for many years among the common people in prison and army barracks, and by the early 1860s he had evolved his most cherished idea: *that supreme value lies in the spiritual, poetic and philosophical culture of the staunch and gifted Russian people, whom destiny has entrusted with the greatest of historical missions.*

'We believe that the Russian nation is an extraordinary phenomenon in the history of mankind,' Dostoevsky wrote in his introduction to his review of the major phenomena in the Russian literature that he loved so eagerly and so deeply. Hence his cult of Russian art in all its forms, from Avvakum to Leo Tolstoy, from Andrei Rublev to Repin and Kramskoi, from street songs and laments to Glinka and Serov, from the Kremlin cathedrals to the eighteenth-century Moscow belfries. All this revealed to him that, deep down, his most precious meditations took their source from 'the mighty ocean that is the land of Russia, an unencompassable and very deep ocean' – a nation great in spiritual questings and creative achievements.

The artist-writer had a special craftsman's esteem for one of the greatest creations of his nation – the sonorous and powerful Russian language, which he had received direct from the lips of country women, wet-nurses from the districts round Moscow with their songs and tales. Here was the first source of his mighty speech, unrecognized by his contemporaries and only properly appreciated in our own time. It was from the very depths of popular speech that this incomparably expressive and forceful literary prose had arisen, the prose of a novelist with an ear for music and verse, who collected from everywhere, but especially from the tradition of song, the Russian folklore that had been lost and forgotten among the masses. Much later, speaking of his ardent love of his native language, he recalled the deep roots of his literary style in the laconic and meaningful aphorism: '*The language is the people.*'

Yet he did not confine himself to his own country or separate himself from other nations. Undeniably, Europe had a strong impact on him. From his youthful love of Shakespeare and Schiller, Balzac and Hugo to his later interest in Flaubert and Émile Zola (whom he simultaneously rejected and accepted), he had a superb knowledge of all the leading figures of European literature. The Italian Renaissance masters in the museums of the West made a tremendous impression on him, and Hans Holbein the Younger and Claude Lorrain inspired some great pages about art in *The Idiot* and *A Raw Youth*. He was struck by the Gothic architecture in Milan, Cologne and Paris. He delighted in Beethoven. Such was the effect of this world of art upon

Dostoevsky throughout his life, such was the inspiration that he drew from the 'land of holy miracles' to which he paid such glowing tribute in his last novel through the lips of Ivan Karamazov. Dostoevsky valued above all in the West, as he did in Russian culture, the world of embodied and spiritualized beauty, which he repeatedly declared to be the basis of all human life and activity: 'Science itself would not last a single minute without beauty.'

Only once in his life did Dostoevsky, master of the social novel, come close to revolution. That was at the beginning of 1849. Prior to that he had feared struggle, and after that he repudiated 'theories and Utopias' for all time. But still he did not repudiate humanism. The great artist's wise and sensitive heart raised him above his own political diatribes against the nihilists. He pities those courageous young men and women who had doomed themselves to death. In *The Devils*, as we have seen, he expressed his compassion for that self-sacrificing generation: 'I solemnly declare that the spirit of life is in the air as before and that living force has not dried up in the younger generation. The enthusiasm of present-day youth is as pure and radiant as it was in our time. The only thing is that there has been a redistribution of objectives, a substitution of one beauty for another.' Thus Dostoevsky unexpectedly admitted that the revolution was a new kind of beauty for Russian youth. Prince Myshkin, his favourite hero, has a fine expression for these Argonauts on a quest for freedom; he calls them 'thirsting and enflamed companions of Columbus', inspired and valiant discoverers of a new world.

To sum up, Dostoevsky's literary path was complex and contradictory. Reactionary views sometimes find graphic expression in his novels, but in the majority of instances they are overpowered by his deep compassion for suffering mankind. His exceptional talents helped him to overcome many questionable tendencies in his philosophical and political thought. His wonderful artistry enabled him to create immortal characters, and the oppressed victims of the regime which he defended at the end of his life hold an important place among them: Siberian convicts, poor students, undernourished and drunken civil servants, girls forced to become prostitutes; all of them hounded down and rejected by the pitiless course of development of the capitalist state. His unforgettable characters and poignant dramas, imbued with social protest, have rightly taken their place among the classics of world literature. Hereby he retains his importance even in our own day. Like Shakespeare, Voltaire, Goethe and Balzac, he surmounted the Utopianism, conservatism and metaphysics of his thinking by the power of his genius, which discarded what was erroneous and sailed full speed ahead towards the ideas of justice, freedom and humanity.

Notes

Chapter I: At the Hospital for the Poor

1. Archives of South-Western Russia, part VI, vol. 1, supplements 71, 73, 74; S. Lyubimov, 'F. M. Dostoevsky (His Origins)', *Literaturnaya Mysl*, no. 1, 1923, pp. 203–10.

2. In an entry for 1876 in *The Diary of a Writer*, Dostoevsky mentioned George Sand's *Venetian Stories* as the source of his early interest in Italy. It was, however in the 1840s, when he was living in Petersburg, that he began to show interest in the works of that French novelist and translated her 'The Last Aldini'. Actually, his early attraction to things Italian stemmed from the novels of Ann Radcliffe: 'How many times since my childhood have I dreamed of visiting Italy!' he wrote to Yakov Polonsky on 31 July 1861. 'Radcliffe's novels, which I began to read at the age of eight, had filled my head with all sorts of Alfonsos, Catarinas and Lucias. Then came Shakespeare – Verona, Romeo and Juliet. The fascination of it all, d–n it. To Italy! But instead, I found myself in Semipalatinsk and, prior to that, in the House of the Dead' (*Letters*, vol. 1, p. 302).

Chapter II: The Engineering Academy

1. V. S. Nechaeva, 'Poezdka v Darovoe' ('A Trip to Darovoe'), *Novy Mir*, 1926, no. 3, pp. 131–2.

2. D. Stonov, 'Seltso Darovoe' ('The Village of Darovoe'), *Krasnaya Niva*, 1926, no. 16, pp. 18–19.

3. V. S. Nechaeva, *V semye i usadbe Dostoevskogo* (*In the Dostoevsky Family and on Their Estate*), Moscow, 1939, p. 59.

4. loc. cit.

5. Heroine of Walter Scott's *St Ronan's Well*.

Chapter III: The Belinsky Whirlwind

1. Here and farther on I have quoted from N. A. Nekrasov's Kamennoe Serdtse ('The Stone Heart'), in which the poet gave a detailed

account of his personal impressions of Belinsky's first meeting with Dostoevsky. Nekrasov's unfinished story was discovered in his archives by Kornei Chukovsky and first published in 1919 (*Niva*, nos. 34–7) For the sake of clarity I have substituted the real names for the invented names and the invented title.

2. I heard this from Dostoevsky's second wife Anna Grigoryevna in the spring of 1917 in Sestroretsk. It was set down at the time and was first published in my *Put Dostoevskogo* (*Dostoevsky's Path*), Leningrad, 1924.

3. See my *Biblioteka Dostoevskogo* (*Dostoevsky's Library*), Odessa, 1919, p. 70. A comparison with Lermontov's unfinished novel is also to be found there.

4. Vs. Solovyov, *Vospominaniya Dostoevskogo* (*Reminiscences about F. M. Dostoevsky*), Petersburg, 1881.

5. Herzen, Panaev and Kavelin, in their recollections of Belinsky, tell of several instances when he spoke in favour of terrorism and the 'holy mother guillotine'.

6. K. Marx, 'Towards a Critique of the Hegelian Philosophy of Law', *Works of Marx and Engels*, 1955, vol. I, p. 415. Belinsky's library contained an edition of the German-French Yearbook that carried this article.

7. In 1878 Dostoevsky told Professor Orest Miller of his arguments with Belinsky about Christianity. 'About three years before Fyodor Mikhailovich died he spoke of this with an indignation that had not faded over the years, and then I understood the reason for *his extreme dislike of Belinsky*, which had hitherto seemed strange to me.' This evidence refutes the many conjectures that in the late 1870s the author of *The Brothers Karamazov* had reconciled himself to the memory of the democratic critic.

8. 'Wad': the soft plug used to retain powder charges.

9. Probably the daughter of L. G. Senyavin, Director of the Asiatic Section and, from 1850, assistant Minister of Foreign Affairs.

Chapter V: The Petrashevsky Circle

1. The year is not correct. Speshnev returned from Europe in 1846 and began to attend Petrashevsky's gatherings in 1847.

2. This was Anna Felixovna Savelieva, *née* Ciechanowecka, the wife of a friend. She died in Vienna in 1844.

3. *Pisma M. A. Bakunina k A. I. Gertsenu i N. P. Ogaryovu* (*M. A. Bakunin's Letters to A. I. Herzen and N. P. Ogaryov*), pp. 46–7.

4. Dostoevsky's italics.

5. Apollon Maikov described this more vividly in a letter to Professor P. A. Viskovatov: 'And I can still remember Dostoevsky sitting in front of his friends like a dying Socrates, in a nightshirt with an unbuttoned collar, exercising all his eloquence to prove the sacredness of that cause and our duty to save the fatherland.'

6. *Istorichesky Arkhiv* (*Historical Archives*), 1956, vol. 3, pp. 224-5.

7. I am referring to the story as it was originally printed in *Otechestvennie Zapiski*, 1849, vols. 62 and 64. A new edition appeared in 1860 with considerable deletions and it served as the basis of the final text.

8. Emile Signole, a French nineteenth-century painter, known chiefly for his paintings on historical themes.

9. 'Let he who is without sin among you be the first to cast a stone at her' (Gospel of St John, viii.7).

10. The verse was read in French. A Russian translation was made later by V. A. Kurochkin.

11. P. M. Kovalevsky, *Vstrechi na zhiznennom puti* (*Encounters on the Road of Life*): *Mikhail Ivanovich Glinka*, Leningrad, 1928.

12. Commandant of the Peter and Paul Fortress.

Chapter VI: The Court Martial

1. They stood in the line behind Dostoevsky. In Siberia, Dostoevsky told his friends that he had had no inkling of the forthcoming reprieve and was fully prepared for death: 'All my life passed through my mind as in a kaleidoscope, quick as lightning and like a picture.'

Chapter VII: The Exiled Convict

1. 'KAT' ('*katorzhny*' – 'convict') was engraved on the convicts' forehead and cheeks in bloody letters with a stamp made of steel needles. Then gunpowder or a special chemical dye was rubbed into the letters to make them indelible. Only members of the privileged classes and women were exempt from this tattoo.

2. M. N. Gernet, *Istoriya tsarstkoi tyurmy* (*The History of the Tsarist Prisons*), Moscow, 1946, vol. 2.

3. Towards the end of his life Dostoevsky saw *Petroushka* at a children's party and said it was an 'immortal folk comedy', 'very jolly, artistic and surprising'. Pulchinella, is a sort of Don Quixote or Don Juan, Dostoevsky explained, whereas Petroushka is a completely Russianized Sancho Panza or Leporello. It is a folk character. 'I always thought that Petroushka could be presented on the stage of our Alexandrinsky Theatre; the public would break down the doors to get into the theatre.'

Rough draft for *The Diary of a Writer* in 1876, *Russian Writers On Literary Work*, vol. 3, pp. 160–61.

Chapter VIII: *The Battalion of the Line*

1. A. E. Wrangel, *Vospominaniya o F. M. Dostoevskom v Sibiri, 1854–6* (*Reminiscences of F. M. Dostoevsky in Siberia*), Petersburg, 1912, pp. 36–7.

2. See the collection of articles 'Pyotr Petrovich Semyonov Tyan-Shansky', edited by A. A. Dostoevsky Leningrad, 1928. Wrangel was something of a scholar, too. A jurist by profession, he had studied archaeology, and took part in scientific expeditions in Central Asia, Eastern Siberia and China. He was planning to translate, besides Dostoevsky, Hegel and also *Psychia*, by Carus, a popular zoologist and physician, interested in natural philosophy.

3. In 1841 Adolf Totleben had shared an apartment with Dostoevsky on Karavannaya Street near the Manège, and his elder brother Eduard, who later became the hero of Plevna and defender of Sevastopol, often came to see him there.

4. Dostoevsky's second wife Anna Grigoryevna Dostoevskaya told me personally several additional details about his first marriage: 'Fyodor Mikhailovich loved his first wife very deeply. This was the first love of his life. His youth had passed entirely in literary work. Under the influence of his first sensational success he became absorbed in his work as a writer and had no time for any real romance. His infatuation with Panaeva was too transitory to count. But with Maria Dmitrievna it was different. This was truly a strong passion with all the accompanying joys and agonies. In the last years the aggravation of her illness made their relationship even more agonizing. From Maria Dmitrievna's physicians I learned that towards the end of her life she was not entirely well mentally.'

5. All these articles were available to Dostoevsky in Semipalatinsk, where he read all the important Petersburg magazines.

6. Dostoevsky wrote in 1861 in his magazine *Vremya*: 'In our second issue we are turning to one of the most pertinent questions of our literature, the question of *the significance of art and of its true relation to real life*.' These words, which Dostoevsky himself underlined, reproduced the title of Chernyshevsky's dissertation with barbed parody: 'its true relation'. This was a challenge and a declaration of war against Chernyshevsky's aesthetics.

7. Dostoevsky's aesthetic views rested mainly on an idealistic philosophy of beauty derived from Kant, Schiller and Hegel. See Chapter III above, 'Dialogue on Art', pp. 86–7.

8. Dostoevsky's letter to a student named Fyodorov about this in 1873 is noteworthy: 'I had not re-read 'My Uncle's Dream' for fifteen years. Having re-read it now, I find it poor. I wrote it in Siberia, the first thing after my time in prison; my only reason for writing it was to re-enter literature, and I was terribly afraid of the censorship (its attitude to a former exile) and therefore I involuntarily wrote a story of dove-like goodness and wonderful innocence.'

Chapter IX: The Magazine Vremya

1. See my article on 'Dostoevsky and the Chartist Novel', *Voprosy Literatury*, 1959, no. 4.

2. Dostoevsky's italics.

3. On this question Dostoevsky adhered to different positions at different periods. In the early 1860s he correctly defined 'artistry': 'as complete as possible *harmony* of the artistic idea with the form in which it is embodied' (*G—bov i vopros isskustva* [*G—bov and the Question of Art*]).

4. B. F. Egorov, 'Apollon Grigoryev – Critic', *Uchonie Zapiski Tartuskogo Gosudarstvennogo Universiteta (Academic Notes of Tartu State University)*, 1960, no. 98, pp. 205–6.

5. Vera Vasilievna Michurina-Samoilova (1824–80): a dramatic actress who played in Griboedov, Turgenev, Molière and Shakespeare. She left the stage in 1853 after her marriage to an army officer.

6. Dostoevsky gives some information about his break with Strakhov in a letter to his wife Anna, dated 12 February 1875. After *A Raw Youth* began to appear in Nekrasov's and Saltykov's *Otechestvennie Zapiski* Strakhov became 'very cold' to him. 'No, Anna, he is a nasty schoolboy, nothing else. He already abandoned me once in my life, when *Epokha* failed, and he came running back only after the success of *Crime and Punishment*.'

7. Anton Petrov: leader of a peasant uprising in the village of Bezdna, Kazan Province, who was captured by General Apraksin's troops and shot on 18 April 1861 by sentence of a court martial. Dostoevsky mentions his name in his manuscript notes for *The Devils*.

8. It is true that Chernyshevsky had nothing to do with 'Young Russia' and disapproved of it. He considered the challenge hurled against the old world by the authors of the proclamation premature and therefore harmful to the cause. He was opposed to the tactic of conspiracy, the principles of which had been developed by P. G. Zaichnevsky in the proclamation. Chernyshevsky did not conceive of a revolution without the decisive participation of the masses of the people.

9. N. G. Chernyshevsky, *Complete Works*, vol. 1, p. 777.

10. Valuev was close to literary circles. He was married to the daughter of P. A. Vyazemsky.

Chapter X: *Abroad and at Home*

1. It should be noted that Bakunin knew and thought well of Dostoevsky as a writer. In a letter to Herzen and Ogaryov (see below) dated 7 November 1860, he mentions the Petrashevsky circle and recalls that 'at times more remarkable people used to appear among them, for example, the not untalented writer Dostoevsky'. (He was referring to his works of the 1870s.)

2. Dostoevsky was forty years old on 30 October 1861. Suslova was twenty-one or twenty-two at the time.

3. Not the free city of Hamburg, as all other accounts of Suslova claim.

Chapter XI: *The Demise of* Epokha

1. Dostoevsky's contributors wrote that *Vremya* had an immediate and decisive success. It had 2,300 subscribers in 1861, the first year of publication, 4,302 in its second year, 4,000 by April of the third year, and would certainly have attained that figure again. The magazine became firmly established at once and brought in a large income. 'My name is worth a million,' Dostoevsky told Strakhov in 1862.

2. *Uchonie Zapiski Tartuskogo Gosudarstvennogo Universiteta*, (*Academic Notes of Tartu State University*), 1963, edn 139, carries B. F. Egorov's materials on Apollon Grigoryev from N. N. Strakhov's archives, preserved in the manuscript section of the library of the Ukrainian Academy of Sciences, Kiev. A. L. Budilovskaya, an undergraduate at Tartu University, discovered in the same manuscript collection six letters from the 'young lady from Ustyug', providing some hitherto unknown data about her, including her surname. Apollon Grigoryev did not break with her in Orenburg in 1862; he continued to live with her in Petersburg until March 1863. In 1864, during the last days of his life, which he spent in a debtors' prison she tried to see him and say goodbye to him: 'I am very sorry for him.' The last information about her is her letter of 8 May 1866 to Strakhov, asking for financial assistance.

3. The final version of *Notes from Underground* has only two chapters: 'The Underground' and 'Concerning Wet Snow'. Apparently, the encounter with school friends that precedes the story of Liza was originally intended as a separate chapter, but in working on it later Dostoevsky must have decided that this episode was not substantial enough for an independent section.

4. First published by A. F. Dolinin in commentaries to *Pisma F. M. Dostoevskogo* (*F. M. Dostoevsky's Letters*), Moscow–Leningrad, 1928, vol. 1, p. 501.

5. *Vospominaniya Andreya Mikhailovicha Dostoevskogo* (*Memoirs of Andrei Mikhailovich Dostoevsky*), Leningrad, 1930.

6. The description and characterization of Anna Korvin-Krukovskaya is based on the memoirs of her younger sister Sophia Kovalevskaya, the noted mathematician (S. V. Kovalevskaya, *Vospominaniya Detstva i Avtobiograficheskie Ocherki* (*Reminiscences of Childhood and Autobiographical Sketches*), Moscow–Leningrad, 1945, Chapter 7: 'Moya Sestra' ('My Sister').

Chapter XII: A Novel of Confession

1. Dostoevsky thought highly of Victor Hugo's *The Last Days of a Condemned Man*. The early version of *Crime and Punishment* draws on that book too: 'I am on trial and I will tell all. I will write everything down.' '*This is a confession, a complete confession.* I won't hide anything.'

2. Dostoevsky mentions Lacenaire's name in *The Idiot* and in the notes for *A Raw Youth*.

3. The rough notes for *A Raw Youth* contain several references to this episode from Dostoevsky's private life, which was to a certain extent reflected in his 1875 novel. (These notes were first published by A. S. Dolinin in his book *V Tvorcheskoi Laboratorii Dostoevskogo* (*In Dostoevsky's Creative Laboratory*), Leningrad, 1947.) The references concern Akhmakova and the young Prince Sokolsky: 'His relationship with the Princess was a bit like mine with E. P. [Elena Pavlovna] when her husband was still alive.' The raw youth tells Anna Andreevna the story of Elena Pavlovna. 'It was a prank. I know that from my own experience.' In the final text the raw youth says: 'Once, when they were abroad, in a moment of joking, she did say to the Prince, that perhaps in the future, when she became a widow . . . How could these be other than lightly spoken words?' Actually, in real life, the matter was much more serious and Dostoevsky considered himself bound to Elena Pavlovna by a promise from which she released him at his request at the end of 1866, after he was already betrothed to Anna Snitkina. 'I am very glad I stood firm last summer and did not say anything definite to you, otherwise I should have perished,' Elena Pavlovna told him.

4. The parts and chapters are given according to the final version, not the magazine version.

5. This letter is published here for the first time.

6. These hopes came true. D. N. Khmyrov was a mathematics teacher and a kind-hearted and cultivated man. He was appointed to a

post in the provinces and later in Moscow. Sonya became completely absorbed in her family and in rearing her children. She died in 1907 at the age of sixty-two.

7. [*Nedra*, 1923], pp. 279–82.

8. G. P. Danilevsky's well-known novel *Mirovich* was written much later. It was first published in *Vestnik Evropy* (*European Herald*) in 1879. Dostoevsky probably read the detailed exposition of the novel, printed in *Russky Vestnik* in 1879 (vol. 143), the issue in which Book Seven of *The Brothers Karamazov* appeared.

Chapter XIII: The Last Love

1. *Crime and Punishment.*

2. Maria-Anna Snitkina's income from her property and the social standing of her tenants in the 1860s are known from the official house-record book that has been preserved. At that time Peski was inhabited mostly by poor people. The book gives the tenants' occupations: cabinet-maker, chimney-sweep, housekeeper and only now and then, a civil servant or a doctor. The monthly rent was from four to ten roubles – quite high for tenants of this kind – and brought in a considerable annual income. The Snitkins also had some cab stables and a general store, which were rented separately by the year. Twenty-year-old Anna had constant dealings with the tenants. It was useful preparation for a life in which she had to enter into combat with creditors, buyers of promissory notes, moneylenders and the like.

3. The dictation of *The Gambler.*

4. At the age of sixteen Anna had jotted down in her mother's house-record book a poem from Nekrasov to which she had taken a fancy: 'A Cheap Purchase'. This was not 'pure lyric', nor was it a love elegy; it was a drama about property, about a young woman who had lost her dowry. It might have been a premonition of her own fate.

Chapter XIV: Beginning of Wanderings

1. The conversation between the two writers is given here from Dostoevsky's accounts, one of which Anna Grigoryevna wrote down in shorthand in her diary a few hours after it had taken place, and the other which Dostoevsky wrote in a letter to Apollon Maikov on 16 May 1867. A transcript of this conversation, taken from Dostoevsky's letter to Maikov, was sent anonymously to P. I. Bartenev, the editor of *Russky Arkhiv* (*Russian Archive*) in September 1867 with the request that it be

preserved for posterity in the Chertkov Library and not published before 1890. Turgenev found out about this and wrote to Bartenev that in the letter Dostoevsky 'ascribes outrageous and ridiculous opinions about Russia and Russians to me . . . I only saw Mr Dostoevsky once. He stayed at my house no more than an hour, and, after unburdening himself of harsh abuse against the Germans, against me and my latest book, departed. I had hardly any time and no desire to argue with him. My attitude to him, I repeat, was as to a sick man.' Turgenev told Y. P. Polonsky in 1871 and E. M. Garshin in 1881 that Dostoevsky had identified Potugin with his creator and had said of *Smoke*: 'This book ought to be burned by the hangman's hand.'

2. A gulden, as is apparent from Anna Dostoevskaya's further account, was equal to ten or twenty francs (half an imperial or an imperial); this sum therefore amounted to 1,660 or 3,320 francs. In either case, this would have supported two people for several months abroad: 'two thousand francs is enough to live on for four months . . . with everything available in Petersburg,' Dostoevsky wrote to Apollon Maikov from Geneva on 16 August 1867.

3. Karamzin, *Works*, Petersburg, 1848, vol. 2, p. 194.

Chapter XV: A Poem-Novel

1. It was only towards the end of his life that Dostoevsky learned the more complete text of the poem he loved. In 1880 P. A. Efremov published in his first collection of Pushkin's works (vol. 3, pp. 260–61) a summary of the latest version of 'The Poor Knight' including the new verse, the key verse, as it were, to the entire legend:

> As he approached Geneva
> He met the Virgin Mary
> Mother of Jesus Christ
> At the foot of a cross.

Dostoevsky entered the four lines into his 1880 notebook (i.e. in the very year of its publication). See *Opisanie Rukopisei F. M. Dostoevskogo* (*Description of F. M. Dostoevsky's Manuscripts*) Moscow, 1957, p. 143.

Chapter XVI: Before the Battle

1. Dostoevsky's italics.

2. Lyubov Fyodorovna Dostoevskaya (1869–1926) wrote short stories and novels, among them *The Woman Lawyer*, *The Woman Emigré* and *The Sick Girls*. A book of reminiscences about her father, published in

Munich in 1921, appeared in an abridged Russian translation: *Dostoevsky vizobrazhenii ego docheri L. Dostoevskoi (Dostoevsky as portrayed by his Daughter L. Dostoevskaya)* Moscow and Petrograd, 1922.

3. Dostoevsky had a very high opinion of the organization of Lermontov's novel (five separate short stories about one hero). In 1846–9 he built *Netochka Nezvanova* upon the same principle, and in 1856 he was already planning 'a long novel . . . about the adventures of one character with a common unifying link running through them, but consisting of completely separate and self-sufficient episodes'. Each episode is a separate story; together they are a complete novel. (Letters to A. N. Maikov, 18 January 1856; to M. M. Dostoevsky, 9 November 1856; and to Y. I. Yakushkin, 1 May 1857).

4. The outstanding philanthropist Dr Haas, whom Dostoevsky mentions in *The Idiot* (see above, pp. 21–2).

Chapter XVII: A Political Pamphlet Novel

1. Cited in *Moskovskie Vedomosti*, 8 January 1870, no. 5.

2. I. A. Khudyakov was a defendant in the Karakozov case, a collector of folklore and a follower of the revolutionary democrats. He went to Geneva to establish political contacts with Bakunin, Herzen and Ogaryov.

3. Published here for the first time.

4. Vladimir Bonch-Bruyevich, 'Lenin on Books and Writers', *Literaturnaya Gazeta*, 21 April 1955.

Chapter XVIII: Dostoevsky as a Journalist

1. I have corrected the memoirist's mistake. She named Kraevsky.

2. 'This is a viewpoint that has already been overcome.'

3. This disproves the statement of V. V. Pochinkovskaya, a proofreader at *Grazhdanin*, who claimed that Dostoevsky had secretly offered his new novel through her to some of the contributors to *Otechestvennie Zapiski*, allegedly asking them to find out whether the editors of the magazine would agree to print his work in it. As is known, Dostoevsky always offered his work to editors openly and directly (for his letter to Katkov with the offer of *Crime and Punishment*, see above, pp. 349–50).

4. There is authoritative proof of this from Anna Grigoryevna: 'There was a painful aspect in this matter for Fyodor Mikhailovich, too: *Otechestvennie Zapiski* was a magazine of the opposing political camp and only very recently, when my husband edited *Vremya* and *Epokha*, that camp had waged a fierce fight against him [a reference to Nekrasov's

and Saltykov's *Sovremennik* – *L.G.*]. Several of Fyodor Mikhailovich's literary enemies were on the editorial board: Mikhailovsky, Skabichevsky, Eliseyev, to some extent Pleshcheev, and they might have required my husband to change his novel to suit their line. But Fyodor Mikhailovich could under no circumstances give up his basic convictions. On the other hand, it was also possible that *Otechestvennie Zapiski* might not want to print some of my husband's opinions, and at the very first serious disagreement Fyodor Mikhailovich would undoubtedly have demanded the return of his novel, whatever lamentable consequences this might have had for us. Worried about these things, he wrote to me in a letter of 20 December 1874: "Now Nekrasov can have full control of me if there is anything against their principles [since *Russky Vestnik*, Dostoevsky's only vehicle, could not print his novel in 1875 – *L.G.*]. But even if we should have to go begging this year, I will not change the political colouring of a single sentence!"' (A. G. Dostoevskaya, *Vospominaniya* (*Reminiscences*), Moscow–Leningrad, 1925, p. 190. Thus although Dostoevsky gave his manuscript to Nekrasov at the end of 1874, he was prepared at any minute to break with the 'hostile' party and editors.

5. This was connected with the intensification of reactionary tendencies in government spheres. On 22 August 1874 Alexander II declared at the opening of the Gentlemen's Boarding School in Moscow that he regarded the gentry as the main bulwark of the monarchy. Katkov in *Moskovskie Vedomosti* (1874, no. 217) lauded the gentry as the living organic tie in the post-reform period between the throne and the people. This happened to be the very time when Dostoevsky started working on *A Raw Youth*.

6. One of the early titles of the novel was *A Raw Youth. Confession of a Great Sinner, Written for Himself.*

7. In Florence Dostoevsky (according to his wife) admired the bronze portal of a small chapel in which infants were baptized, the work of the celebrated Ghiberti. 'My husband told me that were he ever to become rich he would certainly buy life-size photographs of these doors and hang them up in his study so he could admire them' (A. G. Dostoevskaya, *op. cit.*). It was his own artistic taste that he has given to Versilov.

8. '*Tuile*' is French for 'tile', and '*tuilerie*' is 'a tile factory'.

9. Quoted by A. C. Dolinin in *Poslednie Romany Dostoevskogo* (*Dostoevsky's Last Novels*), Moscow–Leningrad, 1963, p. 166.

10. Nekrasov scholars differ about the prototype for 'The Mole', but the italicized lines coincide almost literally with excerpts from a letter Dostoevsky wrote to his brother upon his release from prison (on 22 February 1854): 'Will you believe that there are profound, strong, beautiful characters, and what joy it was to find the gold beneath the

rough crust.' This letter was the first sketch, as it were, for *Notes from the House of the Dead*. It was of great interest and was no doubt well known in literary circles. Nekrasov was personally acquainted with Mikhail Dostoevsky, who might have shown him an outstanding document like this, and it might have influenced Nekrasov's poem of 1856–8 about the 'unfortunates', that is, the Siberian convicts.

11. This name was given to it later ('Unconquerable suffering, unquenchable longing').

12. From A. N. Pypin's notebook, *Literaturnoe Nasledstvo* (*Literary Heritage*), Moscow, 1946, no. 49150, pp. 191–4.

13. *The Physiology of Petersburg* was an anthology Nekrasov had put out in two volumes in 1844 and in 1845. At the end of 1876 Dostoevsky visited the peasant Kornilov in prison. Kornilov had been sentenced to hard labour and permanent exile in Siberia for an attempt to kill his stepdaughter. In *The Diary of a Writer* Dostoevsky printed an article defending the condemned man.

14. In an article, written in 1917 and entitled 'Nekrasov's Funeral,' Plekhanov admitted that his position in the argument with Dostoevsky had been incorrect. 'I began my speech with the remark that Nekrasov had not limited himself to praising the feet of Terpsichore, but had introduced civic motifs into his poetry. The hint was perfectly clear. I had Pushkin in mind. And, it goes without saying, that I *was completely wrong*. Pushkin did much more than praise the feet of Terpsichore, which, incidentally, he only mentioned in passing. But such was our mood at the time. We all more or less shared the view of Pisarev, who 'demolished' our great poet in his well-known article "Pushkin and Belinsky". I have mentioned this part of the speech because *I felt like atoning*; better late than never.' (G. V. Plekhanov, *Iskusstvo i Literatura* (*Art and Literature*), Moscow, 1948, p. 644).

15. From the letters Dostoevsky wrote soon after the Zasulich trial, in April and July 1878, to Moscow students and to Apollon Grigoryev (IV, 17, 33).

Chapter XIX: Before Sunset

1. N. S. Leskov, 'O kufelnom muzhike i proch. Zametki po povodu nekotorykh otzyvov o L. Tolstom' ('On the *Muzhik* in the Kitchen and Other Things. Notes about some opinions about Leo Tolstoy'), *Collected Works*, Moscow, 1958, vol. XI, pp. 146–55.

2. Letter from Leo Tolstoy to L. I. Veselitskaya on 17 November 1892 Leo Tolstoy, *Complete Collected Works*, Moscow, 1953, vol. 66, pp. 274–5. After meeting the author of *Mimochka*, Tolstoy said she was 'a very intelligent and serious woman' (ibid., p. 316).

Chapter XX: A Novel of Synthesis

1. Voltaire developed the principal problems of *Candide* in his poem 'On the Lisbon Disaster'.

2. This obvious resemblance between Ishutin and Nechaev led P. E. Shchegolev (the editor of the three-volume collection entitled *The Petrashevskyites*) to suppose that the revolution in *The Devils* is not based so much on the materials of the Nechaev case as on the testimony in the Karakozov investigation and trial, and that it was not Nechaev but Ishutin who was the real prototype for Pyotr Verkhovensky. This is a controversial statement but it is a fact that Karakozov's name is mentioned repeatedly in the manuscript notes for *The Devils*.

3. Otto Kraus, *Dostoiewsky und Sein Schicksal*, Berlin, 1923, pp. 64–119.

Chapter XXI: Dostoevsky's Epilogue

1. From Pushkin's 'The Gipsies': 'Leave us, proud man.'

Index